Lecture Notes in Computer Scien

T0238796

Commenced Publication in 1973
Founding and Former Series Editors:
Gerhard Goos, Juris Hartmanis, and Jan van Leeuwen

Editorial Board

Sakae Yamamoto (Ed.)

Human Interface and the Management of Information

Information and Interaction for Learning, Culture, Collaboration and Business

15th International Conference, HCI International 2013
Las Vegas, NV, USA, July 21-26, 2013
Proceedings, Part III

 Springer

Volume Editor

Sakae Yamamoto
Tokyo University of Science
Faculty of Engineering
Department of Management Science
1-3 Kagurazaka Shinjuku-ku
Tokyo 162-8601, Japan
E-mail: sakae@ms.kagu.tus.ac.jp

ISSN 0302-9743   e-ISSN 1611-3349
ISBN 978-3-642-39225-2   e-ISBN 978-3-642-39226-9
DOI 10.1007/978-3-642-39226-9
Springer Heidelberg Dordrecht London New York

Library of Congress Control Number: 2013941251

CR Subject Classification (1998): H.5, H.1, K.3, J.5, K.4, H.4, H.3

LNCS Sublibrary: SL 3 – Information Systems and Application,
incl. Internet/Web and HCI

Typesetting: Camera-ready by author, data conversion by Scientific Publishing Services, Chennai, India

Printed on acid-free paper

Springer is part of Springer Science+Business Media (www.springer.com)

Foreword

The 15th International Conference on Human–Computer Interaction, HCI International 2013, was held in Las Vegas, Nevada, USA, 21–26 July 2013, incorporating 12 conferences / thematic areas:

Thematic areas:

- Human–Computer Interaction
- Human Interface and the Management of Information

Affiliated conferences:

- 10th International Conference on Engineering Psychology and Cognitive Ergonomics
- 7th International Conference on Universal Access in Human–Computer Interaction
- 5th International Conference on Virtual, Augmented and Mixed Reality
- 5th International Conference on Cross-Cultural Design
- 5th International Conference on Online Communities and Social Computing
- 7th International Conference on Augmented Cognition
- 4th International Conference on Digital Human Modeling and Applications in Health, Safety, Ergonomics and Risk Management
- 2nd International Conference on Design, User Experience and Usability
- 1st International Conference on Distributed, Ambient and Pervasive Interactions
- 1st International Conference on Human Aspects of Information Security, Privacy and Trust

A total of 5210 individuals from academia, research institutes, industry and governmental agencies from 70 countries submitted contributions, and 1666 papers and 303 posters were included in the program. These papers address the latest research and development efforts and highlight the human aspects of design and use of computing systems. The papers accepted for presentation thoroughly cover the entire field of Human–Computer Interaction, addressing major advances in knowledge and effective use of computers in a variety of application areas.

This volume, edited by Sakae Yamamoto, contains papers focusing on the thematic area of Human Interface and the Management of Information, and addressing the following major topics:

- Learning, Education and Skills Transfer
- Art and Cultural Heritage
- Collaborative Work
- Business Integration
- Decision Support

The remaining volumes of the HCI International 2013 proceedings are:

- Volume 1, LNCS 8004, Human–Computer Interaction: Human-Centred Design Approaches, Methods, Tools and Environments (Part I), edited by Masaaki Kurosu
- Volume 2, LNCS 8005, Human–Computer Interaction: Applications and Services (Part II), edited by Masaaki Kurosu
- Volume 3, LNCS 8006, Human–Computer Interaction: Users and Contexts of Use (Part III), edited by Masaaki Kurosu
- Volume 4, LNCS 8007, Human–Computer Interaction: Interaction Modalities and Techniques (Part IV), edited by Masaaki Kurosu
- Volume 5, LNCS 8008, Human–Computer Interaction: Towards Intelligent and Implicit Interaction (Part V), edited by Masaaki Kurosu
- Volume 6, LNCS 8009, Universal Access in Human–Computer Interaction: Design Methods, Tools and Interaction Techniques for eInclusion (Part I), edited by Constantine Stephanidis and Margherita Antona
- Volume 7, LNCS 8010, Universal Access in Human–Computer Interaction: User and Context Diversity (Part II), edited by Constantine Stephanidis and Margherita Antona
- Volume 8, LNCS 8011, Universal Access in Human–Computer Interaction: Applications and Services for Quality of Life (Part III), edited by Constantine Stephanidis and Margherita Antona
- Volume 9, LNCS 8012, Design, User Experience, and Usability: Design Philosophy, Methods and Tools (Part I), edited by Aaron Marcus
- Volume 10, LNCS 8013, Design, User Experience, and Usability: Health, Learning, Playing, Cultural, and Cross-Cultural User Experience (Part II), edited by Aaron Marcus
- Volume 11, LNCS 8014, Design, User Experience, and Usability: User Experience in Novel Technological Environments (Part III), edited by Aaron Marcus
- Volume 12, LNCS 8015, Design, User Experience, and Usability: Web, Mobile and Product Design (Part IV), edited by Aaron Marcus
- Volume 13, LNCS 8016, Human Interface and the Management of Information: Information and Interaction Design (Part I), edited by Sakae Yamamoto
- Volume 14, LNCS 8017, Human Interface and the Management of Information: Information and Interaction for Health, Safety, Mobility and Complex Environments (Part II), edited by Sakae Yamamoto
- Volume 16, LNAI 8019, Engineering Psychology and Cognitive Ergonomics: Understanding Human Cognition (Part I), edited by Don Harris
- Volume 17, LNAI 8020, Engineering Psychology and Cognitive Ergonomics: Applications and Services (Part II), edited by Don Harris
- Volume 18, LNCS 8021, Virtual, Augmented and Mixed Reality: Designing and Developing Augmented and Virtual Environments (Part I), edited by Randall Shumaker
- Volume 19, LNCS 8022, Virtual, Augmented and Mixed Reality: Systems and Applications (Part II), edited by Randall Shumaker

- Volume 20, LNCS 8023, Cross-Cultural Design: Methods, Practice and Case Studies (Part I), edited by P.L. Patrick Rau
- Volume 21, LNCS 8024, Cross-Cultural Design: Cultural Differences in Everyday Life (Part II), edited by P.L. Patrick Rau
- Volume 22, LNCS 8025, Digital Human Modeling and Applications in Health, Safety, Ergonomics and Risk Management: Healthcare and Safety of the Environment and Transport (Part I), edited by Vincent G. Duffy
- Volume 23, LNCS 8026, Digital Human Modeling and Applications in Health, Safety, Ergonomics and Risk Management: Human Body Modeling and Ergonomics (Part II), edited by Vincent G. Duffy
- Volume 24, LNAI 8027, Foundations of Augmented Cognition, edited by Dylan D. Schmorrow and Cali M. Fidopiastis
- Volume 25, LNCS 8028, Distributed, Ambient and Pervasive Interactions, edited by Norbert Streitz and Constantine Stephanidis
- Volume 26, LNCS 8029, Online Communities and Social Computing, edited by A. Ant Ozok and Panayiotis Zaphiris
- Volume 27, LNCS 8030, Human Aspects of Information Security, Privacy and Trust, edited by Louis Marinos and Ioannis Askoxylakis
- Volume 28, CCIS 373, HCI International 2013 Posters Proceedings (Part I), edited by Constantine Stephanidis
- Volume 29, CCIS 374, HCI International 2013 Posters Proceedings (Part II), edited by Constantine Stephanidis

I would like to thank the Program Chairs and the members of the Program Boards of all affiliated conferences and thematic areas, listed below, for their contribution to the highest scientific quality and the overall success of the HCI International 2013 conference.

This conference could not have been possible without the continuous support and advice of the Founding Chair and Conference Scientific Advisor, Prof. Gavriel Salvendy, as well as the dedicated work and outstanding efforts of the Communications Chair and Editor of HCI International News, Abbas Moallem.

I would also like to thank for their contribution towards the smooth organization of the HCI International 2013 Conference the members of the Human–Computer Interaction Laboratory of ICS-FORTH, and in particular George Paparoulis, Maria Pitsoulaki, Stavroula Ntoa, Maria Bouhli and George Kapnas.

May 2013   Constantine Stephanidis
                                            General Chair, HCI International 2013

Organization

Human–Computer Interaction

Program Chair: Masaaki Kurosu, Japan

Jose Abdelnour-Nocera, UK
Sebastiano Bagnara, Italy
Simone Barbosa, Brazil
Tomas Berns, Sweden
Nigel Bevan, UK
Simone Borsci, UK
Apala Lahiri Chavan, India
Sherry Chen, Taiwan
Kevin Clark, USA
Torkil Clemmensen, Denmark
Xiaowen Fang, USA
Shin'ichi Fukuzumi, Japan
Vicki Hanson, UK
Ayako Hashizume, Japan
Anzai Hiroyuki, Italy
Sheue-Ling Hwang, Taiwan
Wonil Hwang, South Korea
Minna Isomursu, Finland
Yong Gu Ji, South Korea
Esther Jun, USA
Mitsuhiko Karashima, Japan

Kyungdoh Kim, South Korea
Heidi Krömker, Germany
Chen Ling, USA
Yan Liu, USA
Zhengjie Liu, P.R. China
Loïc Martínez Normand, Spain
Chang S. Nam, USA
Naoko Okuizumi, Japan
Noriko Osaka, Japan
Philippe Palanque, France
Hans Persson, Sweden
Ling Rothrock, USA
Naoki Sakakibara, Japan
Dominique Scapin, France
Guangfeng Song, USA
Sanjay Tripathi, India
Chui Yin Wong, Malaysia
Toshiki Yamaoka, Japan
Kazuhiko Yamazaki, Japan
Ryoji Yoshitake, Japan
Silvia Zimmermann, Switzerland

Human Interface and the Management of Information

Program Chair: Sakae Yamamoto, Japan

Hans-Jorg Bullinger, Germany
Alan Chan, Hong Kong
Gilsoo Cho, South Korea
Jon R. Gunderson, USA
Shin'ichi Fukuzumi, Japan
Michitaka Hirose, Japan
Jhilmil Jain, USA
Yasufumi Kume, Japan

Mark Lehto, USA
Hiroyuki Miki, Japan
Hirohiko Mori, Japan
Fiona Fui-Hoon Nah, USA
Shogo Nishida, Japan
Robert Proctor, USA
Youngho Rhee, South Korea
Katsunori Shimohara, Japan

Michale Smith, USA
Tsutomu Tabe, Japan
Hiroshi Tsuji, Japan

Kim-Phuong Vu, USA
Tomio Watanabe, Japan
Hidekazu Yoshikawa, Japan

Engineering Psychology and Cognitive Ergonomics

Program Chair: Don Harris, UK

Guy Andre Boy, USA
Joakim Dahlman, Sweden
Trevor Dobbins, UK
Mike Feary, USA
Shan Fu, P.R. China
Michaela Heese, Austria
Hung-Sying Jing, Taiwan
Wen-Chin Li, Taiwan
Mark A. Neerincx, The Netherlands
Jan M. Noyes, UK
Taezoon Park, Singapore

Paul Salmon, Australia
Axel Schulte, Germany
Siraj Shaikh, UK
Sarah C. Sharples, UK
Anthony Smoker, UK
Neville A. Stanton, UK
Alex Stedmon, UK
Xianghong Sun, P.R. China
Andrew Thatcher, South Africa
Matthew J.W. Thomas, Australia
Rolf Zon, The Netherlands

Universal Access in Human–Computer Interaction

Program Chairs: Constantine Stephanidis, Greece, and Margherita Antona, Greece

Julio Abascal, Spain
Ray Adams, UK
Gisela Susanne Bahr, USA
Margit Betke, USA
Christian Bühler, Germany
Stefan Carmien, Spain
Jerzy Charytonowicz, Poland
Carlos Duarte, Portugal
Pier Luigi Emiliani, Italy
Qin Gao, P.R. China
Andrina Granić, Croatia
Andreas Holzinger, Austria
Josette Jones, USA
Simeon Keates, UK

Georgios Kouroupetroglou, Greece
Patrick Langdon, UK
Seongil Lee, Korea
Ana Isabel B.B. Paraguay, Brazil
Helen Petrie, UK
Michael Pieper, Germany
Enrico Pontelli, USA
Jaime Sanchez, Chile
Anthony Savidis, Greece
Christian Stary, Austria
Hirotada Ueda, Japan
Gerhard Weber, Germany
Harald Weber, Germany

Virtual, Augmented and Mixed Reality

Program Chair: Randall Shumaker, USA

Waymon Armstrong, USA
Juan Cendan, USA
Rudy Darken, USA
Cali M. Fidopiastis, USA
Charles Hughes, USA
David Kaber, USA
Hirokazu Kato, Japan
Denis Laurendeau, Canada
Fotis Liarokapis, UK

Mark Livingston, USA
Michael Macedonia, USA
Gordon Mair, UK
Jose San Martin, Spain
Jacquelyn Morie, USA
Albert "Skip" Rizzo, USA
Kay Stanney, USA
Christopher Stapleton, USA
Gregory Welch, USA

Cross-Cultural Design

Program Chair: P.L. Patrick Rau, P.R. China

Pilsung Choe, P.R. China
Henry Been-Lirn Duh, Singapore
Vanessa Evers, The Netherlands
Paul Fu, USA
Zhiyong Fu, P.R. China
Fu Guo, P.R. China
Sung H. Han, Korea
Toshikazu Kato, Japan
Dyi-Yih Michael Lin, Taiwan
Rungtai Lin, Taiwan

Sheau-Farn Max Liang, Taiwan
Liang Ma, P.R. China
Alexander Mädche, Germany
Katsuhiko Ogawa, Japan
Tom Plocher, USA
Kerstin Röse, Germany
Supriya Singh, Australia
Hsiu-Ping Yueh, Taiwan
Liang (Leon) Zeng, USA
Chen Zhao, USA

Online Communities and Social Computing

Program Chairs: A. Ant Ozok, USA, and Panayiotis Zaphiris, Cyprus

Areej Al-Wabil, Saudi Arabia
Leonelo Almeida, Brazil
Bjørn Andersen, Norway
Chee Siang Ang, UK
Aneesha Bakharia, Australia
Ania Bobrowicz, UK
Paul Cairns, UK
Farzin Deravi, UK
Andri Ioannou, Cyprus
Slava Kisilevich, Germany

Niki Lambropoulos, Greece
Effie Law, Switzerland
Soo Ling Lim, UK
Fernando Loizides, Cyprus
Gabriele Meiselwitz, USA
Anthony Norcio, USA
Elaine Raybourn, USA
Panote Siriaraya, UK
David Stuart, UK
June Wei, USA

Augmented Cognition

Program Chairs: Dylan D. Schmorrow, USA, and Cali M. Fidopiastis, USA

Robert Arrabito, Canada
Richard Backs, USA
Chris Berka, USA
Joseph Cohn, USA
Martha E. Crosby, USA
Julie Drexler, USA
Ivy Estabrooke, USA
Chris Forsythe, USA
Wai Tat Fu, USA
Rodolphe Gentili, USA
Marc Grootjen, The Netherlands
Jefferson Grubb, USA
Ming Hou, Canada

Santosh Mathan, USA
Rob Matthews, Australia
Dennis McBride, USA
Jeff Morrison, USA
Mark A. Neerincx, The Netherlands
Denise Nicholson, USA
Banu Onaral, USA
Lee Sciarini, USA
Kay Stanney, USA
Roy Stripling, USA
Rob Taylor, UK
Karl van Orden, USA

Digital Human Modeling and Applications in Health, Safety, Ergonomics and Risk Management

Program Chair: Vincent G. Duffy, USA and Russia

Karim Abdel-Malek, USA
Giuseppe Andreoni, Italy
Daniel Carruth, USA
Eliza Yingzi Du, USA
Enda Fallon, Ireland
Afzal Godil, USA
Ravindra Goonetilleke, Hong Kong
Bo Hoege, Germany
Waldemar Karwowski, USA
Zhizhong Li, P.R. China

Kang Li, USA
Tim Marler, USA
Michelle Robertson, USA
Matthias Rötting, Germany
Peter Vink, The Netherlands
Mao-Jiun Wang, Taiwan
Xuguang Wang, France
Jingzhou (James) Yang, USA
Xiugan Yuan, P.R. China
Gülcin Yücel Hoge, Germany

Design, User Experience, and Usability

Program Chair: Aaron Marcus, USA

Sisira Adikari, Australia
Ronald Baecker, Canada
Arne Berger, Germany
Jamie Blustein, Canada

Ana Boa-Ventura, USA
Jan Brejcha, Czech Republic
Lorenzo Cantoni, Switzerland
Maximilian Eibl, Germany

Anthony Faiola, USA
Emilie Gould, USA
Zelda Harrison, USA
Rüdiger Heimgärtner, Germany
Brigitte Herrmann, Germany
Steffen Hess, Germany
Kaleem Khan, Canada

Jennifer McGinn, USA
Francisco Rebelo, Portugal
Michael Renner, Switzerland
Kerem Rızvanoğlu, Turkey
Marcelo Soares, Brazil
Christian Sturm, Germany
Michele Visciola, Italy

Distributed, Ambient and Pervasive Interactions

Program Chairs: Norbert Streitz, Germany, and Constantine Stephanidis, Greece

Emile Aarts, The Netherlands
Adnan Abu-Dayya, Qatar
Juan Carlos Augusto, UK
Boris de Ruyter, The Netherlands
Anind Dey, USA
Dimitris Grammenos, Greece
Nuno M. Guimaraes, Portugal
Shin'ichi Konomi, Japan
Carsten Magerkurth, Switzerland

Christian Müller-Tomfelde, Australia
Fabio Paternó, Italy
Gilles Privat, France
Harald Reiterer, Germany
Carsten Röcker, Germany
Reiner Wichert, Germany
Woontack Woo, South Korea
Xenophon Zabulis, Greece

Human Aspects of Information Security, Privacy and Trust

Program Chairs: Louis Marinos, ENISA EU, and Ioannis Askoxylakis, Greece

Claudio Agostino Ardagna, Italy
Zinaida Benenson, Germany
Daniele Catteddu, Italy
Raoul Chiesa, Italy
Bryan Cline, USA
Sadie Creese, UK
Jorge Cuellar, Germany
Marc Dacier, USA
Dieter Gollmann, Germany
Kirstie Hawkey, Canada
Jaap-Henk Hoepman, The Netherlands
Cagatay Karabat, Turkey
Angelos Keromytis, USA
Ayako Komatsu, Japan

Ronald Leenes, The Netherlands
Javier Lopez, Spain
Steve Marsh, Canada
Gregorio Martinez, Spain
Emilio Mordini, Italy
Yuko Murayama, Japan
Masakatsu Nishigaki, Japan
Aljosa Pasic, Spain
Milan Petković, The Netherlands
Joachim Posegga, Germany
Jean-Jacques Quisquater, Belgium
Damien Sauveron, France
George Spanoudakis, UK
Kerry-Lynn Thomson, South Africa

Julien Touzeau, France
Theo Tryfonas, UK
João Vilela, Portugal

Claire Vishik, UK
Melanie Volkamer, Germany

External Reviewers

Maysoon Abulkhair, Saudi Arabia
Ilia Adami, Greece
Vishal Barot, UK
Stephan Böhm, Germany
Vassilis Charissis, UK
Francisco Cipolla-Ficarra, Spain
Maria De Marsico, Italy
Marc Fabri, UK
David Fonseca, Spain
Linda Harley, USA
Yasushi Ikei, Japan
Wei Ji, USA
Nouf Khashman, Canada
John Killilea, USA
Iosif Klironomos, Greece
Ute Klotz, Switzerland
Maria Korozi, Greece
Kentaro Kotani, Japan

Vassilis Kouroumalis, Greece
Stephanie Lackey, USA
Janelle LaMarche, USA
Asterios Leonidis, Greece
Nickolas Macchiarella, USA
George Margetis, Greece
Matthew Marraffino, USA
Joseph Mercado, USA
Claudia Mont'Alvão, Brazil
Yoichi Motomura, Japan
Karsten Nebe, Germany
Stavroula Ntoa, Greece
Martin Osen, Austria
Stephen Prior, UK
Farid Shirazi, Canada
Jan Stelovsky, USA
Sarah Swierenga, USA

HCI International 2014

The 16th International Conference on Human–Computer Interaction, HCI International 2014, will be held jointly with the affiliated conferences in the summer of 2014. It will cover a broad spectrum of themes related to Human–Computer Interaction, including theoretical issues, methods, tools, processes and case studies in HCI design, as well as novel interaction techniques, interfaces and applications. The proceedings will be published by Springer. More information about the topics, as well as the venue and dates of the conference, will be announced through the HCI International Conference series website: http://www.hci-international.org/

General Chair
Professor Constantine Stephanidis
University of Crete and ICS-FORTH
Heraklion, Crete, Greece
Email: cs@ics.forth.gr

Table of Contents – Part III

Learning, Education and Skills Transfer

Social Networking and Culturally Situated Design Teaching Tools:
Providing a Collaborative Environment for K-12 3
Albanie Bolton and Cheryl D. Seals

A Hybrid Model for an E-learning System Which Develops
Metacognitive Skills at Students 9
Maria Canter

Enhancing Information Systems Users' Knowledge and Skills
Transference through Self-regulation Techniques 16
Brenda Eschenbrenner

Articulating an Experimental Model for the Study of Game-Based
Learning 25
*Christina Frederick-Recascino, Dahai Liu, Shawn Doherty,
Jason Kring, and Devin Liskey*

Psychophysiological Assessment Tools for Evaluation of Learning
Technologies 33
Richard H. Hall, Nick S. Lockwood, and Hong Sheng

An Experimental Environment for Analyzing Collaborative Learning
Interaction 43
Yuki Hayashi, Yuji Ogawa, and Yukiko I. Nakano

Transparent Digital Contents Sharing for Science Teachers 53
Thongchai Kaewkiriya, Ryosuke Saga, and Hiroshi Tsuji

Development of a Computer Programming Learning Support System
Based on Reading Computer Program 63
Haruki Kanamori, Takahito Tomoto, and Takako Akakura

The Display Medium, Academic Major and Sex Effect of High School
Students on Visuospatial Abilities Test Performance 70
Yen-Yu Kang and Yu-Hsiang Liao

Video Feedback System for Teaching Improvement Using Students'
Sequential and Overall Teaching Evaluations 79
*Yusuke Kometani, Takahito Tomoto, Takehiro Furuta, and
Takako Akakura*

I See, Please Tell Me More – Exploring Virtual Agents as Interactive
Storytellers..   89
  David Lindholm, Eva Petersson Brooks, and Tom Nauerby

Gamification of Education Using Computer Games..................   99
  Fiona Fui-Hoon Nah, Venkata Rajasekhar Telaprolu,
  Shashank Rallapalli, and Pavani Rallapalli Venkata

New Potential of E-learning by Re-utilizing Open Content
Online – TED NOTE: English Learning System as an Auto-assignment
Generator...   108
  Ai Nakajima and Kiyoshi Tomimatsu

Transferring Tacit Skills of WADAIKO   118
  Makoto Oka, Asahi Mizukoshi, and Hirohiko Mori

A Study of the Crossroad Game for Improving the Teamwork of
Students...   126
  Hidetsugu Suto and Ruediger Oehlmann

Towards Understanding of Relationship among Pareto Optimal
Solutions in Multi-dimensional Space via Interactive System...........   137
  Keiki Takadama, Yuya Sawadaishi, Tomohiro Harada,
  Yoshihiro Ichikawa, Keiji Sato, Kiyohiko Hattori,
  Hiroyoki Sato, and Tomohiro Yamaguchi

Development and Evaluation of a Mobile Search System for Science
Experiments to Connect School Knowledge to Common Knowledge.....   147
  Takahito Tomoto, Tomoya Horiguchi, and Tsukasa Hirashima

Application to Help Learn the Process of Transforming Mathematical
Expressions with a Focus on Study Logs   157
  Takayuki Watabe, Yoshinori Miyazaki, and Yoshiki Hayashi

Learning by Problem-Posing with Online Connected Media Tablets.....   165
  Sho Yamamoto, Takehiro Kanbe, Yuta Yoshida,
  Kazushige Maeda, and Tsukasa Hirashima

Instantaneous Assessment of Learners' Comprehension for Lecture by
Using Kit-Build Concept Map System   175
  Kan Yoshida, Takuya Osada, Kota Sugihara, Yoshiaki Nino,
  Masakuni Shida, and Tsukasa Hirashima

Exploring User Feedback of a E-Learning System: A Text Mining
Approach..   182
  Wen-Bin Yu and Ronaldo Luna

Art and Cultural Heritage

Bodily Expression Media by Dual Domain Design of Shadow 195
  Naruhiro Hayashi, Yoshiyuki Miwa, Shiroh Itai, and Hiroko Nish

Virtual Experience System for a Digital Museum.................... 203
  Yasushi Ikei, Koji Abe, Yukinori Masuda, Yujiro Okuya,
  Tomohiro Amemiya, and Koichi Hirota

Design of Space for Expression Media with the Use of Fog............. 210
  Shiroh Itai, Yuji Endo, and Yoshiyuki Miwa

User Interface of Interactive Media Art in Stereoscopic
Environment 219
  YoungEun Kim, MiGyung Lee, SangHun Nam, and JinWan Park

A Method of Viewing 3D Horror Contents for Amplifying Horror
Experience 228
  Nao Omori, Masato Tsutsui, and Ryoko Ueoka

Digital Railway Museum: An Approach to Introduction of Digital
Exhibition Systems at the Railway Museum 238
  Takuji Narumi, Torahiko Kasai, Takumi Honda, Kunio Aoki,
  Tomohiro Tanikawa, and Michitaka Hirose

Mixed Reality Digital Museum Project 248
  Tomohiro Tanikawa, Takuji Narumi, and Michitaka Hirose

ArchMatrix: Knowledge Management and Visual Analytics for
Archaeologists 258
  Stefano Valtolina, Barbara Rita Barricelli,
  Giovanna Bagnasco Gianni, and Susanna Bortolotto

The Designing Expressions of the Special Visual Effect Film in the
Digital Technology 267
  Tsun-Hsiung Yao and Chu-Yu Sun

Collaborative Work

Lifecycle Support of Automotive Manufacturing Systems through a
Next-Generation Operator Interface Implementation................. 277
  Vishal Barot and Robert Harrison

CoPI: A Web-Based Collaborative Planning Interface Platform 287
  Mohammad K. Hadhrawi, Mariam Nouh, Anas Alfaris, and
  Abel Sanchez

Estimation of Interruptibility during Office Work Based on PC Activity
and Conversation 297
  *Satoshi Hashimoto, Takahiro Tanaka, Kazuaki Aoki, and
  Kinya Fujita*

ARM-COMS: ARm-Supported eMbodied COmmunication Monitor
System 307
  Teruaki Ito and Tomio Watanabe

Interlocked Surfaces: A Dynamic Multi-device Collaboration System.... 317
  Hiroyuki Kamo and Jiro Tanaka

Effects of a Communication with Make-Believe Play in a Real-Space
Sharing Edutainment System 326
  *Hiroki Kanegae, Masaru Yamane, Michiya Yamamoto, and
  Tomio Watanabe*

A Support Framework for Automated Video and Multimedia Workflows
for Production and Archive 336
  *Robert Manthey, Robert Herms, Marc Ritter, Michael Storz, and
  Maximilian Eibl*

Responsibilities and Challenges of Social Media Managers 342
  Christian Meske and Stefan Stieglitz

Digital War Room for Design – Requirements for Collocated Group
Work Spaces 352
  Mika P. Nieminen, Mari Tyllinen, and Mikael Runonen

Detection of Division of Labor in Multiparty Collaboration 362
  *Noriko Suzuki, Tosirou Kamiya, Ichiro Umata, Sadanori Ito,
  Shoichiro Iwasawa, Mamiko Sakata, and Katsunori Shimohara*

Role of Assigned Persona for Computer Supported Cooperative Work
in Remote Control Environment 372
  Yuzo Takahashi

Supporting Group and Personal Memory in an Interactive Space for
Collaborative Work 381
  Mari Tyllinen and Marko Nieminen

Pros and Cons of Various ICT Tools in Global Collaboration – A
Cross-Case Study 391
  Matti Vartiainen and Olli Jahkola

Interpersonal Service Support Based on Employee's Activity
Model 401
  Kentaro Watanabe and Takuichi Nishimura

Business Integration

Situation Aware Interaction with Multi-modal Business Applications in
Smart Environments 413
  Mario Aehnelt, Sebastian Bader, Gernot Ruscher, Frank Krüger,
  Bodo Urban, and Thomas Kirste

Human Factors in Supply Chain Management – Decision Making in
Complex Logistic Scenarios 423
  Philipp Brauner, Simone Runge, Marcel Groten,
  Günther Schuh, and Martina Ziefle

Strategic Study of Knowledge Management Which Led into Furniture
Design Industry – Taking Example by Taiwan Furniture Industry 433
  Chi-Hsiung Chen and Kang-Hua Lan

A Study of Customization for Online Business 443
  Vincent Cho and Candy Lau

Are HCI Issues a Big Factor in Supply Chain Mobile Apps? 450
  Barry Flachsbart, Cassandra C. Elrod, and Michael G. Hilgers

Value Added by the Axiomatic Usability Method for Evaluating
Consumer Electronics 457
  Yinni Guo, Yu Zhu, Gavriel Salvendy, and Robert W. Proctor

Challenges for Incorporating "Quality in Use" in Embedded System
Development 467
  Naotake Hirasawa

Development of a System for Communicating Human Factors
Readiness 475
  Matthew Johnston, Katie Del Giudice, Kelly S. Hale, and
  Brent Winslow

A Method for Service Failure Effects Analysis Based on Customer
Satisfaction 485
  Yusuke Kurita, Koji Kimita, Kentaro Watanabe, and
  Yoshiki Shimomura

Searching Blog Sites with Product Reviews......................... 495
  Hironori Kuwata, Makoto Oka, and Hirohiko Mori

Usability Evaluation of Comprehension Performance and Subjective
Assessment on Mobile Text Advertising 501
  Ya-Li Lin and Chih-Hsiang Lai

Consideration of the Effect of Gesture Exaggeration in Web3D
Communication Using 3DAgent 511
    Toshiya Naka and Toru Ishida

The Relationship between Kansei Scale for Uniqueness of Products and
Purchase Motivation 521
    Yusuke Ohta and Keiko Kasamatsu

Timing and Basis of Online Product Recommendation: The Preference
Inconsistency Paradox 531
    Amy Shi, Chuan-Hoo Tan, and Choon Ling Sia

Research on the Measurement of Product Sales with Relation to Visual
Planning for Commercial Websites 540
    Chu-Yu Sun

Decision Support

Burglary Crime Analysis Using Logistic Regression 549
    Daniel Antolos, Dahai Liu, Andrei Ludu, and Dennis A. Vincenzi

Using Video Prototyping as a Means to Involve Crisis Communication
Personnel in the Design Process: Innovating Crisis Management by
Creating a Social Media Awareness Tool 559
    Joel Brynielsson, Fredrik Johansson, and Sinna Lindquist

Service Evaluation Method for Managing Uncertainty 569
    Koji Kimita, Yusuke Kurita, Kentaro Watanabe,
    Takeshi Tateyama, and Yoshiki Shimomura

On Services and Insights of Technology Intelligence System 579
    Seungwoo Lee, Minhee Cho, Sa-Kwang Song, and Hanmin Jung

Sales Strategy Mining System with Visualization of Action History 588
    Haruhi Satonaka and Wataru Sunayama

An Automatic Classification of Product Review into Given
Viewpoints 598
    Yuki Tachizawa, Makoto Oka, and Hirohiko Mori

User Needs Search Using Text Mining 607
    Yukiko Takahashi and Yumi Asahi

Finding a Prototype Form of Sustainable Strategies for the Iterated
Prisoners Dilemma 616
    Mieko Tanaka-Yamawaki and Ryota Itoi

The Study to Clarify the Type of "Otome-Game" User 625
    Misaki Tanikawa and Yumi Asahi

A Method for Developing Quality Function Deployment Ontology 632
Ken Tomioka, Fumiaki Saitoh, and Syohei Ishizu

Integrating the Anchoring Process with Preference Stability for
Interactive Movie Recommendations 639
I-Chin Wu and Yun-Fang Niu

Application of Ethno-Cognitive Interview and Analysis Method for the
Smart Communication Design 649
Ayako Yajima, Haruo Hira, and Toshiki Yamaoka

Author Index 659

Part I

Learning, Education and Skills Transfer

Social Networking and Culturally Situated Design Teaching Tools: Providing a Collaborative Environment for K-12

Albanie Bolton[1,2] and Cheryl D. Seals[1,3]

[1] Auburn University, Auburn, AL 36849
[2] 364 Weatherford Dr., Madison, AL 35757
atb0010@auburn.edu
[3] Shelby Center for Engineering Technology, Suite 3101M, Auburn, AL 36849
sealscd@auburn.edu

Abstract. For over 25 years, HCI researchers and developers have been challenged with improving usability of products. More recently, the Computer-Supported Cooperative Work (CSCW) community has focused on developing collaborative systems but even though social interaction was recognized the emphasis was on work. The widespread use of the Internet by millions of diverse users for socializing is a new phenomenon that raises new issues for researchers and developers. Just designing for usability is not enough; we need to understand how technology can support social interaction and design for sociability. Moreover, increasing accessibility to Computer Science and Technology is essential for a discipline that relies on creativity and diverse perspectives. With the educational research community having begun to explore the causes behind the underrepresentation of females and students of color in computing courses, outreach efforts have commenced to overcome these enrollment discrepancies.

Keywords: Computer Collaborative Work, user interface, computing, culture, educational gaming, ethomathematics, mathematics, usability, Culturally Situated Design Tools (CSDTs).

1 Introduction

For over 25 years, HCI researchers and developers have been challenged with improving usability of products. More recently, the Computer-Supported Cooperative Work (CSCW) community has focused on developing collaborative systems but even though social interaction was recognized the emphasis was on work [1]. The widespread use of the Internet by millions of diverse users for socializing is a new phenomenon that raises new issues for researchers and developers. Just designing for usability is not enough; we need to understand how technology can support social interaction and design for sociability. Sociability is concerned with developing

S. Yamamoto (Ed.): HIMI/HCII 2013, Part III, LNCS 8018, pp. 3–8, 2013.

software, policies and practices to support social interaction online. Three key components contribute to good sociability [1].

- *Purpose.* A community's shared focus on an interest, need, information, service, or support, that provides a reason for individual members to belong to the community.
- *People.* The people who interact with each other in the community and who have individual, social and organization needs. Some of these people may take different roles in the community, such as leaders, protagonists, comedians, moderators, etc.
- *Policies.* The language and protocols that guide people's interactions and contribute to the development of folklore and rituals that bring a sense of history and accepted social norms. More formal policies may also be needed, such as registration policies, and codes of behavior for moderators. Informal and formal policies provide community governance.[1]

Decisions about *purpose, people* and *policies* by community developers help determine the initial sociability of an online community. Later, as the community evolves an understanding of which social norms and policies are acceptable and which are not gradually becomes established. This is what the CSDT tool base has taken into account for the framework and design.

Culturally Situated Design Tools (CSDTs) allow students and teachers to explore mathematics and computer science with depth and care, using cultural artifacts from specific times, places, and cultures. Ethnomathematics is the study of mathematical ideas and practices situated in their cultural context. The Culturally Situated Design Tools website provides free standards-based lessons and interactive "applets" that help students and teachers explore the mathematics and knowledge systems using ethnomathematics in areas such as African, African American, Youth Subculture, Native American, and Latino. The supporting materials for the CSDTs include lesson plans and evaluation instruments to ensure they are integrated into the curriculum through state and national standards. Based in K-12 schools with significant numbers of African-American, Latino, and Native American students (current locations include Alaska, California, Idaho, Illinois, Michigan, New York, and Utah), preliminary evaluations indicate statistically significant increase in both math achievement and attitudes toward technology-based careers[4].

CSDT in collaboration with CSCW tools, K-12(Kindergarten – 12th Grade) teachers can be encouraged to share and re-use best practices as a community to emulate the business industry that has highly benefited from sharing best practices through collaboration. For example, this can be seen by implementing how the software development industry that successfully utilizes code re-use during software development through collaboration.

The three main goals of the study: (a) Enhance technical skills of novice users, (b) encourage users to adopt the use the technology for collaboration instead of traditional methods, and (c) to introduce new technical skills to novice computer users. The project provides a source for increasing teaching aide in schools. In addition, develop a gaming convention that keeps the student's attention in the field of mathematics. In addition, it evaluates and validates a tool or framework that can be used to encourage sharing of best practices within a community of practice to steadily benefit and enhance member's career aspirations significantly through CSCW as witnessed in the code-re-use within the software development industry. By tapping into CSCW benefits, K-12 teachers benefit and enhance re-use and collaboration using technology. These areas of study scare most students and keep them away from Computing and IT jobs because this is required in the coursework.

2   What Is the Approach of CSCW

By virtue of the first part of its name, the 'CS' part, the professed objective of CSCW is to support via computers a specific category of work - cooperative work. Therefore, the term computer support seems to convey a commitment to focus on the actual needs and requirements of people engaged in cooperative work. Of course, new technologies of communication and interaction necessarily transform the way people cooperate and CSCW systems are likely to have tremendous impact on existing cooperative work practices. Nonetheless, cooperative work can be conceived as a specific category or aspect of human work with certain fundamental characteristics common to all cooperative work arrangements, irrespective of the technical facilities available now or in the future.

By virtue of its commitment to support cooperative work, CSCW should not be defined in terms of the techniques being applied. CSCW is a research area aimed at the design of application systems for a specific category of work – cooperative work, in all its forms. Like any other application area, CSCW, in its search for applicable techniques, potentially draws upon the whole field of computer science and information technology. Accordingly, a technology-driven approach to CSCW inevitably dilutes the field. To some extent, the current lack of unity of the CSCW field bears witness to that.

CSCW, in a sense, should be conceived as an endeavor to understand the nature and requirements of cooperative work with the objective of designing computer-based technologies for cooperative work arrangements. The fact that multiple individuals, situated in different work settings and situations, with different responsibilities, perspectives and propensities, interact and are mutually dependent in the conduct of their work has important implications for the design of computer systems intended to support them in this effort.

The objective of social science contributions to CSCW should not be to cash in on the new wave and do what they have always done but rather to explore exactly how insights springing from studies of cooperative work relations might be applied and exploited in the design of useful CSCW systems. This demand not only raises the issue of how to utilize insights already achieved in related fields to influence the design process. It raises more fundamental issues such as: Which are the pertinent questions being pursued in field studies and evaluations for the findings to be of utility to designers? And how are the findings to be conceptualized? If CSCW is to be taken seriously, the basic approach of CSCW research should not be descriptive but constructive.

On the other hand, as a research area devoted to exploring and meeting the support requirements of real world cooperative work arrangements, CSCW requires that technologists extend out from a strict technical focus and investigate how their artifacts are, or could be, used and appropriated in actual settings. In short, the drive of CSCW should be directed towards designing systems embodying an ever-deepening understanding of the nature of cooperative work forms and practices.

While this conceptualization of the general approach does recommend the CSCW field to focus on understanding the nature of cooperative work so as to better support people in their cooperative efforts, it does not prescribe a particular research strategy. Of course, field studies of cooperative work in diverse domains with the objective of identifying the research requirements of various kinds and aspects of cooperative work is much needed, but the design and application of experimental CSCW systems may also yield deep and valid insights into the nature and requirements of cooperative work. [3]

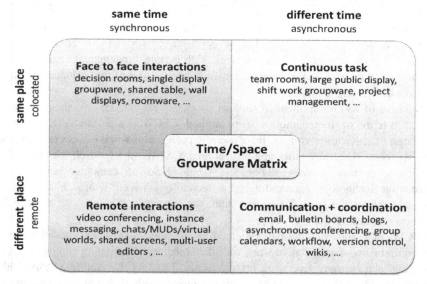

Fig. 1. Computer Supported Collaborative Work Matrix. (Source: Johansen, R. 1988 "Groupware: Computer Support for Business Teams" The Free Press.)

3   Preliminary Data Analysis

The study conducted surveyed 33 teachers in North Carolina city schools with different backgrounds and levels of education using a forum based prototype system. The surveyed group filled the usability survey to express their experiences of the system. The results were encouraging since 70% of those surveyed felt that a forum type virtual tool would be good for K-12 education and expressed confidence in using the proposed tool to teach if it were available. To confirm and validate the preliminary results, this study extends the previous study and focuses on creating a secure and user-friendly environment for a community of practice to share best practices. The proposed system would require the three to entangle to safety and privacy of the community members while on line. For the success of the system, the stakeholder's opinion weighs heavily on the adoption and usability of the system. As stakeholders evaluate the system, they give their opinions and suggestions to improve chances for the future adoption and improved usability of the system. The primary objective of the study were to address the following:

1. Investigate educational tools that are currently available to facilitate and supplement traditional classroom learning.
2. Design an educational style learning environment to provide educators and students with the ability to use and online system that is interactive and open to students.
3. Determine if the educational prototype environment improves effectiveness of educators by providing more interactive lessons and more collaboration among the teaching community.

Participant Experiment Number	Group	Interaction
1	Experiment	CSCW Environment
	Control	------
2	Experiment	CSCW Environment
	Control	--------

Fig. 2. Example Data Table

4 Results

From the preliminary analysis, we gathered that there is a venue for improvement on CSCW networks and teachers would want to use this avenue. It will source teachers with a learning avenue that can pull teachers and students into one unit and encourage collaboration from a broader perspective. Teachers saw this method as a way to resource presentation and increase the usage of educational materials and applications among community of instructors and students. Moreover, grab the attention of students in the early stages before entering a college career. This, in turn, raise the interests of students for these fields and increase retention rate of students going into these areas during their future college careers. Furthermore, raise the awareness of educational tools and bring in alternate form of teaching for the instructor.

The outcome of this research is to have created a novel approach on how to create CSCW environment that attract teachers and students. This encourages opening doors for a new era of teaching STEM methods to enter the classroom. While HCI has continuously made great strides, there is still always room for development and improvement in our new world of technological advancements. This CSCW environment serves as a catalyst toward the continued development of collaboration among the teaching community and students.

5   Conclusion

This study encourages the learning of a new environment for collaboration within groups of communities of practice. The study produces a tool that can be used with Android, Internet, or Wii. It also focuses on the usability of the tool and by doing a comparative study of its usefulness. The data was gathered from the K-12 teacher population in the initial stages of this study to find out if the study was right for the study group.

Moreover, we implemented a better tool for aiding teachers in K-12 environments, facilitating information to their students in a way that is interactive and engaging without losing the goal of education. This shows that there are uses for informal educational environments in the classrooms that serve as content management systems as well as incorporates some of the social networking community features that students are accustomed to today. Social networking has become the norm in regards to students and using social networking technology to provide more intrinsic motivation to educate them is beneficial to keeping their attention.

Acknowledgments. I would like to extend a heartfelt thanks to Dr. Cheryl Seals for being a great mentor during this research. A special thanks to Dr. Ron Eglash and Curtis Cain, for your support and contributions to the subject matter. I would like to thank my family for their continued support in my research activities. All ideas expressed are through research and solely opinions/conclusions of the authors.

References

1. Preece, J.: Sociabilty and usability in online communities: determining and measuring success. Behavior and Information Technology (2001)
2. Collis, B.A.: Collaborative learning and CSCW: research perspectives for interworked educational environments (1994)
3. Grudin, J.: Computer-Supported Cooperative Work: History and Focus" (May 1994)
4. Eglash, R., Bennett, A.,O'Donnell, C., Jennings, S., Cintorino, M.: Culturally Situated Design Tools: Ethnocomputing from Field Site to Classroom. American Anthropologist, http://www.ccd.rpi.edu/Eglash/csdt/teaching/papers/aa.2006.10 8.2.pdf
5. Eglash, R.: Ethnocomputing with Native American Design. Information Technology and Indigenous People, http://www.ccd.rpi.edu/Eglash/csdt/teaching/papers/indig_it.htm
6. Educational Gaming Has to Engage the Students .... but How? http://edutechie.com/2006/11/29/educational-gaming-how/

A Hybrid Model for an E-learning System Which Develops Metacognitive Skills at Students

Maria Canţer

"Lucian Blaga" University of Sibiu, Sibiu, Romania
mcanter10@yahoo.com

Abstract. One of the goals of academic education is to train students in view of acquiring metacognitive skills, thus becoming self-regulated learners prepared for for lifelong learning. The research in this area has proved that metacognition can be taught and learned and that self-regulation behavior can be guided and constrained by the features of the learning environment. In order to become an educational environment, attractive and at the same time efficient for the students and which would enable students to develop their metacognitive skills, the e-learning system needs continuous improvments. This paper presents a hybrid model of an e-learning system, MEM – Metacognitive E-learning system Model, which aims to develop metacognitive skills in students, based on three learning principles of the InTime model, principles which are adapted from Peter Ewell's point of view regarding the complexity of the learning process, and on the metacognitive regulations.

Keywords: self-regulated learning, metacognitive skills, e-learning system, feedback.

1 Introduction

The e-learning systems need continuous improvements in order to become educational environment, attractive and at the same time efficient for the students, where technology is in service to learners. The designing and development of quality e-learning systems, which aim to develop the student's performance, needs a sound scientific foundation concerning learning theories. But improving students' performance does not imply only their knowledge acquisition, but also developing and improving skills necessary for their future workplace or in their lifelong learning process.

Some of these skills are in connection with metacognition and, as McCombs underlines: "Metacognition is thus a key area of research because it shows that if students learn how to control their thinking they become more autonomous and self-regulated learners."[1]

Most of the e-learning systems are not designed to develop metacognitive skills in students, even if "the online learning environment is characterized with autonomy" [2]; for this reason self-regulation becomes "a critical factor for success in online learning." [2]

S. Yamamoto (Ed.): HIMI/HCII 2013, Part III, LNCS 8018, pp. 9–15, 2013.

2   The Metacognitive E-learning System Model (MEM)

This paper presents a hybrid model of an e-learning system, MEM – Metacognitive E-learning system Model, which aims to develop metacognitive skills in students, based on three learning principles of the InTime model, principles which are adapted from Peter Ewell's point of view regarding the complexity of the learning process.

The MEM is the starting point of a research which tries to prove that in case students use the proposed hybrid e-learning system, we expect them to develop meta-cognitive skills and become a self-regulated learner to a higher extent than the students who use a traditional e-learning system during their learning process.

The three chosen principles from the InTime used in the MEM are:

"- the importance of the incentive as well as the corrective role of Frequent Feedback, which students should get from instructors and peers throughout the learning process;
- feedback will be most effective if it is delivered in an Enjoyable Setting that involves personal interactions and a considerable level of personal support.
- Reflection as a subcomponent of Compelling Situation because as a learner discovers new connections while involved in a compelling situation, Reflection is necessary to reach the point of deeper learning required for this information to be used in future situations." [3]

Concerning metacognition and e-learning, MEM is based on the Metacognitive regulation and takes into account the assertion made by Theo L. Dawson as a conclusion of previous researches that:

"Students who have been taught metacognitive (self-regulated learning) skills learn better than students who have not been taught these skills so it is possible to produce better learners by teaching metacognitive skills.

Metacognitive training can increase students' self-confidence and sense of personal responsibility for their own development and this thing may provide motivation for learning." [4]

The MEM model provides an answer to the questions: How can we help students to develop these skills in an e-learning environment? and How should we organize the systematic feedback provided to the learner in order to develop these skills?

As Lai (2011) points out: "Assessment of metacognition is challenging for a number of reasons: (a) metacognition is a complex construct..." [5] so in my opinion not all skills related to metacognition can be developed in an e-learning environment and due to this, the first version of the MEM model is focused only on some aspects of metacognition, namely those connected with self-regulated learning skills.

The following definition of self-regulation was given by Pintrich and al. (2000): ".....self-regulated learning....is an active, constructive process whereby learners set goals for their learning and then attempt to monitor, regulate, and control their cognition, motivation, and behavior, guided and constrained by their goals and the contextual features in the environment."[6]

Table 1. Connections between metacognitive skills and actions performed by the student

Phases of self-regulatory processes	Metacognitive skills (MS) (Self-regulated learning skills and strategies)	Actions performed by the student (SSp)	Tools used
Performance Phase	Task Strategy (TS)	- filling in **Task Management Checklist** - recording and reporting events and process using blogging tools - uploading the results of a task in time	Blog Checklists Student Portfolio
	Help Seeking (HS)	- asking questions on forum - mailing questions to the teacher/tutor - chatting	Forum E-Mail Chat
	Time Management (TM)	- uploading in time the task/homework - monitoring the time spent in the system - monitoring the time spent on each lesson	Student Portfolio Reports from the system
Self-Reflection Phase	Self-Evaluation (SE)	- filling in self-evaluation forms - posting entries in journal - posting comments to blogs - writing and posting revisions of work	Self-assessment forms Journal Blog

This definition comes to support the MEM model in that it recognizes that self-regulation behavior can be guided and constrained by the features of the learning environment, in our case the e-learning system.

The structure of self-regulatory processes was viewed by Zimmerman et al. (2002) in terms of three cyclical phases "The forethought phase refers to processes and beliefs that occur before efforts to learn; the performance phase refers to processes that occur during behavioral implementation, and self-reflection refers to processes that occur after each learning effort."[7] **These three phases are associated by Barnard-Brak et al. (2010) with** self-regulated learning skills and strategies such as: Task Strategy (TS), Time Management (TM), Help-Seeking (HS) and Self-Evaluation (SE).

They also assert that "Individuals who are self-regulated in their learning appear to achieve more positive academic outcomes than individuals who do not exhibit self-regulated learning behaviors."[8]

During the learning process, in an e-learning environment, a student performs a number of actions and a connection can be established between the self-regulated learning skills that we want to develop in student and these actions; in the Table 1 there are some examples showing these in connection with two phases of self-regulatory processes. For actions in e-learning system we used the Andrew Churches - Bloom`s revised digital taxonomy.

The MEM model is designed in order to improve the student's self-regulated learning skills associated with these two phases and with self-regulated learning skills and strategies from above, by providing periodically feedback, through Feedback Module, based on the actions performed by the student in the system. (Fig.1)

We have x students, for each we propose to develop y metacognitive skills - MS_y.

For each metacognitive skill it is established a desirable level based on activities performed by the students, for example: concerning the reflection, the student must have at least 2 entries in the journal per week. Based on this, a desirable profile of the student is built.

The system will deal with two profiles of the student:

- the desirable profile of the student (DSP) – made according to the desirable level of the metacognitive skills to be reached
- the current profile of the student, updated periodically (SPX) The system has a module, Feedback Module, which monitors the students' actions that are in connection with the metacognitive skills to be developed, and scores them in a data base, in order to obtain the current profile of the student.

Both profiles, the desirable profile of the student (DSP) and the current student profile will be composed from a number of sub-profiles ($SSpX_y$), each in connection with a Metacognitive skill (MS) to be developed; MS_y is in connection with SSp_y (see Table 1).

The student's sub-profile SSp is developed in connection with his/her actions which are being scored (see Table 1). For example, a pertinent question on Forum has a bigger score than a simple question on the Forum, but the sub-profile connected with the inquiring takes also in consideration the activity on the forum, as for example the total number of questions asked by a student.

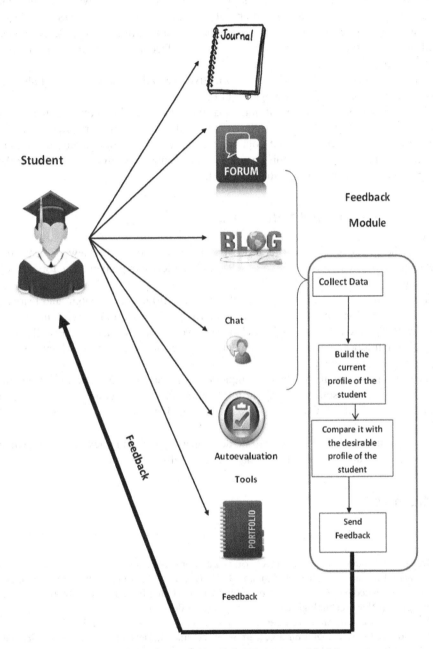

Fig. 1. The Metacognitive E-learning system Model

Each student's current sub-profiles are periodically compared with the desirable level that should have been reached at that moment. For example: if $DSSp_y > SSp1_y$ that means a difference is noticed between the desirable skill level and the developed skill level, and the student number 1 will receive feedback concerning the implied metacognitive skill MS_y.

Based on the same principle and on formative evaluation, the student will also get feedback on the level of knowledge acquired.

The feedback is very important in the learning procces and it is obvious that it can not be provided only by the e-learning system, and this is the reason why the system is hybrid: the feedback is offered both automatically due to programming the system (based on a metacognitive training strategy and Feedback Module), and also by the teacher/tutor and peers, through the same system.

3   Conclusions and Future Work

One of the goals of academic education is to train students in view of acquiring metacognitive skills, thus becoming self-regulated learners prepared for for lifelong learning.

The research in this area has proved that metacognition can be taught and learned, and this can be done in e-learning too, by improving the e-learning environment with new features, which would enable students to develop their metacognitive skills. This paper has introduced such an environment, bringing into attention the Metacognitive E-learning system Model.

The model is now at the stage of implementation and it will be validated on students, from the law school belonging to "Lucian Blaga" University of Sibiu, which attend the seminar of Computer Assisted Instruction, in the second semester of scholar year 2012-2013.

In the future the MEM model will be developed by including new modules, which will have the purpose to enhance metacognitive skills in students.

References

1. McCombs, B.: Developing Responsible and Autonomous Learners: A Key to Motivating Students. American Psychological Association,
   http://www.apa.org/education/k12/learners.aspx
2. Barnard, L., Lan, W.Y., To, M.Y., Paton, O.V., Lai, S.-L.: Measuring self-regulation in online and blended learning environments. Internet and Higher Education 12 (2009)
3. Integrating New Technologies Into the Methods of Education,
   http://www.intime.uni.edu/model/learning/lear.html
4. Dawson, L.T.: Metacognition and learning in adulthood, Developmental Testing Service, LLC (2008), https://dts.lectica.org/PDF/Metacognition.pdf
5. Lai, L.E.: Metacognition: A Literature Review, Pearson's research publications for educators, parents, students, researchers and policy makers (2011),
   http://www.pearsonassessments.com/hai/images/tmrs/
   Metacognition_Literature_Review_Final.pdf

6. Boekaerts, M., Pintrich, P.R., Zeidner, M.: Handbook of self-regulation, p. 453. Academic, San Diego (2000)
7. Zimmerman, J.B.: Becoming a Self-Regulated Learner: An Overview. Theory Into Practice 41(2), 64–70 (2002)
8. Barnard-Brak, L., William, Y., Lan, W.Y., Paton, V.O.: Profiles in Self-Regulated Learning in the Online Learning Environment. The International Review of Research in Open and Distance Learning 11(1) (2010)

Enhancing Information Systems Users' Knowledge and Skills Transference through Self-regulation Techniques

Brenda Eschenbrenner

University of Nebraska at Kearney, Kearney, NE, USA
eschenbrenbl@unk.edu

Abstract. Being able to utilize information systems (IS) to address novel issues continues to be challenging for many IS users. IS training has typically focused on acquiring requisite knowledge and skills to complete routine sets of tasks, and not necessarily transference of this IS knowledge and skills to novel contexts. Being unable to perform this transference can then limit an IS users ability to utilize an IS to address unique problems. Drawing upon Identical Elements and Principles Theories, as well as Social Cognitive Theory, this research study proposes an experiment to assess the effectiveness of utilizing self-regulation techniques (i.e., self-explanations and self-evaluations) to improve IS knowledge and skills transference to unique contexts as well as improve IS performance outcomes. The potential contribution will include suggestions of training modifications to enhance IS usage and providing guidance for future research in the domain of IS users' knowledge and skills transference.

Keywords: IS knowledge transference, IS skills transference, self-regulation techniques, Identical Elements Theory, Principles Theory, Social Cognitive Theory.

1 Introduction

Being able to utilize information systems to solve novel problems or address unique issues is important for many IS users. Although performing routine tasks is necessary, the competitive demands on businesses requires innovative, strategic IS usage. Hence, if IS users are unable to meets these demands, businesses may lose a competitive advantage being sought or one being maintained. However, being capable of doing so requires IS users to apply existing IS knowledge and skills to unique circumstances or situations that are unfamiliar or novel. This can be challenging for those IS users who have not acquired the appropriate cognitive strategies to do so.

IS training has typically focused on IS knowledge and skills acquisition to complete pre-specified tasks or utilize a given set of IS functions. However, when subsequently utilizing IS in their work environment, IS users may struggle to address novel circumstances if they are not capable of applying or transferring their IS knowledge and skills to this new context. Therefore, IS training may consider adding a new component in which IS users are taught strategies to assist with IS knowledge and skills transference.

S. Yamamoto (Ed.): HIMI/HCII 2013, Part III, LNCS 8018, pp. 16–24, 2013.

Previous research has identified the efficacy of techniques such as retention enhancement and symbolic mental rehearsal in the context of developing improvements in software application skills (Davis and Yi, 2004; Yi and Davis, 2003). These skills included rehearsals of specific functions being taught and re-enactments of given sets of tasks, all of which were performed in the same context. Therefore, self-regulated learning techniques have been demonstrated to improve one's knowledge and skills when applied in similar contexts, but what is not clear is the ability to subsequently transfer the acquired IS knowledge and skills to unique circumstances and which self-regulation techniques can facilitate doing so.

Research has noted successful cognitive strategies utilized by IS users included goal-setting, monitoring of learning progression, and self-evaluating levels of comprehension during software training (Gravill and Compeau, 2008). In a decision-making context, suggestions have been made to train the decision maker to utilize appropriate strategies (Payne et al., 1993). Including interventions during training to assist or prompt IS users to reflect on their level of comprehension or explain the materials to themselves to ensure they understand the underlying principles or conceptions may be beneficial in this endeavor of IS knowledge and skills transference. Therefore, research is warranted to identify the potential of self-regulation techniques that can assist IS users in transference of IS knowledge and skills to unique problems or novel situations. Therefore, the research question to be addressed in this proposed research study: Do self-regulation techniques (i.e., self-explanation and self-evaluation) improve IS knowledge and skills transference to novel contexts and improve IS performance outcomes?

To answer this question, this study proposes an experimental study to assess training interventions in which self-evaluations and self-explanations are introduced during software skills training to assist IS users in learning the underlying principles and assumptions, and the overall impact on IS knowledge and skills transference to novel contexts as well as IS performance outcomes.

2   Literature Review and Theoretical Foundation

Previous MIS research has addressed IS knowledge transference from various perspective such as transferring knowledge from IT/IS professionals to users, from consultants to IS users, and between IS users in either an unstructured format or structured, team format (Choi et al., 2010; Ko et al., 2005; Santhanam et al., 2007). However, MIS research is sparse regarding the IS users ability to transfer IS knowledge and skills previously acquired from one context to a dissimilar context. Training is a typical resource utilized to assist IS users in acquiring IS knowledge and skills (Compeau and Higgins, 1995; Sharma and Yetton, 2007) and previous MIS research has studied various factors that influence training outcomes. For instance, research has identified effective trainer behaviors such as training techniques and course design (Compeau, 2002). A paucity of MIS research exists, however, in assessing the application of self-regulation techniques to enhance IS knowledge and skills transference.

Difficulties in learning rich domains have been previously identified (Azevedo, 2005a). However, individuals who were more successful were utilizing more meta-cognitive strategies (Azevedo, 2005b). These strategies included evaluation of one's learning and sense of knowing, as well as self-questioning and monitoring their progress towards achieving their goals, or self-evaluation and self-explanation techniques. To improve knowledge construction and transfer, research has identified the relevance of incorporating variability in problem scenarios to promote thoughtful engagement and motivation (van Merrienboer and Ayres, 2005). Suggestions have also been made to increase interactions with learning materials as well as engage in self-explanations. Also, recommendations have been put forth to explore the potential of prompting individuals to utilize self-explanation or self-constructed explanations in future research (van Merrienboer and Sweller, 2005).

The focus of this research is to assess the influence of self-regulated learning strategies (i.e., self-explanations and self-evaluations) on comprehending underlying principles and transferring existing IS knowledge and skills to novel contexts. Previous MIS research has addressed aspects such as observational learning, symbolizing, and self-efficacy in IS training (e.g., Davis and Yi, 2004), but a paucity of research exists that focuses on enhancing self-regulation mechanisms, in particular self-evaluations and self-explanations. Hence, Identical Elements and Principles Theories are discussed next to address transference of knowledge and skills to different contexts, and Social Cognitive Theory and self-regulated learning literature are discussed subsequently to identify mechanisms (i.e., self-explanation and self-evaluation strategies) that can enhance learning underlying principles and potentially improve knowledge and skills transference.

2.1 Identical Elements and Principles Theories

Identical Elements Theory proposes that transferring knowledge and skills can be facilitated if conditions, inputs, operations, and outcomes in a training context are similar to a subsequent context (Yamnill and McLean, 2001). Essentially, an individual is repeating or practicing applying the knowledge and skills that were acquired. If the *outcome* associated with the application of knowledge and skills to a given set of inputs (e.g., problem variables) is *different* between a training context and a subsequent or new context, then transference is less likely to occur. If the inputs are dissimilar between the training and a novel context, but the *outcomes* are *similar*, trainees are more likely to transfer their knowledge and skills. Therefore, training would need to induce the trainee to apply acquired knowledge and skills to unique sets of inputs that would be associated with or produce identical outcomes. In an IS context, individuals would need opportunities during training to apply their IS knowledge and skills to a context unique to the training context and identify that identical outcomes are achieved.

The ability to transfer knowledge and skills obtained in training to a new context or problem can be influenced by the structure of the training (Yamnill and McLean, 2001). Training is typically focused on acquisition of pivotal knowledge and skills, but not necessarily oriented towards application of this newly acquired knowledge and skill set in a unique or novel context. Hence, modifying the training structure could influence the ability to transfer acquired knowledge and skills to a new context or to solve unique problems. Principles Theory proposes that individuals who have an advanced comprehension of the underlying principles and concepts are more capable of this transference (Yamnill and McLean, 2001). Hence, being able to utilize knowledge and skills in a novel context would first require an individual to understand the rules, principles and assumptions. One potential training structuration modification may entail the introduction of self-regulation techniques, more specifically self-explanation and self-evaluation techniques, to enhance this comprehension of principles and concepts. These techniques may assist individuals in learning the underlying principles and concepts and, therefore, assist them in transferring knowledge and skills to novel contexts. The capability of self-regulation techniques to enhance learning, e.g., comprehension of underlying principles and concepts, is proposed by Social Cognitive Theory.

2.2   Social Cognitive Theory and Previous Research

Bandura's Social Cognitive Theory (which is an extension to Social Learning Theory) provides perspectives on learning (Bandura, 1977, 1986). Social Cognitive Theory (SCT) proposes that human competency and behavior is influenced by the interaction of behavioral, environmental, and cognitive/personal factors. These factors interact as "triadic reciprocal determinants" and influence one's competency or knowledge acquisition and skill development. Another important factor in competency development proposed by SCT is self-efficacy, or one's judgment of their abilities.

SCT proposes that learning occurs through various mechanisms. One such mechanism is the application of one's own cognitive capabilities, which includes self-regulation techniques. Bandura (1991) argues that "human behavior is extensively motivated and regulated by the ongoing exercise of self-influence" (p. 248). Self-regulated learning has been defined as "the learning that results from students' self-generated thoughts and behaviors that are systematically oriented toward the attainment of their learning goals" (Schunk, 2001, p. 125). The three-phase self-regulation model proposes three phases that occur during self-regulation: forethought, performance control, and self-reflection. Forethought entails goal-setting and social modeling. Performance control includes social comparisons, attributional feedback, as well as strategy instruction. Self-reflection encompasses monitoring one's performance and self-evaluating.

SCT has been utilized in various MIS studies that focused on training and learning computer applications. For example, research has assessed the influence of various training styles (e.g., behavioral and observational modeling, symbolic mental rehearsal, and retention enhancement techniques) on self-efficacy, outcome expectations, and subsequent technology-usage performance (Compeau and Higgins, 1995; Davis and Yi, 2004; Yi and Davis, 2001; Yi and Davis, 2003). Previous MIS studies have also identified a variety of self-regulated learning strategies being utilized by participants of a software training session (Gravill, 2004; Gravill and Compeau, 2008). These strategies were found to be significantly related to learning outcomes (which included declarative and procedural knowledge, as well as self-efficacy). Some of the more salient strategies identified were associated with participants who considered the relevancy of what they were learning to complete a task, self-assessed to identify material they didn't master and made adjustments to their learning strategies, monitored their comprehension and the areas needing improvement, evaluated their level of understanding during the training and making sure it was mastered before progressing, and assessed their knowledge and skills acquisition during the training.

Hence, the results suggest that participants were conducting self-regulated learning activities (e.g., self-explanations and self-evaluations). For instance, "I tried to determine the things I didn't understand well and adjusted my learning strategies accordingly." (Gravill, 2004, p. 154). Therefore, an intervention of self-regulated techniques, i.e., self-explanation and self-evaluation, may provide the mechanisms needed for knowledge and skills transference which is proposed in this research study. Previously, self-explanations, operationalized as self-verbalizations, have been found to support learning. For example, students who self-constructed verbalizations of strategies had higher levels of motivation and self-efficacy, as well as improved performance outcomes (Schunk, 1982; Schunk and Cox, 1986). Students who utilized completed examples and self-explanations to solve problems improved performance outcomes and self-efficacy (Crippen and Earl, 2007). This research focuses specifically on self-explanation and self-evaluation and proposes that these self-regulation techniques can be utilized to improve the transference of IS knowledge and skills to novel circumstances and contexts by enhancing the comprehension of underlying principles and assumptions.

In summary, Identical Elements and Principles Theories suggest that fostering the capability to transfer knowledge and skills acquired during training to novel contexts or problems can be accomplished through the structure of training. In particular, transference may be facilitated if individuals comprehend underlying principles and concepts. Social Cognitive Theory proposes that learning can occur through individual cognitive factors, such as self-regulated learning techniques. Hence, self-regulated learning techniques (specifically, self-explanation and self-evaluation techniques) are proposed to improve IS knowledge and skills transference to unique contexts and IS performance outcomes by enhancing the comprehension of underlying principles and concepts.

The following hypotheses are proposed.

H1: IS knowledge and skills transference are greater when users are prompted to utilize self-regulated learning strategies.

H1a: IS knowledge and skills transference are greater when users are prompted to utilize self-explanation strategies.

H1b: IS knowledge and skills transference are greater when users are prompted to utilize self-evaluation strategies.

H1c: IS knowledge and skills transference are greater when users are prompted to utilize both self-explanation and self-evaluation strategies than with just one strategy or no strategy.

3   Research Method

A 2 x 2 experimental design is proposed (see Table 1). The subjects will either receive training for conducting self-explanations, self-evaluations, or both, as well as Microsoft Access training. A control group will only have Microsoft Access training. Each subject will be randomly assigned to one of the four conditions.

Table 1. Treatment Conditions

Self-Explanation only	Both Self-Explanation and Self-Evaluation
Neither Self-Explanation and Self-Evaluation	Self-Evaluation only

3.1   Subjects

Students from Introduction to Management Information Systems classes will be recruited. These students should have no previous experience with Microsoft Access (i.e., creating a query), but the results for those that do will be excluded from the final data analysis. Students who participate will have their names entered into a drawing for a $25 cash prize. To incentivize students to perform well, those students earning a grade of 80% or better on both the exercises and quiz will be entered into a pool to win a $100 cash prize.

3.2   Procedures and Measures

Subjects will first complete a demographic questionnaire which will include measurements of self-efficacy, previous experience with computers and Microsoft Access, existing database knowledge, GPA, and need for cognition. They will then receive the appropriate training based on the condition that they were assigned (see Table 1), or a brief history of Microsoft Access for subjects in the control group (i.e., Neither Self-explanation and Self-Evaluation) so time is consistent between conditions. Subjects in a self-explanation condition will be asked to reflect on the knowledge and skills that they just acquired and to consider how this can be applied to solve a novel problem or how it can be applied in a unique context. Hence, subjects are asked to reflect on the underlying principles and assumptions, and then to apply conceptual knowledge versus memorize or repeat it.

Subjects in the self-evaluation condition will be asked to rate their comprehension of the underlying principles as well as their knowledge and skills (in the context of their ability to apply these to a future task) on a scale of 1 to 7, with 1 being novice and 7 being master. Therefore, self-explanation prompts subjects to elaborate on their comprehension and self-evaluation prompts subjects to judge their comprehension, as well as knowledge and skills. This training will be followed by a brief period (i.e., 5 minutes) to practice self-explanation and/or self-evaluation techniques. Next, they will complete Microsoft Access training.

After the training, subjects will need to complete a set of exercises with Microsoft Access (measuring procedural knowledge), a quiz (measuring declarative knowledge), and a final questionnaire (which is to include a manipulation check). Training, exercises, and quizzes will be administered through an online training application. The exercises will be tailored such that subjects will need to apply the IS knowledge and skills acquired through training in a novel context. For instance, subjects will be taught how to create and run a query, but will then be asked to identify the number of purchases of a specific item from a given vendor such that subjects have to apply what they previously learned to answer the question or complete the exercise. Hence, IS knowledge and skills transference will be essential.

Grading will be automatically completed with the online training software. The final questionnaire will include questions regarding self-efficacy (judging their abilities to utilize Microsoft Access as well as their abilities to conduct self-explanation and self-evaluation), satisfaction with the training(s), perception of challenge and performance, perceived ease of use, perceived usefulness, and future intentions to utilize Microsoft Access and the self-regulated learning techniques. Analysis of the effects of the training interventions will be assessed using factorial ANOVA.

4   Conclusion and Implications

In summary, utilizing IS in novel contexts can be challenging for IS users. Based on propositions of Identical Elements and Principles Theories as well as Social Cognitive Theory, this research plans to address this issue by assessing the efficacy of self-regulation techniques to enhance transference of IS knowledge and skills to novel contexts by enhancing the comprehension of the underlying principles and concepts. The results of this study may provide suggestions to practitioners regarding the feasibility of these interventions to improve IS knowledge and skills transference, as well improve IS performance outcomes. Hence, IS users may be able to utilize IS more effectively to solve unique problems or address novel situations.

Theoretical implications will include extending Identical Elements and Principles Theories into the domain of IS research by elaborating on techniques that can assist with IS knowledge and skills transference in novel contexts. Also, this study extends Social Cognitive Theory, specifically improving one's IS proficiency in novel contexts through self-regulation techniques (i.e., self-explanations and self-evaluation). Therefore, this study extends upon previous MIS research which has assessed other mechanisms (e.g., retention enhancement) to improve IS learning and performance outcomes. This research may also provide guidance for future studies that focus on IS knowledge and skills transference or IS training. Limitations of this research include training with one software application, (i.e., Microsoft Access). Hence, future research can test the generalizability of the results to other contexts, such as expert or decision-support systems. In conclusion, the findings may pose interesting insights into the utility of self-regulation techniques enhancing the transference of IS knowledge and skills to novel circumstances and, ultimately, improving IS usage and performance outcomes.

Acknowledgment. I gratefully acknowledge the reviewers and participants at the 2009 Americas Conference on Information Systems Doctoral Consortium who provided helpful and insightful feedback on a previous version of this paper.

References

1. Azevedo, R.: Computer Environments as Metacognitive Tools for Enhancing Learning. Educational Psychologist 40(4), 193–197 (2005a)
2. Azevedo, R.: Using Hypermedia as a Metacognitive Tool for Enhancing Student Learning? The Role of Self-regulated Learning. Educational Psychologist 40(4), 199–209 (2005b)
3. Bandura, A.: Social Learning Theory. Prentice-Hall, New Jersey (1977)
4. Bandura, A.: Social Foundations of Thought and Action: A Social Cognitive Theory. Prentice Hall, New Jersey (1986)
5. Bandura, A.: Social Cognitive Theory of Self-regulation. Organizational Behavior and Human Decision Processes 50(2), 248–287 (1991)
6. Choi, S.Y., Lee, H., Yoo, Y.: The Impact of Information Technology and Transactive Memory Systems on Knowledge Sharing, Application, and Team Performance: A Field Study. MIS Quarterly 34(4), 855–870 (2010)
7. Compeau, D.: The Role of Trainer Behavior in End User Software Training. Journal of End User Computing 14(1), 23–32 (2002)
8. Compeau, D., Higgins, C.A.: Application of Social Cognitive Theory to Training for Computer Skills. Information Systems Research 6(2), 118–143 (1995)
9. Crippen, K.J., Earl, B.L.: The Impact of Web-based Worked Examples and Self-explanation on Performance, Problem Solving, and Self-efficacy. Computers & Education 49(3), 809–821 (2007)
10. Davis, F., Yi, M.: Improving Computer Skill Training: Behavior Modeling, Symbolic Mental Rehearsal, and the Role of Knowledge Structures. Journal of Applied Psychology 89(3), 509–523 (2004)
11. Gravill, J.I.: Self-regulated Learning Strategies and Computer Software Training. Doctoral Dissertation, University of Western Ontario, Canada, AAT NR00329 (2004)
12. Gravill, J., Compeau, D.: Self-regulated Learning Strategies and Software Training. Information & Management 45(5), 288–296 (2008)
13. Ko, D.-G., Kirsch, L.J., King, W.R.: Antecedents of Knowledge Transfer from Consultants to Clients in Enterprise System Implementations. MIS Quarterly 29(1), 59–85 (2005)
14. Payne, J.W., Bettman, J.R., Johnson, E.J.: The Adaptive Decision Maker. Cambridge University Press, New York (1993)
15. Santhanam, R., Seligman, L., Kang, D.: Postimplementation Knowledge Transfers to Users and Information Technology Professionals. Journal of Management Information Systems 24(1), 171–199 (2007)
16. Schunk, D.H.: Verbal Self-regulation as a Facilitator of Children's Achievement and Self-efficacy. Human Learning, 265–277 (1982)
17. Schunk, D.H.: Social Cognitive Theory and Self-regulated Learning. In: Zimmerman, B.J., Schunk, D.H. (eds.) Self-regulated Learning and Academic Achievement, 2nd edn., pp. 125–151. Lawrence Erlbaum Associates Inc., Mahwah (2001)
18. Schunk, D.H., Cox, P.D.: Strategy Training and Attributional Feedback with Learning Disabled Students. Journal of Educational Psychology 78(3), 201–209 (1986)

19. Sharma, R., Yetton, P.: The Contingent Effects of Training, Technical Complexity, and Task Interdependence on Successful Information Systems Implementation. MIS Quarterly 31(2), 219–238 (2007)
20. van Merrienboer, J.J.G., Ayres, P.: Research on Cognitive Load Theory and its Design Implications for E-learning. Educational Technology Research & Development 53(2), 5–13 (2005)
21. van Merrienboer, J.J.G., Sweller, J.: Cognitive Load Theory and Complex Learning: Recent Developments and Future Directions. Educational Psychology Review 17(2), 147–177 (2005)
22. Yamnill, S., McLean, G.N.: Theories Supporting Transfer of Training. Human Resource Development Quarterly 12(2), 195–208 (2001)
23. Yi, M., Davis, F.: Improving Computer Training Effectiveness for Decision Technologies: Behavior Modeling and Retention Enhancement. Decision Sciences 32(3), 521–544 (2001)
24. Yi, M.Y., Davis, F.D.: Developing and Validating an Observational Learning Model of Computer Software Training and Skill Acquisition. Information Systems Research 14(2), 146–169 (2003)

Articulating an Experimental Model for the Study of Game-Based Learning

Christina Frederick-Recascino, Dahai Liu, Shawn Doherty,
Jason Kring, and Devin Liskey

Department of Human Factors and Systems, Embry-Riddle Aeronautical University
Daytona Beach, Florida, 32119, USA
{christina.frederick,dahai.liu,shawn.doherty,
jason.kring}@erau.edu, liskeyd@my.erau.edu

Abstract. Research related to game-based and technology-enhanced learning lacks a focused experimental method. The present paper articulates a well-defined experimental method for studying game-based learning from pre-learning interventions to post-testing assessment of retention and transfer.

Keywords: Game-Based Learning, Game-Based Testing, Experimental Model.

1 Introduction

There is growing interest in the application of video games to teach, educate, and train. In the military, for example, researchers are modifying commercial games to train soldiers on strategy and interpersonal skills like communication and team coordination [19][26]. In the academic domain, game-based activities are appearing in grades from kindergarten through high school. For instance, Muehrer, Jenson, Friedberg, and Husain [23] found secondary science students performed better on quizzes after playing a science-focused video game in comparison to pre-game scores. This evolving area offers an interesting and socially-relevant topic for HCI research. Numerous Journals are already devoted to this topic or focus their content heavily in this area (e.g., International Journal of Computer Game Research, Journal of Computer Assisted Learning, Computers and Education, Computers in Human Behavior, etc.). The underlying assumption of game-based learning research seems to be that: 1) educational content can be presented within computer games, 2) the context of learning within a highly- interactive gaming environment is engaging to the learner, and 3) learning outcomes associated with game-based learning will be equal to or perhaps superior to traditional presentation of information [7][16][24].

While some or all of these assumptions may be supported, the research related to game-based learning lacks a cohesive experimental focus with which to examine fundamental research about relationships between the game-based context of learning and performance outcomes associated with it. In 2011, Boot, Blakely and Simons drew the same conclusion in a review of the literature examining cognitive outcomes associated with gaming [5]. In their paper, Boot et al. made four recommendations

S. Yamamoto (Ed.): HIMI/HCII 2013, Part III, LNCS 8018, pp. 25–32, 2013.
© Springer-Verlag Berlin Heidelberg 2013

to improve the study of gaming outcomes, including enhancing the articulation of the methods in future studies. It was found from previous the studies that systematic methods and models addressing the effectiveness of game-based learning are extremely limited. This paper presents a systematic and rigorous experimental model for the study of game-based learning. This lays out a framework to incorporate the different factors in game-based learning experiments and method will allow for greater coordination of research efforts and the ability to determine when and how game-based learning leads to effective educational performance. As shown in Figure 1, our basic model for examining game-based learning is simple in design but we believe an important first step in defining a sound empirical approach to uncovering key relationships. The remainder of this paper will focus on defining each of the pieces of the method and defining the variables of study within each element.

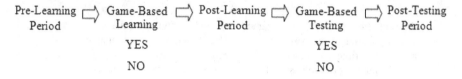

Fig. 1. Proposed Model for Experimental Study of Game-Based Learning

2   Primary Elements: Game-Based Learning and Game-Based Testing

2.1   Elements of Proposed Model

The primary elements of this experimental model are 1) the context in which learning occurs (non-game-based learning vs. game-based learning), 2) the context in which testing occurs (non-game-based testing vs. game-based testing), and 3) the importance of pre- and post-learning measurement of learning achievement or performance.. These elements are important because studies to date have primarily focused upon only the context in which learning occurs. However, research in psychology has shown that learning and its consequent requirement for retrieval can often be context and state dependent [8]. By creating a method that acknowledges the interdependence of learning and testing, findings from empirical studies will have greater generalizability in educational settings. In addition, it is critical to show the change in learning achievement or performance after game-based manipulations with the pre/post test comparison.

Furthermore, it is important to define the variables that might be included or varied within the game-based learning context. Researchers can systematically examine factors such as the type of game used (fantasy, Massively Multiplayer Online Roleplaying Game [MMORPG], social, first-person shooter [FPS], etc.), the domain of learning material embedded within the game (history, math, science), the nature of knowledge presented (declarative, procedural or semantic), as well as factors such as age of the learner, gender of the learner, or usability of the game. Perhaps surprisingly, little research has examined the actual learning environment in gaming. Baker [2] explored the role of the teacher or instructor with technology-enhanced learning, concluding that instructors in this type of learning environment who were perceived as warm and involved positively influenced student perceptions of the class and effectiveness of the learning. Jim [14] and Mayer [20] discussed the need for active learner engagement in an online learning environment rather than passive presentation of information using technology. However, active engagement does need to be purposeful and structured so that the learner does not become confused or overwhelmed by technology to the detriment of learning. Bloom [4] also supports these conclusions adding that game-based learning rather than passive presentation of material via technology can enhance learner engagement. An intriguing finding that contradicts the belief that active game-based learning can be positive for the learner comes from a study by [1]. They found that students participating in a narrative-based game environment to learn did not show any differences in performance than students whose learning was presented in more passively presented learning modules that had no associated story line.

Likewise, the second factor in the model, how testing occurs, includes variables such: as accuracy of performance, the manner in which performance is assessed (recall, recognition or transfer of training), speed of performance, as well as also considering variables such as gender, age and past ability of the learner for the same subject matter. What is fascinating is that to-date we found no studies that focus on how testing is conducted. Specifically, the current model advocates that within game-based learning studies, how testing occurs (within a similar, game-based learning context or not) may influence the results found in these studies. For instance, if game-based learning occurs within a MMORPG should testing also occur within an MMORPG in order to truly assess performance? What happens when learning occurs within the game but the testing environment occurs via a traditional paper and pencil test? Examining all the variations of context within game-based learning and testing will allow researchers to understand technology-enhanced learning environments and create new ones in the future that maximize learning effectiveness. Overall, we advocate for rigorous adherence to this basic experimental method. It will allow for systematic program of research with each study building upon the next and providing a more complete picture of how and when game-based learning is effective.

2.2 Critical Time Periods within the Model

Within the model presented there are also three time periods during which further experimental manipulations can occur to provide an even clearer picture about game-based learning outcomes. The first time period, the pre-learning period, specifies the period prior to learner exposure to a game-based environment. During this period, researchers can investigate the effectiveness of interventions that may influence learning. Some of these can include introducing positive or negative learning expectations, presenting study techniques that may facilitate learning, or even creating a positive or negative mood state in the learner. Some research has focused attention on the pre-learning environment with a focus on the motivational context of learning. Li, Heh, Chen, Wang and Yeh [18] defined three possible motivational contexts that could be created and studied in a gaming context. The first context described as a structured form of autonomy allows players to act freely in a game however limits and directs players to pursue certain desired elements within the game. The second context focuses on creating a motivational gaming environment that acknowledges learning through game-based rewards. The last motivational context focuses on social interaction within the game as a tool to enhance learning. Any of these three motivational environments can be created in game-based learning to compare and contrast their effectiveness in facilitating user learning. Other research studies, rather than establishing a specific motivational climate for game play, focus on understanding the motivational attributes of players prior to entering into actual play. For instance, Jiau, Chen and Ssu [13] and Kong, Kwok and Fang [15] examined differences in extrinsic and intrinsic motivation of players and how these orientations may even factor into team game play. Similarly, Bartle [3] and Lazzaro [17] advocate for grouping players based on their motivational styles and then structuring the game-based learning environment such that challenges and outcomes are different based on initial player motivation. Both Bartle and Lazzaro identified similar player motivational styles that included social players, goal-oriented players, exploratory/fun-based players and winner-take-all players that Bartle referred to as "killers" [3][17].

Yelverton [26] based his work on Dweck's [11] work on goal orientation advocated for establishing pre-learning goals that players must achieve, believing that a strong goal orientation will facilitate learning. Yelverton also acknowledges, however, that creation of a game-based learning environment that establishes public performance goals can be detrimental to learning for individuals who do not want their performance judged by others. In addition, past learning studies have shown that placing substantial focus on performance rather than the process of learning can lead to reduced effectiveness [25][27]. In summary, studies that focus on varying the context of the pre-learning phase of the proposed model can focus on player-based elements of gaming such as motivational styles or player expectations.

The second time period, called the post-learning period, occurs immediately after the learning phase. Again, researchers can systematically study how manipulations occurring during this period may reinforce the learning that has occurred. For example, these may include such activities as: having students read a summary of what they just learned, having students discuss what they learned with a partner or group, or changing the mood state of the learner. Research focusing on post-learning outcomes has examined issues related to how review and practice intervals or spaced learning can impact performance [9][10][12]. Sharing game-related performance data with the player can also allow the learner in his/her next session to better focus on areas of weakness or underperformance in order to facilitate learning. Providing feedback through performance metrics that can be presented visually or in textual forms can assist in creating a more self-directed learner [13][22]. Medler likens player feedback to the statistics that are painstakingly kept and used in professional sports.

A game-based learning "dossier" can be developed with information comparing an individual's current performance to his/her past performance, to group-level performance or to a pre-determined standard of achievement. Each type of comparison and the manner in which the comparison information is presented and shared is a rich area for study in and of itself.

The last time period defined in the model is referred to as the post-testing period. Typically studies end once performance has been exhibited. However, for learning to be truly effective it must be permanent. Acquisition of basic skills and concepts must occur for successful acquisition of more complex skills and concepts in the future. In addition, it is also desirable in some learning situations for skill acquisition to transfer to similar environments and situations. Thus, the learner has to acquire not only the basic skill or knowledge required in the present, but he/she also has to learn when and where it is beneficial to apply the knowledge in the future. The post-testing period can be studied empirically to engage in longitudinal examinations of knowledge, retention and skill transfer.

3   Measures of Game-Based Learning Experiments

One reason for the lack of research in assessing outcomes associated with game-based learning likely stems from the difficulty of measuring performance in game-based learning tasks. Unlike those studies conducted in controlled laboratories, game-based learning is often conducted as a field study in a realistic environment. There are numerous factors that could confound the results. The nature of the dynamic environment adds difficulty for an objective measurement of the outcome.

Establishing criteria for evaluation and assessment of game-based learning tasks is essential in understanding the process of learning in a gaming environment overall. Currently, there is limited research that describes the type of learning, amount of learning and more importantly, the process of how learning occurs in the game environment. What is needed is an understanding of the whole picture of game-based learning, with respect to the effect of different type of games on type of skill and knowledge, and an objective metric to assess the learning outcome in general.

Typical learning outcome measures for game-based learning include:

- Amount of knowledge/skills acquired: To measure whether a person knows something after the learning process, a practical assessment is to compile tests that are representative of the topics learned. Tests could include multiple-choice based or open-ended questions. A second approach is to have the participants provide self-assessment for their level of the understanding of the knowledge, or ask a subject matter expert to evaluate the participant directly without giving a test. The third way to measure learning especially for group learning tasks is to use an anthropological approach to estimate the knowledge of each participant by measuring the pattern of performance consistent among those persons in the same group [6].
- Time taken to learn: There is sometimes a trade-off effect between amount of learning that has occurred and time taken to learn something. However, when

learning efficiency is a factor, time taken to learn something is a critical performance measure for   game-based learning tasks.

- Learning transfer: In either the pre-testing or post-testing phase, measuring the amount of learning that is transferred to a similar task is an important assessment of retention of knowledge.   A positive transfer indicates game-based learning facilitates new learning compared to a traditional learning method. The measure of transfer of learning depends largely on the type of learning tasks involved. Commonly used formula include:

  o Percent transfer. This can be expressed as

$$\frac{Y_t - Y_g}{Y_t} \times \% \tag{1}$$

  where Y_g is the performance measured after the game-based learning post-test and Y_t is the performance for a general test on the subject matter. The learning occurring   in the game-based environment is expected to be transferred positively to performance on a general test.

  o First shot performance (FSP). First shot performance measures the immediate performance after the learning is completed. That is,

$$FSP = \frac{Y_f - Y_L}{Y_f - Y_t} \tag{2}$$

  where Y_1 is the beginning performance of the game-based learning and Y_L is the ending performance of the game-based learning. This measures how much learning is retained on the first transference to a general test on the subject matter.

  o Learning retained (LR). Learning retained measures how much learning is retained on the first post-test trial from the game-based learning compared with that gained from a nongame-based learning.

$$LR = \frac{Y_t - Y_L}{Y_t - Y_{NL}} \tag{3}$$

  where Y_{NL} is the last performance measure for the non-game-based learning

- Assessment of the learning experience. A positive learning experience is believed to facilitate the learning outcome. The learning process and experience can be assessed by using observation, survey, interview or questionnaire, to evaluate the overall experience during, including the flow, usability and workload for the learner.

4   Conclusion

In summary, we advocate for the creation of a rigorous experimental method for the study of game-based learning. The model presented herein offers a comprehensive experimental paradigm to examine the relationship between game-based learning and game-based testing contexts. Further information is infused into the paradigm by introducing systematic manipulation of variables occurring at three different time periods, before, during and after game-based learning or game-based testing occurs. It is only with experimental rigor that researchers, from a multitude of disciplines (education, psychology, human factors, computer science), can assess when, how, and for whom game-based learning is effective and how to optimize the learning environment for the students of today and tomorrow.

References

1. Adams, D.M., Mayer, R.E., MacNamara, A., Koenig, A., Wainess, R.: Narrative Games for Learning: Testing the Discovery and Narrative Hypotheses. Journal of Educational Psychology 104, 235–249 (2012)
2. Baker, C.: The Impact of Instructor Immediacy and Presence for Online Student
3. Affective Learning, Cognition, and Motivation. The Journal of Educators Online 7, 1–30 (2010)
4. Bartle, R.: Hearts, Clubs, Diamonds, Spades: Players Who Suit MUDs. Journal of MUD Research 1, 1 (1996)
5. Bloom, S.: Game-Based Learning: Using Video Game Design for Safety Training. Journal of American Society of Safety Engineers 53(8), 18–21 (2009)
6. Boot, W.R., Blakely, D.P., Simons, D.J.: Do Action Video Games Improve Perception and Cognition? Frontiers in Psychology 2, 1–6 (2011)
7. Borgatti, S.P., Carboni, I.: Measuring Individual Knowledge in Organizations. Organizational Research Methods 10(3), 449–462 (2007)
8. Bower, G.H., Monteiro, K.P., Gilligan, S.G.: Emotional Mood as a Context for Learning and Recall. Journal of Verbal Learning & Verbal Behavior 17, 573–585 (1978)
9. Burguillo, J.: Using Game Theory and Competition-Based Learning to Stimulate Student Motivation and Performance. Computers & Education 55, 566–576 (2010)
10. Cepeda, N., Pashler, H., Vul, E., Wixted, J.T., Rohrer, D.: Distributed Practice in Verbal Recall Tasks: A Review and Quantitative Synthesis. Psychological Bulletin 132, 354–380 (2006)
11. Donovan, J., Radosevich, D.: A Meta-Analytic Review of the Distribution of Practice Effect. Journal of Applied Psychology 84, 795–805 (1999)
12. Dweck, C.: Motivational Processes Affecting Learning. American Psychologist 41(10), 1040–1048 (1986)
13. Janiszewski, C., Noel, H., Sawyer, A.: A Meta-Analysis of the Spacing Effect in Verbal Learning: Implications for Research on Advertising Repetition and Consumer Memory. Journal of Consumer Research 30, 138–149 (2003)
14. Jiau, H., Chen, J., Ssu, K.: Enhancing Self-Motivation in Learning Programming Using Game-Based Simulation and Metrics. IEEE Transactions on Education 52(4), 555–562 (2009)
15. Jim, K.: Stimulation collaboration and discussion in online learning environments. Internet and Higher Education 4, 119–124 (2001)
16. Kong, J., Kwok, R., Fang, Y.: The Effects of Peer Intrinsic and Extrinsic Motivation on MMOG Game-Based Collaborative Learning. Information & Management 49(1), 1–9 (2012)

17. Kuo, M.-J.: How Does an On-line Game Based Learning Environment Promote Students Intrinsic Motivation for Learning Natural Science and How Does it Affect Their Performance? In: First IEEE International Workshop on Digital Game and Intelligent Toy Enhanced Learning (DIGITEL 2007), pp. 135–142. IEEE Press, New York (2001)
18. Lazzaro, N.: Why we Play Games: Four Keys to More Emotion Without Storys. XEODesign Inc., http://www.xeodesign.com/xeodesign_whyweplaygames.pdf
19. Li, K., Huang, J., Heh, J., Chen, C., Wang, H., Yeh, S.: Designing Game-Based Learning Framework - A Motivation-Driven Approach. In: 10th Proceedings of the IEEE International Conference on Advanced Learning Technologies, pp. 215–216. IEEE Computer Society, Washington, DC (2010)

Psychophysiological Assessment Tools for Evaluation of Learning Technologies

Richard H. Hall, Nicholas S. Lockwood, and Hong Sheng

Department of Business and Information Technology,
Missouri University of Science and Technology, Rolla, Missouri
{rhall,lockwoodn,hsheng}@mst.edu

Abstract. Research on the psychophysiological assessment of the impact of information technologies on humans is reviewed, with a particular focus on learning technologies and research carried out in in the Laboratory for Information Technology Evaluation (LITE) at Missouri S&T. Measures of arousal and valence are discussed first, including galvanic skin response (GSR), pupil dilation, and heart rate. This is followed by a discussion of the measurement of eye movement using eye tracking technologies. Lastly, a summary of the LITE lab research is provided. It is concluded that the measures are promising, based on these initial LITE lab results, though further work is needed to more accurately determine the appropriate constructs and contexts for optimizing the use of these tools.

Keywords: Learning Technologies, Psychophysiological Measurement.

1 Introduction

1.1 Psychophysiological Assessment of Learning Strategies

In recent years researchers have expanded their assessment tools for evaluating the impact of technologies on humans to include an array of psychophysiological measures, primarily measures of sympathetic nervous system activity such as heart rate, skin conductance, and pupil dilation. There are a number of reasons for this increased interest in these types of indices. First, subjective measures tend to be post-hoc, relying on learners' memories, or they interfere with experimental tasks, requiring a learner to interrupt an activity to provide self-report. Second, psychophysiological measures are particularly sensitive to the fleeting and non-conscious nature of emotional experience [1]. Third, advances in technology, have made data collection using psychophysiological measurement tools more efficient and user friendly [2]. There is a growing body of evidence that these tools can be more sensitive to some emotional experience than self report [3].

S. Yamamoto (Ed.): HIMI/HCII 2013, Part III, LNCS 8018, pp. 33–42, 2013.

1.2   Laboratory for Information Technology Evaluation

Missouri University of Science and Technology's Laboratory for Information Technology Evaluation (LITE) was founded in 1999. Since that time, LITE lab researchers have carried out a number of large and small-scale assessments of the impact of technologies on humans, with a particular focus on learning technologies. These projects have been sponsored by a number of external funding agencies such as the National Science Foundation; the U.S. Department of Defense, Department of Education, and Department of Energy; and the National Institute for Occupational Safety and Health. Results have been disseminated widely in the literature [4-7].

The LITE lab evaluations have been guided by a principal assumption that user responses are most accurately represented through the triangulation of data, based on multiple measurement and experimental approaches [4]. These measures have always included alternatives to traditional learning measures, such as indices of emotion. In recent years this has included a number of relatively new technologies, which allow for the detailed psychophysiological assessment of emotion, and the micro-behavioral measurement of eye tracking, as a measure of users' attentional focus.

2   Measures of Arousal and Valence

Russell [8] proposed that, fundamentally, emotion consists of two largely orthogonal dimensions, arousal and valance. Arousal represents emotional intensity and valence represents the pleasantness/unpleasantness of an event. Arousal is the dimension most commonly and most easily represented by psychophysiological measures, which measure the activity of the sympathetic branch of the autonomic nervous system. Increased sympathetic arousal results in the characteristic "fight or flight" response, in which many activities occur simultaneously to prepare an organism to flee or fight; including increased blood flow and heart rate to provide blood to skeletal muscles; increased skin temperature and perspiration to provide cooling; and increased pupil dilation to increase visual acuity [9]. Therefore, measures of heart rate, skin conductance, and pupil dilation can all serve as measures of sympathetic arousal. All of these measures demonstrate a human is aroused, though it is difficult to determine, without self-report and/or contextual information, whether or not this arousal represents a positive (e.g., engagement/excitement) or negative (e.g., fear) experience. Valence, on the other hand, is more difficult to measure via these psychophysiological measures, so researchers often use more traditional self-report measures to represent valence as a supplement to psychophysiological measures. However, there is some evidence that some of these psychophysiological measures can provide insight into emotional valence. This will be discussed in more detail below.

2.1   Galvanic Skin Response (GSR)

Overview. Measures of Galvanic Skin Response detect electrical conductance on the skin, caused by moisture, which is indicative of increased sympathetic nervous system activity. Increases in skin conductance are, thus, thought to represent increased emotional arousal [3, 10, 11]. There is some evidence that this arousal is linear, and that it can even provide some information on emotional valence [12].

LITE Lab Research. Measures of Galvanic Skin Response were first used in LITE lab research for the evaluation of a Virtual Reality System, used to train first responders for the aftermath of attacks utilizing weapons of mass destruction [13-15]. The rationale for using this measure of arousal was based on the importance of emotion for this type of "affectively intense learning" [14]. Psychologists have long pointed to the importance of the emotional congruence between learning activities and target performance [16, 17]. Therefore, one important criterion for a tool for teaching learners to perform effectively in emotionally charged environments, is that the learning itself evokes a significant emotional response.

In a pilot study of a desktop version of this virtual reality training system, participants' GSR was measured as they carried out the training. Consistent with expectations, GSR responses increased significantly during more stressful parts of the learning scenario, such as bomb explosions [13]. In a follow up evaluation, those who trained in the virtual reality system, which included emotional events such as bomb explosions, were compared to students who trained in a neutral environment, on learning outcomes. Although those trained in the emotional environment performed best in learning outcomes, GSR recorded during training did not significantly predict training group (emotional training versus neutral) [14].

GSR was also utilized in a more recent study, which consisted of an examination of users responses to web sites [6]. In this study, three types of web sites were evaluated, which differed systematically in degree of vividness and interactivity – low, medium, and high. In this research, users' GSR response again failed to significantly differ across experimental groups. However, the order of the means was interesting, in that those in the low and high vividness/interactivity group had the highest GSR readings, while the medium group had the lowest. It's possible that those in one of those groups were more frustrated, while those in the other were more engaged and excited, demonstrating the challenges of measuring valence via these types of measures, as discussed above.

2.2   Pupil Dilation

Background. Pupil size, as discussed, is a measure of sympathetic arousal, and has been found to predict emotional arousal in a number of studies [18, 19]. Interestingly, there is some evidence that pupil size can provide some insight into valence as well. Dilation size and duration appears to be greater [19] and varies more [20] for unpleasant stimuli.

One advantage of pupil dilation as a measure of emotion is that it appears to be particularly responsive to the granular nature of the emotional response. For example, in one study pupil dilation changed systematically with each successive digit presented in a short term memory task [21]. Due to the non-invasive nature of modern measurement tools, a second advantage of pupil dilation measures is their lack of interference during task performance.

One potential disadvantage of pupil dilation, as a measure of emotion, is that pupil size changes in response to other ambient stimuli as well, such as light intensity, color, and luminosity [22]. To combat this problem, researchers often control for variables such as dimensions of light, by keeping these variables consistent across experimental conditions [23, 24].

One other aspect of measures of pupil dilation is that they've been found to be particularly effective as measures of cognitive load [21, 25]. A number of studies in different contexts have found that pupil dilation increase with task demand or difficulty [21, 26, 27].

LITE Lab Research. The LITE lab carried out the evaluation of a Learning System called the "Rapid Development System", which is an educational technology developed to train Mechanical Engineers about control systems [28-30]. This project was a multi-year project and consisted of iterative evaluation during interface development, utilizing small sample usability testing, followed by evaluation of the system within the context of Mechanical Engineering classes.

As one part of this evaluation, cognitive workload was measured via pupil dilation. Interestingly, pupil dilation proved to be significantly related to learning style. Specifically, verbal learners exhibited a greater cognitive load while utilizing the learning tool than visually oriented learners. This makes intuitive sense, in that the system was graphically oriented, and made use of a number of animations, so it is quite possible that the more visual learners were more challenged and, subsequently, experienced a greater load. This is indirectly supported by the fact that verbal learners also found the interface more difficult to use, and scored lower on measures of perceived learning.

In other research carried out in the lab, researchers examined the impact of wait time and feedback on users responses to a web application [31]. In one group users were provided with feedback indicating a page was loading as they waited; whereas those in another group were not provided with this feedback. Consistent with expectations pupil dilation measures were significantly higher for those in non-feedback condition, representing frustration.

In another study, described above, LITE lab researchers carried out research on students' responses to web sites that differed in vividness/interactivity using a number of outcome measures [6]. In this study, of the three different psychophysiological measures of sympathetic activity utilized, pupil dilation was the only measure on which the groups significantly differed. Specifically, the group of students who experienced the high interactive/vivid web site demonstrated significantly greater measures of pupil dilation than those in the medium or low groups. Presumably, this was the result of the more engaging and arousing nature of the highly vivid and interactive site.

2.3   Heart Rate

Background. The final measure of sympathetic arousal that has been utilized in LITE lab research is heart rate. As with the other measures, heart rate increases and decreases with emotional arousal, however, there is substantial evidence that heart rate can also be used as a measure of emotional valence [3, 32]. First, while heart rate increases with all emotional arousal, the rate of deceleration is greater for responses to negative stimuli [33, 34]. The most promising aspect of heart rate as a measure of valence is the use of heart rate variability, as opposed simple increase/decrease in heart rate. Heart rate variability (HRV) is the oscillation of intervals between consecutive heartbeats. Multiple studies have found that higher HRV is associated with more pleasant emotional experience [35], and lower HRV is associated with unpleasant emotional experience [36, 37].

LITE Lab Research. Heart rate has been utilized in one study thus far conducted in the LITE lab, and this was in the form of heart rate variability (HRV) used to measure users' responses to web sites that differed in interactivity/vividness [6]. Although mean HRV increased systematically as expected, with the lowest level for those in the least vivid/interactive group and the highest level in the most vivid/interactive group, the mean differences among the groups were not significant.

3   Eye Movement

3.1   Background

Though pupil dilation is often measured via the same instruments, the measurement of eye movement is fundamentally different in comparison to the measures discussed above. First, it is not a measure of sympathetic nervous system arousal. Second, it does not represent what is traditionally viewed as a physiological response; rather it is a sort of micro-behavioral measure. However, it also differs from traditional behavioral measures, in that it provides information on non-conscious attention, can be collected without task interference, and is responsive to small gradations in time.

The measurement of eye movement is traditionally used to measure attention [38]. In fact, some researchers have suggested that eye movement is required for any complete theory of attention and visual processing [39, 40]. The measurement of eye movement has been used effectively in the field of psychology to provide insight into problem solving, reasoning, mental imagery and search strategies [38, 41, 42]. Eye tracking is thought to be particularly effective for providing information on moment-to-moment processing.

In order to better understand eye movement measurement, it's important to understand the way in which the eye works mechanically to scan the visual field. The eye views the world with a series of fixations and saccades. Although our visual perceptual experience is continuous, the actual physical activity of the eye is discrete, consisting of a series of momentary fixations connected by very quick movements referred to as saccades. When the eye fixates, it focuses on an object such that the object falls on the fovea which maximizes the perceptual fidelity of the object [43]. The duration of a typical fixation is 250 – 300 ms [44]. Saccades, on the other hand, are rapid eye movements with high acceleration and deceleration rates that last

30 – 120 ms [45]. Most modern eye trackers provide data based on fixations in one form or another as it is fixations, which presumably represent attention.

Typically eye-tracking data is represented visually in two ways. First, a "gaze plot" displays a series of fixations, in the form of circles, connected by lines that represent the saccades. The size of the dots represent the fixation duration, and numbers on the dots represent the order of the fixation. The gaze plot is typically used to represent the data from one individual, but data from a number of users can be combined to create a comprehensive gaze plot. On the other hand a "heat map" uses different colors, much as a weather map, where the colors differ based on the number and duration of fixations, such that an area of high fixation duration/number is represented as red, while green represents levels of low fixation duration/number. Heat maps typically represent the combined data from a number of users [46].

One of the most popular ways of utilizing eye tracking data quantitatively is through the use of "areas of interest" (AOI), which are researcher-defined areas within the visual stimulus. Typically, the total fixation time and/or the number of fixations within that area in proportion to other areas of the stimulus represent attention to the given area [28].

3.2   LITE Lab Research

Eye tracking was used extensively in the study described above, in which a Rapid Development System was evaluated [47]. The method was used in combination with more traditional usability techniques to identify problematic aspects of the interface via a series of iterative evaluations that occurred during development. For example, eye tracking demonstrated that users were not even noticing an important pop-up message, nor did they scroll down to the end of an important help menu. Eye tracking data also identified aspects of the interface that lead to user frustration, based on rapid and extensive saccade movement [48].

In this same study, the quantitative analysis of areas of interest found that students classified a visual learners attended more to the interface animations than the more verbal learners. This finding is consistent with previous research that found visual learners attend more to the visual aspects of a learning technology interface [49].

Another LITE lab study that utilized eye tracking consisted of the examination of the effect of time pressure on task completion strategy [50]. In this experiment, participants examined financial information with or without time constraints. An area of interest analysis supported the research hypothesis that learners under time pressure would tend more to use a non-compensatory solution strategy, which was represented by their reliance on summary tables and other visual information, as opposed to those without a time constraint who attended more to written text.

Lastly, in the study describe above in which users were provided with feedback (or not) while waiting on a web page to load [31], eye tracking data indicated that those without feedback were significantly less focused during the page load time than those in the non-feedback condition. This finding is consistent with the finding mentioned above that the mean pupil dilation measure for the non-feedback group was significantly higher, representing their frustration and boredom.

4 Conclusions

Table 1 is a summary of the LITE lab research reviewed.

Table 1. Summary of LITE lab Research Results

Measure	Study	Construct	Results
GSR	Virtual Reality Pilot [13]	Emotional Intensity	*Significant interface element differences
	Virtual Reality & Affectively Intense Learning [14]	Emotional Intensity	No signification group differences
	Web Site Vividness-Interactivity [6]	Emotional Intensity	No significant group differences
Pupil Dilation	RPS evaluation [28]	Cognitive Work Load	*Significantly related to learning style
	Wait Time and Feedback [31]	Cognitive Work Load	*Significant group differences
	Web Site Vividness-Interactivity [6]	Interest/Engagement	*Significant group differences
Heart Rate	Web Site Vividness-Interactivity [6]	Interest/Engagement	No significant group differences
Eye Movement	Evaluation of RPS [28]	Attention	*Significant learning style differences
	Time Constraints and Problem Solution [50]	Attention	*Significant group differences.
	Wait Time and Feedback [31]	Attention	*Significant group differences

Taking all of these studies together, the techniques applied seem relatively promising; in that seven of the ten studies found some significant effects utilizing these tools, consistent with expectations. Pupil dilation appears to be particularly promising as a measure of arousal, in that significant effects were found in all three studies that utilized this measure. However, it's important to note that this is a relatively small number of studies, and the measures did not always predict and differentiate as anticipated. Future work is needed to determine, more specifically, which measures are most effective for representing given constructs; and in what contexts are they most effectively utilized.

References

1. Eckman, I.: An Argument for Basic Emotions. Cognition and Emotions 6(3), 169–200 (1992)
2. Hudlicka, E.: To Feel or Not to Feel: The Role of Affect in Human Computer Interaction. International Journal of Human Computer Studies 59(1-2), 1–32 (2003)

3. Mandryk, R.K., Inkpen, K., Calvert, T.: Using Psychophysiological Techniques to Measure User Experience with Entertainment Technologies. Behaviour and Information Technology 52(2), 141–158 (2006)
4. Hall, R.H., Philpot, T., Hubing, N.: Comprehensive Assessment of a Software Development Project for Engineering Education. Journal of Learning, Technology, and Assessment 15(5), 4–42 (2006)
5. Luna, R., et al.: A GIS Learning Tool for Civil Engineers. International Journal of Engineering Education 26, 52–58 (2010)
6. Sheng, H., Joginapelly, T.: Effects of Web Atmospheric Cues on Users' Emotional Responses in E-Commerce. Transactions on Human-Computer Interaction 4(1), 1–24 (2012)
7. Truemper, J.M., et al.: Usability in Multiple Monitor Displays. ACM SIGMIS Database 39, 74–89 (2008)
8. Russell, J.: A Circumplex Model of Affect. Journal of Personality and Social Psychology 39(6), 1161–1178 (1980)
9. Brodal, P.: The Central Nervous System: Structure and Function. Oxford University Press, New York (2004)
10. Chanel, G.C., et al.: Boredom, Engagement and Anxiety as Indicators for Adaptation to Difficulty in Games. In: Proceedings of the International Conference on Entertainment and Media in the Ubiquitous Era. ACM Press, Tampere (2008)
11. Ward, R., Marsden, P.: Physiological Responses to Different Web Page Designs. International Journal of Human-Computer Studies 59(1-2), 199–212 (2003)
12. Lang, P.J.: The Emotion Probe: Studies of Motivation and Attention. The American Psychologist 50(5), 372–385 (1995)
13. Hall, R.H., et al.: Virtual Terrorist Attack on the Computer Science Building: A Research Methodology. Presence Connect 4(4), 12–15 (2004)
14. Wilfred, L.M., et al.: Training in Affectively Intense Learning Environments. In: Proceedings of the E-Learn Conference. AACE Press (2004)
15. Hilgers, M.G., et al.: Virtual Environments for Training First Responders. In: Proceedings of the Interservice/Industry Training, Simulation, and Education Conference, I/ITSEC (2004)
16. Ellis, H.C., Moore, B.A.: Mood and Memory. In: Dalgleish, T., Powers, M. (eds.) Handbook of Cognition and Emotion, pp. 193–210. Wiley, Hoboken (1999)
17. Eich, E., Macaulay, D.: Are Real Moods Required to Reveal Mood-Congruent and Mood-Dependent Memory? Psychological Science 11(3), 244–248 (2000)
18. Partala, T., Surakka, V.: Pupil Size Variation and an Indication of Affective Processing. International Journal of Human-Computer Studies 59(1-2), 185–198 (2003)
19. Partala, T.M., Jokiniemi, M., Surakka, V.: Pupillary Responses to Emotionally Provocative Stimuli. In: roceedings of the Symposium on Eye Tracking Research and Applications. ACM Press, Palm Beach Gardens (2000)
20. Janisse, M.P.: Pupil Size, Affect and Exposure Frequency. Social Behavior and Personality 2(2), 125–146 (1974)
21. Kahneman, D., Beatty, J.: Pupil Diameter and Load on Memory. Science 154(3756), 1583–1585 (1966)
22. Beatty, J., Lucero-Wagoner, B.: The Pupillary System. In: Handbook of Psychophysiology, pp. 142–162. Cambridge University Press, New York (2000)
23. Bradley, M.M., et al.: The Pupil as a Measure of Emotional Arousal and Autonomic Activation. Psychophysiology 45(4), 602–607 (2008)
24. Franzen, P., et al.: Sleep Deprivation Alters Pupillary Reactivity to Emotional Stimuli in Healthy Young Adults. Biological Psychology 80(3), 300–305 (2009)

25. Hyona, J., Tommola, J., Alaja, A.: Pupil Dilation as a Measure of Processing Load in Simultaneous Interpretation and Other Language Tasks. The Quarterly Journal of Experimental Psychology 48(3), 598–612 (1995)
26. Payne, D.T., Parry, M.E., Harasymiw, S.J.: Percentage of Pupillary Dilation as a Measure of Item Difficulty. Perception and Psychophysics 4, 139–143 (1968)
27. Wright, P., Kahneman, D.: Evidence for Alternative Strategies of Sentence Retention. Quarterly Journal of Experimental Psychology 23, 197–213 (1971)
28. Chintalapati, A., et al.: Evaluation of a Rapid Development System Using Eye Tracker. In: Proceedings of the American Association of Engineering Education (2010)
29. Tang, L., et al.: Development and Initial Analysis of a Mini CNC Rapid Development System. In: Proceedings of the American Association for Engineering Education (2010)
30. Tang, L., Landers, R.G.: Remote Use of a Linear Axis Rapid Development System. In: Proceedings of the American Association of Engineering Education, pp. 2010–2157 (2010)
31. Sheng, H., Lockwood, N.S.: The Effect of Feedback on Web Site Delay: A Perceptual and Physiological Study. In: Proceedings of the Workshop on HCI Research in MIS, Shanghai, China (2011)
32. Anttonen, J., Surakka, V.: Emotions and Heart Rate While Sitting on a Chair. In: Proceedings of the SIGCHI Conference on Human Factors in Computing Systems. ACM Press, Portland (2005)
33. Bradley, M.M., Lang, P.J.: Affective Reactions to Acoustic Stimuli. Psychophysiology 37(2), 204–215 (2000)
34. Brosschot, J.F., Thayer, J.F.: Heart Rate Response is Longer After Negative Emotions than Positive Emotions. International Journal of Psychophysiology 50(3), 181–187 (2003)
35. Nolan, R.: Heart Rate Variability (HRV). European Heart Journal 17, 354–381 (1996)
36. Jonsson, P.: Respiratory Sinus Arrhythmia as a Function of State Anxiety in Healthy Individuals. International Journal of Psychophysiology 63(1), 48–54 (2007)
37. Brosschot, J.F., Van Dijk, E., Thayer, J.F.: Daily Worry is Related to Low Heart Rate Variability During Waking and the Subsequent Nocturnal Sleep Period. International Journal of Psychophysiology 63(1), 39–47 (2007)
38. Just, M.A., Carpenter, P.A.: Eye Fixations and Cognitive Processes. Cognitive Psychology 8, 441–480 (1976)
39. Findlay, J.M., Gilchrist, I.D.: Visual Attention: The Active Vision Perspective. In: Vision and Attention. Springer, New York (2001)
40. Jacob, R.J.K.: Eye Tracking in Advanced Interface Design, pp. 258–288. Oxford University Press, New York (1995)
41. Yoon, D., Narayanan, N.H.: Mental Imagery in Problem Solving: An Eye Tracking Study. In: Proceedings of the ACM Symposium on Eye Tracking Research & Applications. ACM Press (2004)
42. Zelinsky, G.J., Sheinberg, D.: Why Some Search Tasks Take Longer Than Others: Using Eye Movements to Redefine Reaction Times. In: Findlay, J., Kentridge, R., Walker, R. (eds.) Eye Movement Research: Mechanisms, Processes and Applications. Elsevier, Amsterdam (1995)
43. Pashler, H.E.: The Psychology of Attention. MIT Press, Cambridge (1998)
44. Salvucci, D.D., Goldberg, J.H.: Identifying Fixations and Saccades in Eye-Tracking Protocols. In: Proceedings of the Symposium on Eye Tracking Research and Applications. ACM Press (2000)
45. Palmer, S.: Vision Science: Photons to Phenomenology. MIT Press, Cambridge (1999)

46. Duchowski, A.T.: Eye Tracking Methodology: Theory and Practice. Springer-Verlag, Inc., London (2003)
47. Chintalapati, A., et al.: Evaluation of a Rapid Development System Using Eye Tracker. In: Proceedings of the American Association of Engineering Education, AC 2010-2210 (2010)
48. Goldberg, J.H., Kotval, X.P.: Computer Interface Evaluation Using Eye Movements: Methods and Constructs. International Journal of Industrial Ergonomics 24, 631–645 (1999)
49. Tsianos, N., et al.: The Learning Styles as a Basic Parameter for the Design of Adaptive E-Learning Environments. In: Proceedings of the International Conference on Open and Distance Learning Applications of Pedagogy and Technology (2005)
50. Sheng, H., Pochinapeddi, S.: User Pressure: A Psychophysiological Analysis of the Effect of Temporal Constraints of Information Processing and Decision Making. In: Proceedings of the International Conference on Human-Computer Interaction. Springer, Las Vegas (2013)

An Experimental Environment for Analyzing Collaborative Learning Interaction

Yuki Hayashi, Yuji Ogawa, and Yukiko I. Nakano

Department of Computer and Information Science, Seikei University, Japan
hayashi@st.seikei.ac.jp

Abstract. In collaborative learning, participants progress their learning through multimodal information in a face-to-face environment. In addition to conversation, non-verbal information such as looking at other participants and note taking plays an important role in facilitating effective interaction. By exploiting such non-verbal information in the analysis of collaborative learning activities, this research proposes a collaborative learning environment in which the non-verbal information of participants is collected to analyze learning interaction. For this purpose, we introduce multimodal measurement devices and implement an integration tool for developing a multimodal interaction corpus of collaborative learning.

Keywords: Collaborative learning environment, multimodal interaction, gaze target, writing action.

1 Introduction

Collaborative learning is a learning style in which multiple participants study collaboratively to acquire knowledge about their subjects [1]. Since participants progress their learning through the exchange of ideas, many researchers have focused on analyzing and modeling the learning process in collaborative learning using dialogue data [2, 3]. In a face-to-face environment, participants generally interact with others by not only exchanging utterances but also using non-verbal behaviors such as looking at other participants and note taking [4]. By exploiting such multimodal information in the analysis of collaborative learning, collaborative learning support systems are able to intelligently mediate group interactions more effectively.

While several studies have analyzed group interaction based on non-verbal information such as gaze targets and speech intervals [5, 6] in the research field of computer-supported cooperative work, there is little research that deals with multimodal interaction during learning in order to facilitate a collaborative learning environment. In order to analyze the learning situation in detail, an interaction corpus that includes elaborative non-verbal information is of primary importance. However creating a multimodal corpus requires a large amount of labor. Thus, it would be very useful if the corpus could be generated automatically/semi-automatically.

S. Yamamoto (Ed.): HIMI/HCII 2013, Part III, LNCS 8018, pp. 43–52, 2013.

As the first step for analyzing collaborative learning in terms of non-verbal information, the research objective is to propose a collaborative learning environment for collecting non-verbal information using multimodal measurement devices. The non-verbal information we extract consists of the gaze targets, speech intervals, and writing actions of participants. This exhaustive information allows us to analyze the interaction (e.g., mutual gaze). In order to integrate these primitive data, this research introduces an integration tool and attempts to gather the interaction corpus through collaborative learning in a face-to-face environment. We believe that the corpus can be used to detect learning situations such as when a participant is not actively engaged in the learning process or cannot effectively communicate with others.

2   Collecting Non-verbal Information in Collaborative Learning

In this research, we deal with collaborative learning among participants in small groups (three participants) who study/discuss in face-to-face situations. Through collaborative learning, they try to discuss and share their knowledge of the subject. Each participant has a piece of paper (note) for writing answers/ideas freely.

In collaborative learning, participants progress their learning not only by writing down the answers in their notes as individual learning, but also by looking around at others, listening to what someone is saying, and sometimes expressing his/her own ideas. In order to analyze these various types of interactions in learning, we focus on analyzing the non-verbal information that consists of *(i) gaze direction*, *(ii) speech*, and *(iii) writing action* as multimodal data of collaborative learning. Here, we do not target the verbal information such as utterance content. The following sections describe the methods of acquiring each type of non-verbal data.

2.1   Gaze Direction

The gaze directions of participants afford the clues needed to estimate *gaze targets*; i.e., which participant is gazing at another participant (or their note) at any particular time. The gaze direction of each participant is obtained by eye-tracking glasses[1]. The wearable glasses have a camera that can capture the scene (640*480 pixels, 30Hz) and record what the participant is looking at as coordinate data in the two-dimensional scene into an assistant recording device. In addition, the glasses recognize the identity numbers of infrared (IR) markers based on an IR-ray sensor, when such markers exist in the scene. These data are extracted using the eye-tracking software Tobii Studio[1].

In our learning environment, IR markers were put on each participant's neck and on his/her note. According to the aggregated eye-tracking data, the gaze targets were annotated by calculating the distance between tracked eye coordinates and IR coordinates based on the following equation.

---

[1]   Tobii Glasses Eye tracker and Tobii Studio: Tobii Technology,
     http://www.tobii.com/

$$dist(i,t) = \sqrt{(x_e(t) - x_{ir}(i,t))^2 - (y_e(t) - y_{ir}(i,t))^2} \tag{1}$$

Here, $(x_e(t),\ y_e(t))$ and $(x_{ir}(i,t),\ y_{ir}(i,t))$ represent the coordinates of the eye-tracking position and IR marker i, respectively, for frame t. Fig. 1 shows an example of gaze target detection, representing the image captured by the camera of the eye-tracking glasses at time t. Red points indicate the eye coordinates of a participant, and devices enclosed by yellow circles are IR markers. In this case, two IR markers (IR i and IR j) exist in the view. When $dist(i,\ t)$ is lower than certain threshold (in pixels), the gaze target is detected as the target marked by IR marker i. In this case, the gaze target is detected as participant n since IR marker i is proximate according to the results of the distance calculations. This detection process is conducted for every frame in which tracked eye coordination is normally recognized.

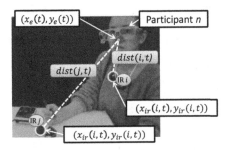

Fig. 1. Example of detection of gaze target

2.2   Speech

In order to detect the duration and identity of speakers at any particular time, the utterances of participants are gathered via a microphone. Audio data stream is transmitted via an audio interface device[2] and recorded independently as audio data (file format: wav, channel(s): 1, sampling rate: 16000 Hz). For speech input/interval detection, we use the Julius adintool software[3], which segments the audio data based on the amplitude level. That is, the start and end times of an utterance are detected when the audio level exceeds certain threshold and by silent intervals. The output is synchronized with the gaze target data. The utterance information gives the number of utterances for each participant and these intervals.

2.3   Writing Action

In order to extract the writing actions of participants, we introduced a digital pen device[4]. The pen performs in two types of modes. One is a mobile mode such that

[2]   UA-1000: Roland Co., http://www.roland.com/products/en/UA-1000/
[3]   Adintool: Julius development team, http://julius.sourceforge.jp/
[4]   airpenPocket: Pentel Inc., http://www.airpen.jp/

the written data are stored into a memory unit. The other is a mouse mode, where the pen is perceived as a computer mouse and the mouse move and click actions are controlled according to the writing motions by connecting the memory unit to a computer. The pen device can use a normal ballpoint-type refill, so that participants can write down his/her notes in the usual manner.

This research uses the mouse mode to judge whether participants are writing or not, expressed as mouse clicking actions based on the pressure-sensitive information collected by the device. In order to synchronize each participant's writing data, we construct a digital pen capturing tool, which sends pen pressed/released data to a writing data receiving tool. Fig. 2 shows an interface image of the pen capturing tool. The writing data stream of each participant is sent to a server computer through a socket connection configured for each participant in advance. Fig. 3 represents the receiving tool. When the data is entered, the tool stores the sequence of the pen pressed/released data with a unique timestamp.

Fig. 2. Digital pen capturing tool   **Fig. 3.** Writing data receiving tool

3   Experimental Environment

We have developed an experimental environment for monitoring the non-verbal behaviors of participants during collaborative learning. Fig. 4 shows the system architecture. In the environment, each participant wears eye-tracking glasses and a microphone (headset or tiepin type) and writes using the digital pen. The eye-tracking glasses record eye movement, IR data, and scene video files into secure digital cards in the assistant recording device. The microphones are connected to an audio interface device to create high-quality audio files. In order to gather the writing data, three computers in which digital pen capturing tools are running are used for the participants. In addition, a high-definition video camera is placed above the learning environment to record the overall learning scene.

Fig. 5 shows the layout of the participants and IR markers, and Fig. 6 shows a snapshot of the collaborative learning environment. Participants are arranged in a triangle formation around a square table (90 cm * 90 cm), and IR markers with unique IDs are placed on each participant and note to detect the gaze targets.

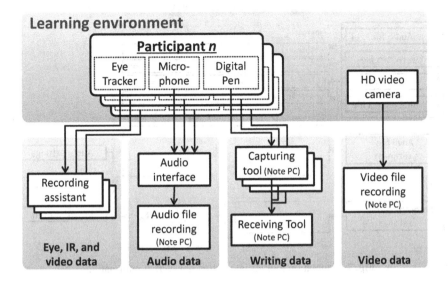

Fig. 4. System architecture of our collaborative learning environment

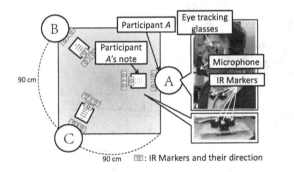 

Fig. 5. Layout of participants and positions of IR markers

Fig. 6. Snapshot of collaborative learning

4   Integration of Multimodal Information

By analyzing the non-verbal information obtained from multimodal measurement devices, we can infer sophisticated meanings from the data array, such as *"who is gazing at the speaker"* and *"who is speaking to another participant who is taking notes"* in collaborative learning. In order to integrate these primitive data types, we developed a tool that integrates the multimodal data of each participant along with the timestamp information.

Fig. 7 represents the main interface of our integration tool. This tool requires a participant's audio file, eye record file, IR record file, and writing record file in the file

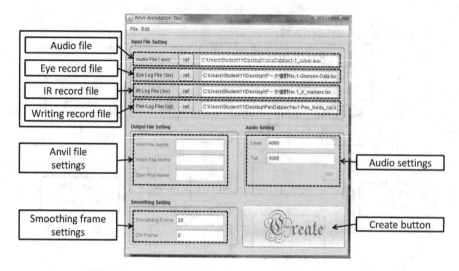

Fig. 7. Annotation tool for integrating non-verbal information

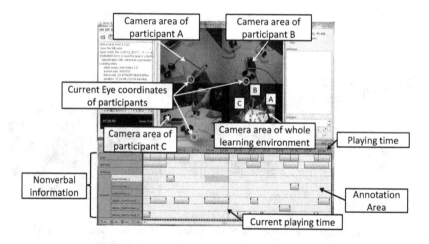

Fig. 8. Example of annotated data visualized using Anvil interface

setting area. Our tool semi-automatically generates an annotated file that can be read by the generic annotation visualization tool, Anvil [7]. In the Anvil file settings, the parameters for the output Anvil file can be set. The audio settings allow the input amplitude level and silent interval to be set for segmenting the audio data as described in Section 2.2. For smoothing the gaze target data, the smoothing frame parameters can be set in the smoothing frame settings. This input is used to combine two gaze data segments if the adjacent same-target data are within the set frame. In addition, for display in the Anvil interface, we manually encode an integrated video file that includes the video stream of the three participants captured by the eye-tracking glasses shown in Fig. 1 and the video stream from the camera that looks at the learning environment.

Based on the created integrated data file and video file, we confirm the interaction in the collaborative learning using Anvil. Fig. 8 shows the integrated multimodal data in the interface. The horizontal axis represents time sequences and the vertical axis shows the ongoing multimodal interactions. The annotation area represents three types of non-verbal information: *gaze target*, *speech interval*, and *writing action* for each participant. Through the interface, we can not only check the annotated non-verbal data by comparing the segments with the video but also modify the data manually if they are incorrectly annotated.

5   Experiments of Data Acquisition

5.1   Experimental Setting

We conducted experiments for collecting multimodal information during collaborative learning. For the experiments, 30 participants (20 males and 10 females) participated in the collaborative learning experiment. Participants consisted of undergraduate and graduate students of our university. Each learning groups consisted of three participants, and 10 groups were created for the experiments.

Each group was asked to study with others for two sessions. In order to obtain various learning situations such as participants who frequently gave their knowledge to others or participants who learned more passively, we arranged the groups such that they contained participants who were both familiar and unfamiliar with the subjects to be learned. Each group consisted of two participants who majored in computer and information science and a participant whose major was in another field such as literature or economics. The groups were asked to work on exercises in the fields of computer and information science. We set two types of exercises: exercises in which participants took notes frequently to derive a unique answer (answer-derived type) and exercise in which participants mainly discussed and shared knowledge with others (open-ended type). Table 1 describes the learning exercises of the experiments. Exercise 1 consisted of radix conversion problems where an n-ary number needed to be converted to another m-ary number. Exercise 2 was a discussion on cloud computing by exchanging opinions for knowledge sharing. In order to avoid the situation where none of the members progressed in their learning, we told the participants who majored in computer and information science the kind of exercises that would be proposed. We asked them to review the exercise domain in advance.

Before the experiment, the participants calibrated their eye-tracking glasses. They were asked to study Exercise 1 and 2 by turns. We gave instructions to use a piece of paper for writing the solutions and answers in Exercise 1, and for writing useful comments in Exercise 2. The discussion times for all exercises lasted for more than 10 min. We observed the learning situation and stopped the discussion when the conversation quieted down.

Table 1. Learning exercises of the experiments

No.	Type	Contents
(1)	Answer-derived	**Radix conversion problems** - $(10101110)_2$ to octal, decimal, and hexadecimal - $(26584)_{10}$ to binary, octal, and hexadecimal - $(164701)_8$ to binary, decimal, and hexadecimal
(2)	Open-ended	**Discussion on cloud computing** - What is cloud computing? - What are the merits and demerits of cloud computing? - Are there any such services?

5.2   Experimental Results

The average times taken for Exercises 1 and 2 were 839 and 817 s, respectively. According to the non-verbal information extracted in the experiments, we created Anvil files of each session using the annotation tool described in Section 4 and the video files for Anvil using video-editing software. We confirmed the intervals of information and the correctness of the annotations using the Anvil interface.

Gaze Target. The average rates of eye-tracking data acquisition of Exercise 1 and 2 were 62.24% and 52.47%, respectively. One of the reasons for failed detection included eye blinking. According to the video observation from eye-tracking glasses of participants whose acquisition rate was low, some of them had certain characteristic eye-movements. For example, some participants looked down at their notes underneath the lenses of the eye-tracking glasses; there were others who only moved their eyes and peered over the glasses with their heads bent down when they looked at others (Fig. 9). The correlation coefficient indicated a positive correlation between the two exercises (0.59). That is, the participants whose acquisition rates were high or low in Exercise 1 tended to also have high or low acquisition rates in Exercise 2. Thus, the mannerisms of the eye movement of participants affected the data acquisition rates.

In addition, we observed many cases where IR markers were not identified even though eye coordination was detected. Our annotation tool does not annotate the gaze target when the IR markers are not identified, even if the acquisition rate of eye tracking is high. Because of these failed eye-tracking detections, often eye targets could not be annotated.

Speech Interval. We confirmed that the speech interval of each participant was almost exactly extracted according to the corresponding voice data. Using an audio interface contributed to the acquisition of high-quality audio data that includes few acoustic noises. Before the start of the experiments, we tuned the amplitude level of the microphones so that they were approximately equal. Depending on participants, however, we had to adjust the amplitude level in order to segment the audio data.

To extract the speech intervals completely automatically, a mechanism of adjusting the amplitude level (e.g., using average amplitude level information) is required.

Writing Action. Since both the eye-tracking glasses and the digital pen used in this research send signals using an IR-based mechanism, there was a risk of interference. In order to avoid IR interference in the experiments, we covered the IR receiver on the memory units for the digital pen (Fig. 10). However, according to the annotated intervals on the Anvil interface, many writing actions were not recorded. In order to improve the detection accuracy, we either need to develop the learning environment so that the interference of IR signals is avoided, or introduce an alternative writing detection device (e.g., tablet-type device with stylus pen).

Fig. 9. Example of failed eye-tracking detection

Fig. 10. Cover for digital pen unit

These results indicate that while the annotation of speech intervals was successfully extracted, the annotations of gaze targets and writing actions were not satisfactorily adequate. In order to extract these types of information accurately, we need to improve the data acquisition method. After the experiment, we annotated the correct eye targets and the writing action intervals based on the extracted eye-coordination points using Anvil to create the plenary annotated data. This collaborative learning corpus includes very exhaustive information regarding the interaction among participants that can be used for analyzing several learning situations.

6   Conclusion

In this research, we proposed an environment for monitoring the non-verbal information of participants to analyze collaborative learning interaction. We introduced various multimodal measurement devices into the environment to gather this non-verbal information. In addition, we proposed an integration tool that synchronized the multimodal data of participants. Experiments for the data acquisition showed that while speech intervals were detected with high accuracy, eye-targets and writing actions were not adequately annotated. This was caused by failed detection of eye-tracking, interference of the IR signal, and so on.

Through manual and automatic annotation of data, we now have an interaction corpus that includes plenary annotated non-verbal information in collaborative learning. Based on this corpus, we are currently implementing a visualization tool for briefly analyzing interaction sequences during learning. For future work, we intend to analyze the differences in the interaction that occurs in particular situations, such as when studying collaboratively or individually, or between the exercise types to facilitate group collaboration. In addition, we intend to consider additional methods for acquiring non-verbal data more accurately for gathering the collaborative learning data automatically.

References

1. Adelsberger, H.H., Collis, B., Pawlowski, J.M.: Handbook on Information Technologies for Education and Training. Springer (2002)
2. Soller, A., Lesgold, A.: Modeling the process of collaborative learning. In: Hoppe, U., Ogata, H., Soller, A. (eds.) The Role of Technology in CSCL, vol. 9, Part I, pp. 63–86. Springer (2007)
3. Inaba, A., Ohkubo, R., Ikeda, M., Mizoguchi, R.: Models and Vocabulary to Represent Learner-to-Learner Interaction Process in Collaborative Learning. In: Proc. of International Conference on Computers in Education, pp. 1088–1096 (2003)
4. Kreijns, K., Kirschner, P.A., Jochems, W.: Identifying the pitfalls for social interaction in computer-supported collaborative learning environments: a review of the research. Computers in Human Behavior 19(3), 335–353 (2003)
5. Brennan, S.E., Chen, X., Dickinson, C.A., Neider, M.B., Zelinsky, G.J.: Coordinating cognition: the costs and benefits of shared gaze during collaborative search. Cognition 106(3), 1465–1477 (2008)
6. Kabashima, K., Nishida, M., Jokinen, K., Yamamoto, S.: Multimodal Corpus of Conversations in Mother Tongue and Second Language by Same Interlocutors. In: Proc. of 4th Workshop on Eye Gaze in Intelligent Human Machine Interaction, Article No. 9 (2012)
7. Kipp, M.: Anvil – A Generic Annotation Tool for Multimodal Dialogue. In: Proc. of Eurospeech 2001, pp. 1367–1370 (2001)

Transparent Digital Contents Sharing
for Science Teachers

Thongchai Kaewkiriya[1], Ryosuke Saga[2], and Hiroshi Tsuji[2]

[1] Faculty of Information Technology, Thai-Nichi Institute of Technology,
1771/1, Pattanakarn Rd., Suanluang, Bangkok, Thailand
thongchi@tni.ac.th
[2] Graduate School of Engineering, Osaka Prefecture University,
1-1, Gakuencho, Naka-ku, Sakai, 599-8531 Osaka, Japan
{saga@,tsuji@}cs.osakafu-u.ac.jp/

Abstract. To support science teachers for preparing their classes, this paper presents concepts and principles on digital contents sharing. The proposed framework is divided into three parts: The first part proposes the maturity levels for science teacher activities based on SECI model and CMMI. The second part designs the system components on DLMS (Distributed e-learning management system) which allows science teachers to share digital contents efficiently. The third part illustrates the scenario how the proposed framework works. The possibility for prototype system based on REST (Representational State Transferred) ful Web service is also discussed. This proposal expects to save time for preparing digital contents for science teachers as they mature on digital contents.

Keywords: e-Learning, Digital content sharing, Knowledge-Network, Maturity Model, Knowledge Management.

1   Introduction

In recent years, the information technology in the education field becomes important especially for the distance learning through the Internet [1]. Such e-learning system basically consists of three components: learning management system [2] (LMS); learning contents; and infrastructure technology which is found as a common part of e-learning system. The volume of digital contents on the Internet has increased day by day for teachers as well as for students. The varieties of digital contents are scattered over schools. Normally each school has provided an LMS for teachers, students, and an administrator. Then one of the problems for teachers is to consume time for creating and sharing digital contents even if there have been already excellent contents in other school. Thus the teacher should create and share digital contents only in his school's LMS. Then, how can a teacher share digital contents with other schools' teachers for preparing classes efficiently.

Our answer is to provide transparent digital contents sharing mechanisms. Let us review the current status on information sharing method. There are still teachers who

S. Yamamoto (Ed.): HIMI/HCII 2013, Part III, LNCS 8018, pp. 53–62, 2013.

hesitate to use information technology. They can exchange tacit idea on teaching materials only based on discussion. Using standalone PC (Personal Computer), some teachers create digital contents as teaching materials which is externalized from his brain. To share them as explicit knowledge, they should copy them into media such as USB memories. Then there is less chance to collect large number of digital contents effectively. If there is an LMS in school which is connected with LAN, each teacher has chance to reuse digital contents which are externalized and to disclose his idea to others. Our discussion occurs at the next stage: each school has its LMS but there is no way to exchange digital contents over schools.

The previous research, digital content sharing could be done in a social network service with maturity level for science teacher [3]. In addition, the design of knowledge-network for Japanese science teachers has been presented [4] to support knowledge sharing among science teachers: 1) relationship 2) reputation 3) personalization. Research in [3] and [4] focused on three factors. However, how to implement the proposal was strongly dependent on social network service. Then it was difficult to describe scenario how teachers mature on digital contents.

Referring concepts of SECI model [5] and CMMI model [6] [7] for considering pioneers followers, this research introduce maturity model for them. Next, this paper will describe what DLMS is and how it works for future digital contents sharing in the future. For prototype, we will use a RESTful web service [8] [9] in order to develop. Then this paper will present scenario how teacher mature and what DLMS should do.

2   Digital Content for Science Teacher

2.1   Pioneer and Follower

To help science teachers, Japanese government has prepared digital contents. Today there are more than 45,000 users and more than 40,000 contents. The examples of digital contents are shown in Fig. 1. The contents are stored in central database and there is keyword query as well as index.

However, there are some problems as follows:

1. While there are pioneers, there are also followers. In fact, some teachers are so active that they are positive to prepare class with digital contents by themselves. They may modify the prepared digital contents for his class because sometimes contents may be too long and too redundant. Then his modification cannot be shared. On the other hand, other teachers may be novice for IT and hesitate to be a leader on digital contents.
2. IT environment of school is different from each other. Some schools may be equipped with up-to-date technology and others may not. On the other hand, it is also true that such environment will be upgraded year by year once the digital contents work well for classes. Then it is still common: when the environment is upgrades, there should be extra tasks such as database moving and usability change.

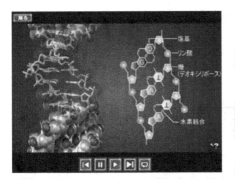 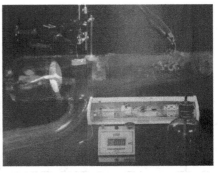

Fig. 1. Example of digital contents sharing

Next, let us consider the initial state and ideal state. At the initial state, there is no IT in a school. Both pioneer teacher and follower teacher has no chance to use digital contents but exchange idea how to start using them at first. At the ideal state, the pioneer teachers will make plan for using digital contents and give lesson at class. They will review the class and may modify both his talk and digital contents. He will be active to open his idea for others. Learning good practice from pioneer teachers, the follower teachers start using digital contents. Even if he hesitates to express his idea, he likes to search digital contents which fit to his class.

Then what we should consider is scenario how we give chance science teachers for transit from the initial state to the ideal state.

2.2   Maturity Upgrade Process

To develop teachers' maturity level higher, let us consider the bias for establishing model for digital contents sharing. This research introduces two biases: CMMI (Capability Maturity Model Integration) [6] [7] and SEKI model.

CMMI is well-known in software development process. CMMI supposes that upgrading maturity level is measured by the existence of process which implies the level of capability. The original CMM includes five maturity levels: initial, repeatable, defined, managed and optimizing.

SEKI model is prepared for knowledge creative company [5]. It includes four spiral processes: knowledge socialization (S), knowledge externalization (E), knowledge combination (C), and knowledge internalization (I). In our context, S can occur even if there is no special tool and I can occur if there is search mechanism. To implement E, there should be at least personal storage and preferable shared storage. For C, there should be computer network for sharing knowledge.

Let us consider the relation between CMMI model and SECI model. At initial stage, all teachers have old-fashioned class and there is no process in school for using digital contents. Then without IT there should be communication in school as socialization. Communication contributes to encourage teacher to improve his class.

Table 1. Table of maturity for science teacher

Level	Detail	Teacher (User)							
		Tool	Rika Network	Own school DB	Other school DB	S	E	C	I
1	No IT	-	-	-	-	○	✗	✗	✗
2	Stand alone	PC	○	-	-	○	✗	✗	○
3	School Network	LMS	○	○	-	○	△	△	○
4	Global Network	DLMS+SNS	○	○	○	○	○	○	○

At final and ideal state, teachers are so active to share good practice on digital contents. They not only use the prepared digital contents but also modify them and disclose their modification. They search the appropriate contents not only from his school but also from other schools. It means that sophisticated digital contents as good practice are transparently accessed by any teacher.

Overview of maturity upgrade process is summarized in Table 1. Let us discuss each level carefully.

Maturity 1

This level is the traditional state before IT is available in school even if a teacher has IT skill. The teachers in this level share knowledge or experience among colleagues. But it is time consuming. Even if one finds good practice, it is not easy to share it with others in another school. There is no space to store it for others. The maturity level process is shown in Fig 2.

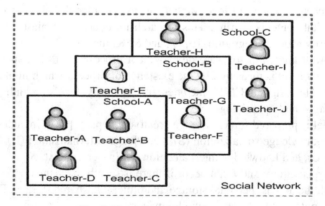

Fig. 2. The maturity level 1 process

Maturity 2

This level is the case that Rika-net appeared. If a pioneer teacher has standalone PC, he has chance to search digital contents stored in central DB. Viewing digital contents, he learns good practice, uses it in his class and stores his experience as his tacit knowledge. He may modify the digital contents for his class. Then even if the modified contents are available by other teachers, there is no chance to share it electronically. What he can do is to communicate with follower teachers on his practice in the meeting. Such socialization allows the follower teacher to start using digital contents. The process of maturity level 2 is illustrated in Fig. 3.

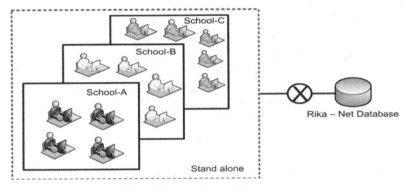

Fig. 3. The maturity level 2 process

Maturity 3

This level is a state where local network is available in a school. Teachers in this level use LMS in his school which allows them to share information electronically. Once one teacher finds good practice in Rika-net, he lets his colleagues know via LMS. Not only sharing knowledge or experience among teachers, pioneer teacher creates own digital contents, save and store in school's DB. Then the followers start using digital contents for their classes. While each school continues to store good practice in its LMS. there is no chance to share them over school unless they use special channel. The process of maturity level 3 is shown in Fig. 4.

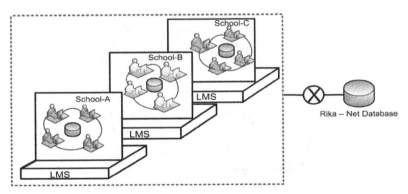

Fig. 4. The maturity level 3 process

Maturity 4

This level is the highest state on digital contents sharing for science teachers. There is DLMS which allows to access database in other school transparently. Once a pioneer teacher stores his good practice in his school LMS, everybody (not only teachers in his school but also teachers in other schools) has chance to access it without difficulty. They feel as if all contents were in one database. This transparency should owe to DLMS. The process of maturity level 4 is shown in Fig. 5.

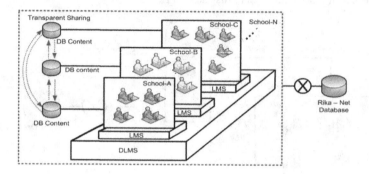

Fig. 5. The maturity level 4 process

3   Distributed LMS

3.1   System Component

Let us describe system components of distributed LMS which allows us to have maturity level 4 process. As shown in Fig. 6, there are more than two LMSs. Each school prepares LMS for science teachers in order to share knowledge based on digital contents. LMS composes of student's module as for student, admin module as for administrator, and section of teacher module. This research focuses on teacher module.

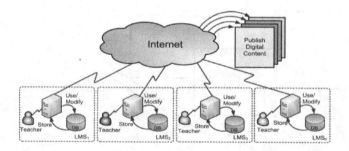

Fig. 6. The system component of DLMS

Then a teacher who is in LMS_1 uses digital contents not only in his LMS of his school but also those in other schools. Under this environment any teacher has chance to externalize his tacit knowledge for other teachers. Once the digital contents are prepared, it can be accessed from any LMS. Thus prepared digital contents are combined as explicit knowledge. Finally, any teacher can search digital contents for his class over schools. If he learns something from new digital contents, it is regarded as internalization.

3.2   Data flow of DLMS

Let us next describe the data flow of DLMS by Fig. 7. Teacher who logins LMS will be able to study new digital contents which other teachers in the system have created. Note that the ability to create digital contents is based on the maturity level of the individual teacher.

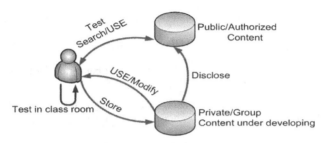

Fig. 7. The data flow of DLMS

Data flow indicates that a teacher is able to search digital contents from database of LMS. In addition, teacher can create digital contents, modify them into a private database of LMS. Also, he can disclose digital contents in private into published digital contents if their maturity level is four (Table 1).

4   Scenario

4.1   Scenario-1

Suppose that teacher-A should prepare class for earth project although he is not a specialist on this topic. Then he will ask his colleagues in his school by face-to-face communication if IT environment is not well organized. Only in the case that there is an expert, he can get solution as shown in Fig. 8.

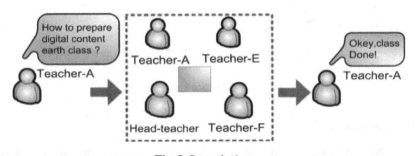

Fig. 8. Scenario-1

4.2   Scenario-2

Assume that teacher-B has PC which is connected to Internet. Then he can search digital contents from DB content (Rika-net) network where there are lots of digital content on planet. He has chance to download digital contents and prepare classroom for his students. When he teaches digital content to students for a while, he may find that digital contents do not suitable to his class. Then he may go to consult with teacher-F and teacher-G who are experts in planet subject and have been doing research about planet subject. After discussion he can modify digital contents to prepare his classroom for the future. Scenario 2 is shown in Fig. 9.

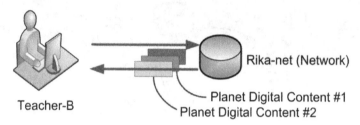

Fig. 9. Scenario-2

4.3   Scenario-3

Suppose that teacher-C would like to use digital contents on plant. He can search for digital contents from DB content (Rika-net) network but is aware that searched digital contents on plant are not enough. Downloading the prepared digital contents, he can modify them and saves them in his local storage for his colleagues. But there is still limitation because teachers in another school have no chance to use his good practice. Scenario 3 is shown in Fig 10.

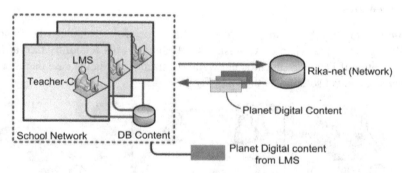

Fig. 10. Scenario-3

4.4   Scenario-4

Assume that teacher-D, J and K would like to use digital contents on Physics, Math and Chemistry respectively. They can search for digital contents from DB content

(Rika-net) but they may fail. To prepare original digital contents for classes, they use DLMS for searching digital contents via Global network to confirm if right contents exist in other schools. If exists, they can down load as if it were in central database. When they download, they modify and save digital contents their local storage. They also use to distribute to those interested to download. Scenario 4 is shown in Fig. 11.

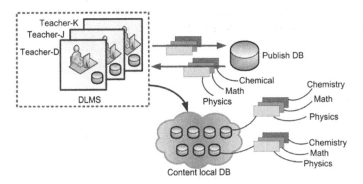

Fig. 11. Scenario-4

5 Conclusion

This paper has proposed a transparent digital contents sharing and knowledge sharing among science teachers. It has been also described how the transparent digital contents sharing occurred based on SECI and CMMI model. The prototype system was developed by RESTful Web service as described detail elsewhere. The scenario how IT contributes to four maturity levels was also illustrated. The results showed that science teacher hoped to use the prototype in order to share their digital contents and knowledge transparently.

References

1. Lester, A., Gerhard, T.: The Future of Distance Learning - The Process and the Product. In: Proc. of Annual International Conference, ITHET IEEE, F1A-K - F2A-2 (2005)
2. Ellis, K.: Field Guide to Learning Management Systems, http://www.astd.org/~/media/Files/Publications
3. Sakoda, M., Wada, Y., Tsuji, H., Seta, K.: Social Network Service with Maturity Level for Science Teachers, pp. 1718–1723. SMC/IEEE, San Antonio (2009)
4. Wada, Y., Sakoda, M., Tsuji, H., Aoki, Y., Seta, K.: Designing Sticky Knowledge-Network SNS for Japanese Science Teachers. In: Smith, M.J., Salvendy, G. (eds.) HCII 2009, Part I. LNCS, vol. 5617, pp. 447–456. Springer, Heidelberg (2009)
5. Nonaka, I., Takeuchi, H.: The Knowledge-Creating Company: How Japanese Companies Create the Dynamics of Innovation. Oxford University Press (1995)
6. Carnegie Mellon University, Software Engineering Institute: The Capability Maturity Model: Guidelines for Improving the Software Process. Addison-Wesley (1995)

7. Chrissis, M., Konrad, M., Shrum, S.: CMMI: Guidelines for Process Integration and Product Improvement. Addison-Wesley (2003)
8. Fielding, R., Taylor, R.: Principled design of the modern Web architecture. ACM Trans, TOIT 2(2), 115–150 (2002)
9. Fielding, R.: Architectural styles and the design of network-based software architectures. PhD Thesis, pp. 76–106. University of California, Irvine (2000)
10. Japan Science and Technology Agency: Rikanetwork (2013), http://www.rikanet.jst.go.jp/

Development of a Computer Programming Learning Support System Based on Reading Computer Program

Haruki Kanamori[1,*], Takahito Tomoto[2], and Takako Akakura[2]

[1] Graduate School of Engineering, Tokyo University of Science, 1-3 Kagurazaka,
Shinjuku-ku, Tokyo 162-8601, Japan
kanamori-haruki@ms.kagu.tus.ac.jp
[2] Faculty of Engineering, Tokyo University of Science, 1-3 Kagurazaka, Shinjuku-ku,
Tokyo 162-8601, Japan
{tomoto,akakura}@ms.kagu.tus.ac.jp

Abstract. In this paper, we describe the development of a support system that facilitates the process of learning computer programming through the reading of computer program. Reading code consists of two steps: reading comprehension and meaning deduction. In this study, we developed a tool that supports the deduction of a program's meaning. The tool is equipped with an error visualization function that illustrates a learner's mistakes and makes them aware of their errors. We conducted experiments using the learning support tool and confirmed that the system is effective.

Keywords: programming learning, flowchart, error-based simulation.

1 Introduction

This paper describes the development of a support system that facilitates the process of learning computer programming through the reading of computer program. In this study, we define reading source code as working backward from the code to determine the original requirement that led to the program. The process of reading code consists of two steps: reading comprehension and meaning deduction (see Fig. 1).

Information technology has spread throughout society, but there is a shortage of information engineers, and it is to train them in great numbers. There is extensive research on learning computer programming through the construction of computer programs [1]. However, gaining a deep understanding of programming requires learners to read source code as well [2].

Programming experts are highly skilled at reading code since this skill is essential in debugging programs and inferring their purpose [3]. Reading code is also important to gain a deeper understanding of programming. Furthermore, posing problems is often useful in understanding the scope of a computer program [4]. Accordingly, we

---

[*] Corresponding author.

S. Yamamoto (Ed.): HIMI/HCII 2013, Part III, LNCS 8018, pp. 63–69, 2013.

developed a support system that facilitates the process of learning programming through reading code.

2   The Process of Programming

In previous research, the process of programming has been considered to consist of two steps: algorithm design and coding. Algorithm design is the step in which structures, such as flow diagrams, are used to construct the abstract process based on the program's requirements. This processing flow is independent of the programming language. In contrast, coding is the step in which the abstract flow is converted into source code, which necessarily depends on the programming language. In learning programming, learners are often given problems as requirements, and write the appropriate source code by first considering the abstract processing flow.

We consider reading code to be an important skill that adds to the process of programming. In this study, we propose that the process of reading code consists of two steps: reading comprehension and meaning deduction (see Fig. 1). Reading comprehension is the inverse step of coding, and meaning deduction is the inverse step of algorithm design. In reading comprehension, learners are required to convert source code into an equivalent abstract processing flow. In meaning deduction, learners are required to deduce a requirement from the abstract processing flow.

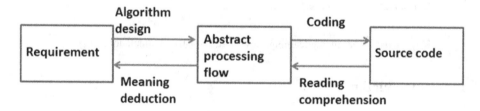

Fig. 1. The process of programming

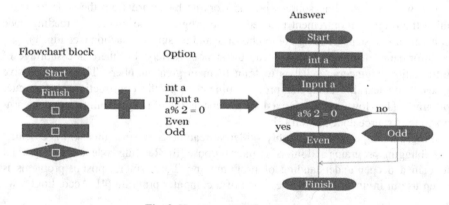

Fig. 2. How to write a flowchart

3   Learning Using a Flowchart

At the reading comprehension step, learners construct flowcharts from given pieces of source code. A flowchart has the advantage of making a problem (requirement) more likely to be discovered by representing it visually. Figure 2 shows the process of constructing a flowchart. A learner chooses a series of flowchart blocks and populates each block with one of several given options. Next, they connect the flowchart blocks with lines. By reducing the degrees of freedom of the answer, it is easier to convey the intent of the program.

4   Deducing Process Requirements

At the meaning deduction step, learners deduce process requirements from flowcharts by choosing statements and concepts from a number of options. By reducing the degrees of freedom of the answer, it is easier to convey the intent of the program.

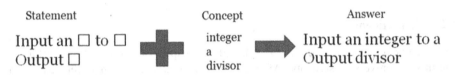

Fig. 3. How to write requirements

5   Error Visualization

Error visualization is the process of illustrating error [5]. Feedback is capable of teaching the correct answer and pointing out errors,   but the learner stops thinking if they are simply shown the correct answer. If a learner is only shown their mistakes, they are not able to understand how and why they erred. In contrast, illustrating the error can make the learner aware of their errors. On this basis, we developed a learning support system that includes an error visualization function.

6   Preliminary Experiment

We conducted two experiments with two different objectives: the objective of Experiment 1 was to examine the reading skill level of learners; and the objective of Experiment 2 was to examine the influence of reducing the degrees of freedom of an answer.

6.1   Experiment 1

In Experiment 1, we spent 10 min explaining the principles of writing a flowchart to 62 second-year university students attending a programming course. The students were asked to solve four reading comprehension problems in 20 min, four algorithm design problems in another 20 min, and four coding problems in a final 20 min. Problems were given in a free-response format, and the maximum score for each problem was 2 points.

Table 1 shows the results of Experiment 1. The average score was 1.20 for the reading comprehension exercise, 1.21 for the algorithm design exercise, and 1.69 for the coding exercise. From these results, we can conclude that reading comprehension and algorithm design were difficult. Although algorithm design is often considered to be more difficult than coding, reading comprehension was found to be as difficult as algorithm design.

Table 1. Experiment 1 Results

	Average score	Standard deviation
Algorithm design	1.21	0.52
Coding	1.69	0.39
Reading comprehension	1.20	0.38

6.2   Experiment 2

In Experiment 2, we took 10 min to explain the principles of writing a flowchart to 12 fourth-year university students. After the explanation, the students were asked to solve six reading comprehension problems in 30 minutes followed by six meaning deduction problems in 15 minutes. How to answer is proposed in sections 3 and 4. The maximum score for each problem was 2 points.

Table 2 shows the results of Experiment 2. The average score was 1.21 for the reading comprehension exercise and 0.64 for the meaning deduction exercise. From these results, we can conclude that the effect of reducing the degrees of freedom of the answer was small, and that meaning deduction was a difficult task. From Experiment 1 and Experiment 2 we confirmed the need to develop a support system that facilitates the process of learning programming through reading code.

Table 2. Experiment 2 Results

	Average score	Standard deviation
Reading comprehension	1.21	0.55
Meaning deduction	0.64	0.21

7   Learning Support System

7.1   Learning Screen

Figure 4 shows the learning screen of the learning support system. The learner uses concept and statement buttons to construct a problem statement. First, a student presses a statement button, which brings the statement with blank to the answer column. Next, a student presses a concept buttons and select blank, which inserts the concept into the blank. When the learner has completed an answer, he or she presses the answer button. If the answer is correct, a message of "Correct answer" is displayed; if the answer is incorrect, the system shows the feedback screen.

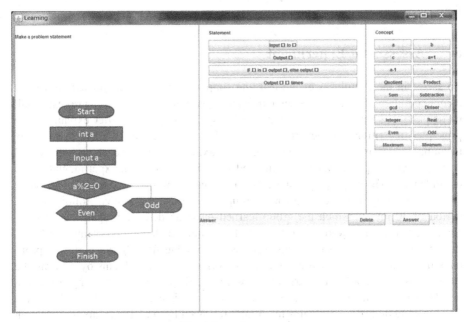

Fig. 4. Learning screen

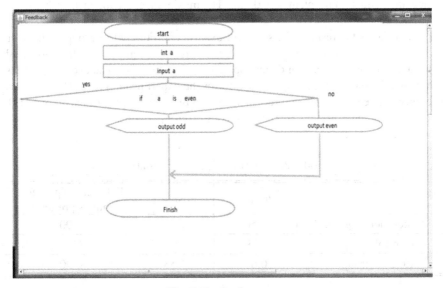

Fig. 5. Feedback screen

7.2   Feedback Screen

Figure 5 shows the feedback screen. If a learner incorrectly deduces a requirement, the system generates an incorrect flowchart based on the incorrect data, and the learner looks for their mistakes by comparing the incorrect flowchart to the correct flowchart.

8   Assessment Experiment

To ascertain the usefulness of the learning support system, we conducted an assessment experiment. In the assessment experiment, we first administered a pre-test for all participants (12 fourth-year university students). In the pre-test, after explaining the principles of writing a flowchart for 10 min, the participants were asked to solve six meaning deduction problems in 15 min. The maximum score for each problem was 2 points. Next, the participants were divided into three groups: an experimental group (4 students), control group 1 (4 students), and control group 2 (4 students). We spent 5 min explaining to the experimental group how to use the system, followed by a period of 30 min in which the group learned meaning deduction using our system. Next, the participants were asked to solve 10 meaning deduction problems in 30 min. In control group 1, the participants were asked to solve five algorithm design problems in 15 minutes, followed by studying algorithm design problems by viewing the correct answer. Finally, the participants were asked to solve 10 meaning deduction problems in 30 minutes. In control group 2, the participants were first asked to solve five meaning deduction problems in 15 min, followed by studying meaning deduction problems by viewing the correct answer. Finally, the participants were asked to solve 10 meaning deduction problems in 30 min. The maximum score for each problem was 2 points.

Table 3 shows the results of assessment experiment. For control group 1, the average post-test score was 1.33 and the average pre-test score was 0.50. This result shows that supporting meaning deduction learning is beneficial. The average post-test score was 1.53 for control group 2 and 1.50 for the experimental group. However, the difference between the average pre-test score and the average post-test score was 1.00 for the experimental group and 0.90 for control group 2. From this result, we confirmed that our system is effective.

Table 3. Assesment Experiment Results

	Pre-test	Post-test	Difference (post-test minus pre-test)
Experimental group	0.50	1.50	1.00
Control group 1	0.79	1.33	0.53
Control group 2	0.63	1.53	0.90

9   Conclusions and Future Work

In this study, we developed a learning support system to provide guidance in meaning deduction, and evaluated the effectiveness of our system. From the results of the assesment experiment, we confirmed that it is necessary to support meaning deduction learning, and that our system is effective. However, the assessment experiment did not include enough participants, and it is necessary to increase the number of participants in future experiments. Additionally, we did not develop a learning support system for guidance in reading comprehension, but believe it is necessary to develop one in the future.

References

1. Matsuda, N., Kashihara, A., Fukukawa, K., Toyoda, J.: An instructional system for constructing algorithms in recursive programming. In: Proc. of the Sixth International Conference on Human-Computer Interaction, Tokyo, Japan, pp. 889–894 (1995)
2. Corbi, T.A.: Program understanding challenge for the 1990s. IBM Syst. J. 28(2), 294–306 (1989)
3. Uchida, S., Kudo, H., Monden, A.: An experiment and an Analysis of debugging process with periodic interviews. In: Proceedings of Software Symposium 1998, Japanese, pp. 53–58 (1998)
4. Lyn, D.: Children's Problem Posing within Formal and Informal Contexts. Journal of Research in Mathematics Education 29(1), 83–106 (1998)
5. Hirashima, T.: Error-based simulation for error-visualization and its management. Int. J. of Artificial Intelligence in Education 9(1-2), 17–31 (1998)

The Display Medium, Academic Major and Sex Effect of High School Students on Visuospatial Abilities Test Performance

Yen-Yu Kang and Yu-Hsiang Liao

Department of Industrial Design, National Kaohsiung Normal University, Kaohsiung, Taiwan
yenyu@nknu.edu.tw, Shon7772002@gmail.com

Abstract. The objective of this study is to evaluate the spatial ability differences and fatigue between three different students on different interface. An experiment was design to compare the differences between using the convention book (C-book) and using tablet computer, and compare the differences between three department students. Fifty-four vocational high school students, age sixteen to eighteen, participated in the study. Response measure included task performance, eye fatigue (measured by critical flicker fusion, CFF), and wrist fatigue (measured by subjective borg 10-CR scale). The result indicate that using the C-book had higher performance and less wrist fatigue than using tablet computer. In addition, on score sequence of task performance, interior design student is first, architecture student is second, and general student is last.

Keywords: Tablet Computer, display.

1 Introduction

In the past, knowledge is often transferred and stored in books form, but with the development of technology, knowledge preservation and presentation have a breakthrough, under the technology advances, rising of environmental consciousness, and promotion of government policies, electronic reader will become the mainstream to get the message in the near future, personalized e-reader is regarded as the most convenient tool in reading [7].

When the obtainment and using of the information is gradually changing towards electronic, computerized tests have gradually been applied in many areas, such as a variety of license test, it may include education entrance exam in the future.

Many studies have pointed out that the level of spatial ability may affect some learning effectiveness, the maturity of the human mind, the computing ability, and language logical thinking ability [1, 2, 3, 4], so spatial ability is also be used as indicator of student ability.

In the past, many research in exploring spatial ability, assume that spatial ability is innate. However, in recent, the related study show that the past experience of

S. Yamamoto (Ed.): HIMI/HCII 2013, Part III, LNCS 8018, pp. 70–78, 2013.

individual may affect spatial ability, or through the strategy or method with elaborately planning can also improve spatial ability [5, 6].

But whether the interface differences cause differences of operating performance is also worth discussing. There are many factors affect the differences between reading a displays and reading a book, there were studies showed that reading performance and efficiency of the books are better than the reading a display.[7]

Belmore (1985)[8] found that, compared to paper reading, poor reading comprehension on the screen, and Mayers et al (2001)[9] pointed out that the screen reader and reading a paper had the same understanding, but the screen reader still spent more time to read, the two studies have different results, this may be because with the advances in technology, also improved the quality of the reading screen.

Therefore, reading conventional book is completely different than reading electronic reader, the reason may includes differences habits, and personal experience of different. Because of the develop of the computerized, whether the different interface will cause operating difference is worth to be investigated. The objective of this study is to evaluate the spatial ability differences and fatigue between three different students on different interface, by using objective measures including task performance, critical flicker fusion, and subjective fatigue.

2 Method

2.1 Subject

Twenty-seven male and 27 vocational high school students participated in the experiment. They average come from three different departments. Someone majors in architecture. Another majors in interior design, others study in general education. Each department student comprised equal female and male. Their age ranged from 16 to 18 years (mean=17.3, SD=0.45). The mean age of male subject was 17.4(SD=0.6). The mean age of female subject was 17.2(SD=0.32). They were required to have at least 20/25 visual acuity with corrective lenses and to be without physical or mental problems. They were also requested not to stay up late, take medicine, alcoholic drinks and any other substance that might possibly affect the test results. All subjects had no previous experience using an E-book.

2.2 Experimental Design

This study employs analysis of variance. The three independent variables are interface type (tablet computer and C-book), departments (architecture, interior design, and general education), and gender (female and male). Subjects were requested to use a tablet computer and a C-book respectively. The tablet computer used in this study is Ipad2 which made in Apple inc., and had the following characteristic: (1) view screen: 241.2mm × 185.7mm, (2) resolution: 1024 × 768(132ppi), and (3) font size: headline: 24-point, content: 18-point. A C-book was prepared in the same format as the E-book so as to minimize differences between the two, it illustrated in Fig. 1.

The aspect ratio and paper size of the C-book was similar to the viewing screen of the tablet computer. The font of both books was Ming type Chinese characters that is the most frequently used font for Chinese textual information and is also known as the standard writing type. The size of each Chinese character was similar to the size of Chinese characters used in the tablet computer. The main difference between reading the tablet computer and the C-book was the interface manipulation. For manipulating the tablet computer, the subjects slide the screen to go to the next page and, used his or her fingers to turn pages in the C-book. The response measures included Task Performance (spatial shorten-memory and spatial ability.) and eye fatigue measure (CFF), and wrist fatigue measure.

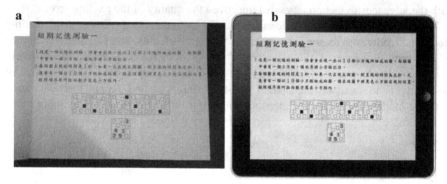

Fig. 1. The Illustration of: (a) C-book and (b) Tablet computer (ipad2) used in this study

Task Performance. In the experiment all subjects had spatial shorten-memory test and spatial ability test. They have both same tests on a tablet computer and C-book, but different quiz sorting. All tests would spend about fifty to sixty minutes. The spatial shorten-memory test contains Corsi block task, arrow span task, and dot memory task, the objective of those tests is to recall position and sorting for each mark. Those test materials is illustrated in Fig. 2.

The spatial ability test contains spatial relation test, card rotation test, and hidden figures test, the objective of spatial relation test is try to match the plane figure to correct three-dimensional figure; the objective of card rotation test is try to figure out the correct card in those rotation card; the objective of hidden figure test is try to cognized correct figures which have the Benchmark line. The test material is illustrated in Fig. 3.

Both score of spatial shorten-memory test and spatial ability test were taken as performance measures.

Eye Fatigue. CFF is a common used measure of visual fatigue because of its characteristic of effective and easy to operate and [10, 11]. It measures the minimal number of flashes of light per second at which an intermittent light stimulus no longer stimulates a continuous sensation. As a highly sensitive and easy-to-use measure, CFF is applied here to evaluate eye fatigue.

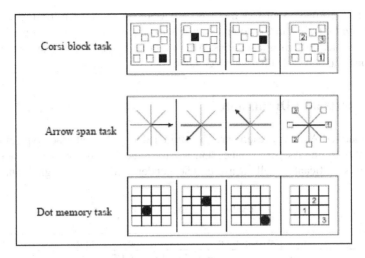

Fig. 2. Spatial shorten-memory test

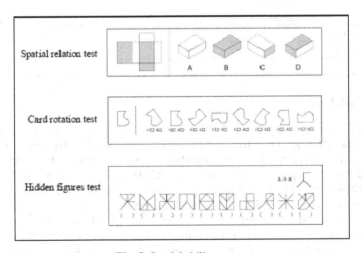

Fig. 3. Spatial ability test

Wrist Fatigue. At the beginning of each experiment session, the subject was required wrist fatigue measure as a baseline for comparison. The subject was asked status of their wrist by their subjective feeling, evaluated it by Borg CR-10 scale.

2.3   Experiment Procedure

A standard classroom desk and chair were provided for experimentation. The experiment environment was standardized. Prior to the experiment each subject was instructed about the purpose and procedure of the study. At the beginning of each experiment session, the subject's CFF was measured as a baseline for comparison. Then, the subject asked to finish the spatial shorten-memory test and spatial ability test, proportion of correction answer for those test were taken as score. Last, each subject was measured CFF again for comparison. Each subject was required to participate in two performance experiment sessions. After completing one performance experiment, another one was scheduled for one week later.

3   Results and Discussion

The summarized ANOVA results are shown in Table 1. The interface type effect was significant both on task performance and wrist fatigue. The department's background effect was significant on all measure. The gender effect is not significant on this study.

Table 1. The ANOVA results

factor	task performance		eye fatigue	wrist fatigue
	spatial shorten-memory	spatial ability	CFF	wrist subjective measure
interface type	**	*		*
department	**	***	*	
gender				

3.1   Task Performance

Task performance was measured by score of spatial shorten-memory and spatial ability. The interface type had a difference affect significantly. Fig.4 shows the performance difference for both interface type. For the C-book the average performance of spatial shorten-memory was 52.95, and the average performance of spatial ability was 51.71. For tablet computer the average performance of spatial shorten-memory was 47.05, and the performance of spatial ability was 48.29. On performance of spatial shorten-memory, using the C-book get 5.9 score more than using the tablet computer. On performance of spatial ability, using the C-book get 3.42 score more than using the tablet computer. The result shows that using C-book had higher performance than using tablet computer. This may be attributed to manipulate habit that people used to take a test by C-book interface type.

The department effect was significant on both task performances, and there was no significant interaction effect. The subjects who major in interior design get 53.63 score on spatial shorten-memory, and get 54.10 score on spatial ability. The subjects who major in architecture get 49.55score on spatial shorten-memory and get 49.81 score on spatial ability. The subjects who study in general education get 46.82 score on spatial shorten-memory and get 46.09 score on spatial ability. The performance differences shows in Fig.5. The subjects who major in interior design had better performance both than the subjects who major in architecture, and the subjects who major in architecture had better performance both than the subjects who study in general education. This may be explained that past experience of individual may affect spatial ability, included of education background.

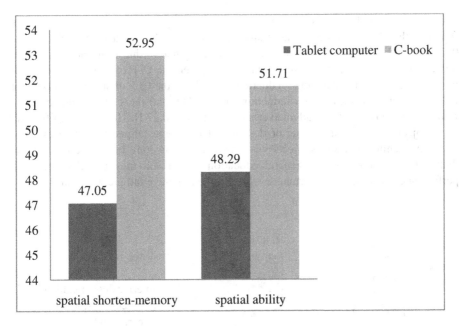

Fig. 4. The task performance for both interfaces

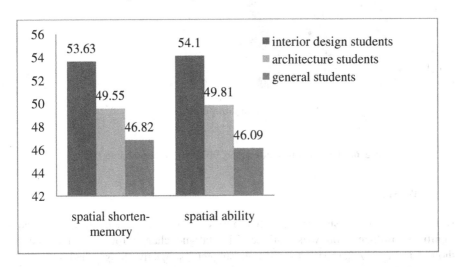

Fig. 5. The task performance for three different background students

3.2   Eye Fatigue

This study measured eye fatigue by CFF. Only department difference had significant influence on eye fatigue, but there was no significant interaction effect to interface. The CFF comparison result of three department show in Fig.6. After using the

C-book, the CFF of subjects who major in interior design had an average reduction of 0.77 Hz, the CFF of subjects who major in architecture had an average reduction of 0.53 Hz, and the CFF of subjects who study in general education had an average reduction of 0.30 Hz. After using the tablet computer, the CFF of subjects who major in interior design had an average reduction of 0.87 Hz, the CFF of subjects who major in architecture had an average reduction of 0.81 Hz, and the CFF of subjects who study in general education had an average reduction of 0.27 Hz. It seems significantly that subjects who major in interior design had more eye fatigue than subjects who major in architecture, and subjects who major in architecture had more eye fatigue than subjects who study in general education. The result may be related to task performance. The better performance who get, the more eye fatigue who had.

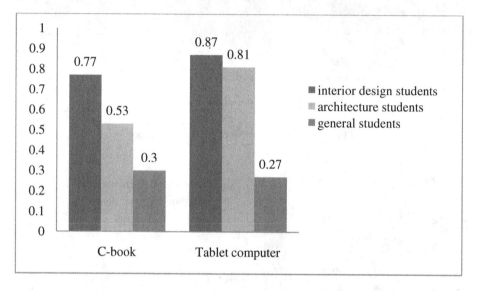

Fig. 6. The department effect on CFF changes for both interface

3.3   Wrist Fatigue

Wrist fatigue was measure by subjective borg CR-10 scale. Only interface type had a significant influence on wrist fatigue. The fatigue change for both interfaces is showed in Fig.7. After using the C-book, subjects' subjective fatigue had an average raise of 0.28. After using the tablet computer, subjects' subjective fatigue had an average raise of 0.81. It seems that using tablet computer would cause more wrist fatigue than using C-book. This may be attributed to usability of computer stylus. In the experiment procedure, many subjects mentioned that they were not accustomed to using the stylus.

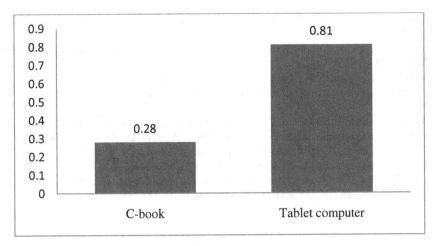

Fig. 7. The wrist fatigue for both interfaces

4   Conclusion

This study is evaluated the spatial ability differences and fatigue between three different students on using the C-book compared with using the tablet computer. The result indicated that using the C-book had higher performance and less wrist fatigue than using tablet computer. This is mainly attributed to using habit. People had more experience of using the C-book on test than using the tablet on test. In addition, on score sequence of task performance, interior design student is first, architecture student is second, and general student is last. The performance difference is due to education al background, the course would create the spatial ability difference, just like past studies said [5,6].

References

1. Carter, C.S., Chi, M.T.H.: Spatial Ability in General Chemistry. NARST, French Lick (1985)
2. Cronbach, L.J., Snow, R.E.: Aptitudes and instructional methods: A handbook for research on interactions. Irvington, New York (1977)
3. Lohman, D.F.: Spatial Ability: Individual Differences in Speed and Level (Tech.Rep.No.9). Aptitude Research Project, School of Education (NTIS No.AD-A075973). Stanford University, Stanford, CA (1979)
4. Pribyl, J.R., Bordner, G.M.: The Role of Spatial Ability and Achievement in Organic Chemistry. ED, 255–393 (1985)
5. Lord, T.R.: Enhancing the Visual-Spatial Aptitude of Students. Journal of Research in Science Teaching 22(5), 395–405 (1985)
6. McCormack, A.: Visual / Spatial Thinking: An Element of Elementary School Science. Council for elementary science international, San Diego State University (1988)

7. Kang, Y.Y., Wang, M.J., Lin, R.T.: Usability evaluation of E-book. Displays 30, 49–52 (2009)
8. Belmore, S.M.: Reading computer-presented text. Bulletin of the psychonomic Society 23(1), 12–14 (1985)
9. Mayers, D.K., Sims, V.K., Koonce, J.M.: Comprehension and workload differences for VDT and paper-based reading. International Journal of Industrial Ergonomics 28(6), 367–378 (2001)
10. Shen, I.H., Shieh, K.K., Chao, C.Y., Lee, D.S.: Lighting, font style, and polarity on visual performance and visual fatigue with electronic paper displays. Display 30, 53–58 (2009)
11. Wang, M.J., Huang, C.L.: Evaluating the Eye Fatigue Problem in Wafer Inspection. IEEE Transactions on Semiconductor Manufacturing 17(3), 444–447 (2004)
12. Chi, C.F., Lin, F.T.: A comparison of seven visual fatigue assessment techniques using three data-acquisition. VDT Tasks Human Factors 40(4), 577–590 (1998)

Video Feedback System for Teaching Improvement Using Students' Sequential and Overall Teaching Evaluations

Yusuke Kometani[1], Takahito Tomoto[2], Takehiro Furuta[3], and Takako Akakura[2]

[1] Graduate School of Engineering
[2] Faculty of Engineering, Tokyo University of Science,
1-3 Kagurazaka, Shinjuku-ku,Tokyo 162-8601 Japan
{kometani,tomoto,akakura}@ms.kagu.tus.ac.jp
[3] Nara University of Education, Takahata-cho, Nara-city, Nara 630-8528, Japan
takef@nara-edu.ac.jp

Abstract. We propose a system that allows university teachers to check the effectiveness of their lecture videos and to grasp points for improvement in the lectures. The system offers two functions: time-series graphing, which visualizes real-time changes in students' evaluation during a lecture, and teaching-behavior estimation, which shows teachers information on their own teaching behaviors estimated from the overall evaluation by students of a lecture. The system was developed and evaluation experiments of each function were conducted. The subjective evaluation of each function by teachers showed the following: (1) the time series graph function was useful to narrow down which portion of the lecture videos contained points for improvement and (2) the teaching behavior estimation function was useful to determine the tendency of teaching behavior in a lecture.

Keywords: Sequential evaluation, Overall evaluation, Teaching improvement, Lecture video, Teaching behavior, Student evaluation.

1 Introduction

We present here a methodology to support university teachers to achieve improvements in lecturing. Our approach is to provide a web-based system that allows teachers to review their own lecture videos. However, teachers often need support to grasp the exact points for improvement in their lectures, thus we propose a system that presents lecture evaluation data obtained from the students in conjunction with a lecture video to make teachers aware of areas for improvement.

The evaluations obtained from students can be roughly divided into the following three timeframes: (1) end-of-term, (2) each lecture, and (3) real-time during a lecture. Here we focus on items (2) and (3), which we refer to as "overall evaluation" and "sequential evaluation," respectively. We have designed a feedback system for teachers that provides lecture videos along with sequential and overall evaluation information. The purpose of this study was to verify the usefulness of this system as a means of support for teachers seeking how their lectures may be improved.

S. Yamamoto (Ed.): HIMI/HCII 2013, Part III, LNCS 8018, pp. 79–88, 2013.

The problems that may arise when a teacher develops a strategy to improve a lecture can be outlined as follows. First, to identify areas to improve, time is required to look through the lecture video. The teacher must check the entire video, including portions of it where information is not directly relevant to improvements. We have therefore designed a function that presents a summary of the sequential evaluation data in order to allow the teacher to narrow down in advance the areas that should be improved. Second, teachers will most likely look for which of their teaching behaviors need to be improved. However, monitoring teaching behavior by watching individual lecture videos is not efficient. To solve this problem, we have constructed a model to estimate the behavior of a teacher from an overall evaluation of each lecture. We have designed and incorporated into the system a function to estimate teaching behavior based on the results of the constructed model.

We formulated the following research questions based on the above considerations:

1. Is the sequential evaluation function useful in aiding teachers to identify areas in the lecture video that need improvement?
2. Which teaching behavior estimation models are applicable to multiple lectures on different topics?
3. Can teaching behavior estimation based on overall evaluations help teachers gain insight into how to improve their lectures?

2   Related Studies

Lecture evaluation feedback methods and student reactions to support lecture improvement have been studied in the past. Stalmeijer et al. explored whether feedback effectiveness improved when physician teachers' self-assessments were added to written feedback based on student ratings[3]. The physician teachers considered the combination of self-assessment and student ratings more effective than either self-assessment or written feedback alone. The authors concluded that self-assessment can be useful in stimulating teaching improvement. However, there was no evidence that the teachers grasped points for improvement by reviewing individual lecture videos. Thus, our proposed method additionally involves an objective evaluation of the teaching behavior based on evaluations obtained from the students and the data are then fed back to the teacher.

Hanakawa and Obana showed that lecture improvement was possible through the use of a Twitter log[4]. They developed a system that supported student-teacher interaction during large-scale lectures. During lectures, this system allowed students to send the teacher their reactions and messages, through a handheld unit, related to the clarity of the lesson. A common pattern between lectures was discovered by analyzing the evaluation log and the students' reactions. The teacher was able to know the points of improvement by comparing the lecture video against the common pattern identified. In addition, after teachers strived to improve their teaching, negative evaluations from the students decreased. Hanakawa and Obana's method identifies a common pattern that emerges across multiple lectures, whereas the present study suggests a method to help teachers understand areas for improvement when watching an individual lecture video.

3   System Design

Different lecture forms, shown in Table 1, were considered in the process of acquiring sequential and overall evaluation information. These forms were applied in actual university lectures. We designed the system as a Web application to support both lecture forms. Figure 1 shows the perspectives of the students and teachers. Evaluation input from student handheld devices such as smartphones is enabled during a lecture through the system interface.

Figure 2 shows the system configuration. The system includes a UI for students and a UI for teachers. Individual students can input their lecture evaluation through the UI and a teacher uses the UI to check the lecture video as well as student feedback from the lecture evaluation.

Table 1. Evaluation forms

Type	FTF	After FTF	VOD	After VOD	Lecture form
A	Sequential	Overall			FTF using mobile terminals[1]
B	Sequential			Overall	Blended Learning(FTF+VOD)[2]
C		Overall	Sequential		
D			Sequential	Overall	e-Learning

FTF : face-to-face, VOD : video on demand

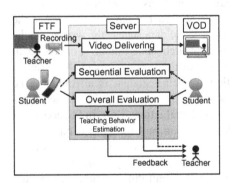

Fig. 1. Overview of evaluation forms

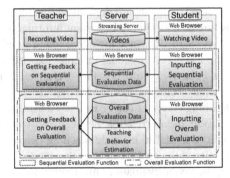

Fig. 2. System Configuration

3.1   Design of the Sequential Evaluation Function

One condition of sequential evaluation is that ratings change as the lecture progresses. A preliminary investigation was carried out to clarify what questionnaire items are suitable for sequential evaluation. We acquired one set of evaluation data during a certain lecture as it progressed and another set at the end of the lecture using questionnaire items from a general student survey. The results showed that six items were available for sequential evaluation: "clarity of the explanation," "degree of understanding of the lecture contents," "degree of interest," "teaching attitude," "ease of hearing," and "ease of seeing writing on the blackboard."

It is necessary to design an input UI which, as much as possible, does not interfere with a lecture. Therefore, the system requires choices that students can choose intuitively. We carried out a preliminary survey to determine the choices, starting first with a prototype, then having students input their evaluation for the six questions while watching a lecture video. As a result, there were many opinions regarding whether a judgment was easy to immediately convey through the choices. For example, choices such as "I can understand" and "I'm not interested" were easy for students to choose. As a result, we decided to use these types of choices, and we developed a system experimentally and performed a preliminary experiment to have multiple students evaluate the six items. As a result of this preliminary experiment, we confirmed the possibility that a teacher could grasp areas for improvement in a lecture by paying attention to changes in the students' evaluation. Thus, it is important that the teacher notices changes in the sequential evaluation information. To meet these requirements, we made a function to graph the time series change in the ratings; we call this function the time series graph function.

3.2   Design of the Overall Evaluation Function

We designed the feedback function of the overall evaluation data. The score of the overall evaluation made by a student does not highlight what the teacher should be paying more attention to. For example, it takes effort to pinpoint a problem with the blackboard demonstration when there are many evaluations saying it is "hard to understand a blackboard demonstration." In contrast, the teacher can pay attention to the action of underlining important information more if the data states "the writing on the blackboard does not include enough emphasis through underlining." For a student who has no professional teaching experience, it is difficult to directly evaluate teaching behavior. However, the overall evaluation from the student is affected by the teaching behavior that the teacher chose. This shows the possibility that the teacher's teaching behavior can be estimated using an overall evaluation. Thus, in Section 4, we analyze the correlation between the overall evaluation and teaching behavior. We build a model to estimate teaching behavior from an overall evaluation based on the results of the analysis. Using this model, we suggest a function to feedback the teaching behavior evaluation information to the teacher. We call this function the teaching behavior estimation function.

4   Correlation Analysis between Teaching Behavior and Overall Evaluation

It is thought that the overall evaluation can be divided into "content evaluation" and "teaching behavior evaluation." Thus, we expect a correlation between the overall evaluation and teaching behavior. We define teaching behavior in order to count it and clarify the correlation between it and the overall evaluation. Next, we check this expectation and build a correlation model of overall evaluations and teaching behaviors. The following questions are examined:

4. Does teaching behavior affect the overall evaluation?
5. Can the model estimate individual teaching behaviors from among the many teaching behaviors displayed?

4.1   Method

We compared two lectures with similar content, one given in 2010 and the other in 2011, in order to determine whether specific teaching behaviors influence the overall evaluation. Overall evaluations were carried out during the information mathematics (IM) lecture given at the authors' universities. Two sets of data were collected: lectures 2–13 in 2010 and lectures 4–13 in 2011. Around 80 students attended each of the lectures. Twenty questionnaire items, such as "degree of content understanding" and "degree of interest," were chosen from an existing general student evaluation. For each item, the students answered using a 5-point Likert scale. The students were given approximately 5 minutes in each lecture to fill out the survey. The lecture was recorded with a video camera.

We first watched the lecture videos to identify the teaching behaviors used, then extracted two lectures of similar content that had a difference in rating level for a particular questionnaire item. We considered we would be able to identify how a specific teaching behavior affects the overall evaluation by comparing the use of the behavior in the two lectures. We performed a t-test to more specifically evaluate any questionnaire item identified. If there was at least one item with a difference in level of significance greater than 0.05, one of the authors watched the two lectures in detail and compared the evaluation results to the actual occurrence of the teaching behavior. In this way we determined which specific teaching behaviors to include in the analysis. We defined the specific teaching behaviors as those that could be counted from the video analysis and then counted each in turn. For example, we saw that changing the color of a phrase or sentence ("Coloring") and underlining a phrase or a sentence ("Underlining") frequently occurred in comparison with other teaching behaviors. Here "Coloring" denotes "the number of times that a color was changed in a word or sentence" and "Underlining" denotes "the number of times a word or sentence was underlined." Based on these definitions, one of the authors watched the paired lecture videos and counted the occurrences of coloring and underlining in each lecture. We confirmed whether a difference emerged in the overall evaluation results between the similar lectures by noting the difference in the number of times each teaching behavior occurred.

4.2   Results and Discussion

In comparing similar lectures, the score for a specific questionnaire item tended to increase if the teacher's activity at the blackboard increased. A specific example of this is the teacher at the blackboard "emphasizing a phrase or sentence" by coloring or underlining, as defined above. Once the teaching behaviors of "Coloring" and "Underlining" were determined, we confirmed whether a difference emerges for the overall evaluation according to a difference in the number of times each teaching behavior occurred. The tenth lecture from the 2011 dataset was compared with the ninth lecture from the 2010 dataset as a large difference in coloring and underlining behavior was observed for lectures on the same topic. The frequency of both "Coloring" and "Underlining" was 0 in the ninth lecture in 2010, while the frequency of "Coloring" had increased to 3 and the frequency of "Underlining" had increased to 18 in the tenth lecture in 2011. T-test results showed the items that varied in the evaluations were "ease of notetaking" ($t=2.79$, $p \leq 0.01$) and "teacher's ability to explain an abstract topic" ($t=2.53$, $p \leq 0.01$). The lecture in 2011 clearly had a higher evaluation than for the similar lecture in 2010, and similarly there was a large difference in the number of times each teaching behavior was observed between the two lectures. Thus, these results indicate that these two different teaching behaviors affected the overall evaluation.

Correlation analysis was performed for all the lectures mentioned above, and models to estimate occurrences of "Coloring" and "Underlining" were developed. The questionnaire items indicating a slight correlation with "Coloring" were "Did the teacher explain abstract concepts plainly?" ($r = 0.60$), "Was the explanation simple?"($r = 0.49$), "Did the example aid your understanding?"($r = 0.46$), and "Was the quiz difficult?"($r = -0.47$). The questionnaire items indicating a slight correlation with "underlining" were "Did you feel the teacher's was motived in teaching?"($r = 0.53$) and "Did the teacher give an explanation that was easy to note down?"($r = 0.41$). The items that correlated to "Coloring" and "Underlining" were different, and therefore "Coloring" and "Underlining" can be estimated individually. A function to estimate "Coloring" and "Underlining" was then generated with those questionnaire items.

5   System Development

5.1   Time Series Graph Function

Based on the system design, a sequential evaluation input function and time series graph function were developed. Figure 3 shows the time series graph. This graph corresponds to conditions selected in the upper part. The values are plotted at the points the students evaluated, then connected by a straight line. The function can overlay evaluation results from multiple items or multiple students, as well as display the average rating.

If there were multiple parts of a lecture video for a teacher to watch, it was difficult to determine which parts should take precedence based only on the time series graph. As a supporting function to determine precedence, we used thumbnails of the lecture video. The thumbnail was connected to the evaluation point in the time series graph. The teacher could quickly confirm the contents of a specific part based on the content of the blackboard. In addition, the teacher could focus on improving areas only in the range of the video that corresponded to the thumbnail.

5.2   Teaching Behavior Estimation Function

Figure 4 shows the UI of the teaching behavior estimation function. Teachers can see messages on the upper portion and a scatter diagram on the lower portion. In the scatter diagram, the x-axis represents the occurrence of a teaching behavior and the y-axis represents the mean rating of the question. Actual data is drawn in the scatter diagram. The teacher can compare current data with past data. The message is changed based on the occurrences of a given teaching behavior measured in the past. The range between 0 and the maximum occurrence of a given teaching behavior is divided into 3 parts: "not performed very often," "performed a little," and "performed," depending on the estimated number of occurrences of the behavior.

"Degree of understanding of the content" and "Satisfaction with the lecture" are important standards as to whether or not a teacher should improve a teaching behavior. Therefore, to support the teaching behavior estimation function, we developed a function to show a rating ratio as a 100% accumulated stick graph for each question item.

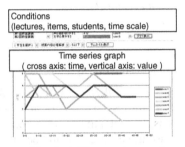

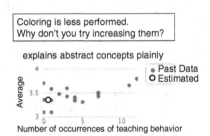

Fig. 3. A Time series graph

Fig. 4. User interface of teaching behavior estimation function

6   Experiments

Although it is true that teachers can grasp the points of improvement of a lecture more efficiently by combining the time series graph function and teaching behavior estimation function, we aim to clarify the usefulness of each function in this research. Therefore, individual evaluation experiments were carried out for the time series graph function and for the teaching behavior estimation function.

This system was designed for use with multiple lecture forms. However, in order to evaluate the functions, we imposed three restrictions in the experimental conditions so that students could perform as many evaluations as possible:

1. Students input sequential evaluation in an e-learning environment.
2. The system specifies the evaluation timing while the students evaluate all six items simultaneously.
3. The video stops while the student is evaluating.

Overall evaluations experiments were carried out in face-to-face (FTF) lectures in order to secure participants.

6.1   Evaluation of the Time Series Graph Function

Evaluation of the function is based on a teacher's subjective evaluations. There are two teachers: Teacher A and Teacher B. We recorded in advance the multiple lectures they were in charge of teaching. We chose one video of a difficult lecture topic from Teacher A (Lecture A), and the corresponding lecture video from Teacher B (Lecture B). Lecture A is 90 minutes long and Lecture B is 45 minutes long, and the evaluation intervals of Lecture A and Lecture B are 10 minutes and 5 minutes, respectively. Fourteen students in all participated in this experiment: seven students evaluated Lecture A and the other seven students evaluated Lecture B. All students were college seniors at the authors' universities.

Teachers A and B then checked the data using the time series graph function. We first gave them directions on how to use the function, then had them use the system individually. They checked whether their lecture had any points for improvement. Finally, we distributed a questionnaire to them to evaluate the function. The questions on the questionnaire were as follows:

Qs1: Do you have any requests regarding the evaluation timing?
Qs2: Do you want to actually use this system?
Qs3: Do you think that a time series graph function is useful?
Qs4: Do you think that a thumbnail function is useful?
Qs5: Can you grasp the lecture points for improvement using this system?

The answers for Qs2 through Qs5 were given using a 5-point Likert scale. Teacher A answered "4" for all questions. Teacher B answered "4" for Qs5 and "5" for all other questions. Both teachers submitted positive evaluations. In explaining their responses to Qs3 and Qs4, they expressed that the system was useful because it would be difficult to notice a bad portion in the video and it would also take time if watch the video from the beginning. These results show the effectiveness of the time series graph to support teachers in pinpointing points for improvement from a lecture video. As for Qs1, their opinion was that it would be even more useful if the timing could be specified as arbitrary time in the lecture video. On Qs5 they said that it takes a little more time to find a clear point for improvement, although it was possible to narrow it down to some extent. Given these comments, a tool for more effective teaching behavior support should be developed in the future. However, as this experiment was conducted under the limited conditions, in future research it is necessary to run the experiment in a more realistic situation with fewer conditions imposed.

6.2   Evaluation of the Teaching Behavior Estimation Function

Overall evaluations of the teaching behavior estimation function were carried out during IM lectures at the authors' universities in the 2012 fiscal year. The evaluation considered 10 lectures. We used 20 items for the construction of the model identical to those described in Section 4. There were an average of 74.1 participants (SD = 5.7), all in either the second or third grade. All the lectures were recorded. Teachers watched all 10 lecture videos, using the teaching behavior estimation function. The subjects were five teachers, consisting of the lead teacher (R) and four coworkers (P1, P2, A1,

A2). R is an associate professor with 10 years of work experience. P1 and P2 are professors with 27 and 31 years of experience. A1 and A2 are assistant instructors with 1 and 4 years of work experience. Each teacher evaluated the teacher behavior estimation function after watching the video. The teachers' subjective evaluations were obtained with a questionnaire. The reason we targeted fellow teachers is to investigate whether the evaluation changed depending on the teacher's background.

Table 2. Results of the teachers' evaluation of the teaching method

#	Question	R	P1	P2	A1	A2
Qo1	The teaching method affects students' understanding of lecture contents.	5	4	4	4	5
Qo2	Students can judge whether a quality of teaching is good or bad.	4	4	4	2	2
Qo3	Student evaluations are useful for improving lectures.	4	4	4	4	5
Qo4	The lesson evaluation acquired after each lecture is effective for lesson improvement.	4	2	3	4	5
Qo5	It is useful for a teaching point for improvement to be estimated by the students' lecture evaluation.	5	3	5	5	5

Table 3. Evaluation of the teacher behavior estimation function by teachers

#	Question	P1	P2	Avg.	R	A1	A2	Avg.
Qo6	Lecture videos with a message and the scatter diagram about "Underlining" help to pinpoint the areas for improvement in the lecture.	2	2	2	3	3	4	3.5
Qo7	Lecture videos with a message and the scatter diagram about "Coloring" help to pinpoint the areas for improvement in the lecture.	2	2	2	3	3	4	3.5
Qo8	The message about "Underlining" served as a reference in examining the points for improvement in the lecture.	2	2	2	3	4	4	4
Qo9	The message about "Coloring" served as a reference in examining the points for improvement in the lecture.	2	2	2	3	4	4	4
Qo10	The scatter diagram about "Underlining" served as a reference in examining the points for improvement in the lecture.	2	2	2	2	3	4	3.5
Qo11	The scatter diagram about "Coloring" served as a reference in examining the points for improvement in the lecture.	2	2	2	2	3	4	3.5
Qo12	The bar graph, message, and scatter diagram about "Underlining" are useful in examining the points for improvement in the lecture.	2	2	2	4	4	5	4.5
Qo13	The bar graph, message, and scatter diagram about "Coloring" are useful in examining the points for improvement in the lecture.	2	2	2	4	4	5	4.5
Qo14	The message about "Underlining" was appropriate.	3	2	2.5	4	3	5	4
Qo15	The message about "Coloring" was appropriate.	3	3	3	4	3	5	4

Table 2 shows the evaluations of using teaching behaviors for lecture improvements submitted by the teachers. Nearly all the teachers answered positively to Qo1 and Qo5. Teachers A1 and A2 answered Qo2 negatively, explaining that although students can perform subjective evaluations, it is difficult for them to evaluate teaching behavior. The Qo3 and Qo4 results show that lecture evaluations alone are not effective for lecture improvement. These results suggest that the teachers support the use of the teaching behavior estimation function.

Table 3 shows the results of the teachers' evaluation of the teaching behavior estimation function. In comparing all items, R has a tendency to rate higher than P, and A has a tendency to rate higher than R. Teacher P1 provided this reason for a negative evaluation: "Although it is advisable, it is not essential." On the contrary, R said "it is useful to know a tendency for a teaching behavior because this leads to enhanced awareness." Moreover, A1 had the same opinion as R. According to these results, although the teachers with long work experience regard the information as important, the teachers with comparatively short work experience tend to view the information as constructive criticism that can be used to improve their lectures. Therefore, the teaching behavior estimation function may be useful, especially for young teachers.

We interviewed R about his intention when underlining and changing the color of a character. He replied that he uses underline unconsciously, but is aware of consciously changing the character color to distinguish a concept. This shows that the correlation between "Coloring" and "explains an abstract concept plainly" is a valid relation.

7   Conclusions and Future Work

We have proposed a function that provides sequential evaluation and overall evaluation information to the teacher as feedback. A system with such functions was developed and an evaluation experiment was conducted on it. We showed through subjective evaluations from teachers that the sequential evaluation and overall evaluation information was helpful. The advantage of the time series graph function was that it was able to pinpoint portions of the lecture videos that should be reviewed. The teaching behavior estimation function was useful in making teachers more aware of their teaching behaviors. A teaching behavior estimation function could possibly be useful, especially for teachers with little work experience.

The evaluation of the time series graph function and the evaluation of the teaching behavior estimation function were carried out separately. In the future we will examine how to combine these functions, increase the types of teaching behavior examined, and build a higher-precision model.

Acknowledgements. This research was partially supported by the Japanese Ministry of Education, Science, Sports and Culture, Grant-in-Aid for Scientific Research, 24300291, 2012–2015.

References

1. Nagaoka, K.: A response analyzer system utilizing mobile phones. In: Proc. of the IASTED International Conference Web-Based Education, pp. 579–584 (2005)
2. Nikolaidou, M., Sofianopoulou, C., Giannopoulos, I.: Assessing the Contribution of Lecture Video Service in the Hybrid Learning Ecosystem of Harokopio University of Athens. In: 2010 Second International Conference on Mobile, Hybrid, and On-Line Learning, pp. 141–146 (2010)
3. Stalmeijer, R.E., Dolmans, D.H.J.M., Wolfhagen, I.H.A.P., Peters, W.G.: Lieve van Coppenolle, Scherpbier, A. J. J. A.: Combined student ratings and self-assessment provide useful feedback for clinical teachers. Adv. Health Sci. Educ. 15, 315–328 (2010)
4. Hanakawa, N., Obana, M.: Lecture Improvement based on Twitter Logs and Lecture Video using p-HInT. In: Proc. of the 18th International Conference on Computers in Education, pp. 328–335 (2010)

I See, Please Tell Me More – Exploring Virtual Agents as Interactive Storytellers

David Lindholm[1], Eva Petersson Brooks[1], and Tom Nauerby[2]

[1] Centre for Design, Learning and Innovation, Aalborg University Esbjerg, Denmark
[2] Development and Evaluation, Municipality of Esbjerg, Denmark
dal@learning.aau.dk, ep@create.aau.dk, tna@esbjergkommune.dk

Abstract. This study explored the effect of a virtual agent, used as a storyteller in an interactive story, with the purpose of distributing information to leaders at the municipal government of Esbjerg, Denmark. The aim was to investigate the influence an agent might have on the user experience, when comparing it to a story with no agent. A simple story was implemented where the user could choose which parts to read. A test was held where ten participants went through the story with and without an agent as a storyteller, and took part in a focus group discussion. Data on story choices and time was saved and analysed along with the focus group data. From the overall findings it can be concluded that a storyteller agent has a positive impact on the experience. Furthermore, that interactive storytelling requires care in placement of important information, so as to avoid it being missed.

Keywords: Storytelling, Agent, Information distribution, User experience, Leadership.

1 Introduction

"Storytelling taps into one of the oldest pastimes, a way of uniting communities, conveying truths and entertaining those we love. Children beg to be told a bedtime story, and so, a small part of us continues to feel comforted and reassured by information presented in the form of a tale" [1].

Storytelling has increasingly been used as a leadership and information distribution tool. "Leadership involves inspiring people to act in unfamiliar and often unwelcome ways. Mind-numbing cascades of numbers or daze inducing PowerPoint slides won't achieve this goal. Even logical arguments for making the changes usually won't do the trick. But effective storytelling often does" [2]. A common element of storytelling is the storyteller herself. "The storyteller, more than other type of sender, manages to capture the attention of the hearer, keeping the energies involved in the process of telling" [3]. A virtual agent [4] is a common way of telling a story in an application. Related work [5, 6] indicates that there is a preference for having a storyteller present visually, even if he/she is unrelated to the story. Furthermore, it hinted at a possible correlation between the length of the material and the strength of the user's desire to

S. Yamamoto (Ed.): HIMI/HCII 2013, Part III, LNCS 8018, pp. 89–98, 2013.

have a storyteller [6]. Other research [7, 8] has indicated that nonverbal behaviour of virtual agents also influences the experience of the user. It has also been determined that an agent with different facial expressions is perceived as more credible [9]. Hertzum [10] emphasizes the importance of trust in a virtual agent for information distribution. While others [11, 12] emphasize the importance of having facial expressions matching the emotions the agent is supposed to be feeling at that moment. Elliott [13] further highlights the benefits of multi-modality in agent perception.

2   Methodology

2.1   Hypothesis and Research Questions

The hypothesis was formulated as: "A virtual agent will not influence the experience of the story, compared to a non-agent situation, when it comes to storytelling for information distribution". Additionally, the following sub-questions were investigated:

- What impact will the virtual agent have on the experience?
- If information is presented as a dialogue tree, is there a risk of information being missed by the user?
- Are there factors that impact the design of an agent for storytelling?

2.2   Case Study

A case study approach [14] was chosen for this work, where the main focus was work environment guidelines in the municipal government of Esbjerg, Denmark (MGoE). The recipients of this information are 25-60 years of age, of both genders, and mainly working in desk jobs at city hall. Specifically the story for the application was aimed at covering a rule in the MGoE for contact with employees who are on sick leave. The rule is titled "1-5-14", where the numbers symbolize the days on which the leader should be in contact with the employee who is ill.

The idea is that sometimes something as simple as having to change desk at an office can sometimes make people ill (MGoE, personal communication, October 2012). If the department leader is in contact with the person in question on the first day, they can work on solving the problem as soon as possible. While this may seem like a reasonable idea, it has caused controversy, where some feel that it is intrusive or patronizing for a leader to be calling an employee the first day they report in ill (MGoE, personal communication, March 2012). The story was constructed to have a morale reflecting the reason behind this rule.

2.3   Test Sample

The test sample consisted of people working in leadership roles, and two people from the health and safety organisation, at the MGoE. Time constraints meant that a sample of ten volunteers in leadership roles at city hall was used. The group consisted of seven women and three men, working in significantly different areas, such as the communication, health, HR, payroll, and environmental departments. The range of participants was chosen to ensure more widely applicable results.

2.4   Prototype

The prototype is implemented as a series of webpages utilizing PHP scripting. At the start of the test the participant is presented with one of two storytelling methods, and after concluding that story, the participant will go through the story again using the other method. The methods have been designated "A" and "B".

Method A utilizes a virtual agent as the storyteller. The story is presented as text, next to a picture of an agent that acts as the storyteller. The agent is animated using a simple animated gif image. The image has two states: "Talking" and "Waiting". When the page is initially loaded, the agent will be in the "Talking" state for nine seconds, which was approximated as the average time it would take to say the dialogue. During this time, the agent will move his mouth every 0,2 seconds to simulate mouth movement while talking. After the initial nine seconds, the agent will go into the "Waiting" state, which is where he awaits the response from the user. During this state the mouth will move every four seconds, to simulate his anticipation of awaiting a response. During both stages the agent blinks every 5 seconds to simulate average human blinking [15]. He will also change his gaze every 10 seconds to simulate random movement of the eyes during speech and waiting.

The story is implemented as a series of screens on which the storyteller will reveal parts of the story and allow the user to ask from a list of predefined questions. Some of these questions move the story along, while others elaborate on the topic most recently covered. For example: One of the first screens introduced the main character and it is explained that the story is about one time when he became ill. The user can then ask either who the person is, how long it took for him to get well, or what was wrong with him. Each response will result in elaboration on the topic, and the question regarding the nature of his illness will also carry the user to the next set of questions. There is no requirement to see all the details of the story, as long as the user makes it to the end. However, in previous research [6] it was found that some young people who play games prefer to see all the bits of the story. So the purpose of including the possibility to skip parts here was to find out if the same idea applies to the leaders at the MGoE. At the end of the test, the list of choices the user made are saved, as well as the time it takes them to make each choice.

In storytelling method B, the story was structured similarly to method A. The same choices were available at the same stages, and this was logged for later analysis. The story text differed a bit due to the lack of a storyteller (i.e. the storyteller would sometimes refer to him as "I" and to the user as "you"), but they were kept as close as possible to eliminate bias. The main difference was in the visual implementation of the storytelling, where the text simply appeared on a virtual display.

2.5   Story Implementation

The story revolves around the fictional Mr Jensen who works in an office at city hall. He goes on sick leave, and his boss decides not to contact him, to give him some peace and quiet in order to recover faster. When Mr Jensen returns after a week and a half, it actually turns out that the illness was related to him getting blinded by the sun due to non-functional solar screening – something that could potentially happen at the real city hall. The problem could have been solved fast, but the boss' hesitation resulted in a prolonged stay away from the office. As a side effect, the other people in the office all had to work harder; as did Mr Jensen when he came back. The morale of the story is that not being in contact with employees on sick leave can have negative consequences and prolong the time away from the office.

2.6   Test Setup and Process

The test was conducted as part of a focus group interview [16] with all participants located in the same room. The participants were split into two groups, and one was asked to start with method A and the other with method B. One participant misunderstood and did the tests in the wrong order, resulting in a total of six people starting with method A, and four with method B.

Before the test began, the participants were given a brief introduction regarding the general purpose of the test, but the specific details were not mentioned. The participants were told to take as much time as they'd like to go through the story. At the end of this test, a researcher asking questions from a prepared structure led a 45-minute focus group discussion. The participants were allowed to talk freely, and the questions were used as a guideline to ensure that important topics were covered.

Though the participants in the two data gathering parts are the same, they are not uniquely linked. For this reason, participants in the application data are designated 1-10 while the ones in the focus group are designated A-J. Participants 1-6 and A-F experienced storytelling method A first, while the remaining four began with B.

One of the participants later revealed that she suspected the purpose actually being to test the leadership capabilities of the people present, by analysing the choices made along the way (e.g. does the participant ask about Mr Jensen first, or are they more interested in when he came back to work). It seems she didn't get this impression until after going through the story. However, she did not participate much during the focus group discussion, and this may be a result of her being unsure about the purpose of the questions.

3   Results

3.1   Application Data

As mentioned earlier, the time spent for each screen was saved, along with the path the participant took through the screens. The time can be seen in Figure 1indicates the number of screens not visited, in each of the storytelling methods. As the structure is the same for both methods, these numbers are comparable. This number is influenced by the design of the application, and the choice early on to experience the story in the first place. The maximum number of screens that can be missed is ten (seventeen if they say no to the story). They also have to miss at least two screens if they accept the story, since those are associated with saying no.

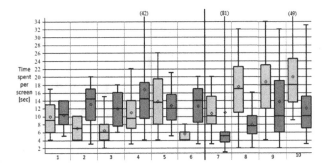

Fig. 1. Time spent per screen. The boxes represent the median, 25th and 75th percentile, average (dot), and outliers (whiskers). For each of the ten participants the left box represents the time spent with method A, and the right box method B.

3.2   Focus Group Interview

The issue the focus group felt strongest about was the fact that the storyteller doesn't speak. The text was meant to appear as a speech bubble, the story is often written in the first person, and the agent moves his mouth as if he is speaking, but there is no audio. This was articulated the firmest by participant B who directly said "I didn't focus on the animation at all, because I didn't have any sound, so I didn't even look at it". When later asked what one thing they would change if they had the option, everyone once again agreed on adding sound. Participant C said, "it would be nice to hear what his voice is like". Several participants mentioned the ability to relax when you have a story read aloud to you, which they felt is different from reading it yourself. One participant brought up the issue of voice, mentioning that people have different preferences. Several participants agreed, and suggested that maybe it would be good to be able to choose from several different voices, perhaps even celebrity voices. A counterpoint was brought up by participant E who said, "if you are sitting in an open office environment, all the storytellers will be talking over each other", to which other participants made motions as if putting headphones on.

When asked about the identity of the storyteller, it was discussed whether the agent should be fictional. The group was presented with the idea that the storyteller could be an animated version of a real leader working at city hall - perhaps the sender of the information. The group laughed out loud at the prospect of seeing one of their colleagues in animated form, and participant I stated that "it would seem disingenuous if it was a real leader standing there moving his mouth [as seen in Monty Python animations]". Participant H added that if the agent were an animated version of a real person, you would focus too much on him and forget about the story.

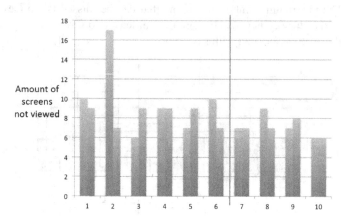

Fig. 2. Screens not viewed for each of the ten participants. The left column represents method A, the right method B.

Several others agreed that it does not matter if the agent is real, since the story is the main focus. This was later clarified by Participant I who stated, "he should look like a leader" when she found out that he was originally designed for another project in which he was a criminal. Participant J mentioned that he became more interested in the application due to the reaction of participant I, who was sitting next to him. During the test, she let out an "ohh" when she saw the storyteller the first time. Participant I said that the exclamation came because she thought the agent looked fun and interesting. Several participants voiced ideas about having a choice of storyteller appearance, or even having the same story told from multiple viewpoints (e.g. the leader, Mr Jensen, or a third person).

A topic of some debate in the focus group was the difference between having the virtual agent as a storyteller (method A), and simply seeing the story as pure text (method B). As mentioned earlier, the stories are structured in the same way in both methods. However, the general consensus of the participants was that method B was more structured and participant A even felt that "it was confusing to choose questions [opposed to topics in method B]". Only participant B said that there was no difference in structure between the two. He did, however, feel that method A was better at leading him to where he wanted to go, and that method B had him running in circles.

Despite the perceived structure of method B, most participants felt that method A was better overall. Participant E said that she normally likes to read things systematically, but in the case of method A she felt more captured by the fact that there was a storyteller. She also felt interested by the fact that the storyteller actually led her to a good reason for working with the "1-5-14" rule. She felt that this topic in particular is good for use with an animation, as it is something that everybody from employees to top management needs to understand if it is to become a success, and an animation can help with that. Several other participants agreed with this. Participant D elaborated "as humans we learn in different ways – by reading, seeing, listening. [...] The way we currently communicate online is by demanding that people read. Many read but don't actually understand, and an animation like this will make sure that some people will understand 100% what the issues are." Participant C added that there have been cases where even a manager of a company doesn't understand what he is reading. Participant A stated that due to the volume of information available on the internal network, some people will not see certain pieces of information unless it is necessary, and in those cases the animation may be exactly the motivation they need. Several other participants agreed.

Participant C said that she felt the question format [opposed to simply topics in method B] were better for covering what the point of the story was, to which participant B added that the questions make the information stick better. The only negative feedback on the questions was in regards to the fact that the same options appear multiple times, to allow for the user to re-read parts previously visited. Several participants stated that they were confused or annoyed by this, and one even said he thought he had made the wrong choice since it was being asked again. He also mentioned that he saw it more as a way to improve leadership abilities by determining which you care about the most; the person, the illness, etc. Because of that, he would have liked for the system to be able to show the "correct" way to go through the story at the end.

Several participants also mentioned that they see this more as a tool for employees than for leaders. Perhaps as a replacement for seminars, where people usually like to hear a good story being told by the presenter. Instead they could experience these stories through the computer. However, other participants cautioned against too much use of this kind of system, as they believe the novelty would then wear off, and reduce the motivation to go through the stories. One participant said that if he was made to sit and listen to stories for a prolonged period (e.g. as part of an introduction) he would fall asleep after 15 minutes. The focus group all agreed that the virtual agent should be an option, and the alternative should not be storytelling without a virtual agent, but rather simply a clear list of requirements (as information is presented today). Interest should then dictate when a person decides to also experience the story.

4   Discussion

The times spent on each screen (Figure 1) show what one could expect: The participants spend less time on the storytelling method they experience as number two. This could be attributed to the fact that the story is the same in both methods. Only participant 5 is unique, in that he/she spent slightly longer (median of 1 second more) on the agent, despite experiencing him the second time through the story. For more accurate data, this part of the test should be repeated with different (but comparable) stories, so all participants experience a story for the first time with one of the methods.

However, it shows that the agent was not interesting enough to motivate the participants to spend significantly more time with him. This was somewhat echoed by some participants in the focus group, who were more interested in speaking about the implications of using storytelling for information distribution, than what the impact of the agent was.

An interesting factor in the time spent on screens is the difference between the storytelling methods for the individual. Those that started with method A spent an average of 7,8 seconds less on method B, while those that started with method B only spent an average of 5,2 seconds less on A. This could be an indication that the agent does add something, which makes people spend slightly more time, but the sample is too small to rule out coincidence [17].

The number of screens missed, does not seem to relate to the storytelling method. Rather, it was mostly around 30-50% of the available screens. In the focus group interview the participants were asked if they felt a need to visit all screens to get every bit of the story, and everybody disagreed. The predominant opinion was that it was up to the user to choose his way through the story, or choose the order in which he wanted to experience the different parts. This was the opposite of previous findings [6], which showed that gamers wanted to explore every part of a story, though these are not comparable due to the vastly different target group. It emphasizes the importance of using this as a secondary information distribution tool, in addition to the way in which information is currently distributed. This was brought up several times by the focus group, who made it clear that if they had the choice they would first go for a simple list of requirements and only use the story if they wanted additional information or couldn't understand the reasoning behind the requirements. If the story is to function as a primary source of information, the mandatory pieces of information could be placed in parts of the story that cannot be missed. In the case of this test, it was impossible to skip several screens (except by saying no to the story in the first place), so the information on these screens would be seen. The optional screens could then be used for information which is "nice to know" but not mandatory.

This would also fit with the focus group's thoughts about using it primarily as a tool for employees rather than leaders. It was a general feeling that this kind of storytelling is best used in smaller portions to keep it feeling special and not boring the users. The visual design of the agent only held a little importance for the focus group, who focused more on the general look. For example, wanting to be able to choose the look and not wanting him to look like a real person. The mentioned desire to have the agent look like a leader is in line with Hertzum [10]. The addition most wanted seemed to be speech from the agent. It was not implemented in the test application to keep the focus on the presence of the agent, but this seems to have been a mistake as it was found that many wanted it. The reasons ranged from making him more interesting, to being able to relax or learn better by listening instead of reading. Many games use agents as storytellers without speech, but as the target group in this project was not selected to be gamers, it is not surprising that they have different expectations. Related work with agents as storytellers [13, 18] also included speech with beneficial results.

Despite the facial expressions being displayed with no connection to the emotional content of the story, the adverse effects reported by others [11, 12] did not occur. This may be a result of the agent not having an emotional stake in the story, and thus the negative effects were not noticeable. The group brought up additional possibilities for using the agent as a mentor for new employees, or an instructor in a tutorial to avoid work-related injuries.

5   Conclusion

The overall hypothesis "A virtual agent will not influence the experience of the story, compared to a non-agent situation, when it comes to storytelling for information distribution", was disproven. While no link could be made between the agent and the time spent on each storytelling method, it was clear from the focus group that the agent was perceived positively. He was seen as an interesting addition that had a positive impact on the story and the information contained within. This is in line with previously mentioned related work [5, 6]. When comparing the storytelling to the current means used to distribute information, the focus group was all but ignoring method B that doesn't have the agent. If information is presented as a dialogue tree, there is a definite risk the user will miss parts of the information. This was clear from the data gathered during the test, which shows that nobody saw all parts of the story about Mr Jensen, and many missed almost half of the details. If information is presented in this manner, it is necessary to ensure that the important details are unskippable.

The factor impacting the agent the most in the test conducted for this work was the lack of audio, which the focus group highlighted several times. Overall they did not have any firm opinions on the visual look of the agent, but they did voice concerns that the content would not be taken seriously or paid as much attention to, if the agent was made to resemble a real leader from city hall.

Acknowledgements. The authors of this paper wish to thank the following people: The municipal government of Esbjerg, Denmark, for funding of the project. Focus group participants at Esbjerg City Hall, for their help in gathering data for the test. Razvan Enescu and Nicolaj Hansen for the original prototype agent design. Yi Gao for software assistance in editing.

References

1. Buckingham, Z.: Truths in Business to Business marketing-How Storytelling Sells (2011), http://zoebuckingham.wordpress.com/2011/03/23/how-storytelling-sells/
2. Denning, S.: The Leader's Guide to Storytelling: Mastering the Art and Discipline of Business Narrative, 2nd edn., p. 5. Jossey-Bass, San Francisco (2011)
3. Gafu, C., Badua, M.: Advantages and Disadvantages of Storytelling in Teaching English at Academic Level: A Case Study in the University of Ploiesti. In: Gouscos, D., Meimaris, M. (eds.) Proceedings of the 5th European Conference on Games Based Learning, pp. 195–201. Academic Publishing Limited, Athens (2011)
4. Sharp, H., Rogers, Y., Preece, J.: Interaction Design: Beyond Human Computer Interaction. Wiley, West Sussex (2007)

5. Bickmore, T.W., Pfeifer, L.M., Paasche-Orlow, M.K.: Health Document Explanation by Virtual Agents. In: Pelachaud, C., Martin, J.-C., André, E., Chollet, G., Karpouzis, K., Pelé, D. (eds.) IVA 2007. LNCS (LNAI), vol. 4722, pp. 183–196. Springer, Heidelberg (2007)

6. Lindholm, D.: TellStory - A Medialogy project about storytelling in handheld games. Aalborg University Esbjerg, Department of Architecture, Design & Media Technology. Unpublished Master Thesis, Esbjerg (2010)

7. Krämer, N.C., Simons, N., Kopp, S.: The Effects of an Embodied Conversational Agent's Nonverbal Behavior on User's Evaluation and Behavioral Mimicry. In: Pelachaud, C., Martin, J.-C., André, E., Chollet, G., Karpouzis, K., Pelé, D. (eds.) IVA 2007. LNCS (LNAI), vol. 4722, pp. 238–251. Springer, Heidelberg (2007)

8. Silva, A., Raimundo, G., Paiva, A.C.R.: Tell Me That Bit Again.. Bringing Interactivity to a Virtual Storyteller. In: Balet, O., Subsol, G., Torguet, P. (eds.) ICVS 2003. LNCS, vol. 2897, pp. 146–154. Springer, Heidelberg (2003)

9. Rehm, M., André, E.: Catch me if you can - Exploring Lying Agents in Social Settings. In: AAMAS 2005: Proceedings of the Fourth International Joint Conference on Autonomous Agents and Multiagent Systems, pp. 937–944. ACM, New York (2005)

10. Hertzum, M., Andersen, H.H., Andersen, V., Hansen, C.B.: Trust in information sources: seeking information from people, documents, and virtual agents. Interacting with Computers 14(5), 575–599 (2002)

11. Walker, J., Sproull, L., Subramani, R.: Using a Human Face in an Interface. In: Adelson, B., Dumais, S., Olson, J. (eds.) Proceedings of the ACM CHI 1994 Human Factors in Computing Systems Conference, pp. 85–91. ACM Press, Boston (1994)

12. Becker, C., Prendinger, H., Ishizuka, M., Wachsmuth, I.: Evaluating affective feedback of the 3D agent max in a competitive cards game. In: Tao, J., Tan, T., Picard, R.W. (eds.) ACII 2005. LNCS, vol. 3784, pp. 466–473. Springer, Heidelberg (2005)

13. Elliott, C.: I picked up Catapia and other stories: A multimodal approach to expressivity for "emotionally intelligent" agents. In: Johnson, W. (ed.) Proceedings of the First International Conference on Autonomous Agents, pp. 451–457. Assn for Computing Machinery, Marina del Rey (1997)

14. Yin, R.K.: Case Study Research: Design and Methods. SAGE, Thousand Oaks (2008)

15. Brandereth, G.D.: Your Vital Statistics: The Ultimate Book About the Average Human Being. Carol Publishing Group, New York (1986)

16. Morgan, D.L.: Focus Groups as Qualitative Research. SAGE, Thousand Oaks (1997)

17. Davies, M.B.: Doing a Successful Research Project: Using Qualitative or Quantitative Methods, p. 54. Palgrave Macmillan, New York (2007)

18. Bleackley, P., Hyniewska, S., Niewiadomski, R., Pelachaud, C., Price, M.: Emotional Interactive Storyteller System. In: Lévy, P., Bouchard, C., Yamanaka, T., Aoussat, A. (eds.) The Proceedings of the Kansei Engineering and Emotion Research International Conference, KEER 2010. Arts et Métiers ParisTech, Paris (2010)

Gamification of Education Using Computer Games

Fiona Fui-Hoon Nah, Venkata Rajasekhar Telaprolu, Shashank Rallapalli,
and Pavani Rallapalli Venkata

Department of Business and Information Technology,
Missouri University of Science and Technology, Rolla, Missouri, USA
{nahf,vtfnd,srvyc,prdn9}@mst.edu

Abstract. We review the literature on gamification and identify principles of gamification and system design elements for gamifying computer educational games. Gamification of education is expected to increase learners' engagement, which in turn increases learning achievement. We propose a gamification framework that synthesizes findings from the literature. The gamification framework is comprised of principles of gamification, system design elements for gamification, and dimensions of user engagement.

Keywords: Gamification, Education, Learning, System Design, Engagement.

1 Introduction

Gamification is the process of game-thinking and game mechanics to engage users and solve problems [1]. It is a strategy to infuse ordinary activities or processes with principles of motivation and engagement based on the gaming concept. Gamification can be used in applications and processes to improve user engagement and learning. By turning an activity or process into a computer game, i.e., through various game design elements such as rewards for achievement, desirable behavioral change can be induced. For example, gamification can be used to improve motivation and learning in informal and formal settings. The trend of gamification connects to a sizeable body of existing concepts and research in human-computer interaction and game studies, such as serious games, pervasive games, alternate reality games, or playful design.

2 Background: Gamification and Its Application to Education

Games and game-like elements have invaded various domains of the real world, including marketing, politics, health and fitness [2]. Gamification can be used to promote a business, a product, a political candidate, or wellness. For example, marketers have used advergames to integrate marketing into games to promote their products and services, and some companies are working with third-party vendors such as Get Heroik to utilize gamification to encourage their employees to keep fit.

Gamification attempts to harness the motivational power of games and apply it to real-world problems, such as the motivational problems of students in schools [2].

S. Yamamoto (Ed.): HIMI/HCII 2013, Part III, LNCS 8018, pp. 99–107, 2013.

The application of gamification in the educational context can help to increase student motivation in learning. As Lee and Hammer [2] explained, schools have been using game-like elements in classroom activities, such as giving points to students for completing assignments; these points are then converted into "badges," more commonly known as grades. Using such an incentive system, students are rewarded for desired behaviors and punished for undesirable behaviors. Students "level up" at the end of every academic year if they perform well.

Despite attempts to use gamification in schools, it remains challenging to fully engage students in classroom-based activities. Computer games, however, excel at engagement. Hence, educational institutions are interested to understand how education can be delivered through computer games. In order to do so, teachers or professors and game designers need to work together. Computer games, if appropriately designed, can keep users (i.e., players) engaged with potentially difficult assignments and learning tasks. This gamification experience can help to give students a clear, actionable task and promise them immediate rewards instead of vague long-term benefits. Games allow repeated failure, and after each failure, the student learns something new. In this way, students can learn from their mistakes while taking failure and the negative experiences in a positive and meaningful way. Thus, gamification has the advantage of reframing failure as a necessary part of learning [2].

3   Development of Gamification Framework

Given the benefits of gamification in education and learning, we propose a gamification framework to provide guidance and suggestions to software designers and researchers in gamifying their educational applications.

3.1   Principles of Gamification

Based on our review of the literature, we identify five main principles of gamification: (i) Goal orientation; (ii) Achievement, (ii) Reinforcement, (iv) Competition, and (v) Fun orientation.

Goal Orientation. It is important for educational games to be structured in such a way that there are various "layers" of goals [3]. For example, to complete the long-term goal of completing an educational game, the player is presented with the medium-term goal of completing the levels in the game, and to complete each of these levels, the player is presented with the short-term goal of completing the missions in each level. Each mission can further be broken down into multiple tasks. As the player advances through the missions and the levels, the challenge of the educational game increases. Player engagement is sustained by balancing the player's knowledge and skills with the challenge required to advance in the game [4-7]. Hence, having a layered goal orientation allows the learner to progress systematically from a beginner to an expert or master as one demonstrates mastery of the skills and knowledge. Having clear and well defined goals of the game also helps to sustain the learners' motivation and engagement.

Achievement. We use the terms, achievement and accomplishment, interchangeably here. When players are recognized for their achievement, their sense of gratification increases which further enhances their motivation and engagement. Hence, recognition of achievement can also be applied in the context of educational games to increase learner engagement and consequently, learning achievement. Achievements can be recognized in the form of badges or other kudos systems (e.g., trophies, ranks, stars, awards).

Reinforcement. The behavioral learning model purports that learning takes place through reinforcement (e.g., verbal praises/compliments or tangible/intangible rewards) [8]. Hence, it is common for games to have a reward structure that is based on player performance and a feedback system to support reinforcement. In the context of educational games, positive reinforcement, in the form of points or virtual currency, offers gratifications to players and can be used to promote learning from the game. Negative feedback (or reinforcement), on the other hand, can offer corrective information, knowledge or skills to help players achieve their learning goals more quickly.

Competition. Competition is not only an important principle but it is also a given in most games. As noted by Liu et al. [9] citing McGonigal [10], a game motivates a player using intrinsic rewards and competitive engagements. In the context of an educational game, competition plays an important role in sustaining or increasing one's engagement and focus on the (learning) task. Rules of the game should be well defined, explicit and strictly enforced in order for the players to develop an internal sense of control [11], which further helps to enhance their level of engagement [12]. To further enhance player motivation and engagement as well as opportunities for learning to take place, an educational game may allow players to generate rules within the game. Generation of rules by players can facilitate discovery learning, an important component of active learning.

Fun Orientation. Fun or enjoyment goes hand in hand with engagement or cognitive absorption [12]. When one is experiencing fun with a game, one can become so engaged in the task that one loses track of time [12], [13]. Fun is a necessary requirement of most, if not all, computer games. Hence, for an educational game to be effective in motivating and engaging learners, having a fun component or orientation is very important.

3.2   System Design Elements for Gamification

For every game application, a set of design mechanisms has to be outlined before its development. Take a simple and well known example of the Carrom board game. The game system comprises the coins, a board, players and a score board. These are the elements which combine and interact to create a game play. The overall experience of a game play depends on how well the system design elements are kept in mind to enhance user experience.

For a system to work properly, some of the elements like input, processing and output are required. Apart from those, it needs users to take control, check out the environment and boundaries, and most importantly, interact through an interface. If we map the design elements to the gaming environment, input and output are the game mechanics which drive the game forward. The process that happens inside the system is required for the users to experience the game play. These are the game dynamics that happen in the background and usually get unnoticed. These hidden elements form the game dynamics that are required for proper functioning of a game. The system needs 'attractive' or 'magnetic' cues to entice people to the game and to continue playing the game. Game components are needed to enhance the players' interest in the game and to make the game meaningful.

A game developer should always keep in mind the interest of the user. When we take the example of the angry birds game, the basic concept is simple. But what drives people crazy to become so engaged or even addicted to the game is how the elements are designed in the game, i.e., the use of the various weapons (i.e., game components). Moreover, the game designer is able to utilize game mechanics that sustain and increase the interest of the users. The quality of the game is one important aspect which amazes the users in getting them captivated by and immersed in the game. The outlying theme of a game is usually tricky to design. It is always best to keep the main theme simple. The sound tracks must be attractive enough to keep the user's mind in the game at all times. However, if the game is simple, it may not be necessary to have a sound track. So, what are the basic mechanics in a game?

Zichermann and Cunningham [1] suggest focusing on seven primary elements in implementing game mechanics: points, levels, leaderboards, badges, onboarding, challenges/quests, and social engagement loops. In this section, we also discuss other game mechanics that can enhance engagement. They are: feedback, teams/social dynamics, rules (explicit and player-generated), marketplaces/economies, avatars, visual/3D space/sounds, customization, narrative context, and roleplay. As a whole, these game mechanics form the core system design elements for gamification.

Points are the basic game component that drives one's goal. Levels indicate progress towards higher-level goals and the fulfillment of intermediate goals. Leaderboards allow players to compare their performance with others. Badges signify the recognition of one's accomplishment or achievement. Onboarding refers to the act of bringing a novice into the system to convey and manage complexity through scaffolding. Quests can be used to create challenges for users. Onboarding and quests work hand to hand to balance challenges and skills, which is a necessary requirement for user engagement. Social engagement loops refer to viral loops that are capable of continually re-engaging users.

Feedback is an important system design element that serves as a form of reinforcement. Competition can be enhanced through social components such as when teams or individuals compete as well as through simulations of an economy where players strive to maximize gains and minimize losses. Competition in a game takes place under explicit rules that are enforced, and these rules can be rules of the game or player-generated rules within the game [11]. To increase the fun component of a game, avatars, visual/3D space/sounds, customization, narrative context, and roleplay can be implemented.

Each of these system design elements is further discussed below.

Leaderboards. The leaderboard brings pride to users in a game. It shows the world the leading scorers of the game. It is possible to personalize the leaderboard to suit specific users' requirements so as to allow them to assess their attainment of specific goals in the game. Having well-defined goals motivate users to stay focused and engaged [4-5].

Levels/Milestones. Levels or milestones signify completion of intermediate goals in the game. They show users their progress during the game. In addition, badges or leaderboards can be offered at every milestone. Hence, levels and milestones not only enhance goal orientation in the game but they also signify achievement.

Points. Points are the basic scoring schema in a game to indicate progress. Using points, users can claim rewards or even cash them to advance in the game. Hence, points are a basic component of the reward system in the game.

Onboarding. Onboarding is a scaffolding method that can help players progress and advance from a novice to an expert or master. When challenges are substantially higher than a player's skills or abilities, anxiety is high which may cause one to give up. Hence, onboarding through scaffolding is important to sustain user engagement.

Challenges/Quests. Challenges are useful to keep users focused on a game, and to stay engaged and interested. Challenges can be introduced in various forms such as time pressure, difficulty, and special quests. A series of challenges in the form of quests can be kept separate and by achieving those targets, players can be well rewarded. In the context of educational games, challenges in the form of quests can offer opportunities for learners to practice what they have learned and be rewarded for doing so.

Badges. Badges serve to reward users as well as recognize their achievement and accomplishment. Users can share and showcase their badges in the game environment as well as in other virtual communities such as Facebook. Badges are social status that can be displayed or showcased to others. Users can also be attracted by the style (graphics) of the badges. Other forms of kudos systems such as trophies, ranks and stars serve similar purposes as badges.

Immediate Feedback. Feedback is a form of reinforcement. The immediacy of feedback is a necessary component of gamification [1]. Points and levels are two examples of the feedback system in a game. However, feedback goes beyond the use of points and levels. It can demonstrate outcomes (i.e., desired or undesired) to reinforce performance. It also shows progress, thus keeping users interested and engaged [4-5].

Social Engagement Loops. Zichermann and Cunningham [1] suggest four components of an engagement loop: (i) motivating emotion – motivation to use an application such as an educational game, (ii) player reengagement – social or other event entices one back to the application, (iii) social call to action – call to participate in a social event, and (iv) visible progress or reward – recognition for, or rewards of, participation that prompts motivating emotion which begins another loop or cycle. Hence, the social engagement loop repeats and reinforces itself such as in the case of Facebook where users are continually enticed back to the application due to prompts and notifications from their social circles and involvement in associated activities.

Teams/Social Dynamics. When teams or individuals compete, their levels of engagement increase [10-11]. The use of social dynamics in a gaming context is very powerful, which is one of the success factors of World of Warcraft. The social dynamics in a team bring a deeper level of richness and involvement in the game where individuals feel a greater sense of responsibility and commitment to each other. Their sense of identity and social positioning is also enhanced. The increased richness and dynamics in a social setting increase their level of engagement in the game.

Rules. Rules of a game need to be explicit and enforced for players to trust the game and perceive them to be fair [11]. Players need to know exactly what it takes to win in order to stay engaged and to continue to play the game. Having clear and explicit rules also increases one's sense of control which increases one's level of engagement [11-12]. In games where the players are also allowed to generate rules of the game, their sense of personal control is enhanced and their level of engagement increases.

Marketplace/Economies. Competition can be enhanced and made more realistic through simulations of a marketplace or economy. To increase the realism of a game, virtual/synthetic currency can be used. A virtual marketplace is created to enable a variety of transactions in the virtual world. Users can perceive the realism of the game and learn concepts of economics in such settings. The realism and intense competition created by the marketplace and economy in the game helps to enhance player engagement and interest in learning.

Visual/3D Space/Sounds. 3D graphic-rich environments are common in gaming. A person can imagine himself/herself in the 3D virtual world by mapping to physical real world existence. For example, one may perceive a high level of telepresence to the point of feeling totally immersed in the virtual environment. Also, the 3D or visual space is particularly helpful for simulating concepts or events that are difficult to or cannot be demonstrated in the real world such as nuclear reactions. Hence, the visual/3D space can be used to simulate and teach abstract concepts or subjects. Sounds can also be used to enhance the presentation of learning material as well as to increase user engagement with the virtual environments.

Avatars. An avatar is an animated character to represent a person in a virtual world. For example, companies can implement real time scenarios of their work place in a game by letting people choose their customized avatars and work in a game environment. Today, online gaming websites are using the avatar concept to give identities and recognitions to individual players. The use of avatars in a gaming environment can be used to enhance player engagement by simulating a real or fantasy world that players can relate to.

Customization. Customization is particularly important in a learning context. In order to maximize learning outcomes, the educational game can be customized to respond to a player based on his or her knowledge, skills and performance. Customization can be general or specific to individuals. General customization includes addressing players by their names, greeting them, and personalizing display to their needs or preferences. Specific customization, on the other hand, leverages on performance assessment of the player in order to present a learning module that is suitable for his or her level of knowledge in the domain. Both forms of customization increase engagement of users.

Narrative Context. "Good games have good backstories" [11, p. 68]. The narrative context or theme of a game keeps people engaged in the game. The narratives guide action, offer hints to fulfillment of goals, and induce psychological responses. Stories can be used to drive fulfillment of goals, give meaning to the tasks in the game, and enhance our social and emotional experience. As stories are a human specialty [11] and an important part of our daily life, we relate better to the game if it is grounded in a narrative context that has a storyline.

Roleplay. Roleplay is an important element of a game. The narrative context of the game offers opportunities for a variety of roleplay. Each player may be given a role in the game or may choose among a set of roles. A central theme will be the common element for all the characters (i.e., taking on a variety of roles) operating in the virtual gaming environment through cooperation and competition. In the context of an educational game, these roles could correspond to the job roles that are most closely related to the learner's domain of specialization or training. Roleplay gives meaning and relevance to a game, and hence, it enhances engagement in learning. For example, learners or players can take on the role of their idealized job to practice and polish their skills or to experience the job role in order to decide whether it is what they want to pursue as a career.

3.3   Outcomes of Gamification

The main goals of gamification of education are to increase cognitive absorption or engagement [1], [11] as well as learning achievement. In this research, the terms, cognitive absorption and engagement, are used interchangeably. Both refer to the degree to which one is in a state of deep attention and involvement and is perceptually engrossed with the experience [12].

In the context of game-based learning, cognitive absorption or engagement is a direct outcome whereas learning achievement is an indirect outcome (i.e., mediated through engagement).

A direct outcome of game-based learning, cognitive absorption or engagement, can be assessed using the following two sets of measures. The first set of measures is presented by Zichermann and Cunningham [1], where the following metrics are used: recency, frequency, duration, virality, and ratings. Recency refers to the time elapsed since the game was last played. Frequency refers to how often the game is played. Duration is the amount of time spent playing the game. Virality refers to the degree to which this game has spread and is adopted by others. Ratings refer to players' subjective evaluations of their level of engagement with the game.

The second set of measures was proposed by Agarwal and Karahanna [12] where cognitive absorption is assessed by subjective evaluations of the following metrics: (i) Curiosity, (ii) Control, (iii) Temporal Dissociation, (iv) Focused Immersion, (v) Heightened Enjoyment. Curiosity refers to the extent to which the experience triggers sensory and cognitive arousal. Control refers to the degree to which users perceive that they are in charge of the interaction. Temporal dissociation refers to the inability to register the passage of time while engaged in interaction. Focused immersion is the experience of total involvement where other attentional demands are largely ignored. Heightened enjoyment refers to the pleasurable aspects of the interaction.

In the context of educational games, we are also interested to assess the players' learning achievement. After playing an educational game, we expect the players' performance or learning achievement to increase. Hence, objective tests and assessments can be used to evaluate the indirect outcome of gamification, learning achievement (i.e., that is mediated by engagement).

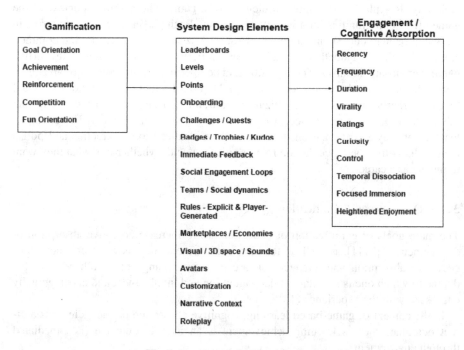

Fig. 1. Framework for Gamification

3.4   Gamification Framework

The proposed gamification framework is presented in Fig. 1.

4   Conclusions and Future Research

In this research, we developed a gamification framework for computer educational games. We review the literature, synthesize the findings from the review, and present a summary of the findings in this paper.

In subsequent and follow-up research, we are interested to assess the gamification framework using laboratory experiments. We plan to use experiments to assess the effects of these system design elements on learner engagement and learning achievement.

References

1. Zichermann, G., Cunningham, C.: Gamification by Design. O'Reilly, Sebastopol (2011)
2. Lee, J.J., Hammer, J.: Gamification in Education: What, How, Why Bother? Academic Exchange Quarterly 15(2), 146–151 (2011)
3. Raymer, R.: Gamification - Using Game Mechanics to Enhance eLearning. eLearn Magazine (2011), http://elearnmag.acm.org/featured.cfm?aid=2031772
4. Csikszentmihalyi, M.: Flow - The Psychology of Optimal Experience. Harper & Row, New York (1990)
5. Csikszentmihalyi, M.: Finding Flow - The Psychology of Engagement with Everyday Life. HarperCollins, New York (1997)
6. Csikszentmihalyi, M., Csikszentmihalyi, I.S.: Optimal Experience: Psychological Studies of Flow in Consciousness. Cambridge University Press, New York (1988)
7. Nah, F., Eschenbrenner, B., DeWester, D., Park, S.: Impact of Flow and Brand Equity in 3D Virtual Worlds. Journal of Database Management 21(3), 69–89 (2010)
8. Skinner, B.F.: The Science of Learning and the Art of Teaching. Harvard Educational Review 24(2), 86–97 (1954)
9. Liu, D., Li, X., Santhanam, R.: Digital Games and Beyond - What Happens When Players Compete? MIS Quarterly 37(1), 111–124 (2013)
10. McGonigal, J.: Reality Is Broken - Why Games Make Us Better and How They Can Change the World. The Penguin Press, New York (2011)
11. Reeves, B., Read, J.L.: Total Engagement: Using Games and Virtual Worlds to Change the Way People Work and Businesses Compete. Harvard Business Press, Boston (2009)
12. Agarwal, R., Karahanna, E.: Time Flies When You Are Having Fun: Cognitive Absorption and Beliefs About Information Technology Usage. MIS Quarterly 24(4), 665–694 (2000)
13. Sackett, A., Meyvis, T., Nelson, L., Converse, B., Sackett, A.: You're Having Fun When Time Flies: The Hedonic Consequences of Subjective Time Progression. Psychological Science 21(1), 111–117 (2010)

New Potential of E-learning by Re-utilizing Open Content Online

TED NOTE: English Learning System as an Auto-assignment Generator

Ai Nakajima and Kiyoshi Tomimatsu

Graduate school of Design, Kyushu University
kamirazio@gmail.com, tomimatu@design.kyushu-u.ac.jp

Abstract. We propose an English learning system "TED NOTE," which automatically generates language training game by re-utilizing open content online. As a first prototype, we use Creative Commons licensed content; presentation video and subtitles; from TED.com as educational materials. In this paper, first, we focused on an educational potential of open content online and researched related projects, which apply the concept of the free culture movement for educational uses. In the second half, we describe the design process of TED NOE as a case study. We illustrate the way to re-use and re-assemble open contents into the new use technically for providing significant learning experiences in TED NOTE.

Keywords: Creative Commons, Open Source, Free Culture, Open culture, e-leaning, learning commons, Gamification, Mash up, Semantic web.

1 Introduction

Nowadays a vast amount of the open content, e.g., open source, public domain and creative commons content (CC content) is available as information materials online. It has been regarded as a potential resource for derivative creation.

This situation promotes new concept of creative and collaborative culture, which has become known as the "free culture movement [1]." On YouTube, Flickr, Wikipedia and so on, user generated content (UGC) is growing by uploading and editing every moment, which result in enormous amount of data.

Although activities of the movement are deployed in various areas, free culture is especially expected as big potential to improve style of education in the future. It will not merely a change in academic trainings, but also realize lifelong education and equality of educational opportunity for everyone, everywhere [2].

S. Yamamoto (Ed.): HIMI/HCII 2013, Part III, LNCS 8018, pp. 108–117, 2013.
© Springer-Verlag Berlin Heidelberg 2013

2   Related Study

2.1   Basic and Academic Education

- The Khan Academy

The Khan Academy (www.khanacademy.org) is the most-used educational streaming service on the Internet with the mission of providing a free world-class education to anyone, anywhere [3]. It consists over 3000 of self-paced video lessons, covering everything from basic addition to advanced calculus, physics, chemistry and biology. It has over 1 million unique students per month.

- iTunes U

iTunes U covers advanced education, which offers a variety of video lectures in world-renowned universities, in order for the new role of a university to the global society.

2.2   Improvement of Digital Divide

- The OLPC

The OLPC (One Laptop per Child) project is a famous educational challenge, which is engaged by a research group of Tufts University and the MIT Media Lab[4]. OLPC's mission is to empower the world's poorest children through education and free culture. They provide children in developing countries with low-cost, low-power durable laptops with open-source software for self-learning.

- Hole in the wall

The project "Hole in the Wall" by an education researcher Sugata Mitra is the research about self-organizing systems of learning [5]. In an urban slum in New Delhi, the research team installed an Internet-connected PC, and left it there with a hidden camera filming the area. The experiments have shown that, without supervision or formal teaching, children teach themselves and each other through the Internet, if they're motivated by their curiosity and peer interest.

2.3   Share Idea

- Open IDEO

Open IDEO (www.openideo.com) is an online innovation platform for creative thinkers, where they share their inspirations, ideas and opinions to solve problems together.

After a challenge is posted at OpenIDEO.com, the three development phases; inspiration, concepting and evaluation; are put into motion. Community members can contribute on various approaches, e.g., from observations, photos, sketches and comments in the form, to business models and snippets of code. Eventually the winning concept goes to final phases "realization."

• TED

TED organizes global conferences devoted to "ideas worth spreading." It invites activists from three worlds: technology, entertainment and design. TED provides the occasion for them to make presentations to the world and it offered the presentation videos for free online, under the Creative Commons license, through TED.com [6].

The TED Global 2012 initiates the concept of "Radical Openness." They mention about the human potential of collaboration and mutual understanding by the ultra-connected world. In fact, after taking open their contents to public, TED became even more famous all over the world. The subtitles of presentation in multiple languages are created in the way of peer production; engaged by worldwide spontaneous volunteers throughout the Internet.

3   Concept Design and Design Objective

3.1   Concept Design

"How to re-utilize the open content for educational use" is our main concept of this development. In the previous chapter, we surveyed some related projects, which offer free educational service and occasion using the Internet. But each of them covers all of the process by themselves; from creating open contents to distribute them and manage them. There are few challenges, which try to re-use open content online and convert them into other, educational use.

Basically, creating content itself require a lot of time and effort. On the other hand, as we mentioned in the introduction, a volume of open contents are growing by the way of UGC every second on the Internet. Relaying on this circumstance, we propose the new approaches to designers and engineers; the way to re-design and the way to re-assembly with utilizing open-information resources into other uses. To create new value, we only need to establish efficient architecture, which customizes information resources.

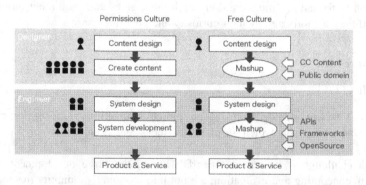

Fig. 1. Difference in development performance

3.2　Design Objective

Whereas it had been difficult to get articles written in foreign languages previously, it now became extremely easy to access them thanks to the Internet. Among the foreign language learners, using the Internet for daily practicing has been one of the popular ways to study them.

But even though the situation gets better, the studying foreign languages by themselves without any introduction are still too much of a bother. So, even now, studying with textbooks is much more popular way. To realize the efficient language learning with the Internet, we need to edit and optimize the data for e-learning style.

We got the idea of the application, which converts raw literal materials in foreign language into the educational material optimized for e-leaning.

We picked English learning up among the foreign language learning as a first design objective for our e-leaning system. Without any doubt, English is the most important and popular language in the world and the core community of free culture is standardized in English as well. Since English is still big barrier for Japanese people, we can gain small benefits from free culture. We need to acquire good English skill to join in the worldwide movement as a necessary precondition.

Also, in terms of digital divide issues, English-language acquisition brings advanced learning opportunity and working chances for the people in developed countries.

4　Design Process

In the stage of designing the TED NOTE, we set two design challenges. One is challenge about user experience; how to design the effective and incentive English learning. The other is technical challenge; how to make the best use of open contents as educational material for the e-learning system.

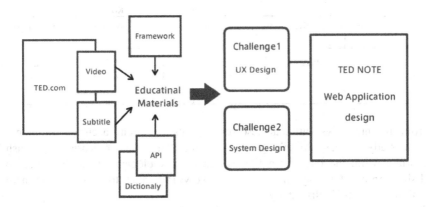

Fig. 2. Design Process

4.1   Educational Material

We chose to use the TED's contents as a main educational material for the application; therefore we named it TED NOTE. The presentation videos are not merely good as English learning itself, but also tell us new exciting knowledge and English expressiveness. Among 1400 TED Talks videos and abundant variety of themes, users can find videos, which meet a specific interest of them. "Switch from studying English to studying WITH English" is a catchword of TED NOTE.

Technically, system architecture of TED.com has favorable style to be re-used. Moreover, TED announced official statement of the expectation for open culture. Also, it provides us the presentation videos and subtitles with the license of creative commons.

4.2   Design Challenge 1: User Experience Design

To design the user experiences: effective and incentive learning experiences, we created *Persona*s: target-user models as a method of user-centered design [7].

To create the realistic *Persona*s and to clarify the problems of current English study, we conducted interviews on 10 expected users who all have international experiences; 2 respondents from EU, 1 from central Europe, 1 from Asia and 6 from Japan. We asked their English learning experiences and international experiences. Based on each personal data and their stories, we created 5 *Persona*s. [Table.1]

Table 1. Profile of 5 *Persona*s

Name	Male/ Female	English Level Country : TOEIC score	Experience abroad	Profile
Eric Q	Male	Native English from UK	rich	English teacher in Japan
Alex S	Male	non-native form Germany: 670	few	University Student in Kosovo
Maria L	Female	non-native form Netherlands: 905	rich	Worker in Internet company in NL
Emiko S	Female	non-native from Japan: 780	few	Japanese English Teacher
Takumi N	Male	non-native from Japan: 655	middle	Japanese Exchange Student in Germany

From the interviews with Japanese respondents, we found a current problem of English study, which doesn't give them the "purpose of learning English." Meanwhile, from the ones from EU, we found key elements to realize incentive English learning. Interests in content are very important to promote the active commitment to self-English study.

We made each story of 5 *Personas* and we planned the English learning system optimized for each usage.

4.3   Design Challenge 2: System Design

In this section, we report on system design of TED NOTE.

After the advent of Web 2.0, the technical circumstance has been developed as favorable environments, where we can utilize tons of qualified open contents, using the architecture of semantic web and APIs (Application Programming Interface). In this development, we dear to include external web contents and APIs as much as possible, to be a good development-example based on free culture movement.

At the first system-design drawing, we found that the system is required 5 core functions. In the current version, we fulfill three of functions.

1. Loading and conversion function
2. Game function
3. Self–study Management function
4. SNS (Social networking service) function : unfinished
5. User generated assignment editor system (UGC function) : unfinished

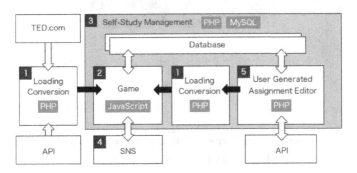

Fig. 3. 5 core functions

We established loading and conversion function in PHP. We built game function in JavaScript. For the dictionary assistant, we use Ajax and APIs offered by WordReference.com and wordnik.com. To monitor the learning effectiveness, we introduced an account system of Facebook API and database in MySQL.

5   User Interface

In this section, we will discuss the current state of our interface design.

Home Screen: Game Interface. The Home screen of TED NOTE is in game interface; while playing, user has to concentrate to listen to what the presenter said in each statement in the presentation video. When the one statement has played, the video is automatically stopped. User is allowed to repeat the statement over and over till he can catch it.

1. Title & Link of the presentation
2. Button for "How to Play" & "Set up"

3. Presentation Video Monitor
4. Subtitle (Translation)
5. Information & Score Monitor
6. Timeline Buttons
7. Re-play Button
8. Game Space

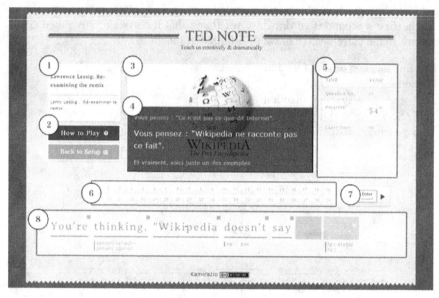

Fig. 4. Home screen: Game interface

Score System. If user completes the typing without any err, user gets high score. The each vocabulary classified 3 levels; junior high, high school and business level. User get additional points depend on the difficulty of each vocabulary. The achievement of user's study habit has been visualized as a total score.

Game Modes. TED NOTE has 3 Game modes.

• typing game mode

Typing the same letters of each word-card

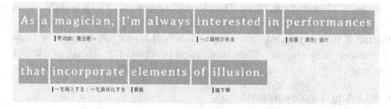

Fig. 5. Typing Game Mode

- Blank game mode

Filling in the blank question with right letters
Some of the words are selected as blank question randomly.

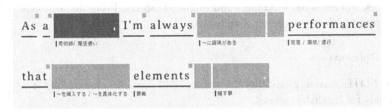

Fig. 6. Blank Game Mode

- Full listening game mode

Filling in all blank questions with the right letters
Most of the words are hidden instead of some difficult words to catch.

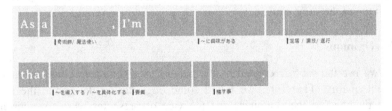

Fig. 7. Full Listening Game Mode

How to Play

1. Login with own user account from the top page of TED NOTE.
   (www.connolab.com/tednote/)
2. Choose study mode among 3 options; Typing game mode, Blank game mode and
   Full listening game mode.
3. Customize your study style with assistant options.
4. Enter the URL of your favorite presentation from TED.com in the URL input box
   of TED NOTE and press the "Next" Button.
5. After the video has loaded into main interface and questions are generated below,
   game starts.
6. The video is stopped automatically at the each end of the presenter's statement.
7. Type the same letters, which you can catch from the statement. Repeat and keep
   listening till user completes each question.
   As user can find the correct answer easily, the subtitle and hints are shown below
   in each word card.   You can cheat the answer easily with right and left keys.
8. After user complete the question, press "Space" key to move on to the next
   question.

6   Feedback

We took user-testing with the first prototype and got the feedback from 4 categorized users; Japanese without international experiences, Japanese who have international experiences, international foreigners and English teachers. From the feedback, we got a lot of opinion. We put some represents below.

Positive Opinions

- TED NOTE has a possibility to reduce the time to prepare the educational materials for English teachers.
- Not only for students, TED NOTE helps also non-native English teachers to improve their English skills.
- Qualified contents from TED.com will be a good motivation to use TED NOTE better than the traditional way of English study based on textbook or non-native English teachers.
- Design of input layout with keyboard is simple and user-friendly.
- If they use the subtitle and dictionary in second foreign language, it is possible to learn it too at the same time.

Negative Opinions

- Since we use the subtitle created by the way of user generated contents, each has different quality. Therefore, we found some bugs during the game; the answer wasn't matched to the statement and the vice of presenter wasn't synchronized with the game.
- Users tend to concentrate typing too much to pay attention to the meaning of the presentation.
- The game need more fancy interaction and rewards.

Requests from Users. We go a lot of user request and suggestion of new ideas. Most of users suggested the necessity of SNS function to encourage their continued learning activity. From English teachers, we got some interesting requests. Some asked editing function of the question part customized for student's level. One asked the function of generator, which help to upload his own lecture-video for his own classes.

Finally, based on users' feedbacks, we found that the main target of TED NOTE is middle to advanced class of Japanese English learners, who want to become active worldwide in the future.

7   Conclusion and Future Prospects

In this paper, we have discussed how to re-utilize the open content for educational use to get the best benefit of free culture movement.

Proposing new approaches to designers and engineers, we illustrate our design process of the TED NOTE; the way to re-design the application and the way to re-assembly the system with utilizing open-information resources. Through the development, we found that the approached are more efficient and rapid way to develop application.

We believe that we have succeeded in developing a working prototype, which shows the one of the challenging case study based on free culture movement. However, the current systems haven't realized two more core functions, which we had planned at the first drawing of the system design. As the future improvements, we will install them; SNS function and user generated assignment editor (UGC function.) Additionally, as an e-learning research, we'd like to analyze users' long-term learning effect by monitoring records of self-study management system.

References

1. Lessig, L.: Free Culture: How Big Media Uses Technology and the Law to Lock Down Culture and Control Creativity, Japan, pp. 328–332 (July 2004)
2. Chen, D.: The guidebook for building a free culture, Japan, pp. 157–169 (May 2012)
3. About Khan Academy (2013), https://www.khanacademy.org/about/
4. One Laptop per Child : Open source vs. dual-boot systems Wikipedia, http://en.wikipedia.org/wiki/One_Laptop_per_Child
5. Mitra, S.: Minimally invasive education: a progress report on the hole-in-the-wall. experiments. British Journal of Educational Technology 34, 367 (2003)
6. Rubenstein, L.D.: Using TED Talks to Inspire Thoughtful Practice (2012) ISSN 0887-8730
7. Nikka (Union of Japanese Scientists and Engineers) Practicing Persona Method to Clarify the Target User - Investigating Utilization of a Blog Service for Communities – (2006)

Transferring Tacit Skills of WADAIKO

Makoto Oka, Asahi Mizukoshi, and Hirohiko Mori

Tokyo City University, 1-28-1 Tamadutumi, Setagaya, Tokyo, Japan
{Moka,hmori}@tcu.ac.jp,mizukoshi@ims.tcu.ac.jp

Abstract. The techniques are acquired through repetition of such copying and passed on in this intuitive way. As even the experts acquired them by intuition, the techniques are difficult to put into explicit knowledge, forms of word or value. To solve the problem, recently there are numerous attempts to turn the techniques into explicit knowledge for preservation and transmission thereof. However, current situation is that not all of the knowledge is conveyed by unsuccessfully forcing tacit knowledge (skills) into the disguise of its explicit counterpart. It is necessary to preserve the tacit knowledge learned by experience and intuition and convey it in a way understandable. Techniques refer to postures and motions of experts. Motions of the experts striking a Wadaiko are extracted as data, which is used in developing an instruction system of passing on the techniques of the experts to novices. Finally, it is verified whether the novices have acquired the techniques through the system.

Keywords: Expert-Novice, Tacit skills, Tacit knowledge.

1   Introduction

In recent years, Japan has declining birth rate and a growing proportion of elderly people. At the forefront of traditional entertainment and crafts, number of expert is decreasing each year and there are few successors. As such, it is a concern that techniques of the traditional skills will be lost together with the experts.

The techniques involve tacit knowledge which is learned by experience and intuition. Tacit knowledge refers to that difficult to convey in written form as it cannot be put into words of text or numbers of value. When learning the traditional techniques, novices do not receive some special training from experts (their masters), but rather are instructed to "see, hear and feel", starting by copying postures and movements of the experts. The traditional techniques are acquired through repetition of such copying and passed on in this intuitive way. Thus, they cannot be conveyed accurately in written form even by the experts, who are well-versed in the practice, and texts in such attempt are vague. As even the experts acquired them by intuition, the techniques are difficult to put into explicit knowledge, format of word or value. As a result, passing them on to successors is also difficult, which may become a reason of the loss of the traditional techniques. Furthermore, it is also a problem that passing on them takes a long time as they have to be learned through repeated copying.

S. Yamamoto (Ed.): HIMI/HCII 2013, Part III, LNCS 8018, pp. 118–125, 2013.

To solve these problems, recently there are numerous attempts to turn the traditional techniques into explicit knowledge for preservation and transmission thereof. These attempts aim to turn tacit knowledge of individuals into written explicit knowledge so that the techniques can be passed on. However, current situation is that not all of the knowledge is conveyed by unsuccessfully forcing tacit knowledge into the disguise of its explicit counterpart. It is necessary to preserve the tacit knowledge learned by experience and intuition and convey it in a way understandable.

2   Related Work

Research of preservation and passing on of traditional skills in ceramic arts has been conducted by the Fujimoto et al.[1]. In their studies, data of movements of a ceramic artist' wrists and fingers was collected by motion capture sensors and data gloves and input into computer to reproduce the movements in CG. Meanwhile, movements of hands of the ceramic artist were captured by two cameras and reproduced in 3D video. Putting shutter glasses on, users could then view the 3D video and see the movements in 3D. The actual hand movements of the potters and transformation of the clay could be understood through the 3D CG animation. Moreover, by setting the clay semi-transparent, movements of the hand on the side in contact with the clay could be viewed which is impossible from ordinary camera angle. This system enabled the techniques be more accurately passed on. However, a problem was raised that how much strength such as the grip strength was applied in fact could not be understood merely by watching the 3D CG animation.

Teaching materials based on motion capture and virtual spaces have been developed by the Ando et al.[2]. They suggested using a virtual reality by 3D space in "observing performance" and "watching video teaching materials", which were basic in conventional practical teaching. They then developed teaching materials in which movements could be observed from any angle with the aid of motion capture technology. Based on the movements captured by motion capture system and incorporated into the teaching materials, together with coordinates of joints calculated, human models were created, which could show differences between movements of novices and experts from various angles. By such comparison, effectiveness of the motion capture technology as practical teaching materials was proved.

Research of comparison between Wadaiko (Japanese drums) experts and novices in terms of techniques was conducted by the Yamaguchi et al.[3], in which movements of upper limbs of experts in striking a Wadaiko and those of novices were compared. The movements, including those of the right side of the head, shoulder, elbow, wrist and waist, and movements of drumsticks were recorded into videos and analyzed through image processing. Also, muscle activities of right anterior part of deltoid, biceps, triceps, musculus extensor carpi radialis and musculus flexor carpi ulnaris were measured by surface electromyography. Results of the analysis showed that change in angle of joints from shoulder toward wrist was to a larger degree in experts and less in novices; drumsticks of experts struck downwards with higher speed; and the two groups also differed in their striking motion. It was found that the experts moved all the muscles monitored while novices moved only those of the upper arms. By their difference in striking motion, it proved that they have different techniques.

3   Proposal

This study aims to extract techniques of experts, including tacit knowledge, for the passing on thereof. If the techniques can be extracted, novices may acquire the techniques quickly even without direct instruction from the experts.

Problems of the related works are that they cannot not show the strength applied by the experts. In this study, in addition to actual motion of the experts, their strength applied and speed of movements are also obtained and extracted. Aiming to extract and pass on techniques of experts, the study is conducted on Wadaiko, one of traditional skills. As the techniques, extracted in the form of data, contain tacit knowledge, they are not handled as explicit knowledge such as text and value, but are passed on by the method of intuition, which is a conventional learning method of "learn by observing".

Techniques refer to postures and motions of experts. Motions of the experts striking a Wadaiko are extracted as data, which is used in developing an instruction system of passing on the techniques of the experts to novices. Finally, it is verified whether the novices have acquired the techniques through the system.

4   Overview of Recording and Playback System

Motions of experts in striking a Wadaiko are extracted by using acceleration sensors, pressure sensors, motion capture sensors and other appliance. By referring to techniques extracting studies of the Ando et al and Fujimoto et al. using motion capture technology; these sensors can extract the motion accurately.

The instruction system avoids as much as possible passing on the techniques to novices in the form of explicit knowledge, in order to prevent the problem of individual differences in interpreting textual information. Instead of value and text, change in colors and shapes are used for instruction.

The studies of the Ando et al. and the Fujimoto et al. created models of human and motions. Merely by watching playbacks of models, one may learn little more than learning by watching video and cannot acquire tacit knowledge behind the motions. Thus, it is important to enable the techniques in the motions be passed on to novices in real time.

A system to pass on techniques extracted from experts to novice is developed (fig.1). The figure 1 shows the whole screen display of the system. Motions of novices are superimposed on motion data of experts saved. When the motions of novices deviated from those of experts, novices are instructed to make adjustments. It is the same for deviations in downward striking speed of and grip strength on drumsticks. When experts and novice take same motion, the novices are considered to have acquired the techniques including tacit knowledge.

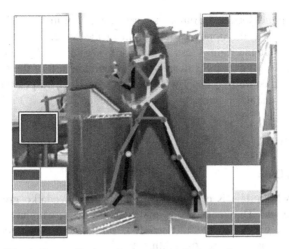

Fig. 1. Screen display of recording and playback system

4.1 Measuring Method and Parameters

Data of motions of the experts striking a Wadaiko extracted includes up-bending angle of arms and wrist indirect and elbow joints movements, as well as speed of downward striking drumsticks. These parameters are determined by referring to the study of the Yamaguchi et al.

3D data of motions are obtained through Kinect, a motion capture sensor of Microsoft Corporation. This sensor calculates depth information by near infrared camera and estimates 3D coordinates of joints of human body. By using Kinect, skeleton data of motions of experts striking a Wadaiko is compiled, and the data of novices is similarly obtained.

Speed of downward striking drumsticks is obtained by using 3-axis acceleration sensors (KXM52-1050), which allow measurement of acceleration and tilt in directions of x, y and z. The sensors can detect acceleration from -2G to +2G.

Grip strength is obtained by pressure sensors (FSR406), which measure 43.69mm and are rectangular in shape. The sensors are installed at where the drumsticks are gripped to detect grip strength. They are controlled by Arduino.

4.2 Motion Based Instruction System

The figure 1 shows the recording and playback system.   Colors of the left side of body in the skeleton data of experts are in deeper shades than those of the right to show depth. Where there are deviations of skeleton data of novices from that of experts, such deviations are indicated by a change of colors.

The graph shows joints on the left, indicated in red, yellow and blue. While looking at the colored joints, novices can rectify their deviations of joint positions. When the deviations are reduced, the indication turns blue, which is showed in the graph. Without any indication on direction of the deviations, the novices have to move their joints up and down, back and forth and left and right, through such efforts it is easier for them to remember where the right position is.

Grip strength and speed of drumsticks are showed by meters. The meters of grip strength are placed at the upper left and right of the screen, and those of speed are placed at bottom left and right. Pressure and speed are showed by colors.

Tempo of strikes of experts is displayed at the middle left of the screen. When left and right drumsticks are in contact with the Wadaiko, their respective indicators turn blue and red, this enables novices to understand the tempo.

5   Evaluation

5.1   Experts Data

Experts, from whom data is obtained, are members of Wadaiko groups which have activities worldwide. They consist of 4 males and females, who have 8 to 27 years of experience. Data was extracted through four one-minute continuous striking, two consist of quarter notes and two of eighth notes.

5.2   Method of Experiment

The figure 2 shows locations of all appliances. Kinect was placed in the front of and 45° right to Wadaiko performers, 0.8m from the ground. Video cameras used for capturing striking motions of the performers were next to Kinect.

The performers struck the Wadaiko with drumsticks equipped with acceleration sensors and pressure sensors, who were instructed to face the acceleration sensors upwards. The screen of the instruction system was set up in the front of and left to the performers.

Effectiveness of the instruction system suggested in the study was subject to verification, in which novices were tested on whether they have acquired techniques of experts and the results were compared with those of conventional instruction methods, where novices are instructed verbally.

The novices consisted of 10 ordinary university undergraduates with no experience of Wadaiko. Five of them received verbal instruction and five used the instruction system in the experiment. After this, they were subject to a test without using both kinds of the instruction to examine to what degree they have acquired the techniques.

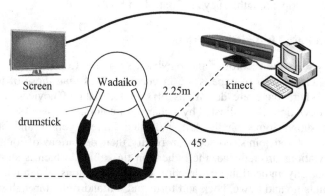

Fig. 2. Experiment environment

5.3   Method of Evaluation

Whether the novices have acquired the techniques is evaluated by comparison of skeleton data. The comparison was on motions in the 0.26 seconds (8 frames) before and after impact of drumsticks striking downwards. Where there were joint deviations from skeleton data of experts over 10cm, the novices were considered not having acquired the techniques.

Subsequent to the instructions, opinion of novices was collected through questionnaire. The performance proceeded and the experts gave subjective assessment on degree of techniques acquired.

6   Result

The table 1 shows percentage of alignment where skeleton data of novices is within 10cm from that of experts.

Table 1. Concordance rate of   skeleton data

Verbal instruction		Proposal instruction system	
Subject	Concordance rate	Subject	Concordance rate
Novice A	34.6%	Novice F	59.5%
Novice B	77.4%	Novice G	70.6%
Novice C	36.0%	Novice H	59.5%
Novice D	46.9%	Novice I	43.5%
Novice E	59.7%	Novice J	51.2%
Average	50.9%	Average	56.9%

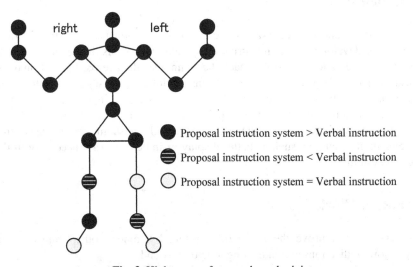

Fig. 3. Higher rate of concordance by joint

The figure 3 shows which method, verbal instruction or the instruction system, resulted in higher percentage of alignment by joint.

7   Discussion

Percentages of alignment were 50.9% and 56.9% for verbal instruction and the instruction system respectively. After calculating the average deviation, there was a significant difference with significance level of 5%. As skeleton data of experts may be compared with constantly, it is considered that its higher percentage of alignment was due to constant modification. Based on the results, it can be said that the techniques of Wadaiko experts which cannot be taught through verbal instruction can be taught by the instruction system.

In grip strength of novices, which was 1631g for verbal instruction and 1371g for the instruction system, there was a significant difference with significance level of 5%. Based on this, the instruction system is better than verbal instruction, as it constantly shows grip strength by colors and is easier for novices to learn as they understand timing and grip strength of strikes of experts. Verbal instruction instructed the novices by utterances of "grip at the instant of strike and loosen the grip when raising the drumsticks", which was not concrete at which instant and how much strength should be applied and led to the bad results.

Novices using the instruction system concentrated on rectifying deviations from motions of the experts in their own motions. As a result, even when they struck, they were not conscious that they struck to make sound. Results of the test showed that sound made by novices receiving verbal instruction was louder.

8   Conclusion

In order to extract and pass on Wadaiko techniques, techniques were extracted from the experts for development of an instruction system, which was then evaluated, with the results that the system can better teach the techniques then verbal instruction does. The results proved the effectiveness of the instruction system suggested. However, problems arose in the experiment that subtle joint bending in skeleton data was indiscernible and too much attention was paid to motions of experts resulting in lower "loudness of sound". Results of the experiment and questionnaire indicated that improvements in accuracy, such as better display of indications, are necessary in the instruction system.

9   Future Work

It is necessary to improve the instruction system by, among other things, better display of joint indications and indicating tempo by sound.

Techniques are not necessarily the same even if extracted from the same person. Also, gender and physique of individuals have effects on the techniques. It is necessary to extract the essence of the techniques by multiple extractions of physical positions of the same person. At present, the data extracted is used for data mining for works of extracting such essence.

References

1. Fujimoto, H.: Passing aspirations on to the next generation: Civil Engineering Consultant, vol. 235, pp. 28–31 (April 2007)
2. Ando, A., Sumikawa, T.: Development and Function Evaluation of Teaching Materials for "sawing" Observation by using Motion Capture and the Virtual World. Japan Society for Educational Technology 36(2), 103–110 (2012)
3. Yamaguchi, M., Horikawa, M., Okai, R., Fujiwara, M.: Japanese Society of Physical Education. Health and Sport Sciences 61, 157 (2010) (in Japanese)

A Study of the Crossroad Game for Improving the Teamwork of Students

Hidetsugu Suto[1,2] and Ruediger Oehlmann[2]

[1] Muroran Institute of Technology,
27-1 Mizumoto-cho, Muroran-shi, Hokkaido, Japan
suto@sdlabo.net
http://www.sdlabo.net
[2] Kingston University, KT12EE, UK

Abstract. The Crossroad game is a social game that is used for learning to deal effectively with difficult situations such as conflicts in teamwork. This paper investigates the characteristics of questions to be used when the Crossroad game is applied to teamwork scenarios. The questions were collected by using questionnaires and dividing them into three groups, high-agreement, low-agreement, and middle-agreement groups using the chi-square method. Results are obtained from students in Japan and the UK, and it is shown that the attitude toward a dilemma within teamwork depended on the background of the students.

Keywords: Teamwork, media biotope, agreement with others.

1 Introduction

The authors are studying the concept of Media biotope (Mizukoshi, 2005) and its applications for vitalizing local communities. Media Biotope refers to gsmallh media such as cable television, free papers, community FM radio, and the communities which are created with these small media. The aim is to support such communities in forming networks, so that they can prosper through their interactions. As examples of communication media, which are based on this concept, we have proposed several systems (Suto, 2011, Suto and Sakamoto, 2011).

A supporting system for teamwork of students is another application based on the media biotope idea. Members of a group in a practice class have to communicate with other members. In many cases, it is difficult for the students to maintain appropriate communication with those members. In addition, they rarely communicate with members of other teams. The objective of the system is to vitalize the communication among members in a group by introducing inter-group communication and forming a structure of a media biotope.

The system implements a social game called Crossroad (Yamori, et al. 2005) as a basis for inter-group communication. In this game, team members discuss several questions related to team relationships which can be answered by *yes* or *no*. The induced discussion is based on the characteristics of these questions.

S. Yamamoto (Ed.): HIMI/HCII 2013, Part III, LNCS 8018, pp. 126–136, 2013.

Especially, whether the players can agree with an answer to the question is important, because controversial discussions would be expected, when the opinions of the players contradict each other.

Hence, this question characteristic is discussed as it has been used in the Crossroad study. The results of the experiments are shown and effects based on the differences between the various backgrounds of the participants are discussed.

2   Crossroad Game

The Crossroad game was invented for considering a wide spectrum of opinions in disaster responses. However it is also useful in other areas that involve communication, such as fostering team relationships. The game involves a facilitator and several players. The facilitator has a stack of cards with questions that are often cast as dilemmas suggesting a particular course of action. Each player has two stacks of cards showing either the word *yes* or the word *no*. The facilitator starts the game by showing the first question from his stack. Each player selects either a *yes* or a *no* card indicating his opinion that the course of action will find a majority support or not. In this way, a given player becomes a member either of a majority of voters or of a minority. If he is a member of the majority, he scores one points. If he forms a minority and he is the only member of that minority, he scores two points and the majority voters score zero points. After each vote, a brief discussion highlights, why the players voted as they did. The player with the highest number of points is declared a winner. However, the exchange of views during the discussion and becoming aware of different opinions are important. It should also be noted that the players are not voting for the best solution, as this could create conflicts. They just predict what solution would attract a majority vote. Therefore the potential for conflicts among players is low. In the teamwork context the Crossroad game is used with reference to inter-personal conflicts in teams to increase inter-team coherence.

3   Question Characteristic

The question classification was based on the chi-square statistics.

It can be assumed that the number of answers to questions, which have the lowest agreement and potentially two alternative answers, are equally divided. Thus, the null hypothesis is that both of the expected values of "*yes* is selected" and "*no* is selected" are 0.5. If the null hypothesis was rejected, the question could be classified into the "high agreement question" group. Therefore the following procedure for classifying the questions was applied:

1. Prepare a question set for the crossroad game.
2. Let the participants answer the questions of the crossroad game.
3. Classify the questions into 3 groups by using Pearson's chi-square test.

(The data are numbers of *yes* and *no* predictions and therefore are nominal.)

The null hypothesis (N0): $P_Y = P_N = 0.5$.

Here for a given question, P_Y means the probability that *yes* has been selected as answer and P_N means the probability that *no* has been selected as answer to that question. The expected values of the numbers of Y and N are $Y : E_Y = (N \times 0.5)$ and $N : E_N = (N \times 0.5)$. In this condition, χ_0^2 is calculated as follows:

$$\chi_0^2 = \frac{(O_Y - E_Y)^2 + (O_N - E_N)^2}{N/2} \tag{1}$$

O_Y and O_N represent the observation values for the numbers of Y and N respectively. χ_0^2 fits the χ^2 distribution with a degree of freedom of 1.

The significance probability P is defined as $P = Pr\{\chi^2 \geq \chi_0^2\}$. If P is less than $0.01(\chi_0^2 \geq 6.63)$, the null hypothesis is strongly rejected and the question is classified as "H: high agreement group." If P is equal to or greater than 0.01 and less than $0.05(6.63 > \chi_0^2 \geq 3.84)$, the null hypothesis is weakly rejected and the question is classified as "M: middle agreement group." If P is equal to or greater than $0.05(3.84 > \chi_0^2)$, the null hypothesis is accepted and the question is classified as "L: low agreement group."

4   Experiments

4.1   Collecting and Grouping Questions

A questionnaire has been developed in order to collect questions for the Crossroad game. 56 questions were collected. Incomplete questions were then eliminated and questions with same meaning were merged. As a result, 35 questions were acquired.

The 35 questions are divided into 6 groups; leadership, health trouble, sense of responsibility, personal matter, communication with others, and commitment to the team.

(Group A) Leadership: Questions related to the participantfs leadership experience. (Group B) Personal matter: Questions about dilemmas between demands caused by health issues and teamwork commitments. (Group C) Sense of responsibility: Questions about the responsibility the participant feels for the team and for the result of the teamwork. (Group D) Personal matter: Questions about dilemmas between the demands of the participantfs personal life and the demands of the teamwork are involved. (Group E) Communication: Questions about communication strategies for resolving intra-team problems. (Group F) commitment: Questions about the commitment of a participant in solving intra-team problems.

4.2   Results and Discussion

The experiments were conducted to investigate the agreements with the obtained questions. Each question was shown to the participants, and they were asked to select *yes* or *no* depending on their own decision. The participants were (I) students of an IT course in the UK (28 males and 5 females), (II) students of an IT course in Japan (33 males and 4 females) and (III) students of a design course in Japan (66 females). The 40 questions have been classified into the 3 groups, H, M and L, described above, in accordance with the results of the experiments.

(A) Leadership. The following six questions are included in this group.

A-1 You are the leader of a team. You have organized many meetings for the team. But one member does not come to any meetings. He also has not contributed at all. Do you discuss the situation with him?

A-2 You are the leader of a team. A team member has not done any work and the deadline is already approaching. Do you ask the lecturer to remove that team member from the project?

A-3 You are the leader of a team. Your team has to submit the assignment tomorrow morning, and you have already finished your parts. However the other members have not done theirs yet, and they highly rely on your help. But you have an important examination tomorrow afternoon. Do you help your members?

A-4 You are the leader of a team. You noticed that one member of the team has not given you his part of the assignment yet. The deadline is the next day. You do not know his e-mail address and telephone number. Do you try to ask your lecturer to resolve this situation?

A-5 You are a member of a team. Your team leader has been involved in an accident and suffered a broken leg. The team has to finish the project the next week. Do you manage your team instead of him?

Table 1. Results of Leadership

	I	II	III		I	II	III
A-1	H (90%)	M (70%)	H (80%)	A-4	H (84%)	L (51%)	H (86%)
A-2	H (72%)	H (10%)	H (31%)	A-5	H (84%)	L (64%)	M (62%)
A-3	L (54%)	H (27%)	H (27%)				

The results of Situation A-2 show that the students of each group could agree with other members' opinion, but the opinion is exactly the opposite. It is expected that Japanese students do not want to remove other members or they do not want to talk about it with a lecturer. In the Situation A-3, Japanese students could agree with other members' opinion of no, but the UK students could not agree. From this results, it is expected that the Japanese students do not want to help others in completing their chores even if they were the leader. In the Situation A-4, only the students of an IT course in Japan could not agree with the other members' opinion of *yes*. It is expected that they do not want to handle other members' personal data. From the results of Situation A-5, it can be seen that the Japanese students tend to hesitate to become a leader.

(B) Health Troubles. The following five questions are included in the group.

B-1 You are a member of a team. You have caught a light cold. You have a doctor's appointment, but your team wants to finish the project because the deadline is the next day. Do you go to see the doctor?

B-2 You are a member of a team. You are very sick. If you do not attend the team meeting, the remainder of your team might fail. But you can pass the module because you get an extension due to your illness. Do you attend the project meeting?

B-3 You are the leader of a team. You are feeling ill and do not want to go to a group meeting. If you do not appear, the other team members are not able to make any decisions. Do you go to the meeting?

B-4 You are a member of a team. You feel tired because you work hard in a part time job. You are considering leaving your task of the project for tomorrow. But your team can not progress until you have completed your part, and they do not want to fall behind. Do you go to bed?

Table 2. Results of health troubles

	I	II	III		I	II	III
B-1	L (39%)	H (21%)	H (22%)	B-3	H (78%)	H (86%)	H (89%)
B-2	L (54%)	H (75%)	H (81%)	B-4	L (33%)	H (16%)	H (16%)

The results of the Situations B-1 and B-2 indicate that Japanese students tend to hesitate to go to see a doctor when they have a team meeting even if they have medical problems. The result of Situation B-4 also shows that the Japanese students tend to hesitate to rest even when they have medical problems. The students of an IT course in the UK could agree with the opinion of *yes* in the Situation B-3 despite being unable to agree with the opinion of *yes* in the Situations B-1 and B-2. One of the most important differences between them is the role of the participant who makes the prediction; in Situation B-3 the participant is the leader and in the Situations B-1 and B-2 the participant is a member. Thus it is expected that they change their attitudes depending on their role.

(C) Sense of Responsibility. The following three questions are included

C-1 You are a member of a team. You have to hand in your team report on a CD. On the way to the student office, accidentally you lost the CD. The deadline is today. Immediately after the submission time, you have another appointment. Do you go home to produce a new CD?

C-2 You are a member of a team. You have to submit the outcome of the project. It is required that all data is recorded on a CD-R disk. However, you have run out blank CD-Rs. Do you buy some new blank CD-Rs for the project?

C-3 You are a member of a team. You have a lot of jobs to do for your employer as a freelance employee at home. You found that the assignment that you were supposed to hand in next week is left and none of the team members did their own part. Will you contact them and try to do the assignment?

In the category "sense of responsibility," the students of the courses agreed with positive opinions in all questions. Thus this kind of question can be classified as a common high-agreement question.

Table 3. Results of sense of responsibility

	I	II	III		I	II	III
C-1	H (93%)	H (100%)	H (89%)	C-3	H (87%)	H (97%)	H (95%)
C-2	H (96%)	H (89%)	H (86%)				

(D) Personal Matters. Personal matters can further be divided into four types; D1: Private events vs. group work, D2: pleasure vs. group work, D3: friendship vs. group work, and D4: other lectures vs. group work.

D1: Private events vs. group work.

D1-1 You are a member of a team. You are looking for a flat. You have an appointment for viewing a house; but your group members need to meet and finish the report at exactly the time of the house viewing. Do you go to view the house?

D1-2 You are a member of a team. You have been invited to an event that you wanted to join today. You also have an assignment which has to be completed by tomorrow noon. If you do not finish it, your team cannot submit the report. Do you attend the event?

D1-3 You are a member of a team. Your family is invited to your aunt's house tonight for dinner because it is her birthday, but you did not manage to finish your tasks yet. Your team has to submit the assignment tomorrow morning and they will work hard tonight. Do you go to your aunt's house?

D1-4 You are the leader of a team. Your have been invited to a free training course event. This course will affect your future work experience and will include the certification by a big company. You have to hand in a report detailing the results of the project on the same day. The other team members either cannot or do not want to come to the University. Do you go to the event?

Table 4. Results of private events vs. group work

	I	II	III		I	II	III
D1-1	L (48%)	L (37%)	H (24%)	D1-3	H (18%)	H (24%)	H (12%)
D1-2	H (18%)	L (35%)	M (34%)	D1-4	H (75%)	H (91%)	H (84%)

In Situation D1-2, the Japanese student could not agree with the opinion of other members. But students of an IT course in the UK could agree with the opinion of no. It is expected that the UK students tend to choose their team work over their own private events.

Both situations of D1-3 and D1-4 ask about the dilemma between group work and other private events. However, the result is exactly the opposite. The event in Situation D1-3 is a family event but the event in Situation D1-4 is of importance for the respondentfs career. Thus it could be said that they tend to choose the private event when it has some relevance for their development.

D2: Pleasure vs. Group Work.

D2-1 You are a member of a team. A close friend invites you and some other friends to the bar for a drink. However your assignment is due tomorrow. Your team wants you to work on the assignment today until it is completed. Do you go to the bar with your close friend?

D2-2 You are a member of a team. A new online multi player game that you wanted to play has come out. Your team has to write a report which is worth 70% of the module. Your team wants to start writing the report tonight. Do you play the game online now?

D2-3 You are a member of a team. Your team members make arrangements to meet in two consecutive days to finish the project. Your friend invites you to an all-night party. Do you go to the party?

Table 5. Results of pleasure vs. group work

	I	II	III		I	II	III
D2-1	H (15%)	H (8%)	H (6%)	D2-3	H (12%)	H (8%)	H (7%)
D2-2	H (6%)	H (5%)	H (3%)				

These results show that all students chose the group work over their pleasure. Thus this kind of questions can also be classified as a common high-agreement question.

D3: Friendships vs. Group Work.

D3-1 You are a member of a team. Your friend is coming to London after 4 years of absence, but the assignment deadline is tomorrow. He is arriving today at 3pm. Do you go to visit him?

D3-2 You are a member of a team. You forgot the appointment with a friend that was scheduled at the same time as a meeting with your team. Do you go to the meeting with your team?

D3-3 You are a member of a team. Your friend broke his leg playing football. He lives in his flat alone. He asked you to visit him, but your team has to present some work tomorrow, and you need to finish the presentation. Do you go and visit your friend?

D3-4 You are a member of a team. There is a team meeting in the afternoon. You are on the way to the University. A team member informs you that he will come later because the train is delayed. The meeting couldn't be started until the member will arrive. You have an appointment with your close friend after the meeting. Do you leave the team meeting earlier to go to the meeting with your friend?

Table 6. Results of friendship vs. group work

	I	II	III		I	II	III
D3-1	L (57%)	L (43%)	L (40%)	D3-3	L (51%)	L (35%)	H (33%)
D3-2	H (84%)	H (94%)	H (77%)	D3-4	L (36%)	L (40%)	L (45%)

It can be seen that it is difficult for participants to agree with each other's opinions in the situations of D3-1, D3-2, and D3-4. In the situations in this group, the protagonists have severe reasons to see their friend except in Situation D3-3. Hence, it is expected that a dilemma of friendship vs. group work is difficult for them, and such questions can be considered as common low-agreement questions.

D4: Other Lectures vs. Group Work.

D4-1 You are a member of a team. You have a very important lecture but at the same time you have to meet with your group to finish the course work, which is due the very same day. Do you go to the lecture?

D4-2 You are a member of a team. You have to meet with your group to finish the project this evening. You have another assignment and the deadline is tomorrow. Do you go to the meeting with your team?

D4-3 You are a member of a team. You have an assignment in another lecture which has to be handed in tomorrow. You also have to work with your team this afternoon. Do you work with your team members?

Table 7. Results of Lecture vs. group works

	I	II	III		I	II	III
D4-1	L (36%)	H (97%)	H (92%)	D4-3	L (48%)	H (81%)	H (31%)
D4-2	L (63%)	H (75%)	H (28%)				

The results of Situation (D4-1) show that many Japanese students agreed with the opinion of choosing the lectures over working with other members. Thus it could be said that the Japanese students are keen to attend lectures. For the situations of (D4-2) and (D4-3), students of each course showed different attitudes. Many students of an IT course in the UK could not agree with the other members whereas many students in Japan could agree. However, the results of (II) and (III) show exactly the opposite result. Central theories in social psychology suggest that group entitativity, i.e. the degree to which a collection of persons is perceived as being bonded together in a coherent unit, depends on common goals (Campbell, 1958) and common social categories (Tajfel and Turne, 1986). A superficial prediction would therefore be that all students should give priority to their group work because they share goals and form a social category. But a closer look would include other social categories such as their family and Lickel, et al. (2000) have shown that intimacy is a strong predictor for entitativity. So the Japanese students would follow the demands of their family rather than those of their team and attend the lecture. The UK students are not very different, but their course has neither a formal requirement nor a formal reward for attending a lecture. It is rather the successful team work that is rewarded with higher scores. Therefore by the same token as the Japanese students, the UK students follow demands of their intimate social context but prioritize the team work. Hence it is expected that the attitude toward a dilemma of teamwork vs. their own assignments depends on their particular study environment and its requirements.

E: Communication with Others. The following five questions are included.

E-1 You are a member of a team. Your relationship to the other team members is not very good. Your printer breaks and the assignment is due tomorrow. Do you ask a team member to print it out?

E-2 You are a member of a team. One group member dominates the group meetings. Do you raise this issue?

E-3 You are a member of a team. In your group, the other members like to do their work in the last minute but you prefer to get started ASAP. Do you talk about it with the other members?

E-4 You are a member of a team. You are aiming for a high mark, but the other team members are satisfied when they just pass the module. Do you talk about it to the other members?

E-5 You are a member of a team. You don't like to talk a lot in front of others. You always agree what others said. You have a great idea that can improve your project. Do you talk to the other team members about your idea?

Table 8. Results of communication with others

	I	II	III		I	II	III
E-1	H (84%)	M (70%)	H (83%)	E-4	H (90%)	M (32%)	M (37%)
E-2	L (54%)	L (62%)	H (69%)	E-5	H (93%)	H (86%)	H (89%)
E-3	H (93%)	M (70%)	H (87%)				

The results of Situation (E-2) show that only the students of a design course agreed with the opinion of *yes*. The reason for this could be that they have received training in expressing themselves. The results of Situation (E-4) indicate that only the students of an IT course in the UK could agree with the opinion of *yes*. It is expected that the students in Japan did not wish to discuss their scores with others.

F: Commitment to the Team.

F-1 You are a member of a team. Your team has to complete a report. The deadline is the next day. One of the team members said that he doesn't want to work tonight. If the report is not finished on time, the team will fail. Do you do the work in his place?

F-2 You are a member of a team. A team member's mother is in the hospital with a severe injury. He feels that he should go to the hospital. However, an assignment is due the next day and he still has a lot of work to do. Your team cannot submit the report until the work is finished. Do you do the work for him?

F-3 You are a member of a team. One of your team members has dropped out. His sections of the presentation must be done by someone else. The rest of your team members are not confident presenters. Do you do the presentation instead of him?

F-4 You are the leader of a team. The day before the deadline you realize that the team assignment involves an additional task that nobody in the team was aware of. Moreover, the other team members have not finished the tasks that were assigned to them earlier. Do you do this new task yourself?

Table 9. Results of commitment for the team

	I	II	III		I	II	III
F-1	H (84%)	H (89%)	H (89%)	F-3	H (87%)	M (70%)	L (57%)
F-2	H (90%)	H (100%)	H (93%)	F-4	M (69%)	H (81%)	H (72%)

The results show that the participants tend to choose the opinion *yes* indicating a preference for commitment to their team, except in the case of the design students in Japan in Situation (F-3). Generally, a student presentation is one of the most important events in that Japanese design course. Thus they might hesitate to make such a presentation because of the high pressure that is associated with that task.

5 Conclustion

In this paper, question characteristics have been investigated for the Crossroad game. The questions were collected by using questionnaires and dividing them into three groups, high-agreement, low-agreement, and middle-agreement using the chi-square method.

The results highlighted that both, the UK students and Japanese students, tend to agree with the opinion of *yes* to questions involving a sense of responsibility or a dilemma between pleasure and demands of the team work or the commitment to the team. By contrast, both, the UK students and Japanese students, could not agree with each other about a dilemma between friendship and team work. Furthermore, the attitude toward a dilemma between teamwork and their own assignments depended on the background of the student. Thus it is expected that discussions in the Crossroad game can be enhanced by adding questions related to dilemmas between friendship and team work or between their own assignments and team work.

Acknowledgements. This work was supported by Grants-in-Aid for Scientific Research from the Japanese Society for the Promotion of Science (No. 20500220 and No. 21360191).

References

Campbell, D.: Common fate, similarity, and other indices of the status of aggregates of persons as social entities. Behavioral Science 3, 14–25 (1958)

Lickel, B., Hamilton, D., Wieczorkowska, G., Lewis, A., Sherman, S., Uhles, A.: Varieties of groups and tghe perception of group entitativity. Journal of Personality and Social Psychology 78, 223–246 (2000)

Mizukoshi, S.: Media Biotope. Kinokuniya publication (2005) (in Japanese)

Suto, H.: Media Biotope: Media Designing Analogous with Biotope. Int. J. Computer Information Systems and Industrial Management Applications 3, 264–270 (2011)

Suto, H., Sakamoto, M.: Local Communication Media Based on Concept of Media Biotope. In: Proc. HCI International 2011, CD-ROM (2011)

Tajfel, H., Turner, J.: The social identity theory of intergroup behaviour. In: Worchel, S., Austin, W. (eds.) Psychology of Intergroup Relations, pp. 7–24. Brooks Cole, Monterey (1986)

Yamori, K., Kikkawa, T., Ajiro, T.: Learning risk communication with protection against disasters game. Nakanishiya Publication (2005) (in Japanese)

Towards Understanding of Relationship among Pareto Optimal Solutions in Multi-dimensional Space via Interactive System

Keiki Takadama[1], Yuya Sawadaishi[1], Tomohiro Harada[1], Yoshihiro Ichikawa[1],
Keiji Sato[1], Kiyohiko Hattori[1], Hiroyoki Sato[1], and Tomohiro Yamaguchi[2]

[1] The University of Electro-Communications
1-5-1 Chofugaoka, Chofu, Tokyo,182-8558 Japan
{keiki,hattori,sato}@hc.uec.ac.jp,
{sawadaishi,harada,yio,keiji}@cas.hc.uec.ac.jp
[2] Nara National College of Technology
22, Yata-cho, Yamatokoriyama, Nara 639-1080 Japan
yamaguch@info.nara-k.ac.jp

Abstract. This paper proposes the interactive system that can help humans to understand the trade-off relationship of Pareto optimal solutions (*e.g.*, good products from a certain aspect) in multi-dimensional space. For this purpose, the following two methods are proposed from the viewpoint of the number of evaluation criteria which should be considered by a user at one time: (i) the two fixed evaluation criteria are employed to evaluate the solutions; and (ii) some evaluation criteria selected by a user (*i.e.*, the number of the evaluation criteria is varied by a user) are employed to evaluate them. To investigate the effectiveness of our proposed system employing either of two methods, we conduct human subject experiments on the motor selection problem and have revealed the following implications: (i) the proposed system based on the two fixed evaluation criteria contributes to helping users to find better motors in terms of all the evaluation criteria, while (ii) the proposed system based on the selected evaluation criteria is more effective to help users to understand Pareto optimal solutions when more evaluation criteria need to be considered.

Keywords: Pareto optimal solution, multi-dimensional space, interactive assistant system.

1   Introduction

In various decision making in human society, we generally have to explore solutions by considering *multiple criteria* rather than *a single criterion*. To derive an optimal decision-making in such a multi-dimensional space, it is necessary to understand trade-off relationship among multiple criteria. Since these relationships become complicated as the number of the evaluation criteria increases, it becomes to be hard to understand all of their relationships. When finding rental apartment, for example, it is

S. Yamamoto (Ed.): HIMI/HCII 2013, Part III, LNCS 8018, pp. 137–146, 2013.

not so difficult to find a good apartment by considering only a room size and a rental cost. However, it becomes to be very hard to find a satisfied apartment by considering a distance from a station, a resistance to earthquakes, and newness/oldness in addition to a room size and a rental cost. This is because it is generally difficult for us to perfectly understand the complicated relationship among many evaluations as the number of the evaluation criteria increases.

For this issue, the multi-objective optimization approach such as NSGA-II (Elitist Non-Dominated Sorting Genetic Algorithm) [1] is useful because it can find Pareto optimal solutions in the multi-dimensional space through an evaluation of solutions by considering all evaluation criteria. As another approach, a visualization of multi-dimensional space [5] is also useful because it can show the relationship among solutions in the two-dimensional space converted from the multi-dimensional space. These approaches can compute good solutions or can visualize the relationship among solutions, they cannot directly support humans to understand the trade-off relationships among them.

To tackle this problem, this paper proposes the interactive system that can support humans to understand the trade-off relationship of Pareto optimal solutions in multi-dimensional space through an interaction between the system and a user. For this purpose, we focus on an influence of changing a number and a kind of evaluation criteria which should be considered by a user at one time, and propose the following two methods: (i) the two fixed evaluation criteria are employed to evaluate the solutions; and (ii) some evaluation criteria selected by a user (*i.e.*, the number of the evaluation criteria is varied by a user according to his or her understanding) are employed to evaluate them. A human subject experiments on a motor selection problem for space exploration rovers as multi-dimensional space problem are conducted to investigate the effectiveness of the proposed system from the viewpoint of the degree of understanding of the human subjects.

This paper is organized as follows. Section 2 explains the non-dominated sorting which is one of the multi-objective optimization, and Section 3 describes the proposed system employing either of both methods. Section 4 explains the human subject experiments on a motor selection problem, and Section 5 shows experimental results. Finally, our conclusion is given in Section 6.

2   How to Evaluate Solutions in Multi-dimensional Space

2.1   Pareto Front

The trade-off relationship among solutions is often occurred when the number of evaluation criteria is more than one. Considering the situation of finding rental apartment, for example, a rental cost increases if a distance between an apartment and a station becomes short, while a rental cost decreases if such a distance becomes long. To evaluate these solutions in the trade-off relationship, the *non-dominated sorting* calculates an order of solutions by finding Pareto optimal solutions [2] (*i.e.*, a solution group which is the most superior to other solution groups) in multi-dimensional space.

Fig. 1 shows how the non-dominated sorting works. In Fig. 1, the points A, B, C, and D are respectively represented as $(x1, y1)$, $(x2, y2)$, $(x2, y1)$, and $(x1, y2)$ with the condition where x1 > x2 and y1 >y2. In such relationship, the point A dominates the points B, C, and D, the point B dominates the point D, and the point C dominates the point D. Concretely, the solutions represented by red circles in Fig. 1 are not dominated by other solutions, and they are called *Pareto optimal solutions* and a set of them is defined as the Pareto front 1. Then, the set of solutions which are not dominated by other solutions except for the solutions in the Pareto front 1 is defined as the Pareto front 2. The Pareto front 3, 4, ..., n are defined by the same way. According to this definition, the solutions in a small Pareto front number are superior to those in a large Pareto front number.

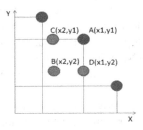

Fig. 1. Image of Pareto front solutions

2.2   Average Pareto Front

Using the concept of the Pareto front, this paper proposes *average Pareto front,* which is an average value of the Pareto front number in the multi-dimensional space. Concretely, the average Pareto front is calculated from all combination of two evaluation criteria. Table 1 shows an example of how the average Pareto front is calculated in the case of three evaluation criteria. For example, the average Pareto front in *x2* (1.67) is calculated by an average of three Pareto front numbers 2, 1, and 2, each of which is an average of the front numbers of 1 and f2, f2 and f3, and f3 and f1.

Table 1. Calculation of average Pareto front

Solution	Value of f1	Value of f2	Value of f3	Evaluation criteria	Front	Average Front
x1	5	5	2	f1&f2	1	(1+1+1)/3=1
				f2&f3	1	
				f3&f1	1	
x2	3	4	4	f1&f2	2	(2+1+2)/3=1.67
				f2&f3	1	
				f3&f1	2	
x3	4	2	5	f1&f2	2	(2+1+1)/3=1.33
				f2&f3	1	
				f3&f1	1	

3   Proposed Interactive System

3.1   Overview

To promote users to understand the trade-off relationship of Pareto optimal solutions in the multi-dimensional space, we take an approach of (1) deleting bad solutions and

(2) reducing/changing the number of evaluation criteria which should be considered by a user at one time. Such a solution deletion and evaluation criteria reduction enables user to easily understand the relationship of evaluation criteria. Regarding the evaluation criteria reduction, in particular, the proposed interactive system starts with two evaluation criteria among them. A sequence of the proposed interactive system shows as follows.

1. Among all solutions displayed in the system, a user selects one solution which he/she thinks it good.
2. The average Pareto front of the selected solution is calculated
3. A certain number of the solutions from the largest average value front (*i.e.*, bad solutions) are deleted. Considering 1000 solutions, for example, the worst 100 solutions are deleted and the top 900 solutions are remained if a certain number of the deleted solutions in 100. Note that if the selected solution is within the 100 bad solutions, the solutions from the worst one to the selected one are deleted instead of the worst 100 solutions
4. The remaining solutions are displayed to a user. In detail, these solutions are displayed from the viewpoint of the different two evaluation functions (described in Section 3.2.1) or they are displayed from the viewpoint of some evaluation functions which are added/deleted (described in Section 3.2.2).
5. Return to 1 until a user determines to find a desired solution.

3.2   Reducing/Changing the Number of Evaluation Criteria

In this paper, we propose the following two methods for reducing/changing the number of evaluation criteria: (1) two evaluation criteria method and (2) changing evaluation criteria method

Two Evaluation Criteria Method. This method decomposes many evaluation criteria that is more than one into a combination of the two evaluation criteria and displays solutions from the viewpoint of one of combinations that a user has not yet understood yet to promote a user to learn the trade-off relationship of such solutions. Since it is generally difficult for us to understand the multidimensional space with many evaluation criteria at the same time, a division of many evaluation criteria into two evaluation criteria makes it easy to understand the multidimensional space. Note that this method displays solutions to a user from the viewpoint of *one* of combinations of the two evaluation criteria, and some bad solutions are deleted from the viewpoint of the *same* combinations of the two evaluation criteria by calculating the average Pareto front value of the selected solution. This indicates that good solutions are displayed with a small number of evaluation criteria to facilitate understanding of the relationship among them, while bad solutions are deleted with the same evaluation criteria to reduce such solutions as fast as possible.

Figure 2 shows an example of the two evaluation criteria method with three evaluation criteria, f1, f2 and f3. The sequence of this method is shown as follows: (1) a user starts to select one solution (*i.e.*, the red triangle dot) from the 2D area of f1 and f2;

(2) the system calculates the Pareto front value from all combination of three criteria, *i.e.*, f1-f2, f1-f3, and f2-f3, and selects one combination of two evaluation criteria that has the highest front value (bad value) as the combination that a user has not yet understood. In this case, the combination of f1-f3 is selected because of the highest front value 3; (3) the system deletes the some bad solutions which are lower than the selected solution's one in the combination of f1-f3; (4) the system displays the remaining solutions in the combination of f1-f3 and return to (1) until a user determines to find a desired solution.

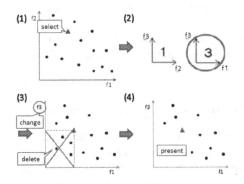

Fig. 2. Sequence of two evaluation criteria method

Changing Evaluation Criteria Method. This method enables a user to change (*i.e.*, increase or decrease) the number of evaluation criteria which a user considers at the same time. A user can freely change it at the timing of the user to adjust his/her understanding of the multidimensional space. Since it is generally difficult to understand many trade-off relations from the beginning, it is reasonable to start by understanding of the simple relationship (*i.e.*, the relationship between two evaluation criteria in this method) and then gradually increases the degree of difficulty of understanding by adding evaluation criterion one by one.

Figure 3 shows an example of the changing evaluation criteria method with three evaluation criteria, f1, f2 and f3. The sequence of this method is shown as follows: (1) a user starts to select one solution (*i.e.*, the red triangle dot) from the 2D area of f1 and f2; (2) the system calculates the average Pareto front of the selected solution from the viewpoint of *two* evaluation criteria, *i.e.*, f1-f2. In this case, the average Pareto front value of two evaluation criteria is calculated as 2; (3) the system deletes the some bad solutions which are lower than the selected solution's one from the viewpoint of the average Pareto front value; (4) the system displays the remaining solutions; (5) a user adds (or deletes) one evaluation criterion and select one solution. In this case, a user adds an evaluation criterion f3 and selects a new solution (*i.e.*, the green square dot); (6) the system calculates the average Pareto front of the selected solution from the viewpoint of *three* evaluation criteria, *i.e.*, f1-f2, f1-f3, and f2-f3, In this case, the average Pareto front value of all combination of three evaluation criteria is calculated as 2.33; (7) the system deletes the some bad solutions which are lower than the

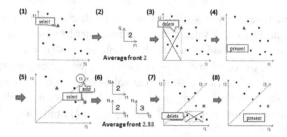

Fig. 3. Sequence of changing evaluation criteria method

selected solution's one from the viewpoint of the average Pareto front value; (8) the system displays the remaining solutions, and return to (5) until a user determines to find a desired solution.

3.3   Comparing the Method by Using Simple Example

We explain how each methods helps user with understanding the relationship by using the simple problem. The example is that there are three evaluate criteria and the number of the solution, (a)-(j), is ten. Table shows the relationship of its solutions, evaluate criteria and average front. Figure is the plot of the solution the combination of f1-f3 f1-f2andf2-f3.In this example, system presents the result of criteria is f1and f2at the beginning, user choice the solution of (d) and the number of deletion is two.

Table 2. Simple example of solution and average front

Solution	Value of f1	Value of f2	Value of f3	Average front
(a)	10	1	6	1.66
(b)	9	3	4	2
(c)	8	6	10	1
(d)	7	9	2	2
(e)	6	10	7	1.33
(f)	5	5	1	2.66
(g)	4	2	8	2.33
(h)	3	7	3	2.33
(i)	2	8	9	1.66
(j)	1	4	5	3

- *Two evaluation criteria method.* When user choice the solution of (d), system calculates the front value which the solution user selected belongs all combination in Figure 4. It shows (d)'s front value are 1, 2, and in the combination f1-f2 f2-f3 and f1-f3, and so system present the result of combination of f1-f3. And then, in this combination, the system deletes the solution which has higher front value. In this case, the solutions of (h) and (j) are deleted. Next, in this evaluation criterion's combination f1-f3, assuming that the solution of (a) is chosen, the result of calculation, the new presentation's combination changes f2-f3 and deleted a certain number.
- *Changing evaluation criteria method.* When user choices the solution of (d), in the presented combination f1-f2, system deletes the solution which has high average

front than selected solution a certain number. In this case, the solutions of (g) and
(j) are deleted. Next, assuming that user become considering the f3 criteria too, user selects the solution considered three criteria f1, f2 and f3. Then the solution of
(c) is selected, and the deleted solutions which have higher average front than (c)
become (f) and (h).

- *Compared method.* This method intends to compare the result of each method. The
way of presentation is that all evaluation criteria are presented at the beginning and
user can change the number of these. Specifically, when user choice the solution of
(d), the system calculates the average front presented all evaluation criteria's combination, in this case f1, f2 and f3. And the solutions which has higher average
front ((g)and (j)) are deleted.

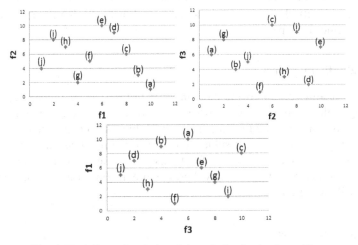

Fig. 4. Two-dimensional plot of the solution in simple problem

4   Motor Selection Problem

In the human subject experiments, we adopt the selection of motors for space exploration rover problem as Multi-Dimensional Space problem. The subjects refer to the
data of the motor and select one motor from seven hundred motors. There are five
evaluation criteria "Weight", "Length", "rpm", "Torque" and "Efficiency". In this
case, the value of each evaluation criteria is important that the value of "Weight" is
low, the value of "length" is low, the value of "rpm" is large, the value of "Torque" is
high, and the value of the "Efficiency" is high.

5   Human Subject Experiment

To investigate the effect of the proposed system, we did human subject experiments.

5.1   Experimental Contents

Subjects consist of nine people, six men and three women of 20s. They chose "most excellent performance" motor in the sequence of one experiment, and do this sequence total of five times. In this experiment, we set the problem special emphasis on the evaluation criteria of "Weight", "Torque" and "Length" in this case and inform user. This is because there are many cases when user searches for some solution, there is priority, so we assume such a situation. Flow of the experiment is as follows. First, we divided nine subjects into three groups, and there are three persons in one group. And we distribute the manual of experiment to subjects. The contents of manual shows that description of the contents of the experiment, the parameters used in the experiment, and how to operate the system. We have subjects read this and explain orally. Then subjects choose the best one motor and that selecting sequence was performed five times for a person.

5.2   Evaluation Criteria

We adopt evaluating the following three items in order to evaluate the degree of understanding of the multidimensional space; (1) average front of the solution chosen by subjects; (2) the time required for the final until subject selects the motor; (3) the similarity of the selected motor. If subject understand the relationship, they can chose the motor which has the low average front. Also, the time is short compared to one which does not understand presumably. Furthermore, if subject understand that, similar motor will be chosen.

5.3   Experimental Result

- *Average front and Time of experiment.* Figure5 shows that the average front of selected solution and time of each method. The horizontal axis shows each system, the vertical axis shows average front (left) and time (right).The difference of color between red and blue shows that the average front of all evaluation criteria and special emphasis on evaluation criteria. In two evaluation criteria method, the average front of special emphasis on evaluation criteria is the best of all. Also in changing the evaluation criteria method, the average front of all evaluation criteria and special emphasis on evaluation criteria is middle value of all methods.
- *Transition of the selected motor.* To examine whether the motor was finally selected by the subjects in each method, has changed how the number of times with each, we shows the distribution of motor in two-dimensional map by Multidimensional scaling method [4] (Figure 6). Multidimensional scaling method is that represented points in the space relationship of the object classification in low-dimensional distribution. Scatter diagram in this way shows that if the distance between the solution and other solutions that are plotted is short, nature of the solution are similar, if it is long, the nature of the solution is different.

In the two evaluation criteria method, motor searching become in the narrow range gradually from a wide range. In the changing the evaluation criteria method, motor searching is always seen only in a narrow range.

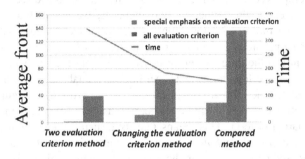

Fig. 5. Average front of selected solution and time of each method

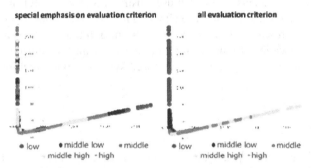

Fig. 6. The distribution of motor and average front by Multidimensional scaling method

5.4 Discussion

In this result, the two evaluation criteria method is that although searching time is long, subjects can choose the best motor in the proposed method and search as efficient transition, this method contribute to understand the multi-dimensional space. the changing the evaluation criteria method is that although it is possible to search a short time, slightly inferior motor has been selected compared with the two evaluation criteria method, this method contribute to understand local understanding of the solution space.

6   Conclusion

In this study, we proposed the interactive system that can help humans to understand the trade-off relationship of Pareto optimal solutions (*e.g.*, good products from a certain aspect) in multi-dimensional space. For this purpose, the following two methods were proposed from the viewpoint of the number of evaluation criteria which should be considered by a user at one time: (i) the two fixed evaluation criteria are employed to evaluate the solutions; and (ii) some evaluation criteria selected by a user (*i.e.*, the number of the evaluation criteria is varied by a user according to his or her understanding) are employed to evaluate them. To investigate the effectiveness of our proposed system employing either of two methods, we conducted human subject experiments on the motor selection problem for space exploration rovers as multidimensional space problem, and investigated the results from viewpoint of the averaged Pareto-front and the time for selecting one motor in order to evaluate the degree of understanding of the human subjects. An intensive analysis of the human subject experiments revealed the following implications: (i) the proposed system based on the two fixed evaluation criteria contributes to helping users to find better motors in terms of all the evaluation criteria. This means that users using this system can learn the trade-off relationship in the *whole* solution space effectively but it takes *long* time; and (ii) the proposed system based on the selected evaluation criteria is more effective to help users to understand Pareto optimal solutions when more evaluation criteria need to be considered. This means that users using this system can learn the trade-off relationship in the *local* solution space although it takes *short* time.

The following research must be done in the near future: (1) a generalization of the obtained implications by increasing the number of human subjects; and (2) a investigation of the effectiveness of the proposed system in other multipurpose design problem.

References

1. Deb, K.: Multiobjective Optimization using Evolutionary Algorithms. Wiley (2001)
2. Hiroyasu, T., Miki, M., Watanabe, S., Sakoda, T., Kamiura, J.: Evaluation of Genetic Algorithm for Objective Computation Methods. The Science and Engineering Review of Doshisha University 43(1), 41–52 (2002)
3. Kuroiwa, T.: Trade-off Analysis Method. Toshiba Special Reports, pp.48–50 (2005)
4. Taguchi, Y., Oono, Y., Yokoyama, K.: A New Eigenvector Technique for Multivariate Direct Gradient Analysis. Proceedings of the Institute of Statistical Mathematics 49(1), 133–153 (2001)
5. Yamashiro, D., Yoshikawa, T., Furuhashi, T.: Grasping the Effects of Genetic Operation and Improvement of Searching Ability through Visualizing Search Process for GA. Information Processing Society of Japan 48, 69–77 (2007)

Development and Evaluation of a Mobile Search System for Science Experiments to Connect School Knowledge to Common Knowledge

Takahito Tomoto[1], Tomoya Horiguchi[2], and Tsukasa Hirashima[3]

[1]Faculty of Engineering, Tokyo University of Science 1-3 Kagurazaka, Shinjuku-ku, Tokyo 162-8601 Japan
[2]Graduate School of Maritime Sciences, Kobe University, 5-1-1 Fukaeminami-machi, Higashinada-ku, Kobe-shi, Hyogo 658-0022, Japan
[3]Graduate School of Engineering, Hiroshima University, 1-4-1 Kagamiyama, Higashi Hiroshima City, Hiroshima 739-8527, Japan
tomoto@ms.kagu.tus.ac.jp

Abstract. In this paper, we propose a method that connects school knowledge to common knowledge through a mobile search system that enables users to think about and perform science experiments relevant to their everyday life. We developed the system and tested it in an evaluation experiment with 15 participants who used the system in everyday life over the course of a week. The evaluation results revealed that the users began to consider appropriate experiments, describe appropriate locations, and understand scientific concepts and methods. Participants' questionnaire responses showed that they became interested in science experiments and formed a strong connection between school knowledge and common knowledge.

Keywords: Common Knowledge, School Knowledge, Learning Science, Science Experiments.

1 Introduction

In this paper, we describe the development and evaluation of a mobile search system for science experiments in order to connect school knowledge to common knowledge. With the rapid development of mobile devices, the learning environment has extended beyond the school's computer room. Mobile learning environments are now being used in classrooms that do not have desktop PCs as well as even outside of the classroom. In the future, we need to discuss not only the wealth of learning resources made available by such environments but also how to use them.

Much of the knowledge in a learner's life comes from school; we refer to the knowledge taught in school as *school knowledge*. Knowledge becomes useful when the learner applies it in everyday life, but school knowledge is known not to be applied often in this way[1]. The knowledge used in everyday life is called *common knowledge*. To convert school knowledge to common knowledge, it is effective to apply

S. Yamamoto (Ed.): HIMI/HCII 2013, Part III, LNCS 8018, pp. 147–156, 2013.

school knowledge to everyday life[2]. It is important, therefore, to develop a system that provides learning resources and allows learners to apply school knowledge to real world situations. In our research, we constructed a database containing various experiments that teach certain scientific concepts and also developed a mobile search system that provides learners with experiments based on their present location when they log into the system.

2   Mobile Search System for Science Experiments

2.1   System Structure

Fig. 1 shows an overview of the learning activities our system provides. In the system, learners are required first to input their present location and then the system provides a list of possible experiments that takes into consideration the possible tools available at the learner's present location. The learners then select an experiment and conduct it. Finally, our system explains the meaning of the experiment so that they can apply various scientific concepts from the experiment to everyday life.

Fig. 1. Example of a Learning Activity in Our System

Fig. 2 shows the structure of our system, consisting of a server and a mobile device. The server program calculates the feasibility of an experiment using database values. The mobile system provides the required interface for searches and displays the experiments through the use of a search module. By inputting their present location, learners are shown a list of science experiments that can be conducted there; the list also shows the feasibility of the experiment with the tools necessary to complete it. The learners select and perform one of the experiments. Next, usage logs are sent to the server.

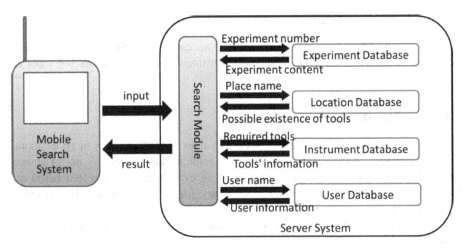

Fig. 2. The Structure of Our System

2.2   Experiment Database

The experiment database contains the experiment number as well as other information on content of the experiment. An example of the content information can be seen below. In the database, there are 61 experiments selected from a book published by Hans Jurgen Press [3].

1. Experiment Number: 0
2. Experiment Name: Floating coin
3. Tools: Water, coin, glass
4. Conditions: none
5. Experimental question:
 What will happen when you put a coin in a glass filled with water?
6. Steps:
 First, fill a glass with water.
 Second, slowly place a coin on the surface of the water in the glass.
7. Result:
 The coin floats in water.
8. Explanation:
 A coin usually sinks because it is made of metal. The coin, however, floats when placed slowly on the water surface in a glass filled with water because the force of gravity of the coin and the combination of upper forces (which consist of surface tension and the force of buoyancy) are in balance.
9. Related scientific concepts:
 Surface Tension, Force of Buoyancy, Equilibrium of Force
10. Related phenomena:
 Pond skater floats in water.

2.3   Instrument Database

The instrument database contains all the tools necessary to complete an experiment contained in the experiment database. The instrument database contains 105 tools in all.

2.4   Location Database

The location database contains the probability values of tools existing in 16 locations that learners visit in their everyday lives; we refer to this probability as "existence probability." In our system, the feasibility of an experiment is calculated based on the existence probability of the tools necessary for an experiment. The existence probability ranges from 0 to 1.0.

The existence probability consists of two types of data: default data and individual data.

The Default Existence Probability

The default existence probability value is calculated through the results of a survey of 56 students who went to various locations and searched for tools. The calculation used is:

$$DEP_{ik} = \frac{s}{56}$$

DEP_{ik}: Default existence probability of a tool k in location i
s: Number of students who can find the tool k in location i

The Individual Existence Probability

In our system, the existence probability of tools is calculated on a per-user basis. If a user conducts an experiment, the individual existence probability for that given location is updated. The existence probability of the tools used in the experiment at the given location is updated to 1.0 because the tools are confirmed to be presently at the location. However, potential dilution of the tools increases with time, so the increased existence probability is decreased to the default existence probability over time. The calculation used is:

$$IEP_{ik} = at + LI_{ik}$$

$$a = \frac{-1.0}{60days * 24hours * 60min.} = \frac{-1.0}{8.64 * 10^4}$$

IEP_{ik}: Individual existence probability of a tool k in location i
LI_{ik}: Last login time associated with the individual existence probability of tool k in location i
t: Time after last login

2.5   User Database

The user database contains each user's name, login time, and the number of experiments the user has conducted with the system.

2.6   Search Module

When learners select their present location, our search module determines the feasibility of the various experiments using the databases. The feasibility values are calculated based on the existence probabilities of the necessary tools for the experiment. The calculation is:

$$FE_{ij} = \prod_{k=1}^{n_j} EP_{ik}$$

$$EP_{ik} = \max\left(DEP_{ik}, IEP_{ik}\right)$$

FE_{ij}: Feasibility of the experiment j in location i
EP_{ik}: Existence probability of a tool k in location i
n_j: Number of required tools for experiment j

Our system calculates all FE_{ij} values for a selected location i and arranges the experiments in descending order of feasibility with the search module.

2.7   Interface

Fig. 3 shows the location selection interfaces. Learners are first required to select their present location.

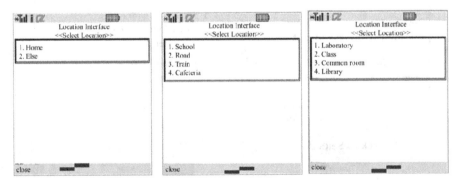

Fig. 3. Location Selection Interfaces

Next, the system calculates the feasibility of each experiment for the selected location (FE_{ij}) and displays experiments in descending order of feasibility (Fig. 4). Learners then select an experiment that they are willing and able to conduct.

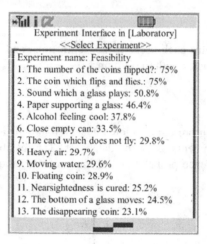

Fig. 4. Experiment Selection Interface

After selecting an experiment, the system shows the learners the experimental question and the tools necessary to complete the selected experiment, as seen on the left side of Fig. 5. When the learners select an experiment, they can check the experimental steps, as seen on the right side of Fig. 5. Finally, they conduct the experiment, as seen in Fig. 6, and check the experimental result and explanation in the system.

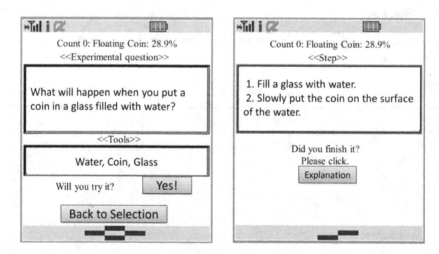

Fig. 5. Experimental question and Tools Interface(left), and Step Interface (right)

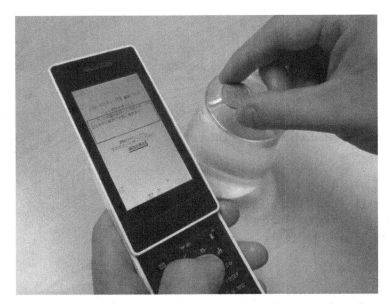

Fig. 6. Performing an Experiment

3   Evaluation Experiments

We report here the results of two experiments (Experiment 1 and Experiment 2). The objective of Experiment 1 was to evaluate the feasibility calculation. In our mobile system, experiments are provided based on feasibility for a given location. The objective Experiment 2 was to evaluate the effectiveness of the system for enabling learners to connect their school knowledge to their common knowledge.

3.1   Experiment 1

In Experiment 1, we evaluated whether the system could provide feasible experiments for various locations.

There were 7 test participants: 6 university students and 1 graduates. The participants tried 10 times to perform the provided experiments in 4 locations around the university (labs, classrooms, cafeteria, and library). Each location was assigned to 2 people, thus 20 evaluations were conducted per location.

We evaluated the experiment feasibility results on a precision basis. Precision was calculated by dividing the number of actual conducted experiments by the number of experiments proposed by our system. The precision results from the laboratory, classroom, cafeteria, and library were 0.9, 0.2, 0.7, and 0.2, respectively. The precision results from the classroom and library were lower than for the laboratory and cafeteria because the classroom and the library do not have as many tools available for experiments.

3.2   Experiment 2

Objective
To evaluate if the system was effective for connecting school knowledge and common knowledge

Subjects
Seven university students and five graduates

Procedure

1. Pre-test (15 min.)
2. Explanation of how to use our system.
3. Use of our system (1 week)
4. Post-test (15 min.)
5. Questionnaire (10 min.)

Contents of the Test
Fig. 7 shows the content of the pre-test and post-test. In the tests, learners are required to describe the experiments that can be conducted in their everyday life. We marked when they described appropriate places, tools, concepts, and methods.

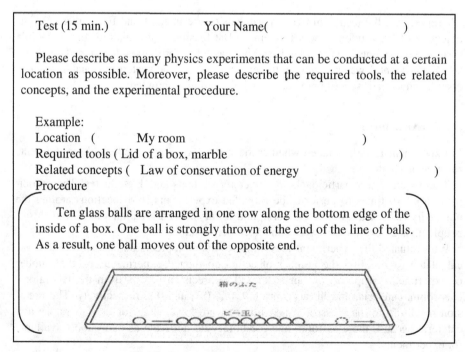

Test (15 min.)   Your Name(   )

Please describe as many physics experiments that can be conducted at a certain location as possible. Moreover, please describe the required tools, the related concepts, and the experimental procedure.

Example:
Location   (My room   )
Required tools (Lid of a box, marble   )
Related concepts (Law of conservation of energy   )
Procedure

Ten glass balls are arranged in one row along the bottom edge of the inside of a box. One ball is strongly thrown at the end of the line of balls. As a result, one ball moves out of the opposite end.

箱のふた

ビー玉

Fig. 7. Content of the Pre-test and Post-test

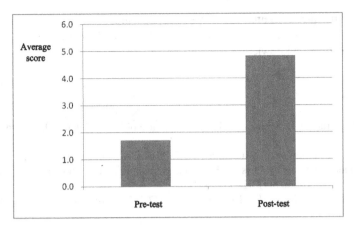

Fig. 8. Average Score of the Pre-test and Post-test

Fig. 8 shows the results of the pre-test and post-test, with an average score of 1.7 for the former and 4.8 for the latter. The statistical difference was determined by paired t test. Table 1 shows that the result of the t test. The average score of post-test was significantly higher($p < 0.01$) than pre-test.

Table 1. The result of t test

degree of freedom	t value	p value
11	2.2	$4.0*10^{-4}$

The participants answered a questionnaire on their thoughts about the system. The participants were asked whether they minded applying school knowledge to their everyday life, to which they responded using a 5-point numerical Likert scale. We found that favorable results: the average score of the item "Did you get more interested in the science experiment?" was 4.42, that for the item "Have you improved your understanding of school knowledge?" was 4.75, and that for the item "Did you start to consider school knowledge in everyday life?" was 4.25.

4   Conclusion

In this paper, we proposed a method to enable learners to use their school knowledge in everyday life. We developed and evaluated our mobile search system for learners to complete science experiments in their everyday lives, finding that they were able to connect school knowledge and common knowledge.

In the evaluation experiment, 15 participants used our system over the course of 1 week. The results indicated that they became able to consider appropriate experiments, describe appropriate locations, and understand scientific concepts and methods. The questionnaire results revealed that they became interested in science experiments and considered school knowledge to be highly applicable to everyday life and thus to common knowledge.

References

1. John, T., Bruer, T.J.: Schools for thought: a science of learning in the classroom. MIT Press (1993)
2. Tomoto, T., Horiguchi, T., Hirashima, T., Takeuchi, A.: Virtual Experimental Environment to Support Learning by Physical Experiment Designing. The Journal of Information and Systems in Education 8(1), 72–83 (2009)
3. Jurgen, H.: Press: SPIEL-DAS WISSEN SCHAFFT, Ravensburger Buchverlag; Neuauflage (20040

Application to Help Learn the Process of Transforming Mathematical Expressions with a Focus on Study Logs

Takayuki Watabe[1], Yoshinori Miyazaki[2], and Yoshiki Hayashi[1]

[1] Graduate School of Informatics, Shizuoka University, Shizuoka, Japan
{gs11055,gs11038}@s.inf.shizuoka.ac.jp
[2] Faculty of Informatics, Shizuoka University, Shizuoka, Japan
yoshi@inf.shizuoka.ac.jp

Abstract. This study proposes a system that helps learners transform mathematical expressions by letting the learners select the part of the original mathematical expression to be transformed. On selection, a list of mathematical expressions is displayed, showing possible transformations. Users select one mathematical expression from the list of displayed candidates. The transformed expressions can be further transformed recursively, step-by-step. In this way, the system supports trial-and-error steps of the transformation process and lets learners transform actively. This study also aims to understand learners' trial-and-error steps by using transformation history.

Keywords: Mathematics education, Mathematical transformation, Study log.

1 Introduction

This study discusses a system that helps learners acquire the necessary skills for transforming mathematical expressions.

The skill of transformation plays a significant role in the study of mathematics. First, transformation is an indispensable tool in more advanced operations such as proving propositions or differentiating/integrating analytically. Second, transformation is helpful for understanding mathematical concepts by observing mathematical expressions from various viewpoints via transformation. However, it is not easy to acquire these skills because in cases where there is a lack of transformation knowledge, it is impossible to use the correct procedures and hence the learning process stalls. Moreover, because transformation proceeds on a trial-and-error basis, it is not easy for learners or educators to understand the entire process or to grasp the types of transformation with which learners experience the most difficulty.

Therefore, this study proposes a system that can help learners understand the transformation process and record the trial-and-error process.

2 Related Work

Computer algebra system (CAS) is widely known and used for transforming mathematical expressions, using commands input by users. However, it is challenging to

S. Yamamoto (Ed.): HIMI/HCII 2013, Part III, LNCS 8018, pp. 157–164, 2013.

learn CAS owing to the low readability of its output format [1]. It is also difficult for users to master their own commands and input format. Furthermore, some mathematics teachers believe that users are not given the opportunity to grasp the process underlying transformation [2]. To solve these problems, some studies that aim to improve the interface have been reported. MathBrush [3] accepts hand-drawn inputs, parses mathematical expressions, and supports transformation using CAS. The interface to select partial expressions in MathBrush is similar to our system in many respects. In our system, we adopt a rectangle selection tool to prevent users from selecting an invalid sub-expression (e.g., "$a +$" and "1" in $a + \frac{1}{2}$). MathBlackboard [4] has a CAS interface for mathematics learners, which enables users to draw mathematical expressions using drag-and-drop and apply transformation and graph drawings to the expressions. STACK [5], another educational application with CAS, accepts answers from students and establishes the corresponding mathematical expressions. Because we aim to make users learn by letting them transform mathematical expressions step-by-step, we do not adopt CAS in our system.

[6] and [7] are works regarding study logs in mathematics education. [6] discusses the significance of hand-written study logs in mathematics learning, while [7] proposes a linguistic analysis methodology of mathematical discourse in tutorial dialog systems. In contrast, study logs involving the transformation process are represented as diagrams in our system.

3   Outline of the Proposed System

This section outlines two functions of our system: step-by-step transformation and transformation history.

3.1   Step-by-Step Transformation

The transformation function consists of "part selection" and "candidate selection." For part selection, users select a part of the mathematical expression to apply transformation from the target expression. For example, users can select an expression such as $\cos \theta$, $1 - \cos^2 \theta$, and so on from $1 - \cos^2 \theta$. For candidate selection, users choose a transformation to be applied from a list of candidate expressions. For example, suppose that the selected expression is $\cos^2 \theta$ and the listed candidates are $1 - \sin^2 \theta$ and $\cos 2\theta + \sin^2 \theta$. Accordingly, the expression is replaced by one of the selected candidates, and thus the one-step transformation is completed.

3.2   Transformation History

Our system can also generate history of transformations, enabling learners and educators to grasp the process of trial-and-error. The history prevents users from trying previously attempted transformations.

Collecting the history of individual learners helps extract the types of transformation with which learners face maximum difficulties. The history of a single learner reveals the transformation in using which he or she is the weakest. For example, if the history shows a learner selects $\cos\theta$ from $\frac{1-\sin\theta}{\cos\theta} + \frac{\cos\theta}{1-\sin\theta}$ and $\log x$ from $\int \sin(\log x)\, dx$, he is likely to focus on a small unit in an expression and may experience difficulties with overviewing the entire expression. The history of learners in a class shows the transformations that the class as a whole finds difficult. For example, suppose that the target expression is $\cos^2\theta$-$\sin^2\theta$. If a number of learners transform $\cos^2\theta$ to $1 - \sin^2\theta$ or $\sin^2\theta$ to $1 - \cos^2\theta$, then most members in the class may recognize the formula as $\cos^2\theta + \sin^2\theta = 1$, but not understand the formula of $\cos 2\theta = \cos^2\theta - \sin^2\theta$. In addition, it is anticipated that educators will reflect the information gained on trial-and-error transformation in both learner evaluation and their education curriculum.

4   Interface

In this section, we discuss the interface and show how the aforementioned two functions are presented to users.

4.1   Step-by-Step Transformation

A screenshot of the interface for step-by-step transformation is shown in Fig. 1.

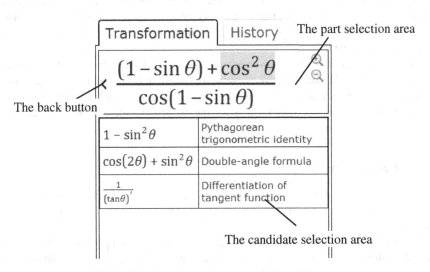

Fig. 1. Interface for step-by-step transformation

The part selection area contains a target mathematical expression that is partially selected using a rectangle selection tool. The candidate selection area holds a list of transformed expressions from various expressions and additional information such as the theorem name of the expressions. The back button can be used to return to the previous step. The "History" tab shown in the upper part of Fig. 1 is described in Section 4.2.

The Part Selection

A rectangle selection tool is used for selecting the mathematical expression, which is in blue font with gray highlight. The target expression can be scaled to select an appropriate expression from the complicated target expression. Furthermore, in cases where it is difficult to select one expression from a complex structured expression (e.g., select $\cos\theta$ from $\cos^2\theta$) by rectangle selection, a list of expressions included in the selected part are shown. The user may optionally show the list by clicking the expression. For example, suppose that a user selects an expression $2\sin\theta + \cos^2\theta$ from a target expression $1 + 2\sin\theta + \cos^2\theta$. When the user clicks the selected expression $2\sin\theta + \cos^2\theta$, a list containing $2\sin\theta$, $\sin\theta$, $\cos^2\theta$, $\cos\theta$ is displayed. These expressions are partial mathematical expressions of $2\sin\theta + \cos^2\theta$. The user can change the selected expression into any expression in the list by clicking on it. Furthermore, the selected expression must be a complete expression (the definition of "complete expression" is elaborated in Section 5.2).

The Candidate Selection

After the expression selection, a list of candidate transformed expressions is displayed in the candidate selection area, and the user can replace the selected expression in a target expression with a candidate expression by clicking on it. Candidate selection is completed when an expression is selected again after a target is replaced, or when a history tab is clicked.

To reduce excessive trial-and-error, candidate selection is not completed when a candidate is just clicked, thereby preventing a learner from replacing target expressions with several candidate expressions. Moreover, if candidate selection is completed by only a click, the user must select the expression again each time a candidate is clicked.

4.2   History View

Fig. 2 shows a screenshot of the history tab. This view is displayed when users click the history tab in Fig. 1 (and Fig. 1 is displayed by clicking the transformation tab in Fig. 2).

In history view, the initial target expression is placed uppermost. When users complete the first step of transformation, the expression obtained is placed below the pre-transformed expression. In this way, the process of transformation is shown by vertically placing the expressions.

The history view also has a function to change the currently focused target expression, which is surrounded by a black border. If users click another expression, the clicked expression is surrounded by a black border and the previous border is deleted, and thus the focused expression is changed.

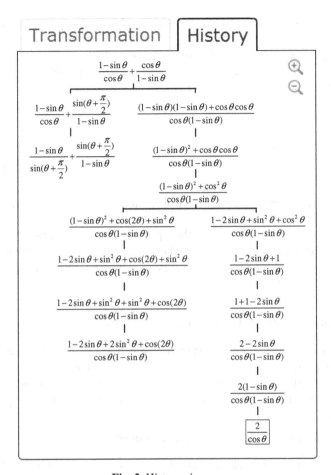

Fig. 2. History view

An identical expression can be transformed to multiple expressions using either the back button or the function to change a focused expression in history view. Such transformation is shown as a branched sequence of an expression to multiple expressions. This branch representation lets learners and educators intuitively grasp the trial-and-error process of transformation.

5   Implementation

This section focuses on the implementation of our system.

5.1   MathML Content Markup

MathML content markup [8], which is one of the XML vocabularies recommended by World Wide Web Consortium (W3C), is used for representing mathematical expressions in our system. Hereafter, we refer to MathML content markup as cmml. In this section, we outline the format.

In cmml, mathematical expressions are represented as a pair of an operator and operands. For example, the expression meaning "applying addition to a and b (addition between a and b)" is represented as shown in Fig. 3.

```
<apply>
    <plus/>
    <ci>a</ci>
    <ci>b</ci>
</apply>
```

Fig. 3. Representation of "applying addition to a and b" using cmml

`apply` is for the application of the operation, while the first child of `apply` indicates the operator and the second or later children indicate the operands. We can also construct nested structures of `apply` to represent complicated mathematical expressions.

5.2   Partially Selectable Expressions

We focus on `apply` in cmml for expression selection. As previously described, only complete expressions can be selected as an expression, and we define complete expressions as single `apply` elements. Consequently, only operations such as "cos" and "+," and operators such as x and 1 are unselectable as expressions.

5.3   Obtaining Candidates in Candidate Selection

Obtaining candidates in candidate selection is based on the algorithm that matches mathematical expressions, proposed by the authors [9]. The system has an equations database consisting of a number of formulae and theorems given in the form of equations. When an expression matches the left- or right-hand side of an equation in the database, the opposite side of the equation is presented as a possible transformation candidate.

For appropriate pattern matching, we represent expressions in the database in a different way than represented for ordinary expressions. There are two particular representations. The first is a generalization of identifiers such as x in $x + 1$ and θ in $\sin \theta$. Identifiers in the database are not assigned by any specific symbols and the identifiers are matched arbitrarily. Consequently, for example, $\sin x$ and $\sin \theta$ are treated as the same expression. It is also possible to distinguish among identifiers. For example, if $\cos^2 x + \sin^2 x$ is partially selected, the expression 1 is displayed. On the other hand, presenting 1 as a replacement of $\cos^2 x + \sin^2 y$ is prevented.

Second, arbitrary mathematical expressions can be represented in the database. We represent an arbitrary expression as an asterisk symbol: $*_i$. The asterisks that have identical i indicate identical expressions. For example, the distributive property of multiplication over addition would be represented as $*_1 (*_2 + *_3) = *_1 *_2 + *_1 *_3$. From this, we perform matching based on the distributive property applicable to not only $x(a + b)$ but also $\cos \theta (1 - \sin \theta)$.

The selected expression is converted to a particular form internally by the matching process. In particular, the system converts $a - b$ to $a + (-b)$, $\frac{a}{b}$ to $a \times b^{-1}$, and so on. The objective of the conversion is to identify different representations that are mathematically identical. This process reduces the number of expressions in the database and the time spent on pattern matching with various candidates.

6   Conclusion

The presented interface has functions to help users smooth the trial-and-error approach. In partial selection, we adopt a rectangle selection tool for intuitive selection. In candidate selection, we add simple information about transformed expressions to assist users. In addition, we optimize the candidate selection process to reduce excessive time and effort. Moreover, the history view is provided to recognize the attempted transformation at a glance. When users transform an identical expression to multiple expressions, the history view visually shows its trace.

In future, we plan to enhance this system with two different approaches. The first is to treat conditions under transformation. Currently, because we adopt simple pattern matching for obtaining candidates, mathematically inappropriate candidates are shown. For example, the system derives $\frac{-\cos^2 x}{\sin x - 1}$ from $\sin x + 1$ by multiplying $\frac{\sin x - 1}{\sin x - 1}$, although it is not true if x equals $\frac{(4n+1)\pi}{2}$ (where n is an integer). To judge the validity of candidates, it is necessary to add a function to treat the condition of expressions. We also plan to treat conditions for not only judging the validity but also displaying it clearly in order to enhance transformation understanding.

Second, user evaluation is needed to consider "implicit transformation." For example, if the database includes $\cos^2 \theta + \sin^2 \theta = 1$ and does not include $\sin^2 \theta + \cos^2 \theta = 1$, the candidate 1 is not displayed for the partially selected expression $\sin^2 \theta + \cos^2 \theta$ because we apply single-pattern matching to obtain candidates. On the other hand, by implicitly applying transformation based on commutative property, the abovementioned transformation can be implemented. However, by applying transformation based on distributive property, $\sin 2x + 2 \sin x$ is shown for $2 \sin x (\cos x + 1)$. In this case, the jump of transformation could lead the users misunderstand a process. That is, implicit transformation increases the number of candidates, but causes user confusion by the jump of transformation. Hence, we plan to let learners use this system and provide us with feedback in order to determine the transformation that should be applied implicitly. Experiments should also be conducted to evaluate the effect of this system compared to paper-based learning in on-site classes.

References

1. Margot, B.: Using CAS to Solve a Mathematics Task: A Deconstruction. Computers & Education 55(1), 320–332 (2010)
2. Bonham, S.W., Deardorff, D.L., Beichner, R.J.: Comparison of Student Performance Using Web and Paper-Based Homework in College-Level Physics. Journal of Research in Science Teaching 40(10), 1050–1071 (2003)
3. Labahn, G., Lank, E., MacLean, S., Marzouk, M., Tausky, D.: MathBrush: A System for Doing Math on Pen-Based Devices. In: IAPR International Workshop on Document Analysis Systems, pp. 599–606. IEEE Computer Society, Los Alamitos (2008)
4. Hiroaki, D., Hirokazu, H.: MathBlackBoard as Effective Tool in Classroom. In: Alexandrov, V.N., van Albada, G.D., Sloot, P.M.A., Dongarra, J. (eds.) ICCS 2006. LNCS, vol. 3992, pp. 490–493. Springer, Heidelberg (2006)
5. STACK, http://stack.bham.ac.uk/
6. McIntosh, M.E., Draper, R.J.: Using Learning Logs in Mathematics: Writing to Learn. Mathematics Teacher 94(7), 554–555 (2001)
7. Wolska, M., Kruijff-Korbayova, I.: Analysis of Mixed Natural and Symbolic Language Input in Mathematical Dialogs. In: Proceedings of the 42nd Annual Meeting on Association for Computational Linguistics. Association for Computational Linguistics, Stroudsburg (2004)
8. W3C Math Home, http://www.w3.org/Math/
9. Watabe, T., Miyazaki, Y.: Framework of a System for Extracting Mathematical Concepts from Content MathML-Based Mathematical Expressions. In: Watanabe, T., Watada, J., Takahashi, N., Howlett, R.J., Jain, L.C. (eds.) Intelligent Interactive Multimedia: Systems and Services. SIST, vol. 14, pp. 269–278. Springer, Heidelberg (2012)

Learning by Problem-Posing with Online Connected Media Tablets

Sho Yamamoto[1,*], Takehiro Kanbe[1], Yuta Yoshida[1], Kazushige Maeda[2],
and Tsukasa Hirashima[1]

[1] Graduate School of Engineering, Hiroshima University, Japan
{sho,kanbe,yoshiday,tsukasa}@lel.hiroshima-u.ac.jp
[2] Elementary School Attached to Hiroshima University, Japan
kazmaeda@hiroshima-u.ac.jp

Abstract. We have developed an interactive environment for learning by posing arithmetic word problems that can be solved by either an addition or subtraction. Through experimental use of the environment on desktop computers, we have confirmed that problem posing with the environment is useful for arithmetic learning. In this paper, as the next step, we implemented the environment on media tablets connected by wireless LAN. Because of this implementation, we have realized development of environment for using usual classroom, visualization of the student's learning performance and suggestion of teaching a method of problem posing. Through this practice, we have confirmed that the first grade students were able to pose problems in the environment, and the teaching and learning by using environment were accepted by the teacher and students as the effective teaching.

Keywords: Problem-posing, Sentence-integration, Media tablet, Interactive learning environment, Online.

1   Introduction

In this paper, learning by problem-posing with online connected media tablets is described. It is pointed out by several researchers that learning by problem-posing is effective activity for promoting to master the use of solution method [1-3]. Targeting arithmetic word problems that can be solved by either an addition or subtraction, we have continuously investigated computer-based learning environment with agent-assessment problem-posing [4]. Currently, we have been developing a type of problem posing environment "MONSAKUN" where problems are posed as sentence integration. MONSAKUN has been practically used in an elementary school [5, 6]. In these previous researches, MONSAKUN was used by students who have already learned the targeted problems. Therefore, problem-posing was an advanced practice for the students and the purpose of the learning with the environment was sophistication of their ability. In contrast, the subjects of this practice were the first grade

---

* Corresponding author.

S. Yamamoto (Ed.): HIMI/HCII 2013, Part III, LNCS 8018, pp. 165–174, 2013.

students who just have finished learning arithmetic word problems that can be solved by one operation addition or subtraction in their class before this practical use. Therefore, a teaching for problem posing and its practice have been needed for the practical use. So, we have to include the learning by using MONSAKUN to the usual class. For this purpose, we required to dedicate three problems as follow: (1) To be used MONSAKUN in the usual classroom, (2) Visualization of the student's learning performance on MONSAKUN, (3) Teaching the method of problem posing for exercising MONSAKUN. In order to solve these problems, we have developed "MONSAKUN Touch" composed of media tablets connected through wireless LAN. In this paper, MONSAKUN touch and its visualization system for monitoring learner's problem posing behaviors are described. Practical use of MONSAKUN Touch is also reported.

2   Problem Posing as Sentence Integration and Its Task Model

In MONSAKUN, the learner poses the problem by selecting three cards to given sentence cards and arranging them in proper order. Proper cards consist of two type card that is expressed by existence and relation. And, one sentence card consists of object, value, and event. Fig. 1 shows the example of problem posing as sentence integration. The learner given sentence cards from S-1 to S5. In this case, by using the Sentence-1, Sentence-5 and Sentence-3 in this order, the learner can pose the problem that can be solved by "8-5". We call this calculation as calculation operation structure. Then, if the calculation is expressed along the cover story of the problem, the calculation is expressed by "5+?=8". We call this calculation as story operation structure. In addition, this problem is expressed by a cover story that called as "combine". Cover story is generally classified "combine", "compare", "increase" and "decrease"[7]. The task of problem posing is set these expression structure and cover story.

The task model of problem posing is shown Fig. 2 [8]. When learner poses the problem, he/she has to decide the calculation operation structure that is addition or subtraction. The calculation operation structure are translated some story operation structure. Learner also decides this structure. Story operation structure has the corresponded cover story. When learner decided these structures, learner decides a sentence cards. Then, learner has to consider the correspondence of object, value and events, and order of each sentence cards for each cover story. This task called as "deciding problem sentence". Actually, in MONSAKUN, the task model that the leaner has to consider is restricting by task of problem posing and given sentence cards. Until now, we have explained the task model of problem posing top-down. However, learner also can consider and pose the problem on the basis of the task model of problem posing bottom up. Therefore, this task model doesn't represent the process of problem posing, but the restriction for posing problem is contained. A level of the task of problem posing in MONSAKUN based on this task model.

In the case of problem posing that can be solved by one operation addition or subtraction, if an operation of calculation operation structure is same as an operation of story operation structure, such a problem called "forward-thinking problem". On the contrary, an operation of calculation operation structure is different from an operation of story operation structure, such a problem called "reverse-thinking problem". Because the cover story doesn't accord with the calculation like "combine" and subtraction, reverse-thinking problem is more difficult than forward-thinking problem. That is, the learner is more required to comprehend the relations between two structures.

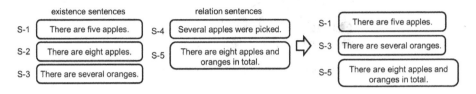

Fig. 1. Example of problem-posing as sentence integration

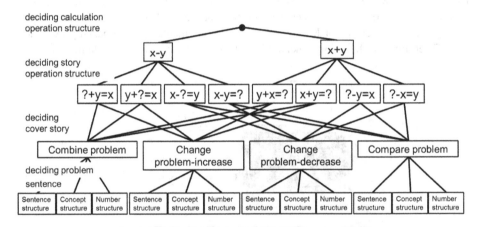

Fig. 2. Task model of problem-posing as sentence integration

3   MONSAKUN Touch and Visualization System

3.1   Framework of Learning Environment

The system architecture is shown in Fig. 3. The students pose problem by using MONSAKUN Touch, then, MONSAKUN Touch send their learning data to server via wireless LAN. After that, the teacher can examine the student's learning data with the visualization system. In this practical use, because there is no significant intelligence infrastructure in usual classroom, we use the laptop as sever. MONSAKUN Touch is developed in Android, visualization system is in PHP, and RDBMS is MySQL. By using this environment, the teacher was able to teach arithmetic word problem by problem-posing in a usual classroom. And, the teacher is able to lecture to his/her stalemate, and consist of next class on the basis of these learning data.

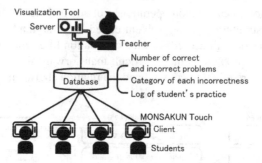

Fig. 3. Framework of learning environment

3.2   MONSAKUN Touch

In this section, we explain about MONSAKUN Touch that can be used in usual classroom. Until previous research, MONSAKUN could be used only in a computer room because previous version of MONSAKUN was implemented on the desktop PC platform. Therefore, we have implemented MONSAKUN on media tablet platform so that

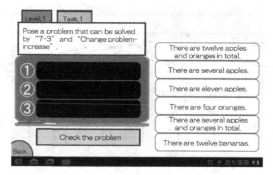

Fig. 4. Interface of MONSAKUN Touch

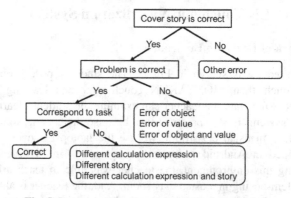

Fig. 5. Processing for diagnosing the posed problem

the teacher was able to use it in usual classroom. This version called as "MONSAKUN Touch". Fig. 4 show interface of MONSAKUN Touch. The left side is problem composition area. On the top of this area, a calculation expression and story is given as problem posing task. Several sentence cards are presented on the right side. The learner poses the problem by moving a simple sentence card with a finger and putting a card into blank on left side. Then, the learner can tap a diagnosis button under the problem composition area. At the same time, the system diagnoses the posed problem based on the flow of Fig. 5, and shows the results of the diagnosis and message to help the learner's problem-posing on another window. The messages composed of two kinds of indications, one is indication of correct or incorrect of the posed problem and the other is indication of wrong points shown in Fig. 5. These errors are also used by visualization system for categorizing student's error.

The flow of exercise of MONSAKUN Touch is, first, the learner login by selecting his/her student number. Second, He/she selects a level from lv.1 to lv.6. Then, he/she also sets ON/OFF of feedback, and moves a specific task. If the learner poses all problems in selected level, this level is end.

3.3   Visualization System

We have also developed a visualization system that is shows a student's learning data to a teacher with graph. As well, the learning data consists of the number of correct and incorrect posed problems, the category of incorrectness, and the log of student's practice. When the teacher input ID and password, he/she can browse the main interface shown in Fig. 6. The main interface shows a number of problems that was posed by the students, the correct one and incorrect one in left side. In right side, this interface shows the rate of incorrectness category with doughnut chart. Also, the visualization system has two interfaces. One is the error check interface that shows the students' error on MONSAKUN Touch. This interface is shown in Fig. 7. The other is the progress check interface that shows the progress of students' problem posing exercise on MONSAKUN Touch. This interface is shown in Fig. 8. The teacher can switch over these interfaces with clicking on a link in the upper part of interface.

First, we describe the error check interface in Fig.7. In this interface, the teacher can browse the student's error on MONSAKUN Touch every level on list. This list shows the kind of problem posing task and the number of student's total errors in each level. When the teacher select one level from the list, the interface show the amount of each error with bar graph in left side and the rate of incorrect category with doughnut graph in right side. Then, the teacher can browse the same data about each task on the selected level by clicking "Check the error of each task" at the bottom. The problem posing task, correct cards and dummy cards are also shown in case of visualized task. Second, we describe the progress check interface. The teacher can browse the number of student who learns each level on MONSAKUN Touch with list like the error check interface. When the teacher select one level from list, the interface show the name of students who learn selected level. Then, the teacher can browse the same data about each task of the selected level by clicking "Check the progress of each task" at the bottom. These data are gathering and visualizing in real time. For this, because the teacher can confirm the student's learning data immediately, he/she can

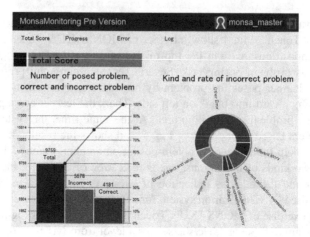

Fig. 6. Main interface of visualization system

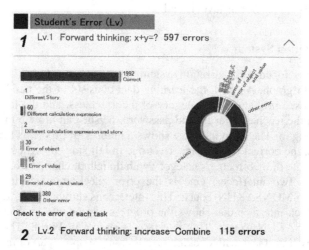

Fig. 7. Interface for confirming incorrectness in each category

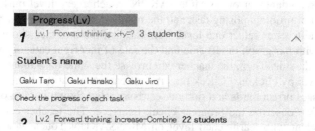

Fig. 8. Interface for confirming progress

adjust their contents and progress of teaching in real time. And the recorded data can be used for consisting next class. As other function, each student's log of problem posing in MONSAKUN Touch is shown.

4 Practical Use of MONSAKUN Touch and Teaching Method

4.1 Procedure of Practical Use

The subjects are 40 students in the first grade of an elementary school attached to Hiroshima University (but one student absent from all classes). The subjects have just learned the arithmetic word problem that can be solved by one operation of either addition or subtraction. The scene of using MONSAKUN Touch is shown in Fig. 9. This practice used nine lesson times (45 minutes per lesson, 3 weeks, 9 days). The students took a questionnaire after the period. One lesson consists of teacher's teaching (30min) and exercise of MONSAKUN Touch (10min), but each time changes depending on the progress of the lesson. Problem-posing exercises on MONSAKUN Touch and teaching by the teacher were divided into 6 levels.

Contents of each level are shown in Table 1. These contents of each level were classified by three scales that are the kind of problem, the calculation of problem posing task, the kind of cover story. These contents of each level were decided by the consultation of the teacher and us on the basis of the task model. In the exercise of MONSAKUN Touch, if the subjects finished problem posing at all tasks, they repeat same level. If the students finished all task of level 5, the teacher allowed students to learn level 6. Three teaching assistants have supported setting of the wireless LAN and operation of the MONSAKUN Touch, but they didn't support learning contents.

Fig. 9. Scene of using MONSAKUN Touch

Table 1. Levels of MONSAKUN Touch

Lv	Thinking	Operation	Cover story
1	Forward thinking	Story	Combine Increase Decrease Compare
2	Forward thinking	Story	Increase-Combine
3	Reverse thinking	Story	Combine Increase Decrease Compare
4	Reverse thinking	Story	Increase-Combine
5	Reverse thinking	Calculation	Combine Increase Decrease Compare
6	Random	Random	Random

4.2 Teaching Method of Problem Posing by Teacher

We designed a teaching method of problem posing based on the task model that requiring the exercise by using MONSAKUN Touch. Class of problem posing by using

MONSAKUN Touch consists of (1) Teaching the method of problem on the basis of the task model, and (2) Exercise by using MONSAKUN Touch. In (1), first, the teacher attaches a task of problem posing and some sentence cards on a blackboard. The task of problem posing consists of calculation and cover story. The sentence cards consist of correct cards and dummy cards. Second, the teacher let the students think about a necessary card and an unnecessary card for posing correct problem. Then, the teacher teach the students a constitution of the sentence cards in the given cover story, a correspondence of the object between the sentence card, a combination of value and an order of sentence cards. The preparing·dummy cards are available for posing problem if the students don't pay attention to these restrictions. However, as necessary, the teacher explain the situation that dummy cards available.   In class, the students learn the problem structure by exercising MONSAKUN Touch after (1). In this research, first, the students use MONSAKUN as introduction of new task of problem posing. Second, the teacher teaches the students about the method of problem posing. Finally, the students use MONSAKUN as confirmation of teaching. This class has been performed belong each level in Table 1.

4.3   Analysis of Log Data

The average number of the posed problems and the rate of correct problems in the learning by problem posing on MONSAKUN Touch are shown in Fig. 10. The time of each practice on MONSAKUN Touch is different because of adjustment of lessons. It is said that the number of posed problem in each practice with MONSAKUN Touch is more than without MONSAKUN Touch. Also, the teacher said that the students posed problem seriously and the suggested class appropriate for him to perform during the nine lessons. Therefore, we believed that learning by problem posing on suggested class was carried out sufficiently. In the class of level 5 (7th lesson), the number of posed problem is high (13.5 per 3 minutes), but the rate of correct problems is extremely low (9%). This indicates that the students posed problem by trial and error for the difficulty of reverse-thinking problem. Because the teacher gives importance to voluntary awareness of students, this tendency continued during this class. After that, in the second class in level 5 (8th lesson), the teacher taught the students that the calculation operation is different from story operation in reverse-thinking problem. This is one of the important features in the reverse-thinking problem. Therefore, the rate of correct problems improves a little in this class. In addition to this improvement, 22 students advanced to level 6 in 9th lesson. It is important that the students can be aware of "the calculation operation is different from story operation in reverse-thinking problem" because it was difficult to let them be aware it by the problem solving practice. This awareness is scaffolding for learning at second grade and above. The problem posing task in level 6 is set random and practice time varies every students. Therefore, Fig. 10 and the following results are analyzed without the level 6.

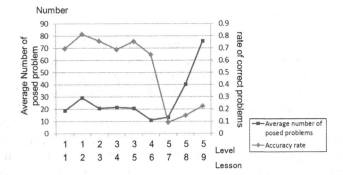

Fig. 10. Result of log (N=36)

4.4 Questionnaire and Students Remark

The results of the questionnaire are shown in Table 2. Almost students agreed with problem-posing exercise by using MONSAKUN and effective to learn. But, we supposed, because of level 5, many students answered the problem-posing is difficult. The teacher agreed that it is easy to teach problem-posing using a media tablet in the usual classroom, and he said that he want to use the MONSAKUN in his class continually. But, he suggested that it is necessary to improve the sentence of feedback and to expand the kinds of feedback. In this practical use, the teacher confirms the utility of visualization system, and he said that this system was effective to adjust the class but its interface and visualized data have still to be improved. Also, he described questionnaire that "it is easy to discuss the problem structure by using the problem posing as sentence integration", "it is important to teach problem posing in usual classroom for using MONSAKUN Touch". These result suggested that the teacher and students agreed that the class of problem-posing exercise by using MONSAKUN Touch. But it is indicated that feedback of MONSAKUN Touch and interface of visualization system needs some improvement.

Table 2. Result of questionnaires (N=38)

Number	Asking	Strongly Agree	Agree	Disagree	Strongly Disagree
(1)	Do you enjoy posing problems in arithmetic?	35	3	0	0
(2)	Are arithmetic word problems easy to pose?	8	7	19	4
(3)	Do you think that posing problems is a good learning method of the arithmetic?	36	2	0	0
(4)	Do you think that posing problems made it easier to solve problems?	20	17	1	0
(5)	Do you think that it easy to use MONSAKUN Touch?	37	1	0	0
(6)	Are feedbacks easy to understand?	20	15	2	1
(7)	Would you like to attend arithmetic classes where problem posing is used?	36	2	0	0

5   Concluding Remarks

In this paper, we have described the practical use of the learning environment for problem posing with online connected media tablets.   For using the interactive environment in the general classroom, we have been required to realize: (1) To be use MONSAKUN in the usual classroom (realized system called MONSAKUN Touch implemented media tablets), (2) Visualization system of the student's learning performance, (3) Teaching the method of problem posing. Then, in this class, the teacher taught the method of problem posing on MONSAKUN Touch on the basis of the task model of problem posing that were implemented MONSAKUN Touch. Before and after this teaching, the teacher was able to monitor the student's learning data on MONSAKUN Touch with visualization system. Through this practice, we have confirmed that the first grade students were able to pose problems in the environment, and the teaching and learning by using environment were accepted by the teacher and students as the effective teaching.

In our future works, improvement of visualization system and constitution of class by using visualization system is very important. Sophistication of the task model of problem-posing and evaluation of learning effect of the teaching method with MONSAKUN is also an important future work.

References

1. Polya, G.: How to solve it: A new aspect of mathematical method. Princeton University Press, Princeton (1957)
2. Ellerton, N.F.: Children's made-up mathematics problems: a new perspective on talented mathematicians. Educational Studies in Mathematics 17, 261–271 (1986)
3. Silver, E.A., Cai, J.: An analysis of arithmetic problem posing by middle school students. Journal for Research in Mathematics Education 27(5), 521–539 (1996)
4. Nakano, A., Hirashima, T., Takeuchi, A.: Problem-Making Practice to Master Solution-Methods in Intelligent Learning Environment. In: Proc. ICCE 1999, pp. 891–898 (1999)
5. Hirashima, T., Yokoyama, T., Okamoto, M., Takeuchi, A.: A Computer-Based Environment for Learning by Problem-Posing as Sentence-Integration. In: Proc. ICCE 2006, pp. 127–130 (2006)
6. Kurayama, M., Hirashima, T.: Interactive Learning Environment Designed Based on A Task Model of Problem-Posing. In: Proc. ICCE 2010, Malaysia, pp. 98–99 (2010)
7. Riley, M.S., Greeno, J.G.: Developmental Analysis of Understanding Language about Quantities and of Solving Problems Cognition and Instruction 5(1), 49–101 (1988)
8. Hirashima, T., Kurayama, M.: Learning by Problem-Posing for Reverse-Thinking Problems. In: Biswas, G., Bull, S., Kay, J., Mitrovic, A. (eds.) AIED 2011. LNCS, vol. 6738, pp. 123–130. Springer, Heidelberg (2011)

Instantaneous Assessment of Learners' Comprehension for Lecture by Using Kit-Build Concept Map System

Kan Yoshida[1,*], Takuya Osada[3], Kota Sugihara[3], Yoshiaki Nino[3],
Masakuni Shida[2], and Tsukasa Hirashima[3]

[1] Faculty of Engineering, Hiroshima University, Japan
yoshidak@lel.hiroshima-u.ac.jp
[2] Science Research Department, Attached Elementary School of Hiroshima University, Japan
mshida@hiroshima-u.ac.jp
[3] Graduate School of Engineering, Hiroshima University, Japan
{osada,sugihara,nino,tsukasa}@lel.hiroshima-u.ac.jp

Abstract. This paper described a practical use of kit-build concept map (KBCM) in science learning class in an elementary school in order to evaluate learners' understanding ongoing the teaching. The responsible teacher of the class reported that the information provided from KBCM is useful to decide complementary teaching ongoing class and improve lesson plan of the next class. We have confirmed that the map scores in KBCM have significant correlation with the scores of standard test of science learning. This case study suggests that KBCM is promising tool to estimate learners' understanding in classroom.

Keywords: kit-build, concept map, instantaneous assessment.

1 Introduction

It is usually difficult for a teacher to estimate learner's comprehension for his/her lecture, although it is indispensable to complement and improve his/her teaching [1]. Concept map [2] is promising way to assess learners' comprehension but it is usually difficult for learners to build and hard for teachers to diagnose. Kit-build concept map is a new framework to build and diagnose concept maps [3,4,5,6]. In this paper, we report a practical use of kit-build concept map system (KBCM) in science lessons in an elementary school as a realization of instantaneous assessment of learners' comprehension for the contents of teaching. In KBCM, a learner makes a concept map by assembling provided parts (we call this method "kit-build"). The parts, then, are generated by decomposing an ideal concept map that is prepared by a teacher as the goal of his/her teaching. Because both the maps made by learners (learner map) and the ideal map made by the teacher (goal map) are composed of the same components, it is possible to compare or overlap them. KBCM provides the teacher with information about learners' comprehension as a map made by overlapping all learner maps (group

---

* Corresponding author.

S. Yamamoto (Ed.): HIMI/HCII 2013, Part III, LNCS 8018, pp. 175–181, 2013.
© Springer-Verlag Berlin Heidelberg 2013

map), differences between the group map and the goal map. The teacher is also able to check each learner map and compare it with the group map, goal map or another learner map.

Through the practical use of KBCM, the responsible teacher of the classes judged that the information provided from KBCM was useful to grasp learners' comprehension and the teacher was able to improve his ongoing and the next teaching based on the information. Then, we found that there was positive correlation between scores of leaner maps calculated by comparing the goal map and scores of a standard assessment test as for learners in the first class. These results suggest that KBCM is a promising approach to realize instantaneous assessment of learners' comprehension for a lecture. In this paper, the practice and results are reported.

2   Procedure of the Practice

Teaching with KBCM was carried out for two classes in the sixth grade in an elementary school. There were 36 learners in the first class and 40 learners in the second one. The procedure of the teaching was as follows.

1. The teacher selected a topic of the lesson and made a teaching plan for the topic. In this practice, the topic is "decomposition of starch made by photosynthesis in leaves into sugar, and transfer of water-melted sugar through stalk". The teacher planned to use two class times (one class time is 45 minutes) for this topic. An experiment to confirm "decomposition of starch in a plant" was included.
2. The teacher creates a concept map that expresses the goal of comprehension of the lessons. The goal map is shown in Figure.1.
3. The teacher taught the topic at the first class.
4. In the middle of the class, the teacher required the learners to make a map with KBCM in order to confirm their understanding. Leaner interface of KBCM is implemented on media tablets. Then, each learner made his/her map with one media tablet. It took ten minutes. When learners made their maps, they walked around freely and talked each other. This is a way to use KBCM in collaborative learning situation [7]. The scene is shown in Figure 2. This is an important benefit to implement KBCM with media tablet [8]. After this collaboration, the learners had improved their understanding.
5. Learner maps were sent to KBCM server through wireless LAN and diagnosed by overlapping and comparing. By comparing the group map with the goal map, it is possible to generate a kind of group map that is composed of lacking links in the learner maps. Figure 3 is the group map composed of the lacking links we obtained in the first class. This map can be generated by comparing the group map and goal map, and then, displaying only lacking links. The bracketed numbers indicate the number of learner maps that don't include the corresponding link. This map informed the teacher that the learners tended to overlook "photosynthesis" link between "leaves" and "starch" (that is, twenty learners in the class could not linked correctly) and "transferable" link between "stalk" and "sugar" (that is, 19 learners could not linked correctly).

6. The teacher examined the information provided from KBCM and found weak points of learners' comprehension of the first class. As mentioned in above step, the teacher found that "photosynthesis" link between "leaves" and "starch" and "transferable" link between "stalk" and "sugar" were weak point of the learners. Therefore, the teacher made supplemental explanation based on the information.

7. At the end of the class, the teacher required the learners to make a map to confirm their final comprehension.

8. The teacher modified the lesson plan of the second class immediately based on the results of the first class in order to emphasis the links that the learners overlooked in the first class. Then, by using the modified lesson plan, the teacher conducted the class.

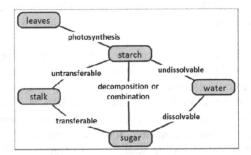

Fig. 1. Goal Map

Fig. 2. Learners Building Concept Maps in Classroom

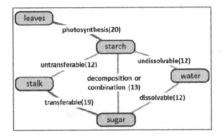

Fig. 3. Group Map Composed with Lacking Links

3   Analysis of the Results

3.1   Comparison Map Scores with Standard Test Scores

The score of the leaner map is calculated by (number of correctly connected links in a learner map) / (number of links in the goal map). It represents the degree of coincidence of learner's map and goal map, and takes the value of 0 to 1. We have compared the learner's map scores with learner's standard assessment test scores of science that were carried out to evaluate general ability of science.

In the first class, average 1st map score was 0.614 (SD=0.245). As for these learners, the correlation coefficient between the scores of the learner maps and the scores of the standard assessment test of science was 0.545. The result was statistically significant (N=36, p=0.0004). This means that higher ability learners in science made better concept maps. It suggests that the map quality would reflect learner's comprehension.

In contract, as for the second class learners, their average 1st map score was 0.792 (SD=0.229) and the correlation coefficient was 0.174. In this class, even learners with low ability in science could understand the lesson enough thanks to the effect of the improvement based on the information provided from KBCM. That caused a celling effect, and it made the correlation coefficient low. The scatter grams of Figure 4 and Figure 5 show the relationship between map scores and science grade of each class.

The celling effect is shown on the scatter gram of the second class. As for the second class, the average of map scores is 0.792 and the standard deviation is 0.229. The sum of these is 1.02. This is higher than the maximum value map score can take. Thus, the ceiling effect of the second class is statistically confirmed.

As for the second maps, similarly to the first ones, there was statistically significant correlation in the 1st class, but wasn't in the 2nd class because of the ceiling effect.

Table 1. Correlative Coefficients Between Map Scores and Standard Test Scores

	1st class	2nd class
1st map score	0.545 (p=0.0004)	0.174 (p=0.283)
2nd map score	0.444 (p=0.005)	-0.219 (p=0.174)

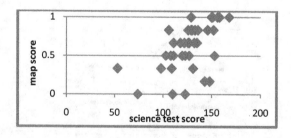

Fig. 4. Standard Test and 1st Map Scores   in the 1st Class

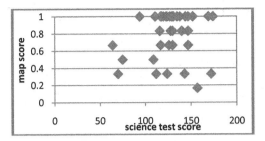

Fig. 5. Standard Test and 1st Map Scores   in the 2nd Class

3.2   Internal-Class Improvement

Figure 6 shows the user interface of the system that the teacher used to check learners' comprehension. Right side is the area to show several kinds of group maps and left side is the area to modify the group map. It is possible to show or hide lacking links and excess links of all learners in the group map. Excess link is a link that is contained in the learner's map but isn't contained in the goal map. It represents the learner's misunderstanding. Contrary, lacking link is a link that isn't contained in the learner's map but is contained in the goal map. It represents where the learner doesn't understand. By moving the sliders on the left side of the interface, it is possible to view only lacking links or excess links of large numbers.

The teacher noted that the system brought meaningful information that the teacher didn't expected, and he reported that it is impossible to gasp such understanding situation of learners without the system. Table 2 shows the number of lacking links in each class and map building time. The teacher checked lacking links in first maps, and conduct complementary explanation for the learners to promote the understanding of the links. In this practice, the teacher modified the visualized links of the group map and showed it the learners directly when he gave supplementary teaching in order to focus their attention. The learners also paid special attention to the shown map and links and accepted they were reflected their comprehension.

3.3   Cross-Class Improvement

The teacher not only conducted supplementary teaching based on the information he grasp from the group maps, but also modify the lesson plan of the second class. Because the second class was scheduled just after the first class, he didn't change the main story or materials but take care to emphasis and explain politely concerning the lacking links. Of course, there was explanation related to the links but the teacher judged that the explanation was not enough.

Table 3 shows averages of science test scores and map scores of each class. The average map scores of the second class were higher than that of the first class. The difference is statistically significant. Besides, there is no significant difference between averages of science test scores of each class. These facts suggest that the improvement of the lesson was effective.

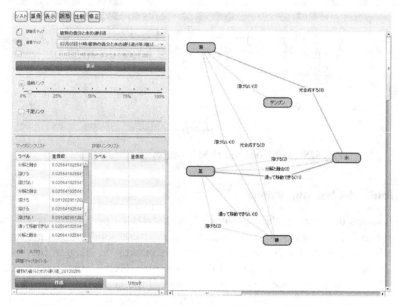

Fig. 6. User Interface for Teacher to Check Learners' Understanding

Table 2. Lacking Links

	1st class 1st map	1st class 2nd map	2nd class 1st map	2nd class 2nd map
photosynthesis	20	11	15	4
transferable	19	13	11	0
untransferable	12	5	9	1
decomposition or combination	13	6	7	0
dissolvable	12	7	6	0
undissolvable	12	7	3	0

Table 3. Map Scores of 1st and 2nd class

	1st class	2nd class
Average Science test score (/200)	126.3	127.2
Average 1st map score (/1)	0.614	0.792
Average 2nd map score (/1)	0.791	0.979

4   Conclusion Remarks

The teacher thinks that assembling a concept map with Kit-Build system and answering to a mini test has the almost same meaning as a method to check students' understanding, and that the former is superior because of its automatic and real-time analysis. Besides, positive evaluations were gained from the students by the questionnaire. From these and the analysis of the results, we conclude that the use of Kit-Build system was useful as a method to check students' understanding. To extend the size of practice and confirm the usefulness of KBCM are our important future wok.

References

1. Royce Sadler, D.: Formative assessment and the design of instructional systems. Instructional Science 18, 119–144 (1989)
2. Novak, J.D., Gowin, D.B.: Learning how to learn. Cambridge University, New York (1984)
3. Yamasaki, K., Fukuda, H., Hirashima, T., Funaoi, H.: Kit-Build Concept Map and Its Preliminary Evaluation. In: Proc. of ICCE 2010, pp. 290–294 (2010)
4. Hirashima, T., Yamasaki, K., Fukuda, H., Funaoi, H.: Kit-build concept map for automatic diagnosis. In: Biswas, G., Bull, S., Kay, J., Mitrovic, A. (eds.) AIED 2011. LNCS, vol. 6738, pp. 466–468. Springer, Heidelberg (2011)
5. Funaoi, H., Ishida, K., Hirashima, T.: Comparison of Kit-Build and Scratch-Build Concept Mapping Methods on Memory Retention. In: Proc. of ICCE 2011, pp. 539–546 (2011)
6. Kouta, S., Takuya, O., Tsukasa, H., Hideo, F., Shinsuke, N.: Experimental Evaluation of Kit-Build Concept Map for Science Classes in an Elementary School. In: Proc. of ICCE 2012. Main Conference E-Book, pp. 17–24 (2012)
7. Hirashima, T., Yamasaki, K., Fukuda, H., Funaoi, H.: Diagnosable Concept Map toward Group Formation and Peer Help. In: CSCL 2011, pp. 880–881 (2011)
8. Sugihara, K., Nino, Y., Moriyama, S., Moriyama, R., Ishida, K., Osada, T., Mizuta, Y., Hirashima, T., Funaoi, H.: Implementation of Kit-Build Concept Map with Media Table. In: Proc. of WMUTE 2012, pp. 325–327 (2012)

Exploring User Feedback of a E-Learning System: A Text Mining Approach

Wen-Bin Yu[1] and Ronaldo Luna[2]

[1] Department of Business and Information Technology,
Missouri University of Science and Technology, Rolla, Missouri, USA
yuwen@mst.edu
[2] Department of Civil, Architectural and Environmental Engineering,
Missouri University of Science and Technology, Rolla, Missouri, USA
rluna@mst.edu

Abstract. Given a collection of survey comments evaluating an E-learning system, the text mining technique is applied to discovering and extracting knowledge from the comments. The purpose is to categorize the comments into several groups in an attempt to identify key criticisms or praises from students using the E-learning system. This study is able to assist the evaluators of the E-learning system to obtain the summarized key terms of major "concerns" without going through potentially huge amount of survey data.

Keywords: E-learning, Text Mining, Survey.

1 Introduction

A GIS learning system [6] was funded by the National Science Foundation (NSF) to introduce GIS to undergraduate students enrolling in a typical civil engineering program. The system consists of five modules with specialties in environmental, geotechnical, surveying, transportation, and water resources, since these topics are standard topics in civil engineering programs nationwide. This GIS learning system enables faculty to bring practical applications to the classroom in ways which are not possible through traditional instruction.

Surveys were conducted a week after each class using the GIS Learning system in a lab environment to evaluate effectiveness of instruction and the learning system itself. Each survey contained both quantitative and qualitative questions. Quantitative questions (i.e., multiple choices, true/false questions) were easy to be analyzed since statistical and scientific techniques can be applied directly to the results. However, the qualitative part including open-ended questions requires human efforts to read all feedbacks from students in order to come up with conclusions.

Text mining is a useful technique which is able to handle unstructured data such as textual data. Therefore, this research aims to apply text mining to the survey comments from students in an effort to assist the evaluation team with the analysis of qualitative data.

S. Yamamoto (Ed.): HIMI/HCII 2013, Part III, LNCS 8018, pp. 182–191, 2013.
© Springer-Verlag Berlin Heidelberg 2013

2   Literature Review

Text mining is a process which attempts to discover and extract hidden knowledge from unstructured text and present it to users in a concise form semiautomatically. It is more art rather than science, and can be defined broadly. Some concepts in computer science, such as information extraction (IE), information retrieval (IR), natural language processing (NLP), and data mining (DM) are also applied in text mining. Text mining optionally inherits some of their techniques to deal with specific problems in each step throughout the entire process.

Text mining process starts from pre-processing which transforms unstructured data into the most structured, meaningful representation of the document collection. The most common way to structure documents is to convert them from qualitative format into quantitative format. Mathematical and statistical methods are useful for term selection and quantitative representation of the documents. Vector-space approach is the conventional model which serves these purposes. Then, the core mining process analyzes the set of documents from the quantitative representation. DM techniques, for instance, classification, clustering, decision trees, or neural networks, can be employed here to extract relations, trend as well as patterns from the document collection, and present the results based on users' requirements.

2.1   Pre-processing

The goal of the pre-processing stage is to create a quantitative representation for the documents. Starting unstructured or partially structured, a document is then proceeded to enrich structure, and finally ended up with the most advanced and meaning-representing features which will be used for the core mining process. Vector-space approach is used to convert and represent the document in quantitative format. The final representation of the collection of documents will be in a term-document frequency matrix.

The resulted matrix is generally sparse and will become much sparse when the size of document collection increases since few terms contain in any single document. Also, only hundreds of documents can yield thousands of terms. Huge computing time and space are required for the analysis. Therefore, reducing dimensions of the matrix can improve performance significantly. Singular Value Decomposition (SVD) is a popular technique to deal with dimensional reduction. It projects the sparse, high-dimensional matrix into smaller dimensional space.

In addition, another way to improve retrieval performance of the analysis is to apply weighting methods. According to Berry and Browne [2], the performance refers to the ability to retrieve relevant information while dismiss irrelevant information. Each element of the matrix ($a_{i,j}$) can be applied weighting and represented as

$$a_{i,j} = L_{i,j}G_iD_j,$$

where $L_{i,j}$ is the frequency weight for term i occurring in document j, G_i is the term weight for term i in the collection, and D_j is a document normalization factor indicating whether document j is normalized.

This equation was originally applied from information retrieval for search engine where longer documents have a better chance to contain terms matching the query than the shorter ones. Therefore, the document normalization factor was included to equalize the length of the document vectors from documents which vary in length [7]. Since this study focused on text mining and the lengths of the documents in the collection were not varied, the third factor was unnecessary and ignored by replacing the variable with 1. Then, the final equation is

$$a_{i,j} = L_{i,j}G_i$$

Defining the appropriate weighting depends on characteristics of the document collection. The frequency weights and term weights are popular weighting schemes which are described in more detail in the following subsections.

2.2   Frequency Weights

They are functions of the term frequency ($L_{i,j}$). This factor measures the frequency of occurrence of the terms in the document by using a term frequency (TF). Common methods include binary and logarithm. Three common weighting schemes are shown below where $f_{i,j}$ represents the original frequency of term i appears in document j.

- Binary: $L_{i,j} = \begin{cases} 1 \text{ if term i is in document j} \\ 0 \text{ otherwise} \end{cases}$
- Logarithm: $L_{i,j} = \log_2(f_{i,j} + 1)$
- None: $L_{i,j} = f_{i,j}$

Sometimes, a term is repeated in a document for a lot of time; thus, it reflects high frequency in the document collection as a whole even though it appears in only one document. To reduce the effect from the repetitive terms, Binary and Logarithm can be applied to the term frequency. The Binary method takes no repetitive effect into account while Logarithm reduces the effect, but still maintains it in some degree. Therefore, the Logarithm is a method in between Binary and None. Moreover, taking log of the raw term frequency reduces effects of large differences in frequencies [4].

According to Berry and Browne [2], the selection of appropriate weighting methods depends on the vocabulary or word usage patterns for the collection. The simple term frequency or none weighting term frequency is sufficient for collection containing general vocabularies (e.g., popular magazines, encyclopedias). Binary term frequency works well when the term list is short (e.g., the vocabularies are controlled).

2.3   Term Weights

Term weights take word count in the document into account. Common methods are:

- Entropy: $G_i = 1 + \sum_j \frac{p_{i,j} \log_2(p_{i,j})}{\log_2(n)}$
- GF-IDF: $G_i = (\sum_j f_{i,j}) / \sum_j X(f_{i,j})$
- IDF: $G_i = \log(n / \sum_j X(f_{i,j}))$
- Normal: $G_i = 1 / \sqrt{\sum_j f_{i,j}^2}$
- None: $G_i = 1$

where $f_{i,j}$ represents the original frequency of term i appears in document j, n is number of documents in the collection, $p_i = f_{i,j} / \sum_j f_{i,j}$ and,

$$X(f_{i,j}) = \begin{cases} 1 \text{ if term i is in document j} \\ 0 \text{ otherwise} \end{cases}.$$

The choice for an appropriate term weight depends on the state of the document collection, or how often the collection is likely to change. This weighting scheme responds to new vocabulary and affects all rows of the matrix. Thus, it is useful when updating of new vocabulary is acceptable or rare such as static collections whereas it is disregarded when updating needs to be avoided by using none weighting. All of the formulas emphasize words that occur in few documents whereas give less weight to terms appearing frequently or in many documents in the document collection. Entropy takes the distribution of terms over documents into account. Normal is the proportion of times the words occurring in the collection.

2.4   Core Mining: Clustering

The stage inherits analysis methods from data mining such as classification, decision trees, and clustering. Since the goal was to cluster comments into several clusters without pre-defined categories, this research only focuses on clustering.

Feldman and Sanger [5] defined clustering as an unsupervised process which classifies unlabeled objects into meaningful groups called clusters without any prior information or pre-defined categories. The labels associated with the groups of objects are obtained from the data.

Clustering determines the features which better describe objects in the set, intra-cluster similarity, while distinguish objects in the set from the collection, inter-cluster dissimilarity [1]. Intra-cluster similarity measures a raw frequency of a term ki inside a document dj, aka TF factor. Inter-cluster dissimilarity measures the inverse of the frequency of a term ki among the documents in the collection, aka inverse document frequency or IDF factor. Term weights, which were introduced in the previous section were derived from this theory. IDF weighting focuses on inter-cluster dissimilarity and tries to reduce the effect when the terms appearing in many documents are not useful for distinguishing documents. The product of TF and IDF (TF-IDF) was proposed as a reasonable measure which tries to balance the two effects, intra-cluster similarity and inter-cluster dissimilarity.

According to Feldman and Sanger [5] clustering can have different characteristics. It can be flat if it produces disjoint clusters, or can be hierarchical if the resulted clusters are nested. Clustering will be hard if every object belongs to exactly one cluster, whereas it will be soft when each object may belong to more than one cluster and have a fractional degree of membership in each cluster. There are three common types of clustering algorithms which are agglomerative, divisive, and shuffling. Starting with each object in a separate cluster, the agglomerative algorithm merges clusters until the criterion for stop is met. By contrast, the divisive algorithm starts with all objects stored in one cluster, and then split it into clusters until stopping criterion is satisfied. The shuffling algorithm redistributes objects into clusters.

The most commonly used clustering techniques are k-Means method and Expectation-Maximization (EM) [5]. Both of them are spatial clustering techniques. However, k-Means is hard, flat, and shuffling while EM is soft, flat, and probabilistic. Unlike k-Means, EM is scalable and allows clusters to be of arbitrary size and shape [3].

3   Experiment and Preliminary Results

The goal of this research was to extract knowledge from surveys conducted after students had accomplished each lab, performing on the GIS learning system. Feedbacks from open-ended questions in the surveys were taken as documents. Thus, each document of the collection to be analyzed in this research contained a few sentences. The nature of the data was not too general since the questions were based on the GIS labs. This led the answers possibly contain jargons as well as specific terms used in the learning system. On the other hand, students could freely express their opinions in the answers which could be anything and then made vocabulary uncontrolled. SAS Enterprise Miner was a tool being used throughout the research.

3.1   Pre-processing

The original data was gathered electronically as texts and no data type conversion was needed. However, it was prepared into a suitable format for feeding into the text miner program during preparatory processing. A CSV file was constructed where rows contained a list of documents and columns represented the author (i.e., the name of the student) of each text and the text itself. The blank cell showed the missing comment from the student.

After the input data file was prepared, the model for text mining was created as a diagram in SAS Enterprise Miner, displayed in Figure 1. The left node was an Input Data node where the data file was imported into and the right node was a Text Miner node where text mining process would be performed to explore information in the document collection. Both nodes were made connected via a line. The direction of the arrow represented the flow of data.

ENV_SP09_Q1   Text Miner (2)

Fig. 1. A Model for Text Mining

The input data was fed into the text mining process. SAS Enterprise Miner took care of tasks automatically based on parameter settings.

A synonym list has been modified from the default provided by SAS Enterprise Miner. A part of the list is shown in Figure 2.

	TERM	PARENT	CATEGORY
1	application	software	noun
2	computer	software	noun
3	program	application	noun
4	gi	gis	noun
5	hands on	hands-on	adj
6	hands-on	interactive	adj
7	interactive	practical	adj
8	borrowsites	borrow site	noun
9	borrow sites	site	noun
10	borrow site	site	noun

Fig. 2. A Part of the Modified Synonym List

Computer, program, application, and software were defined as synonyms. Moreover, the list handled misspellings by defining the correct spelling as the parent of each misspelled word. For example, the fourth and fifth rows of the list in Figure 4 were created since students sometimes spelled 'gis' to 'gi' or forgot a hyphen in 'hands-on'.

Also, a term-document frequency matrix was derived based on the parameters set for the Text Miner node. Table 1 shows some of key parameter settings.

Table 1. Parameter Settings for Term-Document Frequency Matrix Conversion Stage of Pre-Processing

Property	Value
Compute SVD	Yes
SVD Resolution	High
Max SVD Dimensions	100
Scale SVD Dimensions	No
Frequency weighting	Log
Term Weight	Entropy

To improve performance, SVD was computed with high resolution. The higher resolution yields more SVD dimensions, which summarizes the data set better while require more computing resources. The number of SVD dimensions should not be too small to lose concepts and should not be too large to keep noise. Dumais [4] performed information retrieval and found that performance increased over the first 100 dimensions, hitting the maximum, and then falling off slowly. Also, the higher number had been tested in this experiment, but yielded no difference in results. Thus, 100 seemed to be a good start for the maximum number of SVD dimensions. Moreover, since the vocabulary of the collection was not too general and not too controlled, it fit in between Binary and None frequency weights. Therefore, Logarithm was an appropriate frequency weight applying here. Furthermore, the three term weighting techniques were tested which were Entropy, GF-IDF, and None.

3.2   Clustering

Clustering technique was applied to cluster comments from students into clusters. Table 2 shows some key parameter settings for this process.

Table 2. Parameter Settings for Clustering of Core Mining Processing

Property	Value
Automatically Cluster	Yes
Exact or Maximum Number	Maximum
Number of Clusters	10
Cluster Algorithm	EXPECTATION-MAXIMIZATION
Descriptive Terms	7
What to Cluster	SVD Dimensions

Automatically cluster was enabled to allow clustering on the data set. The number of clusters was unknown; thus, it was not possible to define the exact number of clusters. The maximum number was set to 10 since the document collection was small and 10 clusters should be sufficient to cover all ideas. Expectation-maximization (EM) clustering technique was being used. The number of descriptive terms was set to 7 which is reasonable for the size of data. Clustering worked on the term-frequency matrix after dimensional reduction (i.e., SVD) had been applied.

After all required parameters were set appropriately, the Text Miner node was run. Finally, the resulted clusters from text mining, with three different term weighting algorithms, were shown in Figures 3, 4, and 5. The survey comments were collected from 52 students who responded to the question "Please list ways in which the lab activity that covered air pollution sources and transport could be improved."

#	Descriptive Terms	Freq	Percentage	RMS Std.
1		8	0.153846153...	0.0
2	+ instruction, explanation, + good expla nation, why, + good, + do, more	9	0.173076923...	0.1470874...
3	could, + site, would, fill, lecture, + have , on	11	0.211538461...	0.1502967...
4	+ easy, over, air, less, lab, + make, + sh ort	16	0.307692307...	0.1516472...
5	answer, no	4	0.076923076...	0.1481622...

Fig. 3. Clusters from Text Mining with Entropy Term Weighting (Log_Entropy)

#	Descriptive Terms	Freq	Percentage	RMS Std.
1		8	0.153846153...	0.0
2	+ step, + show, on	4	0.076923076...	0.1080237...
3	+ site, would, fill, could, + have, on, + m ake	6	0.115384615...	0.1489361...
4	depth, spend, understand, in, more, + s oftware, + easy	13	0.25	0.1409576...
5	answer, no, + have	3	0.057692307...	0.1161862...
6	do, out of, + complete, + good explanati on, + learn, + not, lab	12	0.230769230...	0.1448537...

Fig. 4. Clusters from Text Mining with GF-IDF Term Weighting (Log_GF-IDF)

#	Descriptive Terms	Freq	Percentage	RMS Std.
1	+ not, + step, + short, + show, + easy, why, + make	29	0.557692307...	0.1329294...
2	depth, answer, spend, more, in, + instr uction, over	18	0.346153846...	0.1521579...

Fig. 5. Clusters from Text Mining with IDF Term Weighting (Log_IDF)

The three weighting methods produced different clusters with different descriptive terms as we as different frequencies in each cluster. Notice that the total number of comments was 52, but the sums of frequencies from all clusters did not reach 52, 48 for Log_Entropy, 46 for Log_GF-IDF, and 47 for Log_IDF. It suggested that some comments were not able to be classified in any cluster. Those comments were ones considered as outliers. Also, there is a cluster carrying no descriptive term. Not only blank comments, comments containing few key terms were classified in this type of clusters.

From the results, human effort is required in order to construct sentences from the resulted key terms to interpret meanings of each cluster. For example, "easy, over, air, less, lab, make, short" may convey the ideas "Make the Air lab easier, shorter with fewer (less) steps." Also, words are stemmed, so analysts have to guess which form should be used to construct the sentence. For instance, "easy" can be "easy" or "easier". The author can either think that the lab is easy, or the lab should be made easier. This variation can change the meaning of the cluster. Moreover, some words which inverse the sentiment of the statement such as 'not', 'never', and 'rarely' are not identified which term is their pair. Thus, interpretation might be misled if the text miners or analysts are not familiar with the domain and document collection. One of the future works for this study is to consult with domain experts to appropriately interpret the meaning of each cluster and to suggest which weighting methods provide the most reasonable clustering outcome.

4   Conclusion

In text mining, the pre-processing stage is very important and dominates the entire process. There are several techniques available to be applied in text mining. Text miners have a chance to adopt or ignore techniques based on the nature of their data sets. From the experiment in applying text mining in survey comments, text mining is able to cluster comments into clusters without pre-defined labels. Attached with each cluster is a set of descriptive terms which summarizes the idea of each one. Analysts are able to read only these descriptive terms, instead of all documents, to obtain the ideas of the entire collection.

Text mining captures only important terms which represent the main focuses or concerns of the document collection as a whole. Some terms which occur only in a few documents will not be included in any specific cluster. The ideas which differ from majority can hardly be captured by text mining. Sometimes, those ideas are important and might be useful since they capture issues which others fail to concern.

Finally, future works may include effective approaches to evaluate the clustering results. Also, sentiment analysis might be helpful for evaluators as well. Classifying the comments by sentiment, not by category, predicts whether each comment from students is positive or negative. This assists system evaluators and developers to understand students' satisfaction towards the learning system.

References

1. Baeza-Yates, R., Ribeiro-Neto, B.: Modern information retrieval, vol. 463. ACM press, New York (1999)
2. Berry, M.W., Browne, M.: Understanding search engines: mathematical modeling and text retrieval. Soc. for Industrial & Applied Math. 8 (1999)
3. Bradley, P.S., Fayyad, U., Reina, C.: Scaling EM (expectation-maximization) clustering to large databases. Microsoft Research (1998)

4. Dumais, S.T.: Improving the retrieval of information from external sources. Behavior Research Methods 23(2), 229–236 (1991)
5. Feldman, R., Sanger, J.: The text mining handbook: advanced approaches in analyzing unstructured data. Cambridge University Press (2006)
6. Luna, R.: Learn-Civil-GIS. Retrieved March 2010, from Learn-Civil-GIS.org (2007), http://learn-civil-gis.org
7. Salton, G., Buckley, C.: Term-weighting approaches in automatic text retrieval. Information Processing & Management 24(5), 513–523 (1988)

Part II

Art and Cultural Heritage

Bodily Expression Media
by Dual Domain Design of Shadow

Naruhiro Hayashi[1], Yoshiyuki Miwa[2], Shiroh Itai[2], and Hiroko Nish[3]

[1] Graduate School of Creative Science and Engineering, Waseda University, Tokyo, Japan
884naruhiro@toki.waseda.jp
[2] Faculty of Science and Engineering, Waseda University, Tokyo, Japan
miwa@waseda.jp, itai@fuji.waseda.jp
[3] Faculty of Human Science, Toyo Eiwa University, Kanagawa, Japan
hiroko@toyoeiwa.ac.jp

Abstract. In an improvised bodily expression, it is important to create the image inside the self. We developed a body expression generator called "shadow media" that generates an image by causing a gap between the body and its shadow. In this study, we focused on the dual residual shadow, a type of the shadow media, which generates a dual gap. Using this aspect of the shadow media, we develop new body expression media by introducing fluctuation and cellar automation to the boundary of the dual residual shadow. Experimental results indicate that these shadow media outputs can effectively support the generation of bodily expressions.

Keywords: bodily expression, image, awareness, co-creation, shadow media.

1   Introduction

In modern societies, the development of non-face-to-face communication technologies such as e-mail allows us to communicate, regardless of time and location. On the other hand, the opportunities to meet and empathize with someone in person are decreasing and existential connections among people are diminishing. However, improvisational bodily expression, by sharing a little bit of the future, allows each individual expression to sometimes become co-creative. In such uniting through bodily expression, it is necessary to respect and accept other people's expressions as having equivalent value for one's own; its irradiation should be accepted within oneself. Opening one's body to gain new awareness of their and others' existence will be facilitated by the reflection of that expression [1].

To explore this concept, we focused on shadows, which are always connected to our bodies but rarely noticed. We conceived of expanding shadows by visualizing the reflected expressions, which are normally sensed inside an individual as an expression of their shadow. To realize this concept, we developed the "shadow media" system with which shadows are artificially deformed into diverse forms; the gaps created between artificial shadows and bodies emphasize bodily awareness. We found that the dual residual shadow, which is a type of shadow media whose outer and inner residual

S. Yamamoto (Ed.): HIMI/HCII 2013, Part III, LNCS 8018, pp. 195–202, 2013.

images are doubly superimposed through subtractive synthesis, effectively supports an improvised creation of the images   [2] [3](Fig. 1). It is anticipated that this shadow media supports an opening of the body image by affecting both the implicit and explicit domains of the self [4].

Thus, in this study, we focused on the boundary generated between the outer and inner residual shadows. We attempted to introduce fluctuation or Cellular Automation (CA), which is known to be simple dynamical systems [5], to the boundary and, by doing so, developed new shadow media, which destabilizes and dynamically changes the boundary and diversifies the gaps generated between the shadow and the body. With the use of new shadow media, we wanted to make it possible for people to co-create bodily expressions with their shadows using the shadow media system.

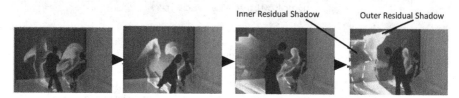

Fig. 1. Dual Residual Shadow

2   Dual Domain Design of Shadow Media

To design the new bodily expression media, we focused on the dual residual shadow, which is a type of shadow media whose outer and inner residual images are doubly superimposed through subtractive synthesis to effectively support an improvised creation of images (Fig. 2). The boundary that is generated between the outer and inner residual shadows of the dual residual shadow are designed with different image processing methods and parameters, such that they reflect bodily motions with time lag, and thus, create gaps between the body and its outer and inner residual shadows. The two gaps in these movements with the shadows change temporally and spatially.

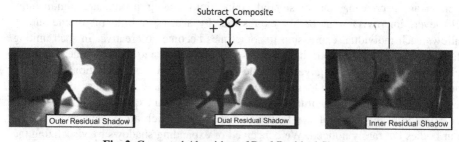

Fig. 2. Generated Algorithm of Dual Residual Shadow

However, we had a problem: embodied movements unambiguously determined how the gaps were generated by the dual residual shadow. This was because the response to the embodied movements did not vary, although the relationship of the double gaps changed both temporally and spatially, depending on the differences in responses to the two residual shadows. Thus, in this study, we focused on the boundary generated between the outer and inner residual shadows and developed a new bodily expression media by trying to dynamically change the boundary as well as destabilize and diversify the gaps generated between the shadows and the body (Fig. 3).

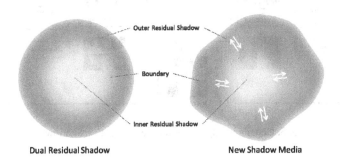

Fig. 3. Design Concept of New Shadow Media

2.1 Fluctuation Shadow

To realize the design concept, we introduced fluctuation to the luminance distribution of both the boundary generated between the outer and inner residual shadows and that generated between inner residual shadows and the background. By doing so, we attempted to diversify the boundaries and focused on dilation and erosion processing, types of morphological operations, which are used for image processing of the dual residual shadow. The processing results are dependent on the shape of the kernel (Fig. 4).

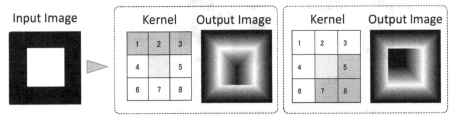

Fig. 4. Relationship between the Shape of the Kernel and Boundary

We changed the shape of the kernel by using fluctuation. More specifically, for each cell 8 that touches the central cell, we generated a random number between 0 and 1. If the number was larger than 0.5, we included the cell in the kernel. We implemented this processing into the generation algorithm for the dual residual Shadow (Fig. 5).

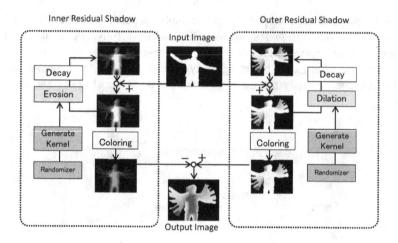

Fig. 5. Generated Algorithm for the Fluctuation Shadow

2.2   Cellular Automation Shadow

We generated the CA Shadow as shown in the flowchart in Fig. 7. By introducing CA, it was expected that the system would dynamically change the boundaries. We manipulated an input image in the same way as we generated the dual residual shadow. Then, we extracted the boundary of the image by the luminance value of the image. To make the image of the boundary affects keep the time evolution of the CA, for each white pixel of input image, the condition of the corresponding cell of CA becomes alive with a fixed probability (Fig. 6).

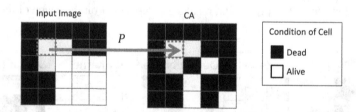

Fig. 6. Method to Affect CA by Input Image

Then we converted the CA to an image using these steps:

1. A dead condition cell is converted into a black pixel and an alive condition cell is converted into a white pixel.
2. The outline of an image is extracted.
3. The output image is a composite of the processed boundary image and the original image, from which the boundary is extracted.

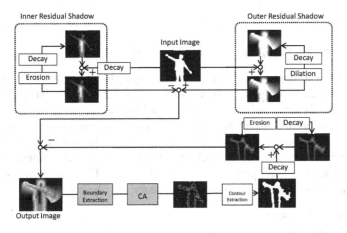

Fig. 7. Generated Algorithm for Fluctuation Shadow

3   System Configuration

The system which is shown in the flowchart in Fig. 8 projects an artificial shadow generated by a PC onto the media space (3600[mm] × 2000[mm] × 2200[mm]). An input image is acquired from Kinect (a motion sensing input device by Microsoft Corporation) and a projective transformation is done so that an artificial shadow can be projected from one's foot similar to a real shadow. The software of this system was developed using "openFrameworks," which is an open source toolkit, and it was coded in C++ programming language.

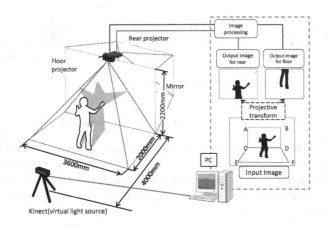

Fig. 8. System Configuration

4   Experiments

4.1   Comparison Experiment of Shadow Media

We performed a comparison experiment to investigate the types of bodily expressions generated from each Shadow medium. Subjects consisted of 10 university students between 21 and 24 years old and one experienced dancer. They were required to stand in a fixed position and wave their hands vertically for one minute in the location where the shadow media was projected. At the time, we measured the 3D coordinates of a subject's hands, elbows, and back by using OptiTrack (NaturalPoint, Inc.). The shadow media that were projected are listed below. These shadow media were projected in random order to eradicate the influence of order effect.

1. Dual Residual Shadow
2. Fluctuation Shadow
3. CA Shadow (Dual)
4. CA Shadow (Boundary)

Fig. 9 illustrates the period distribution of a subject's vertical motion of their right hand. This figure indicates that the period distribution of the shadow media of this study is wider than that of the dual residual shadow. Therefore, it is suggested that the shadow media of this study bring out diversified bodily expressions.

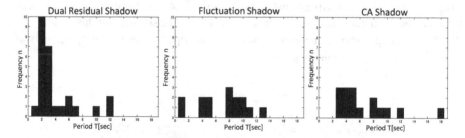

Fig. 9. Period Distribution of Motion of Right Hand

4.2   Bodily Expression Demonstration Using the Shadow Media

We conducted a bodily expression demonstration. Subjects were three experienced dancers. They were required to perform bodily expressions for two minutes in the space where the shadow media was projected. The types of projected shadow media were the same as those in the prior section. Subsequently, we got some comments from the subjects.

Table 1 records the comments from the experienced dancers. The Fluctuation Shadow experience elicited comments about a feeling of vitality. In the CA Shadow experience, subjects reported experiencing feelings similar to those felt in the shadow media.

Table 1. Comments about Bodily Expression Using Shadow Media

Shadow Media	Comments
Dual Residual Shadow	"I felt as if I was a life about to be born." "I felt like I had wings. I felt like flying at the beginning of the performance. Gradually, I began to have an image that made me feel as if I was repainting my own world with a large brush. I painted it in various colors."
Fluctuation Shadow	"I felt a feeling of vitality from the shadow" "I felt warmth because the shadow beat like a heartbeat. "Even if I stopped moving, I could continue to form images"
CA Shadow	"I felt as if my own shadow was not mine but that of another person." "It felt as if I began to be able to see outside of the space. " "I felt as if I was in the room with various other stuff: water, wind, or grass."

5   Summary

In this study, we sought to cultivate sensitivity to the body and support the creation of diverse bodily expressions by raising an awareness of the body acting as a co-creator with its own shadow. We focused on the dual residual shadow which proved to be effective for supporting an improvised bodily expression. We developed new shadow media with diverse boundaries by introducing fluctuation and cellular automation to the boundary between the outer and inner residual shadow. From the results of these bodily expression experiments and the comments of subjects who participated in creating images, we can state with confidence that shadow media brings out diversified bodily expressions and effectively supports continuous image creation.

Acknowledgments. This study was supported by "EU FP7 ICT FET SIEMPRE (Social Interaction and Entrainment using Music PeRformance Experimentation) Project" (No. 250026), the Project Research "Principal of emergence for empathetic "Ba" and its applicability to communication technology" by RISE Waseda University, and "Artifacts/Scenario/Human Institute" of Waseda University. We would like to thank Go Naito, graduate students at Miwa Laboratory (Waseda University), for his valuable suggestion during the course of this project.

References

1. Miwa, Y.: Communicability and Co-Creative Expression. Journal of the Society of Instrument and Control Engineers 51(11), 1016–1022 (2012) (in Japanese)
2. Miwa, Y., Itai, S., Watanabe, T., Iida, K., Nishi, H.: Shadow awareness: Bodily expression supporting system with use of artificial shadow. In: Jacko, J.A. (ed.) HCII 2009, Part II. LNCS, vol. 5611, pp. 226–235. Springer, Heidelberg (2009)
3. Iida, K., Itai, S., Nishi, H., Miwa, Y.: Utilization of shadow media - supporting co-creation of bodily expression activity in a group. In: Smith, M.J., Salvendy, G. (eds.) HCII 2011, Part I. LNCS, vol. 6771, pp. 408–417. Springer, Heidelberg (2011)
4. Miwa, Y., Itai, S., Watanabe, T., Nishi, H.: Shadow Awareness: Enhancing theater space through the mutual projection of images on a connective slit-screen. Leonardo, The Journal of the International Society for the Arts, Sciences and Technology 44(4), 325–333 (2011)
5. Chopard, B., Droz, M.: Cellular Automata Modeling of Physical Systems. Cambridge University Press, Cambridge (1998)

Virtual Experience System for a Digital Museum

Yasushi Ikei[1], Koji Abe[1], Yukinori Masuda[1], Yujiro Okuya[1],
Tomohiro Amemiya[2], and Koichi Hirota[3]

[1] Tokyo Metropolitan University, 6-6, Asahigaoka, Hino-shi, Tokyo 191-0065, Japan
[2] Nippon Telegraph and Telephone Corporation, 3-1, Morinomiyawakamiya, Atugi-shi,
Kanagawa 243-0198, Japan
[3] The University of Tokyo, 7-3-1, Hongo, Bunkyo, Tokyo 113-0033, Japan
`ikei@computer.org, abe@sd.tmu.ac.jp,`
`{masuda,okuya}@krmgiks5.sd.tmu.ac.jp,`
`amemiya.tomohiro@lab.ntt.co.jp,`
`k-hirota@k.u-tokyo.ac.jp`

Abstract. This paper describes a virtual experience system that provides to the participant a new experience of a space and travel for a digital museum. The system creates multisensory stimuli to evoke a sensation of a walk in a tourist site. The virtual walk is introduced as a pseudo voluntary reliving of the experience of the precedent walker at the site.

Keywords: Multisensory Display, Walking Experience, Reliving, Ultra Reality.

1   Introduction

Recently, a museum has had a new possibility of exhibit style by incorporating digital technologies. Digital information provides flexible forms of presentation of the exhibit item and gives new experience relating to the item. We consider that there are two styles of an exhibit that will explore innovative user experience in a digitally enhanced museum.

A virtual representation style of an exhibit item can produce appropriate projection of nature of the item with multimodal information. It also allows a physical interaction of the user to the exhibit item.

A museum is originally directed for the experience of an object. The experience should be a natural and voluntary interactive experience for the participant. However, the reality is usually different. The exhibits in a museum are only seen by the participant prohibiting a touch to them for preservation of objects. In a digital style, the interactivity may be introduced by virtual presentation of exhibits.

Another style of virtual experience is the extension of museum in terms of space presentation. The conventional exhibits are presented in a static display case where the visitor finds the exhibited object in a fixed environment without a context in which the object really existed and used at the time. The object would properly be experienced if the context is presented in a replicated space where it was used. The virtual space experience of a visitor regarding the context of the exhibited object is an

S. Yamamoto (Ed.): HIMI/HCII 2013, Part III, LNCS 8018, pp. 203–209, 2013.

extension of current museum focusing the real object itself. The experience may be applied to a particular space exploration where the space and the visitor interaction are the content of exhibit. In addition, there are too many large things on the earth that cannot be confined in a museum.

In the present paper, we describe a virtual space experience system that might be used in a future digital museum. The ultimate objective of a museum would be a real user experience regarding an object existed in a particular space and time. Here, a space experience system called Five Senses Theatre is discussed for presenting a walking experience at the tourist spot.

2   Virtual Experience System

2.1   System Hardware

A new display system was built incorporating multiple displays that covered five senses with vestibular sensation. Figure 1 shows the devices that are involved in the system, the FiveStar. It is an interactive display system for a single user of home theater size. A three-dimensional visual display, a spatial sound, a haptic/tactile display for a hand and foot, a wind and scent display, and a vestibular display are involved in the FiveStar that is targeted to produce an integrated ultra-reality [1] experience. The scene of a place captured during walking is displayed on the 3D LCD monitor with a 5.1 ch sound. The wind and scent are generated in response to the scene and the virtual motion of the user. In addition to the visual/audio stimuli, the body of a participant is moved by the 3 DOF seat and the foot motion (horizontal/vertical) generator. Vibratory stimuli are produced at the foot sole, the back, the buttocks, and the sigh.

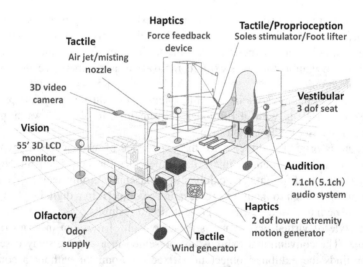

Fig. 1. Overview of the Five Senses Theatre (FiveStar). Multisensory devices are integrated to produce experience of a space of alternative reality.

2.2 System Concept

An experience of a space where the object of interest to exhibit is involved might be a futuristic method to show valuable things and their contexts to the visitors. A digital technology has enabled a three dimensional space experience that is virtually presented to the user by using a stereoscopic monitor with 3D glasses and multi-channel spatial sound displays. Although it presents a remote space in front of the user, the 'walk through' motion of the viewer that is controlled often by a portable controller (sometimes a game controller) does not produce a real walking sensation for the user at all.

It is known that the user of a virtual space can perceive the presented space more accurately and memorably when an actual walking motion is performed with the real body in order to go through the virtual space [2]. It shows that the experience of self-body motion in a space contributes to the perception of the synthesized space as it is analogous to the experience of the real world. On the other hand, a real body motion such as walking in the broad area of interest takes a considerable time for experience that causes a significant fatigue that could normally be eliminated in a virtual world.

We introduce a virtual experience system of a space with a virtual walking of the user. A tourist spot such as a World Heritage site is a good example of the space. Walking in the tourist site would be an attractive content of a future museum. A virtual walking experience is not the real walking nor the walking in place that are used in the conventional virtual locomotion interface [3, 4, 5, 6]. Our system does not force the visitor to walk by him/herself, but moves the visitor's body by the motion chair and the drive mechanisms for the lower extremity to evoke the sensation of walking as if he/she walks in a voluntary control of him/herself.

2.3 Virtual Walk

The space experience by a virtual walk is not discussed so far to our knowledge, and therefore it is the salient feature of our system. A space or location of interest is experienced during a walk of the user, not as physical (standing) walking or cognitive walking, but passive walking. The body of a participant is moved by the display system when the participant sits on the seat and places feet on the foot motion generators. Visual and auditory rendering of the space are concurrently presented along with the wind and scent of the location.

These stimuli provided to the participant are essentially based on the data recorded while the other person (a tourist) walked at the location. Thus, the participant receives the stimuli that were accepted by the tourist. The participant relives the experience of the other tourist's walk by means of the multisensory integrated stimulation. We call it a 'virtual walk' in this sense.

This is a new type of experience in which the participant 'receives' an experience despite the essential voluntariness of a proper experience. It may look inconsistent since the experience is what the participant selects voluntarily by oneself. We consider that it might be resolved by using multisensory displays involving the participant's body as a part of the system displays. Originally, the proprioception of a body may be considered as a display to the brain. The body is usually under control of the central nervous system, and not merely an information source. We assume that pseudo voluntariness might be established where the participant is immersed to the presentation of the location and the walking motion of the original tourist. Normal walking is mostly controlled by the brain stem and the spinal cord which dominate walking autonomously without subjective attention. This is our hypothesis of the design of the virtual walking on the Five Senses Theatre.

3   Virtual Travel System Prototypes

Virtual travel implementation prototypes were built from 2011, and three destinations were installed and demonstrated at the public exhibitions (Digital Content Expo 2011 and 2012 in Japan).

3.1   Overview

Figure 2 shows the virtual travel systems at the exhibits and the laboratory. The FiveStar system represented the recorded travel to Hakodate (3a, 3b) and Milan (3c) to the user. The user experienced the 3D visual image and sound along with winds and scents of the location. The scene of the experience was recorded with a 3D video

a) Climbing stairs, 2011

b) Virtual travel in Hakodate (Japan), 2011.
(3D seat and linear actuators)

c) Virtual walk in Milan (Italy), 2012

Fig. 2. Travel Simulator Systems on the FiveStar

camera (SONY, TD20) during the walk in the location. The sensation of walking was enhanced specifically by the motion of the body and the lower extremities in addition to the tactile sensation on the sole of the user's feet produce by the system. The adequate amount of stimulation was rather small as compared to the real walking motion. The user received multiple modality sensory information in an integrated single experience of walking the tourist spot.

3.2   Presentation of a Walk

Three places were presented as if the user walked through the area of interest. The user walked on a flat alley in the city, climbed stairs, stopped to see a historical building, turned to change the direction, started to walk, went down stairs, and walked looking to the side. These motions need to be presented with a different combination of stimuli by the devices.

While you walk on the flat pathway (Fig. 3a) by the FiveStar system, the reciprocal lifting of lower extremities by pedals (Fig. 3b) was provided concurrently with a horizontal front-back direction movement of the 2-dof motion generator (Fig. 3c). These stimuli to the lower extremities were also synchronized with the 3D seat motion.

  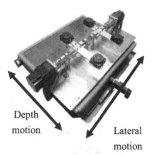

(a) Flat pathway   (b) Pedals with vibrotactors   (c) 2-dof motion generator

Fig. 3. Walking experience on the FiveStar

The presentation of the pedals and the 2-dof motion generator were created by adjusting the amount and the form of the motion referring the real motion of a walk. Figure 4 shows the trajectory of a heel in the body coordinates during a walk of a subject, 172 cm tall, on a treadmill at a velocity of 60 m/min. Figure 5 indicates the trajectory of a heel during the presentation of the FiveStar system. The same data is, plotted in Figure 4 in red. Although the height of the real motion was about 200 mm, the presentation of the system was about 8 mm in height. Only 4 percent (one twenty-fifth) amplitude was adequate to render the sensation of walk in the system. The 3D seat presented an oscillatory motion of the body of about 1.5 mm amplitude as shown in Figure 7 that was about one twentieth of the amplitude in the real walk (Figure 6). The presented stimuli were generally very small in amplitude relative to those observed in a real walk.

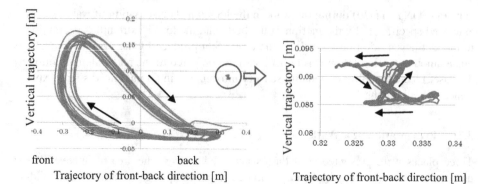

Fig. 4. Real (blue) and presented (red) motions of a heel while walking (in the body coordinates)

Fig. 5. Presented heel motion by the pedal and 2D motion generator

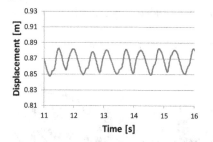

Fig. 6. Motion of the coxal bone during a real walk on the treadmill moving at 60 m/s

Fig. 7. Motion of the 3D-sheat chair body at the left rim

This means that a voluntary walk of the other person may be re-lived by a participant with a small passive motion of the body. The passive reception of a self-body motion as an artificial substitute of a voluntary walking motion may be very sensitive when the body is driven externally. This feature is advantageous when the display for a multisensory theatre is built since the mechanism could be installed with small parts.

4   Conclusion

A new method of display in a digital museum, a virtual space experience, was introduced in the present paper. A working hypothesis of a virtual walk that relives the walk of the other person was presented. A user experience of a virtual walk in a particular place, especially a tourist spot, was developed in the form of a seated multisensory display system where the participant's lower extremities and the body were driven externally in conjunction with other information to the five senses. The external drive of the body and the lower extremity needed for presenting a virtual walk was proved to be a reduced amount as small as less than a twentieth of real motion of actual walk. This implementation suggested a new design of virtual reality, that is, the ultra-reality.

Acknowledgements. This project was supported by a grant for the ultra realistic communication technology by an innovative 3D image technique. We would like to thank National Institute of Information and Communications Technology, Japan.

References

1. Enami, K., Katsumoto, M., Nishimura, R.: Current techniques for Ultra-Reality and the future. The Journal of the Acoustical Society of Japan 64(5), 322–327 (2008) (in Japanese)
2. Slater, M., et al.: Taking steps: the influence of a walking technique on presence in virtual reality. ACM Trans. Comput. -Hum. Interaction 2(3), 201–219 (1995)
3. Hollerbach, J.M.: Locomotion interfaces. In: Stanny, K.M. (ed.) Handbook of Virtual Environments (2002)
4. Iwata, H.: Walking about Virtual Environments on an Infinite Floor. In: Proc. IEEE Virtual Reality Conf. (VR 1999), p. 286 (1999)
5. Souman, J.L., Robuffo Giordano, P., Schwaiger, M., Frissen, I., Thümmel, T., Ulbrich, H., De Luca, A., Bülthoff, H.H., Ernst, M.O.: CyberWalk: Enabling unconstrained omnidirectional walking through virtual environments. Trans. Appl. Percept 8(4), Article 25 (2011)
6. Peck, T.C., et al.: Evaluation of Reorientation Techniques and Distractors for Walking in Large Virtual Environments. Trans. Visualization and computer graphics 15(3), 383–394 (2009)

Design of Space for Expression Media with the Use of Fog

Shiroh Itai[1], Yuji Endo[2], and Yoshiyuki Miwa[1]

[1] Faculty of Science and Engineering, Waseda University, Tokyo, Japan
itai@aoni.waseda.jp, miwa@waseda.jp
[2] Graduate School of Creative Science and Engineering, Waseda University, Tokyo, Japan
y-endo@akane.waseda.jp

Abstract. In this research, we designed and developed a "playground" using fog as a media of expression. The "playground" is a space where children express themselves and connect with others using bodily expressions while playing. To realize this concept, we developed the fog display system to satisfy the following requirements. (1) Everyone has access to the media space created by the fog. (2) Fog displays are scattered all over the space. (3) Images projected on fog displays are visible from various directions inside and outside the space. (4) The expelling, rectification, and diffusion of the fog are controlled. And, we tested the effectiveness of the system through its on-site use. As a result, it was found that this system, which can project an image on the fog that has a naturalness (disappearance, spatiality, and extraordinariness), versatility, and plasticity, has the potential to function as the playground.

Keywords: Bodily expression, Fog, Playground, Open media space.

1 Introduction

In modern society, there has been a remarkable decline in communication skills and the ability to express oneself among children and the young. Furthermore, the opportunity to meet and share experiences with others through expression is becoming increasingly rare. Reports claim that those with more experience with playing during their childhood, and those with more natural experience, tend to have higher levels of motivation, more purpose in life, and better moral and relationship-related skills [1]. Thus, we have investigated assistive technology for extracting bodily expressions through media in order to connect individuals with each other through co-creation of expression [2-5]. In this study, we aim to create a "playground" using media technology for children to create bodily expressions while they play so as to connect with others through their expressions.

To realize this, the authors have focused on the sandbox, which is considered to be one of the best examples of a playground [6]. Characteristics of a sandbox include an "open space" that is "freely accessible by anyone," and a place that allows "improvised play that is produced naturally through embodied interaction." In this context, Minowa have pointed out that sand has the versatility and plasticity to create a variety of playing styles [7]. Based on the above, we suggest that creating a

S. Yamamoto (Ed.): HIMI/HCII 2013, Part III, LNCS 8018, pp. 210–218, 2013.

playground using media technology requires incorporating the function of the audience and nature by opening normally closed media spaces outward, and making use of media with versatility and plasticity.

In this study, we have decided to carry out the design and development of a media space by utilizing the properties of fog. Because people can move through the fog and look through to the other side, we think the opened media space can be realized if images are projected onto the fog. In addition, because of its plasticity and versatility, it is possible for fog to produce complex movements that cannot be predicted by humans through changes in the environment, such as the flow of the air and human touch. For this reason, interaction through fog can allow children to play in a way that is akin to playing in a sandbox, which would allow them to draw out the full originality and creativity of such play. Thus, in this study, we have carried out design and development of a playground by media expression through fog.

A potential issue in carrying out this study is that the media technology to be developed in this study has an inseparable relationship with the children's playgrounds where the technology will be utilized. Therefore, in this study, the engineers have attempted to proceed with device development by bringing the proposed device into the field where play occurs, and reflecting the insights obtained in the design of the device.

Specifically, the fog display [8] we developed was first modified so that it could be brought into the field of play and used by children. Then, based on these results, the playground we designed and developed was arranged in a three-dimensional fog display, and utilized in actual children's playgrounds. The details are reported below.

2   Development of a Portable Fog Display and Its Hands-On Display

The fog display [8] we developed has exhibited problems including: (1) The display is large and heavy, (2) the plane of projection is small, and (3) the device can get the user wet due to water leakage. Thus, it has proved difficult to bring the device to the children's field of play. Therefore, we have developed a new portable fog display consisting of a fog creation unit and fog-expelling unit, which has resolved these issues.

The fog creation unit utilizes an ultrasonic atomizer capable of generating fine fog in the tank and sends it to the fog-expelling unit using the blast of a sirocco fan. The fog-expelling unit is comprised of several fog-expelling devices (width 446 × depth 306 × height 235 [mm], weight 4.7kg). This unit is made of an acrylic material that is 3 mm thick, and was made compact and lightweight so that it could be carried by one person by setting the distance between the inlet and outlet ports at 235 mm. In addition, placing a neodymium magnet (length 10 × width 10, thickness 2 [mm]) on the side of this unit has facilitated the combination and separation of the unit. By producing the above fog-expelling unit, we have solved problem (1) and eased the transportation and installation of the device to the site. Next, in order to solve problem (2), an air outlet (446 × 20 mm) was set up on both sides of the fog expeller (440 × 140 mm) to sandwich the fog in layers of air (air curtains).

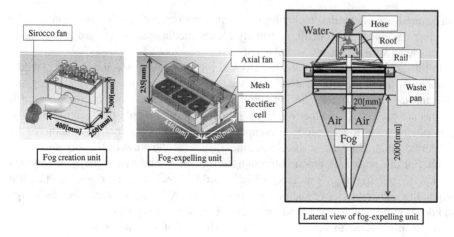

Fig. 1. Fog-expelling device

A swirl flow of an axial flow fan installed to generate the air curtains and the flow of the air curtains is regulated by passing them through a mesh (core size: 4 × 4 [mm]) and a rectifier cell. By sandwiching the fog in the air curtains, the fog is not diffused but injected into a layer 446 mm in width and 20 mm in thickness. As a result, the imaging size of one fog-expelling device was 446 mm in width and 2000 mm in height. Furthermore, a water leakage prevention mechanism was installed to solve problem (3). Specifically, as shown in Fig. 1, a function was added to drain the water that accumulated in the fog-expelling unit towards the water receptacle outside the unit to prevent the water from falling onto the user.

This hands-on display was shown at the Marunouchi Kids Festa (August 15-16, 2011, Tokyo International Forum) and it was intended that the children take advantage of this device in places where they actually play. As for the device composition, four fog-expelling units were connected longitudinally to generate a fog display 1800 mm in width and 2000 mm in height. We also created content that the children could play with by directly touching and interacting with the image projected on the fog display. More specifically, the skeleton data of the user is obtained with Kinect, and based on the position data of the skeleton (head, hands, and feet), the moving trajectory of the right hand touching the fog is left on the fog display as a stroke which can then be moved with the left hand (Fig. 2). In addition, visual representation software has been developed to extend the ripples from the position where the user has touched the fog. The aforementioned fog display system was experienced by more than 300 infants, elementary school students, and parents. As a result, a variety of activities were observed with the fog display, including: 1) situations where they were able to recall/imagine images such as "heart shapes," or "rocket shapes flying above," that they were then able to draw, or 2) collaborations between two or more participants working together to create one object (Fig. 3(a)).

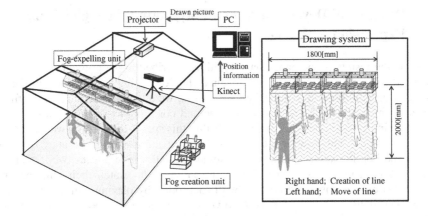

Fig. 2. Drawing system by Fog Display

This has confirmed the possibility that this system can be used to draw out body movements and thus support communication between users. In addition, it is interesting to note that users exhibited behaviors suggesting that they seemed to enjoy touching the fog as well as interacting with images (Fig. 3(b)). Specifically, they seemed to enjoy activities such as passing through the fog, grasping the fog with both hands, eating the fog, and bathing in the fog. This is an indication that the fog itself may allow for the creation of an image and draw out bodily expression. However, the direction of the body and movement is limited by the projection plane of the fog display, which in turn limits bodily expression. The system also gives the impression that the media space is closed off by the fog display. In other words, it was discovered that this system has not yet been able to fully achieve the open media space described in the previous section.

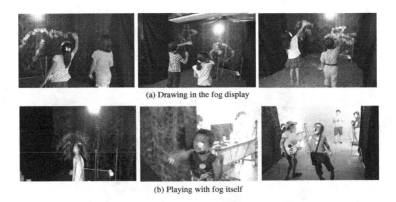

Fig. 3. Pictures of an interactive exhibition at the Kids Festa

3 Design and Development of a Playground through Media Expression with Fog

Based on the results of the hands-on exhibition described in the previous section, we have conceived a playground through media technology using fog as shown in Fig. 4. In other words, in order to realize the open media, we attempt to create a space filled with fog which allows free access to anyone and construct an open media space by projecting images from various directions within this space. In addition, we attempt to change the shape and flow of the fog itself so that the users will be able to create images and bodily expressions through interaction with the fog. Thus, we aim at the realization of a playground where children, parents who watch their children and general visitors can meet and connect with each other by playing with the fog. This will be accomplished by allowing them to voluntarily move their bodies to create new bodily expressions and images.

In order to achieve this concept, we have set the following design requirements and developed a playground using fog:

(1) Anyone can come and go freely.
(2) Fog displays are scattered throughout the space.
(3) Images can be visually recognized from various directions both inside and outside the space.
(4) Expelling, rectification and diffusion of the fog can be freely controlled.

For (1) and (2), a space 2.5 m in width, 2.5 m in depth, and 2.0 m in height was set up assuming 3-5 children enter and exit freely. Sixteen fog-expelling units were then

Fig. 4. Concept for "playground"

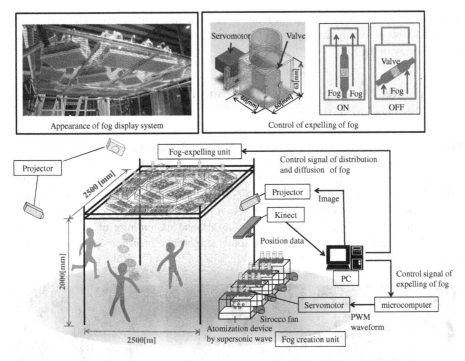

Fig. 5. Expression media space with the use of fog for Playground

placed concentrically in the upper part of this space (Fig. 5). An expanded metal was placed on top of the space (1200 mm horizontally x 1200 mm vertically) enabling the placement of fog-expelling units anywhere on it. Thus, by localizing in space the area where the fogs exists, we aim to diversify the space and support the creation of bodily expression that is not tied to the position and orientation of the fog display. Furthermore, four creation unit units were placed together on the back of one side of the fog space, allowing users to come and go freely in the fog space. Next, in order to achieve (3), images were projected into the fog space using three projectors as shown in Fig. 5. This allowed children and the audience watching them to visually recognize images projected onto the fog display from any direction both inside and outside the fog space. Furthermore, control of the amount of fog expelling was achieved by providing a valve at the supply outlets in the tank to each fog-expelling unit. Note that, in this system, the opening and closing of the valve is performed using a servo motor. Expelling of the rectified and diffused fog has been achieved by turning the air curtains in the fog-expelling unit on and off with a relay circuit.

In addition, the following four items represent content that could be played within the fog space:

(a) Projecting CG and scenery images into the fog space.
(b) Interacting with images in the fog space.
(c) Creating media expressions with the fog by controlling its expelling, rectification, and diffusion.
(d) Exploring the fog space using a light.

By combining the above content, we aim to help the users make new discoveries and create new ways to play through both the creation of mental pictures from images and interaction with the fog.

4   Hands-On Display of a Playground through Media Expression with Fog

We conducted a hands-on exhibition at the National Research Center for Child Health and Development (January 30-February 2, 2012, Tokyo) where parents and the children admitted to this center were able to actually play with the system. This exhibition was experienced by more than 400 people ranging from children to adults. Fig. 6 shows pictures for this exhibition. As the fog is sterically-expelled in a space, we were able to observe the children moving around the entirety of the space (Fig. 6(a)). Since the fog space is open to the outside, parents, guardians and the children they were watching were able to talk to each other, enter and exit the space, and move

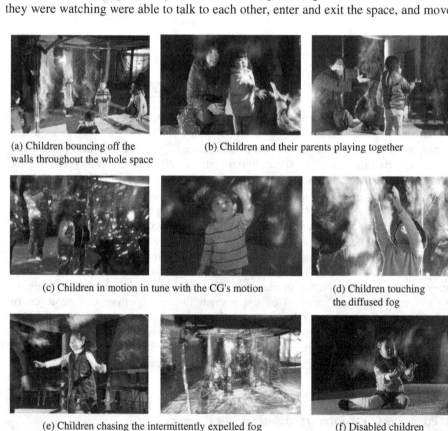

(a) Children bouncing off the walls throughout the whole space

(b) Children and their parents playing together

(c) Children in motion in tune with the CG's motion

(d) Children touching the diffused fog

(e) Children chasing the intermittently expelled fog

(f) Disabled children touching the fog

Fig. 6. Pictures of an interactive exhibition at the National Center for Child Health and Development

their bodies freely (Fig. 6(b)). In addition, since it is possible to visually recognize the three-dimensionally generated image from any direction, we were able to observe the children making bodily expressions in various directions and jumping in response to the movement of the CG image (Fig. 6(c)). The children also created new methods of play by utilizing the fog itself, such as touching the diffused for everyone (Fig. 6(d)), moving around, or chasing the intermittently expelled fog (Fig. 6(e)). Children with cerebral palsy and leg injuries were observed reaching out towards the fog (Fig. 6(f)), voluntarily talking to other children in their surroundings, and moving cooperatively with them. Caregivers that were present made comments such as "The children playing in the fog were full of smiles, not showing signs of their diseases at all" and "It was easy for us to move around with the children according to the image projected in the fog." These results show that bodily expression and communication of children are produced and lively play is created from images projected in the fog space. It is also believed that, by taking advantage of the fog space like this, a connection between people can be created regardless of age, gender, and the presence or absence of disorders.

5   Summary

In this study we constructed an open media space using fog and carried out the design and development of a playground that supports user body expression and the creation of communication. First, we developed a fog display system that can be taken out into the field and carried out a hands-on exhibition of this system at the Marunouchi Kids Festa. Using the results from this hands-on exhibition, we then conducted the design and development of a space for expression media using the fog and incorporated it into the playground. Specifically, we placed 16 fog-expelling units concentrically that can control the amount of fog expelling, and developed a system that can project an image from multiple directions to the fog expelled from these units. We utilized this system at the National Research Center for Child Health and Development and observed children who created images and produced bodily expressions and communication. This allowed us to confirm the prospect that this system can function as a playground. In addition, these results show that play can be drawn out of children by creating a media expression and interacting with fog which has naturalness (disappearance, spatiality, and extraordinariness), versatility, and plasticity. In the future, we would like to further study design methods for a playground that takes advantage of media by focusing on the naturalness of the fog and considering media expression methods that can further extract these function of fog.

Acknowledgments. This study was conducted under the project "Generation and Control Technology of Human-Entrained Embodied Media" and is supported by CREST of JST, Project Research "Principal of emergence for empathetic "Ba" and its applicability to communication technology" by RISE Waseda University, and the GCOE program "Global Robot Academia." We would like to thank Dr. Hidekazu Masaki (National Center for Child Health and Development), Prof. Hiroko Nishi (Toyo Eiwa University), and Dr. Takabumi Watanabe (Waseda University) for their valuable suggestion during the course of this project and conducting the experiment.

References

1. National Institution For Youth Education: Survey research about the reality of children's experience activity (2010) (in Japanese)
2. Miwa, Y., Itai, S., Watanabe, T., Iida, K., Nishi, H.: Shadow awareness: Bodily expression supporting system with use of artificial shadow. In: Jacko, J.A. (ed.) HCII 2009, Part II. LNCS, vol. 5611, pp. 226–235. Springer, Heidelberg (2009)
3. Iida, K., Itai, S., Nishi, H., Miwa, Y.: Utilization of shadow media - supporting co-creation of bodily expression activity in a group. In: Smith, M.J., Salvendy, G. (eds.) HCII 2011, Part I. LNCS, vol. 6771, pp. 408–417. Springer, Heidelberg (2011)
4. Miwa, Y., Itai, S., Watanabe, T., Nishi, H.: Shadow Awareness: Enhancing theater space through the mutual projection of images on a connective slit-screen. Leonardo, The Journal of the International Society for the Arts, Sciences and Technology 44(4), 325–333 (2011)
5. Osaki, A., Taniguchi, H., Miwa, Y.: Collaborative Aerial-Drawing System for Supporting Co-Creative Communication. Journal of Advanced Mechanical Design, Systems and Manufacturing 3(1), 93–104 (2009)
6. Fulghum, R.: All I Really Need to Know I Learned in Kindergarten. Ballantine Books (2004)
7. Minowa, J.: Allure of sandbox. Education of Infant Child 108(5), 13–17 (2009) (in Japanese)
8. Endo, Y., Inazawa, R., Maeda, K., Itai, S., Miwa, Y.: Development of 3D display device by multi-layered structuration of fog screens. In: Proceeding of Human Interface Symposium 2010, CD-ROM (2010) (in Japanese)

User Interface of Interactive Media Art in a Stereoscopic Environment

YoungEun Kim, MiGyung Lee, SangHun Nam, and JinWan Park

Graduate School of Advanced Imaging Science, Multimedia & Film,
Chung-Ang University, Korea
{naankim,sanghunnam}@gmail.com, miklee@naver.com,
jinpark@cau.ac.kr

Abstract. Interactive Media art communicates with audiences using many interfaces. The audience experiences each interface differently. Two different kinds of art experiences can be generated using the same themes. Using a touch screen monitor and Microsoft Kinect motion sensors, in the same gallery environment, we surveyed visitor experiences with both forms of art in a stereoscopic environment. We discovered that motion interfaces are better than touch interfaces for interactive media art, with the changes in depth providing more powerful stereoscopic audience experiences.

Keywords: Interactive Media Art, Natural Interface, Stereoscopic Artwork, Touch Interface, Motion Interface.

1 Introduction

Many artists have been attempting innovative work that emphasizes direct interaction between the audience and the art itself work [1, 2]. The interactive technology used is now much more integrated with the user experience. Viewers know that new technology changes their interaction, as well, because they're familiar with this process in everyday life [3]. Touch screens and better interactive technology has changed the way people interact with many tools, opening the door to new possibilities. For art, possibilities have changed since the era of keyboards, mice and toggles. This new technology, developed originally for commercial and home use, was designed to maximize convenience [4-6]. However, as with all technological innovation, this has also opened the door to a new world for art and the experience of it [7, 8].

Stereoscopic 3D is a technology that makes the viewer feels a stronger sense of space by showing slightly different images to each eye. It's existed in various forms since the 1880's, in the form of stereoscopic glasses and projectors. But as stereoscopic 3D technology has developed, especially since the arrival of the computer age, the potential has radically improved for changing the way we experience 3D spatial interfaces and displays. This has the potential to fundamentally alter the way we experience art, design, and science through 3D interaction [9].

S. Yamamoto (Ed.): HIMI/HCII 2013, Part III, LNCS 8018, pp. 219–227, 2013.

Furthermore, the recent commercial popularity of 3D TVs and movies has created a world in which stereo images are becoming far more familiar. One interesting carryover from the commercial realm is the immediate environment for this new form of art display. Modern media art that uses stereoscopic images requires a darker exhibit environment to maximize viewer immersion, in the same way that movie or other 3D presentations operate [10]. While this technology is liberating in some ways, the result is that the same limitations that affect commercial use apply with its use in art. Interactive displays have to take into account these special limitations. This paper studies audience experiences when dealing with interface changes, when viewing artists' stereoscopic work, via touch and spatial interactions

Section 2 introduces our artwork and related exhibitions using touch and motion interfaces in stereoscopic environments. Section 3 presents a survey that covers the viewer experience of these interfaces and the most powerful factors involved with 3D art. Section 4 draws conclusions and provides scope for further research.

2   Media Art Work in a Stereoscopic Environment

The media art in Figures 3 and 5 are 3D interactive work, titled 'Garden Party 1' and 'Garden Party 2'. They express the same theme and material, exploring the coexistence of nature and human life. The audience colors the sunflower images interactively. If all of the sunflowers are painted, their leaves fly off, as shown in Figure 1. The audience's interaction implies a human interest in nature, which returns a kind of attention or love to its human viewers. 'Garden Party' employed these painted images on canvas in a traditional painting form in order to express this in a comparative analog painting. To deliver the actual feeling of drawing sunflowers, it used a process through which the sunflowers were being painted, changing the sunflowers images through interaction with the audience as shown in Figure 2.

Fig. 1. Garden Party theme

Fig. 2. Sequential sunflower painting

We used natural interfaces in both art forms, designed for intimate use, involving the most current touch and motion interactions. This natural interface is intuitive, not requiring explanations for use, unlike older menu-based interfaces [11]. Since stereoscopic art exhibitions are much darker environments than most exhibition halls, the sensors that can be used are limited in functionality. This reality enforced a resulting simplicity in design. A touch screen monitor is used in 'Garden Party 1' and is good for general exhibitions because images and physical interaction points are matched. However, inexperienced audiences often jump between monitor images and stereoscopic images, which confuses them and inhibits immersion. Microsoft Kinect is used in 'Garden Party 2' for motion interaction, because webcams don't pick up human movement when it's dark.

Figure 3 shows the exhibit image for 'Garden Party 1' and its floor plan, involving a 3D Projector and a touch screen. The touch screen interface is extremely familiar to most audiences at this point, due to the prevalence of smartphones. The touch screen monitor serves as a canvas, and hands as brushes. The parts of the sunflower touched by hands are "painted", which is the reality of direct interaction. When the monitor is touched, the target position is marked on the stereoscopic image, so ideally the audience won't look at the monitor. A butterfly moves to the target position and particles emerge from it. The color "particles" falls onto the sunflowers and "paints" them.

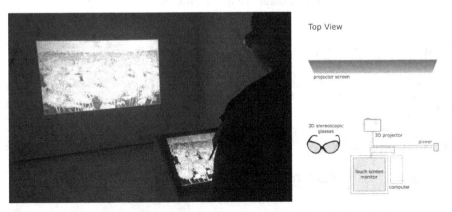

Fig. 3. Garden Party 1 and floor plan

Fig. 4. Butterfly painting sunflowers

Figure 5 illustrates 'Garden Party 2' and its floor plan. A 3D projector is used for stereoscopic images and a Kinect sensor is used for motion detection. The audience can move freely, participating in the artistic creation, because of the spatial interface. As a viewer approaches the work, the viewer's shape appears on the work image in stereoscopic form. "particles" flow out from their hands, "fly" to sunflowers and paint them in accordance with audience movement. The viewer's body becomes a painting tool.

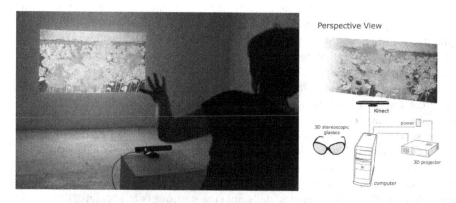

Fig. 5. Garden Party 2 and floor plan

Fig. 6. The body shape painting sunflowers

3   Exhibition Visitors Survey

To carefully examine the touch screen user experience and the motion-based spatial interface used for this interactive media art, a survey of the participating viewers was conducted. The main objective of the survey was to investigate the two methods' effectiveness, the degree of correlating stereoscopic image experiences, and their immersion in and participation with the work.

3.1   Survey Methodology

We surveyed 36 people, 18 male and 18 female, ranging from their early 20s to their 50s (20s: 10, 30s: 14, 40s-50s: 12). No explanations about the interface or details, or instructions, were provided. The average length of the experience for these participants was about around three minutes.

We surveyed the topics listed in Table 1 to evaluate the differences between the two interfaces and the factors involved in this stereoscopic artwork and improvement of this interface. Our questionnaire contains four questions, three with one selection choice and one with multiple selections.

Table 1. Surveyed topics

General	Q1. Which artwork is your favorite?
	① Garden Party 1, ② Garden Party 2, ③ Similar
Interface	Q2. Which interface is easier to control artwork?
	① Touch, ② Motion, ③ Both, ④ Both are difficult.
	Q3. Which interface is better for artwork in stereoscopic environments?
	① Touch, ② Motion, ③ Similar
Elements	Q4. What elements are most impressive? (multiple selection with order)
	① Sketchbooks, ② Butterfly, ③ The hands of participant, ④ Particles from butterflies, ⑤ Particles from hands, ⑥ Sunflower animation, ⑦Flying sunflowers leaves

There were three questions about the influence of the interface and a last question about how the elements affected the audience in this stereoscopic environment. The elements in the art had different characteristics, as shown in Table 2.

Table 2. The characteristic of elements

Element	Characteristics
Sketchbooks	Image change (2D / 3D)
Butterfly	Slow depth change and slow reaction
The hands of participant	Small depth change and fast reaction
Particles from butterfly	Small depth change (downward)
Particles from hands	Fast and large depth change (inward)
The animation of sunflowers	Color change
The flying of sunflowers leaves	Fast depth change (outward)

3.2   Survey Result

First question is about the audience preference for both of the art presentations they experienced. Figure 7 shows that the preferences are similar for 'Garden Party 1' and 'Garden Party 2'.

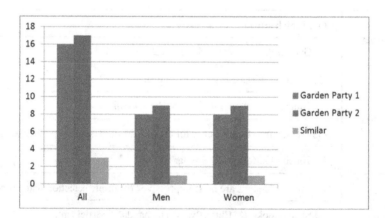

Fig. 7. Art preferences

Figure 8 shows the type of interfaces that they had previously experienced. Most of the audience had previous experience with both interfaces. More men experienced the motion sensor than the touch sensor. Women's responses were similar.

Figure 9 shows the answer for question 3, broken down by gender and age. The participants prefer the motion interface in stereoscopic environments. By gender and age, more men than women preferred the motion interface and more young people than old people liked the motion interface.

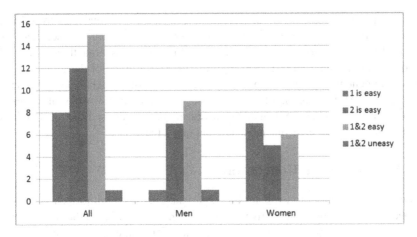

Fig. 8. Easy interface for control artworks in stereoscopic environment

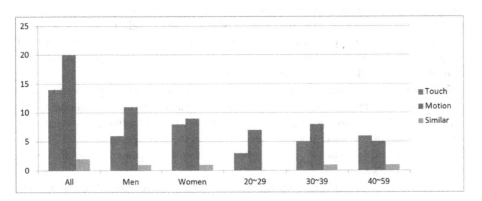

Fig. 9. Preference for interface style in stereoscopic environment

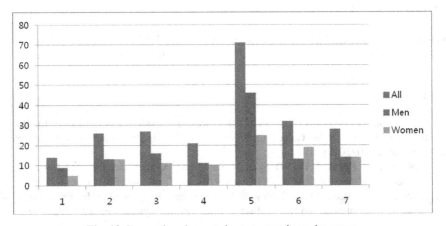

Fig. 10. Impressive elements in stereoscopic environment

Finally, the important factor in stereoscopic artwork was analyzed by selecting what was perceived as the most impressive elements. The audience selected three items in Table 2 in order of preference. The first answer scored three points, the second answer two and the last, one. Figure 10 shows a graph of the totals. The impressive element was particles from hands, and the least, sketchbooks. The second highest score was the painting of the sunflowers, and the third was that of leaves flying toward the audience. Elements that moved in and out aroused the most audience interest. Men preferred elements have that had quick reactions.

4   Discussion and Conclusions

We surveyed 36 visitors to evaluate the experience involved with touch and motion interfaces in stereoscopic interactive artwork. Men were partial to the motion, while women preferred the touch display. The audience found the spatial interfaces using Kinect, rather than the touch screen, more interesting, but at the same time considered them appropriate for this stereoscopic environment. The spatial interface allowed immersion in the work by providing a sense of space, along with movement, whereas the touch screen's weak point was the tendency to split the viewer's attention between the touch screen and the stereoscopic display. The audience was impressed with the elements involving depth and speed of motion.

Media art can use many different technologies, depending on the goals and intentions of the artist, but for stereoscopic images and spatial interfaces, maintaining the appropriate relationships between art and its viewers, and providing a good sense of immersion, requires a good grounding in how the space between these actors is used. Small differences in responses based on gender and age appeared to be the result, according to our survey.

This survey, though small, opens up the field for further research. It hints at questions for further research. It might be fruitful to explore the relationship between the interface used for this type of interactive art and different responses to it stemming from gender and age-related life experience.

Acknowledgements. This work was supported by the National Research Foundation of Korea Grant funded by the Korean Government (NRF-2012S1A5A2A01020337)

References

1. Williamson, B., Wingrave, C., LaViola, J.J.: Realnav: Exploring Natural User Interfaces for Locomotion in Video Games. In: Proceedings of IEEE Symposium on 3D User Interfaces, pp. 3–10 (2010)
2. LaViola, J.J., Keefe, D.F.: 3D Spatial Interaction: Applications for Art, Design, and Science. In: ACM SIGGRAPH 2011 Courses, Article 1, pp. 1–72 (2011)
3. Myers, B.A., Rosson, M.B.: Survey on User Interface Programming. In: Proceedings of the SIGCHI Conference on Human Factors in Computing Systems, pp. 195–202 (1992)

4. Shotton, J., Fitzgibbon, A., Cook, M., Sharp, T., Finocchio, M., Moore, R., Kipman, A., Blake, A.: Real-time Human Pose Recognition in Parts from a Single Depth Image. In: Proceedings of the IEEE Conference on Computer Vision and Pattern Recognition (CVPR), pp. 1297–1304 (2011)
5. Wu, M., Balakrishnan, R.: Multi-finger and Whole Hand Gestural Interaction Techniques for Multi-user Tabletop Displays. In: Proceedings of the 16th Annual ACM Symposium on User Interface Software and Technology, pp. 193–202 (2003)
6. Robles-De-La-Torre, G.: The Importance of the Sense of Touch in Virtual and Real Environments. IEEE Multimedia 13, 24–30 (2006)
7. Sparacino, F.: Natural Interaction in Intelligent Spaces: Designing for Architecture and Entertainment. Multimedia Tools and Applications 38(3), 307–335 (2008)
8. Wilson, S.: Information Arts: Intersections of Art, Science and Technology. MIT Press (2003)
9. Nam, S.H., Chai, Y.H.: SPACESKETCH: Shape Modeling with 3D Meshes and Control Curves in Stereoscopic Environments. Computers & Graphics (2012)
10. Kim, Y.E., Nam, S.H., Park, J.W.: Tracing Time through Interactive Artworks. Future Information Technology, Application, and Service, 147–152 (2012)
11. Valli, A.: The Design of Natural Interaction. Multimedia Tools and Applications 38(3), 295–305 (2008)

A Method of Viewing 3D Horror Contents for Amplifying Horror Experience

Nao Omori[1], Masato Tsutsui[2], and Ryoko Ueoka[3]

[1] Solidray Co., Ltd.
[2] Graduate School of Integrated Frontier Sciences, Kyushu University, Fukuoka, Japan
[3] Faculty of Design, Kyushu University, Fukuoka, Japan
{morio-lp4,ds107766}@gmail.com, r-ueoka@design.kyushu-u.ac.jp

Abstract. Current 3D digital film gives us a realistic sensation. Also adding physical effect with 3D film called 4D film becomes common entertainment system which generates more realistic sensation. So there are many commercial entertainment systems in order to give realistic experience adapted to such as horror contents. However there is still some problem that is unable us to immerse the horror contents. In order to find an effective way to amplify horror experience to viewers, we propose an original film-viewing theater environment. In concrete, we made a locker-type theater environment implementing polarizing filters on peephole of a locker door. This makes a viewer force to stand when to peep a 3d horror movie in a closed space without wearing 3D glasses. And by peeping a screen from a small hole, it is unable to see an edge of a large screen. By evaluating heart rate of viewers and conducting questionnaire-based survey, we confirmed our proposed method amplifies a horror experience especially by producing a closed viewing space.

Keywords: 4D film, virtual reality, virtual horror experience.

1   Introduction

Current 3D digital film gives us a realistic sensation. Also adding physical effect with 3D film called 4D film becomes common entertainment system which generates more realistic sensation. So there are many commercial entertainment systems producing realistic experience such as horror contents. However there is still some problem that is unable us to immerse the horror contents. In order to find an effective way to amplify horror experience to viewers, we hypothesize that obstacles to reduce immersion is

1. Unusual 3d glasses

As we usually have to wear polarizing glasses when to watch 3D contents, this special eye ware may reduce reality of contents.

2. Open space

As most of 3D contents are watched in theater, we sit a seat surrounded by other viewers in a large space. This environment may obstacle the immersion even though the situation of the contents is opposite such as a horror story in a cage.

S. Yamamoto (Ed.): HIMI/HCII 2013, Part III, LNCS 8018, pp. 228–237, 2013.
© Springer-Verlag Berlin Heidelberg 2013

3. Visible edge of screen

We experience 3D contents in theater provided by a large screen. Under this situation, we know 3D contents are played on screen, which implicitly recognize that this is not real.

In order to analyze whether the hypothesis above is obstacles of generating reality, we made a 4D theater environment, which may solve these obstacles and created a horror movie to evaluate the effects. In concrete, we made a locker-type theater environment implementing polarizing filters on a locker door. This makes a viewer force to stand when to peep a 3D horror movie with a closed space without wearing a polarizing glasses. And by peeping a screen from a small hole, it is unable to see an edge of a large screen. By comparing heart rate response and conducting questionnaire-based survey, we evaluated which factors cause to reduce immersion and our proposed theater system amplifies a horror experience.

2 Related Commercial Entertainment System and Researches

3D digital film has become commercially known these days. By adding physical effect that occur in synchronization with 3D film is called 4D film [1] and the first 4D film is known as "Sensorama" [2]. Effects simulated in a 4D film may include rain, wind, strobe lights and vibration of which gimmick is installed above or under seat. Many of the 4D films are presented in custom-built theatres or arcade box such as theme parks or game center [3,4]. There are variety of the contents of 4D films such as adventures story, horror story and time travel story [5,6]. The commercial 4D film theater is seat-type entertainment system and in most cases, he/she experiences it by sitting a seat wearing 3D glasses. Under this environment, especially if the contents of the film is made based on subjective viewpoint, there may be lack of reality. As for the research of combination of film and physical effect, "ants in the pants" gives a novel haptic interface combining video image [7]. And olfactory display presented by Nakamoto et.al. combines scent and image to improve reality of the digital contents [8]. In this paper, we focus on horror contents and propose a method of experiencing 4D horror film. Thus, even though we add physical effect by implementing vibration devices, our main goal of this paper is the design of theater environment to change physical perception, which may cause to amplify horror.

3 Preliminary Experiment: Comparison of Our Proposed Theater System and Conventional One

3.1 Purpose

As a preliminary experiment, we conducted an experiment in a locker-type viewing theater environment as figure 1 shows to examine whether our proposed environment amplifies horror experience. One of the authors created an original horror movie as follows;

Title: "Hide-and-seek at midnight" (scripted and produced by Nao Omori)

Scenario: The movie is created as one situation drama in a locker room at university. Because of a tragic murder during the event, a long time sealed event, a hide-and-seek at midnight is back on the day and you and two friends hide a locker room where the murder had occurred in the past. And you peep outside from the locker seeing that your friends are killed by a zombie and the zombie is seeking you next.

Figure 2 shows captured images from the original movie.

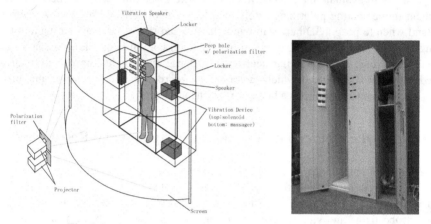

Fig. 1. Locker-type theater system outline (left) and locker(right)

Fig. 2. Horror movie capture image

The movie lasts about 4 minutes. In order to generate horror experience in a closed locker space, we implemented three types of vibration effects on the locker as follows.

A speaker: to give low frequency vibration

A solenoid: to give high-pitch vibration

A hand massager: to give strong vibration

Table 1 shows the categorized scene number and its description, their time durance, sound effect and devices used for vibration effect.

First of all in order to evaluate whether the system really affects viewers' physical state, we compared heart rate of subjects between a standard seat-type theater environment and our proposed system. The standard 3D theater environment consists of a screen, and two projectors with polarization filter, a chair without vibration effect, a surround speaker and 3D glass.

Table 1. Horror movie scene description

Scene No.	Scene	Time(sec)	Surrond–sound effect	Vibration device
1	rest (pre experimemt)	0–240		
2	pre locker vibration	241–293		
3	a subject's locker vibration	294–312		A speaker vibration set on top of the locker
4	a friend being dragged into a locker	335–342		
5	zombie appeared	356–414		
6	another friend is killed	415–427		
7	zombie approched (disappeared to left direction)	429–456		
8	locker vibration from left side	457–463	sound of opening a locker from a left speaker	A DC solenoid
9	zombie murmured	464–472	Zomvie's murmur, "Ready or not"	
10	zombie close–up	476–481	impact sound hitting a locker	A hand massager
11	rest (1–30s)	481–514		
12	rest (31–60s)	515–544		
13	rest (61–90s)	545–574		
14	rest (91–120s)	575–604		

3.2 Procedure

As for a subject experiencing our proposed system, he/she watches a two-minutes pre show movie to understand the context so that the following entering a locker behavior becomes natural. After watching the pre show movie, a subject entered a locker and watched a main movie through a peeping hole of the locker. A subject wore a heart rate sensor (Polar RS800) during the experiment to record RRI (R-R interval). A subject answered questionnaires about how he/she feels in each scene with 5 adjectives (Uneasy, Unpleasant, Astonished, Tensed and Scared) on a one-to-four scale. 9 subjects (4 male and 5 female average age 23.1 years old (SD1.9 years old)) participated the experiment. And as for a subject experiencing a standard seat-type theater environment, 9 subjects (five male and 4 female average age 21.9 years old (SD 1.0 years old)) participated the experiment. The sensor is same as the previous experiment.

3.3 Result

Figure 3 shows the result of the mean heart rate (M-HR) of categorized scene of each subject, which experienced the locker-type theater environment. 7 out of 9 subjects react similar physiological response, which gradually raises heart rate from "zombie approached (7)" to "zombie close-up (10)" scene and maximizes heart rate afterwards. This reaction may relate to the surround-sound and vibration effect as table 1 shows. When the subject started to watch the contents, he/she watched the movie from the third person view but with vibration effect after "zombie approached (7)" scene, the view point becomes more subjective and raises horror experience.

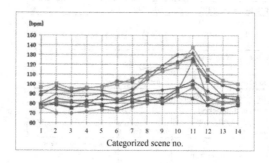

Fig. 3. Result of M-HR(mean heart rate)

Figure 4 shows the baseline comparison of the mean heart rate among subjects(M-HRS) and M-HRS of seat-type theater environment. In all of 13 scenes, we confirmed that two conditions has significant difference (t test 6 scenes: $p<0.05$, 7 scenes: $p<0.01$).

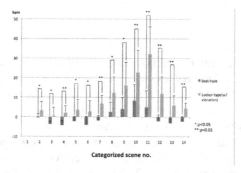

Fig. 4. Comparison of M-HRS (mean heart rate among subjects) between locker-type and seat-type

Figure 5 shows the average score of subjective feelings of each scene. They continuously raise from "another friend killed" scene except for "zombie murmured" scene. "Zombie close-up" scene shows highest score of all five adjectives. The reason why "zombie murmured" scene lowered the subjective horror scale, it is considered that as he/she heard the zombie murmured from the left side of the locker, the zombie was not shown on the screen which did not impact them so much.

In this previous experiment, we confirmed that our proposed theater system succeeds to amplify horror experience. However, we implemented vibration effect as well as designed the theater environment, so it is not clear which factor affects to amplify horror experience. If vibration effect amplifies horror experience, there is no difference between commercial 4D film and our proposed system since vibration effect is already implemented in most of the commercial system.

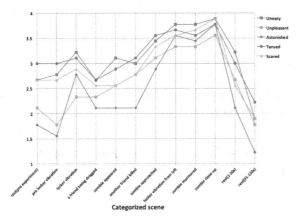

Fig. 5. Average score of subjective feeling of each categorized scene

4   Preliminary Experiment 2: Evaluation of Vibration Effect

4.1   Purpose

In order to evaluate the effect of vibration, we conducted the experiment to measure RRI in the locker-type theater environment with and without vibration effect.

4.2   Procedure

The system is same as the experiment 1. 10 subjects (5 male and 5 female average age 21.8 years old SD 1.69 years) participated the experiment. In this experiment, all the subjects experienced the experiment without vibration effect and its heart rate is measured by the same heart rate sensor used in experiment 1.

4.3   Result

Figure 6 left shows baseline comparison of M-HRS without vibration effect and M-HRS of seat- type theater environment. 7 out of 13 scenes, we confirmed that two conditions have significant difference (t test $p<0.05$). As for the comparison of vibration effect, there is no significant difference between two conditions as figure 6 right shows.

From these results, the factor which amplifies horror experience does not depend on the vibration effect. And this confirms that the factor depends on either of the three hypothesis we defined.

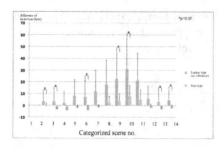 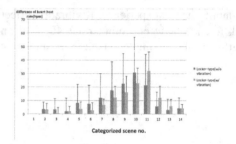

Fig. 6. Comparison of M-HRS between locker-type w/o vibration and seat-type(left) and comparison between w/ vibration and w/o vibration

5   Evaluation of the Effect of Three Factors of the Proposed Theater Environment

5.1   Purpose

In preliminary experiment, we confirmed that our proposed system may amplify horror experience, but it is not clear what affects to amplify horror experience exactly since we included three factors we defined as hypothesis which may effect amplifying horror experience. In order to evaluate the effect of horror experience of each hypothesis quantitatively, we modified the system and conducted three experiments. First one is to compare the effect of wearing and not-wearing 3D glasses. Second one is to compare the effect of open and closed space. And the third one is to compare the effect of visible and invisible edge of the screen. The purpose of each experiment is described as follows.

1. Unusual 3D glasses

In order to compare the effect of wearing and not-wearing 3D glasses whether it affects to amplify horror experience, we took the polarization filter out of the peeping holes of the locker and a subject watches 3D movie by wearing 3D glasses while in the locker.

2. Open space

We use a front door of a locker. A subject watches horror movie through the front door while it is open space.

3. Visible edge of the screen

In order to compare the effect of visibility of the screen, we made two sizes of peeping hole of the locker (large and small). By sizing up the peeping hole, a viewing angle of a subject in the locker broadens so that he/she is able to see the edge of the screen or landscape of the laboratory.

5.2   Procedure

A subject watches a pre-show movie for two minutes. Afterwards, he/she moves to each designated position in a next room. A heart rate sensor (Polar RS800) is worn during watching the horror movie. In experiment 1, 5 subjects (4 male and 1 female (average age 21.6 years old, SD 0.894)) participated. In experiment 2, 5 subjects (4 male and 1female (average age 20.8 years old, SD 0.837)) participated. In experiment 3, 5 subjects (4 male and 1 female (average age 20.8 years old, SD 0.837)) participated.

5.3   Result

1. Figure 7 shows the baseline comparison of M-HRS between wearing 3D glasses and not wearing 3D glasses. The result shows no significant difference between two conditions.

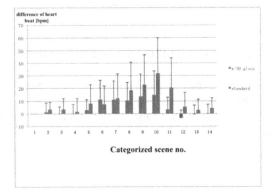

Fig. 7. Comparison of M-HRS between w/ and wo/ 3D glasses

2. Figure 8 shows the baseline comparison of M-HRS between open and closed environment. The result shows significant difference in 4 scenes between two conditions. (t test $p<0.05$)

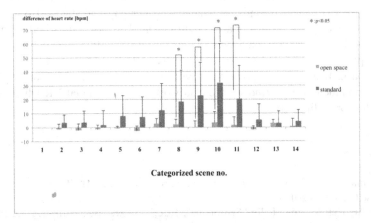

Fig. 8. Comparison of M-HRS between open and closed space

3. Figure 9 shows the baseline comparison of M-HRS between large and small peeping hole size. The result shows no significant difference between two conditions.

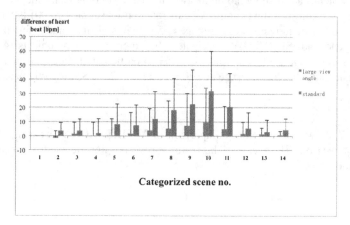

Fig. 9. Comparison of M-HRS between large and small angle

By evaluating the effect of each factor of hypothesis, we found that there is a significant difference between open and closed space of the proposed theater system. Therefore we confirmed that closeness of the space effects to amplify the horror experience of the contents.

6   Discussion

In this paper, we focus on finding the method to amplify reality when to experience a horror movie. We hypothesize three factors reducing the reality in the current 3D or 4D theater environment. By comparing a viewer's heart rate as a baseline of horror emotion, we confirmed that producing a closed space amplifies horror experience. This may relate to the effect of ambience since the closed space compresses a viewer into the small space, which implicitly changes his/her physical state. Also the closed space gives a metaphor of unescapable environment. This also raises horror emotion. In future work, we will work on generating horror virtually. In concrete, we will work on developing system to make a person virtually feel closed space even though it is an open space. If it becomes possible, it will expand this kind of horror amplifying system in commercial use. And we are also working on illusional VR which leads a personal horror feeling virtually.

References

1. Wikipedia "4D film", http://en.wikipedia.org/wiki/4D_film (accessed in March 2013)
2. Media Art Net, Morton Heilig "Sensorama", http://www.medienkunstnetz.de/works/sensorama/(accessed in March 2013)

3. Universal Studio 4D film theater, `https://www.universalorlando.com/Rides/Universal-Studios-Florida/Shrek-4-D.aspx` (accessed in March 2013)
4. Namco 4D arcade game "dark Escape" Trailer, `http://www.youtube.com/watch?v=o03m8IXHVb8` (accessed in March 2013)
5. Captain EO, `http://disneyland.disney.go.com/disneyland/captain-eo/` (accessed in March 2013)
6. Jerusalem Time Elevator, `http://www.gojerusalem.com/discover/item_9983/Jerusalem-Time-Elevator-Tickets` (accessed in March 2013)
7. Nakamoto, Otaguro, Kinoshita, Nagahama, Ohinishi, Ishida: Cooking Up an Interactive Olfactory Game Display. In: Projects in VR, IEEE Computer Graphics and Applications, pp. 75–78 (2008)
8. Sato, K., Sato, Y., Sato, M., Fukushima, Okano, Matsuo, Ooshima, Kojima, Matsue, Nakata, Hashimoto, Kajimoto: Ants in the Pants. In: Abstract for Emerging Technology in Siggraph 2008 (2008)

Digital Railway Museum: An Approach to Introduction of Digital Exhibition Systems at the Railway Museum

Takuji Narumi[1], Torahiko Kasai[2], Takumi Honda[2], Kunio Aoki[2],
Tomohiro Tanikawa[1], and Michitaka Hirose[1]

[1] 7-3-1 Hongo, Bunkyo-Ku, Tokyo, Japan
{narumi,tani,hirose}@cyber.t.u-tokyo.ac.jp
[2] 3-47 Ohnari, Ohmiya-Ku, Saitama, Japan
{kasai,t-honda,aoki}@ejrcf.or.jp

Abstract. Museum is considered as an important application field for digital media technologies. In conventional museum exhibition, museum curators have tried to convey wisdom of mankind to the visitors by displaying real exhibits. Meanwhile, such conventional method for exhibition cannot tell vivid background information about the exhibit such as the social situation where it was made and the mechanism how it worked. Digital media can be used for enhancing delivery efficiency by providing the ability to express background information about exhibits. Based on this idea, we introduced digital exhibition systems, which help us to understand background information of exhibits, into THE RAILWAY MUSEUM (Japan) and held the "Digital Railway Museum" exhibition. In this paper, we describe about the exhibition and report on and knowledge and implication obtained from the exhibition.

Keywords: Digital Museum, Digital Exhibition System, Digital Display Case, Digital Diorama, Sharing Experience System.

1 Introduction

In every museum, a great deal of informational materials about museum exhibits has been preserved as texts, pictures, videos, 3D models and so on. Curators have tried to convey this large amount of information to the visitors by using instruction boards or audio/visual guidance devices within their exhibitions. However, such conventional information assistance methodologies cannot tell or show vivid background information about target exhibits.

Meanwhile, with rapid growth in information technologies, virtual reality and mixed reality technologies had developed and popularized in last decade. Today, we can present a high-quality virtual experience in real-time and in real-environment by using next generation display and interaction system: auto-stereoscopic 3D displays, gesture input devices, marker-less tracking system, etc. Thus, museums are very interested in the introduction of these technologies to tell the rich background information about their exhibits. There are some research projects about this kind of exhibition systems featuring digital technology [1, 2].

S. Yamamoto (Ed.): HIMI/HCII 2013, Part III, LNCS 8018, pp. 238–247, 2013.
© Springer-Verlag Berlin Heidelberg 2013

In this paper, we report on our approach to introduce digital exhibition systems, which help us to understand background information of exhibits, into THE RAILWAY MUSEUM (Ohnari-Ku, Saitama, Japan) [3].

2   The "Digital Railway Museum" Exhibition

Industrial heritages have a great deal of background information such as their behaviors how these worked, their functions, the social situation where these were made, the location where they worked, how people used these, the relationship with other exhibits, historical trail and the process to create these. Especially, the behaviors and functions are essential for explaining a rail vehicle and its mechanism as an industrial heritage. Therefore there are great demands to introduce digital assistance for explaining these essences with real exhibits.   We believe that digital media can be used for enhancing delivery efficiency by providing the ability to express background information about exhibits. Based on this idea, we have developed three types of digital exhibition systems: "Digital Display Case" for conveying the mechanism of exhibits through interaction, "Digital Diorama" for conveying the behaviors of exhibits and surrounding environment where the exhibits were used, and "Experience Sharing System" for conveying the manner of interaction with the exhibits by sharing the interaction which the participant took to others.

Then we held the "Digital Railway Museum" exhibition, and exhibited these systems. The "Digital Railway Museum" exhibition was a special exhibition which held from November 9th, 2011 to January 9th, 2012 at THE RAILWAY MUSEUM. In this exhibition, we aimed to examine the effectiveness and the possibility of our digital exhibition systems by letting visitors try our systems and gathering their reactions. We presented above-mentioned three digital exhibition systems. During the exhibition, all systems kept on running without any accident. The exhibition received over 60,000 visitors.

The following of this paper describes about each digital exhibition system and report on and knowledge and implication obtained from the exhibition and users observations.

3   Digital Display Case

3.1   System Overview

Digital Display Case system [4] enables museums to convey background information about exhibits effectively in an exhibition using interactive techniques and virtual exhibits. While previous studies [4, 5] have examined static exhibits, this study focuses on assisting visitors to understand the mechanisms of the exhibits. In this study, we chose the railway bogie as an example, and implemented a Digital Display Case system with which visitors can interact.

Fig. 1. Digital Display Case for conveying the mechanism of exhibits

The Digital Display Case system composed of three three-dimensional (3D) displays in the shape of a box. The reason why we chose the shape of a three-sided display case was that the appearance of the system would resemble a display case that could be introduced seamlessly in place of conventional display cases in museums. To view the exhibit, a user wears a pair of 3D glasses with a Polhemus sensor, which measures the orientation and rotation of the receptor using magnetic fields generated by the transmitter. Based on the point of view measured by this sensor, the system calculates computer graphics image to display on each 3D display. This enables the user to view a virtual exhibit from many angles as if it were actually inside the case (Fig. 1). Moreover the user can interact with the exhibit by using a controller like a master controller of an electric train.

In this system, a railway bogie was represented as an exhibit which had dynamic mechanisms. The bogie needs to suppress vibration in order to prevent vibration up and down the body when it is running on a rail. Therefore, it has axle and bolster springs. It also has flexible joints consisting of an annular gear, external gears, a spring, and so forth. The role of flexible joints is to transmit driving force from the motor to the wheels and to prevent vibration from being transmitted to the motor. Owing to this joint, trains can remain stable while running. On the other hand, these mechanisms are difficult to understand only with a real exhibit because these cannot be seen from outside when they are really working. Moreover, since the amounts of change of pieces are extremely small, the visitors cannot feel the effectiveness of the mechanisms even if they observe the exhibit working in real scale. Therefore, we intend to convey this mechanism to visitors by using interactive techniques.

In order to convey such mechanisms, the exhibition system requires functionality that enables visitors to interact with the exhibit and see how the mechanism works visually. Therefore, we implemented the system to allow the visitor to operate the railway bogie with acceleration or deceleration. In addition, this system possesses a function to make its parts transparent in six steps, so that visitors can see both the outside and the inside. Using these functions, visitors can observe the hidden parts of the mechanism as if the railway bogie was real and running. In addition, the amplitude of the rail, where the virtual bogie runs on, is defined to be larger than an actual rail since it is necessary to distend the mechanical movement of the bogie in order to convey the mechanism to visitors. Moreover, the system visualizes the friction between parts by representing sparks which emerges at the point of friction with reference to the method by Sreng et al. [6].

3.2   Evaluation of Digital Display Case through the Exhibition

Digital Display Case was exhibited in the exhibition from November 9 to November 14, 2011 and from December 7 to December 19, 2011, excluding December 13. More than 4000 visitors interacted with this system.

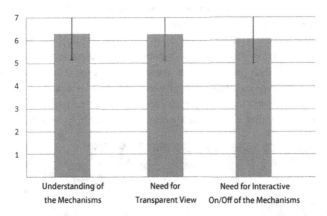

Fig. 2. User Evaluation of Digital Display Case (Average and Standard Deviation)

We asked participants to fill in a questionnaire with a seven-point rating scale and free descriptions after they experienced the exhibition. On the rating scale, higher numbers corresponded to more positive evaluations, and vice versa. Forty eight participants rated the following issues:

- Degree of the understanding of the mechanism how the railway bogie works.
- Degree of the needs for the transparency of the parts in order to understand the mechanism of the bogie.
- Degree of the needs for interactive switching on and off the mechanisms of the bogie to understand their functions.

Figure 2 shows the average and standard deviation of the rates to each item on the questionnaire. These results suggest the interaction with the exhibit in our system enhances delivery efficiency to convey the mechanisms of the bogie. Moreover it is considered that the system satisfied the requirements of THE RAILWAY MUSEUM to easily convey knowledge about the mechanism of the railway bogie to visitors.

In addition, we received many opinions regarding the exhibition in the free description. Among the positive opinions, there were several responses indicating that the exhibition was interesting and useful for understanding immediately the mechanism of the railway bogie, that it was good to experience it in real time with explanations, that both children and adults who were not familiar with the railway could also enjoy it, and so on.

4   Digital Diorama: "Reminiscent Window"

4.1   System Overview

The Digital Diorama system is a mixed reality system which superimposes virtual environment onto real exhibits [7]. In a museum exhibition, a diorama is a technology for showing usage scenes and situations of the exhibits by building a set or painting background image like a film. The Digital Diorama system aims to offer more features than the function of existing dioramas in museum exhibitions. In particular, our proposed system superimposes computer generated diorama scene on an exhibit by using mobile devices. With this approach, the system can present vivid scenes or situations to visitors with real exhibits: how it was used, how it was made and how they moved. Moreover we consider this system can help users to understand the relationship between the real exhibit and its background information in historical materials.

Fig. 3. "Reminiscent Window" to overlay usage scenes onto the real exhibits

Based on this concept, we made the system named "Reminiscent Window," which overlays usage scenes in a video material onto the real exhibits and makes a user to experience how the camera operator captured the scene around the exhibits by inducing them to move as in the same way as the camera operator (Fig. 3). In this system, users can freely observe a spatial expansion of the world reconstructed from a news video, which captured the exhibit worked, by moving the device. At the same time we allow users to experience how the camera operator captured the scene by inducing them to move in the same way as the camera operator did by using visual feedback.

In this study, the video sequences which they were filmed from immutable position were only used; only the orientation of the camera can be changed. First, standing at the point from where the video content was taken relative to the target object, the user points the device camera at the exhibit that is present in the video. Then the system recognizes it by using SURF-based detection method [8], and superimposes the image of the first video frame onto the exhibit. Next, when the user rotates the device to observe the surrounding area without translational movement, the system displays the frame that was taken in the direction in which the user is looking. The system used a gyro sensor embedded in the tablet device to determine the direction in which the user is facing. To determine the direction of the camera in each video frame, we calculated the directions manually in advance.

In order to induce users to move in the same way as the camera operator, the system generates three types of visual feedback: Induction for letting users start moving, Induction for letting them keep on moving, and Induction for letting them stop moving. When users start to move, we give the initial velocity to the overlaid image. Thus, the position of the video content frame moves to the direction the system induces (Induction for letting users start moving). If users try to stop moving the device in the middle of the rotation, the frames move ahead of the user in accordance with the inertial (Induction for letting them keep on moving). This is similar to the movement of the inertial scrolling in GUI. Using this method, not only is the position of the video frames moved in the direction the system aims to induce, but also the directional flow is conveyed in the video screen. Valid effects can therefore be expected to be achieved by means of "vection" effects, which some researchers used to give a change in human behavior [9]. Moreover, when users turn the device beyond the range associated with the image, we keep the frame of the video content to the inside of the range associated with the image (Induction for letting them stop moving). This prevents users from moving the device out of the range, and help users to experience the video content only within the range associated with the image.

4.2   Evaluation of "Reminiscent Window" through the Exhibition

"Reminiscent Window" was exhibited in the exhibition from November 9 to November 14 and from December 14 to December 19, 2011. More than 3500 visitors interacted with this system.

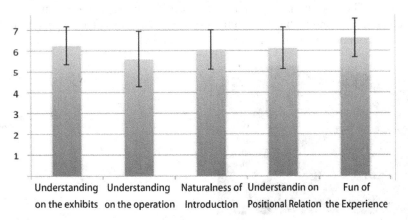

Fig. 4. User Evaluation of "Reminiscent Window" (Average and Standard Deviation)

We asked participants to fill in a questionnaire with a seven-point rating scale and free descriptions after they experienced the system. On the rating scale, higher numbers corresponded to more positive evaluations, and vice versa. Eighty five participants rated the following issues:

- Degree of the understanding on the exhibits.
- Degree of the understanding on how to operate the system.
- Whether the overlaying method which switches from the real exhibits to the past world reconstructed from videos was natural
- Degree of understanding on positional relationship between exhibits and objects in the past world recorded in videos.
- Degree of fun of the experience which the system offered.

Figure 4 shows the average and standard deviation of the rates to each item on the questionnaire. These results suggest the mixed reality exhibition system enhances delivery efficiency to convey the background information such as how it was used and what situation it was used in.

In addition, we received many opinions regarding the exhibition in the free description. Among the positive opinions, there were several responses indicating that they feel full immersion as if they were actually in the past world. This kind of comments indicates that the interaction such as looking around evokes immersive feelings and lets visitors understand the background information intuitively.

5   Experience Sharing System "Time-Leaping Seat"

5.1   System Overview

Experience-based exhibitions are effective in helping people understand the mechanism, functions, and background information on the exhibits. Visitors, however, do not necessarily experience the exhibits in the expected way. A museum cannot prepare explainers for all the exhibits, and the information on description panels is sometimes not enough. Then, we propose a system that records and superimposes past visitors interaction around an exhibit three-dimensionally. Visitors see the behaviors of past visitors, and obtain a better understanding of the exhibit.

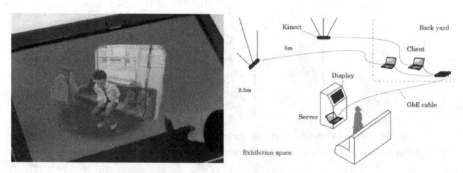

Fig. 5. Experience Sharing System "Time-Leaping Seat"

The proposed system, named the "Time-Leaping Seat" (Fig. 5), consists of the train seat of an exhibit, two depth cameras, two client PCs, a server PC, a touch panel interface, and cables. In our system, a real-time 3D reconstruction technique is used to superimpose images in exhibition space. One of the most effective methods that are capable of real-time 3D reconstruction is to use a combination of image cameras and depth sensors. Wilson et al. [10] developed the "LightSpace" system, which realizes interaction between images and real objects. This system consists of a projector and multiple depth sensors set on the upper side. Our proposed system also uses multiple depth cameras, like LightSpace. The system offers visitors two experiences:

1. Visitors can see a scene in which the exhibit, they themselves, and past visitors are together.
2. Visitors can see a scene where they are sitting on other seats of exhibits (on which they cannot sit in practice).

Visitors sat on the exhibit seat first. The real seat and the current visitors were reconstructed on the touch display in real time. Persons in the exhibit space were recorded as three-dimensional moving data for ten seconds when the visitors tapped a recording button on the display. Past visitors were superimposed on the real-time scene when the current visitors tapped a playing button. In addition, visitors could control the reconstructed scene intuitively with their fingers or a stylus pen, and view it from all directions.

5.2   Evaluation of "Time Leaping Seat" through the Exhibition

The Time-Leaping Seat was exhibited in the exhibition from November 16 to November 21 and from December 21 to December 26, 2011.   More than 1600 visitors experienced this system.

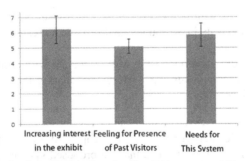

Fig. 6. User Evaluation of "Time-Leaping Seat" (Average and Standard Deviation)

We asked participants to fill in a questionnaire with a seven-point rating scale and free descriptions after they experienced the system. On the rating scale, higher numbers corresponded to more positive evaluations, and vice versa. Thirty six participants rated the following issues:

- How this system increases interest in the exhibit and interaction with it.
- Degree of the feeling for presence of past visitors as if they were along with.
- Degree of needs for this system to introduce interaction method with exhibits.

Figure 6 shows the average and standard deviation of the rates to each item on the questionnaire. The responses showed that we achieved our objectives: visitors understood the exhibit's functions intuitively, the proposed system enhanced their interest in the exhibit, and visitors' experiences could be shared with subsequent visitors.

In addition, we received many positive opinions regarding the exhibition in the free description. On the other hand, some opinions indicated that the system offered visitors an interesting experience that they could sit on past seats; however it did not provide them with enough information about the seat itself although visitors expected them. Therefore the system can be improved by combining other method to giving explanations of exhibits according to the behavior of the visitors.

6   Conclusion

This paper describes about three types of digital exhibition systems, "Digital Display Case" for conveying the mechanism of exhibits through interaction, "Digital Diorama" for conveying the behaviors of exhibits and surrounding environment where the exhibits were used, and "Experience Sharing System" for conveying the manner of interaction with the exhibits by sharing the interaction which the participant took to others, based on the knowledge and implication obtained from the "Digital Railway Museum" exhibition at THE RAILWAY MUSEUM. To summarize the primary findings:

- Digital exhibition systems, which combine real exhibits and background information by using the virtual and mixed reality technology, expand the range of expository activities and enhance delivery efficiency to convey background information about the exhibits.
- Interaction with digital exhibition systems increases visitors' curiosity and interest in the real exhibits and its backgrounds, and provide a greater understanding of its value.
- By sharing the visitors' experience, the way to interact with digital exhibition systems becomes more comprehensive. Moreover, sharing the visitors' experience enhances interest in exhibits.

Both visitors who experienced our systems and museum curators who introduced our systems in their exhibition felt effectiveness and capability of our systems. While the current study is the first step, we believe that the proposed system can help visitors in various situations in museums. For applying these systems to various situations and various exhibits, of course technological improvement is needed. On the other hand, we believe this kind of interaction is most important to develop not only novel, but also useful and effective exhibition systems. The digital exhibition systems in this paper are developed through a deep interaction among researchers, engineers and museum curators. In future, we aim to improve these systems to provide more realistic and sophisticated experiences by not only technical improvement but also schematization of management methods to treat digital exhibition systems and its contents. Then finally we aim to introduce these systems in the museum as a permanent installation.

Acknowledgements. This research is partly supported by "Mixed Realty Digital Museum" project of Ministry of Education, Culture, Sports, Science and Technology (MEXT) of Japan. The authors would like to thank all the members of our project especially staff members of THE RAILWAY MUSEUM.

References

1. Oliver Bimber, L., Encarnacao, M., Schmalstieg, D.: Thevirtual showcase as a new platform for augmented realitydigital storytelling. In: Proceedings of the Workshop on Virtual Environments 2003, pp. 87–95 (2003)
2. Nakashima, T., Wada, T., Naemura, T.: Exfloasion: Multi-layeredfloating vision system for mixed reality exhibition. In: Proceedings of Virtual Systemsand Multimedia (VSMM 2010), pp. 95–98 (October 2010)
3. Japan Railway Museum, http://www.railway-museum.jp/
4. Kajinami, T., Hayashi, O., Narumi, T., Tanikawa, T., Hirose, M.: Digital Display Case: Museum exhibition system to conveybackground information about exhibits. In: Proceedings of VirtualSystems and Multimedia (VSMM 2010), pp. 230–233 (October 2010)
5. Kajinami, T., Narumi, T., Tanikawa, T., Hirose, M.: Digital displaycase using non-contact head tracking. In: Proceedings of the 2011 International Conference on Virtual and Mixed Reality: New Trends - Volume Part I, pp. 250–259 (2011)
6. Sreng, J., Bergez, F., Legarrec, J., Lecuyer, A., Andriot, C.: Using anevent-based approach to improve the multimodal rendering of 6DOFvirtual contact. In: Proceedings of Virtual Reality Software and Technology (VRST 2007), pp. 165–173 (2007)
7. Narumi, T., Hayashi, O., Kasada, K., Yamazaki, M., Tanikawa, T., Hirose, M.: Digital Diorama: AR Exhibition System to Convey Background Information for Museums. In: Proceedings of the 2011 International Conference on Virtual and Mixed Reality: New Trends - Volume Part I, pp. 76–86 (July 2011)
8. Bay, H., Tuytelaars, T., Van Gool, L.: SURF: Speeded up robust features. In: Leonardis, A., Bischof, H., Pinz, A. (eds.) ECCV 2006, Part I. LNCS, vol. 3951, pp. 404–417. Springer, Heidelberg (2006)
9. Kurose, I., Kitazaki, M.: Postural Sway Induced by Visual RadialMotion: spatio-temporal sensitivity to heading direction. Transactionsof Information Processing Society of Japan 8(2), 189–198 (2003)
10. Wilson, A.D., Benko, H.: Combining Multiple Depth Camerasand Projectors for Interactions on, above and between Surfaces. In: Proceedings of the 23rd Annual ACM Symposium on User InterfaceSoftware and Technology (UIST 2010), pp. 273–282 (2010)

Mixed Reality Digital Museum Project

Tomohiro Tanikawa, Takuji Narumi, and Michitaka Hirose

Graduate School of Information Science and Technology, the University of Tokyo, Japan
{tani,narumi,hirose}@cyber.t.u-tokyo.ac.jp

Abstract. In our research, we propose Mixed Reality Digital Museum to convey background information about museum exhibits by using mixed reality technologies. Based on this concept, we construct and demonstrate three types of exhibition system: Digital Display Case, Digital Diorama and Outdoor Gallery. Also to supporting museum activity, we construct and demonstrate several approaches which are acquisition and application of visitor's activity, supporting curator's activity, recalling after visiting, and etc. In this paper, the authors first introduce the outline of "Mixed Reality Digital Museum" project under the sponsorship of MEXT (Ministry of Education, Culture, Sports, Science and Technology). Then, the basic concept and project formation of the project are quickly introduced. After that, among the many project subtopics, the authors introduce two types of museum system using Mixed Reality technology: "Digital Display Case" and "Digital Diorama." Result of the implementation of the first stage prototypes are introduced and future plan is discussed.

Keywords: Digital Museum, Mixed Reality, Digital Display Case, Digital Diorama.

1 Introduction

In this paper, the authors firstly introduce the outline of "Mixed Reality Digital Museum" project which started as a 5 year national project sponsored by MEXT (Ministry of Education, Culture, Sports, Science and Technology). In the digital museum project, following 3 basic concepts are employed.

1. To fuse real (object) and virtual exhibit (event)
2. To support museum visitor's experience as a whole
3. To use digital technology for the sake of museum itself

(1) is a concept focused on the exhibits point of view. Originally, the function of museums is to transfer knowledge from older generation to younger generation beyond long period by using "collection of real (physical) objects" as a media. In other words, working hypothesis of the system called museum is based on convince that most part of knowledge can be transferred only by "objects". Since most of physical objects remains for long period, museum system has been working very well. Of course, there exist various limitations in the museum system. For example, most of

S. Yamamoto (Ed.): HIMI/HCII 2013, Part III, LNCS 8018, pp. 248–257, 2013.

exhibits don't move. It is very difficult for us to imagine dynamic running of steam locomotives from the statically positioned exhibits. If we plan to prepare the exhibits to run, enormous cost will be required. The project call this kind of background information as "event" in contrast to "object". Feature of digital technology will give dynamic "event" aspect to static "object".

(2) is a concept based on the museum visitor's point of view. In order to appreciate exhibits, various background knowledge. If museum visitors study on some exhibit in advance, they will get more information when they actually see the exhibit.   Also, if they make review after going back to their home, they may wish to go to the museum again as repeaters. Appreciation of exhibit is only part of the process or experience of obtaining knowledge. Digital technology can support this process as a whole.

(3) is a concept based on the museum management point of view. Interactive exhibits can accept information from museum visitors. For example, whether the visitor enjoy the exhibit (or not) can be monitored very precisely. This data will be very important for curators to plan next exhibits. Moreover, information directly gathered from the visitor may be useful as an important content for the exhibit.

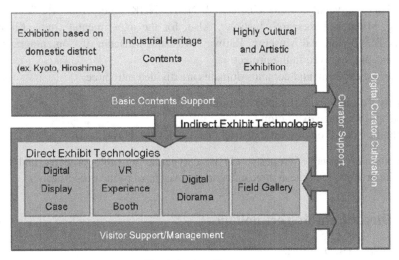

Fig. 1. Project Structure

2   Project Structure of Digital Museum Project

Based on the above mentioned concept, project structure is designed as shown in Fig. 1. Project will develop two kind of technologies; Direct Exhibit Technologies and Indirect Exhibit Technologies.

Direct Exhibit Technologies provide methodologies to implement fascinating exhibits. They relate to concept (1) and   includes the followings:

1. Digital Display Case which provides compatibility to conventional exhibits
2. Digital Diorama which provides context or ambient information to the real exhibits.

3. VR Experience Booth which supports interactive experience related to real exhibits.
4. Field Gallery which provides exhibits outdoor environment with digital equipments.

Indirect Exhibit Technologies provide much broader exhibition environment and can be considered as basic information system of a museum. They relate to concept (2), (3) and includes the followings:

1. Basic Contents Support which is to obtain contents such as shape or motion of real exhibits to digital world from the real world.
2. Visitor Support/Management which is for providing visitor sophisticated museum experience as a whole system
3. Curation Support System which provide methodology to collect information automatically from museum visitors and help curator to design better exhibits.

Project members are composed by researchers from the University of Tokyo, Ritumeikan University, Keio University, NHK, NHK enterprise, NICT, Toppan Printing, Mitsubishi Research Institute. Also, for the experimental study, Museum such as Tokyo National Museum, Railway Museum, Museum of Contemporary Art Tokyo etc. are involved in the project.

Supposed experimental contents domains are divided into three:

1. Highly Cultural and Artistic exhibition
2. Industrial Heritage exhibition
3. Exhibition based on domestic district (such as Kyoto, Hiroshima)

(1) is a static movable property, (2) is a dynamic movable property and (3) is immobile property. So, these three categories cover most of the properties.

3   Direct Exhibit Technologies

3.1   Digital Display Case

There are some researches about exhibition systems featuring digital technology like Virtual Showcase [1]. However, few of them are actually introduced into museums. That is because they are greatly different from conventional display cases in shape. Therefore in this paper, we first construct the system in compatible with conventional display cases and panels [2].

Usually, museum exhibits are preserved inside a display case and cannot be touched, because exhibits will be damaged otherwise. The authors expect digital technologies such as virtual reality technology can solve this problem. Interactive capability of digital technology allows museum visitor to touch and handle exhibits freely.

If we want to illustrate background information by using conventional exhibition method, instruction panels will be used, but as mentioned before, this way is not effective. For example, some visitor may read panels but others don't. This is because most of the visitor see the exhibits in the display case and the instruction on the panel as separate things. Especially, the physical distance between exhibits and panels often makes it difficult to associate the information on panels with the exhibits.

The authors made the first prototype of the digital display case in the similar shape of conventional display cases but it can provide virtual exhibition by using real-time computer graphics. This system consists of four 3D displays assembled as boxshape and two 6DOF (Polhemus) sensors (one is for head tracking the other is for interaction with the virtual exhibit). Fig.3 shows the appearance of the system in operation. User wear glasses with head tracking sensor, and the system measures the position of view point. According to user's viewpoint, the system calculates the images to display and shows proper side of 3D virtual object as if it were in the case. Currently, conventional 3D displays with glasses are used for the prototype, but they will be substituted by glasses-less 3D displays [3-5] such as IP (Integral Photography).

We setup our developed Digital Display Cases at actual museum exhibition, the Railway Museum. This system has a function as same as a simulator. Visitor can drive the train track displayed in the case (Fig.3 left). By making some of the parts transparent, we can understand the functions of the mechanisms.

And the other prototype Digital Display Case was used in the Tokyo National Museum (Fig.3 right). This system enables visitor to interact with very expensive national treasures. In Japan, there are cultural assets called free-motion ornaments. It is a kind of figure model which can change its posture by hand. Since it is a kind of national treasure, almost no one can touch. So it is very difficult to know how it works. By using digital display case, visitor can interact with this kind of exhibit and understand that function.

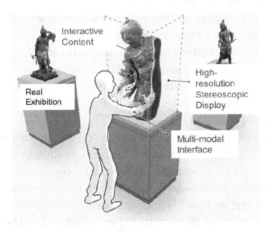

Fig. 2. Concept of Digital Display Case

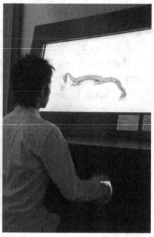

Fig. 3. Digital Display Case (left: the Railway Museum, right: Tokyo National Museum)

3.2   Digital Diorama

In conventional exhibition, diorama is used to show how and under what situation the exhibits are used by building a mockup similar to a movie set.   Digital diorama aims to realize the same function by using mixed reality technology.

In particular, our proposed system superimposes computer generated diorama scene on a exhibits by using HMD, a projector, etc. By this approach, the system can present the vivid scene or situation to visitors with real exhibits: how to be used, how to be made and how to be moved them.   Based on this concept, we implemented prototype system superimposing reconstructed virtual environment from concerning photographs and videos on the real exhibit (Fig. 4).

In order to smoothly connect old photographs or movies with the current exhibit, we have to estimate the relative position where the photos or videos are taken.   This matching system constructed with mobile PC and web camera [6].   The matching system tracking user's assigned feature points on current image and outputs difference vector from old photo view point to current photo view continuously: yaw, pitch, right/left, back/forward and roll.   According to the instruction from the system, we reached the past camera position [7].

To super-imposing old photograph or movies on real exhibits, the authors employed iPad-based AR system. At the estimated camera position, visitors experienced reconstructed past locomotive scene by using image based rendering method [8] (Fig. 5). The evaluation results show that camera position estimation and image matching between current and past images are evaluated very well. Moreover, many subjects said that the system for this experiment was good for knowing the background contexts of exhibits.

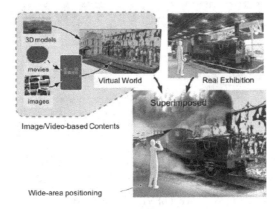

Fig. 4. Concept of Digital Diorama

Fig. 5. Digital Diorama in the Railway Museum

3.3   VR Experience Booth

VR Experience Booth is an immersive VR system in which users can experience large-scale cultural heritages or related event of intangible cultural heritages with high presence by using multi-modal information display, visual, auditory, and haptic displays.

For developing the system, sub-group (Ritsumeikan University) developed following sub-technologies; high-quality interactive character animation and crowd animation technologies, interactive immersive 3D visualization and interaction, presentation of balance sense using motion platform and visual and auditory feedback, interactive immersive sound image reconstruction, dynamic and high-diversity visualization of intangible cultural heritage, sophistication of 4DGIS "Virtual Kyoto[9]", real-time high-fidelity visual-haptic reconstruction. Fig.7 shows Current prototype individual VR experience booth.

We exhibit a part of our research activities, "Multi-band super high-resolution image of accessories of Funaboko", "Reconstruction of street-view using GIS and VR", "Virtual Yamaboko Junko using CG and high-fidelity sound image" at Kyoto City Intangible Cultural Property Exhibition Room [10].

Fig. 6. Concept of VR Experience Booth

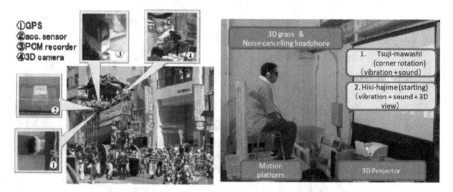

Fig. 7. VR Experience Booth (left: recording "Gion Matsuri", right: prototype VR booth)

3.4 Field Gallery

Field gallery synthesizes a virtual exhibit in the real place. This is a dual relationship to Digital diorama. Digital diorama synthesizes a virtual environment to the real exhibit. By using MR technology, virtual world will be precisely located in the real world. Old buildings which do not exist anymore can be displayed in the actual place. Visitor can enjoy exhibits not only in the gallery but also at the place where they are actually located.

Sub-group (Ikeuchi-Lab, the University of Tokyo) reconstructed the lost buildings of Asukakyo with CG and synthesized them with the real landscape of Asuka Village. To improve the quality of the synthesized image, we worked on the problem of the photometric consistency in MR using fast shading and shadowing method based on shadowing plane and pre-rendered basis images. The system was opened to public in 2009 and 2010, and questionnaire surveys were carried out to evaluate the shadowing method and MR-system [11,12].

Fig. 8. Concept of Field Gallery

Fig. 9. Field Gallery "Virtual Asukakyo"

4   Indirect Exhibit Technologies

Indirect Exhibit Technologies is technologies for realizing "totally supporting museum activities." The technologies are developed for collaboration between the above mentioned direct exhibit technologies and the conventional exhibition technique which are used in general museums.

Our project members consider that total (before and after) services are very important as well as the on-site (at museum) one. For this aspect, sub-group (Kakehi Lab., Keio University, Naemura Lab., the University of Tokyo) developed networked visualization of congestion situation (Breathing Museum), social networking to share visitors' feelings (Post-Visit Board) [13,14], and personalized mementos for each visitor (Peaflet). They are effective for making people want to visit museums and promoting greater understanding.

Furthermore, from museum side, museum curators or officers, it is important visitor's detailed behavior log to design museum exhibition gallery and arrange exhibits. Sub-group (Aizawa Lab., the University of Tokyo) developed a computer vision-based mobile museum guide system named "Navilog" [15]. It is a multimedia application for tablet devices. Using Navilog, visitors can take a picture of exhibits, and it identifies the exhibit and it shows additional descriptions and content related to it. It also enables them to log their locations within the museum. We made an experiment in the Railway Museum in Saitama, Japan.

Fig. 10. left: Post-Visit Board, right: Digital Omoide Note

Fig. 11. Navilog

5   Conclusion

In this paper, first the authors outlined the basic concept and project formation of the digital museum project sponsored by MEXT.   After that, among the many project subtopics, introduced two types of museum system using Mixed Reality technology: "Digital Display Case," "VR Experience Booth," and "Digital Diorama," "Field Gallery." These systems are designed for enhancing the current museum exhibition by presenting the background information of the exhibits. Then, by using implemented prototype systems, the authors demonstrated the effectively to convey synchronic and diachronic background information with their physical exhibits simultaneously. Although these are still an experimental level, both museum curators and subjects of our system feel capability of proposed system.

In future, the project members plan to brush up these prototype system for providing more realistic and sophisticated experiences, by using novel technologies such as auto-stereoscopic display, haptic device, markerless tracking and so on. By integrating with indirect exhibit technologies, which developed as well as the other subtopics R&D, the project will realize and establish useful and practical digital museums for both museum curators and visitors.

Acknowledgement. This research is partly supported by "Mixed Realty Digital Museum" project of MEXT of Japan. The authors would like to thank all the members of our project. Especially, they received generous support from Satoshi Tarashima and Youichi Inoue, the Tokyo National Museum and Torahiko Kasai and Kunio Aoki, the Railway Museum.

References

1. Bimber, O., Encarnacao, L.M., Schmalstieg, D.: The virtual showcase as a new platform for augmented reality digital storytelling. In: Proceedings of the Workshop on Virtual Environments 2003, vol. 39, pp. 87–95 (2003)
2. Kajinami, T., Hayashi, O., Narumi, T., Tanikawa, T., Hirose, M.: Digital Display Case: Museum exhibition system to convey background information about exhibits. In: Proceedings of Virtual Systems and Multimedia (VSMM 2010), pp. 230–233 (October 2010)
3. Doyama, Y., Taniakawa, T., Tagawa, K., Hirota, K., Hirose, M.: Cagra: Occlusion-capable automultiscopic 3d display with spherical coverage. In: Proceedings of ICAT 2008, pp. 36–42 (2008)
4. Jones, A., McDowall, I., Yamada, H., Bolas, M., Debevec, P.: Rendering for an interactive 360deg light field display. In: ACM SIGGRAPH (2007)
5. Yano, S., Inoue, N., Lopez-Gulliver, R., Yoshida, S.: gcubik: A cubic autostereoscopic display for multiuser interaction - grasp and groupshare virtual images. In: ACM SIGGRAPH 2008 Poster (2008)
6. Beier, T., Neely, S.: Feature-based image metamorphosis. Computer Graphics, 262 26, 35–42 (1992)
7. Hayashi, O., Kasada, K., Narumi, T., Tanikawa, T., Hirose, M.: Digital Diorama system for museum exhibition. In: Proceeding of ISMAR 2010, pp. 231–232 (2010)
8. Seitz, S.M., Dyer, C.R.: View morphing. In: Proc. SIGGRAPH 1996, pp. 21–30 (1996)
9. Virtual Kyoto, http://www.geo.lt.ritsumei.ac.jp/webgis/ritscoe.html
10. Kyoto City Intangible Cultural Property Exhibition Room, http://www.city.kyoto.lg.jp/bunshi/page/0000110200.html
11. Kakuta, T., Oishi, T., Ikeuchi, K.: Virtual Asukakyo: Real-time Soft Shadows in Mixed Reality using Shadowing Planes. In: Digitally Archiving Cultural Objects, pp. 457–471 (2008)
12. Virtual Asukakyo, http://www.cvl.iis.u-tokyo.ac.jp/research/virtual-asukakyo/
13. Post-Visit HAYABUSA Board, http://www.xlab.sfc.keio.ac.jp/hayabusa2011/
14. Naemura, T., Kakehi, Y., Hashida, T., Seong, Y.A., Akatsuka, D., Wada, T., Nariya, T., Nakashima, T., Oshima, R., Kuno, T.: Mixed Reality Technologies for Museum Experience. In: 9th International Conference on Virtual-Reality Continuum and Its Application in Industry, VRCAI 2010 (2010)
15. Kawamura, S., Ohtani, T., Aizawa, K.: Navilog: A Museum Guide and Location Logging System Based on Image Recognition. In: Li, S., El Saddik, A., Wang, M., Mei, T., Sebe, N., Yan, S., Hong, R., Gurrin, C. (eds.) MMM 2013, Part II. LNCS, vol. 7733, pp. 505–507. Springer, Heidelberg (2013)

ArchMatrix: Knowledge Management and Visual Analytics for Archaeologists

Stefano Valtolina[1], Barbara Rita Barricelli[1],
Giovanna Bagnasco Gianni[2], and Susanna Bortolotto[3]

[1] Dept. of Computer Science, Università degli Studi di Milano, Italy
[2] Dept. of Cultural Heritage and Environment, Università degli Studi di Milano, Italy
[3] Dept. of Architectural Projects, Politecnico di Milano, Italy
{valtolin,barricelli}@di.unimi.it,
susanna.bortolotto@polimi.it, giovanna.bagnasco@unimi.it

Abstract. The visual representation of large archaeological data sets, especially those related to the subsoil and its stratigraphic units, is a very effective solution for supporting archaeologists' practice. In this paper we present ArchMatrix, a visual analytics tool for Harris Matrices' management that relies on an excavation database and allows the archaeologists to easily perform their analysis tasks by simply adopting a direct manipulation interaction style.

Keywords: Visual Analytics, Archaeology, Harris Matrix.

1 Visual Analytics in Archaeology

Current approaches to Field Archaeology are based on the concept of stratigraphic units, defined and formalized by W. Harris in 1973 [1]. The core concept of the Harris Matrix is that archaeological sites are stratified and the stratigraphic units are linked by geometric, topological and temporal relationships. Stratigraphic units are the result of natural or human action of deposition or erosion and physical relationships among stratigraphic units are necessary to detect the relative chronological sequence of the entire excavation site. However stratigraphic excavations also produce a number of supplemental data that are not included in the concept of the Harris Matrix.

The other side of an archaeological excavation is represented by an enormous amount of data that form the entire range of documentation related to stratigraphic units. For this reason such data are usually stored in the excavation archives because they represent the material evidence of the knowledge accumulated during each excavation phase and deserve the same stratigraphic approach followed in the case of stratigraphic units.

This means that a number of heterogeneous data and analyses addressed to reconstruct different semantic spheres related to the site under observation (ancient productions, environment etc.) need to be assimilated and synthesized in order to produce

S. Yamamoto (Ed.): HIMI/HCII 2013, Part III, LNCS 8018, pp. 258–266, 2013.

integrated results together with stratigraphic units. This situation involves different disciplines and the related activities of comparing and contrasting information coming from different data sources. For example, archaeologists need architectonic or chemical information to support their hypothesis, whilst environmental specialists need information on the nature and status of specific deposits. To support such a complex and interdisciplinary decision-making activity, this paper takes into account a twofold scenario: the contribution of a visual analytics approach to ongoing efforts in archaeological analysis and the affection of a visual analytics approach by aspects of human-computer interaction (HCI).

From the one hand visual analytics focuses on how human perceptual, cognitive, and collaborative abilities are related to the dynamic interactive visual representations of information on the other hand a HCI approach makes it also possible to monitor how individual cognitive and perceptual processes of domain experts involved in the same analytical activities (both innate and acquired through experience with interactive visualization) could affect the ability to share and analyze information between contributing parties through interaction with different visual representation of information.

In this framework interactive systems are meaningful tools both to explore the complexity and diversity of users' abilities and activities in technological contexts and to produce effective results in different fields of research.

Such interactive systems were applied to the complexity of the stratigraphic analysis in the study case of Tarquinia, that will be considered later on. The result of such an experience is a stratigraphic visual representation tool (ArchMatrix) able to integrate data, practices and human decision-making processes through the use of interactive strategies in order to foster individual and collaborative analysis. ArchMatrix creates the condition to support a community of interacting scientists (domain experts, HCI researchers and practitioners) focused on the same archaeological site to produce effective and successful visual interaction solutions on the perceptual, cognitive, and communicative processes in Archaeology.

The aim of ArchMatrix is to fulfil the requirements of the archaeological research in the field of historical interpretation, survey strategies and cultural heritage preservation.

1.1 Harris Matrix

In 1973, the British archaeologist E.C. Harris invented what is known today as "Harris Matrix", a visual representation of stratigraphic sequences using multi-graphs [1]. Data collected during the excavation and registered in the stratigraphic units' forms, are used by the archaeologists to represent the units and the relationships in a drawing on paper that is used in further data analysis.

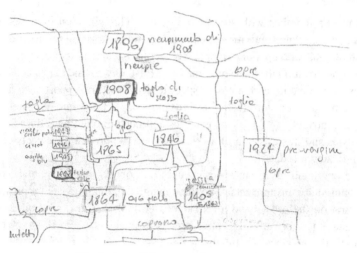

Fig. 1. A small fragment of a Harris Matrix

The resultant Harris Matrix enables the archaeologists to determine the mechanical sequence of the various units (an example is shown in Figure 1). The rectangles represent the stratigraphic units, while lines are used to indicate the existing relationships among them (e.g. "copre" means "covers", "taglia" means "cuts"). After the drawing is complete, the archaeologists can determine the relative chronology of each stratigraphic units, based on such relationships (i.e. stratigraphic units "covering" or "cutting" other units are to be considered superimposing and therefore later).

On the other hand the analysis of the mobile finds belonging to each stratigraphic unit is crucial to determine its real chronological span since mobile finds are good indicators for chronology thanks to the information issued from archaeological literature.

The following activity is the detection of the overlays, i.e. logical levels that are constituted by the stratigraphic units that belong to the same historical period. This activity is usually performed using paper documents, which number increases very fast, according to the quantity of different data sources issued from the excavation. Consequences in data management are heavy and in addition to this the more stratigraphic units are added, the more the Harris Matrix expands and any modification or extension applied to it becomes extremely complicated.

Summing up, a number of disadvantages arise when using a non-digital approach. Among them we can figure out the difficulty to up to date the Harris Matrix documents; to integrate other type of analysis (e.g. geographical, chemical, geological) within the stratigraphic representation offered by the Harris Matrix; to change the representation of the graph according to the ongoing excavation activities and archaeological studies; to allow more than one person to modify the Harris Matrix. Regards this last issue new problems arise whenever many people have access and modification permission to the same resource. Visual interactive systems represent therefore the best choice to support activities and collaboration among experts focused on the same archaeological issues.

1.2   Related Works

We analyzed several existing software tools for Harris Matrices creation. These tools provide simple graphical editors for creating stratigraphic sequences (e.g. Harris Matrix Composer[1]) or offer functions to automatically generate stratigraphic sequences starting from tables filled by users (e.g. Proleg MatrixBuilder[2]). The possibilities offered by these tools are limited, a part from devices addressed to coloring and drawing units and representing relationships through different geometric shapes. These tools do not rely on databases to recover information about the stratigraphy, and in the case they perform some storing strategies, the queries that are allowed are very simple and limited.

Moreover number and typology of relationships are restricted and there is no opportunity to assign further information to stratigraphic units. However the most important limitation is the lack of tools for analyzing data through complex query implementation such as the links among finds and strati-graphic units.

2   ArchMatrix

ArchMatrix, the visual analytics tool we designed and developed, is the result of the analysis of limits and weaknesses of existing software solutions. ArchMatrix is meant to endow archaeologists with a more complete environment able at supporting them in knowledge management and decision making. The innovation in our solution concerns:

- The definition of an interactive visualization tool for efficiently managing archaeological excavation site knowledge;
- The creation of a collaboration strategy in which different domain experts can discuss to produce new ideas and interpretations;
- The automatic updating of the Harris Matrix according to the interaction among different users and ongoing researches both in terms of visualization and storage;
- The definition of visual analytics tool able to support the collaboration activity by putting together different and heterogeneous knowledge sources mediated by a formal ontology.

ArchMatrix enables the archaeologists to represent their acquirements using a graph-based visual environment, by offering a visual representation of archaeological assets and their relationships in order to support intuitive and useful explorations (see Figure 2). With ArchMatrix, node/edge properties and sets of different relationships (covers, fills, leans, cuts, ties, is equal) can be represented by means of different set of colors and shapes.

The edges can be hidden or shown depending on the type of interaction. One of the most useful feature concerns the possibility to design sub-structures of the Harris

---

[1] http://www.harrismatrixcomposer.com
[2] http://www.proleg.com/pmatrixbuilder.htm

Matrix. This improves restricted and localized graph operations and allows selected queries related to specific units in order to increase the explicit knowledge displayed in the graph, without visualizing the Harris Matrix of the entire site. It is possible to organize the graph according to specific properties and/or relationships of the units. A value of ArchMatrix is that the users can modify units and relationships according to their ongoing researches and needs. Different cases might be figured and solved through ArchMatrix:

- a relationship can be changed from its original category (e.g. covers, fills, leans, cuts, ties) to a new one (e.g. "is equal to"); in this case the properties of the related units are updated together with the underlying database and the users are in the condition to re-organize the graph by interacting with nodes and edge in a direct way
- a previous positioning of a stratigraphic unit in the Matrix, based on the mechanical stratigraphic sequence, can shift according to the chronology recovered from the study of the mobile finds
- stratigraphic units containing particular items (for example bronze finds, geological features, etc.) can be sorted out and mapped according the specific needs of the research
- the chronology of a stratigraphic unit (for example a monument like a well) and the mobile finds discovered in it might be very different (for example because the well was sealed by such mobile finds later on and in different periods) therefore there is a strong need to drag and drop the units among different layers.

These type of re-organizations are very useful since they allow experts to visualize the graph according to the modality that better fits their practice. ArchMatrix also supports the integration among domain experts - in discussing their different points of view and ideas to expand the research horizon and to favor the creation and the management of new knowledge - by means of an annotation tool.

This is a new collaboration strategy based on a communication medium for exchanging ideas and impressions. The goal of its use is to enable different experts to make explicit and available to other stakeholders the implicit knowledge they possess. Annotation may be seen as the tool that bridges the communication gap taking place in an interdisciplinary collaboration like the one we are describing in this paper. By inserting an annotation on the graph, an expert is able to describe her/his point of view about a specific matter and to start a discussion with the other experts in order to reach, step by step, a common understanding. Eventually, a last important innovation of ArchMatrix is the possibility to integrate different knowledge sources and make them accessible by means of a visual analytics tool. Specifically, this tool allows to create on-the-fly Harris Matrix and to display related information about the excavation database, other surveys (for example chemical or geological analysis) or the territory (for example using a Geographic Information System – GIS). Making a complete and integrated survey involves the use of a common formalism for representing knowledge and data coming from involved domains. The choice of ontological formalism is driven by formal and applicative reasons.

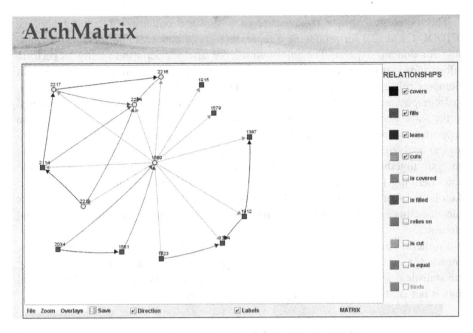

Fig. 2. Part of a Harris Matrix visualized in ArchMatrix

From a formal point of view, ontologies are used to represent knowledge by means of concepts and instances linked by relations. Specifically, our model allows to organize archeological data in a way that is more natural for archaeologists or other experts.

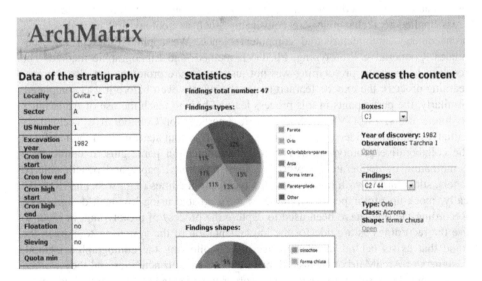

Fig. 3. Further information and statistics about a stratigraphy visualized in ArchMatrix

This ontology exploits the concept of a standard ontology of cultural heritage (CIDOC-CRM [2]) for producing a representation of concepts and relationships suitable for domain experts. The information core also supports the ability to perform information retrieval and to browse the existing knowledge taking in consideration all elements related to the excavation site under study (e.g. data concerning geology, hydrography, altimetry, toponymy or other information related to findings discovered in the same geographic area). The idea is to design an integrated framework able to support the domain experts in studying a wider set of elements during their archaeological analysis but also to collaborate together. For example archaeologists can lead analysis together with geologists who exploit their knowledge about stratigraphic units deriving from natural phenomena (i.e. landslide, flood); chemists can produce data issued from the composition of the finds or of the stratigraphic units; architects can contribute reconstructing the structure of a habitation or other architectural elements.

Furthermore, a statistical analysis module (Figure 3) allows to produce new knowledge on the artifacts (clustering them for example). Improving and integrating the statistical analysis to discover correlation between units and other archaeological data is one of the most challenging issues of our system.

3   Design Methodology and Evaluation

To design and develop ArchMatrix we applied participatory design (PD) techniques [3,4,5]. Specifically, we designed our system in the context of a real Etruscan excavation site placed in Tarquinia. According to the experience we developed in years of collaboration with Etruscologists [6,7,8], we can define the site of Tarquinia as the benchmark of an all-comprehensive investigation upon which multiple disciplinary areas applied to archaeology are converging, such as geology and natural science, archaeometry, architecture and computer science. We applied different PD techniques: Cooperative Prototyping, PICTIVE method, and Ethnographic method. The result of cooperative prototyping was not just a software prototype but also a proper learning process: the experts learned to use the system even before it was completed. Similarly, the participants in this process learned how to teach the use of ArchMatrix to future users. PICTIVE method (Plastic Interface for Collaborative Technology Initiatives through Video Exploration) [9] was carried out starting from the results of the collaborative prototyping and visual communication paradigms. It employed a combination of deliberately low-tech design tools (e.g., paper and pencil, colored labels, sticky notes) with high-tech video recording facilities (e.g., webcam). Specifically, mock-up prototypes of ArchMatrix were created using low-tech design tools. Recording facilities have been used to capture the process of prototyping, in order to use the recordings as a guide for the implementation of the system or to explain the logic that exists behind the design decisions. Following the ethnographic method, designers of ArchMatrix observed domain experts in their activities and they worked with them side by side for some weeks in order to understand their terminology, practices and the tacit knowledge applied in their context of use. The development phase was strongly supported by the activity performed during the design that involved all the stakeholders; this allowed to identify current difficulties and new innovation strategies. Moreover the PD design highlighted several communication gaps existing among the experts and the need to define a formal ontology able to mediate the communication process and the information exchange among heterogeneous data-sources. After the development of ArchMatrix, we set up a user test evaluation carried out both on the field, during the excavations in Tarquinia, and afterwards, during the study of the findings. To this aim, we involved 15 archaeologists all experts in Etruscology. Each user was required to perform a set of tasks. The tasks assigned to the users were all activities that the archaeologists need to perform in analyzing the stratigraphical units and the relationships among them and that most of the time result as time consuming. At the end of the test, a questionnaire, composed by three sets of questions has been submitted to the users. A first set was a SUS (system usability scale), a ten-item attitude Likert scale, the other was a CUSQ (computer usability satisfaction questionnaires), a nineteen-item attitude Likert scale, and the third one was a set of open-ended questions. The results of this evaluation report that ArchMatrix is a usable system and proved that the archaeologists had changed their approach to the working activities and practices. Therefore archaeologists might exploit new possibilities for visualizing the graph according to their needs, better collaborating with each other, integrating and sharing different knowledge sources, and adopting new modalities of interaction and communication

4   Conclusion

What emerges from the user test performed and from the questionnaires, is that ArchMatrix is more powerful than the other systems ever used by the archeologists. They all recognize that ArchMatrix offers more possibilities in terms of modification of a Harris Matrix and that is more helpful in their daily work practice. Moreover, the visual representation of the Matrices and the possibility of directly working on them by using a simple direct manipulation interaction style have been described as the strongest contribution to their daily practice.

In the future we figure out to test ArchMatrix in the field of Architecture since non destructive visual analysis of direct sources (stratigraphic investigations in Architecture) has already been carried out at Tarquinia. The study case of the monument called 'Porta Romanelli' shows that its material and geometric aspect provides considerable information about its historical evolution.

ArchMatrix - adequately translated and transferred from the archaeological practice to architecture - could be applied as a tool for reading monuments, ensuring a common formalism to carry out underground and aboveground research in continuity.

We expect to evaluate results in the same framework by comparing direct observa-tion and indirect sources (i.e. historic documentations, cartography, iconography and bibliography) in order to expand our research and identify new paths and opportunities.

Acknowledgment. Current researches are partially funded by the Italian Ministry of University and Research (MIUR): Mura di legno, mura di terra, mura di pietra: fortificazioni in Etruria (PRIN 2008, coord. naz. G. Bartoloni); Research Unit Mura tarquiniesi (resp. G. Bagnasco Gianni.

References

1. Harris, E.C.: Principles of Archaeological Stratigraphy. Academic Press, New York (1979)
2. Crofts, N., Doerr, M., Gill, T., Stead, S., Stiff, M.: Definition of the CIDOC Conceptual Refe-rence Model,
   http://www.cidoc-crm.org/official_release_cidoc.html
3. Blomberg, J., Giacomi, J., Mosher, A., Swenton-Hall, P.: Ethnographic field methods and their relation to design. In: Participatory Design: Principles and Practices, pp. 123–156. Lawrence Erlbaum, Hillsdale (1993)
4. Bødker, S., Grønbæk, K.: Design in action: From prototyping by demonstration to cooperative prototyping. In: Design at Work: Cooperative Design of Computer Systems, pp. 197–218. Lawrence Erlbaum, Hillsdale (1991)
5. Schuler, D., Namioka, A. (eds.): Participatory Design: Principles and Practices. Lawrence Erlbaum, Hillsdale (1993)
6. Bagnasco Gianni, G., Valtolina, S., Barricelli, B.R., Marzullo, M., Bortolotto, S., Favino, P., Garzulino, A., Simonelli, R.: An Ecosystem of Tools and Methods for Archaeological Research. In: International Conference on Virtual Systems and Multimedia (VSMM 2012), Milano, Italy, September 2-5 (2012)
7. Bagnasco Gianni, G. (ed.): Tra importazione e produzione locale: lineamenti teoretici e applicazioni pratiche per l'individuazione di modelli culturali. Il caso di Tarquinia. In Bollettino di archeologia, 1 edizione speciale, F.5.1 (2011),
   http://151.12.58.75/archeologia
8. Valtolina, S., Mussio, P., Mazzoleni, P., Franzoni, S., Bagnasco, G., Geroli, M., Ridi, C.: Media for Knowledge Creation and Dissemination: Semantic Model and Narrations for a New Accessibility to Cultural Heritage. In: Proc. of the CC 2007, Washington DC, USA, June 13-15, pp. 107–116. ACM (2007)
9. Muller, M.: PICTIVE - an exploration in participatory design. In: Proc. of CHI 1991, pp. 225–231. ACM, New York (1991)

The Designing Expressions of the Special Visual Effect Film in the Digital Technology

Tsun-Hsiung Yao[1] and Chu-Yu Sun[2]

[1] Department of Visual Design, National Kaohsiung Normal University
[2] Graduate School of Applied Design & Department of Animation and Game Design,
Shu Te University of Science and Technology
yaotsun@nknu.edu.tw

1   Introduction

From 1950 when computer technology began to undertake the creation of computer art, the creation of these "digital works" became a new tool and medium for artistic expression. This also had a major impact on visual artistic expression. This paper takes science fiction movies as the textual source of its research and analyzes the commercial messaging and artistic expression of thematic images within the cinematic arts. Science fiction movies have always emphasized the surreal and when they a place beyond our spatio-temporal realm into their form of artistic expression, it is necessary to overcome many technical difficulties before a realistic virtual scene can be built. As such, special effects movies can be said to operate using the newest products of media technology. Through researching various special effects in science fiction movies, we can understand the corresponding period's newest technologies, methods, and advances in movie production and more incisively understand "the entrance of the territory of artistic expression into the digital age."

2   Types of Movie Special Effect Technologies

Movie special effects can be broadly classified into four types: make-up, modeling, animation, and cinematography. The production process can be divided into the two stages. In the earlier stage properties are created such as models, make-up, and man-made sets. Later production includes computer animation and shooting the movie. Among these, shooting can be divided into special effects cinematography and the integrated optical technology of synthesized cinematography.

2.1   Special Make-Up

The greatest difference between modeling and make-up, is that make-up is applied to the actual performers so that they are able to perform the role of a character completely unlike their own. There are many materials which can be used in make-up, and its technical aspects must be able to change constantly in order to satisfy movie scripts. The technical consideration for make-up is that it must cause audience members to

S. Yamamoto (Ed.): HIMI/HCII 2013, Part III, LNCS 8018, pp. 267–274, 2013.

suspend their disbelief and thus must create fictional characters they can accept. Early examples of this technology is The Wizard of Ox (1939), The Exorcist (1973), and An American Werewolf in London (1981), which received an Oscar for best make-up, as well as The Planet of the Apes (1968) which used foam rubber, then a technological breakthrough. Planet of the Apes won a special Oscar to praise its contribution to film history for its makeup, and is part of the permanent collection of the United States National Film Preservation Board.

2.2   Miniature

The early movies used miniature models based on economic considerations. Nowadays movies are willing to use large amounts of capital and see realistic model effect as a necessity. The goal of these models is to provide more stimulation and room for inspiration to modern people an abundant experience of digital visual effects. The value of models lies in "creating reality" and it is not demanded the audience believe the models are real. In early cinema models were often miniatures used for filming, and there were also extremely large models made especially for close-ups. An example of this is the filming King Kong (1933), which in addition to an overall body miniature of King Kong, also utilized an extremely large model of one of King Kong's arms in which the female lead was held. The ILM Company created a whale miniature for the movie Star Trek 4: The Voyage Home (1986).

2.3   Animation

Animation can be classified into two-dimensional, three dimensional, claymation, real people and computer synthesized animation. At present the creation process for animation is already a digital endeavor and is done through "Computer Generated Imagery." In analog movies with explosion scenes, or virtual actions of nature are all places where the work of CGI can be seen. Disney and Pixar are the two animated film producers primarily involved in CGI technology. With its first time synthesis of actual people and animation which lasted 10 minutes in 1964, the classic Marry Poppins was noteworthy in the history of cinema. In 1982, Tron became the first film to use large scale computer generated animation in shooting. In 1995, Toy Story became the first three-dimensional animated movie.

2.4   Composite Photography

The steps in undertaking post production for cinematography can be divided into the first period and the later period. The duties in first period is primarily include "the photography of miniature, in-camera techniques, the stop motion shooting involved in Claymation, projection, regular shooting, and new techniques like motion control. The later stage, by contrast, involves delves into optical printing, and matte, as well as other special effect treatment. Works which notably used lots of cinematic techniques include The Invisible Man, Star Wars, which in 1977 utilized motion control which included repeated reshooting principles; this movie also displayed 30 spaceships along with paintings of space. In 1978 Superman used "blue screen synthesis" and in Alien utilized introjections not long after in 1979. The 1992 film "Honey, I Blew Up the Kinds" utilized forced perspective photography, Tim Burton used stop motion for the Claymation work "Claymation Animation."

2.5   Digital Special Effects in Films

Digital movie effects can be divided into the three areas of compositing, computer graphics, animatronics. The term animatronics is a combination of the terms "animation" and "electronics." At present, many movies are dependent on computer aided technology for their completion, and this means producers are relying more and more on computer aided digital technology in order to achieve believable visual effects. Examples of this include the giant from the 2003 movie Big Fish. In fact the actor who played the giant was already over 2 meters tall. However, digital editing was still used in post production to change his appearance, thus making him stand out as unusually large. Computer art can also utilize electronic computing technologies which "create something out of nothing" with respect to visual effects. Examples of this include the hairy monster in Monsters, Inc (2001). This creature's moving fur was created by computer one hair at a time by the creation team. Another example is the Truman Show's (1999) photomontage graphic collage effect, which was the product of a computer program and, what is more, software such as Arc Soft Photo Montage was developed and marketed based on this technology. Events of nature are also created through the application of CGI technology, as seen in a natural scene from The Day After Tomorrow in which water submerges a city. The virtual fire and liquid metal, as well as ice and other elements created via computer technologies for the Fantastic Four (2005) is an example of the applications of computer technologies in cinema which are already too numerous to count.

3   Application of Digital Technologies in Cinema

The first critical point in movie special effects being permeated by digitalization was the use of motion repeater system technologies by Paramount Pictures. The main principle behind this technology was that movement of a camera's angle could be recorded and then precisely repeated, which made equivalent scale modeling filming more possible. Later this was developed into computer motion control, which created the production effect of allowing the computer to control movie animation and modeling, which represented an epic technological breakthrough and progress. Hereafter, digitalization for cinematic special effects soon became the standard and approached red hot during the 1990 digital age. In the series of "Digital Movie Special Effects" conferences the Autodesk Company held in 2006, Andrew Lesnie, in a talk he hosted entitled "Computer Art in the Digital Age" recalled "from the fifties to the sixties, this period in time, there were many different cinematic and optical production methods which were used in the movie industry. However, in the nineties these different systems slowly became the standard and stable part of the industry, and digital art, which was in its early stages during this period, started to exert an extremely large influence on the movie industry." Lesnie, is a director of photography, which is part of special effects, and won a Best Special Effects for Lord of the Rings (2001) in 2002, and a Best Visual Effects Award from the British Academy of Film and Television Arts, as well as the 2006 Best Visual Effects Oscar for King Kong (2005). Digitalization created a technical frame work for movies and influenced the mode of movie productions. For example, the relatively new digital postproduction system Digital Intermedia can turn traditional linear color grading into non-linear color grading, and the productivity of movie production is improved while through the adoption of digitalization. In recent years there is a trend toward digitalization system research and development being adopted in the movie production process. Many new technology developments are the result of overcoming problems during shooting. Examples of this include the Lustre Color Grading. Because climatic changes at the time of filming Lord of the Rings on location in New Zealand a color difference problem arose. The Lustre system has been used in many special effect movies since the Lord of the Rings.

4   Movie Promotion under the Pursuit of Commercialism

Movie Promotion involves the visually registered image given to audiences of movies being shown; in addition, it also accurately conveys the movie's theme. For this reason, the internal and external aspects which must be considered are many during design. Internal aspects include complicated content such as the spiritual theme, aspirational purpose, narrative structure, content variety, artistic creation, and other aspects. External aspects include: the artistic style of the director, the actors' screen images, properties, costumes, sets and scenery, as well as any particular items related to that film. These are all elements which must be considered in the visual design of a movie.

4.1   Emphasis on Advantages of Movies

Many special effects movies have become box office champions, and watching them is like being present at a rich visual feast. After watching them, audiences have the feeling of having directly experienced in a fantastic visual voyage, and this is the main reason the public loves special effects movies. In cinematic history, the two movies which 11 Oscars happened to be special effects movies. For example, the poster of the movie Ben Hur "Winner of 11 Academy Awards is printed in large letters, thus noting the prizes it has obtained. By contrast, the sentence "From the director of 'Aliens,' 'T2' and 'True Lies'" appears on the poster for Titanic, thus noting the assuredly quality movies the director has undertaken, and these statements appearing on the poster pursue a commercial selling point. Special effects movies are the accomplishment of many expert production departments brought together. For this reason, the aspects and steps involved in them are broader than other types of films.

If a special effects movie is noted as the winner of many awards, its value added will increase and the public will gladly pay to see special effects movies as a result and consumers will feel they got a full return on the ticket price.

4.2   Hollywood Poster's Dominating Visual Effects

Movie posters hide a great deal of forced visual consumption, and this commercial methodology is reflected in Hollywood movies with major stars in the lead. These include the posters for War of the Worlds, Mission: Impossible. In the poster for these movies there is no mention of special effects; rather, all you can see is Tom Cruise's face, and the star's countenance becomes the only piece of information available on the poster. Burt Lancaster stated that: "The audience buys their tickets and goes into the movie theater precisely because they want to see Tom Cruise himself, and not the various characters he plays." In Hollywood's star system, there is a commercial formula in which a group of stars translate into box office success. Hollywood has most definitely classic screen characters in different generations, and these stars certainly have a great impact on the box office. Close-ups of these stars also are utilized for the advertising of movies they play command roles in.

4.3   Multi-version Poster Specifications for Sequels

Science fiction movies have made the sequel very prevalent and, in related promotional material, there is also a mode of operations which is accompanies this promotion. The period before a movie is released is a commercial golden period. Movie makers are becoming ever more generous and refined in both the quantity and quality of poster printing, as posters play an important role in advertising. Multiple versions of stills have become the method in of box office promotion for sequels in the present period. Examples of this include Transformers, which presents fine and exhilarating skills in its posters. These posters utilize computer generated effect, which have already become more advanced and well used, to add cold grey, bluish cold grey, reddish brown and other warm and cold tones. This displays tones of the same style, but with a diverse composition and visually tense effect. Pirates of the Caribbean posters utilize continuous graphic elements to present the film's theme and unique stills of every main character. In addition, there are two uniquely colored poster versions for each actor, as well as a version with all of the actors together, for visual promotional use in various large movie theaters.

4.4   Letter Figure Emblem as Logo Type for Increasing Sale of Peripheral
Commercial Items

Letters can become graphic elements in special effects movie posters, thus providing a graphic notion. On one hand this method can make the audience immediately understand the movie's theme, and on the other hand this element primarily assists in promoting peripheral commercial items extending from the film. An example of this is the Star Wars installment Return of the Jedi, which spent thirty to forty million in its production, and Willow, two movies in which 10 to 20 percent of budget was necessarily spent on visual effects. In addition, the greater benefit of blockbuster films (film rental) lies in the sale peripheral commercial item (including models, toys, and apparel), which can often earn more than the box office itself. Games based on the movie and recreational facilities such as theme parks are also items which can increase the overall profit of a top selling move. It is common to see movies utilize two or more different movie posters, with each one utilizing its own graphic logo. In addition, the script versions all integrate into the graphics. These letters become like pictures and do not perform their original function as a linguistic tool to be read, but rather become an element assisting in the visual affect of the poster. These graphic logos also completely become the face of peripheral commercial items and achieve the movies second wave commercial profit effect.

4.5   Print Promotion Material Visual System as Determined by Directing Style

George Lucas' Star Wars Series, from the 1977 Star Wars Episode IV: A New Hope to the 1980 The Empire Strikes Back, the 1983 Return of the Jedi, the 1999 Star Wars Episode I: The Phantom Menace, the 2002 Star Wars Episode II: Attack of the Clones, and the 2005 Star Wars Episode III: Revenge of the Sith show little variation in the visual style of their scenes. This is as a result of the director's core notions throughout this science fiction series, and well as the exploration of the original driving force throughout. In addition to this, the poster promotion style also evolved into a plain and easy to understand visual vocabulary for the Star Wars series.

5   Conclusion

Presently, cinematic special effects are developing ever more in the direction of digitalization, and many technical processes are already considered from the mode of digital undertakings. At present the CGI sector, which is responsible for the production of visual effects in movies and computer games, is a production structure formed as a result of technological advancements. Computer technology has also transformed production modes in the area of design. As a result, movie posters have seen a change from the early hand produced versions to the present two dimensional and three dimensional artistic works. Changes in publication media have also led naturally to variation in modes and methodologies for product promotion. With respect to "science fiction movie visuals," reasons influencing the fact that the greatest changes appeared between the present and the early period forms of promotional media can be traced two major items:

5.1   Influence of Information Effects

The twentieth century was the information age, and the advent of the internet changed manner in which all people around the world received information. The electronic media plays the role of rapid information dissemination, and people find themselves in a visual age exploding with information, and digitalization makes it easier to obtain, store, and copy images. People can obtain images from digital cameras, the internet, and smartphones, as well as other media devices quickly, conveniently, and often. This means humanity is evermore stimulated by the number of images it experiences, and its visual experiences accumulate over time as a result. The public appears less likely to be satisfied with expressions of mediocre art as time goes on. The information age phenomenon is reflected in movie posters, which resides within the scope of public culture, and this has meant more versions of these posters are produced. On one hand digitalization has made the production of graphic works faster and more economical than traditional hand drawn illustration. On the other hand, science fiction posters particularly emphasize visual effects. In order to avoid the effects involved with perceptual stimulation which is only temporary, movie makers utilize various different visual compositions in describing the same movie theme in creating promotional posters. The goal is to provide the audience with a rich and diverse visually enjoying experience.

5.2   Influence of Commercial Effect

Science fiction movies emphasize visuals, and "special effects" is necessarily a selling point for movies. It follows that, in terms of their surface, the posters for science fiction movies must move toward making the successful conveyance of "visual effects" a main consideration in their composition, and a concern of their design. Science fiction movies have, for a long time, been at the top of box offices. One impact of this fact is that posters for special effects movies must particularly pay close attention to "visual focal points" (key art) in the scenes they depict. These visual focal points also possess commercial selling points. This is the result of the influence which design considerations becoming commercialized and strategic. What is more, in the present information age a movie needs to develop a multimedia market in order to guarantee it will make large profits. Examples of this market include DVD rentals, pay per-view, and peripheral commercial products. This also provides design work with the opportunity to promote a movies from a wide variety of traditional and electronic media including posters, CD covers, DVD covers, script covers, pictures on busses, DM, newspapers, official websites, smartphones, and other items which cross various media platforms, which differ from the traditional hand drawn poster era.

References

1. Li, D.: Hollywood, Movies, and the Dream Factory. Yang Chih Publishers, Taipei (2000)
2. Wei, D.: Science Fiction Cinema: From Outerspace to Cyberspace by Geoff King and Tanya Krywinska. Shulin Publishing, Taipei (2003)
3. World Screen (August 1995)
4. Ye, J.: Intruduction to Digital Art. Artist Publishing, Taipei (2005)
5. Lester, P.M.: Visual Broadcast. Yeh Yeh Book Gallery, Taipei (2003)
6. Hershenson, B.: 100 years of the Cinema. Christie's East, New York (2000)

7. Hershenson, B.: 100 years of the Cinema. Christie's East, New York (2000)
8. Hershenson, B.: Academy Award Winners' Movie Posters (2001)
9. Hershenson, B.: Vintage Hollywood Posters I, California (1999)
10. Hershenson, B.: Warner Bros. Movie Posters at Auction (2004)
11. King, E.: A Century of Movie Posters from Silent to Art House, Barron's (2003)
12. Barton, M.D.: Hollywood Movie Posters 1914-1990. Schiffer Publishing (2003)
13. Osborne, R.: "75 Years of the Oscar", Abbeville Press.Tony Nourmand and Graham Marsh, 2003"Film Posters of the 30s the essential movies of the decade. The Overlook, New York (2003)

Part III

Collaborative Work

Lifecycle Support of Automotive Manufacturing Systems through a Next-Generation Operator Interface Implementation

Vishal Barot[1] and Robert Harrison[2]

[1] School of Electronic, Electrical and Systems Engineering,
[2] Wolfson School of Mechanical and Manufacturing Engineering
Loughborough University
Loughborough, United Kingdom
{V.Barot,r.harrison}@lboro.ac.uk

Abstract. Authors present a novel implementation approach to an operator interface system capable of supporting key phases of the automotive manufacturing machine lifecycle. Review of the lifecycle process realises next-generation requirements which have been addressed through a distributed system components architecture comprising of a Broadcaster, Marshaller and Web-HMI system. This architecture assumes machine control engineering using the Component Based (CB) design approach. Web-HMI system component, the major component serving operator interface systems, is designed using the Blackboard-based methodology, and supported with the Client-Server communication pattern as illustrated in its process runtime description. The proposed approach is assessed through an industrial case study on a web-services based control Ford-Festo test rig. A number of scenarios and demonstrations are applied to investigate the applicability of this approach beyond a theoretical research environment into practice. Importance of this research work is highlighted through identification of potential benefits offered.

Keywords: Operator Interface, HMI, System Architecture, Automotive Systems, Machine Lifecycle, Powertrain Manufacturing.

1 Introduction

The automotive industry (specifically the Powertrain manufacturing sector) is significantly affected by a number of overarching challenges driven by environmental concerns [1], global economies [2] and ICT innovations [3]. These driving factors instigate new demands for shorter machine (and associated product) lifecycles, and require efficient product customisation practices such as agile manufacturing [4]. For clarity, in the Powertrain manufacturing automation process, a product corresponds to a vehicle engine where as a machine corresponds to the production machine system used to manufacture the product.

S. Yamamoto (Ed.): HIMI/HCII 2013, Part III, LNCS 8018, pp. 277–286, 2013.
© Springer-Verlag Berlin Heidelberg 2013

The most agile components within any automation system are the human personnel involved in controlling and monitoring production machines using operator interface systems. Operator interface is defined as a user interface which enables interaction between a human (i.e. typically a machine operator, a diagnostic engineer or a maintenance engineer) and an automotive machine. In industries, this interface is usually termed as a HMI (Human Machine Interface). Section 2 summarises the challenges associated with the current process. Section 3 describes the operator interface approach taken, and its evaluation using an industrial case study is covered in the section 4, the results of which are discussed in the section 5 of this paper.

2   Challenges Associated with the Machine Lifecycle

2.1   Lifecycle Process Description

The engineering process of designing and building a production machine involves an end user, a machine builder and a controls vendor. To appreciate the extent of problems associated with the lifecycle of a production machine, specifically from the operator interface systems' perspective, a brief insight to the design and build process is essential to institute application engineering requirements for next-generation operator interface systems implementation [5, 6]. The lifecycle begins with the concept phase where an end user business needs are addressed through a set of requirements. At this point, operator interface aspect is not given any attention. Specification phase formalises the technology for the machine. Operator interface specification is defined through manual schematic of each individual screen. This process cannot begin until the machine has been roughly designed as interface screens relate specifically to a particular machine's configurations. Operator Interface screens are machine-dependent and therefore cannot be reused or reapplied to other production machines within an engine programme. Operator interface design cannot be completed until the machine control system's logic mapping information is available. The control software is engineered by experienced programmers and then associated operator interface system is added later on using copy-paste techniques. This sequential process contributes significantly to the machine development time – a critical metrics in to-days distributed competitive manufacturing environment. It is extremely essential to compress these times where possible through concurrency and reuse of designs using specialist engineering tools [7].

At the build phase, the machine is physically built and commissioned at a machine builder's site prior to its delivery to the end user premises. Currently, a machine builder cannot evaluate commission activity in a virtually simulated environment prior to the actual machine build process. Simulation can enable physical machine manufacturing to be delayed as long as possible to allow product design to mature, significantly reducing the costs and time associated with the lifecycle process. At the tryout phase, end user witness team travels to the machine builder's site for partial validation. Currently, the whole machine system cannot be validated as there are a large number of components and no tool exists to practically support runtime evaluation of every component. There is no provision of remotely monitoring and controlling machines to reduce or to avoid unnecessary costs incurred in travelling to the machine builder's site. At the commission phase the machine is shipped to, installed and tested at the end user's site. Simultaneously, the operator interface system is now implemented for the first time and operator training can now begin. It is often in the initial ramp up periods when this training occurs, generally reducing the efficiency of production machine. The end user can now produce the first car engine and any maintenance issues can then be addressed by the machine builder's engineers. This support process is usually problematic as it relies on conventional conversations and lacks remote support functionalities (i.e. three-dimensional virtual machine visualisation and emulation) [5]. Any machine reconfiguration activity driven by external factors needs additional programming efforts at the machine as well as operator interface system side due to high coupling between them.

2.2 Requirements Summary

From the above lifecycle description, table 1 summarises the existing limitations and the need to address next-generation operator interface system's implementation requirements.

3 Operator Interface Implementation Approach

3.1 Control and Monitoring System Architecture

To support the operator interface runtime requirements (summarised in the table 1), the traditional PLC/HMI architecture [8] is not sufficient. Authors have designed a novel system components architecture (shown in the figure 1) to support the lifecycle requirements of automation systems. This architecture decomposes the overall control and monitoring responsibility into three system components. It is inherently distributed into Broadcaster, Marshaller and Web-HMI. In a typical configuration, these components can be physically deployed either on a single PC, on networked computers, or within actual control devices (such as PLCs). The architecture assumes the machine control to be engineered using the CB automation approach [9]. This ensures that the CB model has global accessibility to all the three system components. These are:

- **Broadcaster:** This system component is responsible for continuously collecting status data in a timely fashion from shop-floor machines or virtual machines, processing and propagating it to a range of distributed resources, regardless of their geographical locations or their implementation mechanisms.
- **Marshaller:** This system component acts as a channel (bridge) controlling the communication between either the Web-HMI system component (which serves various operator interface client browsers) or other resources and a machine. This also manages historical transactions associated with the machine.
- **Web-HMI:** This is a web server-side system component which serves many operator interface client browsers (i.e. HMI browsers) regardless of their locality, to enable them to control and monitor production machines (real / virtual) with assistance from the Marshaller and the Broadcaster system components.

Table 1. Requirements

Implementation Requirement	Major Benefit(s)
Faster machine design / build / ramp-up, or rapid machine reconfiguration.	New products will be introduced rapidly. This will save the time and costs associated with duplication of efforts.
Increase information transparency and mobility across heterogeneous systems.	Information sharing will shorten the product lifecycles, encourage innovations, and will ease the maintenance process through lessons learned. This will also establish relationships between supply-chain partners, improving business collaboration and support.
Remote real-time collection, dissemination and analysis of production data regardless of underlying machine or control platform.	This will prevent end users from being locked into costly and complex proprietary solutions, and improve overall system productivity. Any reliance on experienced or skilled personal will be unnecessary.
Virtually evaluate machine commissioning prior to its build.	This will verify the machine control logic (i.e. its behaviour) prior to the physical machine manufacturing. It will also enable the product design to mature, saving costs and time associated with frequent machine reconfigurations to match the updated product design.
Verification of operator interface systems early in the lifecycle.	Machines will be rapidly designed and ramped up to full production capacity.
Training machine operators before the actual commission.	Production will begin immediately as soon as the machine has been installed and commissioned at the end user's manufacturing plant. This will also enable firms to use human resources efficiently.

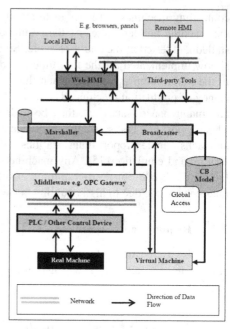

Fig. 1. System Architecture

These three system components have been architecturally designed and described using the Blackboard-based methodology [10]. The design of the Broadcaster and the Marshaller system components is outside the scope of this article; however, interested readers are encouraged to refer to these publications [5] for their detailed explanations. A detailed description of the Web-HMI system component (serving operator interfaces) is discussed next.

3.2 Operator Interface Design and Development

In this research, operator interface systems are supported using the Web-HMI system component implementation. For the operator interfaces to be industrially accepted (i.e. providing the familiar "look and feel" experience to operators accustomed to traditional vendor-specific HMI systems), a set of display standards and accepted practices have been followed [5]. Since this research is driven by industrial requirements, authors have adopted useful principles from a set of design guidelines (presented as standard) directly from the Powertrain manufacturing domain. Consequently, various features from the Siemens Transline standard are utilised for describing the operator interface screen structure, navigational routes, colour schemes, display conventions and standard controls for a production machine. In addition, some operational requirements have been captured through use case descriptions whereas others have been obtained using numerous end user / machine builder interviews, demonstrations, meetings, site visits and available literature. Specifically, the low level interaction requirements have been described through use case diagrams based on standard UML notations, and interface navigational structure is specified using the storyboarding technique. The methodology used to engineer this Web-HMI component is Blackboard-based approach where a set of resources (i.e. knowledge sources) share a common global database (i.e. a blackboard divided into panels) and the access to this shared resource is managed by a control shell. The resulting descriptive model (simplified version shown in the figure 2) can be used to validate that the system has correct data interaction and processing mechanism to support the aforementioned requirements.

As shown in the figure 2, for performance optimization reasons, the blackboard structure of the Web-HMI is divided into three different panels. Monitoring panel is responsible for handling all the tasks associated with machine monitoring by subscribing to the live feeds published through the Broadcaster system. Internally this panel consists of 3 hierarchical levels to support this operation. View panel is responsible for supporting the three-dimensional representation of a machine using VRML model integration, and processing any requests associated with displaying historical machine transactions on operator interface screens. Internally this panel consists of 2 hierarchical levels to support these operations. Control panel plays an important role by managing the access of all the operator interface clients (local as well as remote ones). It administers any conflicts that may arise when a particular operator interface client expresses interest to the Marshaller for controlling and querying an automotive machine (real, simulated or hybrid). This functionality is implemented with a view of providing the necessary level of safety and security within the system components architecture. Internally this panel consists of 3 hierarchical levels to support these operations. To enable machine data transmission within and between panels, and with external sources, a set of dedicated knowledge sources have been designed. Every knowledge source is specialised to contribute knowledge for a specific task. For example, one knowledge source known as "KS2" can carry out necessary processing of events by interpreting and extracting essential real-time machine information from the CB model configurations propagated through the Broadcaster system component at runtime. The controller of this blackboard model operates using event-invocation scheduling to manage contributions of knowledge sources to their respective blackboard panels as well as externally. The model illustrated in the figure 2 is developed into a workable system component using object-oriented techniques. Since the Web-HMI system component supports various distributed operator interface client browsers for control and monitoring purposes, the knowledge sources communicate with these blackboard panels using the Client-Server architectural pattern [11], enabling anytime, anywhere accessibility to operator interfaces at real-time.

Figure 3 illustrates the Web-HMI's process runtime implementation from this Client-Server pattern's perspective. Internally, the Web-HMI has been organized using the MVC (Model View Controller) pattern, and data transmission security has been implemented using the HTTPS (Hypertext Transfer Protocol Secure) and a layered architecture [12]. Initially, an operator interface client browser requests a required webpage (i.e. operator interface screen) from the server using a URL. A TCP/IP socket connection from the Web-HMI caller sockets to the Broadcaster is established (if it is not already initiated) to receive a CB model and current state of a machine. Upon their receipt, the component logic updates the required html page (represented as a reconfigurable template) by populating it with the CB model description and current status of the machine. Furthermore, any necessary navigational information is provided by this logic and the requested html page is returned to the operator interface client browser.

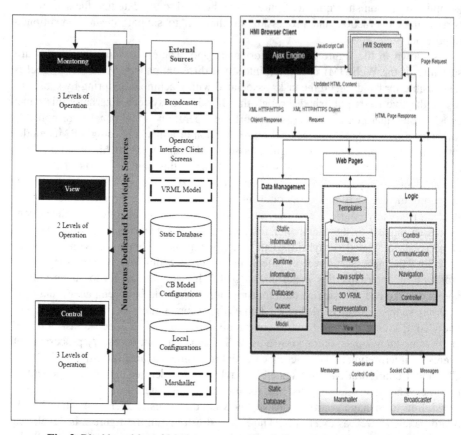

Fig. 2. Blackboard-based Model   **Fig. 3.** Process Runtime Implementation

To avoid the traditional client – server communication issues where a client waits for response from a server after every task, an AJAX (Asynchronous JavaScript and XML) technique is implemented within this system component to improve performance, interactivity of the overall application and provide real-time machine information. Any update request from the operator interface client browser takes the form of a JavaScript call to an AJAX engine (written in JavaScript and tucked away as a hidden frame) instead of a standard HTTP / HTTPs call. This AJAX engine renders the operator interface screens and communicates asynchronously with the server in the client's behalf. If the engine requires any updates from the server to refresh certain HTML content on the browser (for example, retrieving real-time status information such as a machine component state change), the engine makes asynchronous XML HTTP/HTTPS based object calls to the server without stalling operator's interaction with the operator interface browser screen. This technique provides responsive interface experience to operators whilst updating various contents on the screens. Depending on the request, the Web-HMI logic responds to the XML object request, which becomes the updated HTML content of the operator interface client browser screen. In this way, various operator interface screens and their contents can be requested without experiencing any visual interruptions. When the operator interface client browser aims to obtain control of a machine, a request token (represented as an XML object) is propagated to the server where the logic control permits or denies passing the machine control to the client browser that generated the object in the first place. If machine control is permitted, a bi-directional communication channel is established from the operator interface client browser to the Marshaller (via the server component) to enable message transmissions. Any updates that do not require requesting a complete webpage is handled by the AJAX engine. The overall look and feel of the operator interface screens is consistent throughout, thanks to a template-based implementation. The template has editable regions that map to various configurations using the Web-HMI system component's logic at runtime. This provides a consistent set of screens that are reconfigurable and updatable on-the-fly.

4 Industrial Case Study Evaluation

4.1 Assessment Approach

A Ford-Festo test rig has been setup for investigating the proposed research approach. The control modules within this rig have been engineered using the CB approach, and enabled with a web-services based control interface. These interfaces support machine data distribution using a PC-based service orchestration engine. Authors have used relevant scenarios and / or demonstrations to assess the functional properties of the system. Specifically, the following requirements been evaluated:

Reconfigurability and Reuse Support: Operator interface screens must be able to cater for any dynamic changes exercised on the machine modules (i.e. mechanical as well as control ones) when facilitating new requirements. Two major enablers supporting this requirement are; template-based screens (that get populated with latest machine configurations at runtime) and the Broadcaster system which propagates these configurations to Web-HMI at runtime. Any change to a machine is captured in the CB model (i.e. machine configurations) and its dynamic propagation supports this requirement. A scenario corresponding to a process workflow change in an assembly line is applied to the test rig where a three-station rig is replaced with a four-station rig, and operator interface screens are successfully updated to reflect these new configurations through a simple screen refreshing process without any additional programming efforts.

Information Transparency and Mobility: The system architecture must provide a "plug-and-play" integration framework, legacy system support and operate using open standards. Two major enablers supporting these requirements are; the distributed system components architecture operating using standard TCP/IP interfaces and the Broadcaster's ability to propagate machine data using uniform XML format that can be decoded by any third-party system. A demonstration with GmBH's SAP xMII (Manufacturing Integration and Intelligence) tool for shop-floor activity monitoring and fault diagnosis [13] has been undertaken under the SOCRADES project [14]. This application interacts with the test rig using the service orchestration engine (through the Broadcaster's TCP/IP link). Since the orchestrator has a state publication utility and a service invocator, the SAP tool can subscribe to the required machine component's status and invoke operations on the FTB devices successfully. In this way, businesses can have a global view of the entire shop-floor manufacturing process. Similarly, any third-party operator interface system can be plugged-in into the system architecture to monitor machine status through its lifecycle.

Real-Time Remote Control, Monitoring and Maintenance: The web-based operator interfaces must be able to remotely support lifecycle requirements. Three major enablers supporting these requirements are; the web-based technology itself provides any-time, anywhere connectivity, the distributed system components architecture enabling machine configurations to be shared at real-time, and a three-dimensional VRML machine simulation model integrated within the Web-HMI providing visualisation capabilities. Two scenario cases have been setup, the first one aims to investigate remote control and monitoring whereas the second one investigates remote maintenance. For remote monitoring functionality, operator interface client browser is used to supply a set of operational commands to control and monitor the rig at real-time. This functionality is useful especially during the tryout phase of a machine lifecycle as it will reduce travel costs and time. For remote maintenance, two different types of machine faults are introduced in the rig such as; jamming parts and raising sensor's pairs check. Operator interface system can successfully highlight the location of faults and provide clear instructions to troubleshoot issues.

Virtual Machine Evaluation: Operator interfaces must be able to support validation activity of a machine prior to its build to avoid unnecessary costs and time delays later during its lifecycle. Three major enablers supporting these requirements are; the integration of VRML machine model functionality for visualisation, sharing of CB configurations using the system architecture and the ability of operator interfaces to drive both real as well as virtual machines. To verify this, a scenario is setup where some clashes in machine components are introduced at design time. The rig's VRML model is operated using the operator interfaces and successfully inspected for any clashes during its design to avoid any potential issues when physically building it.

Early Operator Interface Verification and Operator Training: While machine needs early validation, the accompanying operator interfaces need to be verified to highlight any operational inconsistencies at the HMI side. Moreover, operators need to be trained before the machine has been commissioned to avoid unnecessary time delays.

Three major enablers supporting these requirements are; the integration of VRML machine model functionality for visualisation, sharing of CB configurations using the system architecture and the ability of operator interfaces to drive both real as well as virtual machines. A scenario has been setup where operator interfaces' consistency and operation is evaluated using a two-step process. In the first step, the rig is operated using default set of components (having unique configurations). The operator interface screens are populated dynamically with these component configurations at runtime. In the second step, an additional machine component is introduced and existing component configurations are modified. These amendments are successfully reflected on the operator interface systems' screens at runtime. Availability of a dynamically updatable operator interface system (that works with a real, virtual or a hybrid machine) successfully supports operator training earlier within the lifecycle.

5   Conclusion

The operator interface implementation approach (coupled with the system components architecture) provides the required level of design, production and maintenance support at various key phases of an automotive machine lifecycle. Adopting the CB approach to Powertrain engineering enables machine configurations (i.e. CB models encoded in a uniform XML format) to be accessible within the system components architecture prior to the actual machine build process. With the help of the Broadcaster system, these configurations can be propagated to local as well as remote clients, including the operator interface systems. Web-HMI system can decode these configurations, populate their dynamic templates, churn out new screens with added functionalities, and thus provides a fully-operational operator interface system at runtime. This is a step towards a vendor-independent ("open") support framework that collectively utilises state-of-the-art in scientific and technical disciplines to address the identified industrial requirements. In a bigger context, this work is anticipated to be beneficial, specifically; it will improvise the production machine design and its development process, provide new ways of supporting automotive machines, and establish stronger relationships between involved supply-chain partners, enabling different classes of people to efficiently interact with automotive machines using operator interface systems. The use of an industrial case study in this paper is used to assess the applicability of the implementation approach beyond a theoretical research environment into practice. However, this approach has been exercised on a small number of case studies, one of which is given by example herein. More thorough investigation of this work against shop-floor production machines' lifecycle is needed to generate new knowledge and complete the migration path to a next-generation operator interface system implementation in industries.

Acknowledgements. The authors would like to acknowledge the support of the EPSRC, IMCRC, BDA and SOCRADES research projects in collaboration with Ford Motor Company, and other industrial partners. In addition, the financial support obtained from the T-Area-SoS FP7 support action is greatly appreciated.

References

[1]   Sutherland, J., Gunter, K., Allen, D., Bauer, D., et al.: A global perspective on the environmental challenges facing the automotive industry: state-of-the-art and directions for the future. International Journal of Vehicle Design 34(2), 86–110 (2004)

[2]   Barot, V., McLeod, C.S., Harrison, R., West, A.A.: Efficient real-time remote data propagation mechanism for a Component-Based approach to distributed manufacturing. International Journal of Aerospace and Mechanical Engineering 4(3), 118–123 (2010)

[3]   Castelli, C., Florio, M., Giunta, A.: The competitive repositioning of automotive firms in Turin: innovation, internationalisation and the role of ICT. Departemental Working Papers (2008)

[4]   Elkins, D.A., Huang, N., Alden, J.M.: Agile manufacturing systems in the automotive industry. International Journal of Production Economics 91(3), 201–214 (2004)

[5]   Barot, V.: Operator Interfaces for the Lifecycle Support of Component Based Automation Systems. PhD Thesis, Loughborough Univesity (2012)

[6]   Haq, I., Monfared, R., Harrison, R., Lee, L., West, A.: A new vision for the automation systems engineering for automotive powertrain assembly. International Journal of Computer Integrated Manufacturing 23(4), 308–324 (2010)

[7]   Interview, Ford Motor Company Control Engineers, Operators and ICT team, Dunton, Essex (2008-2010)

[8]   Da'na, S., Sagahyroon, A., Elrayes, A., Al-Ali, A.R., Al-Aydi, R.: Development of a monitoring and control platform for PLC-based applications. Computer Standards & Interfaces 30(3), 157–166 (2008)

[9]   Harrison, R., Colombo, A.W., West, A.A., Lee, S.M.: Reconfigurable modular automation systems for automotive power-train manufacture. International Journal of Flexible Manufacturing Systems 18(3), 175–190 (2006)

[10] Craig, I.D.: Blackboard systems. Artificial Intelligence Review 2(2), 103–118 (1988)

[11] Al-Ameed, H.: Architecture of reliable Web applications software. Idea Group Publishing, London (2007)

[12] Sommerville, I.: Software Engineering, 9th edn. Addison-Wesley Publishing Company, Reading (2011)

[13] SAP. Sap Manufacturing Integration and Intelligence. (June 20, 2012),
      http://www.sap.com/solutions/manufacturing/
      manufacturing-intelligence-software/index.epx

[14] SOCRADES. Service-Oriented Cross-layer infRAstructure for Distributed smart Embedded devices 2009 (July 15, 2012), http://www.socrades.eu/Documents/
      objects/file1224780946.72

CoPI: A Web-Based Collaborative Planning Interface Platform

Mohammad K. Hadhrawi[1], Mariam Nouh[1], Anas Alfaris[1,2], and Abel Sanchez[2]

[1] Center for Complex Engineering Systems (CCES),
King Abdulaziz City for Science and Technology (KACST), Riyadh, Saudi Arabia,
{m.hadhrawi, m.nouh}@cces-kacst-mit.org
[2] Massachusetts Institute of Technology (MIT), Cambridge, MA, USA
{anas, doval}@mit.edu

Abstract. In this paper we present the Collaborative Planning Interface (CoPI), a web-based multiuser collaboration interface platform for planning of complex systems. The interface provides analytical and visualization components to support decision makers. The Interface is designed using a user-centered design approach, while considering existing tools and environments in the field of decision support systems. The architecture and structure of the Interface are described as well as the flow of the user experience within the system. Finally, a case study explains the use of CoPI in collaborative policy planning for large-scale infrastructures.

Keywords: complex systems, web-technologies, collaboration, multi-user, decision support systems, visualization, HCI.

1 Introduction

The increase in the world's population has led to the increase in the demand of manmade complex systems such as transportation, water and energy systems. In planning such systems many stakeholders need to be involved. However, while each stakeholder improves their particular system, other systems could be affected negatively [2], [7]. Therefore, a collaborative planning approach is required.

Understanding the different stakeholders and their collaboration and activities during the process of making decisions is an essential element toward designing a tool that assists them in making better informed decisions. Current Decision Support Systems (DSS) used by stakeholders provide some analytical modeling or visualization capabilities. However, these DSSs do not provide mechanisms for collaborative decision making. From our user research sessions, a need for a collaborative planning tool was evident.

In this paper we will present the Collaborative Planning Interface (CoPI), a web-based platform that supports multi-user collaborative planning for complex systems. CoPI is intended as a front-end for DSSs providing capabilities for decision management and visualization. The paper is divided into five major sections. Section 1, presents existing DSS systems. Section 2, describes User-Centered Design methods

S. Yamamoto (Ed.): HIMI/HCII 2013, Part III, LNCS 8018, pp. 287–296, 2013.
© Springer-Verlag Berlin Heidelberg 2013

used in designing the platform. Section 3, describes the CoPI Architecture. Section 4, discusses the user experience of the proposed Interface. Section 5, presents a case study of implementing CoPI within the Sustainable Infrastructure Planning System (SIPS).

2   Background

Different tools have been developed to support decision makers in making better-informed decisions within different domains [1], [3], [4], [6], [9]. Some Decision Support Systems (DSS) are Geographical Information Systems (GIS) based [5]. These systems are used to assist decision makers in making spatial planning decisions. They couple the spatial view with different analytical modeling techniques and tools. For example, an integrated simulation environment decision support system was developed, and used to analyze critical infrastructure [6]. The tool is used to assist decision makers in analyzing the impact of disaster propagation on national infra-structures. The amount of information involved in such activity is overwhelming and requires a huge amount of human cognitive capabilities to analyze [6], [7]. Another tool [3] was developed by integrating a GIS with Multiple Criteria Decision Analysis (MCDA) to support land management decisions. Here, the increase of the importance of land and natural resources management derived the demand for such system.

Based on what has been discussed in the previous paragraph, several of these Decision Support Systems do not support multiuser collaboration. In addition, in many of these systems the Interface is either fairly basic or designed for a specific problem or hardcoded within the DSS. This does not provide for reusability of such Interfaces within other DSSs and domains.

Given the use of decision support systems in planning complex systems [6], [10], and the different needs in visualizing, accessing and interacting with the DSS, we designed CoPI to be an interface platform to support different user needs that could be applied to different domains (Fig. 1). In designing the CoPI, we conducted a user research study of the potential users of the platform. The next section discusses briefly the different UCD methods applied in the design, based on best practices in the field [8].

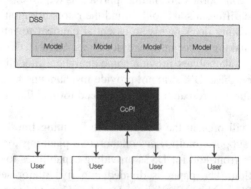

Fig. 1. The collaborative Planning Interface (CoPI) supports multiple users

3   User-Centered Design

To design an interface that supports the collaboration between different stakeholders who make planning decisions, we need to understand their process of making decisions and the tools they use to support their decision process and analysis. To collect this information, we used different User-Centered Design methods during the discovery and design phases. In the discovery phase, we observed the environment in which the stakeholders would likely use the system. We organized a set of semi-structured interviews, which were targeted towards analysts and policy makers within several governmental agencies. During our interaction with the stakeholders, the following sequence of activities was identified. The process starts by an analyst analyzing a specific case and proposing a set of solution scenarios. Each scenario is then evaluated on the basis of predefined indicators. During the analysis, Geographical Information Systems (GIS) or other specialized mathematical models are used. The set of scenarios is then reviewed and new solutions are proposed. This process is repeated until a subset of scenarios is reached whose indicators satisfy a minimum threshold. The list of scenarios is then presented and discussed with decision and policy makers for recommendations and final evaluation (Fig. 2). A popular framework that maps well to the decision analysis process is the Pressure-State-Response (PSR) framework. In the PSR framework, general drivers such as GDP and population are considered as pressures that affect the current state of a system, which is represented by a set of indicators. The response is then carried out to move the existing system into a newer state with a different set of indicator values.

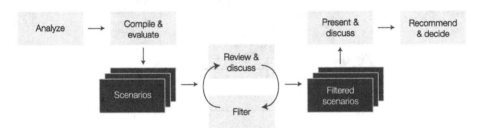

Fig. 2. Sequence of activities during a decision making process

Synthesizing all the results from the observation and user research, we designed the Collaborative Planning Interface to satisfy the expected user needs. It was determined that CoPI will be web-based to allow multiple users to collaborate remotely as well as provide high computation performance within a unified framework. CoPI should enable users to manage their cases and scenarios. To support the analysis and exploration of scenarios, CoPI will provide visualization of outputs that could be spatially and numerically presented. During the design phase of CoPI, we went through multiple iterations of the interface design and collected general feedback from non-domain field experts. The next section describes the architecture and the structure of CoPI in more detail.

4   Collaborative Planning Interface (CoPI) Architecture

The CoPI architecture is focused on the client side. The server side would include the DSS Engine, which consists of the computational server, data warehouse, and mathematical models (Fig. 3). The computational server contains the brain (logic) of the platform. It hosts the models that receive different inputs from users to evaluate. The data that feeds these models resides within the data warehouse. The communication between the client and the server is done through the exchange of messages (AJAX, JSON and XML format). The server receives inputs from the client to evaluate those inputs (decisions/scenarios) and then sends back the results to the client. Later, the client visualizes the outputs for the end users to analyze the results.

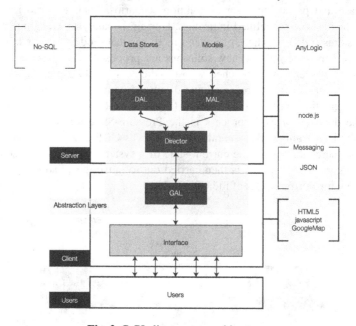

Fig. 3. CoPI client-server architecture

CoPI includes a web interface and visualization elements. The web interface is the portal for the users to interact with the system, simulate their decisions, and interact with other users. The users decisions are encapsulated within a scenario that a user would like to analyze. Charts and outputs representations are part of the visualization on the client side, which uses Data-Driven Document (d3) javascript library.

CoPI is constructed using the model-view-controller architecture. The view holds the html and css files. The controller, is a javascript file that controls the interaction within the CoPI, and the communication with the server side. The model holds the user scenarios before submitting them to the server. In the next section, the components and structure of CoPI are explained.

4.1   CoPI Components

CoPI is divided into six main components (Fig. 4). These components are: the registration system, style components, simulation configuration, real-time communication, Google maps, and visual analytics. The breakdown of CoPI into these components is to simplify the development process and to allow CoPI to be scalable for future features implementation. Each of the components is described in more detail below.

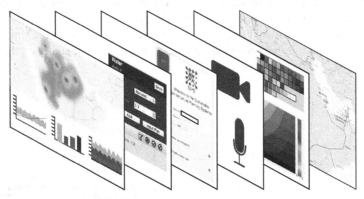

Fig. 4. CoPI Components

Registration System. All the user administration information, such as usernames, passwords, etc. is kept in the same component. Cookies management for multi-user collaboration is also kept within this component.

Style Components. To support different user preferences, we created this component to control the theme. This includes font types, background colors and sizes to be customized by the user.

Simulation Configuration. Generic simulation configuration and scenario setups are kept within this component. Such information includes the simulation time and scale, as well as the categories to be used in each case.

Real-Time Communication. This component is included to support users discussion and negotiation through audio and video channels. For that, we are utilizing WebRTC to include in our development.

Google Maps. The component controls the base map component. It has the country map, regions, and future areas that might be required. In addition, it holds the properties and methods to control the map.

Visual Analytics. This layer holds the visualization elements. Dynamic heat maps and choropleth map visualization are part of map overlays. Plots and charts, such as line, area and scatter plots, are used alongside with the other visualization components, but not as an overly.

4.2   CoPI Interface Structure

At the top level of the content structure of the interface is a case. A case acts as a folder that contains a set of simulation files known as scenarios (Fig. 5). After a case is created, the user creates one or more scenarios to simulate the impact of different decisions on that particular case. Each scenario consists of a set of decision variables (DVs), or inputs; and a set of Key Performance Indicators (KPIs), or outputs. A Decision Variable, is a set of attributes that users can control. Attributes are the smallest element in a DV, which allows the user to modify the values of that decision variable. Those attributes are modifiable before the simulation is started. After the simulation is executed, the outputs are visualized using charts and graphs or spatially on the map or even temporally using a timeline.

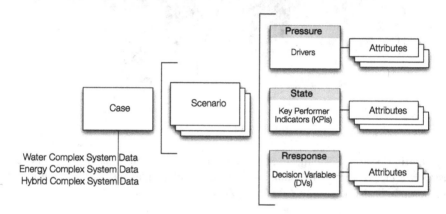

Fig. 5. CoPI interface structure

5   Platform Experience

The user starts interacting with the system by providing their credentials for authentication purposes. After identifying the user's role and authority, the user is granted access to setup, organize and manage cases. Then, the user interacts with the cases by creating scenarios. Finally, a report could be generated by the user(s) to share results and recommendations. This experience is mapped into four main screens/pages (Fig. 6). These are: the login screen, main screen, simulation screen, and reporting screen.

The login screen is the entry point to the platform. Users must be authenticated before they login to the system. The main screen is the first page users see after they

Fig. 6. CoPI overall experience mapped to number of screens

logon to the system. It includes all the cases a user created, or modified, list of shared cases as well as invitations from other users to collaborate on a case. On this screen, the user has the option to create a new case, or modify an existing one.

When a user creates a new case, they have to set it up with the initial configuration. Initial configurations include: the data for the system under study, period of the simulation and the involved users. Infrastructures data (decision variables and KPIs) are stored in the server. The period of simulation is determined to allocate memory space in the server. The user could chose to simulate certain inputs in years, days or hours. Furthermore, users choose the scale of their simulation. They could choose between national scale, regional or city scales.

After users create a new case, or after they select an existing case and modify it, they are directed to the simulation screen. In the simulation screen, users select decision variables, interact with the outputted KPIs, and observe and analyze the visualized results. This screen has four main components: inputs, outputs, temporal and spatial components. The inputs components consist of decision variables and drivers. Users can add as many DVs as required to compose a scenario. DVs are modifiable once they are added to the created scenario container. The outputs component is the list of KPIs that users can select to visualize. These KPIs are visualized after the simulation is run to assist the users in their analysis and decision making. When users specify duration for their created cases, a time slider will appear after the evaluation/simulation is completed. This slider represents the temporal dimension. Users can observe the outputs for every time step that has been simulated.

Finally, the spatial component, which is another visualization element on the screen, shows the map of the selected region of interest. The displayed map is based on the scale that the user has selected when they configured the case. It could show the specified region or the whole country. When there is data associated with geographical locations, this data is visualized on the map as well.

After a desirable scenario (or set of scenarios) is reached, the user has the option to produce a report. On the reporting screen, the user could generate a report form a specific scenario, or all the scenarios within a case. In either case, all the added decision variables, list of KPIs, are displayed. In addition, the user could add snapshots of the different visualization elements on the screen, as well as annotate those images. The users could also write their own recommendations and then export the report into a PDF document for printing. An additional feature is to share that report with other users and decision makers.

6   SIPS: A Case Study

CoPI was implemented for the Sustainable Infrastructure Planning System (SIPS), a decision support system which is currently developed as an integrated modeling framework to assist stakeholders in making informed policy decisions about infrastructure systems planning. At this stage, SIPS is looking at the water Infrastructure in Saudi Arabia.

In this project, CoPI is loaded with water infrastructure data to populate the decision variables and KPIs sections. The variables included are related to demand and supply elements within the system. The KPIs are focused on technical, economic, social and environmental indicators.

The decision variables for example include water plants related data. This group of data describes the physical plants of the infrastructures such as geospatial locations, capacity, status and the types of water it uses. Each plant component has the following variables. Plant latitude and longitude to identify the region of which the plant is located. Plant status, indicates whether it is online or offline. Plant capacity is the amount of water it holds per day, which ranges from 50 m3/day to 880,000 m3/day. Plants types differentiate between solely desalination plants and power/desalination plants. Water sources, define the type of water inputted to the plant. Currently, there are five types of water sources: seawater, brackish/inland water, pure water, river water, and waste water.

The KPIs include economic data such as costs and financial information related to plants. The KPIs could also include environmental data such as the environmental impact on the region or the nation. For example, CO_2 emissions are included to visualize the relation between plants production and capacity and their environmental impact. Users collaborate to generate different scenarios to assess how their current decisions on different inputs impact the future state of the kingdom. In addition, they would indicate policies that should be implemented and decisions/policies that could be modified.

A possible scenario could happen when two or more users such as the ministry of water and electricity (MoWE) and the Saudi Water Company (SWC) want to collaborate to decide whether or not to change water tariff for residential and commercial sectors. An analyst from SWC (user-1) creates a case with a blank scenario after logging on to the SIPS CoPI. The CoPI is loaded with DVs and KPIs. User-1 initiated the case to study the problem on the national scale and for a 30 years span, between 2015 to 2045. The analyst invites two other stakeholders from within his/her organization, and three other stakeholders from the MoWE.

Once everyone is logged onto the system viewing the shared scenario, a shared simulation screen is loaded. User-1 loads his/her decision variables container with the water tariff decision variable for each region, as well as population and GDP. At the same time, a set of KPIs is loaded on charts. The set includes change in demand and normal fractional change per capita. GDP is also included in the output for visualization.

The stakeholders analyze the change in the outputs (Fig. 7), and discuss whether that change is applicable or not. The stakeholders go through multiple scenarios before they achieve a desired result. Finally, User-1 generates a report from the scenarios including everyone's recommendations.

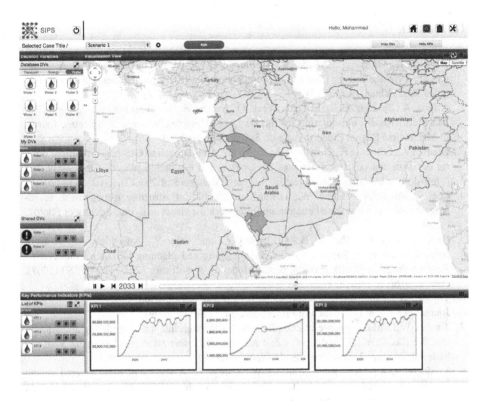

Fig. 7. CoPI prototype in the SIPS project

7   Conclusion

In this paper, we demonstrated the capabilities of the Collaborative Planning Interface (CoPI) platform. With CoPI, a simplified experience for decision management and multi-user collaboration is provided. CoPI assists decision makers in making better informed decisions by dynamically visualizing users' inputs analytically, spatially and temporally. The simple architecture and structure of the platform makes it scalable for the planning of multiple complex systems. As it has been discussed, a current DSS for sustainable infrastructure planning (SIPS) is being developed and utilizes CoPI for multi-user collaboration. We demonstrated how stakeholders utilize the platform for cross planning a sustainable physical infrastructure in Saudi Arabia.

Acknowledgement. The authors want to thank King Abdulaziz City for Science and Technology (KACST) for funding this project. In addition, we want to thank the Center for Complex Engineering Systems (CCES) at KACST and MIT for their support, especially Olivier de Weck, Adnan Alsaati and John Williams.

References

1. Adepetu, A., Grogan, P., Alfaris, A., Svetinovic, D., de Weck, O.: City.Net IES: A Sustainability-Oriented Energy Decision Support System. In: IEEE International Systems Conference 2012, Vancouver (2012)
2. Alfaris, A., Siddiqi, A., Rizk, C., de Weck, O., Svetinovic, D.: Hierarchical Decomposition and Multi-Domain Formulation for the Design of Complex Sustainable Systems. Journal of Mechanical Design (Special issue on Sustainability) (2010)
3. Greene, R., Luther, J.E., Devillers, R., Eddy, B.: An approach to GIS-based multiple criteria decision analysis that integrates exploration and evaluation phases: Case study in a forest-dominated landscape. Forest Ecology and Management 260(12), 2102–2114 (2010)
4. Lee, S., Murty, A., Tolone, W.: Towards sustainable infrastructure management: knowledge-based service-oriented computing framework for visual analytics. Society of Photo-. . . (2009)
5. Rao, M., Fan, G., Thomas, J., Cherian, G., Chudiwale, V., Awawdeh, M.: A web-based GIS Decision Support System for managing and planning USDA's Conservation Reserve Program (CRP). Environmental Modeling & Software 22(9), 1270–1280 (2007), doi:10.1016/j.envsoft.2006.08.003
6. Tolone, W.J.: Interactive visualizations for critical infrastructure analysis. International Journal of Critical Infrastructure Protection 2(3), 124–134 (2009)
7. Tolone, W.J.: Making sense of complex systems through integrated modeling and simulation. In: Ras, Z.W., Ribarsky, W. (eds.) Advances in Information and Intelligent Systems. SCI, vol. 251, pp. 21–40. Springer, Heidelberg (2009)
8. Vredenburg, K., Mao, J.-Y., Smith, P.W., Carey, T.: A survey of user-centered design practice. Presented at the CHI 2002: Proceedings of the SIGCHI Conference on Human Factors in Computing Systems. ACM (2002)
9. Wang, X., Dou, W., Chen, S.-E., Ribarsky, W., Chang, R.: An Interactive Visual Analytics System for Bridge Management. Computer Graphics Forum 29(3), 1033–1042 (2010), doi:10.1111/j.1467-8659.2009.01708.x
10. Zeng, Y., Cai, Y., Jia, P., Jee, H.: Development of a web-based decision support system for supporting integrated water resources management in Daegu city, South Korea. Expert Systems with Applications 39(11), 10091–10102 (2012), doi:10.1016/j.eswa.2012.02.065

Estimation of Interruptibility during Office Work Based on PC Activity and Conversation

Satoshi Hashimoto, Takahiro Tanaka, Kazuaki Aoki, and Kinya Fujita[*]

Graduate School, Tokyo University of Agriculture and Technology
2-24-16 Nakacho, Koganei, Tokyo 184-8588, Japan
{takat,kazuak,kfujita}@cc.tuat.ac.jp

Abstract. The chances of being interrupted by online communication systems, such as email, instant messenger, and micro-blog, are rapidly increasing. For the adequate control of interruption timing, the real-time estimation of the interruptibility of the user is required. In this study, we propose an interruptibility estimation method using PC activity and conversational voice detection based on the wavelet transform. The offline estimation was applied to a dataset of 50 hours obtained from 10 users. The results indicated the feasibility of improving the interruptibility estimation accuracy by the automatic detection of the existence and end of conversations.

Keywords: interruptibility, availability, voice detection, office work, interruption.

1   Introduction

A wide variety of online communication systems, such as email, instant messenger, and micro-blog, have been growing in popularity with the growth of the Internet. Although such systems pose a risk of inconveniently interrupting the users, such interruptions are not controlled in present systems. Studies of human multitasking have suggested that the suspension and resumption of a working memory related to active tasks occurs when task switching is forced by an external interruption. This set of suspensions and resumptions causes a lag at task switching [1, 2]. Furthermore, it has been pointed out that a "resumption lag" can be potentially increased by interruption timing and the relationship between switching tasks [3, 4]. Therefore, frequent inter-ruptions regardless of the user's status risk the fragmentation of the user's working time and decrease intellectual productivity [5]. Therefore, automatic user status estimation and interruption timing control can be expected to reduce the chance of inappropriate interruptions and to enhance online communication quality.

One potential method to estimate a user's status is user activity monitoring by using sensors. For example, counting keystrokes and mouse clicks has been utilized during PC work [6], and various sensors have been installed in the work space or have

---

[*] Corresponding author.

S. Yamamoto (Ed.): HIMI/HCII 2013, Part III, LNCS 8018, pp. 297–306, 2013.

been attached to the users [7, 8]. These methods estimate interruptibility based on PC activities or recognized events, such as having a guest or a telephone call [9, 10]. These methods are expected to adequately estimate a user's status during tasks that have observable physical activity. However, the mental workload during a task or intellectual activity, such as deep thinking, has no measurable output. Moreover, it is practically difficult to install sensors on users or in the work space.

Another approach is to estimate the breakpoints of a task. Several studies have reported the relationship between the resumption lag and breakpoint. These studies have experimentally demonstrated that resumption lags at breakpoints are shorter, because the breakpoint is the end of a subtask, and therefore, suspension and resumption of a working memory is not required, even if the task requires significant intellectual activity [11, 12]. Iqbal and Bailey have also proposed a breakpoint detection method based on the structural analysis of the tasks [13].

However, this approach requires task-structure analysis to determine interruptibility levels at breakpoints. Therefore, a real-time breakpoint estimation method, which can be performed by an information system, is desired for automatic interruption timing control.

We consider that focused application switching (AS), which is the transition of the active application window, is a potential breakpoint in PC work. Our experimental results demonstrate that the interruptions at AS are significantly more acceptable than those during continuous work. Finally, we propose a user interruptibility estimation method at AS [14]. However, for office workers, there are social factors that affect their interruptibility, such as communication and collaboration during work. Although the interruptibility during communication would be low, the proposed method estimates high interruptibility in such a situation, because there are no, or very few, observable PC activities. Therefore, we need to consider social activities in addition to PC activities to improve the estimation accuracy.

In this study, first, we experimentally collected PC activity, environmental sound, and subjective interruptibility data of participants during work in a laboratory. Second, we analyzed the relationship between conversational status and interruptibility. Third, we proposed an interruptibility estimation method based on conversation status in addition to PC activity. Finally, we experimentally confirm that estimation accuracy is improved by considering conversational status.

2 Real-Time Estimation of User Interruptibility Based on PC Activity

We used focused AS, which is the transition of the active application window, as a breakpoint in PC work [14]. AS is considered as the user's intentional switching of the working space or working target. Therefore, the user's concentration at AS is expected to be instantaneously weakened compared with that during continuous work. Moreover, AS commonly and frequently occurs in PC work and is easily detected. Thus, AS is a potential source of information presentation timing with less risk of task disturbance.

To examine this assumption, we experimentally collected and analyzed PC operation records and subjective interruptibility scores. The experimental results demon-strated that interruptions at AS are significantly more acceptable for users than those during continuous work ($p < 0.01$, t-test). Moreover, the resumption lags caused by interruption at AS were significantly shorter than those during continuous work.

We analyzed the relationship between the interruptibility scores and features, which were calculated from the operation records and were expected to reflect the interruptibility at AS. Finally, we defined an estimation rule, which estimates user interruptibility at three levels on the basis of the occurrence probability of each index at a particular interruptibility level.

On the other hand, the frequency of AS during PC work depends on the user's task and situations. Therefore, the opportunity of information presentation may significantly decrease in some cases. Thus, we proposed an interruptibility estimation method during continuous work (Not Application Switching (NAS)) based on four PC-activity-related indices. The estimation method demonstrated a level of accuracy almost comparable with that of the estimation method at AS.

However, the accuracy was susceptible to change because of non-PC work and conversation during work. In both cases, the indices based on PC activity do not reflect the actual user activity; therefore, the proposed method estimated the numbers of low interruptibility status as high. In particular, 50% of these serious errors in the office environment were caused by conversation. We needed to consider the conversation state to improve the estimation accuracy.

3   Collection of Interruptibility Data during Deskwork

3.1   Experimental Setup and Conditions

To investigate the effect of conversation on the interruptibility of office workers while using PCs, we conducted experiments to interrupt the participants during work. The participants were requested to subjectively score their interruptibility at interruption. The configuration of the experimental system is shown in Fig.1. The experiment program remained in the "task-tray" and recorded the PC operation information and the sound at 500-ms intervals. The recorded data are keystroke, mouse click, mouse wheel, clipboard update, window number, and foreground application name.

The experiment program intermittently interrupted the participants when one of the preprogrammed interruption conditions was satisfied. The participants were requested to score their subjective interruptibility in five grades through a "dialog-box." The participants were instructed to assume that the interruption is the request of a five minute conversation with their colleagues. The interruption conditions are set as follows to obtain the interruptibility scores during conversation, after finishing the conversation, and in the quiet state:

1. Continuous sound detection (potential conversation): The rate of samples in which the sound pressure exceeded the threshold is between 25 and 90 percent in the last 20 seconds and more than 15 percent during the period between 10 and 20 seconds before the interruption.

2. End of continuous sound (potential conversation ending): Condition 1 had been satisfied at the previous sample and is not satisfied at the current sample.
3. Quiet (potential not conversation): Conditions other than 1 and 2.

Furthermore, the minimal interruption intervals, between 30 and 900 seconds, were imposed on each condition to avoid excessive interruption and bias in data. The participants were eight university students and two faculty members. All participated in the five-hour experiment at their own desks. No restrictions in activity were imposed. The observed PC activities were programming, document editing, data analysis, email, and net surfing; and the non-PC activities were reading from a printed paper, conversation, smartphone operation, and eating. The conversational contents were research-related matters, hobbies, and daily news.

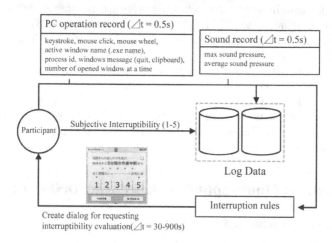

Fig. 1. Experimental system for collecting interruptibility data during deskwork

3.2   Detection of Conversational Statuses

We defined three types of status—"During conversation," "Conversation ending," and "Quiet"—to investigate the effect of conversation on interruptibility. The decision rules were as follows:

1. During conversation: human voice had been detected in the last 10 seconds.
2. Conversation ending: human voice had been detected in the last 20 seconds and had not been detected for 10 seconds including interruption timing. The cases in which a keystroke or mouse click is detected have been excluded, because PC operation implies the participants' resumption of the task.
3. Quiet: conditions other than 1 and 2.

The conversational voice was detected by the Wizard-Of-Oz (WOZ) method and an automatic method based on the wavelet transform [15]. In the WOZ method, the experimenter judged the conversational status from the recorded sound based on the described rules. Therefore, "During conversation" included both the conversations in which the participant was included and not included.

In the automatic method, the conversational voice was detected on the basis of the features in the frequency and time domains. In the frequency domain, voice has a pitch frequency and the first formant frequency. The first formant frequency is about two times the pitch frequency. In the time domain, the pitch frequency gradually changes during conversation. To detect these features, the following detecting rules were defined by using wavelet transform in reference to a method for speech detection [16].

- Frequency domain conditions:

    (a) The pitch frequency is between 80 and 360 Hz.
    (b) The first formant frequency is similar to two times the pitch frequency.
    (c) The power at the dip is sufficiently smaller than that at the pitch.

- Time domain condition:

    (d) The number of the divided-into-eight subsamples that have stable pitch frequency is greater than three. The stability index was the variation of the pitch frequency.

Samples that satisfied both conditions were regarded as conversational voice.

3.3   General Trends of Experimental Results

The general trends of the obtained data are shown in Table 1. Because the PC operation might influence the effect of conversation on interruptibility, the data was categorized by the existence of PC activity as well as the conversational status. PC activity was detected as a keystroke or mouse click within the last 30 seconds.

Table 1. Average subjective scores and frequencies at various interruption timings

	During conversation	Quiet	Conversation ending
PC activity	2.19 (159)	2.80 (150)	3.96 (25)
No PC activity	2.71 (156)	3.39 (76)	3.98 (51)

The result of multiple comparisons revealed that the interruptibility "During conversation" is significantly higher and that at "Conversation ending" is significantly lower than that during the quiet state, regardless of PC activity. Therefore, "During conversation" and "Conversation ending" are promising indices for interruptibility estimation. The interruptibility with PC activity is detected was significantly lower than that without PC activity.

The average interruptibility values "During conversation" and at "Conversation ending" were 0.61 lower and 1.16 higher, respectively, than that during the quiet state, when PC activity was detected. The differences changed to 0.68 and 0.59 in the cases without PC activity, respectively. These differences suggest that conversation ending has a larger effect on interruptibility.

4   Offline Estimation of Interruptibility

4.1   Interruptibility Estimation Equation

We introduced two conversational indices into the estimation equation during NAS in reference to a previous study [17]. The PC operation indices that were proposed in the previous study are shown in Table 2. Equation 1 represents the estimation equation. If the data meet the condition for each index, the index takes the value 1, otherwise 0. The value of function f ranges from 0 to 1. Interruptibility is classified into three levels using Equation 2.

Table 2. Indices based on PC operation

ID	Indices	Interruptibility
A	Keystroke in last 20 seconds.	Low
B	PC activity detection in more than 30% of the last 2 minutes.	Low
C	Use of both keyboard and mouse in the last 2 minutes.	Low
D	Transitioned from shell (desktop) within 5 min.	Low

$$f(x) = (2A + B + C + D)/5 \tag{1}$$

$$\text{Interruptibility} = \begin{cases} \text{Low} & 0.7 \le f(x) \le 1 \\ \text{Medium} & 0.2 \le f(x) < 0.7 \\ \text{High} & 0 \le f(x) < 0.2 \end{cases} \tag{2}$$

The added conversational indices in this study are shown in Table 3. Equations 3 and 4 show the estimation equations. In Section 3.3, it was suggested that the effects of "During conversation" and "Conversation ending" on interruptibility are different in the cases PC activity and No PC activity. Therefore, the coefficients in the two equations differ. The coefficients were experimentally decided with reference to the results of a multiple linear regression analysis. After calculating the function f, interruptibility was classified into three levels using equation 2.

Table 3. Added indices of conversational statuses

ID	Indices	Interruptibility
E	During conversation	Low
F	Conversation ending	High

$$\text{PC activity:} \quad f(x) = (2A + B + C + D + E + 2\bar{F})/8 \tag{3}$$

$$\text{No PC activity:} \quad f(x) = (2A + B + C + D + 2E + \bar{F})/8 \tag{4}$$

4.2   Interruptibility Estimation Results

Fig.2 (a) shows the estimation result using the already proposed PC operation indices. Figs.2 (b)–(d) show the offline estimation results with "During conversation," "Conversation ending," and both indices, respectively. The conversational voice was de-tected by the WOZ method. In Fig.2 (a), the precision for high interruptibility was 40%. The indices "During conversation" and "Conversation ending" increased the precision to 48% and 42%, respectively, as seen in Fig.2 (b, c). The use of both indices further improved the precision to 59%. Especially, the rate of high-risk error esti-mation, which means the unacceptable status was mistakenly estimated as interrupti-ble, decreased from 40% to 18% by applying the two indices. On the other hand, the improvement in precision for low interruptibility was from 66% to 69%. The im-provement of the total recall was from 36% to 40%. The conversational indices ap-pear to be more effective for the improvement of accuracy for high interruptibility.

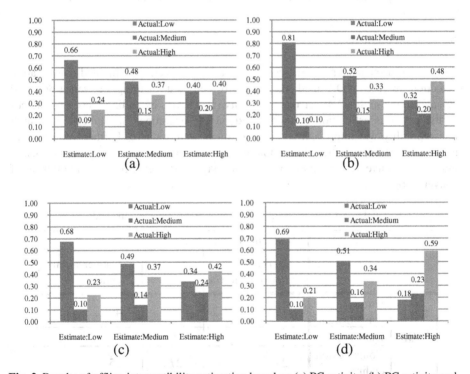

Fig. 2. Results of offline interruptibility estimation based on (a) PC activity, (b) PC activity and conversation, (c) PC activity and conversation ending, and (d) PC activity and both conversational indices

Fig.3 shows the estimation results based on automatic conversational voice detection. The precision for high interruptibility was slightly increased to 42% compared to the PC-activity-based method. The rate of high-risk error estimation was reduced to 34%. The precision of high interruptibility was also increased to 68%. Even though the current automatic voice detection algorithm still needs to be improved, the use of conversational information in combination with PC activity appears promising.

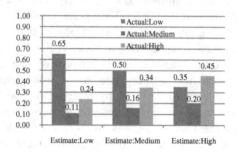

Fig. 3. Estimation results based on the automatic conversation detection

5   Discussions

As a result of the analysis of the correlation between interruptibility and conversation detection by the WOZ method, we confirmed that "During conversation" and "Conversation ending" affect interruptibility. Moreover, by adding these two indices to the previous estimation method based on PC operations, the precision of high interruptibility was improved, and serious errors were reduced. Further improvement is expected by using other indices that correlate with interruptibility. One promising index is "Conversation duration," which may correlate with the importance of conversation.

Table 4. Comparison of conversation status detection methods

		Automatic detection		
		During conversation	Quiet	Conversation ending
WOZ	During conversation	162	103	49
	Quiet	12	207	7
	Conversation ending	24	27	25

Among the "During conversation" samples that were judged by the WOZ method, 103 samples were categorized as "Quiet," and 49 samples were detected as "Conversation ending." It implies that the automatic detection method tends to fail for the detection of conversational voice. Therefore, an improvement of the detection rule is required. As for the computational time of the automatic method using the continuous wavelet transform, it took 0.86 s for 0.5 s sound data. For real-time estimation, it is necessary to reduce this computational time. The reduction of time and frequency resolutions and the use of the discrete wavelet transform may be potential solutions.

In this study, the introduction of two conversational indices improved the accuracy of the interruptibility estimation method based on PC operations. It suggests that the reflection of social factors in addition to task-related factors will enable a more accurate estimation. The task-related factors utilized in the present study are only PC activity features, suggesting that the target task of the present method is limited to office work with PC usage. However, other types of office activities exist, such as paperwork. The introduction of additional indices, reflecting the working density or user's working attitude during office works without PC, is expected to extend the applicable office activities. Head motion is one potential index, because it reflects the gaze that is tightly related with the worker's information acquisition behavior.

6   Conclusions

In this study, we analyzed the correlations between the conversational features and interruptibility during office work. Two conversational indices "During conversation" and "Conversation ending" improved the estimation accuracy of the interruptibility estimation method based on PC activity. The improvement of automatic conversation detection accuracy and the reduction of the computational time are required for adequate interruptibility control toward better online communication.

Acknowledgement. This work was partly supported by Grants-in-Aid for scientific research from the Japan Society for the Promotion of Science and the National Institute of Information Technology (NICT).

References

1. Altman, E.M., Trafton, J.G.: Memory for Goals: An Activation-based Model. Cog. Sci. 26, 39–83 (2002)
2. Salvucci, D.D., Taatgen, N.A.: Threaded Cognition: An Integrated Theory of Concurrent Multitasking. Psychol. Rev. 115(1), 101–130 (2008)
3. Cutrell, E.B., Czerwinski, M., Horvitz, E.: Effects of instant messaging interruptions on computing tasks. In: Extended Abstracts on Human Factors in Computing Systems, pp. 99–100 (2000)
4. Monk, C.A., Trafton, J.G., Boehm-Davis, D.A.: The Effect of Interruption Duration and Demand on Resuming Suspended Goals. J. Exp. Psychol. Appl. 14, 299–313 (2008)
5. Mark, G., Gonzalez, V.M., Harris, J.: No Task Left Behind? Examining the Nature of Fragmented Work. In: Proceedings of the SIGCHI Conference on Human Factors in Computing Systems, pp. 321–330. ACM, New York (2005)
6. Honda, S., Tomioka, H., Kimura, T., Oosawa, T., Okada, K., Matsushita, Y.: A Home Office Environment based on the Concentration Degrees of Workers: A Virtual Office System Valentine. Trans. Inform. Process. Soc. Jpn. 39(5), 1472–1483 (1998) (in Japanese)

7. Avrahami, D., Fogarty, J., Hudson, S.E.: Biases in Human Estimation of Interruptibility: Effects and Implications for Practice. In: Proceedings of the SIGCHI Conference on Human Factors in Computing Systems, pp. 50–60. ACM, New York (2007)
8. Fogarty, J., Hudson, S.E.: Toolkit Support for Developing and Deploying Sensor-based Statistical Models of Human Situations. In: Proceedings of the SIGCHI Conference on Human Factors in Computing Systems, pp. 135–144. ACM, New York (2007)
9. Danninger, M., Stiefelhagen, R.: A Context-Aware Virtual Secretary in a Smart Office Environment. In: Proceedings of the 16th ACM International Conference on Multimedia, pp. 529–538. ACM, New York (2008)
10. Lu, H., Pan, W., Lane, N.D., Choudhury, T., Campbell, A.T.: SoundSense: Scalable Sound Sensing for People-Centric Applications on Mobile Phones. In: Proceedings of the 7th International Conference on Mobile systems, Applications, and Services, pp. 165–178 (2009)
11. Borst, J.P., Taatgen, N.A., Van Rijn, H.: The problem state: A Cognitive Bottleneck in Multitasking. J. Exp. Psychol. Learn. Mem. Cognit. 36(2), 363–382 (2010)
12. Monk, C.A., Boehm-Davis, D.A., Trafton, J.G.: Recovering from Interruptions: Implications for Driver Distraction Research. Hum. Factors 46, 650–663 (2004)
13. Iqbal, S.T., Bailey, B.P.: Leveraging Characteristics of Task Structure to Predict Costs of Interruption. In: Proceedings of the SIGCHI Conference on Human Factors in Computing Systems, pp. 741–750. ACM, New York (2006)
14. Tanaka, T., Fujita, K.: Study of User Interruptibility Estimation Based on Focused Application Switching. In: Proceedings of the ACM 2011 Conference on Computer Supported Cooperative Work, pp. 721–724. ACM, New York (2011)
15. Juang, C.-F., Cheng, C.-N., Tu, C.-C.: Wavelet Energy-Based Support Vector Machine for Noisy Word Boundary Detection with Speech Recognition Application. Expert Syst. Appl. 36(1), 321–332 (2009)
16. Juang, C.-F., Cheng, C.-N., Che, T.-M.: Speech detection in Noisy Environments by Wavelet Energy-based Recurrent Neural Fuzzy Network. Expert Syst. Appl. 36(1) (2009)
17. Tanaka, T., Fukasawa, S., Takeuchi, K., Nonaka, M., Fujita, K.: Study of Uninterruptibility Estimation Method for Office Worker during PC Work. Inform. Process. Soc. Jpn. 53(1), 126–137 (2012) (in Japanese)

ARM-COMS: ARm-Supported eMbodied COmmunication Monitor System

Teruaki Ito[1] and Tomio Watanabe[2]

[1] The University of Tokushima, 2-1 Minami-Josanjima, Tokushima 770-8506 Japan
[2] Okayama Prefectural University, 111 Tsuboki, Souja Okayama 719-1197 Japan
ito@me.tokushima-u.ac.jp, watanabe@cse.oka-pu.ac.jp

Abstract. Remote communication systems are getting popular these days, which makes it possible to enjoy audio/video communication over the network in high quality. However, remote communication using these systems is still not identical to face-to-face meeting due to several reasons which are still open issues. This study focuses on two of the issues. One is lack of tele-presence and the other one is lack of connection in communication. In order to tackle these issues, this study proposes an idea of connecting remote individuals through augmented tele-presence systems called ARM-COMS: ARm-supported eMbodied COmmunication Monitor System. ARM-COMS is composed of a desktop robotic arm and a tablet PC which is attached to it. The tablet PC presents audio/video images of a remote person just as typical video conference. However, ARM-COMS controls the physical movement of the tablet PC during the video conference to be consistent with physical motion of the remote participant as if the remote person were there and behaved in a face-to-face conversation. ARM-COMS also considers the meaningful physical position in space to show the connection with other person or topics. The tablet PC approaches to the speaking person as if embodied communication occurs. This paper shows the idea of ARM-COMS and presents some of the on-going work of the study to show the feasibility of the idea.

Keywords: Embodied communication, augmented tele-presence robotic arm manipulation, human interface.

1   Introduction

Network-based communication has been popular these days according as the development of video conference systems [Abowdm 2000]. Even though remote communication is getting popular over the network using these systems, several drawbacks are still regarded as open issues as opposed to a face-to-face meeting, such as lack of tele-presence and lack of relationship in communication [Greenberg 1996]. Using a mobile robot for remote communication with multimodal information, the experimental results in several studies show the effectiveness of these remote controlled robots in communication [Kashiwabara 2012]. Embodiment of an agent using anthropomorphization of an Object [Osawa 2012] is also an interesting idea to

S. Yamamoto (Ed.): HIMI/HCII 2013, Part III, LNCS 8018, pp. 307–316, 2013.

show the presence. There robots could provide tele-presence of the operator in the remote site and even enables some kinds of tele-operating tasks from distance. These robots provide basic function to suppose distance communication using several critical functions such as face image display of the operator [Otsuka 2008], drivability to move around, tele-manipulation on remote objects as well as basic communication functions including talk/listen/see [Kim 2012]. Even a smaller robot is now available on the market for these purposes as well. However, there are still a gap between robot-based video conferences/meetings and face-to-face ones, which is an open issue to be solved for better communication. A new challenge is undertaken by a robotic arm type system with mobile function [Tariq 2011; Wongphati 2012]. For an example of non-mobile arm type system, Kubi [Revolve Robotics] allows the remote user to "look around" during their video call by commanding Kubi where to aim the tablet using intuitive remote controls over the web. However, non-verbal movement of the remote person is still an open issue.

This study proposes an idea for connecting remote individuals through augmented tele-presence systems called ARM-COMS(ARm-supported eMbodied COmmunication Monitor System), focusing on the two issues; lack of tele-presence and lack of relationship in communication. ARM-COMS is composed of two sub-systems: a tablet PC for video communication and a robotic arm to control physical motion of the tablet PC as an avatar. As opposed to the manual control of Kubi, ARM-COMS makes the tablet PC physically behave as if the remote person were actually there by way of movement and positioning of the tablet PC. Fig.1 shows an illustrative image of ARM-COMS, which enables the behavior of a tablet PC as an avatar of a remote person.

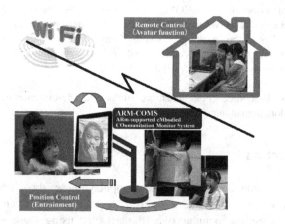

Fig. 1. Overview of ARM-COMS application in vide conference

This paper shows the basic idea of ARM-COMS and presents the on-going work of this study.

2   A Proposal of an Idea ARM-COMS

This study proposes an idea of ARM-COMS, which is capable of movements similar to a human neck and is used for mimicking a person's movements. ARM-COMS traces the head movement of a person during conversation, understands the meaning of motions and makes the tablet PC physically behave as if the person were actually there. As opposed to the conventional tele-presence robots, ARM-COMS pursues the realization of entrainment in video conversation with a remote person. The idea of ARM-COMS challenges two types of issues. One is motion-control to mimic the movement of a remote person and to enable entrainment in conversation. The other one is position-control to show the dynamic relationship with participants in conversation [Okada 1994] or to show the status of interest in topics under discussion.

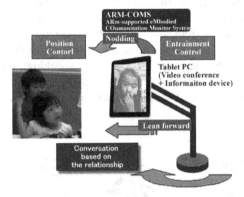

Fig. 2. An overview of ARM-COMS to support remote communication

— Challenge 1: Entrainment movement control

It has been reported that entrainment among participants emerges during conversation if the participating persons get together in the same physical space and engage in the conversation. [Okada 1994; Watanabe 2011] Tracking the head movement of a speaking person, ARM-COMS mimics the movement using a tablet PC by a robotic arm and challenges to enable this control function in remote communication.

— Challenge 2: Entrainment position control

In a face-to-face meeting, each person takes a meaningful physical position to represent the relationship with the other participants, or to send a non-verbal message to others. A closer position would be taken for friends, showing close relationship, whereas a non-closer position would be taken for strangers, showing unfriendly relationship [Osawa 2012]. ARM-COMS controls a tablet PC to dynamically locate an appropriate position in space and to explicitly represent the relationship with other participants, sending a non-verbal message. The tablet PC would be approaching to the speaking person to show that the remote person is interested in the talk.

This study tackles these two types of challenges to implement the proposed idea as ARM-COMS. However, this paper mainly focuses on the challenge 1 and presents the on-going work. The challenge 2 will be presented in a separate paper.

3   ARM-COMS: Motion Control Experiment

3.1   Basic Structure of Motion Control

During conversation, various types of body/head movements can be observed. In order to mimic some of these movements, this study focuses on three types of head movements, namely, nodding, head-tilting, and head shaking movements. All of these are very typical non-verbal expression in Japan during conversation. Nodding means affirmative, agree, listening, etc. Head-titling means ambiguous, not sure, impossible to answer, etc. Head shaking means negative, disagree, no way, etc. Fig.3 shows the corresponding physical motions implemented by the robotic arm control. If the monitor behaves like these in conversation, it is assumed that the physical movements could send a non-verbal message. Technically speaking, these three types of movements can be regarded as the rotation around each axis as shown in Fig. 3. Therefore, the rotation angles of these three motions can be calculated as in Scheme (1), (2) and (3).

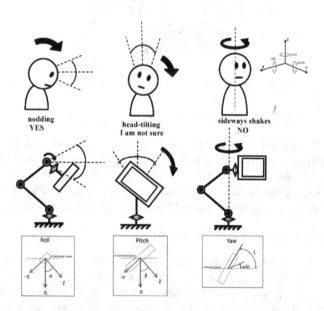

Fig. 3. Three types of target head motion

For nodding movement, roll angle can be calculated by scheme (1), where α is the rotation angle around y-axis, and X,Z are the acceleration value for each direction.

$$\alpha = \sin^{-1}\left(\frac{-X}{\sqrt{X^2 + Z^2}}\right)(3-1) \qquad (1)$$

For "I am not sure" movement, pitch angle β can be calculated by scheme (2), where$\beta$is the rotation angle around x-axis, and Y,Z are the acceleration value for each direction.

$$\beta = \sin^{-1}\left(\frac{-Y}{\sqrt{Y^2 + Z^2}}\right)(3-2) \qquad (2)$$

For sideway shaking movement, yaw angle ξ can be calculated by scheme (3), where ξ is the rotation angle around z-axis, ω is the angle subtracted from the horizontal angle and Δt is the sampling interval, which was 100[ms] here.

$$\xi = \sum \omega \Delta t \quad (3-3) \qquad (3)$$

3.2   Prototype System

A prototype robotic arm system was built to mimic the head motions based on the scheme (1), (2) and (3). Fig. 4 shows the overview of the system architecture of the prototype.

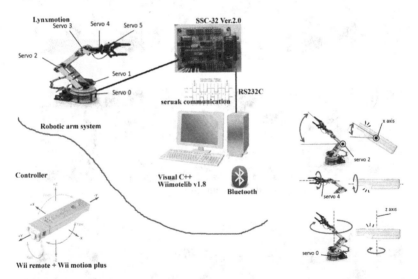

Fig. 4. An overview of ARM-COMS prototype and its motion by Wii remote

The robotic arm system is composed of a table top robotic arm (Lynxmotion) with motor controller board (SSC-32 Ver.2.0) which is connected to PC (Windows 7) by serial cable. The robotic arm is controlled by PC using a remote controller (Wii Remote + Wii Motion Plus) through Bluetooth connection. The combination of Wii Remote and Wii Motion plus makes it possible to trace the acceleration for three axis and three rotation angle around these three axis. Software to control the arm was developed by Visual C++ with library Wiimotelib v.1.8. As a result, the robotic arm is wirelessly controllable by Wii Remote manipulation.

3.3   Study 1: Embodied Proxy Platform Using a Robotic Arm

According to the feasibility test of the prototype, it was recognized that the prototype could mimic the head motion if the Wii remote is attached to the head. However, Wii remote is not suitable to attach to the body of human. Therefore, another type of wireless acceleration sensor (WAA-001, ATR-Promotion, Bluetooth type) was used. Since this sensor detects only acceleration value for three axes, a pair of sensors was used to cover the target three motions. One was attached to the ear portion of the head, while the other one was attached to the neck. Fig.5 shows the nodding, head-tilting and lean forward motion, all of which were mimicked by the prototype ARM-COMS.

Nodding motion

Head-tilting motion

Lean forward motion

Fig. 5. Master-slave motion of ARM-COMS system to demonstrate the physical behavior

ARM-COMS mimicked the basic motions as shown in Fig.5, where a pseudo-display attached to the arm follows the head's motion. However, head-shaking motion was not available. Therefore, another type of sensor (TSND-121, ATR Promotion)

was applied. TSND-121 is an integrated sensor composed of InvenSence MPU6050 which covers acceleration and angular velocity, as well as AMI306 which covers gyro motion. By modifying the control software to be applicable to TSND-121, the ARM-COMS prototype enabled the target three-motion only by a single TSND-121, was used for the experiment in Study 2 presented in the next section.

3.4 Study 2: Feasibility Study of Video Communication Using ARM-COMS Idea

Study 2 was designed to compare the video communication with and without ARM-COMS to make clear the effectiveness of the idea of ARM-COMS.

4 pairs of participants were recruited from students and two sets of video conversation were conducted by those paired students. One conversation is just a regular Skype communication and the other one is based on ARM-COMS idea. Fig.6 shows the overview of the experimental setup. The video communication was conducted between Site-A and Site-B by a pair of Subject-A and Subject-B, who were located in separate places.

Site-A is regarded as a local site where ARM-COMS is installed. For a tentative purpose, a smart phone is equipped to the robotic arm to be used as a pseudo-active display. Subject-A communicates with Subject-B via Skype on the smart phone. A magnetic sensor (Fastrak, POLHEMUS) is attached to the head of Subject-A during conversation to detect the head motion of subject-A.

Site-B is regarded as a remote site where Subject-B communicates with Subject-A in Site-A through video communication (Skype) on a laptop PC. A multi-sensor TSND-121 was attached to the head of Subject B to trace the head movement during conversation, which was also used to control ARM-COMS in Site-A. The sensing data from the multi-sensor was transmitted to the client program in the laptop through Bluetooth. The socket program communicates with the server program in desktop PC on Site-A, and controls the ARM-COMS via Wi-Fi network. The collecting data from the multi-sensor was also used to analyze the head movement of Subject-B during video conversation.

Subject-A and Subject-B were video-recorded in both Site-A and Site-B during the whole conversation, which was used to synchronize the head movements of Subject-A and Subject-B in the conversation.

Several types of topics for video conversation were prepared from daily conversation. For example, "Which animal do you like?", "What did you eat for the breakfast?", "How did you come to the university today?", "Which convenience store do you often go? ", etc. Each pair of subject was asked to perform one-minute video conversation about one of the selected topics twice. First conversation was without the robotic arm manipulation, which was similar to regular Skype conversation, and the second one was with arm manipulation, which was identical to the idea of ARM-COMS.

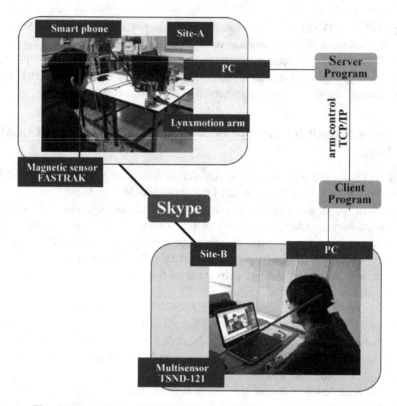

Fig. 6. An overview of ARM-COMS to support remote communication

3.5   Results and Discussion

Video conversation was smooth in any of the four pairs with or without AMR-COMS. It was observed that most of the four pairs conducted their conversation without using dynamic head movement simply because it was what they normally do in regular conversation.

Figure 7 shows an example of comparison data between with and without ARM-COMS during conversation. As opposed to the dynamic head movement of Subject B, that of Subject A was stable. Entrainment of the head was not significantly observed. However, synchronization of the two subjects was observed in the bowing at the beginning and at the ending of the conversation.

For smooth conversation, a topic memo was given to each subject. As a result, each subject quite often looked down the memo in the conversation, rather than looking at the counterpart in the video screen. Subject did not use the memo at the greetings in the beginning and in the end. This made it possible to perform the conversation in a smooth manner. However, this might have hindered the entrainment with the counterpart. Future works needs further discussion on the experimental setup.

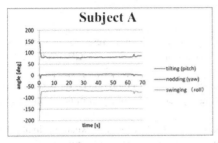
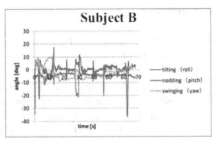

Video conference without ARM-COMS

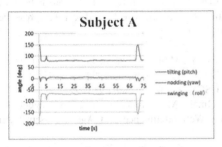
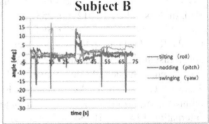

Video conference with ARM-COMS

Fig. 7. Comparison data of video communication with and without ARM-COMS

4 Concluding Remarks

The original idea of this study is aiming at how to control the physical position and movement of a tablet PC in such a way that a remote participant would most likely behave if he/she were actually there. Active display presents the tele-existence of a remote object shown in the display by physical movement. However, ARM-COMS not only presents the tele-presence of a remote person, but also explicitly shows the relationship between the remote person and the local participants by way of the entrainmental behavior of a table PC.

ARM-COMS employs only a general tablet PC attached to the sub-system of robotic arm, which will be specifically designed and built for this purpose. ARM-COMS not only presents a new idea for remote communication system, but also opens a potential new market for non-industrial robotic arm design and products.

This paper proposed the basic idea of ARM-COMS, which is based on the combination of entrainment movement and entrainment positioning, and showed the preliminary result of feasibility in entrainment movement. The future works include the design and manufacturing of sub-system for ARM-COMS robotic arm, development of the entrainment movement/positioning algorithm and its feasibility study.

References

1. Abowdm, D.G., Mynatt, D.E.: Charting past, present, and future research in ubiquitous computing. ACM Transactions on Computer-Human Interaction (TOCHI) 7(1), 29–58 (2000)
2. Greenberg, S.: Peepholes: low cost awareness of one's community. In: Conference Companion on Human Factors in Computing Systems: Common Ground, Vancouver, British Columbia, Canada, pp. 206–207 (1996)
3. Kashiwabara, T., Osawa, H., Shinozawa, K., Imai, M.: TEROOS: a wearable avatar to enhance joint activities. In: Annual Conference on Human Factors in Computing Systems, pp. 2001–2004 (May 2012)
4. Kim, K., Bolton, J., Girouard, A., Cooperstock, J., Vertegaal, R.: TeleHuman: Effects of 3D Perspective on Gaze and Pose Estimation with a Life-size Cylindrical Telepresence Pod. In: Proc. of CHI 2012, pp. 2531–2540 (2012)
5. Kubi, http://revolverobotics.com/meet-kubi/
6. Okada, K., Maeda, F., Ichikawa, Y., Matsushita, Y.: Multiparty videoconferencing at virtual social distance: MAJIC design. In: SCW 1994 Proceedings of the 1994 ACM Conference on Computer Supported Cooperative Work (CSCW 1994), pp. 385–393 (1994)
7. Osawa, T., Matsuda, Y., Ohmura, R., Imai, M.: Embodiment of an agent by anthropomorphization of a common object. Web Intelligence and Agent Systems: An International Journal 10, 345–358 (2012)
8. Otsuka, T., Araki, S., Ishizuka, K., Fujimoto, M., Heinrich, M., Yamato, J.: A Realtime Multimodal System for Analyzing Group Meetings by Combining Face Pose Tracking and Speaker Diarization. In: Proc. of the 10th International Conference on Multimodal Interfaces (ICMI 2008), Chania, Crete, Greece, pp. 257–264 (2008)
9. Sirkin, D., Ju, W.: Consistency in physical and on-screen action improves perceptions of telepresence robots. In: HRI 2012, Proceedings of the Seventh Annual ACM/IEEE International Conference on Human-Robot Interaction, pp. 57–64 (2012)
10. Tariq, A.M., Ito, T.: Master-slave robotic arm manipulation for communication robot. In: Proceedings of 2011 Annual Meeting on Japan Society of Mechanical Engineer, vol. 11(1), p.S12013 (September 2011)
11. Tomotoshi, M., Ito, T.: A study on awareness support method to improve engagement in remote communication. In: The first International Symposium on Socially and Technically Symbiotic System (STSS 2012), Okayama, vol. 39, pp. 1–6 (August 2012)
12. Watanabe, T.: Human-entrained Embodied Interaction and Communication Technology, Emotional Engineering, pp. 161–177. Springer (2011)
13. Watanabe, T., Okubo, M., Nakashige, M., Danbara, R.: InterActor: Speech-Driven Embodied Interactive Actor. International Journal of Human-Computer Interaction 17(1), 43–60 (2004)
14. Wongphati, M., Matsuda, Y., Osawa, H., Imai, M.: Where do you want to use a robotic arm? And what do you want from the robot? In: International Symposium on Robot and Human Interactive Communication, pp. 322–327 (September 2012)

Interlocked Surfaces: A Dynamic Multi-device Collaboration System

Hiroyuki Kamo and Jiro Tanaka

University of Tsukuba, 1-1-1 Tennodai, Tsukuba, Ibaraki, Japan
{kamo,jiro}@iplab.cs.tsukuba.ac.jp

Abstract. In this research, we propose "Interlocked Surfaces", which supports cooperation work between different devices. The system offers to connect different devices wirelessly and allow multiple users to view and edit documents simultaneously. We have developed a technique to share and view documents between different devices even they have difference screen sizes and resolutions. In a user study, we conducted experiments to evaluate the usefulness of the system. The result shows that users can perform the document inspection task more comfortably using the proposed system.

1 Interlocked Surfaces

We propose "Interlocked Surfaces" in this paper. The main function of "Interlocked Surfaces" is to allow users to share, browse and edit information content effectively and smoothly, when they are working together with different devices. The system permits users to connect many different devices and to share the contents among them.

When using the system, a user can use a tablet or smartphone device that has a camera to capture video on other devices and tap on a particular device to make connection. Depending on the functions of the devices, we call the devices as "operating device" and "target device" respectively. See Figure 1.

After the user selected and connected a target device, then the information of a target device will show on an operating device. After this step, the user can operate the connected device remotely. And we call the connected target device as "pairing device".

1.1 Selecting Target Device for Pairng

Depending on whether the device has a camera or not, two different methods for selecting a target device were developed.

If the operating device has a camera, then the user can capture the video on a target device and select it on the image that shown on the operating device. All available devices on the camera video will show as highlighted icons. The name and owner information of the devices are also shown on the screen of operating device (see Figure 1). The pairing action is intuitive that, the user can see the

S. Yamamoto (Ed.): HIMI/HCII 2013, Part III, LNCS 8018, pp. 317–325, 2013.

Fig. 1. The pairing through the video image

target device on the video image and simply taps on that device, and then the pairing will complete. The augmented reality technique adopted here is helpful to user when making device pairing. This technique is also proved by Gaze-line metaphor [1].

While, on the other hand, if the operating device has no camera, the user can select a target device from a list on the operating device screen.

In general, each of the devices can be a target device of the pairing. Thus, many devices can connect together at the same time and share the same contents. After a device connected to the target device, the contents of target device will show on the operating device (see Figure 2). In that time, when new devices want to make connection, no matter it selects either device as the target device, it can get the same contents (see Figure 3).

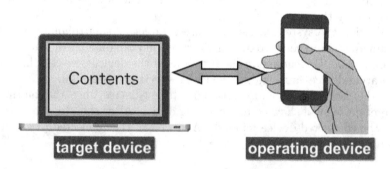

Fig. 2. Shairing contents at the first pairing

1.2 Display Areas of Pairing Devices

In the first pairing of two devices, the content displayed on the operating device (Figure 4(a)) will be shared with the target device(Figure 4(b)). And then, in the next pairing, another operating device (Figure 4(c)) is able to connect to the same target device (Figure 4(b)). In this time of pairing, the content shared in

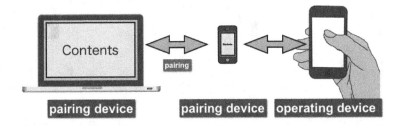

Fig. 3. Shairing contents after the second pairing

the first pairing will be shared with the new operating device again (Figure 4(c)). Meanwhile, the frame of content displayed on each device is depending on the resolution and size of the device screen. The display areas of pairing devices are represented by rectangles (Figure 5). The red frame in the device A (Figure 4(a)) represents the displaying area of the device B (Figure 4(b)). The icon of a lock is shown on the upper right of the frame. When the user taps on the icon, the lock state will change. In the lock state (Figure 5(a)), the operating device cannot be operated by other pairing devices. In the unlocking state (Figure 5(b)), the operating device can be operated by other pairing devices.

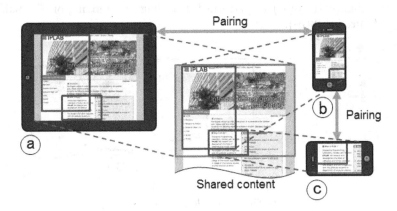

Fig. 4. Display of each device

1.3 Interlock Manipulation

The user can perform many operations on the operating device even after it is paired with another device. When a click or a tap is performed on the operating device, the operation will also be performed on other pairing devices in the same time.

In general, the scrolling and scaling operation are needed, and usually it is not easy to be implemented. Therefore, we develop a technique to support these two functions.

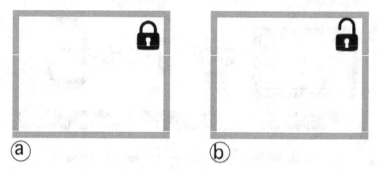

Fig. 5. Frame

In the case of two pairing devices and a scrolling action is performed on the smaller size device. First, the scroll positions of the both pairing devices are located at the topmost part of the screen area (Figure 6(a)). After the user started the scrolling, the display area on the smaller device moves continually to the bottom of the display area on the bigger size device (Figure 6(b)). Finally, the display area of the both pairing devices is interlocked and can be scrolled together (Figure 6(c)).

In the same time, the user is able to change the scaling of pairing device by using drag action (see Figure 8(b)). User can drag the sides or the corners of the frame (Figure 7(a)8(a)) to perform the scaling and moving on the pairing devices (Figure 7(b)8(b)).

Fig. 6. Interlock scroll

Fig. 7. Moving of pairing device's view   **Fig. 8.** Scaling of pairing device's view

2   Use Case

As an example, we assume a situation of four people who are gathered in a conference room for reading and editing documents together. After each participant paired own personal mobile device with large display of the conference room, they read and edit documents collaboratively. When a participant edits documents on the own device, the change will be reflected on the other devices. Furthermore, participants can see the overview of documents effectively on the large display.

3   Evaluation

We evaluated our proposed system to investigate its usability with the help of 10 subjects. All the subjects are graduate students of information science and familiar with viewing documents on a touch panel.

3.1   Experiment Description

The subjects carried out the task of finding targets in the content by operating the smart phone provided. The size of the smart phone screen is 3.5 inches. On the screen, the combination of the alphabet of two characters is arranged in the shape of a grid as shown in figure 9. The combination of alphabets is listed from

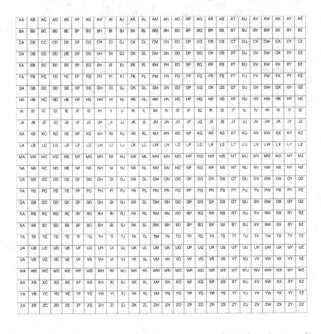

Fig. 9. Combination of the alphabet arranged in the shape of a grid

left to right as AA, AB, AC,..., AZ, and top to bottom as AA, BA, CA, ...,
ZA. The width and height of the mass outside the combination of the alphabets
is 50 pixels and the total size of the content is 1300 pixels. The questionnaire
was performed after the end of the experiment. The items of a questionnaire are
as follows.

1. Do you feel it difficult to see while inspecting documents using a smart
   phone?
2. Is the inspection comfortable while applying the proposed system?
3. Is the inspection comfortable without applying the proposed system?

To answer the question we use five-level likert scale and asked the reason of
answer for each item in the questionnaire. The first level denotes worst evaluation
and fifth level denotes the best evaluation. We defined two scenarios for subjects
to operate with smart phone. In scenario A, the subject performs the task only
using a smart phone (figure 10). In scenario B, a subject performs the task using
the proposed system in which the smart phone is cooperated with a 23-inch
display (figure 11). Before starting the task, all the subjects performed practice
for getting used to the system.

Fig. 10. Signs that the task is carried out
on the conditions A

Fig. 11. Signs that the task is carried out
on the conditions B

3.2   Result of Experiment

The result of the questionnaire is shown in figure 12. We show standard deviation
using the error bar. The average points for the first question were 4.5, while for
the second and third question we obtained 3.8 and 2.4 respectively. The result
of the questionnaire shows that the subjects were able to perform the inspection
of the document more comfortably using the proposed system.

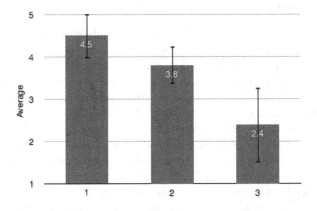

Fig. 12. The result of questionnaire

3.3 Consideration

Many smart phone users feel that the inspection of the documents by using the smart phone only is uncomfortable. Therefore, it is useful to extend the screen area of the smart phone. Our experiment showed that users are convinced with the idea of using the extended screen.

4 Implementation

This system is implemented as an add-on of a web browser in order to make available on variety of devices regardless of the Operating System. Pairing devices connects and communicates with each other through the server application.

5 Related Work

5.1 Studies Used Multiple Devices as One Screen

Many systems which cooperate multiple devices and utilize as one screen were proposed in [2]. Kurihara, et al. [3][4] proposed the system which cooperate multiple devices for presentation. This system is suitable for a one-way transmission of information from a presentor to audience. Our system can transfer documents bidirectionaly as well as used for collaborated work within multiple people. Nam, et al. [5] proposed the system which constructs one large screen by multiple display in the form of tiles. This system focuses on the presentation of documents. Our system can also edit documents by multiple people.

5.2 Collaboration Technique of Multiple Device

Collaboration techniques of a private device and public device are researched in
the past. Touch Projector [6] is the system which can operate another devices
remotely through the video image of the smart phone. Virtual Projection[7] is the
system which can view and edit documents by cooperating smart phone and large
display. The main features of previous research include expanding the view area
and facilitating information browsing of multiple users by collaborating private
device with public device. We take advantage of these features in our research.
Furthermore, we built a system which facilitates content browsing and operates
processes between multiple users by performing hybrid collaboration of multiple
personal devices. Shoot & Copy[8] is the system that can transfer contents from
public large display to private smart phone by touching large display through
video image of smart phone. This system is only able to get documents from
public devices to personal devices. Our system can ransfer documents mutually.

6   Conclusion

In this paper, we described the development of "Interlocked Surfaces". The system supported users to connect different devices wirelessly, and view and edit
documents by multiple users. The augmented reality approach was used for making device pairing, which is effective and intuitive for users. We also conducted
experiments to evaluate the proposed system. The results showed that our system is feasible and useful in a cooperation work scenario.

Acknowledgements. The authors would like to thank Shaowei Chu and Mohsin
Ali Memon for providing useful comments on an earlier draft.

References

1. Ayatsuka, Y., Matsushita, N., Rekimoto, J.: New Real-World Oriented User Inter-
   afaces with "Gaze-Link" Metaphor. In: Interaction 2000, pp. 181–188 (2000)
2. Ni, T., Schmidt, G.S., Staadt, O.G., Livingston, M.A., Ball, R., May, R.: A Survey
   of Large High-Resolution Display Technologies, Techniques, and Applications. In:
   Proc. Virtual Reality Conference, pp. 223–236 (2006)
3. Kurihara, K., Igarashi, T.: A flexible presentation tool for diverse multi-display
   environments. In: Baranauskas, C., Abascal, J., Barbosa, S.D.J. (eds.) INTERACT
   2007. LNCS, vol. 4662, pp. 430–433. Springer, Heidelberg (2007)
4. Kurihara, K., Mochizuki, T., Oura, H., Tsubakimoto, M., Nishimori, T., Nakahara,
   J., Yamauchi, Y., Nagao, K.: Linearity and synchrony: quantitative metrics for slide-
   based presentation methodology. In: Proc. ICMI-MLMI 2010, pp. 33:1–33:4. ACM
   (2010)
5. Nam, S., Deshpande, S., Vishwanath, V., Jeong, B., Renambot, L., Leigh, J.: Multi-
   application inter-tile synchronization on ultra-high-resolution display walls. In: Proc.
   MMSys 2010, pp. 145–156. ACM (2010)

6. Boring, S., Baur, D., Butz, A., Gustafson, S., Baudisch, P.: Touch projector: mobile interaction through video. In: Proc. CHI 2010, pp. 2287–2296. ACM (2010)
7. Baur, D., Boring, S., Feiner, S.: Virtual projection: exploring optical projection as a metaphor for multi-device interaction. In: Proc. CHI 2012, pp. 1693–1702. ACM (2012)
8. Boring, S., Altendorfer, M., Broll, G., Hilliges, O., Butz, A.: Shoot & copy: phonecam-based information transfer from public displays onto mobile phones. In: Mobility 2007, pp. 24–31. ACM (2007)

Effects of a Communication with Make-Believe Play in a Real-Space Sharing Edutainment System

Hiroki Kanegae[1], Masaru Yamane[1], Michiya Yamamoto[1], and Tomio Watanabe[2]

[1] Kwansei Gakuin University, Japan
[2] Okayama Prefectural University, Japan
{chd70752,bre74974,michiya.yamamoto}@kwansei.ac.jp,
watanabe@cse.oka-pu.ac.jp

Abstract. Recently, e-learning has become widely used. We have already developed an edutainment system named GOSAL (GOkko-asobi Supporting system for Active Learning) in which we introduce distinctive CG characters and communication support functions to enhance user communication for group work. We also confirmed that an element of make-believe play promotes the utterance of users. In this study, we evaluated the effectiveness of the system through an experiment in comparison with real group work, and confirmed the effectiveness for creative and laugh-filled learning.

Keywords: Embodied communication, embodied interaction and edutainment.

1 Introduction

In recent years, information technology has been used to develop various e-learning systems that enable users to study anywhere and at any time. However, with such systems, it is difficult to check the process and the depth of understanding achieved because the communication between the teacher and the students is not adequately smooth or intuitive. To solve this problem, the authors developed a speech-driven CG-embodied character called InterActor [1], which performs the functions of both speaker and listener by generating expressive actions and movements in accordance with the speech input. In addition, the authors developed a speech-driven embodied group-entrained communication system called SAKURA, which introduces multiple InterActors [2]. Furthermore, InterActors can be employed for various purposes, such as education and entertainment. For example, the authors have developed an edutainment system called LEAP (Learning with Embodied entrainment Animal Partners) that uses teacher and student InterActors, in which the user plays a double role, acting as both the teacher and student, and have demonstrated the effectiveness of this system [3].

The authors then expanded these systems to group learning, and developed an edutainment system called GOSAL (GOkko-asobi Supporting system for Active Learning), in which the user's learning is facilitated by engaging in make-believe play with CG characters [4]. In addition, they confirmed that the make-believe play of GOSAL

S. Yamamoto (Ed.): HIMI/HCII 2013, Part III, LNCS 8018, pp. 326–335, 2013.

encourages users to speak more freely during group learning [5]. In the present study, we performed an experiment to confirm the effects of communication using GOSAL, by comparing group learning that takes place in a meeting room both with and without GOSAL.

2 GOSAL

2.1 Concept

We learn many important things when playing, in the process of growing up [6]. GOSAL is a system in which students can enjoy their learning process by engaging in make-believe play in a group learning setting. Students communicate by playing a learning role as a distinctive character in real space, via a sharing edutainment system in which they enjoy shared make-believe play (Fig. 1). Teachers can also play the role of a character and enjoy learning along with their students. In this way, users can exchange knowledge or information more freely, thus enhancing the group's education process.

Fig. 1. Concept

2.2 System Configuration

When using GOASL, all the students sit around a table, each with their own PC and microphone. Students play a character role using InterActor [1], which generates communicative motions and actions based upon the student's speech from the microphone while immersed in the virtual space. The students share real space in the same room at the same time, as well as enjoy face-to-face learning with their teacher and fellow students (Fig. 2). Here, we used five microphones (audio-technica AT810F), five PCs (HP Elite-Book 8730w) equipped with Windows 7, an Ethernet, and an LCD TV (SHARP LC-52RX5) or a 100-inch screen and a projector (EPSON LC-52RX5).

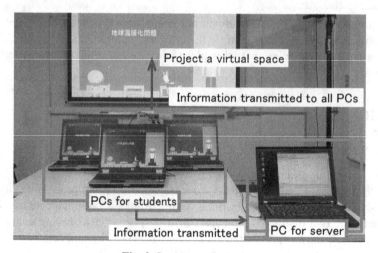

Fig. 2. System configuration

2.3   Virtual Classroom and Characters

We prepared a virtual classroom and eight characters whom students can enjoy in their make-believe play (Fig. 3, Fig. 4). Each student determines the character that he will play. For each character, a distinctive expression was prepared so that the character can be easily identified. For example, when a user chooses the "Samurai" character, the user speaks like "—- de gozaru," and enjoys this mode of communication. In this way, we support each student's make-believe play by keeping everybody informed of the appearance and expression of the characters. This approach promotes the speaking of all participants since they can feel a sense of unity, based on the communication used by these characters in the virtual space.

Fig. 3. Virtual classroom

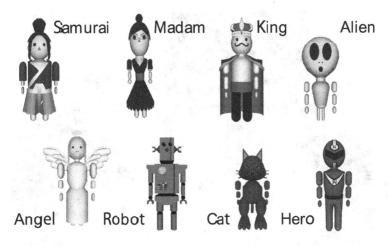

Fig. 4. The eight characters

3   Communication Experiment

3.1   Experimental Setup

In our experiment, considering group learning both with GOSAL (w/ G) and without GOSAL (w/o G), we compared four subjects acting as students and one subject acting as a teacher (Fig. 5, Fig. 6). We made slides showing educational materials that were configured as an explanation section, a discussion section, and a debate section (Fig. 7). We prepared two kinds of content—"Japanese and Western food" and "Chinese and French food"—to make the students to discuss familiar meals in various ways.

Fig. 5. Experiment scenery (w/ G)

Fig. 6. Experiment scenery (w/o G)

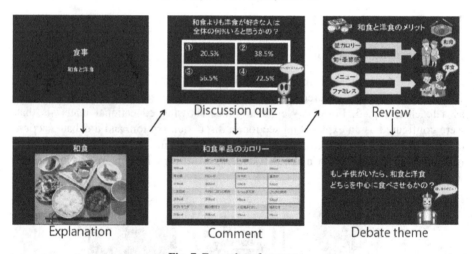

Fig. 7. Examples of contents

The procedure of the experiment is shown in Fig. 8. First, the teacher explained the experiment. Then, we had the users initiate the group learning by introducing themselves, which they did via the characters in the w/ G mode. After these introductions, the teacher gave a lecture to the students using the slides. During the lecture, students discussed their answers to a discussion quiz for 3 min, which they repeated a second time. They also each debated the theme of the debate for 6 min. Finally, the students answered a questionnaire that included a seven-point bipolar rating scale and a free description. These flows constituted one set for one mode, after which we went through the same set of flows in the w/o G mode. In the experiment, we assigned the w/ G and the w/o G modes and the lecture contents randomly. Before beginning the experiment, we explained the system and the educational materials to the teacher, and prescribed the lectures that would be given in the same way in both modes. The role of the teacher was to give a lecture in the same way using slides, and to ask one of the students to make a comment. All the participants wore a microphone during the experiment, and we recorded their conversation during the group learning process. We used a portable multi-track recorder (TASCAM DR-680) to record the conversation. The experiment was performed by one 23-year-old Japanese student who acted as the teacher, and 8 pairs drawn from 32 Japanese students, 19–23 years old, who acted as students (16 men, 16 women, with each group composed of the same gender).

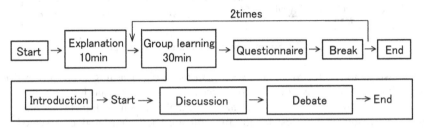

Fig. 8. Procedure of the experiment

3.2   Results

Fig. 9 shows the results of the seven-point bipolar ratings. As shown by the results of a Wilcoxon signed-rank test, there were no significant differences in any of the items. We then divided the results of the seven-point bipolar ratings by gender, and performed a Wilcoxon signed-rank test and a Mann-Whitney U-test. Fig. 10 shows the results. In terms of "easy communication," there was a significant difference, at a significance level of 1%, and the w/o G mode was rated higher by the men. In addition, in terms of "enjoyment," "active participation," "easy communication," the women rated the system higher than the men in the w/ G mode. At a significance level of 5%, for "active participation," "lively conversation," the women rated the system higher than the men in the w/ G mode, at a significance level of 1%.

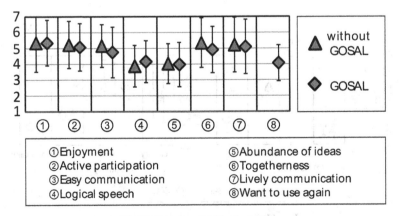

Fig. 9. Seven-point bipolar rating

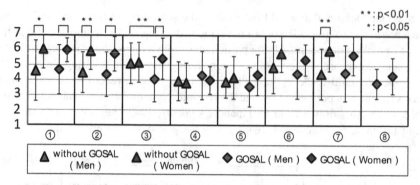

Fig. 10. Seven-point bipolar rating, by gender

Next, we analyzed the voice and speech in the group-learning event that we recorded using ELAN [7]. We divided the voices into utterances and laughter, and analyzed these in terms of time of occurrence and number of times. Fig. 11(a) shows the results. The result of the t-test for the time of utterances and laughter revealed that there was a significant difference at a significance level of 5%. In addition, for the number of times of utterances and laughter, there was a significant difference at a significance level of 1%. To analyze the speech, we investigated the degree of creativity expressed using the S-A creativity test by G. P. Guilford. Using this test, we could categorize the words spoken in the group learning event, and could calculate the scores for creativity in terms of the frequency of the appearance of the words used. First, we noted the words that appeared for the first time in conversation, and the person who had uttered these words. The number of the words was 1,176 of 755 kinds. Next, two experimenters categorized these words and determined a total of 18 categories. Next, we constructed a table to calculate the scores for the words according to the frequency of their occurrence. Using this table, we were able to calculate the scores for fluency, flexibility, originality, and creativity, which was the sum of the first three scores. Fig. 11(b) shows the results. As shown by the results of the t-test, there was no significant difference in the scores for creativity. However, for the original scores, there was a significant difference at a significance level of 1%.

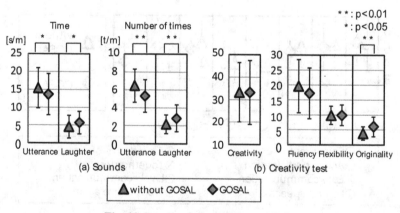

Fig. 11. Results of conversation analysis

In addition, we divided the results of the creativity test by gender. Fig. 12 shows the results. As shown by the results of the t-test, there was a significant difference at a significance level of 5% for time of men's laughter in the w/o G mode, and at a significance level of 5% for the number of times of men's utterances. Moreover, in terms of men's fluency scores, the w/o G mode was rated higher than the w/ G mode at a significance level of 5%. In terms of the fluency scores, in the w/ G mode, the women rated higher than the men, at a significance level of 5%. Furthermore, in terms of men's and women's scores for originality, the w/ G mode was rated higher than the w/o G mode, at a significance level of 1%.

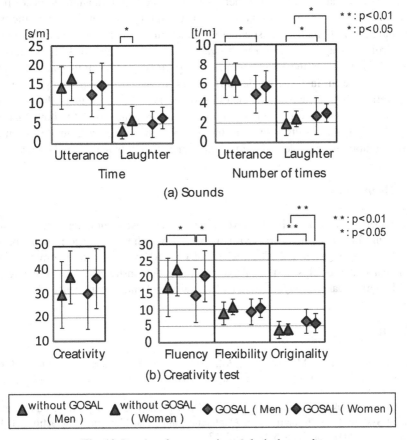

Fig. 12. Results of conversation analysis, by gender

3.3   Discussion

The results of our voice and speech analysis show that GOSAL produces more laughter and creative discussion than ordinary group work. The reason for this is that learners enjoy the group learning process in which they flexibly share ideas utilizing the different characteristics of the CG characters. For example, one learner said, "You should use the search function of ROBOT," which showed that this promoted the other learners' interaction in the quiz mode. This is but one example of how ideas and interactions using GOSAL provoked the learners' laughter and made their communication more pleasurable.

On the other hand, the learner's utterances decreased in the w/ G mode. This reflects the decrease in men's utterances, as their fluency scores were low. This result is also reflected in the seven-point bipolar ratings, in terms of "easy communication" and the other items. These results suggest that the men had a harder time getting used to enjoying role-play talk. On the other hand, there were significant differences in the seven-point bipolar rating in terms of gender, though the women evaluated the w/ G mode and the w/o G mode almost equally. In fact, the women were readily able to get used to role-playing, and gave a high evaluation to the group work. In addition, in terms of laughter time, there were significant differences between men and women in the w/o G mode. In fact, the gender differences displayed in the seven-point bipolar ratings reflect the fact that the women talked and laughed much more than the men. However, the laughter time and the originality scores increased for both men and women. In fact, the results show that the group work in the w/ G mode essentially becomes a more pleasurable and unique experience than it is in the w/o G mode.

4   Summary

In this paper, we first describe the development of GOSAL, which facilitates pleasurable learning for users who share a virtual space in which they engage in make-believe play. Next, we evaluated the effectiveness of GOSAL by means of a communication experiment that used this system. As a result, we demonstrated the effective-ness of GOSAL, which makes group learning a pleasurable and unique experience.

References

1. Watanabe, T., Okubo, M., Nakashige, M., Danbarao, R.: InterActor: Speech-Driven Embodied Inreractive Actor. International Journal of Human-Computer Interaction 17(1), 43–60 (2004)
2. Watanabe, T., Okubo, M.: SAKURA: Voice-Driven Embodied Group-Entrained Communication System. In: 10th International Conference on Human Computer Interaction (HCI International 2003), vol. 2, pp. 558–562 (2003)
3. Yamamoto, M., Watanabe, T.: Development of an Edutainment System with InterActors of a Teacher and a Student in which a User Plays a Double Role of Them. In: Proceedings of the 17th IEEE International Symposium on Robot and Human Interactive Communication (RO-MAN 2008), pp. 659–664 (2008)
4. Yamane, M., Yamamoto, M., Watanabe, T.: Development of a Real-Space Sharing Edutainment System based on Communication Support with Make- Believe Play. In: Proceedings of SICE Annual Conference 2011, pp. 2571–2574 (2011)

5. Kanegae, H., Yamane, M., Yamamoto, M., Watanabe, M.: Evaluation of a Real-Space Sharing Edutainment System based on Communication with Make-Believe Play. In: The 12th SICE System Integration Division Annual Conference, pp. 0148–0149 (2011) (in Japanese)
6. Vygotsky, L.: Play and its role in the Mental; Development of the Child. Voprosy Psychologii (6) (1966)
7. ELAN Description,
   http://www.lat-mpi.eu/tools/elan/elan-description
8. Study group of psychology experiment instruction: Experiment and test = Basis of psychology exposition section; BAIFUKAN, ch. 4 (1985)

A Support Framework for Automated Video and Multimedia Workflows for Production and Archive

Robert Manthey, Robert Herms, Marc Ritter, Michael Storz, and Maximilian Eibl

Technische Universität Chemnitz,
Chair Media Informatics,
Straße der Nationen 62, D-09111 Chemnitz
{robert.manthey,robert.herms,marc.ritter,
michael.storz,maximilian.eibl}@informatik.tu-chemnitz.de

Abstract. The management of the massive amount of data in video- and multimedia workflows is a hard and expensive work that requires much personnel and technical resources. Our flexible and scalable open source middleware framework offers solution approaches for the automated handling of the ingest and the workflow by an automated acquisition of all available information. By using an XML format to describe the processes, we provide an easy, fast and well-priced solution without the need for specific human skills.

Keywords: Ingest, Framework, XML, Archiving, Middleware.

1 Introduction

Today's archives of audiovisual media, especially video tapes, are still at least partly insufficiently documented. Making this media searchable is a challenging task concerning capacity and time. The more specific the metadata vocabulary is, the greater are the possibilities for information retrieval and the automation of processes [1, p.94]. A comprehensive description of the media requires the collection of as many as relevant metadata [2].

This challenge can be overcome by an early intervention into the workflow, for instance during the ingest process. Ingest means transferring media into a system including encoding and file creation. The automated ingest is a complex workflow, which requires appropriate hard- and software components. [3]

We assume that metadata concerning technical constraints of the ingest process is a benefit for the media lifecycle. This includes the used technologies as well as hard- and software. Based on this approach, media can be documented more comprehensively by enabling an increasing transparency for the end user. Furthermore, more available options concerning search requests are provided like searching for original video tape formats or video software and their requirements, for instance, devices that naturally only supports low bandwidth only would get low bandwidth results. An established workflow yields the opportunity to detect faulty equipment or to correct errors automatically in the ingested material, because the type of the video tape or the video player is known that may have caused a specific noise. [4]

S. Yamamoto (Ed.): HIMI/HCII 2013, Part III, LNCS 8018, pp. 336–341, 2013.

Nowadays, commercial systems in production and ingest often use proprietary standards, closed and fixed black boxes or are very expensive like Multicam [5] or Airspeed 5000 [6]. On the other side non-commercial systems like Ingex [7] are open source and therefore modifiable, but more focused on production processes. In contrast to that our solution allows an automated tape-ingest and the extraction of metadata to support further processing.

2   Imtecs-Framework

As a part of our research, a flexible and open source framework called Imtecs (*I*ngest *m*iddleware including extraction of metadata from *te*chnical *c*onstraints) has been developed providing a collection of components in order to implement an automated ingest workflow, which in addition enables the extraction of metadata of the technical constraints for each job. Basically, the framework is extensible and can be integrated into existing workflows, such as archiving. Furthermore, it can be applied individually or in combination with an automatic content analysis as well as intellectual annotation to grant a holistic solution.

In order to adapt to such an ingest workflow, as much information as possible should be acquired. For this purpose, we define the Ingest Workflow Description Format (IWD), an XML format to describe all devices and services that are involved in the workflow as well as their properties and relationships to each other.

Using this description, the framework works as a middleware layer for an ingest workflow scenario storing the collected metadata of the technical constraints of each ingested job.

2.1   System Architecture

The Imtecs-Framework provides a collection of software components to meet the requirements to be open source, modifiable, using an extensible format as well as gathering as much information as possible. The handling of external devices and services is included in the system core. After configuring the framework, it acts as a middleware-layer to control the participating devices and services. Basically, also devices can provide any kind of services like a webservice. The classification at user level facilitates the configuration of workflows making them more transparent, especially for other people in the collaboration.

The architecture of the framework (Fig. 1) prescribes that devices are represented by Device Objects and services by Service Objects. Device and Service Classes are abstractions of devices. Each class provides metadata parameters which are set by each corresponding object. The adjusted Controller takes over the control of the workflow and arranges the scheduling of the devices and services, so that one or more audiovisual media can be are successfully ingested. The Metadata Collector gathers all the metadata of each Device and Service Objects that are involved in the ingest process of a certain medium. [4]

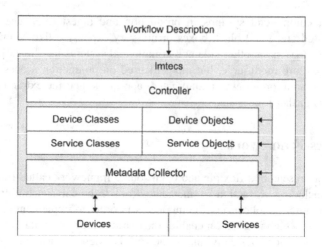

Fig. 1. Scheme of our framework

2.2   Ingest Workflow Description Format (IWD)

To describe a given workflow, the components and relations between them, we need a flexible, customizable, scalable and easy to handle format. We decided to create a format based on XML which fulfills these requirements. We separate these descriptions into several files to allow their distribution through several hosts and administrative authorities. Because of this, one file handles the configuration of relatively general settings as shown in Fig. 2. Others hold the workflow-dependent settings for the given workflows like in Fig. 3. This distribution and the possibility to use any kind of network to operate the framework, provides the opportunity and adaptivity to realize any given ingest workflow as presented in the next section, for instance.

Fig. 2 shows a configuration file from our Imtecs-framework. It contains relatively general, workflow-independent settings. For example, the amount of time that can be added to each ingest operation to be robust against overlong input materials or unpredictable timing issues. The *TestController* is used to operate the whole framework in a simulation mode with communication between the components, workflow operation, metadata acquisition and so on, but without interaction to real hardware devices or external services. After this manner, configurations of all kinds of workflows can be tested and verified, easy and fast and without any touch to the valuable material. Because of the distributed nature of the framework all locations occurs as local or remote paths, as shown in the entries *Devicelist*, Log and *PathList*. Here, they point to the descriptions of the workflow and the location of the logging file. The final destination of each ingest, the *Storage*, displays the connection to other systems pointing to different hosts with different destination paths on that hosts, to allow them to be used by different workflows or stages of workflows.

```xml
<?xml version="1.0" encoding="utf-8" ?>
<Configuration>
  <TestController>false</TestController>
  <RecordTolerance unit="minutes">10</RecordTolerance>
  <DeviceList id="1">C:\Users\validax\Imtecs\Imtecs\WorkflowDescription.iwd</DeviceList>
  <Log id="40">\\validax.informatik.tu-chemnitz.de\ingest\Log.txt</Log>
  <PathList>
    <Path id="51" type="Storage">
    \\validax-storage1.informatik.tu-chemnitz.de\validax\ValidaxIngest</Path>
    <Path id="52" type="Storage">
    \\validax-storage2.informatik.tu-chemnitz.de\validax\ValidaxIngest</Path>
    <Path id="53" type="Storage">
    \\validax-storage3.informatik.tu-chemnitz.de\validax\ValidaxIngest</Path>
    <Path id="70" type="Metadata">
    \\validax-metadata.informatik.tu-chemnitz.de\validax\ValidaxMetadata </Path>
  </PathList>
  <Source_Identification type="manual"/>
</Configuration>
```

Fig. 2. General configuration file

```xml
<?xml version="1.0" encoding="utf-8" ?>
<WorkflowDescription>
  <DeviceList>
    <List name="Robot">
      <Robot id="1" active="true" controllable="true">
        <Address type="TCP/IP">123.110.220.121:8001</Address>
        <DeviceInfo>
          <Name>L2012</Name>
          <Type>Lego</Type>
          <Interface>
            <Input>Bluetooth</Input>
          </Interface>
        </DeviceInfo>
      </Robot>
    </List>
    <List name="Camera">
      <Camera id="31" active="false" controllable="true">
    </List>
    <List name="Player">
      <Player id="62" active="true" controllable="false">
        <DeviceInfo>
          <Name>Panasonic AG-7700</Name>
          <Type>SVHS</Type>
          <Interface>
            <Output>SVideo</Output>
          </Interface>
        </DeviceInfo>
        <Workflow position="2">
          <Next type="Device">92</Next>
        </Workflow>
      </Player>
    </List>
    <List name="Converter">
      <Converter id="92" active="true" controllable="false">
        <DeviceInfo>
          <Name>Electronic-Design TBC-Light</Name>
          <Type>Time Base Corrector</Type>
          <Interface>
            <Input>SVideo</Input>
            <Output>SVideo</Output>
          </Interface>
        </DeviceInfo>

      <Workflow>
        <Previous type="Device">62</Previous>
        <Next type="Device">93</Next>
      </Workflow>
      </Converter>
      <Converter id="93" active="true" controllable="false">
        <DeviceInfo>
          <Name>Blackmagic Design Mini Converter</Name>
          <Type>Analog to SDI</Type>
          <Interface>
            <Input>SVideo</Input>
            <Output>SDI</Output>
          </Interface>
        </DeviceInfo>
      <Workflow>
        <Previous type="Device">92</Previous>
        <Next type="Device">122</Next>
      </Workflow>
      </Converter>
    </List>
    <List name="CaptureDevice">
      <CaptureDevice id="122" active="true" controllable="true">
        <Address type="HTTP">123.110.220.66:8004</Address>
        <DeviceInfo>
          <Name>Telestream Pipeline HD</Name>
          <Type>HD Hardware-Network-Encoder</Type>
          <Interface>
            <Input>SDI</Input>
            <Output>Ethernet</Output>
          </Interface>
        </DeviceInfo>
      <Workflow>
        <Previous type="Device">93</Previous>
        <Next type="Storage">53</Next>
      </Workflow>
      </CaptureDevice>
    </List>
  </DeviceList>
  <ServiceList>
</WorkflowDescription>
```

Fig. 3. XML description of a workflow

The sample in Fig. 3 shows the description of one of our workflows used for the automated ingest of video tapes. The *WorkflowDescription* is divided into two parts the *DeviceList* and the *ServiceList*. The *DeviceList* contains information to the devices and their part of the workflow. In a similar way a *ServiceList* is organized and used. They contain for instance lists of groups of similar devices that are uniquely identified by the name of the group. Each device also has a unique id to be identified within the workflow. The attribute *Active* enables or disables the device. The term Controllable describes the capability to control and receive information on-demand in order to be stored as metadata. If the device is uncontrollable the metadata must be predefined. Besides, the name, the type of the device and information about the connectivity are stored. The *ID*s of the previous and subsequent devices complete the description.

As shown in the example, the robot-device is a part of the workflow, because it changes the tapes, but it is not connected to the chain of devices operating the ingest itself to get the content of the tapes.

3   Application in the Field of Digital Archiving

We use the proposed framework within a complete automated workflow from ingest over analyzation and distribution to storing operations. The ingest of our application domain comprises a big amount of VHS, DV and Betacam tapes. About one thousand hours of content combined with associated technical constrains and metadata have already been processed.

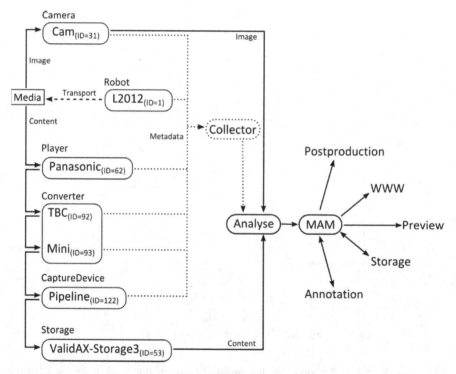

Fig. 4. Scheme of the workflow and its application inside our media management process

The left side of Fig. 4 shows the workflow described in the XML of Fig. 3. The dotted line represents the flow of the metadata extracted during the ingest, the collection and transfer to our analysis system. Together with the content of the media and the images from the envelop of the media, a comprehensive analyzation is realized.

The results are passed to our Media Asset Management System (MAM) and prepared to support subsequent steps like postproduction, distribution to Websites or to store in archiving systems.

4 Future Work

The results in this paper indicate that our framework can be used for automated pre-processing and distribution of the audiovisual media. Since the description of the ingest-workflow is separated, the applicability of the framework appears very flexible in creating arbitrary even non-linear processing chains that can be interactively altered during run-time.

The next steps include investigations of the human-machine interface concerning monitoring and controlling of a workflow with the intention to distinguish between professional and non-professional users by certain characteristics and parameters. At last, there is also a need for the examination of the deployment to mobile applications.

Acknowledgements. This work was partially accomplished within the project ValidAX – Validation of the AMOPA and XTRIEVAL framework (Project VIP0044), funded by the Federal Ministry of Education and Research (Bundesministerium für Wissenschaft und Forschung), Germany.

References

1. Hercher, J., Mitzscherlich, A., Sack, H.: Bestandsanalyse, Metadaten und Systematisierung. Digitalisierungsfibel, Leitfadenfüraudiovisuelle Archive. transfermedia, Potsdam, pp. 82–101 (2011)
2. Airola, D., Boch, L., Dimino, G.: Automated Ingestion of Audiovisual Content (2003), http://www.broadcastpapers.com/whitepapers/IBCRAIAutoIngestAVContent.pdf (February 15, 2013)
3. Borgotallo, R., Boch, L., Messina, A.: Automated Industrial Digitizationof Betacam tapes - with MXF generation andvalidation (2011), http://tech.ebu.ch/docs/techreview/trev_2011-Q4_betacam_digitiztion_borgotallo.pdf (July 10, 2012)
4. Herms, R., Manthey, R.,Eibl, M.: A Framework For Media Ingestion- Adding Data About Technical Constraints. (2012), http://nbn-resolving.de/urn:nbn:de:bsz:ch1-qucosa-103912 (January 15, 2013)
5. EVS Broadcast Equipment SA: Multicam - Version 11.01 – Operating Manual (2012), http://www.evs.tv/sites/default/files/download_area/package/compatible_11.01.77_addon/Multicam%2011.01.77/MULTICAM_operationman_11.01_ENG_121221_web.pdf (January 21, 2013)
6. Avid Technology Inc.: AirSpeed 5000 Datenblatt (2012), http://www.avid.com/static/resources/common/documents/datasheets/airspeed_5000/AirSpeed_5000_ds_A4_sec_de.pdf (February 5, 2013)
7. Tudor, P.N., McKinnell, J.S., Pinks, N.P., Casey, S.: Developments in Automated Tapeless Production for Multi-Camera Programmes (2010), http://www.bbc.co.uk/rd/publications/whitepaper186.shtml (February 10, 2013)

Responsibilities and Challenges
of Social Media Managers

Christian Meske and Stefan Stieglitz

University of Muenster, Department of Information Systems
Muenster, Germany
{christian.meske,stefan.stieglitz}@uni-muenster.de

Abstract. Within the last years enterprises massively began to adapt social media for internal usage. They do so in order to increase their knowledge management as well as to make collaboration and communication more efficient. However, until now, very little is known about employees who are responsible for adaption processes and the management of the internal social media. In our study we conducted 15 interviews with "social media managers" of 15 large German enterprises. We found that the role of a social media manager is faced with enormous challenges (e.g. providing information about the added value of social media) while on the other hand they lack the power to make decisions (e.g. regarding staff and budget).

Keywords: social media, manager, Mintzberg, manager roles.

1   Introduction

Due to the increasing importance of internationalization, project work, and expert knowledge in enterprises the demands on company-internal communication and collaboration processes grows as well. Companies have recognized the potentials of social media applications and started to use inter- and intranet-based social media such as e.g. microblogging and wikis [1, 2]. While the introduction of social media in the past was rather decentralized – on departmental level (e.g. introduction of a wiki) - companies are now striving for the implementation of company-wide solutions. Technology suppliers like IBM or Microsoft react by supplying new social media applications (such as Lotus Connections or Jive) or extending existing products with respective features (e.g. Microsoft SharePoint).

A targeted use of this so-called social business software, which comprises components such as wikis, discussion rooms, and profile pages (similar to social networking sites), can facilitate the externalization of expert knowledge, make experts more easily identifiable and approachable, and support the creation of social capital [3, 4].The emergence of "Social Business Software" (e.g. Jive, Lotus Connections, Microsoft SharePoint) has been a noticeable driver for this. At the same time, the company-wide introduction and usage bears new challenges for companies. The internal use of social media does not only lead to a series of legal, technical, and socio-cultural obstacles,

S. Yamamoto (Ed.): HIMI/HCII 2013, Part III, LNCS 8018, pp. 342–351, 2013.

but also faces a high pressure for justification since the "return on investment" in the context of the traditional cost-benefit-analysis is difficult to measure [5, 6]. So far these new challenges on management level of companies have only received marginal attention. The emergence of social business software suggests a strategic control of the introduction and usage processes by the higher management levels. Yet, very little is known about social media managers who take responsibility for those processes. Throughout the course of this article we therefore explore the role of social media managers based on a series of interviews. A special focus lies on the findings about the organizational positioning as well as the responsibilities and rights of social media managers. As a first step we analyzed current literature and discuss the state-of-the-art of research on this matter. We then continue by introducing a role model for the evaluation of our study. Afterwards the results are presented and discussed before we end with a conclusion and an outlook for further research.

2   Related Work

2.1   Social Media Managers

The phenomenon of social media has been an intensively discussed subject of the academic world within the last years. Kaplan and Haenlein [7] provided a frequently used definition of social media. According to them *"social media is a group of Internet-based applications that build on the ideological and technological foundations of Web 2.0, and that allow the creation and exchange of user generated content"*. In this sense, social networking sites (SNS), file sharing platforms, wikis, and blogs are understood as social media. Most studies focus on the use of a certain type of web 2.0-technology in companies such as e.g. blogs or microblogs [8-11], wikis [2, 4, 12], social bookmarking [13, 14] or social networks [15, 16]. Wenger, White and Smith [17] discussed how to organize the creation of virtual communities. Based on their work, life cycle approaches were used to describe different stages of community building and how managers could support the success of those communities. However, his work does not reflect the role of social media managers. Montalvo [18] focuses on the impacts of social media on the corporate landscape. According to him, *"social media management, at a business enterprise level, is the collaborative process of using Web 2.0 platforms and tools to accomplish desired organizational objectives"*. Following him, social media management influences several core areas of companies such as brand awareness, brand reputation, strategy development, analytics, creativity, and collaboration. He does however not explicitly discuss the role of the manager but rather the range of activities of social media management. Furthermore, he does not differentiate between the internal tasks (addressing the employees) and the external tasks (addressing the customers).

Following Bottles and Sherlock [19], it is a crucial task to implement a social media manager in order to lead the effective and appropriate use of social media (see also [20]). Furthermore, they highlight that an organization can eliminate potential obstacles by taking responsibility for the (social media) strategy. They suggest that this is independent from specific departments, as employees are going to be using social media as part of their jobs. Regarding the role of the social media manager, Bottles and Sherlock [19] suggest that it should not be located in the IT department, because technical matters do not cause the main challenges. Instead, social media managers should report directly to senior management. However, Ter Chian Tan and Vasa [20] found that in contrast to this, the responsibility of a social media strategy often falls largely in the hands of the owners (for small firms) and the marketing departments (for medium and large firms). Literature also mentions that a major problem of social media managers is to prove that social media brings any benefits to the enterprise. Therefore CEOs ask them to measure the return on investment (RoI). Following Stieglitz et al. [5], measuring the RoI of virtual communities and other collaboration tools is a difficult task since costs can be easily measured while benefits can hardly be operationalized and monetized.

2.2   Management Roles

In the context of managerial work there has been a variety of normative studies that investigate the conception of managerial behavior and coherent activities that are aligned to managerial effectiveness [21]. In detail they describe idealistic objectives in connection with prerequisite actions that require effective and efficient allocation of resources that will lead to the best output [22]. In contrast, inductive studies in this scope of research focus on accurate descriptions of what managers actually do, identifying characteristics, work patterns, and tasks that constitute managerial work by conducting empirical investigations [23]. Both approaches, normative as well as the inductive one, have been widely discussed in respect to their capability of giving comprehensive insight into managerial work [22, 24, 25]. The choice of the inductive approach seems to be appropriate for our study as it is based on empirical methods and sees the managers as *"affected by such realities of organizational life as politics, the actual distribution of power and authority, the pressures which managers face to manage conflict and limits on human rationality (...)"* [22]. In this context, Mintzberg [26] conducted an empirical study of managerial roles. Based on this he identified three different categories, comprising ten different manager roles that each person in a leadership position more or less adheres to [26]. The respective roles can be described as follows:

Interpersonal Category. *Figurehead:* The manager in this case is the symbolic head of the organization or department, having representational duties of legal and social kind (e.g. sign legal documents or host receptions). *Leader:* Leading is one of the most important tasks of managers. Their main tasks lie in the motivation and guidance of employees as well as their allocation and personal development. *Liaison:* Here the establishing and maintenance of internal and external contacts is of importance, which can develop formally as well as informally. This can be realized through horizontal and vertical communication.

Informational Category. *Monitor:* The goal of the manager is to increase the understanding of the company's operations and field of work by seeking and acquiring related information. _Disseminator:_ The manager is responsible for the passing of internal and external information towards the members of the organization.

Spokesman: As a spokesperson, the manager keeps influential and other interested groups of people informed about the performance, policies and plans of his organization, department or team.

Decisional Category. _Entrepreneur:_ As an entrepreneur, the manager acts as initiator and designer of a major part of the controlled change within the organization. He is responsible for finding useful innovations or the change of impulses, and the initialization of related optimization processes. _Problem Solver:_ While the manager handles voluntary changes in his role as an entrepreneur, as a problem solver he is responsible for handling unforeseen crisis situations. The center of this function is defined by coping with unexpected and important disturbances in the company's business processes. _Resource Allocator:_ The manager has to make decisions about the allocation of monetary resources, staff or organizational units. Beyond this, he is charged with the control of interrelationships of different decisions. _Negotiator:_ The last role describes the manager as a participant in negotiating activities. This can also comprise company-internal negotiations like e.g. setting work standards.

3   Empirical Study

3.1   Methodology

In this research paper our goal is to exploratively investigate social media managers' roles. We therefore conducted a series of interviews with social media managers in companies, which are listed in the DAX30 (German stock exchange index of the 30 largest companies regarding the market capitalization). Altogether 15 people have been interviewed, which, according to the companies, manage the internal social media processes. The interviews have been conducted between October 2011 and April 2012. Each interview took between 60 and 90 minutes. The majority of questions have been open-ended questions following a previously developed interview guide. We based the guide development on the theoretical work of Mintzberg. In the interviews we therefore addressed the topic of the formal position in the company as well as the roles and responsibilities allocated to a social media manager. The majority of interviews have been recorded (if agreed by the interviewee) and subsequently transcribed and analyzed by the open coding method.

3.2   Results

Based on the ten managerial roles described before, we present our findings in the following chapter.

Interpersonal Roles. _Figurehead:_ The task of representation is usually appropriated to the higher or top level of management. Our interviews have shown that social media managers mostly belong to the line of middle management. Since social media is used as a tool for communication, the responsible people have been from the area of internal communication in eight cases and in three cases from the human resources department. In four cases, the IT department has been involved in the contextual design and execution, while in the other cases it was mainly responsible for the commissioning of the systems. *"The responsible for our social media project is a double lead, composed of the department of internal communication and IT, where internal communication is the designer and IT the enabler."* Only in one case a top manager (CIO) is the main responsible for social media. <u>Leader:</u> We obtained mixed results concerning this aspect. Social media managers are usually already members of existing teams in the areas of company communications, human resources (HR) or IT. The positions reported were amongst others "Head of Internal Communications", "Assistant Team Leader of Internal Communications", "Digital Media Manager", "Enterprise Community Manager", "Global Collaboration and Knowledge Manager", "Social Director Collaboration Application" or "Senior Manager eCollaboration". The interviews revealed that while the leaders of existing groups are now also responsible for the implementation of social media, additional positions are also being created to include social media experts in existing teams. Only in two cases an autonomous social media team has been implemented which in turn required a lead of its own. Altogether we can conclude that newly created social media positions are seldomly created in leading management positions, but rather existing department and team leaders gain social media expertise and hence take over new responsibilities. <u>Liaison:</u> All interviewees indicated that they have to communicate and coordinate both on a vertical and horizontal level. Other departments on the same hierarchy level are included in the organizing of the platform, such as e.g. the IT department participating in the commission of the systems. In addition to this, there are often several departments that want to use social media in their operations. *"Next to us* [as internal communications] *also the departments of HR, marketing and finances are interested in using social media."* Furthermore, the workers council has often been included in the planning and implementation at an early stage to be able to consider e.g. legal questions concerning personnel. *"There is a responsibility to communicate with different institutions within the company like the workers council, the IT-Security or the division for data protection."* Additionally, the communication with different user groups has a great influence for social media managers on supporting the adoption of social media. *"We used the knowledge of promoters and Early Adopters to configure our platform and to support the process of introduction."* Besides that, the establishing of contacts on a vertical level is also of high relevance to promote the social media project internally and find supporters (e.g. the CIO). According to the case studies mentioned in section 2, one of the most important factors of success for the introduction and usage of social media is to convince the management to participate actively and act as role models. Therefore a certain influence of the social media manager on the higher levels of management seems to support that goal. *"The growth of our platform benefits from the promotion by the top management. With the participation of our CIO and other IT managers, the activity among the users of our platform increased rapidly."*

Informational Roles. _Monitor:_ Our interviews show that all social media managers are expected to have a solid understanding of the operations and field of work of their company. According to them this information is important since the implementation of social media is not comparable to that of conventional IT applications. _"I need to know about the subtleties of our corporate culture, the structure and organization of important business processes as well as the major aspects of our IT landscape."_ Outside the company the interviewees especially pay attention to the trend developments in the area of social media, monitor the legal situation concerning data protection, and educate themselves. Also the search for information about success factors and best practice scenarios is part of it since the use of social media is still a relatively young research topic. Furthermore, the monitoring of other companies is a common practice and is used as a benchmark for the success of internal social media activities. _" We compare our data with experience values from other companies, e.g. the percentage of active users, and exchange our experiences on conferences."_ _Disseminator:_ This role only applies very rarely to social media managers. Although they gather information (refer to the role of monitor), this is not an essential part of their role according to 13 of the interviewed. _"The gathered information is mainly used for the improvement and development of our social media project and not to supply other parts of the company with it."_ _Spokesperson:_ The interviewees stated that they represent this function especially towards three groups: the higher management, the users, and the (interested) public. Social media managers are, like other project leaders, obligated to keep the management up-to-date about the status quo, performance, development, problems, and further plans. This is also true for social media projects, since the added value for the company is often hard to measure and the use of social media is frequently associated with a "waste of time". Interviewees stated _"The management defines writing of e-mails clearly as a natural part of working time. But to use social media to communicate with colleagues instead of writing an email is viewed skeptically."_ and _"We do not have the real support of the management, primarily because the added value is not visible."_ Towards the interest group of users, i.e. employees of the company, the social media managers also have the role of a spokesperson. _"We inform and educate our users about new guidelines, future plans, current measures and the reasons for those."_ Seven interviewees added that they contacted the public to inform it about their current project in the form of articles or presentations. The reason for this is often an intended exchange of knowledge and experiences with science as well as other companies. Furthermore in four cases a _"positive influence on the company image to be perceived as modern and progressive"_ was expected.

Decisional Roles. _Entrepreneur:_ The majority of the interviewees stated that social media can not only change the way to communicate within a company, but also workflow processes and the corporate culture. Social media managers, in their role as entrepreneurs, design and conduct such social media projects and are constantly looking for new possibilities for adding value. _"One of the main reasons for the introduction of social media within our company is that we constantly need to simplify our processes and have to bring our new products faster to the market."_ Here they are supported by the above-mentioned information that is gathered inside and outside the company due to their monitor role. Yet in 12 cases it was mentioned that it is imposs- ible to dictate the potential and value adding changes that are expected by the use of social media. This is why the extent of organizational change, that is associated with the entrepreneurial role, can only be controlled with very difficulty. *"Due to the often found bottom-up-processes in social media it is very difficult to implement our ideas in a controlled manner."* This makes the role of the entrepreneur even harder for the social media manager since it lies in the tension field between innovation, the difficult steering and control as well as justification towards the top-management.

Problem Solver: Our interviews indicate that the traditional role of a crisis manager only applies very slightly to the social media managers. Yet in social media new dis- turbances may also emerge, such as the occurrence of a "social crisis", such as a mas- sive and immediate surfacing of negative customer critique [27].

Resource Allocator: 13 participants of our interviews stated to control a social media related budget, which is usually approved by the higher management level, e.g. the CIO. In three cases we found a sponsorship by the departments of HR and internal communication. *"Basically the budget is used for software procurement, customizing or consultancy."*

Negotiator: In three cases the interviewees were part of the IT department and in leading positions, due to which they also acted in their function as a negotiator. The remaining interviewees indicated that they are *"acting in a consulting function but [are] not actively participating in the negotiation processes"*. One person stated that due to changes in the workflows and the topical sensitivity regarding data security and legal employee matters, such close coordination with the employee representation has been necessary, *"that it could actually be called negotiation"*.

4   Discussion

Based on the interviews and the role model of Mintzberg, we were able to analyze responsibilities and challenges that social media managers are confronted with. At the same time we could also identify problems that social media managers face.

Positioning: Social media managers are mostly located in the internal communications department. Therefore, social media managers are seen as coordinators of communica- tion and collaboration systems. At the same time this raises the problem that the internal communication department, in contrast to HR and e.g. Knowledge Management, has so far rather been considered as a "soft" support function, which did not directly contribute to the value of the company. In some companies it could be observed that the social media manager has been repositioned and e.g. been migrated from the internal commu- nication to the HR department. According to the respective companies, this led to an increased acceptance of the responsible. *"[it is an] essential success factor, that they are not part of internal communications, so that they are taken more seriously"*. Often the social media responsible reports directly to the top management.

The position of the social media managers itself is either created as an enrichment to an existing or as a completely new position in the middle management level. Our interviews show that social media managers have a greater impact on the internal development of a company than other managers on the same hierarchical level, and also than originally anticipated by the higher management. The reason for this lies in the profound change possibilities which the social media manager has on the communication and collaboration in the company, through which e.g. knowledge management, collaboration, search for experts, creation of social capital, and a common corporate culture are reinforced.

Roles, Tasks, and Power of Decision Making: According to the results of our empirical study the major roles of social media are those of the coordinator, spokesperson, entrepreneur, and monitor.

Social media managers take a strong liaison role between the different perspectives and departments of the company (e.g. workers council, board, internal communication, HR, IT). At the same time they are under pressure to justify that their projects contribute value to the company. Here, social media managers often meet their limits since on the one hand the board demands clear KPIs and operational measurements for the degree to which the goals are reached, but on the other hand barely any methods for community controlling and measurement are known. The interviews have further shown that the managers are aware of this tension field and intensively look for possibilities to quantify the added value of social media. Another way to increase and retain the acceptance of the CEO is e.g. to prove that competing or similar companies use company-wide social media strategies as well. *"Benchmarking with other companies is a means by which I argue towards my CEO that we have to further intensify our social media activities"*.

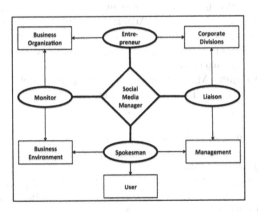

Fig. 1. Roles of Social Media Managers

5   Conclusion and Outlook

The interview series has shown that social media managers are often part of the middle management level and are either rooted in the internal communication or HR department. The position titles vary significantly since the extension of responsibility of an existing position can be done formally but also informally.

Besides always having up-to-date knowledge about social media, they furthermore require knowledge about the company's organization, corporate culture as well as communication and organizational skills due to their often mediating and coordinating function. It has to be considered as a limitation of this study that the series of interviews did only include managers of German companies. It must also be noted that the companies are partially in very different stages of implementing social media internally in their companies.

This article represents a first important step to scientifically discuss the current, and possibly the future role of the social media manager in companies. Our conducted interviews served for a broad overview that helped in uncovering central problems. Furthermore, a contribution to practice is given, since companies can derive their own relative position and estimate the challenges of a social media manager better.

One of the main problems of social media managers is the imbalance of high expectations and relatively low discretionary power. Further research should therefore cover the aspect how social media managers can best face this tension field, and whether the discretionary power of the social media manager has to be redefined. Especially the lack of possibilities to evaluate projects and determine their success has been stated as a central problem by the interviewed. Concerning this, research should aim at developing a theoretical basis and provide empirical studies of best practices.

References

1. Zhang, J., Qu, Y., Cody, J., Wu, Y.: A Case Study of Microblogging in the Enterprise: Use, Value, and Related Issues. In: Proceedings of the 28th International Conference on Human Factors in Computing Systems, Atlanta, USA, pp. 123–132 (2010)
2. Stocker, A., Tochtermann, K.: Exploring the Value of Enterprise Wikis - A Multiple-Case Study. In: Proceedings of the International Conference on Knowledge Management and Information Sharing, Funchal (2009)
3. Saldanha, T.J., Krishnan, M.S.: Organizational Adoption of Web 2.0 Technologies: An Empirical Analysis. In: AMCIS, Proceedings, Paper 103 (2010),
http://aisel.aisnet.org/amcis2010/
103drivingfactorsbehindadoptionofWeb2.0
4. Mansour, O., Abusalah, M., Askenäs, L.: Wiki collaboration in organizations: an exploratory study. In: Proceedings of the 19th European Conference on Information Systems, Helsinki, Finland, pp. 9–12 (2011)
5. Stieglitz, S., Lattemann, C., vom Brocke, J., Sonnenberg, C.: Economics of Virtual Communities - A Financial Analysis of a Case Study at the Berlin Stock Exchange. In: Proceedings of the 21st Bled eConference (2008)
6. Stieglitz, S., Dang-Xuan, L.: Adoption and Use of Corporate Wikis in German Small and Medium-sized Enterprises. In: Proceedings of the 17th Americas Conference on Information Systems, USA, Detroit, Paper 235 (2011)
7. Kaplan, A., Haenlein, M.: Users of the world, unite! The challenges and opportunities of Social Media. Business Horizons 53(1), 59–68 (2010)

8. Efimova, L., Grudin, J.: Crossing boundaries: A case study of employee blogging. In: 40th Annual Hawaii International Conference on System Sciences, pp. 86–96 (2007)
9. Riemer, K., Richter, A., Diederich, S., Scifleet, P.: Tweet Talking - Exploring The Nature Of Microblogging at Capgemini Yammer. Business Information Systems Working Paper-WP2011-02, University of Sydney, Australia Link (2011),
   http://ses.library.usyd.edu.au/handle/2123/7226
10. Yardi, S., Golder, S.A., Brzozowski, M.J.: Blogging at work and the corporate attention economy. In: Proceedings of the 27th international Conference on Human Factors in Computing Systems, pp. 2071–2080 (2009)
11. Seebach, C.: Searching for Answers - Knowledge Exchange through Social Media in Organizations. In: Proceedings of the 45th Hawaii International Conference on System Sciences, pp. 3908–3917 (2012)
12. Hasan, H., Pfaff, C.C.: The Wiki: an environment to revolutionise employees' interaction with corporate knowledge. In: Proceedings of OZCHI 2006, pp. 377–380 (2006)
13. Laurie, E., Damianos, D.C., Griffith, J., Hirst, D.M., Smallwood, J.: Exploring the Adoption, Utility, and Social Influences of Social Bookmarking in a Corporate Environment. In: 40th Annual Hawaii International Conference on System Sciences (2007)
14. Millen, D.R., Yang, M., Whittaker, S., Feinberg, J.: Social bookmarking and exploratory search. In: ECSCW 2007, Limerick, Ireland, September 26-28 (2007)
15. Riemer, K., Overfeld, P., Scifleet, P., Richter, A.: Oh, SNEP! The Dynamics of Social Network Emergence - the case of Capgemini Yammer. Business Information Systems Working Paper-WP201201, University of Sydney, Australia. Link (2012),
   http://ses.library.usyd.edu.au/handle/2123/8049
16. DiMicco, J., Millen, D., Geyer, W., Dugan, C., Brownholtz, B., Muller, M.: Motivations for social networking at work. In: Proceedings of the ACM 2008 Conference on Computer Supported Cooperative Work, pp. 711–720 (2008)
17. Wenger, E., White, N., Smith, J.D.: Digital Habitats; stewarding technology for communities, Portland, CPsquare, p. 228 (2009)
18. Montalvo, R.E.: Social media management. International Journal of Management and Information Systems 15(3), 91–96 (2011)
19. Bottles, K., Sherlock, T.: Who Should Manage Your Social Media Strategy? Physician Executive 37(2), 68–72 (2011)
20. Ter Chian Tan, F., Vasa, R.: Toward a Social Media Usage Policy. In: Proceedings of ACIS 2011, Paper 72 (2011), http://aisel.aisnet.org/acis2011/72
21. Leslie, J.B., Dalton, M., Ernst, C., Deal, J.: Managerial Effectiveness in a Global Context. Greensboro, Center for Creative Leadership, NC (2002)
22. Burgaz, B.: Managerial roles approach and the prominent study of Henry Mintzberg and some empirical studies upon the principals work (1997)
23. Noordegraaf, M., Stewart, R.: Managerial behaviour research in private and public sectors: distinctiveness, disputes and directions. Journal of Management Studies 37(3), 427–443 (2000)
24. Hales, C.P.: What do managers do? A critical review of the evidence. Journal of Management Studies 23(1), 88–115 (1986)
25. Fondas, N., Stewart, R.: Enactment in Managerial Jobs: A Role Analysis. Journal of Management Studies 31(1), 83–103 (1994)
26. Mintzberg, H.: The nature of managerial work. Harper & Row, New York (1973)
27. Urban Dictonary,
   http://www.urbandictionary.com/define.php?term=shitstorm

Digital War Room for Design

Requirements for Collocated Group Work Spaces

Mika P. Nieminen, Mari Tyllinen, and Mikael Runonen

Aalto University School of Science, P.O. Box 15400 FI-00076 Aalto, Finland
{mika.nieminen,mari.tyllinen,mikael.runonen}@aalto.fi

Abstract. In this paper, we describe the requirements elicitation for a digital war room – a group work facility to support people interacting with digital (and analog) materials. The target user group is product design teams and construction engineers/architects. Main requirements for an interactive group work space include fluent sharing of documents within the facility and ability to comment on them, support for both analog and digital sketching and writing by hand, minimum of three displays allowing parallel tasks and comparison of different alternatives and the importance of the physical properties of the facility.

Keywords: Requirements elicitation, user-centred design, group work, design project room, working with digital materials, collaboration spaces.

1 Introduction

Product or service design leverages participants' skill set and past experiences with available information about the task at hand in order to create a new solution to a given problem. It is characterized by highly interactive processes among multidisciplinary project groups. As more and more design artifacts and documents are digital, the designers also want to use and share these digital documents among themselves in their collaboration situations. Making changes to the working habits and environments is hindered by traditional, yet outdated, work practices and tools. Earlier learned or used methods are often hard to change. Product design also requires working with very complicated stakeholder networks both within a company and across subcontractors and marketing channels. And above all, the employees' ability and willingness to cope with the fast changes in their working environment is limited.

Some of the often tried remedies to these ailments are to promote and adopt digital processes to accelerate work flow and introduce new information and communication technology (ICT) tools and systems to the workers. Some of the proposed solutions include dedicated ubiquitous group work facilities with large visual displays [1], combining digital and analog tools to support meetings [2] and use of large multi-display arrays [3]. Lately these kinds of solution have been referred to as blended spaces [4].

This paper describes the research conducted in the DiWa – Digital War room project aiming to develop an interactive digital collaboration space that enables fluent

S. Yamamoto (Ed.): HIMI/HCII 2013, Part III, LNCS 8018, pp. 352–361, 2013.
© Springer-Verlag Berlin Heidelberg 2013

group interaction with digital, mainly visual, contents. It will act as an active tool for design, collaboration and assessment. Our primary design drivers are 1) a better inclusion of rich media about the actual end-users and their experiences [5] to user-centred design (UCD) process, 2) natural interaction with large visual displays and digital artifacts, 3) leverage the synergies between physical and digital design practices and 4) to finally update the omnipresent "one data projector and a flip chart" meeting room standard design to the 21st century.

This paper describes the first half of our project where our goal was to find out and understand our stakeholders' needs and expectations towards the use of interactive group work spaces. We will ground this knowledge with current state-of-the-art through a systematic literary review and validate the resulting solutions with our target users to receive directions for our next steps.

2   Literary Review

Group work and collaboration taking place in technologically enhanced spaces is a combination of multiple disciplines and almost unlimited topics. We did a systematic literature review to act both as a foundation for our project and as a source for validation and justification for our final requirements. With 49 search terms applied to five academic publication indexes (ABI/Inform, ScienceDirect, ACM Digital Library, IEEE and Google Scholar) we found total of 13,6 million hits, of which 907 most relevant where browsed through and for 168 of these written summaries were created. The written summaries were used to group the papers into eight categories with variable strength interconnections between them.

Group Work. Understanding group work or collaboration practices among designers is important in order to be able to design new technology to support them. Working in a group, in general, seems to be a messy event to understand. According to Cross and Clayburn [6] even if there is a plan for the design session, the designers tend to pursue unplanned activities also in collaboration. They also claim that the main challenge in such sessions is to reach a shared understanding about the problem; this is not what happens naturally, there can be misunderstandings even in the apparently shared concepts.

The basic activities designers do in a collaborative design meeting are sketching and talking e.g. telling design stories. Sketching, however, is not the most used tool. It seems that verbalizing (spoken and written) is more dominant. But it could be that the combination of sketches and speech is actually the most powerful way of communication. Linking these two design artifacts is generally done by gesturing. [7]

Work Practices. Poulsen & Thøgersen [8] conclude that the whole human body is engaged in the sense making process. They further argue that designers' communication and thinking cannot be understood with only words, and it cannot be reduced to gesturing. Also Tholander et al. [9] observed this in design activities where walking was used as a way to shift the focus in the design. Sketching and gesturing are done also for the sake of the person's own understanding rather than merely as tools for communication

[10]. According to Vyas et al. [11] also other material artifacts beside sketches are important in the communication of collaborative design. These artifacts mediate the experience of other designers in the group and are not just interaction aids.

Space Design. The design environment is an important part of the design process. By surrounding themselves with sketches, design models etc. designers get inspiration for new ideas and communicate existing ones. Especially important seems to be the ability to communicate multimodal information. [12]

Vyas et al. [13] also state that it is important to understand the physicality of design and its social aspects. Plaue et al. [14] observed real collaboration in companies and found that physical aspects of the spaces affect how people feel about the space. Their findings also indicate that technological changes were not required as often as environmental ones. Also Magadley and Birdi [15] have found that environment appears to be equally important as technology for the users.

System Design. Simultaneous actions in multi-surface, multi-user environments cause problems. Voice commands should be avoided [16] as well as individual mouse cursors as they cause confusion [17]. According to Tse et al. [16], small gestures help parallel individual work and large gestures increase collaboration, mode awareness is crucial if modes are used, container marking and location affect viewing them as group or personal territories and there are two types or joint multimodal commands. Jiang et al. [17] suggest that using a multi-touch screen promotes task awareness. Tse et al., Jacucci et al. [18] and Cesar et al. [19] agree that users should be presented with an option for transitioning between individual work and collaborative work. Tang et al. [20] promote the idea of using analogous technology to ease transitions. In their study a whiteboard was used to support users' existing work practices with new large display applications. Large collaborative displays however are often supplemental technologies as opposed to primary tools [21].

Interaction. In general, the bigger the display, the more physical its navigation is. Findings about physical navigation are however contradictory. According to Ball et al. [22] it increases the users' performance and is preferred by users compared to virtual navigation. When manipulating objects, planning time is shorter and users are able to perform more efficiently and are able to rotate objects around all axes [23]. However, according to Forlines et al. [24], users can perform better when using a mouse for one-handed input and fingers for two-handed input with large horizontal displays. Reilly [25] argues that immediate feedback is not necessarily needed when pointing at objects that are familiar and that users don't even need to look at them.

Requirements. It is paramount that the users of a multi-touch setup are aware of what is happening and what other users are doing. According to Carroll et al. [26], awareness is the key for mediated collaboration and tools. This can be translated to system requirements: fluid and fast interaction, users have to be aware which display is being controlled at all times, related objects are drawn together and users must be able to work on separate sub-tasks without interfering with others [27].

System Possibilities. Drag-and-drop has been advanced from mouse-only use to other environments. For large display tabletop interfaces users face a problem of reachability. A virtual grabber can be used to manipulate objects that are beyond user's immediate reach [28]. Authors argue that the virtual grabber could be used to interact with objects in wall screens from the tabletop in intelligent and responsive spaces. Hopmann et al. [29] have tried to bring tangibility back to drag-and-drop. In their study a remote control that detects gestures was used to transfer a picture from a TV to a digital photo frame. Their findings show that more feedback in the process is needed.

Video. Video indexing is the most popular subject for studies, since automated process for describing certain aspects of video would be preferable to laborious human annotation. Hu et al. [30] describe state-of-the-art of video indexing in their work covering topics such as shot boundary detection, key frame extraction, feature extraction from static key frames, objects and motions as well as video navigation.

Annotations are a good way to provide possibilities for navigation [31]. Also other strategies are reported in studies for navigating videos, from affective annotation timelines [32] to a more classic database solution where multiple ways of searching are supported [33].

Different approaches to help in searching video information have been suggested. Cordeiro and Ribeiro [34] have identified what they call low-level descriptors which can be analyzed for similarity and used for a retrieval system. Li and Wang [35] have created a method for searching videos based on faces, the information is automatically created combining visual and temporal video information to separate similar faces. By augmenting a video with other data (e.g. sensor data) and then providing search possibility for the combination of video and other data makes finding significant shots more easy [36]. Halvey et al. [37] on the other hand have created a collaborative tool that supports different search approaches.

3   Field Study

After the literature review, we performed a field study to gain a sufficient understanding of our stakeholders' operations and most importantly of their everyday collaboration situations and practices. The field study included observations (as a complete observer [38 pp. 228]) from 12 collaboration situations, five group interviews with total of 22 participants and six individual interviews. The analysis was based on Contextual Design [39] and it produced detailed descriptions and flow models for each stakeholder and a consolidated physical model of the shared aspects of the collaborative work environments.

Results. Our analysis indicated that all units had unique collaboration goals. On a detailed level there were only a few similarities in the everyday activities. However, on a higher abstraction level the collaborative work practices seem to coalesce and are elaborated on in the following sections.

From the field study it was clear that one of the key aspects in everyday collaboration was the versatility of situations ranging from working in pairs and tight collaboration in small teams to more formal meetings with agendas and schedules. In formal meetings making decisions was the main objective while the role of collaboration situations was mostly to share information, make decisions and distribute tasks. The amount of actual tasks done together in these situations differed in the studied units. Sketching and drawing were important co-creation activities. The role of external participants varied extensively from merely passing out information to creating new material together with the other participants.

The processed or viewed media in collaboration situations was mainly digital documents in several different formats, but also videos and digital photographs were used. Handled artifacts included drawings and sketches, very large plans and physical prototypes. The participants also more often than not had their own laptops as well as pen and paper for making notes in the collaboration situations. Documenting decisions and making notes of the work done were considered both difficult and cumbersome to do properly. It was also almost impossible to efficiently share these notes in real time to the collaborators.

The current facilities provided for collaboration were much alike for all studied units and thus it was possible to present them in one consolidated model. Several concerns were found with video conference systems; they require configuration before use and working software had to be installed on the computers. There are also severe incompatibility issues. Connectivity issues are also relevant for teleconference systems. With whiteboards and flip charts the most common problem was saving made notes. In the field study we found several strategies for saving the notes, for instance, photographing the flip charts or transcribing the notes by hand. In all meeting rooms there were only one projector or display, but in many cases participants would have needed to see several projections at the same time. Participants also had the need to point at things on the screen and in many cases a mouse pointer was used. The mouse pointer, however, was difficult to see by all participants.

4   Requirements for Collocated Group Work Spaces

After the field study, its results were integrated to the findings of the literary review in order to compile a list of 82 individual requirements for an interactive collocated group work space. These requirements were grouped into five common categories: space and layout, work practices, ICT and technology, remote collaboration, and interaction. The requirements were validated by presenting them to the stakeholders in a full-day workshop during which the participants rated the suggested features. At that time remote collaboration was considered out of scope for this project and it was not studied further.

The following paragraphs describe the interactive group work space based on the explicit requirements in the remaining four themes as well as summarize the stakeholder-specific requirements.

Space and Layout. The interactive group work space is intended for collaborative activities for three to six people, while the space still accommodates ten to twelve persons. The space is furnished to support the activities, but it also must be pleasant to be in. The importance of environmental aspects of the room was also found very significant for users in the literature [14-15].

Basic elements in the space are furniture, screens and equipment for controlling the system. The screens are placed so that all users are able to view them. According to one study users mostly prefer the screen which is in a 45 degree angle straight in front of them [27]. The table size and placement of all furniture can be modified depending on activity and needs. Conventional pen and paper collaboration tools are available.

Work Practices. The interactive group space supports all customary existing work practices [20], but also offers the possibility for multiple users to interact with digital and physical materials at the same time. The collaboration situations to be supported include formal meetings as well as real collaborative work. The space enables comparing several alternatives effectively which is essential in most team work (e.g. software development [40]). Other normal collaboration activities include sketching, commenting and comparing alternatives. The need to support sketching, both as individual and group activity, was also evident from literature [16, 41-42].

ICT and Technology. The interactive group work space and its equipment are operated as an independent system. This system provides versatile connectivity for personal devices as well as access into corporate data systems. Personal devices can be used to share documents and specific applications with the system. Biehl et al. [43] describe a framework for sharing applications and input in a multiple display environment.

The screens connected to the system are large and have adequate resolution. The placement and type of screens in the room can affect group interaction [44] and should thus be considered carefully. The system enables viewing and modifying several documents or materials by multiple users at the same time. The system also saves all activity and produced documents for later reference, and the system can digitalize physical documents and objects (e.g. [45]). The system manages different groups' and stakeholders' data separately from each other.

Interaction. The system supports several different ways for interaction to meet different needs arising from the activities and users' preferences. These different input methods include touch, mouse and keyboard. Multiple ways for interaction are encouraged by literature [46-47]. The interaction with the system can be done locally from the screens or remotely through the system with a separate device. Controlling the displays while seated is important [14]. Providing multiple sets of input devices and tablets also supports switching between different working styles [45].

Interacting with the system and different materials can be done by several users at the same time. When multiple users work simultaneously they have to be able to work without interfering with each other and at the same time be aware of what they are controlling [27]. The system also has efficient tools for handling visual material, such as zooming and panning, as well as pointing at the materials.

Stakeholder-Specific Requirements. All activity within the space, especially decision making and the reasoning behind them, is saved for future reference. The system enables presenting and sharing documents to other users in the interactive space. Also viewing, sharing and editing multimodal materials, especially user research findings, is possible within the space. Vyas et al. [12] point out the importance of designers surrounding themselves with multimodal materials. Commenting and drawing on presented materials is possible.

The interactive space supports innovation by supporting specific ideation methods if needed, as well as enabling more free-form activities. Regarding design and other creative endeavors, researchers have recognized the need to support a wide range of methods so that users can choose the one that fits them and the task at hand [14].

5   Conclusions

After a field study on collaborative work with four stakeholders in addition to an extensive literature review covering both design and interaction with digital artifacts, we were able to define generic requirements for an interactive collocated group work space. With the aid of an abstract requirements specification [48] our technology and implementation independent description of the system's features and functionalities were understood and committed to by our various stakeholders.

The highest rated requirements fall into four distinct groups of: 1) collaboration: fluent sharing of documents within the facility and ability to comment on them, 2) supporting conventional work practices: support for both analog and digital sketching and writing by hand, 3) parallel and uninterrupted use: minimum of three screens allowing parallel tasks and comparison of different alternatives, and 4) physical properties of the facility: flexible and adaptive furniture and lighting, fast Internet connection and above all well-functioning ventilation and lighting.

Our design principles share the requirements for robustness and extendibility with other similar facilities referred in literature (e.g. [15, 27]). Our goal of defining a general purpose interactive space equally useful for all of our stakeholders may prove challenging during the implementation phases. But still due to the wide scope of interests within our stakeholders, the relatively high abstraction level of our requirements and the strong supporting evidence from literature, we argue that most of the described requirements are generalizable to most instances of collocated group activity in relation to digitally supported design activities and large displays.

Acknowledgements. This research has been made possible by the funding from Tekes – the Finnish Funding Agency for Technology and Innovation, and the participated companies Kemppi, Konecranes, the City of Vantaa and Suomen Yliopisto-kiinteistöt.

References

1. Borchers, J., Ringel, M., Tyler, J., Fox, A.: Stanford interactive workspaces: a framework for physical and graphical user interface prototyping. IEEE Wireless Communications 9(6), 64–69 (2002)
2. Haller, M., Leitner, J., Seifried, T., Wallace, J.R., Scott, S.D., Richter, C., Brandl, P., Hunter, S.: The NiCE Discussion Room: Integrating Paper and Digital Media to Support Co-Located Group Meetings. In: Proc. CHI 2010, pp. 609–618. ACM Press (2010)
3. Jagodic, R., Renambot, L., Johnson, A., Leigh, J., Deshpande, S.: Enabling multi-user interaction in large high-resolution distributed environments. Future Generation Computer Systems 27(7), 914–923 (2011)
4. Benyon, D., Mival, O.: Blended Spaces for Collaborative Creativity. In: Designing Collaborative Interactive Spaces: An AVI 2012 Workshop (2012)
5. Nieminen, M.P., Runonen, M.: Designer Experience - Designing in Experience. In: Proc. IASDR 2011, IASDR (2011)
6. Cross, N., Clayburn, A.: Observations of teamwork and social processes in design. Design Studies 16(2), 143–170 (1995)
7. Brown, J., Lindgaard, G., Biddle, R.: Stories, Sketches, and Lists: Developers and Interaction Designers Interacting Through Artefacts. In: Proc. AGILE 2008, pp. 39–50. IEEE (2008)
8. Poulsen, S.B., Thøgersen, U.: Embodied design thinking: a phenomenological perspective. CoDesign 7(1), 29–44 (2011)
9. Tholander, J., Karlgren, K., Ramberg, R., Sökjer, P.: Where all the interaction is: sketching in interaction design as an embodied practice. In: Proc. DIS 2008, pp. 445–454. ACM Press (2008)
10. Reid, F.J.M., Reed, S.E.: Conversational grounding and visual access in collaborative design. CoDesign 3(2), 111–122 (2007)
11. Vyas, D., Heylen, D., Nijholt, A., van der Veer, G.: Experiential role of artefacts in cooperative design. In: Proc. C&T 2009, pp. 105–114. ACM Press (2009)
12. Vyas, D., Heylen, D., Nijholt, A., Popescu-Belis, A.: Physicality and cooperative design. In: Popescu-Belis, A., Stiefelhagen, R. (eds.) MLMI 2008. LNCS, vol. 5237, pp. 325–337. Springer, Heidelberg (2008)
13. Vyas, D., van der Veer, G., Heylen, D., Nijholt, A.: Space as a resource in creative design practices. In: Gross, T., Gulliksen, J., Kotzé, P., Oestreicher, L., Palanque, P., Prates, R.O., Winckler, M. (eds.) INTERACT 2009. LNCS, vol. 5727, pp. 169–172. Springer, Heidelberg (2009)
14. Plaue, C., Stasko, J., Baloga, M.: The conference room as a toolbox: technological and social routines in corporate meeting spaces. In: Proc.C&T 2009, pp. 95–104. ACM Press (2009)
15. Magadley, W., Birdi, K.: Innovation Labs: An Examination into the Use of Physical Spaces to Enhance Organizational Creativity. Creativity and Innovation Management 18(4), 315–325 (2009)
16. Tse, E., Greenberg, S., Shen, C., Forlines, C., Kodama, R.: Exploring true multi-user multimodal interaction over a digital table. In: Proc. DIS 2008, pp. 109–118. ACM Press (2008)
17. Jiang, H., Wigdor, D., Forlines, C., Shen, C.: System design for the WeSpace: Linking personal devices to a table-centered multi-user, multi-surface environment. In: Proc. Tabletop 2008, pp. 105–112. IEEE (2008)

18. Jacucci, G., Morrison, A., Richard, G.T., Kleimola, J., Peltonen, P., Parisi, L., Laitinen, T.: Worlds of information. In: Proc. CHI 2010, pp. 2267–2276. ACM Press (2010)
19. Cesar, P., Bulterman, D.C.A., Geerts, D., Jansen, J., Knoche, H., Seager, W.: Enhancing social sharing of videos: fragment, annotate, enrich, and share. In: Proc. MM 2008, pp. 11–20. ACM Press (2008)
20. Tang, A., Lanir, J., Greenberg, S., Fels, S.: Supporting transitions in work: informing large display application design by understanding whiteboard use. In: Proc. GROUP 2009, pp. 149–158. ACM Press (2009)
21. Huang, E.M., Mynatt, E.D., Trimble, J.P.: When design just isn't enough: the unanticipated challenges of the real world for large collaborative displays. Personal Ubiquitous Computing 11(7), 537–547 (2007)
22. Ball, R., North, C., Bowman, D.A.: Move to improve: promoting physical navigation to increase user performance with large displays. In: Proc. CHI 2007, pp. 191–200. ACM Press (2007)
23. Hippler, R.K., Klopfer, D.S., Leventhal, L.M., Poor, G.M., Klein, B.A., Jaffee, S.D.: More than speed? An empirical study of touchscreens and body awareness on an object manipulation task. In: Jacko, J.A. (ed.) HCII 2011, Part II. LNCS, vol. 6762, pp. 33–42. Springer, Heidelberg (2011)
24. Forlines, C., Wigdor, D., Shen, C., Balakrishnan, R.: Direct-touch vs. mouse input for tabletop displays. In: Proc. CHI 2007, pp. 647–656. ACM Press (2007)
25. Reilly, D.: Reaching the same point: Effects on consistency when pointing at objects in the physical environment without feedback. International Journal of Human-Computer Studies 69(1-2), 9–18 (2010)
26. Carroll, J.M., Rosson, M.B., Farooq, U., Xiao, L.: Beyond being aware. Information and Organization 19(3), 162–185 (2009)
27. Wigdor, D., Shen, C., Forlines, C., Balakrishnan, R.: Effects of display position and control space orientation on user preference and performance. In: Proc.CHI 2006, pp. 309–318. ACM Press (2006)
28. Abednego, M., Lee, J.-H., Moon, W., Park, J.-H.I.: Grabber: expanding physical reach in a large-display tabletop environment through the use of a virtual grabber. In: Proc. Tabletop 2009, pp. 61–64. ACM Press (2009)
29. Hopmann, M., Thalmann, D., Vexo, F.: Tangible drag-and-drop: Transferring digital content with a remote control. In: Chang, M., Kuo, R., Kinshuk, Chen, G.-D., Hirose, M. (eds.) Learning by Playing. LNCS, vol. 5670, pp. 306–315. Springer, Heidelberg (2009)
30. Hu, W., Xie, N., Li, L., Zeng, X., Maybank, S.: A Survey on Visual Content-Based Video Indexing and Retrieval. IEEE Transactions on Systems, Man, and Cybernetics, Part C: Applications and Reviews 41(6), 797–819 (2011)
31. Pimentel, M.G., Goularte, R., Cattelan, R.G., Santos, F.S., Teixeira, C.: Enhancing Multimodal Annotations with Pen-Based Information. In: Proc. ISMW 2007, pp. 207–213. IEEE (2007)
32. Chen, L., Chen, G.-C., Xu, C.-Z., March, J., Benford, S.: EmoPlayer: A media player for video clips with affective annotations. Interacting with Computers 20(1), 17–28 (2008)
33. Hauglid, J.O., Heggland, J.: Savanta - search, analysis, visualisation and navigation of temporal annotations. Multimedia Tools and Applications 40(2), 183–210 (2008)
34. Cordeiro, M., Ribeiro, C.: Reuse of video annotations based on low-level descriptor similarity. In: Proc. WIAMIS 2009, pp. 193–196. IEEE (2009)
35. Li, J., Wang, Y.: Face indexing and searching from videos. In: Proc. ICIP 2008, pp. 1932–1935. IEEE (2008)

36. Ivetic, D., Mihic, S., Markoski, B.: Augmented AVI video file for road surveying. Computers & Electrical Engineering 36(1), 169–179 (2010)
37. Halvey, M., Vallet, D., Hannah, D., Feng, Y., Jose, J.M.: An asynchronous collaborative search system for online video search. Information Processing & Management 46(6), 733–748 (2010)
38. Lazar, J., Feng, J.H., Hochheiser, H.: Research Methods in Human-Computer Interaction. John Wiley & Sons Ltd. (2010)
39. Beyer, H., Holtzblatt, K.: Contextual Design: Defining Customer-Centered Systems. Morgan Kaufmann Publishers, Inc., San Francisco (1998)
40. Petre, M.: Insights from expert software design practice. In: Proc. ESEC/FSE 2009, pp. 233–242. ACM Press (2009)
41. Youmans, R.J.: The effects of physical prototyping and group work on the reduction of design fixation. Design Studies 32(2), 115–138 (2011)
42. Mann, P., Aczel, J., Scanlon, E., Cooper, M.: Supporting computer-supported collaborative work (CSCW) in conceptual design. In: Proc. ARCOM 2008 (2008)
43. Biehl, J.T., Baker, W.T., Bailey, B.P., Tan, D.S., Inkpen, K.M., Czerwinski, M.: Impromptu: a new interaction framework for supporting collaboration in multiple display environments and its field evaluation for co-located software development. In: Proc. CHI 2008, pp. 939–948. ACM Press (2008)
44. Rogers, Y., Lindley, S.: Collaborating around vertical and horizontal large interactive displays: which way is best? Interacting with Computers 16(6), 1133–1152 (2004)
45. Hartmann, B., Morris, M.R., Benko, H., Wilson, A.D.: Pictionaire: supporting collaborative design work by integrating physical and digital artifacts. In: Proc. CSCW 2010, pp. 421–424. ACM Press (2010)
46. Collomb, M., Hascoët, M.: Extending drag-and-drop to new interactive environments: A multi-display, multi-instrument and multi-user approach. Interacting with Computers 20(6), 562–573 (2008)
47. Do-Lenh, S., Kaplan, F., Sharma, A., Dillenbourg, P.: Multi-finger interactions with papers on augmented tabletops. In: Proc. TEI 2009, pp. 267–274. ACM Press (2009)
48. Heitneter, C.L., McLean, J.D.: Abstract Requirements Specification: A New Approach and Its Application. IEEE Transactions of Software Engineer SE-9(5), 580–589 (1983)

Detection of Division of Labor in Multiparty Collaboration

Noriko Suzuki[1], Tosirou Kamiya[2], Ichiro Umata[3], Sadanori Ito[3],
Shoichiro Iwasawa[3], Mamiko Sakata[4], and Katsunori Shimohara[4]

[1] JSPS/Doshisha University, Japan
[2] Kyoto University, Japan
[3] National Institute of Information and Communications Technology, Japan
[4] Doshisha University,
1-3 Tataramiyakodani, Kyotanabe, Kyoto, 610-0394 Japan
nosuzuki@mail.doshisha.ac.jp

Abstract. In the research field of human-computer interaction, there
are many approaches to predicting interactive roles, e.g., conversational
dominance or active participation. Although interactive roles have been
predicted for entire tasks, little attention has been given to evaluating
how such roles are reorganized during a task. This paper explains how
to construct a model for predicting emergent division of labor and the
reorganization of labor in multiparty collaboration using verbal and non-
verbal cues. To build the model, we adopted stepwise multiple-regression
analysis, which is a type of statistical model analysis, using both behavioral data and third-party evaluations. We confirmed useful verbal and
non-verbal parameters for predicting interactive roles and their reorganization through this model.

Keywords: Emergent division of labor, reorganization, statistical
model analysis, verbal and nonverbal behavior, third-party evaluation.

1   Introduction

Recent human-computer studies have focused on a framework for CG characters
or communication robots participating in multiparty interaction among people
[1, etc.]. Predicting emerging interactive roles in group collaboration is a key
task for constructing such a framework.

In group work among people, the interactive roles of leaders and followers
emerge and reorganize themselves. Participants participate in group work while
perceiving the emerging interactive roles and their reorganization from each
other's verbal and non-verbal behaviors [2,3,4,5,6].

The purpose of this study is to develop a ubiquitous computing technique
that can automatically predict the players of interactive roles in multiparty interaction. This paper focuses on how verbal and nonverbal behaviors contribute
to natural leader and follower emergence and role-reorganization during interaction. In this study, a participant who has the ability to motivate other group

S. Yamamoto (Ed.): HIMI/HCII 2013, Part III, LNCS 8018, pp. 362–371, 2013.

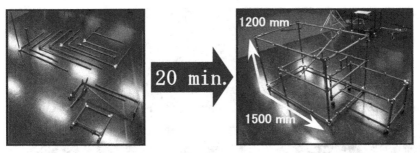

(a) Materials used in the task of assembling a structure: twelve kinds of components (left) and completed figure (right).

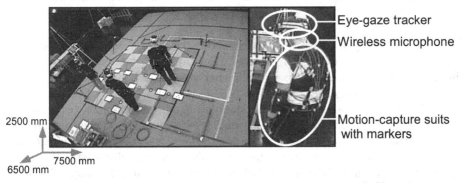

(b) Large-structure assembly task in shared physical space (left) and devices worn by participants (right).

Fig. 1. Materials used in assembly task: twelve components (upper left) and completed figure (upper right), large-structure assembly task in shared physical space (lower left), and devices worn by participants (lower right)

members to achieve the task is considered a leader. Similarly, a participant who has the ability to effectively follow and support a leader is regarded as an active follower, while a less able follower is regarded as a passive follower, based on Bjugstad's definitions [7].

Conventional studies on multiparty conversations with positionally fixed participants have pointed out the crucial role played by verbal and nonverbal behaviors in the process of natural leader emergence [8,9]. Previous studies on the relationship between dominance and conversational behavior show that gaze, as well as speech, contributes to the establishment of higher-status persons [10,11,12]. Related works on conversational dominance have also tried to detect a single interactive role, either dominance or activeness [13,14].However, no research has yet shown what kinds of verbal and nonverbal behaviors contribute to the development of multiple interactive roles in multiparty collaboration.

In this study's task, people assembled a large structure consisting of pipes. No participant was assigned a particular role. As the participants moved in a

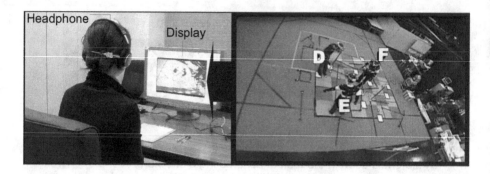

Fig. 2. Third-party rating experiment (left) and movie scene used for third-party evaluation (right)

shared physical space to assemble the structure, their gaze, speech, motion, and position data were captured by sensors. The captured data were analyzed to investigate the relationships between verbal/nonverbal behaviors and natural interactive role emergence [15,16,17].

In our previous analysis results, we found no significant difference between the leading and supporting roles in a task from the self-evaluations of the participants [16]. To examine the co-occurrence relation between an observer's judgment and verbal/nonverbal behaviors in the task, we asked neutral third parties to select the participant playing the leading role and the one playing the supporting role in the assembly task [18,19].

This paper presents a method of constructing a model for detecting the interactive roles of leader, active follower, and passive follower. We perform stepwise multiple regression on the model by using the results of both behavioral data and third-party evaluations. This model could be useful for detecting interactive roles and their reorganization in multiparty interaction.

2   Method

2.1   Task of Assembling a Large Structure

We focused on how both verbal and nonverbal behaviors help us to understand emerging leadership and followership through group work while the participants are moving. A preliminary experiment was conducted on the task of assembling a large structure in a shared physical space while checking a picture of the completed structure.

Figure 1(a) (upper left) shows twelve types of components, and Fig. 1(a) (upper right) shows the picture of the completed structure (PCS) used in this experiment. Gaze, speech, and distance among participants were captured within a space of 7500 × 6500 × 2500 mm (width/depth/height) (Fig. 1(b) (lower left)). Each participant wore an eye-gaze tracker attached to a cap, a close-proximity microphone, and optical markers on a body suit for use by the motion-capture device (Fig. 1(b) (lower right)).

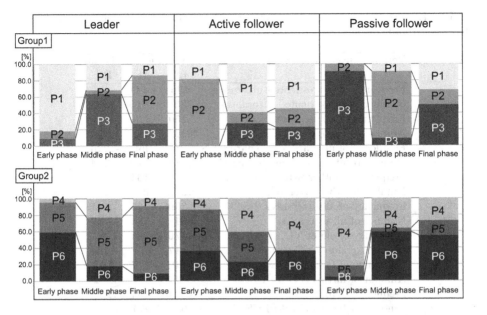

Fig. 3. Results of third-party evaluation: (a) leader (left), (b) active follower (middle), and (c) passive follower (right)

Two groups (C1 and C2), each consisting of three participants, took part in this preliminary experiment. Before the task, the participants had never met each other. No participant was assigned a particular role, such as leader or follower. At the start, all participants shared equal status. Group C2 successfully assembled the large structure in just over 13 minutes, but group C1 failed to complete the task within 20 minutes. For details, please refer to the previous work [15,16,17].

2.2   Method of Third-Party Evaluation

We conducted a third-party rating experiment on predicting the emergent interactive roles of leaders and followers to investigate the relationship between an observer's judgment and the participants' verbal/nonverbal behaviors.

Twenty-two people from 20 to 38 years old were recruited as raters. These raters consisted of eleven males and eleven females. They did not take part in the task of assembling the large structure.

We used movies made by recording the task of assembling the large structure (Fig. 2 (right)). The raters watched the movies of both C1 and C2 groups. In the rating experiment, the order of watching the movies was counterbalanced between the two groups. Each movie was evenly split into thirds: early, middle, and final phases of the task. Each rater was assigned to a computer with headphones (Fig. 2 (left)) and told that they would watch a movie of an assembly task and then select the task's leader as well as its active and passive followers.

Table 1. Correlation coefficient between results of third-party evaluation and verbal/nonverbal behaviors

Verbal/nonverbal behavior	Correlation coefficient		
	LD	AF	PF
Frequency of task-oriented utterances	.484*	-.441	-.111
Number of task-oriented utterances	.735**	-.413	-.362
Frequency of response utterances	.150	.126	-.232
Number of response utterances	.172	.021	-.173
Frequency of utterances for sharing CS	.035	.256	-.225
Number of utterances for sharing CS	.214	.105	-.274
Frequency of other utterances	.163	-.134	-.048
Number of other utterances	.263	-.045	-.206
Frequency of all utterances	.300	-.123	-.182
Number of all utterances	.631**	-.186	-.437
Frequency of closer VC with PCS	.270	-.085	-.183
Amount of closer VC with PCS	.417	.071	-.434
Frequency of farther VC with PCS	-.301	-.117	.363
Amount of farther VC with PCS	-.235	.004	.212
Frequency of total VC with PCS	-.111	-.134	.202
Amount of total VC with PCS	.095	.050	-.124
Total moving distance	-.138	-.084	.189
Distance to other participants	-.237	-.103	.294
Frequency of facing each other	.181	.167	-.291
Frequency of overlapping utterances	.022	-.062	.026
Number of overlapping utterances	-.047	-.039	.072
Frequency of gaze to others	.122	-.064	-.064
Amount of gaze to others	-.072	.249	-.121
Frequency of mutual gaze	-.112	.035	.076
Amount of mutual gaze	.068	-.025	-.043
Frequency of gaze to components	.244	-.216	-.061
Amount of gaze to components	.042	-.050	-.001
Frequency of JA to components	.108	-.059	-.054
Amount of JA to components	.070	.016	-.077
Frequency of JA to PCS	.029	-.026	-.007
Amount of JA to PCS	.046	-.010	-.035

LD: leader, AF: active follower, PF: passive follower, VC: visual contact, CS: current status, PCS: picture of completed structure, JA: joint attention
**: $p < 0.01$, *: $p < 0.05$

In this experiment, the determination of which participant takes over the leadership of the task is based on that person's asking for the support of the other participants. As for the other roles, the participant who best shows the ability to effectively follow and support the leader is regarded as the active follower, while the other is regarded as the passive follower. For details, please refer to the previous work [18,19].

Figure 3 shows the third-party evaluation results for the emergent interactive roles of leader, active follower and passive follower with temporal alterations in

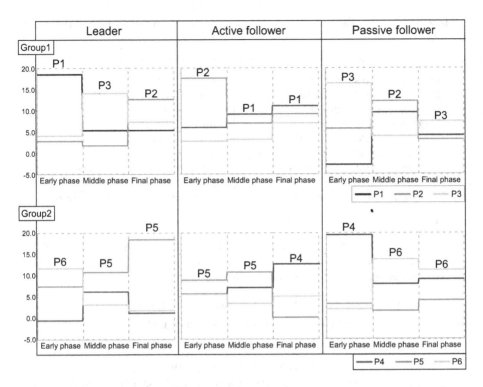

Fig. 4. Results of detecting emergent division of labor using a statistical model analysis: (a) leader (left), (b) active follower (middle), and (c) passive follower (right)

the assembly task. Table 1 shows the correlation coefficients between interactive roles and 31 sets of verbal and nonverbal behaviors.

3   Results and Discussion

We applied stepwise multiple regression for detecting the interactive roles of leader, active follower, and passive follower. We used 18 sets of verbal and nonverbal behavior data as independent variables (see 1) and the results of third-party evaluation as dependent variables. The 18 sets of behavioral data were selected from 31 such sets after deleting variable candidates with stronger correlation coefficients (0.7 or more). Table 2 shows the verbal and nonverbal behaviors as independent variables in stepwise multiple regression.

The regression equations for the interactive roles are as follows:

$$
\begin{aligned}
(\text{Leader}) = {} & 3.241 \times (\text{Number of task-oriented utterances}) \\
& + 1.424 \times (\text{Number of all utterances}) \\
& + 0.291 \times (\text{Amount of gaze to components}) \\
& - 0.039 \times (\text{Total moving distance}) + const. \quad (1)
\end{aligned}
$$

Table 2. 18 sets of verbal and nonverbal behaviors as independent variables in stepwise multiple regression

Number of task-oriented utterances	Distance to other participants
Frequency of response utterances	Frequency of facing each other
Frequency of utterances for sharing CS	Number of overlapping utterances
Number of other utterances	Amount of gaze to others
Number of all utterances	Frequency of mutual gaze
Frequency of closer VC with PCS	Amount of mutual gaze
Frequency of farther VC with PCS	Amount of gaze to components
Frequency of total VC with PCS	Amount of JA to components
Total moving distance	Amount of JA to PCS

CS: current status, PCS: picture of completed structure, JA: joint attention

The equation (1) shows that number of task-oriented utterance, number of all utterances, amount of gaze to components and total moving distance from the 18 sets of behavioral data contribute to "leader".

$$\text{(Active follower)} = -3.563 \times \text{(Number of task-oriented utterances)}$$
$$- 0.004 \times \text{(Distance to other participants)}$$
$$+ 1.129 \times \text{(Frequency of facing each other)}$$
$$+ 1.168 \times \text{(Frequency of gaze to others)}$$
$$+ 0.245 \times \text{(Frequency of utterances for sharing current status)}$$
$$+ 0.056 \times \text{(Total moving distance)} + const. \tag{2}$$

The equation (2) shows that number of task-oriented utterance, distance to other participants, frequency of facing each other, frequency of gaze to others, frequency of utterances for sharing current status and total moving distance from the 18 sets of behavioral data contribute to "active follower".

$$\text{(Passive followers)} = -1.492 \times \text{(Number of task-oriented utterances)}$$
$$- 1.306 \times \text{(Frequency of facing each other)}$$
$$+ 0.003 \times \text{(Distance to other participants)}$$
$$+ const. \tag{3}$$

The equation (2) shows that number of task-oriented utterance, frequency of facing each other, and distance to other participants from the 18 sets of behavioral data contribute to "passive follower".

We obtained the above regression equation models for detecting leader (adjusted $R^2 = 0.706$, $p < 0.01$), active follower (adjusted $R^2 = 0.482$, $p < 0.05$), and passive follower (adjusted $R^2 = 0.427$, $p < 0.05$). The adjusted R^2 value shows the percentage of overall contribution of the above selected variables in the regression equations for each interactive role.

Figure 4 shows the scores for interactive roles as calculation results of the above equations. P1 to P6 means the participants of group 1 (P1 to P3) and group 2 (P4 to P6). In this figure, the participants with the highest scores are shown in three phases: early, middle and final. When compared with the results of third party evaluation (fig. 2), it seems to show a better recall. Nevertheless, P5 in the middle phase of group2 is selected as both a leader and an active follower.

In comparing the results of correlation coefficients in Table 1 with regression equations (1) to (3), behavioral data with correlation coefficients of 0.2 or more are mostly selected, e.g., number of task-oriented utterances, frequency of utterance for sharing current status, and number of all utterances. On the other hand, frequency of visual contact with the picture of the completed structure is not selected as a parameter for higher contribution, even though it has a moderate correlation coefficient. We should examine the adequacy of the model for application to other groups under similar experimental conditions.

4   Conclusions

We captured, analyzed, and evaluated verbal and nonverbal behaviors in group collaboration in an effort to find a method for automatically predicting the emergent division of labor.

To construct a model for detecting the emergent division of labor in the roles of leader, active follower and passive follower, we applied stepwise multiple regression as a statistical model. We used both the results of raters' judgments and verbal/nonverbal behaviors in an assembly task as variables for the model. Consequently, we obtained a model with a moderate contribution ratio.

These models helped to reduce the costs of capturing and analyzing multiparty cooperation. In the future, we will conduct an assembly task using more groups with simpler equipment than in our first trial. Using these data, we will again investigate the effectiveness of our findings for predicting leaders.

In our preliminary multiparty cooperation task, we created groups of strangers without checking their capacity for assembly tasks or their spatial cognition ability. In future work, we will also conduct a similar task and control the familiarity among participants or address their task adequacy. Accordingly, we will examine the performance of the model in predicting interactive roles when it is applied to various types of groups.

If we could make a model of the structure of interactive roles, including leader and followers in multiparty cooperation, and then automatically predict these roles from captured data, such an approach would be useful in the design of various future collaborative systems: (1) face-to-face cooperation-support systems that enhance the emergent division of labor through visualization of the status of interactive roles, or that optimize the performances and the contributions among participants [20, etc.]; (2) evaluation systems that control multiple cameras according to the detection results of the key person in multiparty cooperation [13, etc.] or that conduct comparative quality evaluation between remote and face-to-face meetings in relation to the emergent division of labor; and, needless to say, (3) communication robot systems that participate in and activate multiparty conversation [1, etc.].

Acknowledgments. The authors thank Kazumi Asai, Takugo Fukaya, Hiroaki Noguchi, Naho Orita, Dr. Kohei Suzuki, and Tetsushi Yamamoto for their technical support. This work was partly supported by funds from the Grant-in-aid for Scientific Research (C) (Grant No. 20500247 and No. 23500338) and the Grant-in-Aid for JSPS Fellows (Grant No. 24·40261).

References

1. Matsuyama, Y., Taniyama, H., Fujie, S., Kobayashi, T.: Framework of communication activation robot participating in multiparty conversation. In: Proceedings of AAAI Fall Symposium, Dialog with Robots, pp. 68–73 (2010)
2. Carter, L., Haytorn, W., Shriver, B., Lanzetta, J.: The behavior of leaders and other group members. The Journal of Abnormal and Social Psychology 46, 589–595 (1951)
3. Cartwright, D., Zander, A.: Group dynamics, 2nd edn. Harper & Row, Publishers (1960)
4. Strickland, L.H., Guild, P.D., Barefoot, J., Paterson, S.A.: Teleconferencing and leadership emergence. Human relations 31, 583–596 (1978)
5. Kelly, R.: The power of followership. Doubleday, New York (1992)
6. Forsyth, D.R.: Group dynamics, 5th edn. Wadsworth, Cengage Learning (2009)
7. Bjugstad, K., Thach, E., Thompson, K., Morris, A.: A fresh look at followership: a model for matching followership and leadership styles. The Journal of Behavioral and Applied Management 7, 304–319 (2006)
8. Otsuka, K., Yamato, J., Takemae, Y., Murase, H.: Quantifying interpersonal influence in face-to-face conversations based on visual attention patterns. In: Proceedings of CHI 2006, pp. 1175–1179 (2006)
9. Jayagopi, D., Ba, S., Odobez, J., Gatica-Perez, D.: Predicting two facets of cosial verticality in meetings from five-minute time slices and nonverbal cues. In: Proceedings of ICMI 2008, pp. 45–52 (2008)
10. Dovidio, J., Ellyson, S.: Patterns of visual dominance behavior in humans. In: Ellyson, S.L., Dovidio, J.F. (eds.) Power, Dominance, and Nonverbal Behavior. Springer, New York (1985)
11. Burgoon, J., Dunbar, N.: Nonverbal expressions of dominance and power in human relationships. In: Manusov, V., Patterson, M.L. (eds.) The Sage Handbook of Nonverbal Communication. Sage publications (2006)
12. Fukuhara, Y., Nakano, Y.: Gaze and conversation domination in multiparty interaction. In: Proceedings of IUI 2011 (2011)
13. Rienks, R., Heylen, D.: Dominance detection in meetings using easily obtainable features. In: Renals, S., Bengio, S. (eds.) MLMI 2005. LNCS, vol. 3869, pp. 76–86. Springer, Heidelberg (2006)
14. Sumi, Y., Yano, M., Nishida, T.: Analysis environment of conversational structure with nonverbal multimodal data. In: Proceedings of ICMI-MLMI (2010)
15. Suzuki, N., Umata, I., Kamiya, T., Ito, S., Iwasawa, S., Toriyama, T., Kogure, K.: Nonverbal behaviors in cooperative work: a case study of successful and unsuccessful team. In: Proceedings of CogSci 2007, pp. 1527–1532 (2007)
16. Suzuki, N., Kamiya, T., Umata, I., Ito, S., Iwasawa, S.: Verbal and nonverbal behaviors in group work: a case study of leadership through the assembling process. In: Proceedings of ICCS 2008, pp. 262–265 (2008)

17. Suzuki, N., Kamiya, T., Umata, I., Ito, S., Iwasawa, S.: Nonverbal behaviors in cooperative work: a case study of successful and unsuccessful team. In: Proceedings of ICCS 2010, pp. 448–449 (2010)
18. Suzuki, N., Kamiya, T., Umata, I., Ito, S., Iwasawa, S.: Analyzing the structure of the emergent division of labor in multiparty collaboration. In: Proceedings of ACM CSCW 2012, pp. 1233–1236 (2012)
19. Suzuki, N., Kamiya, T., Umata, I., Ito, S., Iwasawa, S., Sakata, M., Shimohara, K.: Analysis of emergent division of roles and its reorganization. In: Proceedings of ICHS 2012 (2012)
20. Oehlmann, R., Syed, Z.: Supporting intra-team communication based on psychological tagging and indirect communication. In: Proceedings of KES, pp. 1602–1608 (2012)

Role of Assigned Persona for Computer Supported Cooperative Work in Remote Control Environment

Yuzo Takahashi

Ergonomics Laboratory, Graduate School of Information Sciences,
Hiroshima City University, Japan
3-4-1, Ozuka-higahi, Asaminami-ku, Hiroshima City, Japan
y-taka@hiroshima-cu.ac.jp

Abstract. In the case of cooperative work through networks, non-verbal communication is obstructed. The purpose of this study is to examine the role of assigned persona for the computer supported cooperative work in remote control environment. This experiment scenario was the workplace and set the user scenario for the real subjects. The superior persona and the subordinate persona which affects the "psychological reward" and the "partner's evaluation" were assigned to the subjects. The experimental task that was the simulated chemical plant required to operate two subjects during 90 minutes. Results of primary and secondary task performances, the difference among the assigned persona was observed to execute the computer supported cooperative task. It is necessary to manage a basic design of the interaction between the person and the task concerned about the partner's honor information and the behavior information adequately.

Keywords: persona, nonverbal communication, cooperative behavior, organizational ergonomics, computer supported cooperative work.

1 Introduction

In the case of cooperative work through networks, non-verbal communication (e.g. exchanging the strategy, understanding of own role, synchronizing the timing for operation) is obstructed. Therefore, it is predicted that work performance of the computer supported cooperative work in remote control environment is deteriorated in comparison with normal cooperative work environment. In the study of the efficiency of the behavioral information, it was examined the process of inducing mutual cooperation among workers in a remote work environment (telework) experimentally. Subjects were not given information regarding their partners' reputations and knew only which buttons their partners pushed, i.e., their behavior in the remote work environment. The gambling task developed by Payne [1] was used, and cooperative behavior arose as subjects saw which buttons their partners pushed. Overall, the results suggest that an exchange of nonverbal behavioral information was necessary for inducing cooperative behavior [2].

S. Yamamoto (Ed.): HIMI/HCII 2013, Part III, LNCS 8018, pp. 372–380, 2013.

In general, the following are generally thought to be necessary for cooperative behavior to be induced: (1) an incentive for cooperation, (2) appropriate information about the reputations of cooperative partners, and (3) a clear role structure among partners. Moreover, in scenarios with two-participant decision making (e.g., Prisoner's Dilemma), research has indicated that participants would devote resources to gathering the information that they needed and accommodating the other participant's actions in their decision making [3].

It is considered that the "psychological reward" and the "partner's evaluation about own behavior or decision making" are the factors of an incentive for cooperation. Then, we examined experimentally the "partner's evaluation" concerned about the process of sharing strategy. This study was set at the communication style restricted environment. Because, it was thought that sharing correct strategy under the restricted communication situation was difficult. In this study, the subjects were made to play a game on the network with exchanging their environmental noise or partner's voice. As the results, it was suggested that subjects could achieve the cooperative behavior at the restricted communication situation using the "partner's evaluation" through the partner's environmental noise [4].

Meanwhile, it was suggested that the "psychological reward" was a function of the number of the cooperative behavior. In a social dilemma, participants are considered to show more reciprocal behavior as the game progresses, responding more sensitively to how much others cooperated in the previous round. That is, the frequency of cooperative behavior has an important role in the quality of decision making, which can foster the formation of a cooperative relationship [5].

Because the "psychological reward" depends on the participant's reputations, it is difficult to examine whether the "psychological reward" affects the work performance and the decision making quality. In addition, it is difficult to manage the structure of participant's role experimentally. Then, in this study, we focused on the structure of participant's role influencing the incentive for cooperation. The participants were assigned the persona. In this experiment, we assigned the persona to the task environment with the user scenario [6]. The assigned persona were the superior persona and the subordinate persona which affected the "psychological reward" and the "partner's evaluation about own behavior or decision making".

The purpose of this study is to examine the role of assigned persona for the computer supported cooperative work in remote control environment.

2   Method

2.1   Subjects

The subjects of this study were sixteen university students (male = 8, female = 8, 19-23 years; 20.9 ± 1.5 years). Before participation to this experiment, the informed consent was established with each subject. All subjects were paid for the participation of this experiment.

氏名	吉田　浩司			
性別	男性	家族構成	妻，娘 1 人	
年齢	40 歳	趣味	ゴルフ	Photo Image
役職	部長	性格		
	(入社 18 年目)	仕事には厳しいが，非常に部		
年収	約 800 万	下想い．正義感が強い．		

化学プラントの運転操作に関しては社内で 3 本の指に入る優秀なオペレーターである．同僚とは職場以外でもコミュニケーションを持ち，彼を慕う部下も多数存在する．会社では次期取締役候補とされている．また，非常に家族想いで，休日には家族 3 人で頻繁にレジャーに出かける．

普段は本社工場の化学プラント施設で働くとともに，オペレーター養成施設にて教官も務めているが，今回は会議への出席のため，東京に出張することとなった．しかし，本社の化学プラント施設の運転操作から外れるわけにはいかないため，東京の支社ビルのコントロールルームから遠隔操作でプラント施設のオペレーションを行うこととなった．

Fig. 1. Example of the user scenario (the "male" superior persona, written in Japanese)

2.2   Assigned Persona

Our experiment scenario supposed the workplace. We set the user scenario [6], the use case scenario [7] and persona core [8] for the real subjects. Subsequently, the superior persona and the subordinate persona which affects the "psychological reward" and the "partner's evaluation about own behavior or decision making" were assigned to the subjects. All subjects were required to participating two experiments: the superior persona part and the subordinate persona part. He or she was required to play the assigned persona as described in the user scenario (e.g. Fig. 1).

2.3   Experimental Task

The experimental task (taking some sort of reference [9]) that is the simulated chemical plant is required to operate two subjects. This task is constructed in three tasks; the primary task is the mixture task of raw material, the goal operation is the heat treatment task, and the secondary task is the gauge reset task. The secondary task was prepared to examine the focus of attention and the influence of the assigned persona. Task screenshot is shown in Fig. 2. In this experiment, two participants were required for operating the task as a team during 90 minutes.

The trouble events were also set in the experimental scenario. The trouble events were inserted to induce the cooperative behavior. And the degree of difficulty was set in each 30 minutes; the first 30 minutes was easy phase, subsequently the mid 30 minutes was difficult phase, and the last 30 minutes was easy phase. The degree of difficulties was controlled by the failure probability in the trouble events and the frequency of the gauge reset demand. In this study, the subject played the two personas (the superior persona and the subordinate persona). To execute the primary task reliably, two subjects were required to the cooperative behavior controlling three valves each other (see Fig. 3).

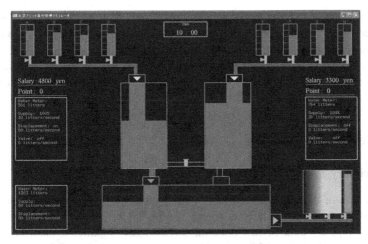

Fig. 2. Screen shot of experimental task

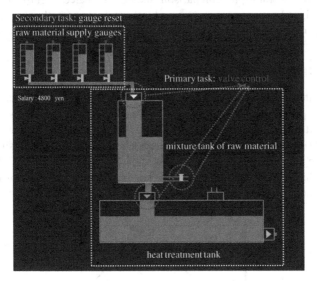

Fig. 3. Primary task control and secondary task control

2.4   Evaluation Indexes

The evaluation index for the primary task was the error rate of the mixture tank of raw material. Each subject was required to maintaining the material level from 50 % to 80 % by operating the three valves. The secondary task evaluation indexes were the success rate of the gauge reset, the reaction time to push the given buttons, and the error rate to find the reset demand. The evaluation index for the team's task performance was the ratio of the heat treatment tank of mixed material. The cooperative behavior was defined by two type of the observed behaviors: a) to use the valve for recovering the partner's material shortage, b) to control the own valve for compensating the partner's material. Six experiment pairs were divided into the cooperative group and the other experiment pairs were divided into the non-cooperative group. And the evaluation indexes of the cooperative behavior were the rate of the cooperative behavior in the primary task, the assist rate of the partner's gauge reset and the reaction time to assist the partner's gauge reset.

3   Results

3.1   Primary Task Performance

The error rate of the mixture tank of raw material among the assigned persona as a function of experiment period was shown in Fig 4. Two-way ANOVA of the error rate of the mixture tank of raw material revealed two significant main effects: assigned persona ($F(1,11) = 6.24$, $p < 0.05$) and experiment period ($F(2,22) = 5.59$, $p < 0.05$). *Bonferroni's* multiple comparison method revealed significant differences among the assigned persona (superior > subordinate). During all experiment periods, the superior persona's error rate was higher than the subordinate persona's error rate.

3.2   Secondary Task Performance

The success rate of the gauge reset behavior among the assigned persona as a function of experiment period was shown in Fig 5. Two-way ANOVA of the success rate of the gauge reset task revealed significant main effect of the assigned persona ($F(1,11) = 9.80$, $p < 0.05$). *Bonferroni's* multiple comparison method revealed significant differences among the assigned persona (subordinate > superior). It was observed that the success rate on the subordinate persona was higher than the superior persona during all experiment periods.

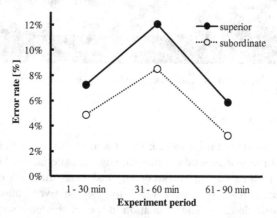

Fig. 4. Error rate of the primary task performance as a function of experiment period

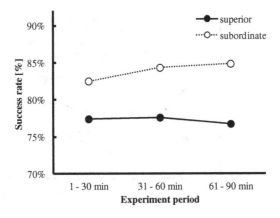

Fig. 5. Success rate of the gauge reset task behavior as a function of experiment period

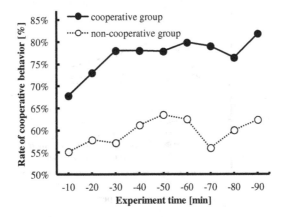

Fig. 6. Rate of the cooperative behavior as a function of experiment time

3.3   Effects of Cooperative Behavior

Rate of Cooperative Behavior. The rate of the cooperative behavior in each 10 minutes among the cooperative group and the non-cooperative group as a function of experiment time was shown in Fig. 6. Two-way ANOVA of the rate of the cooperative behavior revealed two significant main effects: observed behavior ($F(1,5)$ = 82.54, $p < 0.0001$) and experiment time ($F(8,40) = 2.26$, $p < 0.05$). *Bonferroni's* multiple comparison method revealed significant differences among the observed behavior (cooperative group > non-cooperative group). It was observed that the rate of the cooperative behavior on the non-cooperative group was around 60 % during experiment. Meanwhile the rate of the cooperative behavior on the cooperative group was increased about 12 % or more with experiment progression.

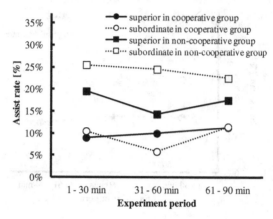

Fig. 7. Assist rate of the partner's gauge reset as a function of experiment period

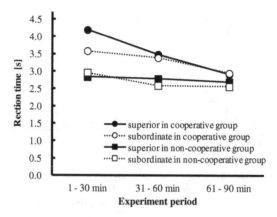

Fig. 8. Reaction time to assist the partner's gauge reset as a function of experiment period

Assist Rate for the Partner's Gauge Reset. The rate of cooperative behavior in the cooperative group had occurred higher than the non-cooperative group. Therefore it was examined the assist rate for the partner's gauge reset behavior. The assist rate for the partner's gauge reset among the assigned persona (the superior and the subordinate) and the observed behavior (the cooperative group and the non-cooperative group) as a function of experiment period was shown in Fig. 7. Three-way ANOVA of the assist rate for the partner's gauge reset revealed significant main effect of the observed behavior ($F(1,5) = 19.85$, $p < 0.01$). *Bonferroni's* multiple comparison method revealed significant differences among the observed behavior (non-cooperative group > cooperative group). The assist rate for the partner's gauge reset showed no significant difference between the assigned persona, but the assist rate of the subordinate in the non-cooperative group was higher than other group in all experiment periods.

Reaction Time to Assist the Partner's Gauge Reset. The same tendency was observed in the reaction time to assist the partner's gauge reset. The reaction time to assist the partner's gauge reset among the assigned persona (the superior and the subordinate) and the observed behavior (the cooperative group and the non-cooperative group) as a function of experiment period was shown in Fig. 8. Three-way ANOVA of the reaction time to assist the partner's gauge reset revealed significant main effect of the observed behavior $(F(1,5) = 7.94, p < 0.05)$. In addition, the experiment period's main effect was revealed $(F(2,10) = 4.01, p < 0.05)$. *Bonferroni's* multiple comparison method revealed significant differences among the observed behavior (cooperative group > non-cooperative group).

4   Discussion

The results of the primary task performance and the secondary task performance, the difference among the assigned persona were observed to execute the computer supported cooperative task through the network. During the first 30 minutes (period: 1 - 30 min), the error rate was increasing moderately. At the high difficult condition of mid 30 minutes (period: 31 - 60 min), the error rate was increased drastically. After the high difficult condition, the rate was recovered near the level of the first 30 minutes. And all experiment periods, the superior persona's error rate was higher than the subordinate persona's error rate. Similarly, the same tendency was observed in the success rate of the partner's gauge reset behavior at the secondary task. To summarize those results, if the person assigned the superior persona, the main task performance deteriorated because of the required follow-up behavior to the subordinate persona. But, it was also considered that the reason of the bad decision making to do the task was the expectation to the "psychological reward" from the subordinate persona for the assist behavior.

To examine the role of the assigned persona, twelve pairs divided two observed behavior groups. And all experiment periods, the assist performance to the partner of the subordinate in the non-cooperative group was higher than the other group. In this experiment, a subject executed two personas, the superior and the subordinate. Therefore, it was considered that the same subject selected different behavior to operate the task. That is, it was thought that the subordinate persona induced the subsidiarity attitude to the task. The subsidiarity attitude to the task diverted the focus of attention to the primary task and mistook the secondary task for the primary task. For the inappropriate attitude to the task, the assigned superior persona had to perform independent management to compensate low task performance in the assigned subordinate persona. In other words, it is able to say that the superior persona could understand the reward from the subordinate persona in their mind. Meanwhile, the subordinate persona could not understand the superior's overload from the result of their performance deficiency. That is, it is considered that the role of persona leads the operator into the misunderstanding state to infer the "partner's evaluation about own behavior or decision making" under the condition of inhibited the non-verbal communication.

5   Conclusions

In conclusion, these types of problem are not able to solve optimizing the interface design only. Therefore, it is necessary to manage a basic design of the interaction between the person and the task concerned about the partner's honor information and the behavior information adequately. This point of view may apply the ambient or the ecological interface design to manage the interaction.

Acknowledgments. This work was supported by a Hiroshima City University Grant for Special Academic Research (General Studies: 0215). The author would like to thank Mr. Masaya Shimooka whose comments enormously contributed to my work.

References

1. Payne, J.W., Bettman, J.R., Johnson, E.J.: Adaptive strategy selectionin decision making. Journal of Experimental Psychology: Learning, Memory, and Cognition 14(3), 534–552 (1988)
2. Takahashi, Y.: Induction of cooperative behavior through exchange of nonverbal information. Journal of Advanced Computational Intelligence and Intelligent Informatics 15(7), 904–910 (2011)
3. Akiyama, M.: Cooperative decision-making process: An analysis of information search processes and recall of alternatives after choice. Cognitive Studies 5(4), 65–77 (1998)
4. Nakata, M., Takahashi, Y., Tanaka, H.: Experimental study of the process of sharing strategy under the restricted communication situation. In: Proceedings of the human Interface Symposium 2011, pp. 985–986 (2011)
5. Shinada, M., Kameda, T.: Emergence of frequency-dependent cooperative strategies in iterated social dilemma: An experimental study. The Japanese Journal of Psychology 74(1), 71–76 (2003)
6. Yamazaki, K., Yokota, Y., Imao, M.: Proposal for advanced user interface on mobile phone. Annual Design Review of Japanese Society for the Science of Design 13(13), 62–66 (2007)
7. Sonehara, A., Shirataka, Y., Kodate, A., Namikawa, D., Minami, H., Shimomura, M.: Disclosure control based on persona information for image sharing on the Web, IEICE Technical Report, LOIS2011-89(2012-3), pp.97–102 (2012)
8. Watanabe, S., Uyama, M., Sashida, N., Otsuka, I., Nakamura, A., Ishigaki, K.: The improvement of persona method: Between the risk of rubber and the strategies for long-term use, IPSJ SIG Technical Report, vol.2010-HCI-140 (19), pp.1–8 (2010)
9. Vicente, J.: Multilevel interface for power plant control rooms I: An integrative review. Nuclear Safety 33(3), 381–397 (1992)

Supporting Group and Personal Memory
in an Interactive Space for Collaborative Work

Mari Tyllinen and Marko Nieminen

Aalto University School of Science, P.O. Box 15400, FI-00076 AALTO, Finland
{mari.tyllinen,marko.nieminen}@aalto.fi

Abstract. This paper reports the findings from our research on constructing the memory functions of DiWa (Digital War room), an interactive collaboration environment to support work especially with digital information. The aim is to identify the current organizational and personal practices of storing and retrieving meeting information. We report findings from a field study conducted in selected units of four organizations and results from the initial stage of a survey on the users of our collaboration environment. Our findings include that organizational practices and systems for storing meeting information are varied and they are not used systematically; personal practices still largely involve pen and paper notes; and the need to return to meeting information exists.

Keywords: Collaborative work, Interactive collaboration environment, User study, Meeting capture.

1   Introduction

Working in teams is business as usual in most organizations and companies regardless of the field of work. The level of collaboration in teams may vary depending on the work culture or objective. In our work, special consideration is put into studying the capabilities of the interactive space to support the capturing and recalling of events and issues that have been addressed during the joint meetings.

Researchers have been interested in team work from many perspectives during the last decades. Working in teams in office-type surroundings has also been the subject of studies e.g. in computer-supported collaborative work. From the technological perspective several projects over the years have involved constructing technologically enhanced meeting rooms or interactive spaces to support working in teams (e.g. [1-3]). Researchers have also focused their efforts on building systems to support meeting capture and later browsing and retrieval of the captured data (e.g. [4-5]). However, these systems and facilities have still not become part of everyday activities in the industry. It has been suggested that this is in part due to a lack of a user-centred approach in the development [6].

In this paper we describe research activities involving the user-centred development of an interactive collaboration environment. Our DiWa project involves four public and private organizations from industrial manufacturing as well as construction

S. Yamamoto (Ed.): HIMI/HCII 2013, Part III, LNCS 8018, pp. 381–390, 2013.

and zoning. The project started with a literature review, continued with a field study and requirements elicitation after which the first prototype of the environment was constructed.

This prototype implemented the infrastructure that provided the initial facilities to support collaborative work. Instead of being considered as the final solution, the technical realization of the interactive space has provided us a modifiable research instrument that can be used to study various features in an iterative and interactive way. The initial features of our enhanced co-located collaboration environment originated from the literature review and the initial findings or the field study. The first components of the interactive space were large interactive touch-screens with remote presentation capabilities, an environment-specific wireless networking infrastructure with shared file storage. The prototype also implemented the basic functionality of logging user actions such as saving information on opened documents. (See Figure 1)

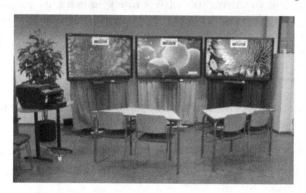

Fig. 1. Our co-located collaboration environment

During fall 2012 our interactive environment and software prototype was used in the university premises. During this time our interactive space was used by students and researchers for different purposes such as software development team work, research workshops, presentations, and teaching.

In this paper, we focus on our research activities that aim at defining the meeting capture, browsing and retrieval functionality which are intended to help the collaborating group in their recurring work. More specifically, we aim at gaining increased understanding on how to supplement and expand personal and organizational practices for storing and retrieving information from meetings. We aim to do this by identifying those aspects of collaborative work that are important for recalling recurring group activity and by finding ways of technologically enhancing current memory aiding practices such as note-taking. The specific research question of our study is as follows:

What are the current personal and organizational practices for storing and retrieving meeting information?

The answers to this question help us in defining user-originated memory support features for the interactive collaboration environment. We will also conclude and discuss such prerequisites that would enable the introduction and broader utilization of memory support functions in collaborative environments.

2 Related Research

Technologically enhanced meeting rooms that support working in teams have been studied by several researchers. The iRoom [3] is a meeting room enhanced with large touch displays both on walls and on a table. The room includes support for multiple personal computing and communication devices that integrate with each other. The IMPROMPTU interaction framework [7] supports collaborative work in a multi-display environment. The framework enables sharing of information across multiple displays concurrently. WeSpace [2] is an interactive space combining a large display wall and a multi-user multi-touch table for use by scientists. The space is especially designed for easy access with personal devices and applications to begin a shared situation where visual data from multiple participants is examined collaboratively. The NiCE Discussion Room [1] takes a slightly different approach in focusing on integrating digital and paper tools into a meeting room design.

Our focus is in supporting the memory of meeting participants with specific functionality within our interactive collaboration environment. A number of previous works have implemented memory supporting functionality for capturing and retrieving meeting data. Whittaker et al. [6] have presented a categorization of retrieval systems or meeting browsers. They present four categories: audio focused, video focused, artifact focused and discourse focused. TeamSpace [4] is a team interaction space that among other things supports capture and access of virtual meetings. The capturing and access is time-based. Jaimes et al. [5] have constructed a meeting retrieval system based on a visuospatial user interface and dynamic queries into the data. The MemTable [8] is a system based on a custom-built interactive tabletop. The retrieval is based on both searching and temporal browsing. A special feature is the ability to include information from the retrieval into a current meeting.

Whittaker et al. [6] have done research on the current practices of creating meeting records. Jaimes et al. [5] conducted a survey study on the reviewing of past meeting data especially regarding video capture. Plaue et al [9] researched the in-meeting sharing of information and found that the sharing practices with own laptops varied and appropriation of new technology depends on whether it adds value to existing practices. Our study focuses on current organizational and personal practices for capturing and retrieving meeting data.

3 Methods and Data

3.1 Field Study

The results in this paper represent a subset of a larger field study that contained the following themes: different everyday collaboration situations, their progress and significance, collaboration facilities and their use, media and artifacts related to collaboration as well as problems with collaboration. The field study consisted of observations, interviews and group interviews. The participants of our field study were employees from the organizations involved in our DiWa project including product development engineers, industrial designers, project managers, planning engineers and architects.

Our data for this paper originates from seven collaboration situations in which the participants were either completely internal (4) or involved external participants (3). The number of participants in these situations ranged from five to eight. The observations from the situations were written notes on the following viewpoints: (a) participants; (b) technology and its use; (c) layout of the space; (d) participants' movement within the space; (e) interaction between participants; (f) handled media and artifacts; (g) role of meeting in the decision making process; (h) references to shared past situations of information. Especially viewpoints (b) and (f)-(h) are relevant regarding the research question of this paper.

Additionally, our data consists of four individual interviews and four group interviews that had 18 participants. These interviews were conducted with employees in different roles in the studied units. Some of the participants were present in the earlier observed meetings. The interviews were conducted by two researchers; one researcher was responsible for transcribing and making detailed notes in real time while the other moderated the interview. The interviews were also audio recorded.

The themes of the semi-structured interviews were: (a) role and background of participants; (b) work tasks; (c) everyday collaboration situations; (d) facilities for collaboration; (e) media and artifacts used in the collaboration; (f) informal collaboration; (g) problems with collaboration.

The aims of our analysis that are reported in the results section of this paper were to identify: (a) current organizational practices of saving records; (b) the types of records saved; (c) the systems used for preserving and sharing records; (d) reasons and practices of creating personal records; (e) reasons and occasions for returning to past records. We classified 80 findings for (a), 60 findings for (b), 31 findings for (c), 14 findings for (d) and 19 findings for (e) from the field study data.

3.2   User Survey

In addition to the field study we conducted a user survey on personal memory support and managements practices with the users of our interactive space in the university premises. This survey is the initial stage of a survey study that will be continued during the piloting of our interactive space in the organizations involved in the DiWa project.

The survey is divided into before-meeting and after-meeting sections. It includes questions on the reasons, tools and forms of personal note-taking as well as reasons and strategies for returning to past meetings both at general and meeting-specific levels. The questionnaire consisted of open-ended questions (5) as well as questions about the frequency of different note-taking practices (4) including the returning to previous notes and memos. The questions of our survey are in part based on the study reported by Jaimes et al. [5] which focused on the use of different tools and strategies to review past meetings.

The questions in the before-meeting questionnaire were: 1) Do you take personal notes in meetings? 2) How often do you use these tools to make personal notes? 3) How often do you use the following ways to make notes? 4) Do you return to past meetings (i.e. to recall the event details, decisions, …)? 5) How often do you use the following tools or strategies to return to past meetings?

The questions in the after-meeting questionnaire were: 1) How did you take the notes? 2) What information from your meeting would you imagine using/needing afterwards? 3) If you could access a complete record of everything that happened in meetings, would you be interested in returning to past meetings? Please evaluate the importance of the following reasons to return to past meetings.

Out of the 19 participants to the before-meeting-questionnaire, 7 represented the zoning organization and the rest were students and researchers of our university. Out of the 11 participants to the after-meeting-questionnaire, 3 represented the zoning organization and the rest were students and researchers.

4   Results

4.1   Field Study

Current Organizational Practices of Saving Records. Our field study reveals that in principle the studied organizations have ways and systems for saving records of meetings. However, these systems are not used systematically mostly due to a lack of commonly agreed upon practices which is reflected in the following answers:

"All project files are accessible where ever, there is no one specific way"
"There is a project folder, but there are no instructions for using it"
"You don't get caught for not documenting".

A significant amount of work is written or drawn on paper during meetings. These documents can be digitalized by scanning or photographing, but often these documents remain to be filed by individuals that collect them in personal binders.

The practice of writing minutes or a memo is not common, and even when it is done there are several problems involved in the process. The quality of the minutes is considered to be the responsibility of the secretary. There is always the risk of the secretary having a different understanding of the meeting than other participants. The minutes are usually written by hand and misunderstandings are only visible afterwards to the other participants. In two of the organizations consultants are usually responsible for writing the minutes. However, they are considered to be poor at producing them on time or at all. Good practices involved with minutes and memos were writing the memo together at the end of the meeting and saving it to the system as the meeting ended.

The practices involved in documenting decisions and action points also varied. Usually it was the responsibility of the persons in question to make note of the action points. Following comment illustrates this: "It varies whether they are written down or not. Even clear decisions are not always documented."

In general, meetings involve a lot of discussion and comments that are not saved in any way. The documenting of "right things" is considered difficult. However, our field study suggests that there is interest in being able to return to this information.

The Types of Records Saved. Based on our field study, the material that is handled in meetings can be in various digital file formats, digital files printed on paper, physical objects such as prototypes and drawings or writings on a flip chart or white board. The digital file formats are used so that the contents are not evident based on the format: examples of these are web links in a PDF or memo in a spreadsheet. The way to save public records varied: saving to some system or sending by email.

The Systems Used for Preserving and Sharing Records. Through our field study it was evident that most organizations have several different systems for saving and sharing records ranging from network drives to different types of systems for different types of records such as for project management and for ideation. Some of these systems have support for collaborative activities. Email was used commonly as a way to share and save information. These systems have several problems including: network drives easily become disorganized, documents in the systems are not up-to-date, management of user rights is difficult, finding relevant information afterwards is hard.

Reasons and Practices of Creating Personal Records. Based on our field study only few people take notes from collaborative situations consistently; most people take notes occasionally. Notes are taken especially when there are matters that concern the individual personally, most commonly such issues are action points. The notes taken by people are most often done by hand, either to personal notebooks or material that was distributed on paper during the meeting, such as agendas.

Reasons and Occasions for Returning to Past Records. In our field study people expressed the hope of being able to return to the documentation of past meetings. This documentation would also give structure to the next meeting, which was utilized in some organizations by following on the progress of previous decisions. However, most often than not, these documents were not available or not found easily. Based on our study it also seems that special pictures, conceptualizations or meaningful ideas that have been developed in earlier meetings and have raised special interest leave a memory trace without the details. This prompts the need to return to the documents.

4.2   User Survey

Taking Personal Notes in Meetings. Ten out of the 19 respondents answered that they do take notes, five take notes sometimes, three don't take notes and one did not answer. The reasoning that they offered for taking notes seem to fall in two categories: for remembering (7) and collecting personal action points or tasks (3). Two respondents answered that taking notes interferes with participating in the meeting.

Some people also feel they need to take notes to get an overview of the meeting for learning in the moment or for checking afterwards.

In the after-meeting questionnaire, however, only four out of 11 respondents reported taking notes. The main reasoning for not taking notes was that the meeting involved hands-on work.

Used Tools and Ways for Making Notes. Out of the five options (computer, digital camera, pen and paper, phone and other) the most used tool was pen and paper: 12 respondents answered that they use it often or always. The least used tool was phone: 11 respondents answered that they use it rarely or never. One respondent identified the iThoughts HD application for iPad as something he uses always. Out of the six options (drawing, taking pictures, video recording, voice recording, writing and other) the most used way of taking notes was writing: 17 respondents use if often or always. The least used ways of taking notes were video and voice recording: 19 and 17 respondents respectively use them rarely or never. One respondent identified his way of making notes to be mind maps.

In the after-meeting questionnaire, however, from the four out of 11 respondents that took notes three reported having used a computer and only one taking notes by hand.

Returning to Past Meetings. Twelve out of the 19 respondents answered that they return to past meetings, four return sometimes, one does not return and two did not answer. The reasoning that they offered for returning fell into the following categories: remembering details or discussions (6), preparing for the next meeting (3), checking for personal action points (2) and sharing information to others (1). Two respondents also review their notes for reflecting their thoughts further.

Out of the nine options (asking someone, common notes, distributed documents, images of white board/flip chart, personal notes, photographs, video recordings, voice recordings and other) for returning to past meetings, the most used tool was personal notes: 14 respondents answered that they use it often or always. Distributed documents were also quite common for returning: 9 respondents used them often or always. The least used tools were video and voice recordings: 18 respondents answered they use them rarely or never.

In the after-meeting questionnaire ten respondents identified the following possible reasons and ways for returning: needing details and discussions (6), using the presented or produced documents (3) and checking personal action points (1).

Possible Reasons for Returning to Past Meetings. Finally, respondents were asked to imagine that they would have a complete record of everything that happened in the meeting in different media formats (text, voice, pictures…) and rate the importance of reasons to return to past meetings. They were given ten options: (a) have accurate record of meetings; (b) keep in mind what customers or key persons said; (c) verify the truth when memory and descriptions are inconsistent; (d) reexamine other person's speech and its context to correctly understand meaning or intention; (e) listen to a portion of speech not understood; (f) listen to a portion of speech not heard; (g) know the results of discussions of ideas from earlier meetings with respect to current interest or problem; (h) obtain proof when someone denies having said something; (i) recall an idea that I had during a meeting; (j) check the consistency between present and earlier presentations.

Out of the 10 respondents to this question, seven respondents rated options (b) and (i) as strong or very strong reasons to return. Eight respondents rated option (h) as the least likely reason for returning.

5   Memory Support Functionality

From Personal to Shared. Despite the finding that only few persons in meetings tend to take notes there are usually some that do. Without too much additional burden to the participants this provides a possibility to improve the documentation level with little effort through transforming the personal note-taking into a shared activity. In addition to sharing personal notes with other participants, the note-taking activity in itself may be transformed into group activity. In a group setting, shared note-taking may be considered as less burdening for an individual. Our collaboration environment is designed to support this in several ways: by making sharing files with others easy through a shared repository, by providing an easy two-click solution to marking important moments from all devices and by allowing everyone to contribute to the editing of files.

From Analog to Digital. Despite the increase of digital material, paper-based documents and pen-and-paper-note-taking are part of current work practices and meetings, too. However, effective sharing can mainly be done with digital material. Therefore, smooth transition between paper-based and digital documentation appears important. In our collaboration environment we try to support this by providing possibilities for digitalizing paper documents within the room. Our facility includes a scanner and a digital camera with an Eye-Fi memory card that both transfer documents automatically to the shared repository.

Logging Document Handling. No meetings happen without supporting documentation, either digital or printed. As these documents are handled during the meeting, they provide both the content as well as the timeline of the meeting. Through the logging of the usage of the handled documents, memory aids about the content and the events can be created as a byproduct of the work. Meeting participants may refer to topics and concepts presented in earlier meetings and, therefore, the availability of these documents and logs about their handling provide additional support for later retrieval of the past issues. Our collaboration environment includes these logging features. There is also an internet browser interface to accessing the logged activity in a timeline and artifact centered presentation.

Human-Recorded Timestamps. Even though no human resources are needed to produce automatic logging of handled documents, the meaning and accuracy of these "timestamps" may be imprecise and require extended effort in later retrieval. The human participants are capable of spotting conceptually and semantically important issues and events. The possibility to record human-created timestamps on these moments in the meetings with content snapshots and context data would enable later retrieval of presentations and notes. In our collaboration environment this is supported by providing an easy two-click solution accessible by all devices for marking these important events and automatically recording the context around the moment with snapshots.

Snapshots. In our collaboration environment the "snapshot" concept around important events provides means for recording and retrieval of past issues. The events around timestamps provide both content and context for the timestamp that is the point-of-interest in the meeting timeline. Recording the presentation context (screenshots) as well as the physical context (overall picture of the space) provides means for navigating the meeting timeline afterwards. Additional content-temporal context is stored through audio recording as most of the elaboration on the topics dealt within a meeting happens through discussions.

6   Discussion

Our results indicate that there are not well established common practices for capturing, storing, and saving information created in collaborative meetings. Even very basic activities such as note-taking are, after all, not that widely performed. As a consequence of this lack of basic activities, there are also no advanced practices and tools in retrieving data for later use. Due to these, we see many opportunities in developing the interactive collaborative environments further by examining the group memory support functions.

The results of our note-taking and retrieval study are based on a rather small sample. Despite this, however, many of the results appear to be well aligned with other recent studies in the field [5-6]. These relate to the very basic issues such as the lack of meeting minutes as well as their accuracy and personal nature.

In addition to these findings on memory support functionality, there are also interesting extensions worth examining in further studies. Until recently, extensive recording of audio has not widely been technically feasible. Contemporary solutions, however, enable even the recordings of whole meetings. These make it possible to rewind to an earlier discussion and statements and make shorter snapshot recordings (e.g.[8]).

While the technological developments seem to offer straightforward solutions for memory functions, the human practices constrain the possibilities. Therefore, we aim at continuing our studies from the user-centered viewpoint in the development of memory support functionality of interactive collaboration environments. Our future work deals with experiences and evaluation of this functionality.

Acknowledgements. The work reported in this paper has been funded within the Spaces and Places programme by the Finnish Funding Agency for Technology and Innovation (Tekes) and the collaborating organizations. The authors would like to thank Mikael Runonen and Mika P. Nieminen for contributing to the data gathering and Nick Eriksson for technical implementation.

References

1. Haller, M., Leitner, J., Seifried, T., Wallace, J.R., Scott, S.D., Richter, C., Brandl, P., Gokcezade, A., Hunter, S.: The NiCE Discussion Room: Integrating Paper and Digital Media to Support Co-Located Group Meetings. In: CHI 2010, Proceedings of the SIGCHI Conference on Human Factors in Computing Systems, pp. 609–618. ACM, Atlanta (2010)
2. Wigdor, D., Jiang, H., Forlines, C., Borkin, M., Shen, C.: WeSpace: the design development and deployment of a walk-up and share multi-surface visual collaboration system. In: CHI 2009, Proceedings of the SIGCHI Conference on Human Factors in Computing Systems, pp. 1237–1246. ACM, New York (2009)
3. Johanson, B., Fox, A., Winograd, T.: The Interactive Workspaces Project: Experiences with Ubiquitous Computing Rooms. IEEE Pervasive Computing 1(2), 67–74 (2002)
4. Geyer, W., Richter, H., Fuchs, L., Frauenhofer, T., Daijavad, S., Poltrock, S.: A team collaboration space supporting capture and access of virtual meetings. In: 2001 International ACM SIGGROUP Conference on Supporting Group Work, pp. 188–196. ACM, New York (2001)
5. Jaimes, A., Omura, K., Nagamine, T., Hirata, K.: Memory cues for meeting video retrieval. In: 1st ACM Workshop on Continuous Archival and Retrieval of Personal Experiences, pp. 74–85. ACM, New York (2004)
6. Whittaker, S., Tucker, S., Swampillai, K., Laban, R.: Design and evaluation of systems to support interaction capture and retrieval. Personal and Ubiquitous Computing 12, 197–221 (2008)
7. Biehl, J.T., Baker, W.T., Bailey, B.P., Tan, D.S., Inkpen, K.M., Czerwinski, M.: IMPROMPTU: A New Interaction Framework for Supporting Collaboration in Multiple Display Environments and Its Field Evaluation for Co-located Software Development. In: CHI 2008 Proceedings of the SIGCHI Conference on Human Factors in Computing Systems, pp. 939–948. ACM, New York (2008)
8. Hunter, S., Maes, P., Scott, S., Kaufman, H.: MemTable: An Integrated System for Capture and Recall of Shared Histories in Group Workspaces. In: CHI 2011 Proceedings of the SIGCHI Conference on Human Factors in Computing Systems, pp. 3305–3314. ACM, New York (2011)
9. Plaue, C., Stasko, J., Baloga, M.: The Conference Room as a Toolbox: Technological and Social Routines in Corporate Meeting Spaces. In: 4th International Conference on Communities and Technologies, C&T 2009, pp. 95–104. ACM, New York (2009)

Pros and Cons of Various ICT Tools in Global Collaboration – A Cross-Case Study

Matti Vartiainen and Olli Jahkola

Virtual and Mobile Work Research Unit, BIT Research Centre,
Department of Industrial Engineering and Management, Aalto University School of Science
{matti.vartiainen,olli.jahkola}@aalto.fi
http://www.vmwork.net/

Abstract. Collaboration in global distributed teams is only possible by using various information and communication technology (ICT) tools, because team members only seldom meet face to face. This study focuses on studying the types and usage of ICT tools in twelve global teams of Finnish companies. We formulated the following research questions: What ICT tools are used in global virtual teams to support group processes and collaboration, and what are their experienced pros and cons?

Keywords: collaboration environments, tools, group processes, hindrances, facilitators.

1   Introduction

Collaborating only via ICT tools with no face-to-face meetings is often referred to as 'full virtuality'. In total, there are two main approaches to defining the degree of full virtuality in teams [12]: the technology-oriented approach and the system-oriented approach. In the technology-oriented approach, the degree of 'virtuality' is defined and measured as the amount, frequency and quality of electronically mediated communication. This measure is often complemented with the amount and frequency of face-to-face contacts as the other basis for categorization [e.g., 8]. The rather narrow perspective of the technologically-oriented approach to only look at the immediate virtual relationships and the quality of their outcomes is avoided when virtuality is seen as just one feature of dispersed teams as work systems in their context [11, 13] and as the outcome of several factors. The system-oriented approach uses contextual factors such as the multiplicity of geographical locations, time zones, organizational affiliations, cultures and work practices in addition to technology use to define the virtuality index. This is justified by saying that these factors are related to the cohesion of a group or an organization, to the needs to communicate virtually and to the types of information technology needed to support work activities. Jarvenpaa and Leidner [3] define global virtual teams as "temporary, culturally diverse, geographically dispersed, electronically communicating work group[s]." All of the twelve studied cases meet this definition, though their 'virtuality' varies: some teams are more

S. Yamamoto (Ed.): HIMI/HCII 2013, Part III, LNCS 8018, pp. 391–400, 2013.

temporary, geographically dispersed, and culturally diverse than other teams are. Although both the communication media and contextual factors influence the functionality of intra-team collaboration, this study focuses specifically on finding what ICT tools are used in collaboration of global companies and what are their pros and cons.

2   ICT Tools and Support of Collaboration Processes

2.1   Factors Influencing Collaboration Outcomes

Many factors have been found to influence the outcomes of global virtual teams. These factors are frequently presented as input-process-output –models (I-P-O) [e.g., 4, 9] consisting of:

- **Inputs,** including design, culture, technical expertise, and training.
- **Socio-Emotional Processes,** including relationship building, cohesion, and trust.
- **Task Processes,** including communication, coordination, and task-technology-structure fit.
- **Outputs,** including performance and satisfaction.

Bosch-Sijtsema, Ruohomäki and Vartiainen [2] presented an I-P-O model of knowledge work productivity in distributed teams complemented with *contextual factors*, many of which are ultimately based on the concept of *ba* [7]. The categories of the model are:

- **Task-related factors** subdivided into task content and mode of working. Task content refers to things like interdependence, ambiguity, and complexity of tasks.
- **Workplaces** made up of layered mental, physical, virtual, and social spaces.
- The **organizational context** referring to organizational strategy, culture, policies, and structures.
- **Team structure** and **composition** including things like role and goal clarity, proximity of team members to each other, and the diversity of team members.
- **Team processes** including e.g. planning, action and interpersonal processes.
- **Outcomes**, the nature of which obviously depends on tasks, contexts and intra-team processes.

This study concentrates on one of the contextual factors, the virtual space, which refers to electronic working environments used for collaboration [11].

2.2   ICT Tools and Collaboration Processes

This study uses for its analysis Andriessen's [1, see also 5] ICT tools categories based on the basic interaction or group processes that they should support. The group processes are: communication, co-operation, co-ordination, information sharing, and group-oriented processes. Classifying ICT tools by these processes yields the following groups of tools [1, p. 11]:

- **Communication systems** "make the communication between geographically distributed people easy, fast and cheap". E-mail and instant messaging are typical communication tools.
- **Information sharing systems** "make the storage and retrieval of large amounts of information quick, reliable and inexpensive". Document repositories and Share-Point sites are typical information sharing tools.
- **Co-ordination systems** "support the co-ordination of distributed teamwork by providing synchronizers i.e. tools to synchronize the work processes of a team". E.g. group calendars and workflow management systems fall into this category.
- **Co-operation systems** "are tools to improve teamwork by providing document-sharing and co-authoring facilities". Google Docs is a good example of a co-operation tool.
- **Tools to support social encounters**: "people at geographically distant places can meet each other unintentionally, such as near the coffee machine." We changed the name of Andriessen's fifth category to *"Group maintenance systems"*. Virtual worlds and social media tools exemplify this group.

Andriessen points out that the five process categories aren't entirely discrete or exhaustive, but function as a heuristic device for analyzing group processes. He combines the five group process categories with three variants of time and space: "asynchronous electronic encounters", "synchronous electronic encounters", and "synchronous face-to-face meetings".

Today, systems that integrate many kinds of functionality appear to be very common. Unlike Andriessen, Mittleman et al. [6] responded to this fact by including a category of aggregated systems in their classification. In this study, we redefined the communication systems category to include many such systems: systems that support multiple interaction processes (as defined above), and which aren't used predominantly to support one of the other processes, are categorized as communication systems.

3   Data and Methods

3.1   Data Collection

The data was collected from twelve globally distributed teams (in eleven companies based in Finland) of varying sizes and degrees of virtuality. The case companies represent multiple industries, e.g. telecommunications, electronics manufacturing, IT services, industrial manufacturing, and technical consulting. The twelve studied teams varied quite a bit in terms of size, from a three-person sales team to a software development team of a few dozen people. Some of the teams were affixed to a specific project, while others were more permanent. Some of the teams consisted solely of managers while others only had a single manager. Some of the virtual teams had very high interdependence between locations while others were only involved with a small amount of non-critical information sharing that happened virtually.

A single virtual team was selected for study in each of the companies except one company in which two teams were selected. Semi-structured interviews were conducted with members of each of the teams, and with key personnel outside of the teams (e.g. HR and IT managers). A total of 94 interviews were conducted between 2008 and 2011. The interviews lasted between 40-90 minutes and were conducted either face-to-face or via phone. The interviews were recorded and transcribed.

3.2   Data Analysis

The first perspective to analyze and describe the type and prevalence of ICT tool use concerns the main five group processes to be supported. Respectively, the ICT tools in use were categorized as 'communication systems', 'information sharing systems', 'co-ordination systems', 'co-operation systems' or "group maintenance systems". The second analytical perspective concerns time and space. We analyzed and described when and where tools were used: asynchronously or synchronously from different places, or synchronously face-to-face.

Interviewees' experiences of pros and cons of specific tools were identified from their verbal citations. Interviewees made some comments that weren't about any specific ICT tool, e.g. comments about mediated communication in general. These were omitted. Additionally, only tools that the interviewees explicitly said are in use by themselves or by the team were considered.

The interviews were analyzed with open and axial coding [10]. The analysis began with identifying and categorizing open codes explicitly concerning any specific ICT tool (or face-to-face communication) into several somewhat arbitrary groups, e.g. Phone/VOIP, document repositories/FTP, Instant Messaging and so on. The exact categories are fairly inconsequential, because they were used simply to slightly speed up the next analytical phase: going over each case individually and constructing tables for each team in the format of Table 1. The tables were constructed based on the codes, not the code categories. The uses for each of the ICT tools were also described textually based on the codes, and double checked against initial case reports to help tease out possible errors of oversight. When a tool was used for multiple team processes, the tool is categorized according to the process that it predominantly supported. Intranet sites, for example, were typically used mainly for information sharing. Similarly, some tools could be categorized into multiple columns, e.g. instant messaging tools can be used more or less synchronously, and occasionally even in face-to-face meetings! Once again, the tools are classified based on the predominant way in which they were used in the case. If no predominant interaction process could be found for a tool, then it was classified as a communication system.

The twelve case-specific tables were then aggregated into a single large table (Table 1). For the aggregated table, the individual tools were once again put into a single cell, even if they were used in differing ways and for differing purposes across the cases.

The most central 'pros' and 'cons' were identified in a similar manner. First, interviewees' negative ('cons') and positive ('pros') experiences related to different tools were identified. Next, team level summaries were made, and based on them the cross-case outcomes were finally arrived at.

4   Findings

4.1   ICT Tools Used in Global Virtual Teams

As shown in Table 1, communication systems in particular were mentioned frequently by interviewees across the twelve cases. Tools were needed for both distributed asynchronous and synchronous communication. Face-to-face communication also took place in each of the cases. So, the teams were not fully virtual. Information sharing and coordination seemed to predominantly happen by using asynchronous tools. Regularly scheduled teleconferences and web conferences were common, and these were often used to share information, to keep people updated on others' activities, and to coordinate work. No systems were found that were used primarily for co-operation! Systems that primarily served group maintenance purposes were also very rare. Both co-operation and group maintenance were frequently done in a face-to-face setting and via various communication systems. No ICT tools were identified that seemed to predominantly support face-to-face meetings.

The following observations concerning the use purposes of tools were made:

- E-mail was used predominantly as a formal and slow asynchronous communication channel, but occasionally similarly to instant messaging (with higher synchronicity). E-mail was also frequently used for sharing files (e-mail attachments).
- Instant messaging (IM) was used for informal communication ("chit-chat"), for asking quick questions, for scheduling phone calls and videoconferences, and in one case for sharing files. IM was occasionally also used for initiating contact with others concerning specific issues, after which the discussion would be taken to a richer medium. Instant messaging was mostly used for one-to-one communication. Most IM tools display also availability information.
- Calls were mostly used for work-related matters, but some informal communication also reportedly occurred.
- Teleconferences were often used for regular (planned) meetings, although ad-hoc teleconferences were also mentioned. Teleconferences were often used in conjunction with screen sharing tools.
- Web conferences were used for online meetings. They usually include text, audio, and video functionality as well as possibilities for application or screen sharing. Some web conferencing tools also included document co-editing functionality.
- Dedicated videoconferencing facilities such as Halo rooms were also used mainly for small group meetings.
- SharePoint sites were often used as corporate-level intranet sites. Files and information were stored on these sites, particularly related to corporate policies, standardized processes, and best practices. Some teams and projects had their own private SharePoint sites. Such sites were used for a variety of purposes.
- Blogs were said to be used for e.g. sharing best practices. Wikis were used for information sharing, giving directions, and project-level status updates.
- Document repositories and FTP servers were used for storing and sharing files, particularly sending large files that can't be sent via E-mail. Network drives were used in similar ways, albeit within a single office.

Table 1. Aggregated list of ICT tools used in the 12 cases, with counts in parentheses

Systems	Asynchronous/different place and time	Synchronous/ different place/ same time	F-t-F/ same place and time
Communication	• E-mail (12) • SMS (4) • Message board (2)	• Phone/VOIP (12) • Instant messaging (11) • Teleconferences (8) • Web conferences (8) • Dedicated videoconferencing rooms (8)	•
Information/ knowledge sharing	• SharePoint/ Intranet (9) • Separate Document repository (7) • Wiki (4) • Social media tool (4) • Newsletters/mailing lists (3) • Blogs (2) • FTP (2) • Network drive (2) • SAP (2) • CRM tool (1)	• Document/screen/ application sharing for web conferences (7)	•
Coordination	• Shared calendars (6) • Availability/status information (6) • Miscellaneous tools (3) • Shared task list (1) • Project management tool (1) • Ticketing system (1)	•	•
No **Co-operation tools** were named!			
Group maintenance	• "Phonebook" with photos, titles and interests of team members (1)	• Permanently open Skype/ webcam link between two sites (1)	• Face-to-face (12)

- Social media, for example a tool called *"Socialcast"*, was used for discussions and networking.
- Face-to-face kickoff meetings were relatively common, and their primary role in globally distributed teams seemed to be one of group maintenance: team building, forming relationships, and building trust.

4.2   Experienced Pros and Cons of the Tools

One of the most common experiences was an excessive amount of e-mail, which was closely related to the frequently mentioned overly liberal use of the CC-field (Table 2). Communication problems were often directly attributed to e-mail communication. Consequently, people were often urged to use alternative tools whenever possible. E-mail was said to remain a dominant communication channel because people are accustomed to it. Another plausible explanation for the popularity of e-mail is that asynchronous communication was particularly important in the twelve case teams, and e-mail is particularly suitable for asynchronous communication.

Table 2. Pros of cons of using ICT tools, frequencies in parenthesis

Systems	Pros	Cons
Communication	• E-mail (12): allows asynchronicity, automatic documentation, file sharing, easy to use. • Phone/VOIP/Skype (12): instant, availability. • Instant messaging (11): fast, effective and convenient, easy to use, less formal, status information, sense of presence. • Teleconferences (8): cost effective, suitable for internal issues, informality. • Web conferences (8): possibilities to share screen and/or application, webcam reduces multitasking and makes interaction less anonymous. • Dedicated videoconferencing rooms (8): almost f-t-f, easier attention to cultural differences, easier to non-native English speakers, trust building, reduced multitasking, engagement. • SMS (4): easy, able to quickly reach people whenever/wherever	• E-mail: too many, somewhat slow, distracting, emotions and reactions not available, exacerbates language barriers, misunderstandings. • Phone/VOIP/Skype: accessibility and poor UI, Skype banned, quality of connections. • Instant messaging: not automatically archived discussions. • Teleconferences: background noises, poor lines, low voice quality, working outside working hours, missing use practices, missing body language. • Web conferences: technical issues, webcam quality varies, availability, background noise, managing over time zones, extra effort needed, less lively. • Dedicated videoconferencing rooms: availability, more formal than f-t-f, technical expertise needed.

Table 2. (*continued*)

	• Message board (2): can support some informal communication.	
Info/knowledge sharing	• SharePoint/ Intranet (9) and separate document repository (7): easy to use, good for storing and sharing large files, creating "we" feelings, reducing data security risks, increasing efficiency. • Document/screen/application sharing for web conferences (7): easy to use, makes meetings more effective and interactive, good for going through documents together, good for knowledge sharing. • Wiki (4): easy to use, reliable. • Social media tool (4): good for (informal) discussions, information sharing, and networking • Newsletters/mailing lists (3): choosing which newsletters to subscribe to is an easy way to control information flow	• SharePoint/ Intranet/Document repository: hard to find information, hard to get feedback, no user-friendliness/ ease of use, missing version control, slow servers, no online document editing, slow file synchronization. • Document/screen/application sharing for web conferences: technical and availability issues. • Wikis: can crash and be slow, currency of information unclear, information redundancy, difficult to find information. • Social media tool: resistance: some people see no benefit to using social media tools at work. • Newsletters/mailing lists: no negatives mentioned.
Info/knowledge sharing	• Blogs (2): good for practice sharing. • FTP (2): suitable for sharing large files, often as a plan B solution. • Network drive (2): easy to use. • SAP (2): good for its narrowly defined purpose. • CRM tool (1): suitable for sharing information about customers.	• Blogs: can be "boring". • FTP: no negatives mentioned. • Network drive: only used locally. • SAP: rigid structure restricts what kind of information can be shared, complex. • CRM tool: very crude system (excel file).
Coordination	• Shared calendars (6): integration with other tools. • Availability/status information (6): makes coordination of communication easier, improves visibility, automated status info. • Unnamed project management tool (1): vastly improved visibility between locations, makes project management much easier. • Miscellaneous idiosyncratic tools mentioned in individual cases:	• Shared calendars: lacking support for changing time zones. • Status information: no complaints. • Project management tool: No negative aspects mentioned.

Table 2. (*continued*)

Coordination	shared task list, ticketing system, .ppt file with people's responsibilities, sales case tracker, SAP workflow module.	
	• No **Co-operation tools** were named!	
Group maintenance	• Face-to-face (12): Group maintenance appeared to particularly be associated with informal communication, which mostly happened face-to-face, via telephone/VOIP, and via IM. • "Phonebook" with photos, titles and interests of team members (1): helped people to get to know each other early on in the project.	• Face-to-face: interaction was considered a necessary prerequisite, but not always possible, mainly because it's very expensive. • "Phonebook" with photos, titles and interests of team members (1): No negative comments.

Instant messaging was widely used and said in multiple interviews to be fast, effect-ive, and convenient. They were said to be great for asking quick questions, and its slightly informal nature made it one of the few tools that were used for "chit-chat". Status information was also said by many of the interviewees to be useful.

Background noises were said to disrupt telephone calls, teleconferences, and web conferences. Technical issues like connection errors and varying audio quality were also mentioned in many cases. As mentioned in multiple cases, synchronous communication across time zones can be problematic.

Availability issues were mentioned concerning web conferences and particularly concerning videoconferencing. Dedicated videoconferencing rooms were said to be good or very good, and they were compared with face-to-face communication. The main difficulty seemed to be their limited number.

Giving globally distributed teams a chance to meet face-to-face was said by many of the interviewees to help subsequent mediated communication. Many interviewees felt that face-to-face kickoffs alone aren't enough: intermittent face-to-face meetings are also needed.

5   Discussion and Conclusions

The ICT tools used by the twelve case teams can be divided into ones with highly specific uses and into more general-purpose communication tools. The tools that were classified as communication systems were generally used for fairly varied tasks, as were some information/knowledge sharing tools, whereas the rest of the tools general-ly served a more specific function in the teams' interaction. For example, SharePoint and Intranet sites, advanced document repositories, wikis, social media tools, and document/screen/application sharing tools are all examples of ICT tools that were predominantly used for information/knowledge sharing, but that also had other uses.

The conspicuously empty cells of both the aggregated tables raise some interesting questions; one might wonder why there are so few co-operation and group maintenance systems. The lack of group maintenance systems could partially be explained by the fact that the oldest interviews are from 2008, and many companies have only recently begun to utilize social media instead of restricting its use. Be that as it may, the lack of group maintenance tools among the twelve case teams might represent a real challenge: group maintenance might be difficult without proper group maintenance tools. Most of the group maintenance activities mentioned by interviewees seemed to be linked to informal communication, which seemed to be somewhat scarce: informal communication mostly happened face-to-face or via certain communication tools like instant messaging and phone/VOIP calls.

References

1. Andriessen, J.H.E.: Working with Groupware – Understanding and Evaluating Collaboration Technology. Springer, London (2003)
2. Bosch-Sijtsema, P.M., Fruchter, R., Vartiainen, M., Ruohomäki, V.: A Framework to analyze Knowledge Work in Distributed Teams. Group & Org. Manag. 36, 275–307 (2011)
3. Jarvenpaa, S.L., Leidner, D.E.: Communication and Trust in Global Virtual Teams. J. Com.-Med. Comm. 3, 1–38 (1998)
4. Martins, L.L., Gilson, L.L., Maynard, M.T.: Virtual Teams: what do we know and where we go from here? J. Manag. 30, 805–835 (2004)
5. McGrath, J.E.: Groups: Interaction and Performance, vol. 14. Prentice-Hall, Englewood Cliffs (1984)
6. Mittleman, D.D., Briggs, R.O., Murphy, J., Davis, A.: Toward a taxonomy of groupware technologies. In: Briggs, R.O., Antunes, P., de Vreede, G.-J., Read, A.S. (eds.) CRIWG 2008. LNCS, vol. 5411, pp. 305–317. Springer, Heidelberg (2008)
7. Nonaka, I., Toyama, R., Konno, N.: SECI, Ba and Leadership: a Unified Model of Dynamic Knowledge Creation. L. Ran. Plan. 2, 5–34 (2000)
8. Niederman, F., Beise, C.M.: Defining the "Virtualness" of Groups, Teams and Meetings. In: Proceedings of the 1999 ACM SIGCPR Conference on Computer Personnel Research, New Orleans, Lousiana, USA, April 8-10, pp. 14–18 (1999)
9. Powell, A., Piccoli, G., Ives, B.: Virtual Teams: A Review of Current Literature and Directions for Future Research. The Data Base for Ad.Inf. Sys. 35, 6–36 (2004)
10. Strauss, A.L., Corbin, J.M.: Basics of Qualitative Research: Grounded Theory Procedures and Techniques, 2nd edn. Sage, Thousand Oaks (1998)
11. Vartiainen, M.: Mobile Virtual Work – Concepts, Outcomes and Challenges. In: Andriessen, E., Vartiainen, M. (eds.) Mobile Virtual Work: A New Paradigm?, pp. 13–44. Springer, Heidelberg (2006)
12. Vartiainen, M.: Full Virtuality as the Challenge of Global HRM. In: Conference Proceedings of HRM Global 2008, Sustainable HRM in the Global Economy, August 27-29, pp. 357–365. Turku School of Economics, Turku (2008)
13. Vartiainen, M.: Facilitating Mobile and Virtual Work. In: Wangel, C. (ed.) 21st Century Management, A Reference Handbook, vol. II, pp. 348–360. Sage, Thousand Oaks (2008)

Interpersonal Service Support
Based on Employee's Activity Model

Kentaro Watanabe and Takuichi Nishimura

National Institute of Advanced Industrial Science and Technology,
Center for Service Research, Tokyo, Japan
{kentaro.watanabe,takuichi.nishimura}@aist.go.jp

Abstract. To improve the productivity of services and satisfy both customers and employees, the activity support by means of IT systems is effective. However, it is rather difficult to support employees' activities in interpersonal services such as nursing care with IT systems. One of the main reasons is that they are required to respond to requests from customers or coworkers flexibly and their activity cannot be described in a formal and sequential manner. To develop a effective system to support such activities, analysis on triggers to perform tasks, criteria to prioritize them, and concrete means to perform them are necessary. However, there are few methods to determine which aspects of employee's activities should be supported in a simple manner.

In this report, the authors propose an employee's activity model and its usage for the support of interpersonal services. In addition, the authors introduce an example case of activity analysis and support planning of a nursing care service by means of the proposed model.

Keywords: Intelligent systems, Humanization of work, Service Engineering, Employee's activity model.

1 Introduction

Service industry takes a dominant role in most of developed countries. Meanwhile, many services are still labor-intensive and working environments tend to be hard. Generally, the activity support by means of IT systems is effective to improve the productivity of services and to satisfy not only customers, but also employees. However, it is rather difficult to support employees' activities in interpersonal services such as nursing care, retailing and restaurant services with IT systems. One of the reasons is that employees for these services should respond to requests from customers or coworkers flexibly [1] and their activity cannot be described in a formal and sequential manner, which makes the adaption of ordinary Systems Engineering approach difficult (For example, [2]). In addition, it is not usually acceptable for customers to replace human-to-human interactions in interpersonal services with IT systems. Therefore, an indirect support for employees' activities is preferable in many cases.

S. Yamamoto (Ed.): HIMI/HCII 2013, Part III, LNCS 8018, pp. 401–409, 2013.

To develop an effective system to support employees, it is important to understand how they perform their complicated tasks. For this purpose, the deep analysis on their way of work, such as triggers to perform tasks and criteria to prioritize them is necessary. Though various models and methods to describe characteristics of human behavior such as its cognitive process for designing interfaces between users and systems (For example, [3-5]), there are few methods to determine which aspects of employee's activities should be supported in a simple manner.

In this report, the authors propose an employee's activity model to describe these aspects, and its usage for the support of interpersonal services. In addition, the authors introduce an example case of the activity analysis and support planning of a nursing care service by means of the proposed model. Based on the case study, the authors discuss the effectiveness of the proposed model and future researches.

2   Employee's Activity Model and Its Usage

2.1   Employee's Activities in Interpersonal Services

In this report, the authors focus on interpersonal services that are to create value through interactions between a person and a person (in most cases, an employee and a customer). A nursing care service in a hospital or a facility for elderly people is a typical example of interpersonal services. In addition, interactions with customers in a retail store or a restaurant are also categorized into interpersonal services.

In such interpersonal services, activities of each employee directly influence the quality of the service and satisfaction of their customers. Human behaviour is not necessarily stable. Human errors easily cause the dissatisfaction of customers and even crucial in medical services for example [6]. Meanwhile, the judgement of situations by humans and human-to-human interactions are not easily replaced with machines or automated systems. Therefore, the role of IT systems in interpersonal services tends to support employees' activities.

2.2   Existing Models on Employee's Activities

To support employees' activities, it is necessary to determine the tasks to be supported and how to support them. For that purpose, various analysis and modeling methods have been proposed.

Sequential process modeling methods are commonly applied in software or systems engineering. For example, the activity diagram in the Unified Modeling Language (UML) [7] can describe human activities as sequential processes. Business Process Modeling Notation (BPMN) is also a famous modeling method for reengineering business processes [2]. These process modeling methods are useful to analyze stable and common processes and to replace them with automated process of IT systems. However, the support for employees' activities in response to various requests and situations is not within the focus of these models.

Meanwhile, there are numerous analysis and modeling methods on characteristics of human behavior. For example, Card et al. [5] describe the information process of humans. Such an information process model is useful to provide standards for the interface of IT systems such as responsiveness. There are also researches on physical features of human behavior [8]. They are effective to lighten the load of a certain movement in a service activity. However, there are few methods to determine which kinds of employee's activities should be supported in a simple manner. A holistic model of human activities would be effective to determine a concept of a support system, especially for interpersonal services.

2.3 Employee's Activity Model

In this section, the authors introduce an employee's activity model (see Fig.1). To develop this model, the authors focus on employees' information processing sequence and their actual activities. The proposed model is developed based on the information process model such as [5] and the result of informal interviews and observation in three kinds of interpersonal service fields.

In this model, triggers of employees' activities are given by two types of 'input', which are 'plan' and 'event'. Plan is information on activities scheduled beforehand. Event is information from customers or other employees to trigger a new activity which is not scheduled in advance. An activity corresponding to each plan or event is called as a 'task.'

Contents of a planned task that is a task corresponding to a plan are usually determined beforehand. Meanwhile, an event task that corresponds to an event depends on the requests and situation. Event tasks can be categorized into the following two types. One of the types is an explicit event task that is performed in response to explicit requests from other employees or customers. The other type is an implicit event task that is performed based on the employee's own awareness on the situation in a service field or an attitude of others.

These tasks are retained in the memory of the employee, which is named as 'pool.' The tasks in the pool are prioritized based on the employees' judgment using "operational information" and "priority rule." Operational information is about customers,

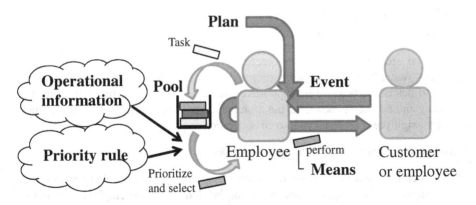

Fig. 1. Employee's activity model

employees and related issues in a service field for service activities, such as characteristics of customers. Priority rule is a fundamental rule to determine the priority of tasks. After the prioritization of tasks, a selected task is actually performed to a customer or a coworker. To perform a task, a certain means is applied.

The employee's activity model provides a basic framework to analyze tasks performed in a service field. The result of analysis is utilized to determine the specification of a support system for interpersonal services as is explained in the next session.

3   Activity Analysis and Support Based on the Employee's Activity Model

3.1   Approaches

In this report, the authors propose an approach of activity analysis and support based on the proposed model. This approach consists of the following three steps.

1. Observing employees' activities

The first step is to observe employees' activities in a service field and to record them. Manual observation methods of human activities such as time and motion study [9] will be effective. In addition, sensing devices of human behaviors and methods to estimate actual activities are also applicable, such as [10]. The items to be observed and recorded are time, frequency and period of each task, its performer and the elements of the employee's activity model such as events and means. In addition, supplemental information such as an activity's importance for customers and physical or mental costs to perform a task are effective to determine tasks to be supported at the later step. Since the information process to determine tasks are not necessarily visible, questionnaire, interviews and other qualitative research approaches should be applied if necessary. When recording the activities, it is also important to develop codes to determine the classification and description of employees' activities for the statistical analysis [1].

2. Specifying tasks to be supported

The second step is to analyze the recorded activities for specifying tasks to be supported. According to the concern of a service field or its manager, the evaluation criteria to determine tasks to be supported should be determined. In addition to the frequency and period of each task, the aforementioned importance for customers and costs for employees can be taken into consideration.

3. Making concepts to support the specified tasks

The last step is to make a concept to support the specified tasks. For this purpose, the authors suggest typical support approaches for the elements of the employee's activity model as are summarized in Fig.2. In these support approaches, training and education for employees are not included. Though they are important and effective supports for employees, the authors focus on the system development for the direct implementation to a service field in this report.

- Plan

A plan for services should be correctly notified to adequate employees and its result should be managed. The plan management is a common approach for this purpose. As concrete support functions, announcement of future tasks and mechanisms to confirm the completion of tasks can be developed.

- Event

An explicit event which is a clear request from other employees and customers can be handled or at least noticed even by novices. Meanwhile, it is more difficult to notice an implicit event and react to it. Visualization of events mainly focuses on implicit events which require employees to acknowledge the necessity to perform certain tasks. A nurse call button is a typical example to express requirements of patients who cannot show their requests.

- Pool

The human memory has a limited capacity and tends to lose its content. In the interpersonal services, interruptions to tasks occurs often [11]. After several interruptions occurred during a certain task, it is difficult to remember doing it again after the interruptions. To externalize the memory is effective not only for novices but also for those who have sufficient experiences. For example, voice recording is useful for this purpose.

- Operational information

In addition to information included in plan or event, various kinds of operational information are required to perform tasks. For example, customers' previous experience on services is valuable information for better services. A system to search for and view required information on customers or tasks and to leave messages on tasks for other employees would be effective for this purpose.

- Priority rule

The priority rule of each employee can be various, which affects the quality and efficiency of his / her service. The decision support for each employee may decrease the variability of his/her activities. For example, task recommendation would be effective during a service activity, though its implementation for on-time support is quite difficult.

- Means

In interpersonal services, tasks are basically performed by humans. However, it is preferable to support high-load tasks to prevent injury. The support for such tasks can be realized by mechanical systems. For example, the robotics technology is a promising technology for this purpose.

Elements in employee's activity model	Support concepts for employee's activities

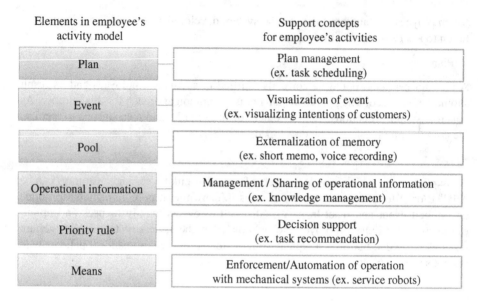

Fig. 2. Support concepts for employee's activities

By applying these steps, concepts of support systems for interpersonal services can be extracted.

3.2   Case Study

As a case study, the authors applied the proposed model and approach to the observation results of an actual nursing care service in a nursing care facility named as Wakoen and extracted some concepts for employee's activity support. This observation results consist of seven employees' activity data: four care workers, two nurses and one occupational therapist. The information on tasks was gathered by the time and motion study performed for three days.

According to the aforementioned approach, the authors extract tasks with higher frequency and make the concepts to support them using the employee's activity model.

3.3   Results

Table 1 shows ten most frequent tasks of each kind of employee. First, "information sharing", "making records" and "confirming records" are the common tasks for several kinds of employees. These tasks are especially expected to be improved by information systems. "Talking to residents" is also a common task for all the kinds of employees. This task is a characteristic one in a nursing care service to extract implicit events from elderly people. Meanwhile, the specialized tasks for each kind of employees were also extracted such as "measurement of vital signs" for nurses, "physical therapy" for occupational therapists and "wheel chair guidance" for care workers.

Table 1. Frequently performed tasks in the nursing-care service

	Planned task	Event task	
		Explicit	Implicit
Care worker	(none)	- Information sharing	- Wheel chair guidance - Transfer assistance - Talking to residents - Watching residents - Hand washing - Making records - Confirming records
Nurse	- Maintenance of gastric fistula - Measurement of vital signs (temperature, SpO2, others)	- Information sharing	- Talking to residents - Making records - Confirming records
Occupational therapist	- Physical therapy (massage, walking training, standing training)	- Information sharing	- Wheel chair guidance - Transfer assistance - Talking to residents - Making records - Confirming records

Table 2. Concepts of an activity support system for occupational therapists

Target operations	Elements in employee's activity model	Concepts of activity support
Physical therapy	Plan	Management system of therapy plan
Information sharing	Operational information	Mobile device for information sharing
Transfer assistance	Means	Transfer support robots
Talking to residents	Event	Indication system of residents' intent
Making / confirming records	Operational information	Mobile device for information sharing
	Pool	Voice recording

Next, support concepts for these tasks of each kind of employees were extracted. Table 2 shows the support concepts for occupational therapists. For "physical therapy" as a planned task, a management system of a therapy plan was considered. For "talking to residents" to extract implicit events, a sensing system or an interface to detect the residents' demands and to visualize them was considered. It should be noted that this concept is just a supplemental system and cannot replace the basic communication between residents and employees. A mobile device system for information sharing was considered to support "information sharing", "making records" and "confirming records." In addition, voice recording is effective approaches to make temporary records instantly. A transfer support robot would be an effective approach to help a high-load task as "transfer assistance."

4   Discussion

As can be seen in Table 2, various kinds of support concepts can be obtained from the aspect of the proposed model. A mobile system for information sharing is actually under development. Meanwhile, it is preferable to consider multiple criteria to determine a support target such as customer value, cost for employees, and risk in tasks, though the frequency of tasks is also an effective criterion. How to determine such criteria would be an important strategy to improve interpersonal services.

In the proposed model, a task is described as a single, inseparable one. Meanwhile, Tukker and Spear [6] noticed that the nurses in hospitals use three strategies to complete their tasks: separating, interweaving and reprioritizing their tasks. How to analyze a large portion of tasks within the proposed model is a remaining issue in the future.

As another issue to be discussed, how to describe an interpersonal service as teamwork should be considered. In the proposed model, interactions between employees are taken into consideration. However, how employees work as a team dynamically and how these processes can be improved are not mentioned sufficiently. This issue remains also as a future research.

Currently, the employee's activity model is used as a framework to determine support concepts of employees' activities. When more information on the employee's activity model can be gathered, the numerical evaluation of support concepts such as changing the priority rules and applying IT systems to a service field can be performed by computational methods such as the multi-agent simulation [12].

5   Conclusion

In this study, the authors proposed the employee's activity model to analyze an employee's activity and to support it. In the future research, the authors will refine the related methods based on the proposed model, and validate them through actual system development.

Acknowledgement. We appreciate the sincere support for this study by Wakoen and our colleagues, Hiroyasu Miwa and Tomohiro Fukuhara.

References

1. Miwa, H., Fukuhara, T., Nishimura, T.: Service Process Visualization in Nursing Care Service Using State Transition Model. In: 4th International Conference on Applied Human Factors and Ergonomics, CD-ROM (2012)
2. Havey, M.: Essential Business Process Modeling. O'Reilly Media (2005)
3. Davis, F.D.: A Technology Acceptance Model for Empirically Testing New End-User Information Systems: Theory and Results, Doctoral Dissertation. MIT Sloan School of Management, Cambridge (1986)
4. Lin, C.J., Yang, C.-W., Lin, S.-B., Lin, S.-F.: A Human Factors Model for Enterprise Resources Planning System Implementation. In: Smith, M.J., Salvendy, G. (eds.) HCI International 2009, Part I. LNCS, vol. 5617, pp. 123–130. Springer, Heidelberg (2009)
5. Card, S.K., Moran, T.P., Newell, A.: The Model Human Processor: An Engineering Model of Human Performance. In: Boff, K.R., Kaufman, L., Thomas, J.P. (eds.) Handbook of Perception and Human Performance, vol. 2, pp. 1–35. Wiley-Interscience, New York (1986)
6. Tukker, A.L., Spear, S.J.: Operational Failures and Interruptions in Hospital Nursing. HSR: Health Services Research 41(3), 643–662 (2006)
7. Object Management Group (OMG): OMG Unified Modeling Language (OMG UML), Infrastructure Version 2.3 (2010)
8. Nemeth, C.P.: Human Factors Methods for Design. CRC Press, Boca Raton (2004)
9. Zheng, K., Guo, M.H., Hanauer, D.A.: Using the Time and Motion Method to Study Clinical Work Processes and Workflow: Methodological Inconsistencies and a Call for Standardized Research. J. American Medical Informatics Association 18, 704–710 (2011)
10. Pentland, A.: Automatic Mapping and Modeling of Human Networks. Physica A: Statistical Mechanics and its Applications 378(1), 59–67 (2007)
11. Kasahara, S., Ohno, Y., Ishii, A., Numasaki, H.: Visualizing the Impact of Interruptions in Nursing Workflow using a Time Process Study. IT Healthcare 5(2), 124–134 (2010)
12. Ferber, J.: Multi-Agent System: An Introduction to Distributed Artificial Intelligence. Addison-Wesley, New York (1999)

Part IV
Business Integration

Situation Aware Interaction with Multi-modal Business Applications in Smart Environments

Mario Aehnelt[1], Sebastian Bader[2], Gernot Ruscher[2], Frank Krüger[2], Bodo Urban[1], and Thomas Kirste[2]

[1] Fraunhofer IGD, Joachim-Jungius-Strasse 11, 18059 Rostock, Germany
{mario.aehnelt,bodo.urban}@igd-r.fraunhofer.de
[2] University of Rostock, Albert-Einstein-Strasse 22, 18059 Rostock, Germany
{sebastian.bader,gernot.ruscher,frank.krueger2,
thomas.kirste}@uni-rostock.de

Abstract. A consistent user experience in combination with proactive assistance may improve the user performance while interacting with heterogeneous data sources as e.g., occurring in business decision making. We describe our approach which is based on inferring the user intentions from sensory inputs, providing a situation aware information assistance, and controlling the environment proactively by anticipating future goals. Our system has been realized within a smart meeting room and has in parts been evaluated. In this paper, we describe the core ideas underlying our approach and report on first findings from the evaluation.

Keywords: intelligent environment, proactive assistance, self-explanation, information assistance, interaction design, usability.

1 Introduction

Business decisions require substantial and interconnected information. However, in real world's environments - as we face them in today's manufacturing industries for example - this information is derived from heterogeneous company resources and systems, e.g. enterprise resource planning systems (ERP) or manufacturing execution systems (MES). Thus, presentation of and interaction with required information follows diverse strategies and metaphors used by underlying devices, applications and user interfaces. The growing use of novel mobile or display devices with completely different interaction metaphors like touch gestures or voice recognition raises further problems. It leads to alternating user experiences and influences the efficiency of decision making processes [1].

In this paper we explore how far recent approaches from HCI and intention recognition can be used to improve the efficiency of business processes. It is our goal to increase process reliability and decrease process costs through improving homogeneity and quality of interacting with data and information using business applications embedded in smart environments. In order to work with realistic business

S. Yamamoto (Ed.): HIMI/HCII 2013, Part III, LNCS 8018, pp. 413–422, 2013.

scenarios we start our exploration by illustrating a specific use case which will serve as basis for our further consideration.

2   Use Case: Smart Business Applications in Manufacturing Industries

In manufacturing industries we find a vital demand for decision making on all company levels. Even on the shop floor a growing amount of structured and unstructured data requires aggregation, interpretation and decision making to guarantee a timely and qualitative delivery of industrial goods. This data reaches from work order information and product specifications to customer data and correspondence as well as information on the current state of production, issues and work plans. Within this general scenario we want to address decision making processes on operational level where the monitoring and controlling of all manufacturing and assembling activities takes place. Our use case here involves different roles: assembling team manager, technical supervisor, constructing engineer and purchaser. In a daily routine they watch over the current and planned state of production and assembling in order to identify upcoming problems and solve them through an early adoption of prior plans. Their decision making here will build the theoretical and practical testbed for our further work.

We transfer the described meeting into a smart control room with a multi-touch table surrounded by an instrumented multi-display environment including a position sensor system. There the assembling team manager is meeting with his supervisor in order to discuss the team's recent progress and problems. They use their private laptops and the multi-touch table to work through the plans and work sheets. In discussion they face a critical issue with a pump in a cooler engine. One of the purchasers is immediately needed to check a replacement. As soon as he enters, the small screens are not sufficient anymore and the presentation is moved to a larger public display next to the table. It shows a detailed model of the pump to replace in parallel to the current work plan. To discuss further technical issues, a constructing engineer is required. He is connected via Skype remote conferencing and shown on a public display to interact with all the other team members simultaneously. In order to start an individual discussion on technical details and on pricing the purchaser moves to another room corner. This movement is recognized by the smart control room and as a result the video chat is transferred onto another screen in this corner. Meanwhile, team leader and his supervisor are discussing further work plans on the table display. As soon as purchaser and constructing engineer have finished their discussion, the room transfers their chat back to the public display. The supervisor can finally estimate delays based on his team's feedback and decide next steps in order to solve the issue. After leaving the smart control room is set back. All described steps of the team meeting can be repeated in arbitrary order.

This setup has been implemented in the *SmartLab* as described in [2] using the *Plant@Hand* system which provides monitoring, planning and documentation functions for manufacturing or maintenance companies (see Figure 1).

Fig. 1. Plant@Hand multi-touch user interface with linked information and in use during a team discussion

3   Preliminaries

Some preliminary evaluation and work results with respect to specific aspects of our approach are discussed below.

3.1   Dynamic and Heterogeneous Smart Environments

For our research, we do not assume any fixed setup of the environment. On the contrary, it is assumed to be a dynamically changing ensemble of heterogeneous devices and services. Our middleware [3] allows connecting all components dynamically. In addition it realizes the idea of *goal-based interaction* as described in [4]. Instead of a command on a given device, it suffices to specify a goal. The component itself will realize this goal. A possible goal for a projector is *"show Input VGA 1"*, depending on the current state different actions are necessary to reach this goal (switch power, mute, input source, etc.), but these details are handled by the device itself.

3.2   Multi-modal Interaction

Based on the heterogeneous and dynamically changing ensemble of devices where we cannot rely on any central component, we developed a multi-modal interaction system [2]. *Dialogues* can be described as flows of interactions between user and system, composed of actions, choice, loops and sequences, and entirely independent of the equipment of the underlying environment. User-system interaction is realized by *Interaction Components* which encapsulate different modalities such as GUI, speech, and also sensor data. User-initiated interaction is handled by components which broadcast events as soon as a user interaction has been noticed. Whenever system-initiated interaction is necessary this can be done using three different interaction performatives: ASK presents an arbitrary question to the user, CHOICE asks questions with limited sets of answers, and VERIFY is used to query yes-no questions. The main advantage of this system is its ability to allow a natural interaction between the user and a distributed, dynamic and heterogeneous ensemble of devices and services.

3.3   Visual and Semantic Information Linking with Plant@Hand

On architectural level we use enterprise service bus (ESB) technologies to interface with heterogeneous software applications holding data required for our decision making process. These applications are coupled with the bus using application specific connectors. Then pre-configured information flows process the incoming data using our own context model. In this step a semantic filtering, which a) works implicitly through the structure of the context model and b) automatically identifies connections between structured and unstructured data using contextualized network graphs [5], generates additional links which are finally used to visually link the data on presentation layer. This way we give for example work sheets a specific location on the construction plan although there did not exist an explicit link before.

The final visualization in Plant@Hand follows known metaphors in engineering and production in order to reduce the cognitive effort of interpreting presented information. Key of our visual representation, as well as the users mental model of work to monitor, is the construction plan and the time schedule (see Figure 1). All other information is linked with both. Selecting a specific work task highlights the corresponding sections in both plans for example. On-site documentations are located exactly in the construction plan where they refer to.

3.4   Sensor Systems

To acquire context information regarding the users' current activities within our environment, we utilize various sensor systems. Among the most important sensor data is location information, i.e. positions and movements of persons which are then transformed to their symbolic equivalents. With this we can recognize e.g. the movement of the purchaser to another room corner.

Location data can be estimated by two different types of location systems: Passive and active location systems. With the latter require specific technical devices – mostly called tags – on part of the users to be able to estimate the location, the former work without them. However, they are not able to distinguish persons standing close to each other, which makes it impossible to determine the number of persons in the room solely based on those systems. To overcome this problem, we have developed a sensor data fusion system which models the sensor data of both systems together with the persons in the environment as a joint conditional density function and estimates the number of all persons together with their respective positions [6]. Thus, we have a unified location system able to deliver location estimations regardless of the underlying location systems, which may be active (e. g. Ubisense RTLS®) or passive ones (e. g. SensFloor®).

4   Approach

When building smart business applications we have to consider significant challenges:

- **Consistent user experience.** Business data and logic is typically located in heterogeneous information systems. Each comes with a different interaction strategy and metaphor, but smart business applications need to work with integrated information and to provide a consistent user experience.
- **Situation awareness.** Interacting with smart environments can be demanding for the user. Therefore, a situation aware assistance system should simplify the interaction. Instead of controlling available devices explicitly, the system should infer the current user goals and act proactively to support them. This allows the user to concentrate on his task instead.
- **Help users to understand.** Business applications provide complex functions for fulfilling work tasks. Smart business applications need to reduce learning efforts and cognitive load of users working with them.

Our use case application (see Figure 1) applies HCI research in order to improve the homogeneity and quality of working with data and information in business decision processes. We used a threefold approach consisting of situation modeling and intention recognition components, providing a consistent multi-touch interaction metaphor, and building the users' mental model of interaction accordingly.

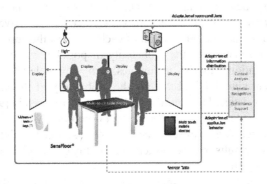

Fig. 2. Configuration of smart control room for providing smart business applications

We make use of the user's mental model in order to link work locations with work details and performance figures visually. The interaction takes place using well known gestures from working with paper documents but translated into their digital counterparts using multi-modal and multi-touch technologies. Our Plant@Hand application is finally embedded into a smart environment which provides us with sensors and opportunities to follow the user's movements, activities and their interaction as well as to estimate the user's intentions and thus next requirements with respect to the visual presentation of required data and information using multiple displays.

The next sections give a brief overview on our adoption of HCI research supporting the previously described decision making use case.

4.1   Situation Modeling and Intention Recognition in Smart Environments

Modern smart environments are equipped with various sensors and actuators. While actuators like projectors, canvases and audio equipment are used to present information, sensors are used to access the current state of devices and users. Intention recognition aims at inferring the current user goals from a sequence of sensor data [7]. For this, probabilistic models are constructed that are able to interpret noisy sensor data appropriately. To construct our intention recognition components, we employ causal behavior models, business process models, and sensor models [8]. These are automatically converted into a probabilistic model that can recognize the current abstract situation as well as the underlying user intentions and allows to support the users accordingly.

These causal models, used for translation to probabilistic models, are based on abstract action specifications. An action specification consists of a list of preconditions and effects to the environment. Together with a description of an initial environment state, such as "a critical issue appeared in the production process" and a description of a possible goal environment state, as "the issue has to be discussed and solved", an probabilistic model that includes all possible action sequences leading from the initial state to the goal state can be generated. A mapping of possible environment states, such as "team-leader and supervisor are at the multi-touch table, the purchaser is moving to a private corner and there is an active Skype call", to sensor data, including the current location of each user and the current Skype activity provides further information on the probability of possible environment states with given sensor information. Filtering techniques such as particle filter are then applied to determine current situation and thereby the probability of this initial state - goal state combination. A detailed description of this process is given in [9].

To recognize the intention of the team several combinations of initial states and goal states are selected and followed. Each hypothesis is then weighted as described and combined which results in a categorical probability distribution over possible goal states - the intention [10].

To reduce the number of possible intentions (combinations of initial and goal situations) sensor fusion techniques as described earlier are applied. If the prior probability that two persons are in the room is high for example, the system can skip all hypotheses that contain different numbers of acting agents. If later a third person (the purchaser in our case) enters these hypotheses have to be started again. The result of the intention recognition phase is a probability distribution of possible intentions, which is the base for further assistance decisions.

4.2   Multi-modal and Multi-touch Interaction with Information

In our use case the decision making takes place on the basis of structured and unstructured data from heterogeneous sources, e.g. ERP, MES, product data management systems (PDM), work sheets, or content management systems (CMS). The connection of data is seldom obvious as there are independent infrastructural software applications holding and providing it. Each application comes with a different user experience and requires a varying interaction style. This leads to additional cognitive loads required to switch between application contexts and usage metaphors [1].

In order to ensure a consistent user experience on multi-modal devices and to reduce the cognitive load of working with different applications required to draw conclusions and allow for decision making, we followed a two-folded approach:

- **Information integration.** We model, collect and interlink all required information prior to their further usage in our application. Starting with a context model of information as well as the process specific information requirements, we use *enterprise service bus technologies* to request the data from their native systems and aggregate it into our own model. So we bring together work plans from planning systems with construction data from product data management systems as well as shift reports from content management sources. The reports are semantically linked with work tasks which may have a location on the construction plan.

- **Context aware presentation and interaction metaphors.** If we want to reach a consistent user experience on multi-modal devices we have to provide a familiar way of presenting and interacting with information. So we combined the metaphors of industrial engineering (e.g. working with construction plans) with monitoring activities (e.g. controlling work sheets) in order to found a common experience. Our presentation and interaction modalities further address changing states of decision making, e.g. when we transfer certain information on public displays to allow an situational and adequate working.

The information integration takes place on data level. On top of this we built with the Plant@Hand application a consistent multi-touch user experience on multi-modal devices. In our stationary control room scenario we transferred the metaphor of using paper documents on a table into an implementation on a multi-touch table interface where this familiar way of interacting can be found again. Touch gestures or digital pen annotation known from the classical paper metaphor are used to interact with construction plans, time figures as well as text, image, or video documents. The same interaction is made available through Plant@Hand in a mobile decision making scenario, where we transferred the visual and interactive part of our application onto mobile devices, e.g. smartphones or tablets.

The intention recognition allows us finally to adapt the visual representation and smart environment accordingly. Dependent on a recognized situation during the team discussion (monitoring, briefing, planning, problem solving) , room conditions (light, acoustics, projection modes, display usage) and application behavior (presentation mode, information distribution) are modified (see Figure 1).

4.3   Shaping the User's Mental Model of Interaction

Efficient interaction with intelligent environments is a challenge, due to the number of possible options and offered functionality. Novice users are often overwhelmed while entering our lab, a smart meeting room equipped with various sensors and actuators, which served as a hardware platform for this work. A consistent user experience is needed to simplify the interaction. In [1], some design principles have been identified to reduce learning efforts and cognitive load, in particular observability, transparency, and tangibility. Those principles were applied while developing the system described here.

In smart environments both user and application need to understand the counterpart's actions and intentions to align own actions accordingly. Analyzing the user's intentions has been discussed above, here we concentrate on how to shape the user's mental model of the environment. A sufficiently correct mental model is necessary to understand and predict the behavior of the system. Usually, the behavior of such systems is described in manuals provided by the manufacturers. But this is not possible in our setting, because the environment, i.e., the system itself, is dynamic – devices, services and users can enter and leave the ensemble at any time. Therefore, the overall behavior can neither be fixed at the time of the installation, nor can it be described in a manual. Nonetheless, the behavior must be understandable for the user. We believe that a solution to this problem is the system's ability to explain its behavior and the ability to teach the user. As a result, the user's mental model is shaped and updated by the environment itself. The self-explanation capability enables the users to learn more about the system without referring to external sources [11]. A realized controller with self-explanation capabilities is described in [12].

Most people tend to understand technical systems as "simple" stimulus-response systems (e.g. normal software applications, ticket machines). To achieve a goal, they need to perform an explicit triggering action, e.g., to switch on the projector, they need to use the corresponding interface. This mental model influences their expectations and interaction. Earlier work in psychology [13, 14] showed this impact on learning to operate new devices, for example. Instead of this automata model, we would like the user to perceive the environment as being controlled by a proactive intelligent assistant. To achieve this goal, the environment should be able to answer questions with respect to its current state and it should be able to teach the user to use it efficiently. For example, if the system recognizes that the user performs a number of actions to prepare a presentation on a public display as needed in the simple automata model, a message could be generated describing how to use the room more efficiently. Here we can adopt scripting approaches from computer supported cooperative work research (CSCW). There scripting is a well-known approach to structure the learning of new methods. It is also used to guide as well as organize cooperative interactions between people [15]. Unfortunately, and to the best of the authors' knowledge, research in this direction is just about to evolve but no real solutions exist so far.

5   Results and Evaluation

Evaluating the overall performance increase of such a complex system is hard or even impossible without long term studies pursued on-site. Instead, we evaluate different aspects of the system independently.

The evaluation of the situation recognition was done in [9] based on a similar problem from the meeting domain. The location data of three persons was recorded during several different meetings and later used as input for the inference engine. The evaluation illustrated that the described approach is (1) competitive with probabilistic models built from training data, (2) able to provide activity recognition with 90% accuracy and (3) reusable in different applications within the same domain. The intention recognition based on these causal models was introduced in [10]. A live demonstration showed that recognizing the intention based on activity recognition with causal models is valid and provides accurate results.

Additionally we brought our Plant@Hand business application on-site into a manufacturing company for cooling devices and evaluated there with staff under field conditions. The results show a positive effect of picking-up the user's mental model with our chosen visualization and interaction styles. After a short learning phase of basic touch gestures (move, resize) the assembly team worked autonomously with the application. With respect to efficiency the main benefit was seen in the information integration avoiding time consuming search in paper documents or opening different applications to collect the required data. The evaluation also showed a fast adoption of our provided information linking methods. After working a while with the application the team was requesting a construction plan manipulation on design level which shows a seamless transition from monitoring and controlling towards re-planning.

6   Conclusion and Future Work

Research in HCI progresses continuously towards a fast adoption of novel device generations which vice versa enable new interactions with the user. With addressing a specific use case from manufacturing industries we focused on bringing together different HCI approaches to improve the efficiency and quality of assistance in business decision making. By realizing the system within our smart lab environment, we showed the principal applicability of this approach. First evaluation results, especially with respect to intention recognition and the multi-modal interaction with information, demonstrate not only a general usability but also a growing user acceptance. Nevertheless, there is more research needed to provide proactive and self-explanatory abilities within such smart environments. Here we will address with our future work the role of mental models on the contextualization of visualization and interaction technologies as well as on the learnability of autonomously working systems.

Further work and research is also addressing the transfer of our results into other usage scenarios. Here we aim to support mobile on-ship monitoring as well as local control rooms to track and manage fishing fleets and their by-catch.

Acknowledgment. Sebastian Bader is supported by the DFG within the GRK1424 MuSAMA.

References

1. Aehnelt, M., Peter, C., Müsebeck, P.: A Discussion of Using Mental Models in Assistive Environments. In: Proc. of the 5th ACM International Conference on Pervasive Technologies Related to Assistive Environments (PETRA 2012). The 5th Workshop on Affect and Behaviour Related Assistance (ABRA), Crete, Greece, June 6-8 (2012)
2. Bader, S., Ruscher, G., Kirste, T.: Multimodal Interaction in Dynamic and Heterogeneous Smart Environments. In: Proc. of the 1st International Workshop on Language Technology in Pervasive Computing (LTPC) at the PerCom, UK (2012)
3. Bader, S., Kirste, T.: An Overview of the Helferlein-System. Rostock, Germany, Technical report CS-03-12 under (2012) ISSN 0944-5900
4. Heider, T., Kirste, T.: Supporting goal-based interaction with dynamic intelligent environments. In: Proc. of ECAI, pp. 596–600 (2002)
5. Ceglowski, M., Coburn, A., Cuadrado, J.: Semantic search of unstructured data using contextual network graphs. National Institute for Technology and Liberal Education 10 (2003)
6. Ruscher, G., Kirste, T.: Estimating User Number and Location from a Multi-Modal Localization Sensor Setup. In: Proceedings of the UPINLBS 2012, Helsinki, Finland (2012)
7. Krüger, F., Ruscher, G., Bader, S., Kirste, T.: A Context-Aware proactive Controller for Smart Environments. I-COM 10, 41–48 (2011)
8. Yordanova, K., Krüger, F., Kirste, T.: Strategies for Modelling Human Behaviour for Activity Recognition with Precondition-Effect Rules. In: Proc. of the 35th German Conference on Artificial Intelligence, Saarbrücken, Germany (2012)
9. Krüger, F., Yordanova, K., Hein, A., Kirste, T.: Plan Synthesis for Probabilistic Activity Recognition. In: Proceedings of the ICAART 2013, Barcelona, Spain (2013)
10. Krüger, F., Yordanova, K., Kirste, T.: Tool support for probabilistic intention recognition using plan synthesis. In: Paternò, F., de Ruyter, B., Markopoulos, P., Santoro, C., van Loenen, E., Luyten, K. (eds.) AmI 2012. LNCS, vol. 7683, pp. 439–444. Springer, Heidelberg (2012)
11. Bader, S.: Probably Asked Questions: Intelligibility through Question Generation. In: Mandl, S., Ludwig, B., Michahelles, F. (eds.) Proc. of the 2nd Workshop on Context Aware Intelligent Assistance, Berlin, Germany (2011)
12. Bader, S.: Explaining the Reactions of a Smart Environment. In: Proc. of Exact 2012, Montpellier, France (2012)
13. Johnson-Laird, P.N.: Mental models: towards a cognitive science of language, inference, and consciousness. Harvard University Press (1983)
14. Kieras, D.E., Bovair, S.: The role of a mental model in learning to operate a device. Cognitive Science 8, 255–273 (1984)
15. Aehnelt, M., Hambach, S., Müsebeck, P., Musielak, M., Hoog, R., de, K.J., Lindstaedt, S.: Context and scripts: supporting interactive work-integrated learning. In: O'Malley, C., Suthers, D., Reimann, P., Dimitracopoulou, A. (eds.) CSCL 2009: In Proc. of the 9th International Conference on Computer Supported Collaborative Learning, vol. 1, pp. 144–146. International Society of the Learning Sciences (2009)

Human Factors in Supply Chain Management

Decision Making in Complex Logistic Scenarios

Philipp Brauner[1], Simone Runge[2], Marcel Groten[2], Günther Schuh[2,3], and Martina Ziefle[1]

[1] Human-Computer-Interaction Center (HCIC)
[2] Institute for Industrial Management (FIR)
[3] Laboratory of Machine Tools and Production Engineering (WZL)
RWTH Aachen University, Germany
{Simone.Runge,Marcel.Groten}@fir.rwth-aachen.de,
G.Schuh@wzl.rwth-aachen.de, {brauner,ziefle}@comm.rwth-aachen.de

Abstract. Human behavior in supply chains is insufficiently explored. Wrong decisions by decision makers leads to insufficient behavior and lower performance not only for the decision maker, but also for other stakeholders along the supply chain. In order to study the complex decision situation, we developed a supply chain game in which we studied experimentally the decisions of different stakeholder within the chain. 121 participants took part in a web-based supply chain game. We investigated the effects of gender, personality and technical competency on the performance within the supply chain. Also, learnability and the effect of presence of point-of-sale data are investigated. Performance depended on the position within the chain and fluctuating stock levels were observed in form of the bullwhip effect. Furthermore, we found that risk taking had an impact on the performance and that the performance improved after the first round of the game.

Keywords: Supply Chain Management, User Diversity, Gamer types, Human Behavior, Beer Game, Serious Gaming.

1 Motivation and Related work

If your local supermarket spontaneously offers groceries at a discount, you might be happy about the bargain. Supply chain managers, however, might worry about the consequences a discount has on the downstream supply chain. One crucial consequence is the so-called *"bullwhip effect"*: The bullwhip effect is a phenomenon in which a relatively small variation in the orders of a customer at one end of a supply chain causes escalating fluctuations in the stock levels and orders along a supply chain. Increasing demand at the nth tier in a supply chain is usually over-compensated by an even grater increase of the demand at the $n+1^{th}$ tier of the chain. As a result, the curve mapping the stock levels along the time looks similar to a whiplash, hence the name *"bullwhip effect"*. It has been first described by Forrester in the 1960s [5] and

S. Yamamoto (Ed.): HIMI/HCII 2013, Part III, LNCS 8018, pp. 423–432, 2013.
© Springer-Verlag Berlin Heidelberg 2013

replicated in a series of studies and was found in real world companies, such as Procter & Gamble or Hewlett Packard [6, 7].

Typical symptoms caused by the bullwhip effect are the following: First, excessive inventory and safety stocks, which – while lowering the amplitude of the bullwhip effect – cause additional costs for storing goods. Second, production forecasts are poor, resulting in unsatisfactory production planning. Third, production capacities are insufficiently utilized. Finally, service rates descent, meaning that requested products are not delivered in time.

According to Lee et al. [6] key reasons of the bullwhip effect are the existence of lead times of information and material in a supply chain. A member of the supply chain will not be able to follow a change of the final demand directly, because of the following three reasons: First, s/he will not receive the information immediately, as information is not delivered in real time. Second, safety stocks along the supply chain also delay the information flow. Third, supply chain members are not able to adapt their capacity, demands and deliveries immediately.

Other factors causing or magnifying the bullwhip effect are *demand forecast updating, order batching, price fluctuations* and *rationing and shortage gaming* [6]. *Order batching* refers to the strategy of companies to order sub-components at fixed rhythms or fixed quantities and not directly when an order comes in. Hence, an additional delay or further fluctuations occur. The *demand forecast* is predicted by each supplier along a supply chain individually. This is based on the data and experience of the past, received information from its customers, individual estimation of e.g. the economic situation and an internal safety stock. Mistakes in these individual forecast planning transmit upwards and can cause a higher variability. This variability will even further increase, if the lead times of the resupply along the supply chain grow. *Price fluctuations* also contribute to the bullwhip effect, as outlined in the beginning of this paper. When components are offered in a special promotion, customers may be inclined to order larger quantities. Also, the price level is usually linked to the order size. Therefore, often more components than needed are procured. *Rationing and shortage gaming* also increase security stocks and the bullwhip effect. If the capacity of a supplier is lower than the current demand, only a share of a given order will be delivered. Therefore, orders are typically increased to counterbalance this reduction. Though, if the orders can be fulfilled by the supplier, e.g. because the capacities have been increased, this gaming behavior causes again increasing stocks and a magnified bullwhip effect.

Possible counter-measures against the fluctuations along the supply chain are presented in [6]. They include the sharing of point-of-sale data, inventory data and capacities and therefore simplifying the demand forecast, faster ordering systems and the reduction of lead times, as well as Everyday Low Prices to reduce variations induced by special promotional offers. Another approach to reduce the bullwhip effect is the implementation of High Resolution Supply Chain Management (HRSCM) [9]. HRSCM aims on high information transparency between the stakeholders in a supply chain in combination with decentralized, independently acting and self-optimizing control loops. While many shortcomings of traditional supply chains are bettered. Still, this approach focuses solely on technical optimizations of supply chains and not on humans in the loop, who also usually take a great part in forecasting the demand and deciding what quantities to order from which supplier.

The bullwhip effect is described well in literature and many counter-measures from the side of industrial management are proposed to avoid or reduce the bullwhip effect (see [6]). Still, the underlying human factors are not yet sufficiently explored.

The beer distribution game was originally developed at the MIT in the 1960 [7]. It is used to simulate a dynamic build-to-stock (in contrast to build-to-order) supply chain. The chain consists of four tiers and is used to explain the approach of system dynamics and the bullwhip effect.

Nienhaus, Ziegenbein und Duijts investigated the human influence on the Bullwhip effect [7]. They compared models of supply chains that were purely based on independently acting computer agents with supply chains with humans as co-players. A central finding of the study was that both supply chains differed. Hence, humans and computer agent acted differently and human factors have to be considered as a factor influencing supply chains. Furthermore, they did a post-hoc classification of human strategies in a "panic" and a "safe harbor" strategy. In their study some humans played a "safe harbor" strategy, which means that they always tried to maintain a specific stock level, whereas others tried to keep the stock level as low as possible, resulting in panic reactions as soon as the customer demand rises ("*panic strategy*").

2   Method

In order to understand how human factors influence the individual stakeholder performance as well as the overall performance in a supply chain, we pursued an experimental approach, in which participants acted as different stakeholders within the supply chain. Before interacting with the supply chain we measured several personality factors and related them to the outcome of the game. In the following the model of the supply chain, the experimental variables and the sample is detailed.

2.1   Model of the Beer Game

We implemented a web-based version of the Beer Game, that allows users to participate in a supply chain and to experience the difficulties to balance stock levels while incoming orders and deliveries are subject to variations.

The game reassembles a supply chain for one specific good (e.g. in this case for beer crates). The supply chain consists of the four positions *retailer, wholesaler, distributor* and *factory* (see Fig. 1 for a schematic overview). Each position has a number of this good in its stock. If the predecessor in the supply chain (e.g. the predecessor of the distributor is the wholesaler) is ordering goods, the number of goods is removed from the stock and transferred to the predecessor. To replenish the stock, the position orders a number of goods from its successor (e.g. the distributor orders from the factory). A computer-simulated customer that orders goods from the retailer triggers the supply chain.

As in the original Beer Game (and in real-world supply chains) the difficulty arises from the time delay between submission of an order and its fulfillment. It takes one week until a submitted order reaches the successor in the supply chain and additional two weeks until the goods arrive at the ordering position. Notable exception is the customer: His/her order is instantly available to the retailer and she/he also instantly receives the purchased goods.

Even if a player's stock level is lower than the request, the request is still fulfilled. However, the stock will then get negative and penalties have to be paid (*1.00$* per good). Also, each position has to pay stock keeping costs for surplus of goods in stock (*0,50$* per good). Therefore, each player has to minimize the stock level while at the same time ensuring that orders can be fulfilled.

The computer-simulated customer acts according to a fixed order function: At the beginning of the game the customer is ordering 4 goods in each of the first 5 rounds. After that, the order increases to 8 goods per round for the rest of the game.

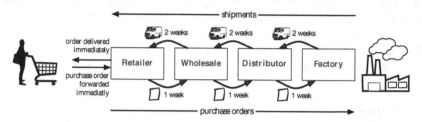

Fig. 1. Schematic diagram of the supply chain

2.2   Independent Variables

A series of demographical and psychometrics were assessed before the experiment. All ratings were measured with 4-level Likert scales.

Demographics and personality factors: As independent variables gender, age and highest formal educational attainment were collected.

Expertise: The study was targeted at novices that have no or limited experience in the logistics domain. To check this precondition, the subjects had to subjectively rate their experience in logistics and related domains, such as economics.

Technical Self-Efficacy (TSE) [2]: This scale has shown to be valuable in understanding performance and learning in many computer mediated environments [1, 3].

Personality type: To analyze the effect of personality traits on the performance we used the Five Factor Model (FFM)[4]. This model describes the human personality by five dimensions: Openness (openness to new experiences vs. cautiousness), conscientiousness (self-discipline vs. easy-going), extraversion (sociability vs. solitariness), agreeableness (friendliness vs. unkindness) and neuroticism (self-confident vs. sensitive). Also, the subscale "need for security" was used. These factors were measured with a German version of the Big Five inventory[8]. For test-economy the number of items was reduced from ten to three by a factor analysis.

Player types: Furthermore, we measured the motives for playing board or computer games with questions such as "*I like to understand the underlying strategy of a game"* or *"I like to play games because it is popular among my friends"*. This scale is based on Yee's study of player types found in online games [10] and categorizes gamers along the three main dimensions *Social*, *Achievement* and *Immersion*. People who like to socialize, either within or outside the game, rank high on the *Social* scale. Players who are driven by understanding the game mechanics or like collecting material and money rank high on the *Achievement* scale. If diving into roles or customizing their characters drives people they get high values on the *Immersion* scale.

2.3   Experimental Variables

The position within the supply chain was varied as a between-subjects variable (e.g. the position in the supply chain was chosen randomly, still it was the same for both rounds of the game). To control interactions across individuals we substituted the other players by computer players with a fixed strategy. Previous studies showed that the availability of point-of-sale data lowers the bullwhip effect. In this study we varied the availability of this data as a within-subject variable: Participants played both with and without point-of-sale data and the order of both conditions was randomized.

2.4   Dependent Variables

Performance within the supply chain. Behavior and performance within the game was measured through interaction logs of the web application. We looked at costs and stock levels of each position in each round and the total costs of the supply chain.

2.5   Experimental Setup

The participants were asked by email, social networks and personally to visit our beer game website. There, a survey assessed the demographics and personality factors as described above. Then, two rounds of the beer game were played. 173 people started the online survey, 128 have completed both rounds of the game and 126 people finished the post-survey. We revised the dataset and eliminated 5 cases with duplicated data or without meaningful gameplay (e.g. greatly exaggerated orders). The final dataset contains the gameplay and the questionnaire data from 121 people. The game was played for 25 rounds and as the players could optimize his/her strategy towards the end. Hence, only data from week 1 to 20 will be presented.

2.6   Participants

Of the 121 participants 61 (51%) were male and 57 female (48%). The age mean is 27.1 years (±6.1 years). The youngest participant is 19 years old and the oldest participants 54 years. The majority (68%) reported having no substantial prior knowledge in the areas of logistics, supply chain management, economy or business administration. 32% reported at least some knowledge either of these domains.

Gender has a significant effect on the participant's subjective technical competency (TSE), with women having a lower TSE ($M_{\female}=3.15$, ±.58) than men ($M_{\male}=3.53$, ±.45) ($F(1,117)=14,363$, p=.000<.05). This finding is in line with prior research [3]. Regarding the five factor model, our sample is also consistent with common findings: Men are less extraverted than women and show lower levels of neuroticism (see Table 1). Significant gender differences were found regarding the *Achievement* Scale in Yee's player types with men being more attracted to achievement ($M_{\male}=2.84$, ±.48) than women ($M_{\female}=2.53$, ±.54) ($F(1,108)=10.014$, p=.002 < .05). No differences were found on the *Social* ($M_{avg}=2.55$, ±.42) and *Immersion* dimension ($M_{avg}=2.67$, ±.65).

Table 1. Gender differences regarding the Five Factor Model ((* significant at p<.05, (*) at p<.1))

	Openness	Conscientiousness	Extraversion	Agreeableness	Neuroticism	Need for Security
Men	3.30	2.89	3.01	3.29	1.96	3.02
Women	3.29	3.10	3.27	3.43	2.23	3.13
F(1,108)	.003	3.413	4.287	1.283	3.601	.871
p	.957	.067$^{(*)}$	.041*	.260	.060$^{(*)}$	.353

3   Results

The data was analyzed using bivariate correlations, χ^2-tests, uni- and multivariate analyses of variance (ANOVA/MANOVA) with a significance level of $\alpha=.05$. Pillai values were used for the significance of the omnibus F-tests in the MANOVAs.

3.1   Bullwhip Effect

The Bullwhip effect is clearly observable (see Fig. 2). After the 5th week the customer increases his order from 4 to 8 good/week. This immediately affects the retailer's orders that increase from 5.1 to 7.5. Each week this increase is observable at the next position in the supply chain and eventually reaches the factory in week 9.

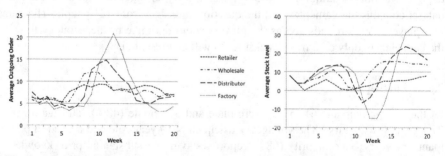

Fig. 2. Average stock level (left) and average outgoing orders (right) by week and position

3.2   Effect of Position in the Supply Chain

As expected the position within the supply chain had a significant effect on the total cost of a player and the average costs increase along the supply chain: Retailers accumulated less costs (C_R=87,95, ±46.5) than wholesalers (C_W=156,14, ±124.0), distributors (C_D=158,76, ±84.4) and factory players (C_F=223,76, ±101.6) (see Fig. 3, left). This effect is significant ($F(3,108)$=9,807, p<.001). A post-hoc Tukey-HSD test revealed that the mean scores from the retailer differ significantly from all other positions. Factory and distributor scores differ significantly. However, factory and wholesaler score closely miss the significance level with $p=.052>.05$. The mean scores of the wholesaler and the distributor do not differ significantly. Likewise the average spread ($max(stock_{Week\,j}) - min(stock_{Week\,i})$) differed significantly along the supply chain ($F(3,108)$=13.105, p<.001). A post-hoc test revealed that the spread differed significantly for all positions but wholesaler and distributor (see Fig 3, right).

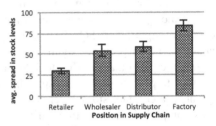

Fig. 3. Average costs (left) and average stock level spread along the supply chain (right)

3.3   Effect of Point-of-Sale Data

Contrary to numerous previous studies, the presence of point-of-sale (POS) data did not lower the costs in the supply chain. In the first round players without POS data actually produced slightly lower costs (C_{noPOS}=198, ±144) than player with POS data (C_{POS}=221, ±154). Yet, both differences are not significant, when the position is statistically controlled ($F(1,104)$=2.368, p=.075>.05, n.s.; $F(3,104)$=1.993, p=.120>.05, n.s.). However, we found that the POS data reduced the fluctuations of the supply chain: It was easier for players with POS data to maintain positive stock levels and avoid peaks (e.g. in week 14 the average stock level for factory players without POS was -14.1, while factory players with POS data had stock levels of -1.6 (see Fig 4). Still, the reduced variations did not reduce the final costs generated in the game.

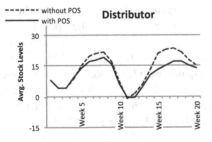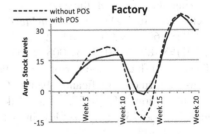

Fig. 4. Effect of Point-Of-Sale data on avg. stock levels of for distributor (l.) and factory (r.)

3.4   Effect of Repetition

There is a strong significant correlation between player's cost in the 1st and the 2nd round of the game ($r=.628$, $p=.000<.05^*$). With the position in the supply chain controlled the partial correlation between the costs in the 1st and 2nd round is also strong and significant ($r=.560$, $p=.000<.05^*$). Hence, factors must exist that explain good or bad performance in the supply chain, otherwise, if no such factors would exist, the costs of the 1st and 2nd round would be uncorrelated. Furthermore, the player's average cost decreases significantly between the first ($C_{1st}=160$, ±64) and the 2nd round of the game ($C_{2nd}=143$, ±47) when the position within the supply chain is controlled ($F(1,111)=4.204$, $p=.043<.05^*$).

3.5   Effects of User Diversity

Effects of gender: Women generated more costs than men ($C_{♀}=621$, ±276, $C_{♂}513$, ±122). Although women's cost were higher on all four positions of the chain, this effect is not significant ($F(1,102)=4.732$, $p=.110$, n.s.). We suspected that the large standard deviation prevents significant results, thus we used a different metric for analyzing the performance: The stock level spread ($max(stock_{Week\,j}) - min(stock_{Week\,i})$). In contrast to players with a low spread, players with a large spread have difficulties to maintain a constant stock level. They are not only victims of the bullwhip effect, but also amplify it, as variations in the stock level usually cause wriggly outgoing orders. Indeed, gender actually influences the spread ($F(1, 102)=8.897$, $p=.065<.1$) and men have a lower stock level spread ($S_m=35$, ±29) than women ($S_w=39$, ±28).

Effect of technical self efficacy: Technical self-efficacy (TSE) influenced the performance and players with low TSE performed worse ($C_{low}=167$, ±141) than players with high TSE ($C_{high}=124$, ±101) ($F(1,109)=4,018$, $p=.048<.05$). The same result was found for the spread in stock levels.

Effects of need for security: The "need for security" subscale of the personality inventory shows significant differences ($F(1,103)=4.872$, $p=.030<.05$) with players having a high need for security having a higher spread ($S_{high}=45$, ±29) than players with a   low need for security ($S_{low}=33$, ±37). Again, this difference fades if total costs are considered ($F(1,103)=2.623$, $p=.108$, n.s.) ($C_{low}=128$, ±113; $C_{high}=173$, ±135).

3.6   Effect of Gamer Type

Analyzing the effect of the gamer type on the game performance. Contradicting expectations, the *Desire for achievement* did not impact the performance ($F(2,101)=.060$, $V=.001$, $p=.942$, n.s.). However, desire for *Social* interaction ($F(2,101)=5.489$, $V=.098$, $p=.005 < .05$) and *Immersion* ($F(2,101)=3.203$, $V=.060$, $p=.045<.05$) influences the performance. Participants with high interest in social interactions performed significantly better ($C_{soc}=131$, ±76) people with low interest in social interaction ($M_{asoc}=177$, ±120). Likewise, high immersion players performed better ($M_{imm,high}=137$, ±67) than low immersion player ($M_{imm,low}=165$, ±120).

4   Discussion

The experimental approach used to study the complexly linked factors and to uncover human factors involved in supply chains revealed to be very useful. The supply chain was hit by the bullwhip effect and the effect increases with the distance from customer to player. Players performed equally well respective bad in the 1st and the 2nd round of the game. Hence, underlying factors must exist that explain player's performance. The data gives an insight in these factors, however they are not yet fully understood.

Social behavior increases performance, while focussing on his/her own interests is punished by the market. Also, immersing in the task of managing a supply chain was rewarded by low costs. The player's personality, modeled by the Five Factors Model did not impact performance within the supply chains, showing a high universality of the findings. Gender and technical self-efficacy influenced performance, with women and persons with lower self-efficacy performing worse. As gender and technical self-efficacy are connected [3], the lower performance of women can be referred to their lower self-efficacy levels. Corroborating previous findings in other contexts, we see once more the strong power of technical self-efficacy as a cognitive control mechanism that immensely controls human behavior [1].

The expected finding of a softening effect of point-of-sale data on the turbulences in supply chains could not be replicated as players performed equally well with and without the presence of this data. This can be referred to two major sources: First, our participants were novices with no prior knowledge about the game or supply chain management. Getting familiar with the complexity of the supply chain over the experimental phase may have veiled effects. Future studies will clarify effects with experts having higher domain knowledge. Second, as only a comparatively small sample size was given here, the non-linear nature of the costs and stock levels and the strong influence of the position on the performance, make the current dataset vulnerable regarding statistical rigidity. Hence, further studies have to be carried out in which more linear metrics are utilized or only one or two positions are considered, increasing the sample size for the remaining position.

To rule our effects by interactions with other human players, we modeled the co-players by artificial agents in this study. We noticed though that our agents performed very well and that the supply chains showed less turbulence than usual. Further studies will investigate the interaction of human players and different personality traits.

5   Summary, Limitations and Outlook

We presented a first glimpse on human behavior in supply chains. Still our research is just at the beginning with many influential factors not varied as an experimental condition or even discovered. We used a linear supply chain with four different positions. Reality is though more complex and more interactions between stakeholders occur that have to be investigated. Furthermore, the co-players were modeled by computer agents and it is unclear if our results are transferable to games, where all positions are played by humans and what interactions might occur when different personality types cooperate in a supply chain. Consequently, further research must evolve in four directions: First, identify and investigate additional factors that influence decision making along the model of a linear supply chain. Possible factors include, but are not limited to, the spread between penalty payments and stock keeping costs, variations in delivery reliability in regard to time or quantity and variations in the order function of the customer. Second, develop and evaluate an ecologically valid supply chain network, which extends to both additional positions horizontally as well as vertically. Decision conflicts, such as choosing the right supplier, have not been investigated in a model like this before. Third, evaluate how results from the "clean" experimental conditions can be transferred to either more realistic scenarios with multiple human players or how the results perform in real life to ensure external validity. Finally, investigate if this game is a suitable educational tool to train future managers and to evaluate if these trainings strengthen the competitiveness of companies.

Acknowledgements. The authors thank Manfred Ihne and Ralf Philipsen for research support. This research is funded by the German Research Foundation (DFG) as part of the Cluster of Excellence "Integrative Production Technology for High-Wage Countries".

References

1. Arning, K., Ziefle, M.: Understanding age differences in PDA acceptance and performance. Computers in Human Behavior 23(6), 2904–2927 (2007)
2. Beier, G.: Kontrollüberzeugungen im Umgang mit Technik [Locus of control when interacting with technology]. Report Psychologie 24(9), 684–693 (1999)
3. Brauner, P., Leonhardt, T., Ziefle, M., Schroeder, U.: The effect of tangible artifacts, gender and subjective technical competence on teaching programming to seventh graders. In: Hromkovič, J., Královič, R., Vahrenhold, J., et al. (eds.) ISSEP 2010. LNCS, vol. 5941, pp. 61–71. Springer, Heidelberg (2010)
4. Costa, P.T., McCrae, R.R.: The Revised NEO Personality Inventory (NEO-PI-R). In: Boyle, G.J., et al. (eds.) The SAGE Handbook of Personality Theory and Assessment, pp. 179–198. Sage Publications Ltd. (2008)
5. Forrester, J.W.: Industrial dynamics. MIT Press, Cambridge (1961)
6. Lee, H.L., et al.: Information distortion in a supply chain: the bullwhip effect. Management Science 43(4), 546–558 (1997)
7. Nienhaus, J., et al.: How human behaviour amplifies the bullwhip effect. A study based on the beer distribution game online. Production Planning & Control 17(6), 547–557 (2006)
8. Satow, L.: B5T. Psychomeda Big-Five-Persönlichkeitstest. Skalendokumentation und Normen sowie Fragebogen mit Instruktion. Leibniz-Zentrum für Psychologische Information und Dokumentation (ZPID)(Hrsg.), Elektronisches Testarchiv
9. Schuh, G., et al.: High resolution supply chain management: optimized processes based on self-optimizing control loops and real time data. Production Engineering 5(4), 433–442 (2011)
10. Yee, N.: Motivations for play in online games. Cyberpsychology & Behavior: The Impact of the Internet, Multimedia and Virtual Reality on Behavior and Society 9(6), 772–775 (2006)

Strategic Study of Knowledge Management Which Led into Furniture Design Industry – Taking Example by Taiwan Furniture Industry

Chi-Hsiung Chen[1,2] and Kang-Hua Lan[1]

[1] Graduate School of Design Master & Doctoral Program,
National Yunlin University of Science and Technology, No.123, University Road,
Section 3, Douliou, Yunlin 64002, Taiwan
[2] Department of Product Design, Chungyu Institute of Technology,
No. 40, Yi 7th Rd., Keelung 20103, Taiwan, R.O.C
chenchs@yuntech.edu.tw, chenchs@cit.edu.tw

Abstract. With changing times, the furniture industry in Taiwan has gradually transformed into a design service industry that integrates set design and manufacturing, and its design development has become increasingly intensive and closely linked, enabling many design information to emerge and accumulate as a result of the process. Henceforth, it is up to businesses to utilize knowledge management measures for effective integration. However, the backbone of the industry is product development process management application, and a majority of Taiwan's current furniture design industry is unable to advance alongside the industry's transformation trend. In terms of operations, many mechanism problems, such as knowledge management, still await resolution. Therefore, this research hoped to determine developmental strategies for industrial application of knowledge management and success factors for the industry's development, and to offer a reference to furniture developers with operation management and transformation strategies. Through the **supplementing** in-depth interviews with multiple case studies, the researcher first explored Taiwan's furniture developers' current use of and thoughts on knowledge management in the process of product development. Thereafter, data collected from the interviews and studies were analyzed, and based on knowledge management concepts proposed by scholars, the results were summarized according to four major influencing dimensions, namely business organization, product development process, information technology and cultural system. Using cross-analysis and data generalization, the following conclusions were made regarding knowledge management strategies in the development of related industries in furniture design: (1)Establish a knowledge management model using the development process of the industry as the core, and tailor the model according to the needs of the industry; (2) A complete plan is needed to enable those in charge to have awareness and measures to implement knowledge management; (3) It is more difficult to establish storage mechanisms for some of the tacit knowledge and diversified market survey data in development; and (4) In the furniture industry, the process of creative product thinking and human power will become programmed, making policies and mechanisms for employee training and experience teaching even more important.

S. Yamamoto (Ed.): HIMI/HCII 2013, Part III, LNCS 8018, pp. 433–442, 2013.
© Springer-Verlag Berlin Heidelberg 2013

Keywords: knowledge management, furniture design industry.

1   Introduction

Furniture design industry is an important industry in Taiwan. Due to its leading technology and insistence in its use of materials, Taiwan enjoyed a reputation of Furniture Kingdom during its early days of export. However, with changing times and domestic and foreign threats, Taiwan's furniture industry has gradually moved from OEM to ODM to Own Branding & Manufacturing (OBM), and industrial competitive edge has moved from Made in Taiwan (MIT) to Designed in Taiwan (DIT). Many furniture industries have gradually transformed from furniture manufacture to design and processing. To integrate personal design into the development of related products, they have further transformed from design and processing to overall field planning. Furthermore, manufacture and orders are based in one's own factory, thereby increasing the added value of a single product through the whole design and marketing process. This industrial trend has gradually transformed set designing, production and manufacture into a single design services industry. Moreover, diversified developments in the industry are also beginning to integrate talents and technologies from many different fields. Given this trend, strategies for incorporating internal organization and knowledge management are particularly important to enterprises. Management requires flexibility and measures to comprehensively integrate corporate resources and enable proper coordination among different jobs and departments, and thereby create the most efficient process and competitive edge.

However, for the most part, current organization and knowledge management model in Taiwan's furniture design industry is unable to advance alongside the transformation trend in the industry, and in its operations, many problems still await exploration and resolution. Undermined by the inability to innovate and master the trend in management strategies, many medium and small-scale furniture developers are also stalled in their development. In addition to external strategies such as industrial marketing and promotion, if industries hope to increase their market competitiveness and upgrade their enterprises, they must strengthen the development of their internal core competencies, and focus on the industry's management, storage and application of industrial knowledge. Only by commanding the development of design and core competencies of enterprises, and establishing internal and external entrepreneur mechanisms such as comprehensive production process and marketing, can the industry sustain innovation and progress.

Thus this research hoped to determine developmental strategies for industrial application of knowledge management and success factors for the industry's development through relevant investigations, and determine theoretical basis undergirding these concrete concepts and strategies, and thereby offer a reference to furniture developers for operation management and transformation strategies.

2   Literature Review

Definition of Knowledge Management. Wiig (1997) first comprehensively defined knowledge management as a set of clearly defined procedures or methods that are used to examine and manage knowledge pertinent to different fields, approve new products or strategies, and strengthen human resource management in order to achieve corporate goals. On the other hand, Gartner Group (1997) pointed out that knowledge management is the organizational and technological foundation of enterprises for facilitating knowledge sharing and re-use. Moreover, it is the capability of enterprises to integrate operations in order to verify, manage and share all the organization's information assets such as databank, documents, organizational policies and procedures, and potentially harvest implicit skills and experience of knowledgeable workers. Based on the above-mentioned definitions, scholars can recognize that knowledge management is the basic element in industrial management. In addition, it is also effective for improving organizational performance, and an important impetus behind industrial value. As such, integrating the advantages of one's industry and incorporating appropriate measures for knowledge management have become the most important subject in knowledge innovation and industrial renovation for enterprises.

Knowledge Management Model. Laurie (1997) proposed that in the model, knowledge management is a series of knowledge creation, acquisition and application that enhances management activities such as organizational performance. Arthur Anderson (2001) believed that knowledge management is the foundation of value construction, and proposed four critical structural elements in knowledge management formula, namely Technology, People, Share, and Knowledge. He further proposed a model for organizational knowledge management, and believed that the comprehensiveness of organizational knowledge management depends on the management of its processes, including the following seven actions: Identify, Create, Collect, Adapt, Organize, Apply and Share, while factors influencing the effectiveness of knowledge management implementation are Leadership, Culture, Technology and Measurement (Fig. 1). If enterprises appropriately command these factors, the process of knowledge management will be fluent, thereby affecting performance and also enhancing the accumulation of organization knowledge and increasing competitiveness.

Process of Furniture Product Development. The core knowledge of corporations lay within their work content and process, and in this research, the furniture product development process and content of relevant industries in furniture design constitute the important core of their industrial knowledge management. Furniture design development is a multi-step and repetitious process. In the Design Analysis Method, Huang (1995) discussed the importance of the cyclical nature of the design process, and proposed five stages, namely Statement of Problem, Analysis and Research, Possible Solution, Experimentation and Final Solution. Interactions among these five stages enable the completion of the design process to produce results. In furniture product development, orderliness of work flow and the completeness of the process are not only important factors affecting the smoothness of job implementation; at the same time, they are the key to whether a design can eventually be transformed into mass production. Although differences in design development processes exist due to differences in social, cultural, entrepreneur and individual factors, their goals and basic content remain consistent with the three major elements of design, namely creativity, expression and value. As shown in Fig. 2, based on the abovementioned design analysis method, elements and longstanding furniture design practices of related domestic and foreign industries, this research classified the design process into five major steps: (1) Design Positioning, (2) Information Analysis, (3)Design Development, (4) Production Management, and (5) Marketing and Sales

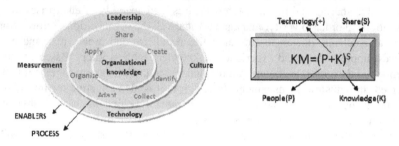

Fig. 1. Organizational knowledge management model and critical structural elements (Source: Arthur Andersen, 1995 / 2001)

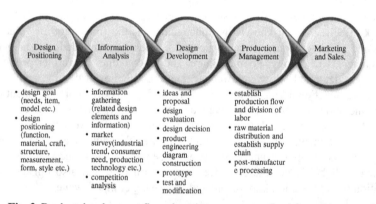

Fig. 2. Product development flow chart (source: summarized from this research)

Summary. Based on the final summary of Arthur Anderson's interpretation of knowledge management formula and his proposed factors affecting the effectiveness of knowledge management implementation, the four major elements facilitating industrial knowledge management are: Organizational Leadership, Product Development Process, Information Technology and Cultural Systems. In terms of the core knowledge of management, by integrating Laurie and Arthur Anderson's proposed knowledge management and creation process, four major processes of knowledge application are delineated, namely Creation, Storage, Transfer and Share, and Application. Hence in incorporating knowledge management strategies, the above four major influencing dimensions must be taken into complete consideration. More importantly, the core and unique developmental tasks and relevant process of the industry, such as design positioning, analysis and research, design development, production and manufacture and marketing and sales, must be completely integrated with industrial knowledge management and application process in order to further synthesize innovative industrial knowledge and become a knowledge-based industry that have greater competitive and innovative power.

3   Research Method and Procedure

Research Method. The subjects in this research were three furniture design development companies that have been fairly successful in innovations in the furniture design industry in Taiwan. The purpose of the study was to determine the industry's development strategies for knowledge management application and success factors for its development. The research used methods such as case analysis and in-depth interviews to first gather raw data. The obtained data were then summarized and conceptualized, and common concepts among the cases were integrated and summarized to derive a more easily understood theoretical basis underlying the industrial concepts and strategies. Figure 3 shows the analytical framework of the research.

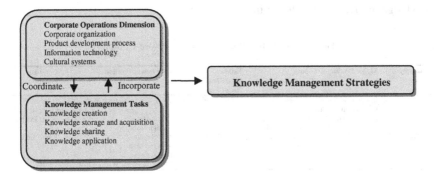

Fig. 3. Research analytical framework (Source: summarized from this research)

Research Procedure. This research involved three major steps, namely literature review, case study and in-depth interviews. In Stage 1, relevant literature and studies on current domestic and foreign knowledge management were collected and current and future trends in furniture development industry were analyzed. Results of the analysis formed the major basis for the research theory. In Stage 2, three Taiwan furniture design development companies were studied, and the operations of domestic furniture design industries were surveyed. After relevant industrial literature and information on the case examples were obtained, a structured interview was constructed to conduct in-depth interviews with the supervisors and employees of professional departments of the companies. In Stage 3, the content of the in-depth interviews and collected information were summarized using comparisons and analysis, and the knowledge management strategies of related furniture design development industries were delineated.

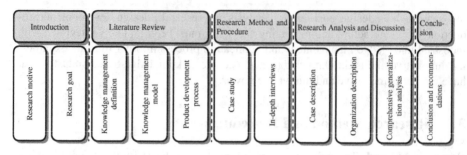

Fig. 4. The Research Flow Chart

4   Research Results and Analysis

4.1   Case Description and Organization Condition

Within the limitations of this study, three Taiwan furniture design developers, Sunwhite, Strauss and Formosa, were selected as subjects. The basic interviewee and company information, general organization description, and cognitive survey of corporate knowledge innovation are shown in Tables 1 and 2.

Table 1. Basic information of Interviewee Company

Company Name	Major Product Attribute	Established/Total No. of Years	Interviewee/Position	Company Location
Sunwhite	furniture design and development using composite materials	1981/33years	Tseng Ren-ju /General Manager	Hsichou, Changhua County,
Strauss	furniture and home decor development using wood and composite materials	1951/63years	Li Jian-shing /Design Manager	Wuri, Taichung City
Formosa	integration and design development of systems furniture	1981/33years	Shie Hau-lin /Plannng Manager Jau Guo-tan /Deputy General Manager	Xitun, Taichung City

Table 2. Organization description and cognitive survey of corporate knowledge innovation

Name of Case Dimension/Item		Sunwhite	Strauss	Formosa
Organization Description of Corpora-	Primary Production Model	ODM	ODM/OBM	ODM/OBM
	Primary Sales Model	B2B	B2B/B2C	B2c
	Primary Sales Market/Ratio	International(Europe, United States, Canada, Australia, Japan etc.) 100%	Taiwan 90%/Others 10%/China(future goal)	Taiwan region 100%
	Annual Operating Income	300-500 million	200-300 million	1.3-1.6 billion
	No. of Employees — Total No.	200	100	70
	No. of Employees — R&D Ratio	15%	10%	8%
	Department Organizational Structure	Business Department; Design Department; Production Department; Quality Control Department; Management Department	Research and Development Center; Sales Center; Spatial Center; Management Center	Management Department; Plant Operations Department; Research and Development Center; Design and Business Center; Marketing Planning Department
	Industrial Alliance	Complete and self-sufficient in technology, hence few industrial technology alliances.	Coordinate with assisting partners for assistance based on production needs	Coordinate with material suppliers and assisting processing plants based on design needs
	Corporate Philosophy on Research and Development	Experience furniture in living	Create aesthetics in furniture space	Integrate residence and craft

Table 2. (*continued*)

Features of Research and Development Information Gathering	International market analysis	Design information library	Internet platform for employee learning
Awareness of Importance of Industrial Knowledge	Important. Market information analysis and content of developed products are especially important company knowledge asset content in development	Important. Content of developed products are important company knowledge asset and source of experience accumulation.	Important. During design services, the process and cooperative experiences of relevant tasks are the most important.
Incorporation of Knowledge Management System	Yes, especially in work process	Yes, especially in sales process	Yes, especially in overall service process
Whether knowledge management can be comprehensively applied in the corporation	Still lack comprehensive application. Much tacit knowledge in development and production, and many details that require employee experience.	Still lack comprehensive application. Much tacit knowledge in development and production, and many details that require employee experience.	Still lack comprehensive application. Much tacit knowledge in development and production, and many details that require employee experience.

Table 3. Comprehensive **Analysis and Summary of Case Examples**

Dimension/Item			Name of Case	Sunwhite	Strauss	Formosa
Organization Leadership			Management and Decision Method	Directed and integrated by the operator	Directed and integrated by the operator and high level managers	Directed and integrated by the operator and management department
			Incorporation of Knowledge Management/Extent	o Has a personal operation management method, combined with concepts of knowledge management.	o Has a personal operation management method, combined with concepts of knowledge management.	o Knowledge management concepts built into management model.
			Measures for Promoting Management Policies	o	o	o
Industrial Development Process	Product Development Model		Design Positioning	o	o	o
			Information Analysis	o	o	o
			Design Development	o	o	o
			Production and Manufacture	o	o	o
			Marketing and Sales	x(no particular sales measure)	o	o
			Others	o(Customer development)	x	o(Design Center services)
	Materials Used			Composite	Wood(coordinated with composite materials)	Boards and systems furniture materials
	Types of Product Development			Develop composite furniture and all kinds of foreign furniture design	Develop wood furniture, all kinds of composite material furniture and home decor	Integrate systems furniture and design development
	Product Development Cycle			Based on nature of development	Based on nature of development	Based on nature of development
	Degree of Work in Product Development			High	Medium(part of the task is combined with space planning services)	Low (currently most tasks are integration planning services)
	Development Limitation		Difficulty in teaching technology	o	o	o
			Requires cooperation with outside technology	X	o	o
Information Management Technology			System Incorporation	o(partially incorporated, mainly in production and manufacture development)	o(partially incorporated, mainly in sales)	ocompletely incorporated
			Tool Selection	Both traditional electronic forms and ERP	Both traditional electronic forms and ERP	Cloud ERP system/Webpage platform
			Research and Development Method	Process drafted by supervisory staff and developed by professional IT staff	Process drafted by supervisory staff and developed by professional IT staff	Process drafted by supervisory staff and developed by professional IT staff
			Systemization of Documents/Forms	o	o	o

Table 3. (*continued*)

	Knowledge Storage and Protection Mechanism		o	o	o
	Establishment of Cloud Knowledge Bank		Partial(only for work forms)	Partial(only for work forms)	Complete(both design information and work forms)
Systems Knowledge Classification		Market survey information	X(stored separately)	X((stored separately)	o(links established from official website)
		Technological knowledge	o	X((stored separately)	o
		Outcome knowledge	o	o	o
		Development experience	X(difficult to store)	X(difficult to store)	o(can be partially recorded and stored)
		Customer knowledge	o	o	o
	Regulations for Use(Storing and Obtaining/Sharing)		o	o	o
	Application extension (Statistics/Analysis)		o	o	o
Cultural Systems	Education and Training		o(documents available for references)	o(departments conduct their own training)	o(documents available for references)
	Job Standards		o	o	o
	Awards and Demerits Mechanism		o(no award and demerit mechanism)	o	o
	Cultural Sharing		o	o	o
	Activity Sharing		o(lectures	o(exhibits, lectures)	o(exhibits, lectures, sharing sessions)

Note: In the charts and tables, o and X indicate whether the corporation implemented and agreed with the particular item

4.2   Comprehensive Analysis and Summary of Case Examples

In the analysis and discussion of the cases, the research used analysis and comparisons to obtain important dimensions and relevant elements that affect the construction of knowledge management strategies for furniture design industry (Table 3). Moreover, after summarizing the commonalities and differences among the three case examples, the different dimensions were respectively discussed.

1. Organization Leadership: From the table, it can be seen that in the organization leader, the promotion and establishment of knowledge management are best planned and promoted by high level supervisors for a more comprehensive overall design process. Following the completion of the overall framework, attention must be given to promotion and employee education. If knowledge management concepts can be introduced early in the development rather than merely promoting integrated work process, the effectiveness of management integration can be greatly enhanced, thereby enabling more effective use of industrial knowledge.
2. Product Development Process Dimension: The construction of knowledge management process must be built upon the core product development process of the enterprise.   Product development processes are relatively similar, and the importance lies in establishing differentiation process to complement different production and development focus.   Only a process that is constructed according to the company's development attributes and details can best meet the needs of the enterprise's system.
3. Information Technology Dimension: From the tables, it can be seen that among the interviewees, only one operator has more complete systems incorporation. In their knowledge management systems development, the other two companies, though

having a higher level of research and development, had relevant ERP information software in only some of their work content while other industrial tasks are yet to be completely integrated into the electronic systems. In terms of systems development, the case examples for the most part did not directly utilize packaged software from relevant software developers; rather, company supervisors first formulated relevant processes, and then had professional IT personnel develop the model. Moreover, their knowledge classification generally comprised content such as market survey information, technological knowledge, outcome knowledge, and development experience and customer feedback knowledge. Operators stated that market survey information and development experience are more difficult to integrate, possibly because the diversities of survey data are difficult to organize and certain employee knowledge is inherent and thus difficult to store in the form of files and documents.

4. Cultural System Dimension: Influencing factors in the cultural system dimension include education and training, job standards, awards and demerits mechanism, cultural sharing and activity sharing. In the interviews, the example companies showed certain level of standards and identification. Therefore it is evident that these elements must be taken into full consideration in the development of knowledge management strategies.

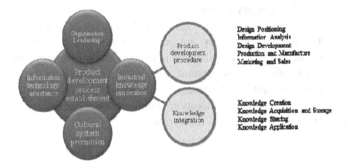

Fig. 5. Relational diagram of knowledge management impact

From the above analysis, the core development process of the enterprise itself must be the primary foundation on which the framework for the mechanisms of integrating industrial knowledge management is constructed while concepts of knowledge integration are secondary. In addition, the impact of the above four major dimensions must be comprehensively considered. Figure 5 is a relational diagram showing the impact of knowledge management.

5   Conclusion and Recommendations

5.1   Research Conclusion

The above research and analysis of the development strategies for knowledge management application, and elements and limitations of industry development among furniture design development industries yielded the following results:

1. The establishment of a knowledge management model must be centered on the industry's own development process and tailored to the demands of the industry.
2. Supervisors Need Comprehensive Planning For Awareness and Promotion Measures For Knowledge Management.
3. Difficulty in Constructing Storage Mechanism for Certain Tacit Development Knowledge and Diversified Market Survey Information.
4. In Work Procedure, Work Processes and Human Power Involved in Product Creativity Make Policies and Mechanisms For Employee Education and Training and Experience Teaching Even More Important.

5.2   Research Recommendation

1. Knowledge management form and system establishment vary with industrial characteristics. Particularly in innovative product development related industries, operations and management processes depend on the content and content connectivity of the development tasks. Therefore, if the furniture design industry wants to incorporate knowledge and management systems, it is less suitable to directly use related packaged software developed in the market. Instead, it is best that company management and decision-makers first construct its own management process, and then seek the help of IT engineers to construct the system.
2. The difference between furniture design industry and other innovative product development is that complete machinery automation is not possible in its work process. During production, human assistance is needed in the processing process, and these processing requires a large amount of training and wealth of experience. Therefore, except for relevant explanations and construction in the work forms, employee education, training and cultivation are more important than in other related innovative product development industries.

References

1. Andersen, A.: APQC, The Knowledge-Management assessment Tool, Prototype Version. Released at the Knowledge Imperative Symposium, Houston, Texas, Developed by Arthur Anderson and the American Productivity and Quality Center (1996)
2. Anderson, A.: Business Consulting. Zukai knowledge management. Toyo Keizai, Japan (1999)
3. Bair, J., Fenn, J., Hunter, R., Bosik, D.: Foundations for Enterprise Knowledge Management. Gartner Group (1997)
4. Hansen, M., Nohria, N., Tierney, T.: What's Your Strategy from Managing Knowledge. Harvard Business Review (1998)
5. Laurie, J.: Harnessing the power of intellectual capital Training & Development. Management Accounting, 49–53 (June 1997)
6. Wiig, K.M.: Integrating intellectual capital and knowledge management. Long Range Planning 30(3), 399–405 (1997)

A Study of Customization for Online Business

Vincent Cho and Candy Lau

Department of Management and Marketing
The Hong Kong Polytechnic University
Hong Kong
msvcho@polyu.edu.hk, dr.cando@candotimes.com

Abstract. The ever-expanding Internet and fast-growing pace of online shopping push companies to implement online customization. Rather than customizing on the information delivery, transaction handling, and product features, companies also start to offer different specific privileges to different types of customers. In this regard, we would like to examine how these different forms of customization affect customer satisfaction.

1   Introduction

With the advancement of production flexibility, logistic efficiency, and customer behavioral tracking, many online businesses are now focusing on customization strategies for building up customer satisfaction. Early customization relies on assembly of modular parts for a customized product which begins the era of mass customization (e.g. Syam et al., 2005; Dellaert & Strmersch, 2005; and Gilmore & Pine, 2000). Coming along with sophisticated logistic and scheduling arrangement with suppliers and distributors in supply chain management, companies are capable to launch the "build to order" strategy (e.g. Volling and Spengler, 2011; Brabazon, et al. 2010). Nowadays, customer relationship management enables companies to pay more attention to the preferences and needs of an individual customer (e.g. Palmatier et al., 2006; Darley, Blankson & Luethge, 2010; Fornell, Rust & Dekimpe, 2010; Thirumalai & Sinha, 2009, 2011).

Integrating all the above developments together, companies are now in full swing towards customization and are capable to deliver a customized product within a short time frame. Along this vein, this study attempts to investigate the impacts of customizations. In our framework, we classify customization according to information delivery, transaction handling, product features, and preferential treatment. We will testify our framework using data collected from an online jewelry company in China. Based on the situation in the current online marketplace, a tremendous opportunity now exists for online businesses. More consumers are buying their jewelry online than ever before, especially if they believe that they have found a reliable Website. Moreover, testing our research model in the context of an online jewelry business will provide executives in the online businesses on luxury products in China some helpful insight for possible future marketing strategies. Investigating different types of

S. Yamamoto (Ed.): HIMI/HCII 2013, Part III, LNCS 8018, pp. 443–449, 2013.

customers will also allow marketing practitioners to gain a better understanding of how different customization practices affect customer satisfaction.

2   Theoretical Framework

Information customization signifies the multiple ways in which companies can arrange and organize online information (in terms of display and content) to reflect their customers' preferences (Berry et al., 2002). Often, customers are overwhelmed with the plethora of products and services available. With an established customer database, a company would easily keep track the behavior and preference of its customers. Upon the login of a customer, the online store can tailor information content to help customers identify their needs and facilitate their decision making in an effective way.

Oliver (1997) stated customer satisfaction is related to two stimuli—an outcome and a comparison referent. A customer feel satisfied when he/she has greater experience than his/her expectation. Hence, we expect that a tailor-made and well-arranged presentation of information on an online store will induce high customer satisfaction and we propose the following hypothesis:

2.1   H1: Information Customization Has a Significant Positive Impact on Customer Satisfaction

Transaction customization refers to different logistic and payment conveniences and options for customers in handling a transaction. It also allows customer to trace a transaction conveniently. Berry et al. (2002) hypothesized that transaction inconvenience is a factor contributing to the high abandonment rates of shopping carts in electronic retailing. The frustration that the customers encounter in the online transaction experience with inconvenient electronic shopping carts or processing speed is similar to that of waiting in long lines at a retail store. Ultimately, as Srinivasan et al. (2002) explained, customizing the transaction process for customers allows "individuals [to be] able to complete their transactions more efficiently." The speed of the transaction is also a vital component of transaction customization. Based on the profile of a customer in the customer database, an online store would save the customer's effort filling in the address and payment details of an order. We argue that for a company providing convenience for customers in handling and tracing their transactions in terms of payment and logistic arrangement in a more customized way, the higher will be the satisfaction of the customers. Hence, we put forth the following hypothesis.

2.2   H2: Transaction Customization Has a Significant Positive Impact on Customer Satisfaction

Product customization provides a means for customers to specify their products according to a wide variety of options and accessories in specifying a product. It relies on advanced manufacturing using modular design in a product. Product customization is the adaptation of products to the individual tastes and needs of consumers

(Thirumalai & Sinha, 2009). Involving customers in the process creates a sense of ownership for the customers. When customers design a unique product, they feel a sense of accomplishment (the "I designed it myself" effect) (Franke, Schreier, & Kaiser, 2010). Buying a ready-made product generally provides the customer a lower degree of psychological ownership (Pierce et al., 2002). Therefore, many companies consider the "I designed it myself" effect and allow customers to design their unique products (Dellaert & Stremersch, 2005; Franke & Piller 2004; Randall et al., 2007; Ulrich, 2009).

This is consistent with the literature on empowerment in general: when people are allowed to participate actively in decision-making that may influence the final outcome, the decisions become their decisions (Hunton, 1996). In other words, people assume psychological ownership of such decisions because they are partly responsible for the outcome, and this tends to elicit positive feelings of satisfaction (Barki & Hartwick, 1994; Hui &Bateson, 1991). This would bring the happiness and pleasure during the process. Therefore, a highly customized product increases the likelihood of customer satisfaction. This leads to the following hypothesis:

2.3   H3: Product Customization Has a Significant Positive Impact on Customer Satisfaction

Preferential treatment focuses on serving customer preferentially and in different manner. It is a kind of customization because it caters for the unique wants and needs of different customer types by providing them with specific privileges, social benefits and special treatment (Tam & Ho, 2005) and is for building, developing and maintaining targeted customer types (Morgan & Hunt, 1994; Hennig-Thurau et al., 2002; Gwinner et al., 1998). For instance, while VIP members get an extraordinary discount on prices because of their status, ordinary members will also get excited about receiving a special discount during their birthday month. It offers unique services to customers, such as tailored personal recognition, discounts, price breaks and extra attention (Gremler et al., 1997; Gwinner et al., 1998). Preferential treatment would help companies build and stabilize the relationship between different types of customers and the company (Lacey et al., 2007).

It is not difficult to understand why customers welcome preferential treatment. Some researchers have suggested that customers typically compare themselves with "similar others" (Xia et al., 2004). This need for comparison is pervasive, even though customers make the comparisons unintentionally (Gilbert et al., 1995) and without self-awareness (Stapel & Blanton, 2004). With time, preferential treatment may make customers feel special and entitled to adulation (Boyd & Helms, 2005). When preferential treatment is highly apparent to customers, it becomes even more important for them to understand the stipulations behind these disproportionate levels of treatment (Schneider & Bowen, 1999). Ridgeway and Walker (1995) also pointed out that status structures are formed by "patterned inequalities" among a group of people. People compare themselves to someone who is either better off (upward comparison) or worse off (downward comparison). Everyone engages in each comparing type at one time or another, and sometimes in both simultaneously (Taylor & Lobel, 1989). Because of social comparisons, customers in high tiers enjoy extraordinary levels of privilege and attention (Brady, 2000). Numerous researchers have concluded that people feel better when they perceive themselves to be superior (Giordano et al., 2000; Locke & Neckich, 2000). People wish to be better off than others (Taylor & Brown, 1988), and comparisons with others who are less privileged can boost their self-esteem (Brown & Lohr, 1987; Giordano et al., 2000; Locke & Nekich, 2000; Olson & Evans, 1999; Wills, 1981). Such a feeling might enhance the relationship with the company (Klemperer, 1987; Wernerfelt, 1985). Research has confirmed that preferential treatment can be used to enhance and augment products and services (Crosby, 1991; Berry, 1983), which may also lead to customer satisfaction. Hence, we predict the following hypothesis:

2.4   H4: Preferential Treatment Has a Significant Positive Impact on Customer Satisfaction

Control Variables
Perceived value is defined as the net benefits customers gain in proportion to their costs, including the amount paid and the related transactional cost (Woodruff, 1997; Holbrook, 1994; Zeithaml, 1988). What constitutes value seems to vary widely from one person to another (Holbrook, 1994; Zeithaml, 1988). However, the impact of perceived value on satisfaction cannot be neglected; a considerable amount of research has focused on identifying the impact of perceived value on customer satisfaction (Anderson et al., 1994; Ravald & Grönroos, 1996; Bolton & Drew, 1991). This study also considers perceived value as a control factor on customer satisfaction.

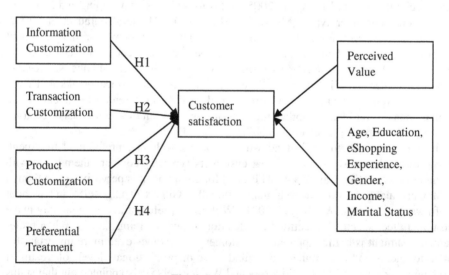

Fig. 1. Research Model

The backgrounds of users may influence their online shopping behavior. Prior online shopping experience, for example, may be proportionate to satisfaction. Moreover, the education of users sometimes increases with their understanding of online shipping. Different levels of understanding result in different presumptions, influencing user satisfaction. Therefore, it was necessary to control the possible effects of gender, age, prior shopping experience and education on satisfaction.

3   Conclusion

In sum, this study investigates the impacts of customizations on customer satisfaction in an online jewelry business and observes the differences between the two groups of customers (ordinary and VIP members). Our framework is testified using the online jewelry store in China. It is an expanding market and gaining widespread popularity among high-income earners.

References

1. Anderson, E.W., Fornell, C., Lehmann, D.R.: Customer satisfaction, market share and profitability: Findings from Sweden. Journal of Marketing 58, 53–66 (1994)
2. Barki, H., Hartwick, J.: Measuring user participation, user involvement, and user attitude. MIS Quarterly 18, 59–79 (1994)
3. Berry, L.L.: Relationship marketing. In: Berry, L.L., Shostack, G.L., Upala, G.D. (eds.) Emerging Perspectives on Services Marketing, pp. 25–80. American Marketing Association, Chicago (1983)
4. Berry, L.L., Seiders, K., Grewal, D.: Understanding service convenience. Journal of Marketing 66, 1–17 (2002)
5. Bolton, R.N., Drew, J.H.: A multistage model of customers' assessment of service quality and value. Journal of Consumer Research 54, 69–82 (1991)
6. Boyd, H.C., Helms, J.E.: Consumer entitlement theory and measurement. Psychology & Marketing 22(3), 271–286 (2005)
7. Brabazon, P.G., MacCarthy, B., Woodcock, A., Hawkins, R.W.: Mass customization in the automotive industry: comparing interdealer trading and reconfiguration flexibilities in order fulfillment. Production and Operations Management 19(5), 489–502 (2010)
8. Brady, D.: Why service stinks. Business Week 23, 118–128 (2000)
9. Brown, B.B., Lohr, M.J.: Peer-group affiliation and adolescent self-esteem: An integration of ego-identity and symbolic interaction theories. Journal of Personality and Social Psychology 52(1), 47–55 (1987)
10. Crosby, L.A.: Building and maintaining quality in the service relationship. In: Brown, S.W., Gummesson, E., Edvardsson, B., Gustavsson, B., Lexington, B. (eds.) Service Quality: Multidisciplinary and Multinational Perspectives, pp. 269–287. Lexington Books, Lexington (1991)
11. Darley, W.K., Blankson, C., Luethge, D.J.: Toward an integrated framework for online consumer behavior and decision making process: A review. Psychology and Marketing 27(2), 94–116 (2010)
12. Dellaert, B.G.C., Stremersch, S.: Marketing mass-customized products: striking a balance between utility and complexity. Journal of Marketing Research 42(2), 219–227 (2005)
13. Franke, N., Piller, T.P.: Value creation by toolkits for user innovation and design: The case of the watch market. Journal of Product Innovation Management 21, 401–415 (2004)

14. Franke, N., Schreier, M., Kaiser, U.: The "I designed it myself" effect in mass customization. Management Science 56(1), 125–140 (2010)
15. Gilbert, D.T., Giesler, R.B., Morris, K.A.: When comparisons arise. Journal of Personality and Social Psychology 69(2), 227–236 (1995)
16. Gilmore, J.H., Pine, J.B.: Markets of one: Creation customer-unique value through mass customization. Harvard Business School, Cambridge (2000)
17. Giordano, C., Wood, J.V., Michela, J.L.: Depressive personality styles, dysphoria, and social comparisons in everyday life. Journal of Personality and Social Psychology 79(3), 438–451 (2000)
18. Gremler, D.D., Brown, S.W.: Towards a conceptual model of service loyalty. In: Marketing Theory and Applications AMA Winter Educators' Conference, pp. 218–219. MCB UP Ltd., Chicago (1997)
19. Hennig-Thurau, T., Gwinner, K.P., Gremler, D.D.: Understanding relationship marketing outcomes: An integration of relational benefits and relationship quality. Journal of Service Research 4(3), 230–247 (2002)
20. Holbrook, M.B.: The nature of customer's value: An axiology of service in consumption experience. In: Rust, R.T., Oliver, R.L. (eds.) Service Quality: New Directions in Theory and Practice, pp. 21–71. Sage, Thousand Oaks (1994)
21. Hunton, J.E.: Involving information system users in defining system requirements: The influence of procedural justice perceptions on user attitudes and performance. Decision Sciences 27(4), 617–669 (1996)
22. Lacey, R., Suh, J., Morgan, R.M.: Differential effects of preferential treatment levels on relational outcomes. Journal of Service Research 9(3), 241–256 (2007)
23. Locke, K.D., Nekich, J.C.: Agency and communion in naturalistic social comparison. Personality and Social Psychology Bulletin 26(7), 864–874 (2000)
24. Morgan, R.M., Hunt, S.D.: The commitment–trust theory of relationship marketing. Journal of Marketing 58, 20–38 (1994)
25. Oliver, R.L.: Satisfaction: A behavioral perspective on the consumer. McGraw-Hill, New York (1997)
26. Olson, B.D., Evans, D.L.: The role of the big five personality dimensions in the direction and affective consequences of everyday social comparisons. Personality and Social Psychology Bulletin 25(12), 1498–1508 (1999)
27. Palmatier, R.W., Dant, R.P., Grewal, D., Evans, K.R.: Factors influencing the effectiveness of relationship marketing: A meta-analysis. Journal of Marketing 70(4), 136–153 (2006)
28. Pierce, J.L., Kostova, T., Dirks, K.T.: The state of psychological ownership: Integrating and extending a century of research. Review of General Psychology 7, 84–107 (2002)
29. Randall, T., Terwiesch, C., Ulrich, K.T.: User design of customized products. Marketing Science 26(2), 268–280 (2007)
30. Ravald, A., Grönroos, C.: The value concept and relationship marketing. European Journal of Marketing 30(2), 19–30 (1996)
31. Ridgeway, C.L., Walker, H.A.: Status structures. In: Cook, K.S., Fine, G.A., House, J.S. (eds.) Sociological Perspectives on Social Psychology, pp. 281–310. Allyn & Bacon, Needham Heights (1995)
32. Schneider, B., Bowen, D.E.: Understanding customer delight and outrage. Sloan Management Review 41(1), 35–46 (1999)
33. Stapel, D.A., Blanton, H.: From seeing to being: Subliminal social comparisons affect implicit and explicit self-evaluations. Journal of Personality and Social Psychology 87(4), 468–481 (2004)

34. Syam, N.B., Ruan, R., Hess, J.D.: Customized products: A competitive analysis. Marketing Science 24, 569–584 (Fall 2005)
35. Tam, K.Y., Ho, S.Y.: Web personalization as a persuasion strategy: An elaboration likelihood model perspective. Information Systems Research 16(3), 271–291 (2005)
36. Taylor, S.E., Brown, J.D.: Illusion and well-being: A social psychological perspective on mental health. Psychological Bulletin 103(2), 193–210 (1988)
37. Taylor, S.E., Lobel, M.: Social comparison activity under threat: Downward evaluation and upward contacts. Psychological Review 96(4), 569–575 (1989)
38. Thirumalai, S., Sinha, K.K.: Customization strategies in electronic retailing: Implications of customer purchase behavior. Decision Sciences 40(1), 5–36 (2009)
39. Thirumalai, S., Sinha, K.K.: Customization of the online purchase process in electronic retailing and customer satisfaction: An online field study. Journal of Operations Management 29(5), 477–487 (2011)
40. Ulrich, E.: Avoiding market dominance: Product compatibility in market with network effects. The Rand Journal of Economics 40(3), 455–485 (2009)
41. Volling, T., Spengler, T.S.: Modeling and simulation of order-driven planning policies in build-to-order automobile production. International Journal of Production Economics 131, 183–193 (2011)
42. Wernerfelt, B.: Brand loyalty and user skills. Journal of Economic Behavior and Organization 6(4), 381–385 (1985)
43. Wills, T.A.: Downward comparison principles in social psychology. Psychological Bulletin 90(2), 245–271 (1981)
44. Woodruff, R.B.: Customer value: The next source of competitive advantage. Journal of the Academy of Marketing Science 25, 139–153 (1997)
45. Xia, L., Monroe, K.B., Cox, J.L.: The price is unfair! A conceptual framework of price fairness perceptions. Journal of Marketing 68, 1–15 (2004)
46. Zeithaml, V.A.: Consumer perceptions of price, quality, and value: A means-end model and synthesis of evidence. Journal of Marketing 52, 2–22 (1988)

Are HCI Issues a Big Factor in Supply Chain Mobile Apps?

Barry Flachsbart, Cassandra C. Elrod, and Michael G. Hilgers

Missouri University of Science and Technology, Rolla, MO, USA
{barryf,cassa,hilgers}@mst.edu

Abstract. A previous survey about the use of iPhone and/or iPad apps in supply chain operations learned that the use of such apps varies greatly among different individuals and different organizations, with many respondents using apps, but not for supply chain operations [1]. In product design, an aspect of growing importance is its usability. This raises the question that is the focus of the paper. Namely, are human-computer interaction (HCI) issues a factor being addressed in the mobile apps for supply chain management? It appears that addressing HCI issues for most any kind of commercial mobile app seems to have had little focus, even though some usability problems are well-known. Nielsen summarized this as "the user experience of mobile websites and apps has improved since our last research, but we still have far to go" [2].

1 Introduction

As a starting point, it is appropriate to distinguish between a browser-based mobile website and a mobile app. A mobile website application works as on a desktop. Webpages are developed in a language such as HTML, which interlinks text data, images, videos, and other files. A browser is used to download the pages from the Internet across a wireless network and renders them for the display on the phone or tablet. The primary difference for mobile websites is the pages are designed with the smaller screens in mind. However, the advantages of the mobile web application (or browser-based app) are mostly the same as for the desktop version. Webpages are device independent. It is only the browser, which normally comes with the phone or tablet, that depends on the underlying hardware. The web applications are instantly accessible, easily updatable, sharable, searchable and the like.

A mobile application (app) is an executable program that is downloaded and installed on the device such an iPhone or iPad. Once there, the Internet may no longer be needed, unless the application requires access to online data. Mobile apps can be highly interactive and capable of performing high-level calculations. They can generate personalized reports. They can work with the supporting platform to use native capabilities such as a camera. Of course, an application must be developed for and compiled on a particular platform. That is, an application may not be able to run on both an iPhone and an Android, for example.

S. Yamamoto (Ed.): HIMI/HCII 2013, Part III, LNCS 8018, pp. 450–456, 2013.
© Springer-Verlag Berlin Heidelberg 2013

A visit to the Apple apps store provides an overwhelming number of choices for mobile apps to add to one's iPad, iPhone, or similar device. Furthermore, the devices themselves have become almost ubiquitous, being everywhere you look. This means that employers can assume that an employee possibly has and or at least understands the iPhone and iPad. It follows that involving this technology in the execution of co-operative tasks should not present a challenging learning curve to overcome.

Of particular interest in this research is the application of mobile technology to the vastly complex notion of a supply chain. Fundamentally, a supply chain is the inter-linking collection of elements and actions required to fulfill a customer's order. It can begin with raw materials and the transportation of those raw materials to facilities for storage and/or manufacture. It incorporates distribution nodes and retail locations, ultimately placing the product in the customer's hands. Each unit involved in the chain may include functions such R&D, logistics, operations, marketing, sales, finance, and customer service. This is a vastly complex organism. Any efficiency found or optimization that occurs can save large amounts of money and resource. Hence, research into any means to improve supply chain operations is relevant and important.

Simple observation recognizes that mobile technology should be well-positioned to introduce efficiencies into the supply chain. For example, rather than making employees move to centralize computing locations, mobile technology allows them to bring the computing to them. Kalakota, et al., note a number of compelling reasons why mobile apps would be important to supply chain operations: fulfillment velocity, inventory visibility, supplier coordination, and versatility. They further note that customers expect real-time information about orders, information about location of product, and accurate delivery commitments [3]. However, others characterize the field as still in the early phases of providing competitive advantage [4].

One might wonder why so little is being done with mobile apps when they have so much promise for solving supply chain operation problems. There are issues that range from human behavior to complex IT demands. From the computing perspective, the integration of mobile apps across a supply chain is proposing changes to the underlying information system infrastructure. Studies have shown that over 49% of IS projects finish over-budget, late, and with fewer features than specified. Nearly 28% of all IS projects are cancelled [5]. This is quite daunting; yet corporations routinely carry the risk, provided the return on investment promises to be great enough. Estimating this ROI of mobile apps impact on IT infrastructure is not a focus of this research but does have promise for further work.

On the other hand, the interest in this research is on the human side. Will people be willing to accept the new technology? The adoption of information technology is a heavily studied problem, since the technology acceptance model (TAM) was proposed [6]. It is not the intention of this work at this time to provide an in-depth analysis of mobile apps technology in supply chain operations in the light of the TAM. Rather the two main external variables in the model, perceived usefulness and perceived ease of use motivate some of the discussion to follow.

Once a company decides to put a new technology into operation, there is the possibility it will fail because of the employee's reception of it. According to a simple view of the TAM model, if the employees do not perceive it as a useful technology or perceive it as not easy to use, then they may not accept it. This raises the question that is the focus of the paper. Namely, are usability issues a factor being addressed in the development of mobile apps for supply chain management?

This research will look further at the use of mobile apps to aid supply chain operations, then consider aspects of human-computer interaction that are important, especially for mobile apps. Next, anecdotal information relative to recent searches specifically for mobile apps applied to supply chain will be considered, followed by conclusions, especially with respect to whether HCI aspects are presently important for mobile apps in the supply chain area, and then thoughts about likely future scenarios.

2   Mobile Applications in Supply Chain

Given the complexity of supply chains already discussed, a common theme that emerges from looking at published literature about supply chains is that the flow of information is critical. It is here that mobile apps have the potential to accelerate that flow and improve its accuracy. Figure 1, Siau and Shen [7], illustrates the broad scope of the information flow in dealing with supply chain operations, stretching from supplier relationship systems to customer relationship systems, and flowing in both directions. Facilitating this flow of information can provide a much needed efficiency. Examples of this follow.

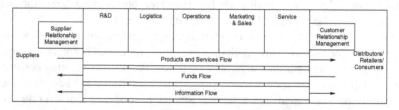

Fig. 1. Extended Supply Chain and Supply Chain Flow (Source: Siau and Shen [7])

Some supply chain areas are actively moving toward mobile apps. Transportation and logistics is one of these, Rowe reports, for functions like route planning, carrier and price selection, tendering, load board visibility, and updates of shipping location status. There are still concerns, though, especially around security, and the drawback of less screen real estate is also recognized [8].

With such a broad scope present in a supply chain, it is not surprising that there are many different mobile applications possible. Doolin and Ali, for example, prepared an extensive review of three companies in New Zealand who implemented aspects of mobile technology in supply chain: a food company who used mobile sales force automation (sales force information downloads, updated product information, customer information, sales promotion, territory management, stock levels, and replenishment dates) to speed up input ordering and invoicing information; a freight company, who used mobile freight tracking systems; and a power company, who used mobile service support to send information about faults to field crew PDAs, including information on the job status, fault location, work required, and billing [9]. This type of case-by-case analysis will likely increase as researchers attempt to understand the return on investment of mobile app technology in supply chain operations.

As developers seek appropriate uses of mobile apps, one might wonder what characteristic and requirements will offer a perceived usefulness to the mobile app. Siau, et al., tried to identify characteristics of a "killer app" for mobile-commerce: it should provide service directly relevant to mobile needs as well as benefit users in immediacy and efficiency. The inherent characteristics of mobile-commerce (ubiquity, personalization, flexibility, and dissemination) provided reason to believe such apps could be developed. However, perhaps presaging the next section in this presentation, some of the limitations of the devices, including impeded user-friendly interfaces, were a concern [10].

3 Human-Computer Interaction and Its Applicability to Mobile Apps

One of the goals of HCI is to address the perceived ease of use of a technology, or said in another way, its usability. This then, as mentioned, addresses one of the factors behind technology acceptance. The general principles of usability can be drawn from Nielsen as:

- Ease of learning: How fast can a novice user learn the interface sufficiently well to perform basic tasks?
- Efficiency of use: Once an experienced user has learned to use the system, how fast can he or she accomplish tasks?
- Memorability: Can a past user remember enough to use the system more effectively the next time?
- Error frequency and severity: How often do users make errors, how serious are these errors, and how easy is it to recover from an error?
- Subjective satisfaction: How much does the user *like* using the system? [11]

It seems addressing issues of usability connected with mobile apps can be improved, although many shortcomings are known and documented. There is a long history of accessing and improving usability of websites. Similar effort toward increasing usability of mobile apps is being made. Nielsen summarized this as "The user experience of mobile websites and apps has improved since our last research, but we still have far to go" [2].

Today, most the technological solutions available for supply chains are still browser-based web apps designed to run on desktop browsers and not on smaller devices. Nielsen found that, "empirically, websites see very little traffic from feature phones, partly because people rarely go on the Web when their experience is so bad." As is typical in usability analysis, Nielsen's tests involved seeing if users could successfully carry out specific tasks. The average success rate was only 62%. However, he notes, this is about the same as the rate for desktop Web use in 1999. That low success rate for use of smart phones led to the recommendation to design a separate site for mobile phone users, but the research also found that iPad users fared reasonably well using a standard website. However, designing a specific app worked even better: 76%. This suggests moving in the direction of mobile web apps for areas such as supply chains wherein accurate and timely flow of information is critical.

Some of the usability issues for websites are the same as those as those for apps, yet some difference remain. For example, providing clear text on a contrasting background and using "real estate" effectively are true for both platforms, but websites usability reviews usually lead to strong guidelines to avoid horizontal scrolling, while app users expect to use horizontal swiping as a normal action. Further, the selection process for a mouse on a website is similar to the use of a finger touch on a mobile device, but a finger can't be used to select as precisely (sometimes called the "fat finger" problem), so usability suffers if selection points are too small on a mobile device [2]. The use of a stylus can overcome the "fat finger" problem, to a large degree, but a stylus is easier to "carry along" on an iPad than it is on an iPhone, so it is likely to continue to be a problem. Of course, zooming is relatively easy on a mobile device, but it requires additional effort and distracts from the task at hand.

Also it is not surprising that there are usability issues specific to tablets. After several years of testing by the Nielsen Norman Group, it found consistent usability issues for iPads:

- Read-tap asymmetry when using browser-based sites, with content that was large.
- In general, touchable areas too small or too close together.
- Accidental activation due to unintended touches.
- Low discoverability, with active areas that didn't look touchable.
- Difficulty with entering information (typing was disliked on the touchscreen).
- Further, some apps featured too much navigation [12]

Dealing with the global issue, in another report, Nielsen reinforced the need for separate and distinctly different user interfaces for websites and mobile devices. "Most complex tasks have vastly better user experience on the desktop and thus will be performed there," he states. Thus he urges implementation of multiple user interfaces [13].

Chan and Feng address practical concerns with the development of mobile apps. They point out that multiple form factors are constraints in terms of the amount and format of content presentation, navigation, and site structure. Further, they believe that developers will be challenged to adopt new methods and design guidelines that take into account contextual variations. And they also note that mobile-commerce users are likely to have experienced e-commerce technology and thus have heightened expectations [14].

The sum of these reports is to realize that there are a number of usability issues that tend to impede the success of mobile apps or of browser-based apps made available on tablets. The designers of mobile apps are not always the same people who have been designing websites, so some of the usability lessons will have to be learned anew; other lessons are more unique to mobile devices and will have to be addressed.

4   The Kinds of Mobile Apps That Dominate Supply Chain Today

A previous survey about the use of iPhone and/or iPad apps in supply chain operations learned that the use of such apps varies greatly among different individuals and different organizations. While most respondents to that survey indicated that they believed that apps would be of value in an organization's operations and supply chain, and over half were using apps in some form at the workplace, most were not using them for supply chain operations [1]. Recent queries of exhibitors at an APICS (The Association for Operations Management) conference provided a simple survey of mobile apps available in the marketplace. It indicated that little has changed in the last year or so -- only a few mobile apps were being used in supply chain applications, although a number of supply chain applications were available for browser-based usage, especially for iPads and equivalent devices. The vendors reported little to no user unhappiness with the use of browser-based applications. This might be due to the prior experience of most users, which was with desktops and laptops, and which apparently had a lower level of perceived ease of use than the mobile apps. Furthermore, the mobile apps that were in use tended to be in areas with longer histories of mobile use, such as logistics (tracking of shipments, for example) and in calculations related to quality (six sigma calculations, for example). Likewise, industries with specialized supply chains such as health care use mobile devices to manage financial information and product scanning.

In a study by Barlow, it was noted by one respondent that, "There's a significant amount of supply chain related business activities, such as product evaluation or purchase negotiations that occur outside of the typical office environment, such as trade shows, dinners and/or site visits. Mobile apps allow instant access to information, which can significantly impact the outcome of the activity" [15]. This suggests the value of information collected from mobile apps, which ties in well with the information flow view of supply chains, as was illustrated in Figure 1. However, it also highlights the continued scarcity of mobile apps designed specifically for supply chain activities.

5   Conclusions

For mobile apps in general and supply chain apps in particular, it seems clear that HCI issues have not yet become a big factor in development. The usage of true mobile apps in supply chains is small, although growing in some specific areas. It appears that the predominant use of mobile devices for supply chains operations favors the iPad using browser-based mobile websites. Usability of iPads has been studied; the question remains as to whether developers for supply chain apps will put increased usability into practice.

The evolution of web development shows websites that put usability principles into practice are more successful with users. This, then, raises the expectation of users when surfing, thereby driving other websites to improve usability to survive. The authors expect and anticipate that the use of mobile apps will follow the same course, with mobile apps increasing in usability over time. The ones generally most popular will show the way. As Minda Zetlin put it, "today's enterprise apps must be as user-friendly and inviting as those found in a mobile app store in order to entice users who, increasingly, can choose whether or not to bother with them" [16].

References

1. Elrod, C.C., et al.: iPhone and iPad Applications: Perceptions of Use in an Organization's Supply Chain. Issues in Information Systems XII(1), 170–180 (2011)
2. Nielsen, J.: Mobile Usability Update, Alertbox (September 2011)
3. Kalakota, R., Robinson, M., Gundepudi, P.: Mobile Applications for Adaptive Supply Chains: A Landscape Analysis. In: Lim, E.-P., Siau, K. (eds.) Advances in Mobile Commerce Technologies. Idea Group Publishing (2003)
4. Eng, T.: Mobile Supply Chain Management: Challenges for Implementation. Technovation 26, 682–686 (2006)
5. Legrisa, P., Inghamb, J., Collerettec, P.: Why Do People Use Information Technology? A Critical Review of the Technology Acceptance Model. Information & Management 40, 191–204 (2003)
6. Davis, F.D.: Perceived Usefulness, Perceived Ease of Use, and User Acceptance of Information Technologies. MIS Quarterly 13(3), 319–340 (1989)
7. Siau, K., Shen, Z.: Mobile Commerce Applications in Supply Chain Management. Journal of Internet Commerce 1(3) (2002)
8. Rowe, D.: Mobile Tech and the Supply Chain. Transport Topics 3975 (December 5, 2011)
9. Doolin, B., Al Haj Ali, E.: Adoption of Mobile Technology in the Supply Chain: An Exploratory Cross-Case Analysis. International Journal of E-Business Research 4(4) (2008)
10. Siau, K., Lim, E., Shen, Z.: Mobile Commerce: Current States and Future Trends. In: Lim, E.-P., Siau, K. (eds.) Advances in Mobile Commerce Technologies. Idea Group Publishing (2003)
11. Nielsen, J.: What is Usability? (2001), http://www.zdnet.com/devhead/stories/articles/0,4413,2137671,00.html
12. Nielsen, J.: Pad Usability: Year One. Alertbox (May 2011)
13. Nielsen, J.: Design for the 3 Screens (Make That 5), Alertbox (August 2011)
14. Chan, S., Fang, X.: Mobile Commerce and Usability. In: Lim, E.-P., Siau, K. (eds.) Advances in Mobile Commerce Technologies. Idea Group Publishing (2003)
15. Barlow, R.: What's Your apptitude? Healthcare Purchasing News, 36.2 34, 36–37 (2012)
16. Zetlin, M.: The New Rules for Enterprise Apps. Computerworld, 46.2, 18–19, 14–16 (2012)

Value Added by the Axiomatic Usability Method for Evaluating Consumer Electronics

Yinni Guo[1], Yu Zhu[2], Gavriel Salvendy[1,3], and Robert W. Proctor[1,4]

[1] School of Industrial Engineering, Purdue University, West Lafayette, IN
[2] Department of Statistics, Purdue University, West Lafayette, IN
[3] Department of Industrial Engineering, Tsinghua University, Beijing, China
[4] Department of Psychological Sciences, Purdue University, Lafayette, IN
Yinni.Guo@gmail.com, {yuzhu,Salvendy}@purdue.edu,
proctor@psych.purdue.edu

Abstract. In this paper we demonstrate how to use the axiomatic evaluation method to evaluate usability of consumer electronic products. The axiomatic evaluation method examines three domains of a product: customer, functional, and control domains. This method collects not only usability problems reported by the users, but also usability problems found through the mapping matrix between the three domains. To determine how well this new usability evaluation method works, an experiment was conducted to compare the axiomatic evaluation method with a think-aloud method. 60 participants were randomly assigned to use one method or the other to evaluate three popular consumer electronic devices. Number of usability problems discovered and completion time were collected and analyzed. Results showed that the axiomatic evaluation method performed better than the think-aloud method at finding usability problems for the mobile phone and about user expectation and control.

Keywords: axiomatic evaluation, consumer electronics.

1 Theoretical Background of Axiomatic Evaluation

The axiomatic evaluation method is a usability evaluation method developed based on axiomatic design theory. In a prior paper [1], we introduced the conceptual model of the axiomatic evaluation method. In the current paper we demonstrate the potential value of using the method to evaluate usability of consumer electronic products. Axiomatic design consists of four domains and two axioms [2]. The four domains are customer domain, functional domain, physical domain and process domain (see Fig. 1). The customer domain ([CA]) consists of the needs for which the customers are looking in a product. The functional domain ([FR]) consists of functional requirements, which are the minimum independent requirements that completely characterize the functional needs of the product. The physical domain ([DP]) consists of design parameters, which are the key variables in the physical domain that characterize the design that satisfies the specified functional requirements. Finally, the process domain ([PV]) consists of process variables, those in the process domain that characterize the

S. Yamamoto (Ed.): HIMI/HCII 2013, Part III, LNCS 8018, pp. 457–466, 2013.

process that can generate the specified design parameters. For successive domains in Fig. 1, the domain to the left represents "what we want to achieve", whereas the domain to the right represents the design solution of "how we propose to satisfy the requirements specified in the prior domain."

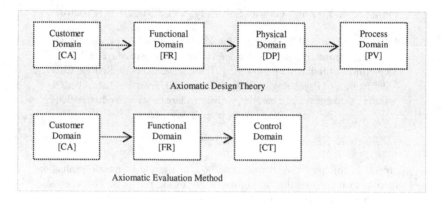

Fig. 1. Axiomatic Design Theory and Axiomatic Evaluation Method

The design flow suggested by axiomatic design theory consists of mapping from one domain to the other. The mapping process between domains can be expressed mathematically in terms of vectors. For example, a set of functional requirements in the functional domain can be written into a functional requirement vector ([FR]). Similarly, a set of design parameters has been chosen to satisfy the functional requirements constitutes the design parameter vector ([DP]). The mathematical expression can be then written as [FR] = [A][DP] or as the following equation, where [A] is the mapping matrix that characterizes the product design:

$$\begin{bmatrix} FR_1 \\ FR_2 \\ FR_3 \end{bmatrix} = \begin{bmatrix} A_{11} & A_{12} & A_{13} \\ A_{21} & A_{22} & A_{23} \\ A_{31} & A_{32} & A_{33} \end{bmatrix} \begin{bmatrix} DP_1 \\ DP_2 \\ DP_3 \end{bmatrix}$$

The axiomatic design theory examines the design quality with respect to two axioms, identified by Suh [2] through examining common elements always present in good designs. The first axiom, the *independence axiom*, states that the independence of functional requirements that characterizes the design goals must be maintained. In other words, when there are two or more functional requirements, the design solution must be such that each functional requirement can be satisfied without affecting others. The second axiom, the *information axiom*, states that among those designs that satisfy the independence axiom, the design that has the smallest information content is the best. In a real design scenario, there can be many designs that satisfy the independence axiom. However, one of those designs is likely to be superior. The information axiom provides a quantitative measure of a given design, and it is useful in selecting the best among those designs that are acceptable.

The axiomatic design theory helps to overcome shortcomings of the product development process based on a recursive "design/build/test" cycle, which requires continuing modifications and changes as design flaws are discovered through the testing [3]. The axiomatic design theory has been applied to a variety of products and systems such as mechanical design, software design, organizations management, and materials design. Although the meanings of the four domains are quite different from one product area to another, the axiomatic design theory successfully enhances the performance, robustness, reliability and functionality of products in different fields.

2   Conceptual Model of the Axiomatic Evaluation Method

The core idea of the axiomatic design theory is to start designing from understanding "what do the customers need", and to continue from there to specify "how could we achieve it" through providing the right functions, the appropriate design parameters for the functions, and the proper process variables for the design parameters. Similarly, in usability evaluation we try answer the questions of "what do the users want in the product" and "how well does the product satisfy user requirements". Therefore it is feasible to apply the framework of axiomatic design theory to usability evaluation, and three domains are set up for the usability evaluation process: customer domain ([CA]), functional domain ([FR]) and control domain ([CT]) (Fig. 1). Customer domain ([CA]) consists of customer requirements of the product, and they can be retrieved by an open-ended questionnaire. Functional domain ([FR]) consists of existing functions of the product, which can be easily retrieved by reading the product manual. Control domain ([CT]) consists of the control keys of the product; these also can be retrieved by examining the product or reading the product manual. The use of the two axioms is similar, but the axiomatic evaluation method also includes constraints for human-computer interaction design to examine the mapping matrix, such as maintaining stimulus-response compatibility [4], following Hick's Law [5] and adhering to Fitts's Law [6]. The biggest difference between the original axiomatic design theory and the axiomatic evaluation method is that in the latter the third domain is the control domain ([CT]) instead of the physical domain ([DP]). The main reason for this change is that, in the evaluation process, one is more interested in evaluating how the existing design parameters with which users interact (the control keys) support the functions, rather than in figuring out how the design parameters with which users will not interact perform. Usability problems can be found by examining the mapping between the three domains. The mapping can be expressed as matrices [X] and [Y]:

$$[CA]=[X][FR] \text{ or } [Customer Requirements] = [X] [Functions]$$

$$[FR]=[Y][CT] \text{ or } [Functions] = [Y] [Control Keys]$$

The mapping matrix [X] between customer domain ([CA]) and functional domain ([FR]) can provide an index of function sufficiency, which can be beneficial to prototypes at the beginning stage of product development. If the index is high, the current product could satisfy most customers. If the index is low, designers may want to reconsider the design direction. The mapping between functional domain ([FR]) and control domain ([CT]) shows how easy it is to control the device. Usability problems can be found by checking the mapping matrix [Y] between the functional and control domains which is determined by users' operation. According to the independence axiom, an ideal mapping matrix should be a diagonal matrix or a triangular matrix. The former means that users need only one step to control the function, and each function has its own control key. The latter means that users may need more than one step (press more than one key) to complete the task, but the keys used are not conflicting with the ones used in other functions. So if the [Y] matrix is a diagonal matrix or a triangular matrix, it means there are no conflicting controls between different functions. If the [Y] matrix is neither diagonal nor triangular, the designers should reconsider the control design to avoid possible usability problems (e.g., high error rate caused by using the same combination of keys for two functions).

However, only meeting the requirement of a diagonal matrix or a triangular matrix is not enough. According to the information axiom, the design that has the smallest information content is the best alternative. Therefore, designers should also make sure that users do not need to take too many steps in order to complete a certain task. Other constraints like stimulus-response compatibility, Hick's Law, and Fitts's law for movement times, mentioned previously, can be used to determine usability problems as well. For instance, Hick's law describes the time it takes for a person to make a decision as a result of the number of possible choices that he or she has. In axiomatic evaluation, if the mapping matrix [Y] shows that there are too many options under one menu, it may take users a long time to select the option they want. Another example is Fitts's law, which is used to model the time to move the hand or a cursor from a current position to a target position. In axiomatic evaluation, if the mapping matrix [Y] shows that the keys used for one function are located far away from each other, it is possible that Fitts's law was not followed well.

The proposed axiomatic evaluation method could be used in the formative stage of product development before a final design is accepted for release. Compared to traditional usability evaluation methods, the axiomatic evaluation method is likely to discover more usability problems related to user requirement and control. Examining the mapping matrix between customer domain ([CA]) and functional domain ([FR]) will reveal what the customers need and what is barely used. Examining the mapping matrix between functional domain ([FR]) and control domain ([CT]) will reveal the problems about control.

3   Experiment

3.1   Experimental Design

Because the axiomatic evaluation method is a new tool for usability evaluation, we conducted an experiment to assess how well this evaluation method worked and in which aspect it would perform better or worse than other usability evaluation methods. Since the axiomatic evaluation method is task-specific and intended to be used in the formative stage before the design is finalized, we chose another task-specific evaluation method used at the same stage for comparison, the think-aloud method. This method was selected also because it did not require participants to have much knowledge about usability. The experiment used a between-subjects design: 60 participants were recruited and randomly assigned to the group using the think-aloud method or the group using the axiomatic evaluation method. Three popular consumer electronic devices: music player, digital camera and mobile phone representing different levels of complexity were evaluated by each participant in a randomized order.

Using the Axiomatic Evaluation Method. Participants in the axiomatic evaluation group were first asked to complete a background questionnaire. Then, the experimenter introduced the purpose of the study and encouraged the participants to raise any problems or questions regarding to the test products. Although the participants were not required to tell the experimenter everything in their mind, as in the think-aloud method, they were encouraged to voice any problem or question relating to the test device. This way, the experimenter could collect usability problems found by the participants without interfering with their performing the tasks. As the experiment started, participants were asked to fill out a questionnaire of what functions they really used and their expectations of the product. After that, participants were asked to evaluate the product's functions that they said they would really use. The order of the tasks was randomized for each participant. The evaluating procedure was videotaped, and the problems raised by the participants were written down by the experimenter. After evaluating each test product, participants were asked to fill out a satisfaction questionnaire. Upon completion of the experiment, the experimenter went through the videos to fill out the mapping matrix [Y] between function and control keys according to participants' action—which keys did they click in order to perform a certain task. By examining the errors participants made, and by examining the mapping matrix, usability problems not reported by the participants could be identified, as well as the reasons for the usability problems.

Using the Think-Aloud Method. The think-aloud method is widely used in the same stage of product development in laboratories and industries. This method, developed by Lewis [7] and refined by Ericsson and Simon [8], has proved to be successful in collecting qualitative data from a small number of users [9]. The think-aloud procedure involves participants thinking out loud as they perform a set of specified tasks. In a think-aloud evaluation, users describe whatever they are looking at, thinking, doing, and feeling, as they go through their task. This allows the experimenter to understand how the task is completed. The experimenter records everything the participant says, without attempting to interpret the actions and words. Test sessions are usually videotaped or audiotaped so that experimenter can go back and refer to what participants did and how they reacted. However, there is a limitation of the think-aloud method: it seems unnatural to test users and may influence users' problem-solving behavior.

In this study, we employed the specific think-aloud procedure that has been used in more than 30 studies (e.g. [10]). After the experimenter introduced the purpose of the study, participants were asked to fill out a background questionnaire. Then, printed instructions of how to perform "thinking aloud" were given to the participants. The instructions were based on the methodology developed by Lewis [7]: "The basic idea of thinking aloud is that you ask your users to perform a test task, but you also ask them to talk to you while they are working on it. Ask them to tell you what they are thinking: what they are trying to do, questions that arise as they work, things they read." After this, participants were asked to watch a video of how to perform the think-aloud method and to do a warm-up practice. When the experiment formally started, participants were given a list of tasks to perform—to use a set of functions of a product. The experimenter videotaped the whole procedure and took notes of the thinking reported by the participant. The participants' thinking included not just the problems they encountered, but also whether they thought a certain function was well designed, or what kind of design they liked, or their suggestion for the product. After the evaluation, participants were asked to fill out a satisfaction questionnaire.

3.2   Participants and Test Products

The number of participants was determined by statistical power analysis and experiment design requirements. In this experiment, each participant would use one of the two methods to evaluate all three products in one of the six testing orders. Assuming the standard deviation of the number of usability problems found would be approximately 5, and the maximum difference between the means of usability problems found would be 20, we calculated that having 4 participants in each testing order can give us a power value of 0.9 (given $\alpha = 0.05$). Thus, we decided to have 5 participants in each of the 6 testing orders for both evaluation methods, 60 participants in total.

Participants who had experience with at least 2 of the 3 consumer electronic products (music player, mobile phone and digital camera) were recruited through e-mail from an electronic product company located in Xiamen, China. More than 90% of the participants had used more than 1 music player for at least 2 years, and over 70% of them had used at least 3 mobile phones for more than 5 years. The participants had less experience of using digital cameras, but still more than half of them had used at least 2 models for more than 2 years. Participants in the think-aloud group and the axiomatic evaluation group had similar distribution in gender, age, education, job category, and experience of using the 3 consumer electronic products.

Three widely used consumer electronics were chosen as the test products: music player, mobile phone and digital camera. The music player had eight major functions (playing music, recording, playing recorded soundtrack, radio, games, e-book, picture display, address book) and six control buttons. The digital camera offered multiple photo shooting modes (automatic, manual, portrait, landscape, moving mode, night mode, video recording) and the button layout was similar to most point and shoot digital cameras. The mobile phone had all common smart phone features. It had a touch screen and a key pad of 21 keys including the 12 number keys.

3.3   Results

Number of Usability Problems Found. The number of usability problems found was the total number of different usability problems discovered by all participants using the same evaluation method. To obtain this number, the experimenter first collected all usability problems found by all participants using the same evaluation method and then filtered out all the different ones. Each usability problem may have different weight, but in this study we weighted them equally. The usability problems found by the two evaluation methods were then sorted into eight main categories: content, menu, panel, display, control, functions, technology and appearance. A summary of usability problems is shown in Table 1. For the music player, the axiomatic evaluation method found 245 problems, which is slightly more than the think-aloud method (212 problems). For the digital camera, the axiomatic evaluation method found 193 problems, a value slightly smaller than the think-aloud method (215 problems). For the mobile phone, the axiomatic evaluation method found over twice as many problems as the think-aloud method (404 vs. 161). A closer look reveals that the "extra" usability problems found with the axiomatic evaluation method were mainly from four categories: content (lack of information, incorrect information, and ambiguous information), panel (location of the keys, shape of the keys), display, control (don't know which key to press, control bug) and functions.

The comparison of the two evaluation methods for the mobile phone showed an advantage of the axiomatic method in finding usability problems of user requirement and usability problems about control. This advantage was not evident for the music player and digital camera. One possible reason is that in recent years the mobile phone has become more complex than the music player or digital camera and is likely to have more usability problems. Also, nowadays people use mobile phones so often that they may become more stringent in their evaluation of the phones and thus point out more usability problems. Both reasons lead to the conclusion that participants would discover more usability problems in the mobile phone than the music player or digital camera (as the data in Table 1 show). According to Ericsson and Simon's research [11], think-aloud participants retrieve information from short-term memory. When evaluating a mobile phone (a complex device with more usability problems), a participant may not have been able to report all of the usability problems noticed while performing the task, possibly because doing so would break the flow of performance or because he/she forgot some usability problems after explaining the first few (limit of short term memory). Although a participant was evaluating a complex device when using the axiomatic evaluation method, similar to the think-aloud method, not all of the usability problems s/he noticed could be spoken aloud, but some of the hidden usability problems were caught by examining the mapping matrix (how the participant interacted with the device) recorded in the video. That is why the axiomatic evaluation method could find more usability problems than the think-aloud method on a complex device.

Table 1. Summary of Total Number of Problems Found

Category	Music Player		Digital Camera		Mobile Phone	
	TA*	AE*	TA	AE	TA	AE
About content						
Lack of information	14	5	12	9	2	18
Incorrect information	0	1	2	2	0	5
Ambiguous information	3	5	5	9	3	12
Redundant information	0	1	0	0	8	16
Lack of description in Chinese	0	3	5	7	0	0
Sub-total	17	15	24	27	13	51
About menu						
The sorting	8	7	1	1	21	29
The order or priority	0	0	0	0	0	7
Sub-total	8	7	1	1	21	36
About panel						
Position/location of the keys	5	17	6	13	0	7
Shape	3	3	3	3	0	4
Material/touch feeling	16	9	15	10	6	9
Label on the keys	19	12	9	8	3	4
Lack of keys	0	1	4	2	3	5
Sub-total	43	42	37	36	12	29
About display						
Font size, style, color	8	9	2	2	3	10
Screen or display	3	3	1	1	0	3
Icon	5	1	1	1	3	3
Format	11	10	0	0	2	7
Sub-total	27	23	4	4	8	23
About control						
Don't know which key to press	41	38	3	7	14	23
Control bug	16	17	1	3	14	37
Not convenient design	22	16	6	6	33	47
Sub-total	79	71	10	16	61	107
About functions	11	42	16	20	20	121
About technology	27	35	62	59	20	36
About appearance	0	10	61	30	6	1
Total	212	245	215	193	161	404

* TA stands think aloud, AE stands for axiomatic evaluation.

Completion Time. The completion time was measured by the timer on the video recorder. The experimenter started the recording when the participant was ready to perform a task, and stopped it when the participant said that s/he was finished. The elapsed time was the completion time. Statistical analysis of completion time is listed in Table 2. Normality tests conducted on each of the respective time measures showed no violations of normality, $p > 0.10$. For the think-aloud method, the total completion time, consisting of the time of training, evaluating the products, and filling out the satisfaction questions, was 51.13 minutes. For the axiomatic evaluation method, the total completion time, for which there is no training time but time for the experimenter to review the videos and identify usability problems, was 52.85 minutes. An analysis of variance (ANOVA) showed this small difference in total completion time to be nonsignificant (bottom row of Table 2).

Table 2. Statistical Summary of Completion Time (in min)

Test Segment	Think-Aloud Mean (std)	Axiomatic Evaluation Mean (std)	F	p
Training	6.47 (0.68)	-	-	-
Background questionnaire	0.80 (0.20)	0.83(0.02)	0.27	0.626
Evaluate music player	15.67 (2.80)	9.78 (2.83)	59.80	<0.0001
Evaluate mobile phone	20.75 (3.03)	15.93 (2.78)	35.86	<0.0001
Evaluate digital camera	6.33 (0.68)	5.07 (1.27)	16.17	0.0002
Satisfaction questionnaire	2.05 (0.33)	2.23 (0.22)	2.40	0.1266
Video review	-	20.2 (5.38)	-	-
Total	51.13 (4.75)	52.85 (7.10)	1.19	0.2791

A generalized linear model was used to test the interaction between type of evaluation (think-aloud and axiomatic) and product (music player, mobile phone, digital camera), and the interaction was significant. The benefit in evaluation time for the axiomatic evaluation method over the think-aloud method was larger for the music player (5.89 min) and mobile phone (4.82 min) than for the camera (1.26 min). However, individual ANOVAs for each product showed evaluation time to be shorter with the axiomatic evaluation method than with the think-aloud method in all cases (Table 2). Because participants spent much less time evaluating the camera than the other two products, the percentage improvement with the axiomatic evaluation method was still 80%, compared to 77% for the mobile phone and 62% for the music player. From the participants' point of view, the axiomatic evaluation method is more efficient than the think-aloud method because they are finishing their part in less time.

4   Discussion and Future Research

This experiment showed that the axiomatic evaluation method performed better at finding usability problems for a mobile phone than did the think-aloud method. But the axiomatic evaluation method did not show advantages in finding usability problems for the music player or digital camera. In particular, when used to evaluate the mobile phone, the axiomatic evaluation method was able to identify more usability problems about user requirement and control. Therefore, we suggest using the axiomatic evaluation method for evaluating products similar to mobile phones, e.g., tablets and laptops that have a lot of features and a high level of complexity, and thus are likely to have more usability problems. On the other hand, axiomatic evaluation may not benefit evaluation of products with a lower level of complexity and just a few features, like web cameras. This experiment also compared the completion time using the two evaluation methods. Although there was no significant difference between the total time for the methods, the axiomatic evaluation method required significantly less time than the think-aloud method for participants to evaluate each individual product.

The ultimate goal of usability evaluation is to improve user experience of products. What is unique about the present study is that it develops and validates a systematic evaluation method that can discover usability problems from "what do the users want" to "how well does the product satisfy user requirements". This type of evaluation procedure could reduce the time and energy of the "design-test-redesign" cycle. The new evaluation method also complements finding usability problems about control. One limitation of the study is that only two usability evaluation methods and three testing products were compared. In the future, the axiomatic evaluation method needs to be applied to more products with a larger range of complexity, and compared with other evaluation methods on more devices.

References

1. Guo, Y., Proctor, R.W., Salvendy, G.: A conceptual model of the axiomatic usability evaluation method. In: Smith, M.J., Salvendy, G. (eds.) HCII 2011, Part I. LNCS, vol. 6771, pp. 93–102. Springer, Heidelberg (2011)
2. Suh, N.P.: The Principles of Design. Oxford University Press, New York (1990)
3. Suh, N.P.: Axiomatic Design: Advances and Applications. Oxford University Press, New York (2001)
4. Proctor, R.W., Vu, K.-P.L.: Selection and Control of Action. In: Salvendy, G. (ed.) Handbook of Human Factors and Ergonomics, 3rd edn., pp. 89–110. John Wiley, Hoboken (2006)
5. Schneider, D.W., Anderson, J.R.: A Memory-based Model of Hick's Law. Cognitive Psychol. 62, 193–222 (2011)
6. Guiard, Y., Beaudouin-Lafon, M.: Fitts' Law 50 Years Later: Applications and Contributions from Human–Computer Interaction. Int. J. Hum.-Comp. St. 61, 747–750 (2004)
7. Lewis, C.: Using the" Thinking-Aloud" Method in Cognitive Interface Design. IBM Research Report RC 9265. IBM TJ Watson Research Center, Yorktown Heights, NY (1982)
8. Ericsson, K., Simon, H.: Verbal Reports on Thinking. In: Faerch, C., Kasper, G. (eds.) Introspection in Second Language Research, pp. 24–54. Multilingual Matters, Clevedon (1987)
9. Nielsen, J.: Usability testing. In: Salvendy, G. (ed.) Handbook of Human Factors and Ergonomics, 2nd edn., pp. 1543–1568. John Wiley & Sons, New York (1997)
10. Magliano, J., Millis, K.: Assessing Reading Skill with a Think-Aloud Procedure and Latent Semantic Analysis. Cognition Instruct. 21, 251–283 (2003)
11. Ericsson, K.A., Simon, H.A.: Protocol Analysis: Verbal Reports as Data, rev edn. The MIT Press, Cambridge (1993)

Challenges for Incorporating "Quality in Use" in Embedded System Development

Naotake Hirasawa

Otaru University of Commerce, Hokkaido, Japan
hirasawa@res.otaru-uc.ac.jp

Abstract. Challenges for incorporating "quality in use" in embedded system development were discussed. In the Japanese embedded system industries the foundation of the quality in use management is not necessarily established because of their various backgrounds and histories. In the paper three key points to introduce the quality in use into the design process in the industries were proposed. These were implementation of user requirement process, understanding of "service" as final outcome and synchronization to functional safety.

Keywords: Quality in use, Usability, System quality, ISO 25000 series, Functional safety.

1 Introduction

As the importance of user experience design has recognized, try-and-error methods for incorporating it in the development process are being deployed. The typical method is process approach as human-centered design represented by ISO 9241-210 [1]. On the other hands, product quality approach for promoting quality in use can be recognized as another method. The method related to the quality in use can be referred to ISO/IEC 25000 -Software product Quality Requirement and Evaluation (SQuaRE) series [2].

The quality in use is a part of system/software quality. Owing to some automotive safety issues and other critical accidents, the influence of software quality is being recognized so that the impact to society may be very large. In Japan the audit system for software quality has been studied in order to avoid the incidences caused by software malfunctions in industries in attempt to achieve higher safety, reliability and usability during the software operation [3]. In parallel MITI in Japan has already launched high reliability software project [4]. In these Japanese situations regarding to software quality, it would be concerned about that various software quality concepts would exist conflicted. Consequently that would cause the difficulties to introduce those new quality concepts into development environments respectively. Especially as the quality in use is relatively new concept, it would be easy to understand the difficulties of the introduction into product development.

S. Yamamoto (Ed.): HIMI/HCII 2013, Part III, LNCS 8018, pp. 467–474, 2013.

User Experience Research Division in CBC from Otaru University of Commerce has been consulted about human-centered design by various types of companies such as home-appliance makers, office appliance makers or car-related companies. These companies are preparing the human-centered design processes to assure the usability for their systems or products. They accept the importance of human-centered design process approach, however quite a few companies are concerned with introducing the quality in use into their quality management system.

Considering the circumstances above, the objective of the paper is to clarify the challenges for introducing the quality in use into the embedded system development processes in Japan.

The research project began with collecting the literatures, standards, papers and technical reports regarding software quality and usability and so on. Secondly the project analyzed the qualities from the viewpoint of the concept and vision, the quality model, the positioning against the other qualities and the timing to intervene the development processes. As the basement of embedded development process model, ESER (Embedded System development Process Reference) [5] by SEC/IPA was used. Finally the workshop that was consisted of the specialists related to system engineering, usability engineering and quality management was held and then they were asked to elicit the challenges for incorporating quality in use in embedded system development.

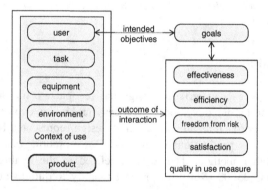

Fig. 1. Quality in use framework based in 9241-11

2   The Challenges for Quality in Use Management

(1) The difficulty to understand the way of thinking of quality in use "Quality in use" is defined in ISO25010 [6] as the following,

> *"Quality in use is the degree to which a product or system can be used by specific users to meet their needs to achieve specific goals with effectiveness, efficiency, freedom from risk and satisfaction in specific contexts of use."*

ISO9241-11 [7] defines "usability" as same thing. According to these definitions, the targets for the quality in use are the outcome of interaction between user and system. (Fig.1) The "outcome" is not necessarily the clear entities comparing to the targets for the system or the software quality. As quality manager has to start with the definition of the targets for controlling the quality, it would be difficult to envision the management strategy about the quality in use.

Furthermore the mapping between the quality in use and the system quality is not always one to one. (Fig.2) For the control of the quality it is an ideal that the mapping could be clear and fixed. For example, it would be easy to control the quality in use if the effectiveness of the character of the quality in use would be improved indeed whenever the functional suitability of the character of the system quality was improved. Moreover the quality in use sometimes depends on the context of use. Consequently that might cause the discords between the quality the developer made with a struggle and the quality in use. Then it might happen that CS score could not rise although the system qualities are improved expressly.

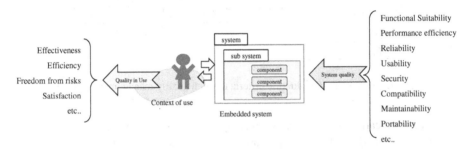

Fig. 2. Relation between quality in use and system quality

In the case of a car or airplane which is consisted of the sub-systems, the management for the quality in use requires more complicated. The structure of the quality in use for the system, called as system of systems, has multi-layered. One layer is to the each sub-system and another is to the total system. User does not exist respectively for the every sub-system, so the all quality in use should be managed coherently through all sub-system and system.

(2) Lack of foundation for quality in use management

System quality can be evaluated and judged by measuring the property with the measurement. Specifically the system quality would be managed by the following step [8];

1. Establish the evaluation requirements,
2. Specify the evaluation,
3. Plan the evaluation,
4. Execute the evaluation,
5. Conclude the evaluation.

In the second step, "Specify the evaluation", the quality model and property, the quality measurement and measure, and its criterion should be identified. And to do these, historic data has been collected based on the quality metric management lifcycle organized by the company. Then in the third step, "Plan the evaluation", the evaluation activities should be defined based on the method which are certified by the organization.

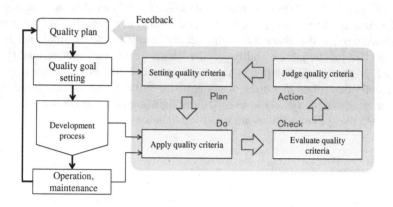

Fig. 3. Improvement of evaluation criteria through quality management lifecycle

In order to carry out the quality management, a lot of preparation is needed actually. Particularly, additional preparations are required for the quality in use management because its quality model is very different from the system's or the software's one. Especially regarding to define the measure of the quality in use, it must take long time till the proper criteria are obtained because it is difficult to accumulate them without try and error approach. (Fig.3) As far as the proper criteria have been accumulated through the development lifecycle, it is difficult to prove the necessity of the quality in use management to senior managers.

(3) Lack of resources and infrastructures for quality in use management
Evaluation skill based on psychology or sociology is necessary for specialty found for quality in use management other than the skill about the quality management. The evaluation skill for the quality in use is not familiar for the embedded engineer or the quality engineer. That causes their job transfer to the quality in use management difficult. As result, the lack of human resources can be evitable.

Furthermore the development environments for supporting the quality in use management activities, such as a usability testing room, a prototyping tool or a informant data-base and so on, would be necessary to be built if these are not equipped.

Consequently in order to start up the quality in use management, the investment budget for ensuring the resources and preparing the infrastructure must be required to be persuaded for those who will be in charge for setting up the quality in use management framework.

(4) non-existent of user requirement process

In general, system or software quality management begins with making the quality plan and setting the criteria for the quality property prior to system development. Next the quality is evaluated in every development process respectively and then is judged whether the criteria are reached. The quality in use follows the same process. So in what kind of design process is the quality in use management carried out?

As the management is required to validate whether the outcome from use of product or system could reach the criteria to be expected in the presumed context of use, it should be carried out in the user (stakeholder) requirement process. In ESPR, the user requirement process is out of the scope of the development processes. That is, the quality in use management would not be assumed in ESPR. Consequently the validation plan would have been uncertain based on arbitrary intention till the end of development. (Fig4)

Furthermore, since many system engineers tend to think they could design the system without the user requirement, the user requirement process might often be passed in their mind [9]. Consequently in Japanese embedded development environment, the quality in use management would lose their position in the development environment.

(5) Immaturity of system lifecycle management

The metrics of quality in use is planned in the top stream of development process and controls the outcome from every development process throughout the development lifecycle process. This means in the every process the quality in use should be checked and ensured through the whole development processes. In other words, the quality in use management should ensure the traceability from the quality planning to the validation of the system.

On the contrary, in Japanese manufactures there is a term "process completion" that means for a process the pre-process must be done completely. The idea would be applicable for manufacturing process, however for the system development process it is very difficult to be finished completely because it cannot avoid the incomplete requirement. Although it is unlikely, the mindset of "process completion" would succeed to the embedded system engineer in Japan. As a result, for many embedded system engineer it could be unimaginable to manage the total development lifecycle by looking down at it from higher layer view. If they could try to do it, they have to face the difficulties how the user requirement process would be implemented in their development processes. Without the lifecycle management from the user or customer view, the information related to user or customer cannot be circulated and consistent in the development lifecycle. For example, the misconnection between the target user in planning process and the informant in system validation or usability testing often happens.

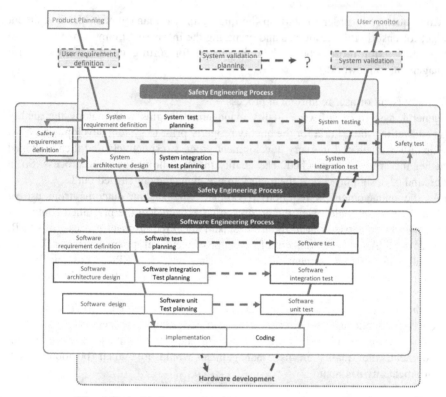

Fig. 4. Embedded system development process based on ESPR

3　Discussion – To the Next Step

In Japanese manufactures of embedded system, the causes why quality in use is not managed in development process were discussed based on the consultation experiences of our institute. The author's research institute, User Experience Research Division has been making some suggestions to the manufactures up to the present. A couple of key points from the suggestions would be proposed in the following.

(1) Implementation of user (stakeholder) requirement process
It was discussed above that in most of Japanese embedded system manufactures user requirement process does not exist in their development process. It might be caused that the system development begins with the system requirement process. In this case the development project often faces the trouble of redesign related to the user interface design. For the trouble our institute recommends to introduce the user requirement process by having the company understand that user interface design process needs the information about user, such as a target user profile or a use case scenario and so on. By implementing the user requirement process, it becomes to be possible to kick off the quality in use management.

(2) Understanding of "service" as final outcome of embedded system
The goal of an embedded system development is changing from offering the product to providing the services with using the system. If the developers recognize the outcome from the development is the product itself, the perception to quality is enough to understand that the quality is just only system quality. But if they recognize that offering the service is final goal, they have to assure the service quality consequently. The quality need to be evaluated from the viewpoint of quality in use.

In this way changing the mindset of the final outcome for system engineer from the product to the service persuades to change the mindset of the quality.

(3) Synchronization to functional safety
Recently the demand for assuring the functional safety such as IEC 61508 [10] in embedded system industries is increasing. Implementing the functional safety into development process must require the process and lifecycle management. (Fig5) To support the management it is necessary to ensure the traceability of processes at least.

As a safety is positioned as very significant in the quality in use, the managements that are required in the functional safety certification would be needed in the quality in use similarly. Therefore by introducing the management for the functional safety, the foundation for the quality in use management can be established in parallel.

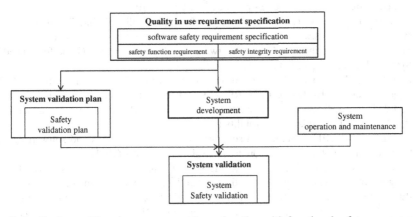

Fig. 5. Quality in use lifecycle management in conjunction with functional safety management

4   Summary

Considering recent movement for the software quality, the challenges for incorporating "quality in use" in embedded system development were discussed. The possibility that the system could improve the usability or the user experience is expected to be increased by introducing the quality in use into the development process. However, in the Japanese embedded system industries the foundation of the quality in use management is not necessarily established because of their various backgrounds and histories. Consequently it seems very difficult for the companies to understand the certainty and the urgency of it.

In the paper three key points to introduce the quality in use into the design process in the industries were proposed, implementation of user requirement process, understanding of "service" as final outcome of embedded system and synchronization to functional safety were introduced.

Eventually the commitment made by the administration should be needed to build the institution for the management of the quality in use. For the example of the institution, enhanced quality assurance, development for the human resource for quality in use, arrangement of the development environment and so on are required.

Our institute is studying to make some business model to persuade the quality in use in to the companies.

References

1. ISO/IEC 9241-210:2010 Ergonomics of human-system interaction - Part 210: Human-centred design for interactive systems (2010)
2. ISO/IEC 25000:2005 Software Engineering - Software product Quality Requirements and Evaluation (SQuaRE) - Guide to SQuaRE (2005)
3. IPA/SEC, Proposal for institutional framework to enhance accountability of soft-ware quality - an interim report (2011) (in Japanese),
   http://sec.ipa.go.jp/reports/20110930.html
4. Ministry of Economy, Trade and Industry, Information Policy. Reliability of Information system, http://www.meti.go.jp/policy/it_policy/softseibi/
5. SEC (Software Engineering Center) Software Development Process Guide for Embedded System (2007) (in Japanese)
6. ISO/IEC 25010:2011 Systems and software engineering - Systems and software Quality Requirements and Evaluation (SQuaRE) - System and software quality models (2011)
7. ISO 9241-11:1998 Ergonomic requirements for office work with visual display terminals (VDTs) - Part 11: Guidance on usability (1998)
8. ISO/IEC 25040:2011 Systems and software engineering - Systems and software Quality Requirements and Evaluation (SQuaRE) - Evaluation process (2011)
9. Hirasawa, N., Ogata, K., Kawai, K.: Empirical Analysis for Effectiveness of HCD Integration. Economic Review (Bulletin of Otaru University of Commerce) 61(1) (2010)
10. IEC 61508-1 ed2.0 Functional safety of electrical/electronic/programmable electronic safety-related systems - Part 1: General requirements (2010)

Development of a System for Communicating Human Factors Readiness

Matthew Johnston, Katie Del Giudice, Kelly S. Hale, and Brent Winslow

Design Interactive, Inc.
1221 E Broadway, Ste 110, Oviedo, FL 32675 USA
{Matthew,Katie,Kelly,brent.winslow}@designinteractive.net

Abstract. While human factors has been recognized as a key component in re-search and development efforts, there is a lack of systematic guidance as to how to insert human factors evaluation outcomes into system development processes. The current effort proposes a systematic scale comparable to existing Technology Readiness Level scales to objectively quantify and track human factors readiness throughout the system development lifecycle. The resultant Human Factors Readiness Levels (HFRLs), iteratively developed with input from government and industry human factors practitioners across a variety of domains, prioritize each identified human factors issue based on its risk level and by the status of any resolution. The overall scoring method utilizes a scale of 1 to 10, with a higher score indicating a higher level of human factors readi-ness. The HFRL scale has been integrated into a software tool, the System for Human Factors Readiness Evaluation (SHARE), that supports tracking and cal-culation of system level HFRLs that can be quickly and easily shared to support acquisition decision making and product development in an effort to realize re-turn on investment through early identification, prioritization and rectification of issues avoiding expensive, late design changes..

Keywords: Human Factors Readiness, Risk Assessment, Acquisition Decision Support, Human System Integration.

1 Introduction

There is an increasing importance of incorporating sound Human System Integration (HSI) methods in systems acquisition decision-making. HSI analysts focus on opti-mizing the human part of system interaction by integrating and inserting manpower, personnel, training, human factors, safety, occupational health, habitability, and per-sonnel survivability considerations into the Defense acquisition process [1]. System acquisition policy requires that total system performance be optimized and total own-ership costs be minimized through a "total system approach" to acquisition manage-ment [1]. Nevertheless, there are several limitations that make this hard to achieve, these include: 1) decision makers who are not formally trained in HSI practices, 2) lack of agreed upon definitions of performance metrics to use for comparing impact of HSI decisions on systems acquisition, and 3) it is difficult to quantify impact of

S. Yamamoto (Ed.): HIMI/HCII 2013, Part III, LNCS 8018, pp. 475–484, 2013.

HSI decisions. Hence, there is a need for an automated decision support system that allows novice and expert HSI decision makers to assess human factors maturity and readiness of operational systems.

In the broadest sense, HSI focuses on the human considerations in system design. The HSI process aims to ensure systems are designed and developed that enhance operational capability, while affordably and seamlessly integrating with human capabilities and limitations. The HSI process considers interdependent multi-disciplinary aspects of multiple domains within the systems engineering lifecycle, including: manpower; personnel; training; human factors engineering; environment; safety; occupational health; survivability; and habitability. While HSI research has become recognized as a critical area that needs to be addressed during the research and development (R&D) process, there is a current lack of consistency throughout the multi-disciplinary communities of how to quantify HSI impacts and associated human-system readiness status. The transition from research to operation is complex, and it is important to have specific criteria that define a concept's operability readiness with respect to HF to seamlessly transition from one state to the next or between collaborating agencies. Specifically, through the use of human factors readiness assessment, HSI can become institutionalized within the systems engineering lifecycle.

By implementing human factors readiness assessment early and often within a system's development cycle, risks to operator and public safety, operator acceptance, and maintenance and training costs can be reduced. If human factors issues are identified later in the system's operational phase, deployment of "quick fixes" or additional training to overcome design shortfalls may occur, resulting in a non-optimal overall design. Further, if human factors issues remain unresolved, users often eventually reject the system and a replacement must be sought. Identifying a non-optimal human-system interface implementation during development can save up to 10 times the cost of repairing after release [2]. For example, design issues that are non-intuitive can be appropriately addressed, saving on back-end training time to properly train system use [3]. Failing to identify, track, and resolve such human factors design issues can threaten the success of a system.

While there are numerous tools available to track technical issues in a system (e.g., Sun's BugDB; [4]), there are currently no tools available that are specifically designed to measure the human factors readiness of the system that focus on the outcome of thorough human factors evaluations. Previous attempts to create human readiness levels have resulted in complimentary frameworks to the existing Technology Readiness Levels with a process orientation as opposed to a focus on the state of existing issues [Phillips, 2010].

The FAA has recognized the need for a tool that provides for human factors issue tracking and which allows users and managers to easily identify those issues that pose the greatest risk to the success of the system. The tool should not only store and track issues, but quantify the human factors readiness of a system, such that human factors related research and development progress can be aligned with the commonly used TRL scale for reasons of compatibility and easy comparison by acquisition communities. Further, such a tool should provide decision support such that human factors can be used as an explicit evaluation component. Such a system would therefore support both point in time decision making as well as an iterative product development schedule resulting in a tool that could meet the needs of government agency acquisition arms through product development in industry providing a foundation for standardized human factors readiness assessment and simplifying detection of human factors gaps.

2   Background

Human Factors is "a multidisciplinary effort to generate, compile, and apply information about human capabilities and limitations" [6]. Human Factors anchors are those elements for which human-system capabilities and limitations should be carefully assessed, although not all anchors are necessarily relevant to every application. HF readiness assessment can utilize existing anchor categories, such as the 24 Human Factors study areas listed in [7], which were originally taken directly from the FAA Human Factors Job Aid [6], as a foundation for an assessment tool. Table 1 outlines the original anchor categories grouped into six main areas. Such classification schema may be used to form the foundation for human factors assessment, as there is no current mechanism to ensure that all appropriate human factors study areas are evaluated, and that system evaluations address relevant objectives.

Table 1. Issue Categories

Group Headings	Issue Categories	
Physical Working Environment	Anthropometrics and Biomechanics Displays and Controls Environment	Input/Output Devices Safety and Health Work Space
Organization and Staffing	Knowledge, Skills, Abilities Staffing	Culture Workload
Procedures, Roles, &Responsibilities	Allocation of Function	Procedures
Training and Development	Documentation Special Skills/Tools	Training
Teams and Communication	Communications	Teamwork
Human – System Interaction	CHI Functional Design Human Error Information Presentation	Information Requirements Situational Awareness Operational Suitability Visual/Auditory Alerts

Further, while a human factors analysis may result in a list of issues and recommendations, programs often select a subset of recommendations or issues to address (perhaps due to limited cost for implementing changes), and develop solutions without further testing to validate whether the implemented changes are indeed effective at reducing HF issues.

Typically, system engineers are responsible for identifying technical issues related to system safety and functionality during the development process. To support this task, Technology Readiness Levels (TRLs; [8]) have been developed to quantify and communicate system technical readiness. TRLs are an established assessment method that has proven useful in providing significant insights into potential program problems and risks with technology maturity. The wide-spread model of TRL, however, does not provide explicit means for assessing potential HF issues and risks, and there is a lack of systematic methods to measure Human Factors readiness. Further, system engineers may lack the knowledge and skills needed to evaluate a system for human factors readiness.

Thus, there is a need to build explicit shared representations of human factors readiness that could be used to communicate effectively across HSI components and achieve common ground among stakeholders. These representations would provide traceability of HSI objectives, supporting data structures, decision points, and the rationale for decisions across the system development lifecycle. This will establish a shared language that supports communication across the HSI components, makes relationships and trouble points apparent, and facilitates common ground and understandings. Specifically, a tool is needed that will allow system acquisition decision makers the ability to assess whether a proposed system addresses relevant HSI components and how these elements impact total system performance. Put another way, the tool will define and assess HSI maturity of systems, where HSI maturity is defined as the degree of the transfer process from R&D to deployment.

3   Human Factors Assessment

The objectives of implementing Human Factors Readiness Assessment are very similar to those that surrounded the advent of TRLs, which were an attempt at approaching technology development and infusion in a more systematic way - one that would increase the likelihood of innovation success. Although TRLs were initially developed to assess maturity of technology developed for space, the TRL scale relates very well to other capability assessment scales (including ISO 9241-210:2010), and many organizations have since chosen to adapt the same approach for maturity assessment of their specific domain with just minor changes in definitions or terms (e.g., Software Readiness Levels, Manufacturing Readiness Levels). However, the TRLs are incapable of capturing the human readiness of a system or product. The underlying assumption of the TRL scale is the more mature a technology the more "ready" the technology is. This matches typical product development schedules in which a process is followed that supports incremental changes in maturity governed or assessed at periodic reviews of system status. Although many in industry include human factors or ergonomic input in such reviews, it is rare for this input to be based on a consistently applied framework for communication human factors status.

3.1 Development of a Scale for Measuring Human Factors Readiness

In an effort to develop a scale capable of measuring human factors readiness consistently across industry and government agencies to support point in time evaluations and iterative development processes interviews were conducted with human factors practitioners in product development industries including automotive, medical, telecommunication and consumer electronics and government agencies such as the Federal Aviation Authority (FAA). These interviews were supplemented by review of documentation provided by these individuals with respect to their procedures for integrating human factors assessment.

The first insight gained from this analysis was the consistent application of some for of risk assessment. The risk for each human factors issue, regardless of industry or government agency included some form of severity and probability rating. Table 2 provides an example in use by the FAA to guide risk assessment.

Table 2. Severity and Probability Ratings

	Code	Definition
Severity	1	CATASTROPHIC – Death, system or aircraft loss, permanent total disability
	2	HAZARDOUS - Severe injury or major aircraft or system damage
	3	MAJOR - Minor injury or minor aircraft or system damage
	4	MINOR – Less than minor injury or aircraft or system damage
	5	NO SAFETY EFFECT
Probability	A	PROBABLE - Likely to occur
	B	REMOTE – Possible
	C	EXTREMELY REMOTE – Unlikely
	D	EXTREMELY IMPROBABLE –not expected

FAA Order 8040.4 [8] establishes the safety risk management policy and prescribes procedures for implementing safety risk management.

Table 3. Risk Assessment Table

Severity	A- Probable	B- Remote	C- Extremely Remote	D- Extremely Improbable
1- Catastrophic	4- Extreme Risk	4- Extreme Risk	3- High Risk	3- High Risk
2- Hazardous	4- Extreme Risk	3- High Risk	3- High Risk	2- Medium Risk
3- Major	3- High Risk	2- Medium Risk	2- Medium Risk	1- Low Risk
4- Minor	2- Medium Risk	1- Low Risk	1- Low Risk	1- Low Risk
5- No Safety Effect	0- Acceptable	0- Acceptable	0- Acceptable	0- Acceptable

According to this order, "each risk assessment should first analyze the two elements of risk: severity of the hazard and likelihood of occurrence. Risk assessment is then performed by comparing the combined effect of their characteristics [...]." This approach is further illustrated in Appendix B of the FAA System Safety Handbook [10]. Based on the above, a risk assessment approach was considered for identifying and prioritizing research issues. It was determined that that the risk of an existing human factors issue should form that basis for communicating human factors readiness.

The second insight came from interviews with multiple practitioners in industry, particularly product development. Communication of risks associated with an issue is not sufficient to support product development. Communication of any risk is typically followed by a plan to resolve the risk. Decision makers, particularly in product development, are tasked with resolving conflicts in an effort to implement or launch a product. To accomplish this, a plan must be proffered that resolves the risk to the satisfaction of the development team or the end customer. This second insight may be the most significant observation made during the development process as it was the key to developing an outcome focused human factors readiness assessment scale that could be mutually exclusive from technology maturity. Previous attempts to create human readiness scales have been so coupled to TRLS (5) that they assume human readiness increases as maturity increases. However, these concepts needed to be decoupled as a significant human factors issue identified or left unresolved at a high maturity level is possible and carries greater risk to the development or acquisition of a product and possibly to the end user.

Building upon the second insight is that each plan for resolution carries with it a certain confidence that it will address the outstanding issue. This may seem counterintuitive to have a resolution that may not fully address an issue however considering that solutions are often recommended by multiple parties and human factors practitioners are often required to evaluate each, the outcome of the evaluation could be a resolution that may only partially address an outstanding issue. Further the recommended resolution may lack validation and be based on expert guidance or it may be the result of an objective validated test. The validation is key in this regard, not the test itself. Human factors practitioners did not desire a system that evaluated their process but rather focused on the outcome of their evaluation as often the process in governed by external factors beyond their control. For example that lack of a validated computer aided design tool or a procedure based on federal regulations. For the resulting human factors readiness system to be valid across industries the focus had to be on the outcome of the process not the quality of that process. Decision makers will often ask for the recommended plan and balance the projected risk resolution with costs and timing.

3.2   Human Factors Readiness Levels

Feedback from human factors practitioners summarized above identified a number of considerations for quantifying human factors readiness, including the need to capture risk associated with outstanding issues, consideration of available and proposed recommended solutions for identified issues, and the degree and confidence to which recommendations are expected to minimize or eliminate the issue [11]. The Human Factors Readiness Levels Scale was developed to prioritize each identified human factors issue based on its risk level (as with FAAs risk matrix) and by the status of any resolution. The overall scoring method utilizes a scale of 1 to 10, with a higher score indicating a higher level of human factors readiness. In addition, HFRL ranges were created to provide a quick understanding of readiness, ranging from low (red), moderate (yellow), and high (green) (Table 4). While concerns such as cost and schedule impacts can influence decisions regarding system selection, it was determined that such factors are not reflective of "readiness". A solution that costs more or takes more time to implement does not make a system's current state more "human factors ready" than one that costs less and takes less time.

Table 4. HFRL Score Matrix

	Issue Resolution					
	Proposed			Tested		
	Does not resolve	Partially resolves	Completely resolves	Does not resolve	Partially resolves	Completely resolves
Extreme Risk	1	1	1	1	2	10
High risk	1	2	3	1	3	10
Medium Risk	4	5	6	4	6	10
Low Risk	7	7	8	7	8	10
Negligible Risk	9	9	9	9	9	10

As outlined in Table 4, the left of the HFRL scoring matrix is the risk level that maps to FAA's current risk matrix that includes probability and severity of issues (see Table 3). At the top is Resolution Status. Resolutions are divided into two categories, those that have been tested and those that have been proposed. It was determined from the observations that this delineation followed typical human factors behavior in product development. A resolution recommendation can be determined to not resolve the issue, partially resolve the issue, or resolve the issue completely. The more a countermeasure or resolution addresses an issue, the higher the HFRL score could eventually become. By using this method, SHARE's HFRL matrix supports both iterative development and point in time evaluations.

3.3   System for Human Factors Readiness Evaluation (SHARE)

The above HFRL scoring method has been fully instantiated into an assessment tool known as the System for Human Factors Readiness Evaluation (SHARE). SHARE enables HFRL tracking over time by calculating an HFRL for each issue identified, each issue category of relevance, and the system as a whole based on user input. SHARE computes a HFRL for each issue based on user input concerning the risk and resolution level of the issue. SHARE also computes an HFRL score for each relevant Issue Category, based on the worst issue-level HFRL score among the issues in that category, and for the overall system, based on the worst issue-level HFRL score among the issues present in the system. As issue information is updated, SHARE automatically re-calculates HFRL's, providing real-time indication of system human factors readiness.

Figure 2 provides a conceptual overview of SHARE. Human factors issues are typically identified during evaluations of varying fidelity (e.g., paper and pencil heuristic evaluation through high fidelity user testing). SHARE enables tracking of these issues by allowing for storage and manipulation of the following data surrounding each issue: data about the issue itself, the issue's level of risk, associated issue category(s), and resolution recommendations.

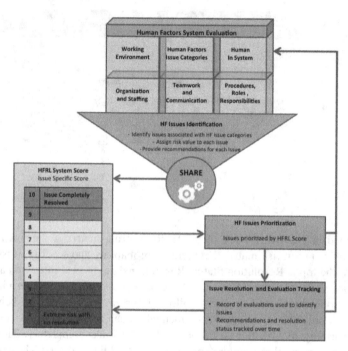

Fig. 1. SHARE Conceptual Model

SHARE provides a repository for storing information about the issues identified in a system, including an issue description, its associated issue category(s) (see Table 1), and the use case(s) under which the issue is identified. Each issue identified during an evaluation carries a certain level of risk which can be defined by its severity (e.g. propensity to cause injury, reduced efficiency, and diminished satisfaction) and the probability with which it is expected to occur. Further, in response to an issue, a human factors practitioner, engineer or team members of a responsible party within product development or acquisition will develop a single resolution recommendation or set of countermeasures thought to be able to resolve the issue. SHARE allows cost, timing, and other information to be associated with each resolution recommendation to support the practitioner in the decision-making process. SHARE uses both the practitioner's risk assessment for the issue and status of the chosen resolution recommendation to automatically compute an HFRL for the issue (see Table 4).

Dependent upon the available validation techniques or the fidelity of the system, a human factors practitioner or other party may empirically test the countermeasure and validate that the selected recommendation did indeed resolve the issue. Examples of these types of tests might be usability evaluations with relevant end users, measurements taken with CAD data, or other means of empirical validation. The extent to which the issue is resolved based on this measurement or test generates an updated HFRL score. As seen in Table 4, empirical testing that proves resolution of an issue progresses the score toward an HFRL of 10, which allows issue closure.

SHARE also provides tools to support management of a system with respect to HFRLs. In particular, SHARE provides a System Dashboard (Figure 3) that provides a summary of the status of a system with respect to HFRLs. A user can quickly view the current HFRL status of a system, the HFRL status of each Issue Category, and a graph representing the recent history of the system with respect to both HFRLs and TRLs. In addition, the System Dashboard also provides a master list of all the issues currently in the system, including their current HFRL.

SHARE enables the user to track all issues and associated resolution recommendations for a system over time to support the development process and provide historical information regarding the human factors issues that have been addressed.

4   Conclusion

The increasing importance of incorporating sound HSI methods in systems development and acquisition decision making is borne out of the observed impact human factors engineering can have on both safety risks to the end user or consumer of a product and the potential return on investment. Existing technical and manufacturing readiness levels and tracking systems do not adequately address human factors nor appreciate the financial impact human factors can have in the development or acquisition process. This impact calls for a quantification of human factors readiness within development and acquisition that adequately captures the risks of outstanding human factors related issues and the status of their proposed countermeasures. The HFRL scale employed by the SHARE system is designed to quantify this status and supports communication throughout the design or acquisition lifecycle in an effort to realize return on investment through early identification, prioritization and rectification of issues avoiding expensive, late design changes.

Acknowledgment. The research was sponsored by the Federal Aviation Authority under contract Number DTRT57-10-C-10028.

Any opinions, findings, and conclusions or recommendations expressed in this material are those of the authors and do not necessarily reflect the views or the endorsement of FAA.

References

1. Defense Acquisition University DAU, ch. 6: Human Systems Integration, in Defense Acquisition Guidebook. Fort Belvoir, Virginia (2004)
2. Gilb, T.: Principles of Software Engineering Management. Addison-Wesley (1988)
3. Bias, Mayhew: Cost-Justifying Usability: An Update for the Internet Age. Mogan Kaufmann Publishers, San Francisco (2005)
4. Bug Database, http://bugs.sun.com/bugdatabase/ (accessed on September 25, 2012)
5. Phillips, E.L.: The Development and Initial Evaluation of the Human Readiness Level Framework. Unpublished Master's Thesis Naval Postgraduate School (2010)
6. Federal Aviation Administration. Human Factors Acquisition Job Aid (2012), http://www.hf.faa.gov/HFPortalNew/Uploads/supoladb/ HFAcqJobAid2012.pdf (viewed September 26, 2012)
7. Krois, P., Rehmann, J.: Assessing Human Factors Risks in Air Traffic Management Research. Final Report Number DOT/FAA/TN- AR-05/1. Submitted to Federal Aviation Administration, Washington, DC 20590 (2005)
8. Sadin, S.R., Povinelli, F.P., Rosen, R.: TheN technology push towards future space mission systems. Acta Astronautica 20, 73–77 (1989)
9. FAA. Order 8040.4: Safety Risk Management (1998), http://www.faa.gov/library/manuals/aviation/risk_management/ ss_handbook/media/app_g_1200.PDF (viewed September 25, 2012)
10. FAA (2000). FAA System Safety Handbook, Appendix B: Comparative Risk Assessment (CRA) Form (December 30, 2000)
11. DelGiudice, K., Johnston, M.R., Hale, K.S.: System for Human Factors Readiness Evaluation. Final Report. Submitted to Federal Aviation Authority under Contract DTRT57-10-C-10028 (2012)

A Method for Service Failure Effects Analysis Based on Customer Satisfaction

Yusuke Kurita[1,*], Koji Kimita[2], Kentaro Watanabe[3], and Yoshiki Shimomura[1]

[1] Dept. of System Design, Tokyo Metropolitan University, Tokyo, Japan
kurita-yusuke@sd.tmu.ac.jp, yoshiki-shimomura@center.tmu.ac.jp
[2] Dept. of Management Science, Tokyo University of Science, Tokyo, Japan
kimita@ms.kagu.tus.ac.jp
[3] Center for Service Research, National Institute of Advanced Industrial Science and Technology, Tokyo, Japan
kentaro.watanabe@aist.go.jp

Abstract. Recently, the importance of service is widely accepted. Service Engineering that aims to design a service from the engineering viewpoint has been proposed. In order to achieve a successful service, service providers should maintain service quality and always satisfy their customers. To be specific, the provision of highly reliable service is essential. To realize highly reliable services it is important to minimize the occurrence of service failures. This paper proposes a method for analyzing service failure effects in the service design phase. Specifically, we define service failure and propose a procedure to analyze service failure effects with models that are proposed in Service Engineering. The proposed method is verified through its application to a nursing-care service.

Keywords: Service reliability, Service failure, Service Engineering.

1 Introduction

Recently, customer demands have become more varied due to the maturing of economy. It is difficult to satisfy such customer demands purely with physical products; thus, an approach that combines physical products and intangible services is widely accepted. Manufacturing companies have been making a fundamental shift away from selling only physical products towards providing a combination of products and services. For example, Rolls-Royce is selling energy to an airline, rather than selling engines [1]. Clearly, service is an important aspect of many industries.

Service has been the subject of extensive research in the academic field. Recently, service has been discussed from the engineering or scientific perspective rather than from the perspective of traditional service marketing [2, 3] that focuses on the characteristics of service. For example, service engineering [4] has been proposed from an engineering point of view in Japan and focuses especially on the design of

---

* Corresponding author.

S. Yamamoto (Ed.): HIMI/HCII 2013, Part III, LNCS 8018, pp. 485–494, 2013.

services. In other locations, particularly Europe, product-service systems (PSSs) [5, 6] that aim to provide value by coupling physical products and intangible services have been actively discussed. On the other hand, service science [7] has been proposed in the United States. This aims to create the basis for systematic service innovation.

In general, in order to make a service successful and profitable, service providers need to establish long-term relationships with their customers. That is to say, the provision of highly reliable service that is able to consistently satisfy customers' expectations is important. In the product field, the approach to minimizing product failures for customers is widely accepted as a means of realizing highly reliable products. In order to prevent product failures, it is important to identify potential failures and their causes, and take them into account in the design phase. These processes are also useful apply to services because service is also an artifact created by humans. Failure mode and effects analysis (FMEA) [8] or fault tree analysis (FTA) [9] are recognized as effective engineering methods to support the above processes of failure analysis and are applied in various fields. The service field requires an engineering evaluation against service reliability like FMEA. Although failure effect analyses such as FMEA focus on upper-level functions, it is more important to focus on the influence on customer satisfaction because customers evaluate services subjectively. In addition, the degree of influence on customer satisfaction is different for each customer, even if the kind of service failure is the same. Based on this background, we aim to support analysts who analyze service failure effects in order to determine the priority number of service failures. In this paper, we propose a procedure to analyze service failure effects using the analytic hierarchy process (AHP) [10] and models proposed in service engineering. The AHP is utilized to quantify service failure effects and is explained in the detail in section 2.3.

2   Existing Study

2.1   Failure Modes and Effects Analysis

Failure mode and effects analysis is a systematic method of identifying and preventing product and process problems before they occur. This is focused on preventing defects, enhancing safety, and increasing customer satisfaction [11]. Failure mode and effects analysis is a deductive technique that consists of failure identification for each component, its causes and consequences on the equipment and on the whole system. This analysis proceeds with a table called an FMEA worksheet. Elements of this worksheet are flexible and may be changed according to the subject being analyzed. Table 1 shows an example of an FMEA worksheet.

As mentioned in chapter 1, this paper focuses on the effects of service failure. In the case of a traditional FMEA, failure effects are not changed. However, in the case of services, failure effects change according to the customer's sense of value. Therefore, the FMEA worksheet should be extended.

Table 1. An example of FMEA worksheet

Item	Function	Failure mode	Failure effect		Occurrence frequency	Critically	Action
			First-order	Second-order			

2.2   Service Realization Structure

Service engineering aims to consolidate the methodology for the representation, design, and evaluation of services. Service is defined as "an activity between a service provider and service receiver to change the state of the receiver" [4] in service engineering. According to this definition, a receiver is satisfied when his/her state changes to a new desirable state. Namely, service design should be based on the desired change in the state of the receiver. The target receiver's state is represented as a set of parameters called receiver state parameter (RSP). In service engineering, a sub-model called a view model is proposed to represent a realization structure for changing an RSP. This model consists of functions and entities. Each function has one or several function parameters (FP) that show the degree of functional expression. Function parameters are associated with attribute parameters (APs), which represent the attributes of entities. Figure 1 presents an example of a view model that describes part of the realization structure of a coffee shop service. As shown in Figure 1, functions are described hierarchically in order to change the RSP.

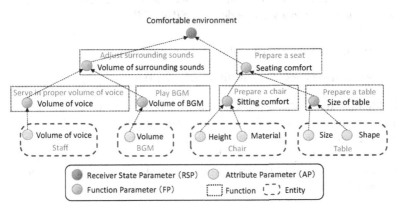

Fig. 1. An example of a view model

2.3   Analytic Hierarchy Process

The AHP is a process of deriving relative scales using judgment or data from a standard scale, and performing the subsequent arithmetic operation on such scales to avoid extraneous number crunching. The judgments are given in the form of paired comparisons. One of the uses of a hierarchy is that it allows us to focus judgment separately on each of several properties essential for making a sound decision. The most effective way to concentrate judgment is to take a pair of elements and compare them with respect to a single property, without concern for other properties or other elements. This is why paired comparisons in combination with a hierarchical structure are so useful in deriving measurements. This technique is applied to many kinds of cases, and its effectiveness is widely accepted.

In this study, AHP is utilized to quantify service failure effects. Although a view model has hierarchical structure and shows relationship between functions and a customer satisfaction factor, how each function contributes a customer satisfaction factor is not clear. Whereat, this degree of contribution is quantified by AHP.

3   A Method for Analyzing Service Failure Effects

3.1   Outline

In order to determine the influence of service failure on customer satisfaction, a method for analyzing service failure effects using AHP and models from service engineering has been developed. In the product field, analysts can proceed to analysis using the generalized evaluation axis. However, in the service field, it is difficult to define the evaluation axis compared to the product, since customer evaluation of service is subjective. In this study, the analyst analyzes service failure effects with evaluation axes based on each the customer's sense of value in each category. In addition, service failure effects analysis that considers multiple customer categories is achieved by allocating each customer's value rating by category with respect to intensity of importance in a view model for RSP and FP.

3.2   A Procedure for Service Failure Effects Analysis

The proposed method consists of the following four steps:

Step1: Identification of Target Customer Category. In this method, a persona model is constructed to identify target customer categories [12]. A persona model consists of demographic data, such as age and family structure, and psychological data, such as personality and values. Figure 2 shows a persona model for a coffee shop service. The number of persona models in this step is decided based on the cause and purpose of the analysis.

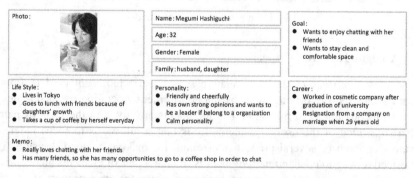

Fig. 2. A persona model; coffee shop service

Step 2: Identification of Service Failure. Understanding of service failure differs according to the research field or objective. For example, service marketing explains service failure as an operational miss; it has many discussions on service recovery and how to recover from an operational miss [e.g., 13, 14]. In the reliability engineering field, some researchers define service failure as service defects [15]; others define it as the dissatisfaction that customers experience during the service offering [16]. In this study, the fundamental interpretation of product failure and service failure is essentially the same, because services, like physical products, are also artifacts created by humans. Therefore, services and physical products should not be considered as different things. In this study, the definition of failure by the International Electrotechnical Commission, is applied to service. In this case, the difference between product failure and service failure is in understanding of the word "item" in the IEC's definition. Specifically, an "item" refers to a part of a physical product or system, such as any part, component, or functional unit. Human beings should also be included in the term "item" when we focus on services: a human being is one of the most important elements since the quality of services depends on activity by human beings. Human beings here means not only service providers but also customers, because if the activity of a customer has a negative influence on other customers or a whole service, in general, this case is recognized as a failure. In addition, an entity's functional loss is divided into functional loss that impacts customer satisfaction and functional loss that has no negative influence on customer satisfaction.

Based on the above, in this study a service failure is recognized as an item's failure to perform a function intended by its designer in order to meet a customer requirement. The word "item" here refers to human beings, physical products, systems, services, etc.

To describe a view model, functions that are required to change an RSP, which is identified through the construction of a persona model, are deployed hierarchically; the lowest functions have an entity that is needed to exert the function. An "entity" in a view model corresponds to the term "item" in the definition of service failure in this study. In addition, functions in a view model can be recognized as functions, i.e. the functions designed in order to meet a customer requirement. Therefore, the lowest function's loss can be recognized as a service failure. In this step, service failures are identified by converting the lowest functions in a view model into a negative expression.

Step 3: Quantification of Service Failure Effects on Customer Satisfaction. Service failure effects on customer satisfaction are structured using the described view model in step 2. The importance value, based on each persona's sense of value, is allocated from RSPs to the lowest functions in an integrated view model in order to quantify service failure effects on customer satisfaction. However, it is not easy to quantify the importance of RSPs and functions. Therefore, AHP is adopted in this study in order to determine the importance of each RSP and function. As mentioned in section 3.3, AHP is a structured technique for organizing and analyzing complex decisions. Total importance is 100 in this study. This importance value is allocated from RSPs to the lowest functions based on the results of paired comparisons. Here, paired comparison is carried out from each persona viewpoint. The importance of the lowest function is recognized as the degree of influence on RSP, which is a customer satisfaction factor, and is called the effect value on customer satisfaction.

Service designers use the scale shown in Table 2 when pairing comparisons. In addition, Table 3 presents the results of a calculation in the case of three RSPs. In this step, service failure effects on customer satisfaction are quantified by determining the importance of RSP and functions using AHP.

Table 2. The scale for intensity of importance

Intensity of importance on an absolute scale	Definition	Explanation
1	Equal importance	Two activities contribute equally to the objective
3	Moderate importance of one over another	Experience and judgment strongly favor one activity over another
5	Essential or strong importance	Experience and judgment strongly favor one activity over another

Table 3. An example of paired comparison

	RSP1	RSP2	RSP3	Geometric mean	Importance (total 100)
RSP1	1	3	5	2.47	62
RSP2	1/3	1	5	1.19	30
RSP3	1/5	1/5	1	0.34	8

Step 4: Service Failure Effects Analysis. In this step, information obtained from steps 1 through 3 is inserted into a template, as shown in Table 4. First, entities and service failures identified in step 2 are filled out in part (a). Second, identified personas are filled out in part (b). Finally, effect value on customer satisfaction is filled out in part (c). Analysis of service failure effects considering multiple customer categories is realized through the above four steps.

Table 4. A template for service failure effects analysis

Entity	Service failure	Persona	Effect value on customer satisfaction
(a)		(b)	(c)

4   Application

In this chapter, the proposed method is applied to a nursing-care service. The purpose of this application is to clarify whether service failure effects are quantified appropriately. First, in order to determine target customer categories, two types of persona models were constructed: (1) an elder woman who wants to enjoy living in an elder care facility (see Figure 3); and (2) an elder man who wants to maintain a sense of self-esteem (see Figure 4).

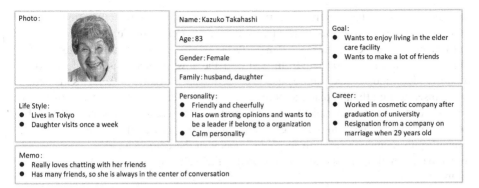

Fig. 3. Persona model of an elder woman

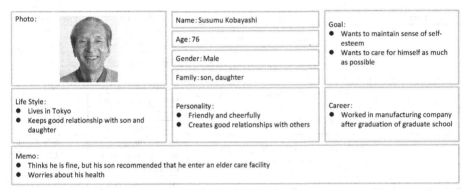

Fig. 4. Persona model of an elder man

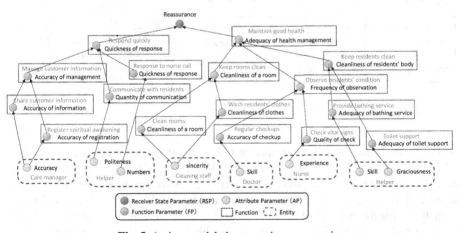

Fig. 5. A view model about nursing-care service

Next a view model is constructed. In this application, "reassurance" is identified as an RSP. Therefore, functions that are needed to change this RSP were deployed and entities were associated with the lowest functions. Figure 5 shows the described view model. Service failures were identified by converting the lowest functions in the integrated view model into a negative expression. For example, "share customer information" was converted to "inability to share customer information." The importance value is allocated from RSPs to the lowest functions based on AHP. Finally, identified service failures and their influence value on customer satisfaction were inserted into the template, as shown in Table 4. Table 5 presents the results: the effect value on customer satisfaction is completely different by persona, even if the service failure is the same. For example, the effect value of the service failure "inability to communicate with residents" was 9 in the case of an elder man. On the other hand, in the case of an elder woman, the value was 29, which is a critical number.

Table 5. Deployment result of service failures and effect value

Entity	Service failure	Persona	Effect value
Care manager	Inability to share customer information	Kazuko Takahashi	5.2
		Susumu Kobayashi	10.1
	Inability to register spiritual awakening	Kazuko Takahashi	1.8
		Susumu Kobayashi	3.4
Helper	Inability to communicate with residents	Kazuko Takahashi	29.0
		Susumu Kobayashi	9.0
	Inability to respond to nurse call	Kazuko Takahashi	14.0
		Susumu Kobayashi	27.5
	Inability to provide bathing service	Kazuko Takahashi	19.5
		Susumu Kobayashi	2.3
	Inability to conduct toilet support	Kazuko Takahashi	6.5
		Susumu Kobayashi	6.7
Cleaning staff	Inability to clean a room	Kazuko Takahashi	6.0
		Susumu Kobayashi	6.8
	Inability to wash residents' clothes	Kazuko Takahashi	6.0
		Susumu Kobayashi	6.7
Doctor	Inability to conduct regular checkups	Kazuko Takahashi	3.0
		Susumu Kobayashi	20.6
Nurse	Inability to check vital signs	Kazuko Takahashi	9.0
		Susumu Kobayashi	6.9

5   Discussion

As shown in Table 5, even if the service failure is the same, its effect on customer satisfaction differs by persona. For example, the service failure "inability to communicate with residents" was the most critical failure for the persona of an elder woman, since she places great value on conversation, as shown in Figure 3. On the other hand, for the persona of an elder man, "inability to respond to nurse call" was the most critical failure, since he worries about his health, as shown in Figure 4. That is to say, the proposed method can reflect each persona's characteristics in the analysis results. Therefore, analysis of service failure effects considering multiple customer categories is achieved.

In this paper, paired comparison is based on a three-level scale, as shown in Table 2, in order to decrease the amount of work. Specifically, if the scale is different on one level, the allocation result is quite different. Therefore, we must reconsider the number of levels within the scales. For example, Saaty [10] proposes a five-level scale, as shown in Table 6. In addition, this paper only focuses on two values: service failure or no service failure. However, the degree of functional loss should also be considered. If we can identify the relationship between the degree of functional loss and the influence value on customer satisfaction, we expect to realize a refined analysis of service failure effects.

Table 6. The fundamental scale proposed by Saaty [10]

Intensity of importance	Definition	Explanation
1	Equal importance	Two activities contribute equally to the objective
3	Moderate importance of one over another	Experience and judgment strongly favor one activity over another
5	Essential or strong importance	Experience and judgment strongly favor one activity over another
7	Very strong importance	An activity is strongly favored and its dominance demonstrated in practice
9	Extreme importance	The evidence favoring one activity over another is of the highest possible order of affirmation
2, 4, 6, 8	Intermediate values between the two adjacent judgments	When compromise is needed

6   Conclusion

The purpose of this paper is to quantify the effects of service failure on customer satisfaction, in order to realize highly reliable services. To achieve this purpose, we proposed a method of analyzing service failure effects. Specifically, we proposed a procedure to analyze service failure effects using AHP and models proposed in service engineering. We applied the proposed method to a nursing-care service. The result of this application showed a realization of service failure analysis considering multiple customer categories. Future works will reconsider the number of levels in the multi-level scale in order to improve the quality of the results. In addition, the degree of functional loss should be considered in order to realize a more exhaustive analysis of service failure effects.

References

1. Harrison, A.: Design for service –harmonizing product design with a services strategy. In: Proceedings of GT 2006, ASME Turbo Expo 2006: Power for Land, Sea and Air, Barcelona, Spain (2006)
2. Parasuraman, A., Zeithaml, V.A., Berry, L.L.: A conceptual model of service quality and implications for further research. Journal of Marketing 49, 45–50 (1985)
3. Parasuraman, A., Zeithaml, V.A., Berry, L.L.: Servqual: A multiple item scale for measuring consumer perceptions of service quality. Journal of Retailing, 22–40 (1988)

4. Arai, T., Shimomura, Y.: Proposal of Service CAD System: A Tool for Service Engineering. Annals of the CIRP 53(1), 397–400 (2004)
5. Tukker, A., Tischner, U.: Product-services as a research field: past, present and future. Reflections from a decade of research. Journal of Cleaner Production 14(17), 1552–1556 (2006)
6. Morelli, N.: Product-Service Systems: a Perspective Shift for Designers. A Case Study – The Design of a Telecentre-, Design Studies 24, 73–99 (2003)
7. Maglio, P.P., Kreulen, J., Srinivasan, S., Spohrer, J.: Service systems, service scientists, SSME, and innovation. Communications of the ACM 49(7), 81–85 (2006)
8. IEC 60812, 2edn. Analysis technique for system reliability –Procedure for failure mode effects analysis (FMEA) (2006)
9. IEC 61025, 2 edn. Analysis technique for system reliability –Procedure for fault tree analysis (FTA) (2006)
10. Saaty, T.: How to make a decision: The Analytic Hierarchy Process. Journal of Operational Research 48, 9–26 (1990)
11. Robin, T.M., Raymond, J.M., Michael, R.B.: The Basics of FMEA, 2nd edn. Productivity Press (1996)
12. Hosono, S., Hasegawa, M., Hara, T., Shimomura, Y., Arai, T.: A Methodology of Persona-centric Service Design. In: Proceedings of CIRP Design Conference 2009, pp. 541–546 (2009)
13. Tax, S.S., Brown, S.W.: Recovering and Learning from Service Failure. Slone Management Review, 75–88 (Fall 1998)
14. Kelly, S.W., Hoffman, K.D., Davis, M.K.: A Typology of Retail Failures and Recoveries. Journal of Retailing 64(4), 429–452 (1993)
15. Masuda, A., Iwase, T., Suzuki, K.: Development of Three Element FMEA Considering the Interaction between Human, Environment and Equipment for Reliability and Safe Analysis. The Japanese Society for Quality Control (JSQC) 24(1), 122–135 (1999) (in Japanese)
16. Yokoyama, S.: FTA for Service Reliability Evaluation. Journal of Reliability Engineering Association of Japan (REAJ) 34(1), 24–29 (2009) (in Japanese)

Searching Blog Sites with Product Reviews

Hironori Kuwata, Makoto Oka, and Hirohiko Mori

Tokyo City University, 1-28-1, Tamadutumi, Setagaya, Tokyo, Japan
{g1181811,moka,hmori}@tcu.ac.jp

Abstract. Recently, buzz marketing sites gives the information that is useful for consumers and companies. They want to customer feedbacks of feeling and experience. However, the searched results contain huge numbers of commercial sites when user search review with traditional search engine. We search blog site that include review sentence. We need to decision whether document of blog site include review sentence. Thus we think that two process to decide blog site whether review blog site. The first process creates to data set for certain product that viewpoint feature word. In this paper, feature word is tow term in the evaluated perspective word and evaluated value word. Data set is information for making decision sentence whether review sentence. Second process is a search for review sentence. This process decided blog site whether review blog site. This process use extracted opinion tuples from one sentence of blog site document and created data set to decide sentence whether sentence is review sentence. This process decided review blog whether document of blog site include one and more review sentence. We proposed review blog site searching system that system have two process.

Keywords: natural language, opinion extraction.

1   Introduction

Recently, buzz marketing sites gives the information that is useful for consumers and companies. Consumers watch buzz marketing sites such as Amazon.com when they want to buy some items. For consumers the reviews can be used as the reference information in purchasing a product, and for companies they are useful to develop the products of the next generation by watching reputations of their and another companies' products. However, word-of-mouth is difficult to search with traditional search engine. They are looking reviews for some media.

Buzz marketing comments are contained in many review sites, blogs and twitters so on. On the review sites, we can collect a lot of reviews but, the reviews are often short and do not contain much detail information. On the other hand, review blog sites sometimes include more detail information, such as long-term reviews, but traditional search engines by the keywords matching find too much sites. For example, when we want to find blog sites where the reviews about a compact digital camera, the searched results contains huge numbers of commercial sites and we must spend much time to find review blog site among them. Commercial site are online shop site, new

S. Yamamoto (Ed.): HIMI/HCII 2013, Part III, LNCS 8018, pp. 495–500, 2013.

products information and so on. We think that review blog site is an efficient media to get review if we can find only review blog sites.

We propose searching system that detects review blog site. User wanted information for blog site that information is customer feedbacks sentence of feeling and experience. Commercial sites not contain customer feedbacks of feeling and experience. We define a review blog site that contains one or more customer feedbacks sentence of feeling and experience.

2 Related Works

Kuwata[1] proposed method to organize free written review of review site with the use of other review site. How to organize this study is classification review sentence into viewpoint given review sentence of item. Viewpoint is that of camera, such as design, function and battery so on. Typically, training data are created manually when classified sentence. His system substitute reviews of like Viewpoints.com for training data. He created training data automatically extracted review for each viewpoint, as shown in figure 1. These reviews will be referred to as review corpus in this paper. They created data set that is pair viewpoint and feature word. They have extracted feature word from the review corpus that feature word is occurring frequently word only certain viewpoint. He classified review sentence into each viewpoint with the use of data set. He showed review corpus is substitute for the training data.

Fig. 1. Viewpoints.com's review

Table 1. Five syntax opinion pattern

1	X→Y
2	(X→Y1)→Y2
3	X1→(X2→Y1)
4	((X1→Y1)→X2)→Y2
5	YX (modification relation)

X:evaluated perspective word Y:evaluated value word   →: dependency relation

Sugiki[2] proposed new presentment of search results of accommodation review site that method to sort from does not quantification point of view. His system sorts review in descending order of relation between user query of natural language and review sentence. His measured the relevance of opinion tuples (evaluated perspective word and evaluated value word). His system extracted opinion tuples with the use of syntax opinion pattern. Using syntax opinion pattern can be extracted opinion tuples when review sentence had the same sentence structure as five syntax opinion pattern (Table 1.). His study showed that these five patterns can use extracted opinion tuples. However, using syntax opinion pattern has a problem. Syntax opinion pattern considers the category of sentence in order to extract the structure of sentence. His study has solved this problem through abounded scope for search page.

In this paper searched review blog site from searched results by traditional blog search engine. We think that it is difficult to use a syntax opinion pattern for blog site. We adapt to blog site for combination of syntax opinion pattern and data set.

3   Searching System

In this paper, we proposed system that searched review blog site that is contained one or more review sentence in blog site. Our system classified blog site that are extracted by traditional blog search engines whether review blog site. We create a system that determined one sentence whether review sentence (Fig.2). Processing of this system consist of two processes. The first process creates to data set for certain product that viewpoint and opinion tuples from review corpus. This process is a preparation to classify one sentence. Opinion tuples are two term in the evaluated perspective word and evaluated value word. Data set is information for making a decision sentence whether review sentence of blog site. Thus we choose opinion tuples for product feature. Second process is a search for review sentence. This process decided whether sentence of blog site is review. This process use extracted opinion tuples from one sentence of blog site document and created data set. Discrimination circuit of this process classified sentence whether review sentence.

We determine blog site when second process classified one or more review sentence from blog site documents. This study targets domain of the digital single-lens reflex camera. Sentences are pre-multiplied by morphological analysis for the words to deal with Japanese.

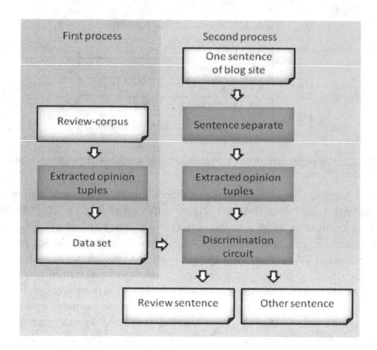

Fig. 2. System to decide whether review sentence flow

3.1   Data Set

We create data set of the product in order to determine whether review sentence. This study can't be to extract data set of the production from the general corpus. We need corpus that written about a certain product. However, handmade corpus is costly alternative. Review corpus is low cost because it can be generated automatically that review corpus written for each viewpoint. We create data set from review corpus.

Our system extracted data set from one sentence of review corpus with the use of five syntax patterns. Data set have viewpoint and opinion tuples (evaluated perspective word and evaluated value word). Review corpus is review sentences of review site written for each viewpoint. Our system extracts the opinion tuples one sentence for each viewpoint. Opinion tuples are extracted when one sentence has the same syntax as the five patterns. Our system checks sentence for sentence structure with the use of syntax analysis. Our system extracted opinion tuples when the sentence has same sentence structure as one of five syntax opinion patterns. Our system erases unnecessary word class from extracted opinion tuples. In this paper, view point is "Design" , "Image quality", "Ease of use", "Battery", "Portability"," Function", "LCD" and "Grip" of digital single-lens reflex camera review corpus. These viewpoints have opinion tuples that have been extracted in the above.

We define that feature word of certain product is like "functional" and "button" (Table 2.) We calculate the frequency of these extracted viewpoint, evaluated perspective word and evaluated value word. Word set is a collection of high frequency only in a viewpoint.

Table 2. Frequently-appearing evaluated value word

		Viewpoints								Total
		Design	Image quality	Ease of use	Battery	Portability	Function	LCD	Grid	
evaluated value word	think	1089	1516	1166	851	925	1175	705	694	8121
	big	136	302	438	529	1283	1392	1719	2301	8100
	good	705	981	658	489	497	605	402	620	4957
	shoot	45	932	475	1111	138	1214	442	212	4569
	use	125	578	620	632	166	725	257	136	3239
	functional	120	104	533	52	120	1823	98	42	2892
	feel	321	619	352	193	363	313	196	326	2683

3.2 Classification Review Blog Site

Our system classified blog site that extracted by traditional blog search engine whether review blog site. We define a review blog site that contains one or more review sentence. We create a system that determined one sentence whether review sentence.

Our system need to perform a process separated one sentence document of blog site. There is a one sentence that did not end with a period Japanese document of blog site. For example, one sentence ends with line breaks. Japanese used verbs such as “desu” and “masu” so on at the end of case one sentence. We consider sentence end whether sentence ends verbs and line breaks.

Our system extracted opinion tuples (evaluated perspective word and evaluated value word) with the use of five syntax opinion pattern from separated one sentence. Opinion tuples are extracted when one sentence has the same syntax as one of the five patterns. Our system checks sentence for sentence structure with the use of syntax analysis. Our system extracted opinion tuples when the sentence has same sentence structure as one of five syntax opinion patterns.

The sentence comes up for review sentence that had same sentence structure as the one of five syntax opinion pattern. Sentence of blog site mixed certain review sentence and other sentence.

We define that review sentence when it is discovered that there is opinion tuples of the digital single-lens reflex camera. This system decides opinion tuples whether about the digital single-lens reflex camera with the use of data set. This system determine review sentence when the same extracted opinion tuples and data set. Our system determined to be a review blog when document of blog site include review sentence.

4 Discussion

Sugiki[2] use syntax opinion pattern on sentence of review site. We have not been able to confirm that syntax opinion pattern adapt to free description sentence. We verified effect of syntax opinion pattern to extract opinion tuples of free description sentence. This study use sentence that mixed review sentence and other sentence. We need to determine five syntax opinion pattern can be extract evaluated perspective and evaluated value of the digital single-lens reflex camera.

Test data is free description review on Amazon.com. This data include 250 review sentence and 250 other sentence. We have verified manually to decision extracted opinion tuples whether evaluated perspective and evaluated value word. We get the results of precision rate 93.5% and recall rate 62.8%. Although it is at the discretion of the manually, we think that our system can be classified review sentence with data set and extracted opinion tuples of blog site. Recall rate is low because the sentence is not the correct structure. We think syntax opinion pattern work poorly when reviewer written sentence of very short and spoken language. Many short sentence is itemize as "DESIGN: VERY NICE!!". Many of the spoken language are not subject word and mistake grammar. Japanese spoken language is often omitted the subject word. We need to think of solution for sentence is not subject word.

As it stands, data set is viewpoint, evaluated perspective word and evaluated value word. We expect the results of high compliance rate and low recall rate with the use of its data set. We should consider new data set to determine many review sentence.

5   Conclusion

In this paper, we have proposed system that searched review blog site. Our system classified blog site that are extracted by traditional blog search engines. We create a system that determined one sentence whether review sentence. Sentence of blog site contain many sentence other than review unlike document of review site. Thus we solve two processes. The first process creates to data set for certain product that viewpoint and opinion tuples from review corpus. Data set is information for making a decision whether sentence of blog site is review. Second process is a search for review sentence. This process use extracted opinion tuples from one sentence of blog site document and created data set to decide sentence whether sentence is review sentence. We think system can search for review blog site if there are two processes.

6   Feature Works

We have three challenges. First, we need examine again the effect of such as very short sentence and spoken language because we deal with free description in this study. Second, we create new data set. In the current word set is expected to increasingly not given review sentence. Third, we need to create a new classifier when the foregoing has been improved. We think to be classified in two stages. First stage, system classifies certainly review sentence. Second stage, system classifies dropped review sentence of first stage with the use of new data set.

References

1. Hironori, K.: An evaluation viewpoint distinction automatic classification of a review. IPSJ Processing, 2.399–2.400 (2011)
2. Sugiki, K, Matsubara, S.: Natural language search based on information extraction from the reputation of review sentences. IPSJ SIG Technical Reports, Research Report of Natural Language Processing (124) (2006)

Usability Evaluation of Comprehension Performance and Subjective Assessment on Mobile Text Advertising

Ya-Li Lin and Chih-Hsiang Lai

Department of Statistics, Tunghai University,
40704 Taichung, Taiwan
{Ya-Li.Lin,Chih-Hsiang.Lai,yllin}@thu.edu.tw

Abstract. The effects of text presentation applied to mobile advertisings were examined in the context of the explosion of small-screen devices. Presentation mode of text advertising visual structure, position of layout, moving speed, format of segmented presentation, and luminance contrast of text/background window are used as design factors. Ad comprehension, user interface satisfaction, and overall workload would be collected using an orthogonal array experiment. The results indicate the interaction effects of presentation mode and position as well as presentation mode and speed on Ad comprehension are statistically significant. In addition, the interaction effects of presentation mode and format as well as presentation mode and position are statistically significant on user interface satisfaction. It also indicates the interaction effects of presentation mode and format as well as presentation mode and luminous contrast are statistically significant on overall workload. In summary, the interaction effects between text advertising visual structures have to be taken into account for the user-centered usability of mobile text advertising presentation.

Keywords: Mobile Text Advertising, NASA-TLX, Leading Display, User Interface Satisfaction (UIS), Rapid Serial Visual Presentation (RSVP).

1 Introduction

In recent years, electronic commerce is getting to expand towards mobile commerce. Mobile advertising is a rapidly growing sector providing brands, agencies and marketers the opportunity to connect with consumers beyond traditional and digital media and directly on their mobile phones [24]. It is a form of advertising via mobile (wireless) phones or other mobile devices. As the internet is reinvented on mobile devices — smaller, more personal and personalized, ubiquitously accessible — established forms of interactive advertising will also evolve as they migrate from PCs to mobile devices.

Mobile Advertising refers to advertising or marketing messages delivered to mobile devices, either via a synchronized download or wirelessly over the air [14]. Although this broad definition potentially included advertisings delivered to laptops, media players, and other classes of mobile device, in practice the most interesting and potentially

S. Yamamoto (Ed.): HIMI/HCII 2013, Part III, LNCS 8018, pp. 501–510, 2013.

revolutionary part of the mobile advertising market line in delivering messages to non-PC devices—primarily mobile phones, but also including mobile devices.

Mobile interactivity is in some ways similar to the PC-based internet, and these similarities will speed advertisers' ability to take advantage of the mobile medium. The key findings in Lin and Chen focused on the click-through rate for the advertising effectiveness to examine the effects of design factors on animated online advertisings [7]. Their findings showed order effect, two-factor interaction effect of ad types and presentation positions, as well as presentation position and animation lengths are s tatistically significant. In addition, the report of IAB indicated that text-based advertising remains the most common creative format on both the web and other applications like short message services (SMS) [2,3]. Mobile Marketing Association (MMA) has published mobile advertising guidelines, but it is difficult to keep such guidelines current in such a fast-developing area [8]. Leveraging accepted Web advertising best practice will facilitate building a successful mobile advertising business. At the same time, the user experience, interactivity, and expectations of consumers on the mobile web differ from their PC counterparts, and simply transplanting PC-optimized advertising onto mobile device is unlikely to yield optimal results.

As small screen interfaces become more and more popular, especially mobile display advertising, an important usability problem is how best to display mobile text advertising on small screen. One possibility is to use dynamic presentation methods involving the movement of text on the screen. These methods have been shown to be viable alternatives for displaying text information on small screen of non-PC devices or limited screen space of PC-based devices [4-6, 9-10]. These studies focused on investigating users' visual performance, readability, and reading comprehension of dynamic or continuous texts. However, it lacks of providing the guideline of the user experience, interactivity, and expectations of consumers on the mobile web, including the current trends in advertising as delivered to mobile phones. The objective of this study is to evaluate the reading comprehension performance of mobile text advertising using static and dynamic moving display on the interface of mobile phone. The usability evaluation is used to achieve specified goals with efficiency, preference, and user interface satisfaction.

2   Methods

2.1   Participants

Twenty-seven undergraduate and graduate students (13 females and 14 males) from Tunghai University participated individually in the experiment.

2.2   Materials

Macromedia Flash CS3 and SWiSHzone SWiSHmax are used to design the simulated mobile text advertising interface. The simulated interface contained search results and visual structure of text advertising. The size of mobile text advertising is categorized as large image banner (216×36 pixels) in accordance to MMA guidelines [8]. Mobile advertising of one line of text up to 18 Chinese words is adopted. The font was "New Thin Ming Ti", font size was 12 points. In addition, CyberLink StreamAuthor 3.0 is used to record the process of screen operation during the experiment. A digital video camera recorder (SONY DCR-PC330) is used to record the overall process of experiments and after-experiment questionnaire. In addition, the luminance of experimental lab is 487~611 lux measured by Lutron LX-101 Lux meter.

2.3   Experimental Design

A design of $L_{27}(3^{13})$ orthogonal array experiment is used to collect the comprehension performance. A questionnaire for user interface satisfaction (QUIS) and National Aeronautics and Space Administration Task Load Index (NASA-TLX) task load index [1] will be implemented and analyzed after the experiment. Five design factors are: (1) presentation mode (M) --Rapid Serial Visual Presentation (RSVP), Leading, and Static, (2) presentation position (P)--Top, Bottom, End-of-Search position, (3) presentation speed (S)--80, 170, and 260WPM, (4) format (F)--keyword-by-keyword, phrase-by-phrase, and sentence), and (5) luminance contrast (C)--2/3, 4/5, and 8/9 for mobile text advertisings would be investigated. There are two-hundred forty-three treatment combinations for the five design factors and each factor has 3 levels. Based on L_{27} orthogonal array design, one-ninth of complete factorial design, that is, twenty-seven treatment combinations will be implemented. One of twenty-seven treatment combinations is randomly assigned to a participant.

2.4   Procedure

The experiment session lasted roughly one and half hours. Firstly, participants read instructions displayed on the computer screen. Participants were informed that they had to read the search results and mobile text ads in order to perform a reading comprehension test. A predesigned simulated system including search results and text ad is shown within 30 seconds. Participants were asked to answer five propositions based on the contents of searching results and associated mobile text advertising for previous pages. Twenty search topics are randomly assigned in the experiment. Fill in QUIS and NASA-TLX after completing the reading comprehension test.

3   Results

3.1   Comprehension Performance

Reading comprehension score (RCS) is the number of propositions correctly answered in a given time limit (total=100). Summary statistics of reading comprehension score is shown in Table 1. It indicates Leading Mode has the best reading comprehension (mean of RCS=96.0, SD=4.6), Bottom position has the best reading comprehension (mean of RCS=97.7, SD=1.3), Presentation speed of 170WPM has the best reading comprehension (mean of RCS=96.3, SD=4.2), Keyword-by-Keyword format has the best reading comprehension (mean of RCS=95.8, SD=3.2), and Luminance contrast of 4/5 has the best reading comprehension (mean of RCS=96.1, SD=3.3). Since reality must be reduced to manageable proportions whenever we construct models, only a limited number of factors and their interactions should be included in a regression model. Some evidence of the internal validity of these fitted models can be obtained through an examination of the various model-selection criteria. Table 2 summarizes the fits of the five candidate models. As a consequence of the concerns, Model (3) and Model (5) were eliminated from the consideration of normality about model assumptions. While Models (1), (2), and (4) performed comparably in the R^2, R^2_{Adj}, and Akaike's information criterion (AIC), Models (2) and (4) performs better than Model (1) in R^2, R^2_{Adj}, and AIC. The final selection was based on the principle of parsimony, Model (2) achieves this level of performance with one fewer parameter than Model (4). For this reason, Model (2) is ultimately chosen as the final model. The fitted regression model of RCS is expressed in Equation (1) as following:

$$\hat{\mu} = 89.96 + 0.33M_1 + 3.56M_2 + 6.33P_1 + 6.67P_2 - 3S_1 - 4.67S_2$$
$$+ 1.78C_1 + 2.33C_2 - 0.67M_1 \times P_1 - 1.33M_1 \times P_2 - 1.33M_2 \times P_1$$
$$- 7.33M_2 \times P_2 + 7M_1 \times S_1 + 2.67M_1 \times S_2 \tag{1}$$

where:

$$M_1 = \begin{cases} 1, \text{if Leading} \\ 0, \text{otherwise} \end{cases}, \quad M_2 = \begin{cases} 1, \text{if RSVP} \\ 0, \text{otherwise} \end{cases}$$

$$P_1 = \begin{cases} 1, \text{if Bottom} \\ 0, \text{otherwise} \end{cases}, \quad P_2 = \begin{cases} 1, \text{if End - of - search} \\ 0, \text{otherwise} \end{cases}$$

$$S_1 = \begin{cases} 1, \text{if 170 WPM} \\ 0, \text{otherwise} \end{cases}, S_2 = \begin{cases} 1, \text{if 260 WPM} \\ 0, \text{otherwise} \end{cases}$$

$$F_1 = \begin{cases} 1, \text{if Keyword} \\ 0, \text{otherwise} \end{cases}, F_2 = \begin{cases} 1, \text{if Phrase} \\ 0, \text{otherwise} \end{cases}$$

$$C_1 = \begin{cases} 1, \text{if LC} = 2/3 \\ 0, \text{otherwise} \end{cases}, C_2 = \begin{cases} 1, \text{if LC} = 4/5 \\ 0, \text{otherwise} \end{cases}$$

To understand the meaning of the regression coefficients, M1=1 and M2=0 would be substituted for the presentation of Leading mode in Equation (1), M1=0 and M2=1 for RSVP mode, and M1=0 and M2=0 for Static mode. Similarly, P1=1 and P2=0 would be substituted for the presentation of Bottom position in Equation (1), P1=0 and P2=1 for End-of-Search position, and P1=0 and P2=0 for Top position; S1=1 and S2=0 would be substituted for the speed of 170 WPM, S1=0 and S2=1 for 260 WPM, and S1=0 and S2=0 for 80 WPM; F1=1 and F2=0 would be substituted for the presentation format of keyword-by-keyword, F1=0 and F2=1 for phrase-by-phrase, and F1=0 and F2=0 for sentence-by-sentence; C1=1 and C2=0 would be substituted for the luminance contrast of 2/3, C1=0 and C2=1 for 4/5, and C1=0 and C2=0 for 8/9.

In Table 3, the results indicate the interaction effects of presentation mode and position as well as presentation mode and speed on Ad comprehension are statistically significant. Interaction plot of presentation mode and position (M×P) is illustrated in Fig. 1(a). It indicates that mobile text ad of the Bottom position outperforms than ones of the Top position for all the three presentation modes. The combination of RSVP mode and End-of-Search position has the worst reading comprehension performance. There is only little difference between Leading and static modes on reading comprehension performance. In addition, interaction plot of presentation mode and speed (M×S) is illustrated in Fig. 1(b). It indicates that the combination of Leading mode and 170 WPM has the best reading comprehension performance, however, the combination of RSVP mode and 260 WPM has the worst reading comprehension performance.

Table 1. Summary statistics of reading comprehension score (RCS)

Factor	Level	n	Mean	SD	Min	Q_1	Q_2	Q_3	Max
Mode	RSVP	9	93.8	4.0	88	90	96	97	98
	Leading	9	96.0	4.6	85	96	97	99	100
	Static	9	95.7	3.6	90	93	97	97	100
Position	Top	9	92.0	4.3	85	90	92	93	99
	Bottom	9	97.7	1.3	96	97	98	98	100
	End-of-Search	9	95.8	3.9	89	96	97	97	100
Speed	80WPM	6	95.8	1.5	93	96	96	97	97
	170WPM	6	96.3	4.2	90	92	99	99	100
	260WPM	6	92.5	5.8	85	88	93	98	98
Format	Keyword	9	95.8	3.2	90	93	97	98	100
	Phrase	9	95.2	3.9	89	92	97	97	100
	Sentence	9	94.4	5.2	85	91	96	98	100
Luminance Contrast	2/3	9	95.6	3.2	89	93	97	97	99
	4/5	9	96.1	3.4	90	96	96	98	100
	8/9	9	93.8	5.4	85	90	96	97	100

Table 2. Regression results based on model-selection for RCS

Model	R^2	R^2_{Adj}	AIC	Kolmogorov-Smirnov	P-value
(1)M,P,S,M×P,M×S	0.74	0.52	138.82	0.128	>0.150*
(2)M,P,S,C,M×P,M×S	0.80	0.57	135.39	0.15	0.148*
(3)M,P,S,C,M×P,M×S,M×C	0.86	0.53	135.16	0.17	0.055*
(4)M,P,S,F,C,M×P,M×S	0.82	0.54	136.67	0.15	>0.150*
(5)M,P,S,F,C,M×P,M×S,M×F	0.91	0.59	127.33	0.17	0.044

Note: "*" indicates that Kolmogorov-Smirnov test doesn't violate normality at α=0.05.

Table 3. Analysis of parameter estimates for RCS

Parameter	Estimate	t	P-value
Intercept	89.96	6357.30	<.0001
Leading	0.33	0.04	0.8415
RSVP	3.56	4.55	0.0329*
Bottom	6.33	19.25	<.0001*
End-of-Search	6.67	21.33	<.0001*
170WPM	-3	4.32	0.0377*
260WPM	-4.67	10.45	0.0012*
2/3	1.78	4.55	0.0329*
4/5	2.33	7.84	0.0051*
Leading×Bottom	-0.67	0.11	0.744
Leading×ESR	-1.33	0.43	0.5136
RSVP×Bottom	-1.33	0.43	0.5136
RSVP×ESR	-7.33	12.91	0.0003*
Leading×170WPM	7	11.76	0.0006*
Leading×260WPM	2.67	1.71	0.1914

Note: "*" denotes t reaches statistical significance at $\alpha=0.05$.

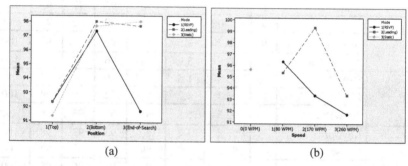

(a)   (b)

Fig. 1. Interaction plots: (a) presentation mode and position (M×P), and (b) presentation mode and speed (M×S) for RCS

3.2   User Interface Satisfaction (UIS)

The quality of user experience is rated using the questionnaire of user interface satisfaction (UIS) based on the Likert's ten-point scale from 1 (extremely dislike) to 10 (extremely like). UIS score is the total of fifteen usability criteria rated after the experiment. Table 4 summarizes the fits of the five candidate models. Model (2) is ultimately chosen as the final model. The fitted regression model of UIS is expressed in Equation (2) as following:

$$\hat{\mu} = 118.67 - 60.22M_1 - 16.44M_2 - 10P_1 + 17P_2 + 4.5S_1 + 11.17S_2 - 6.67F_1 + 4.67F_2$$
$$- 3.67C_1 + 33.33C_2 + 11.67M_1 \times P_1 + 13.67M_1 \times P_2 + 11.67M_2 \times P_1 + 40.33M_2 \times P_2$$
$$+ 51M_1 \times F_1 + 2M_1 \times F_2 + 0.67M_2 \times F_1 - 39.33M_2 \times F_2$$
$$+ 7.67M_1 \times C_1 + 41.33M_1 \times C_2 + 25.67M_2 \times C_1 + 34.67M_2 \times C_2$$

$$(2)$$

It indicates the interaction effects of presentation mode and position, presentation mode and format, as well as presentation mode and luminance contrast are statistically significant on user interface satisfaction.

Interaction plot of presentation mode and position (M×P) is illustrated in Fig. 2(a). It indicates that the combination of Static×End-of-Search position has the highest UIS score; however, the combination of RSVP and End-of-Search position has the lowest UIS score. There is only little difference among Leading mode interacted with three positions. Interaction plot of presentation mode and format (M×F) is illustrated in Fig. 2(b). It indicates the combination of Leading and Keyword format has the highest UIS score; however, the combination of Leading and Sentence format has the lowest UIS score. There are only little differences between RSVP and Static modes with Keyword and Sentence formats. The combinations of Static×Sentence and RSVP×Sentence outperform than one of Leading×Sentence. In addition, the combination of Static×Phrase outperforms than the ones of Leading×Phrase and RSVP×Phrase. Interaction plot of presentation mode and luminance contrast (M×C) is illustrated in Fig. 2(c). It indicates that the combinations of Static×luminance contrast of 2/3 and Static×luminance contrast of 8/9 have the higher UIS out of other combinations. There is only little difference among the combinations of Leading, RSVP and Static modes interacted with luminance contrast of 4/5.

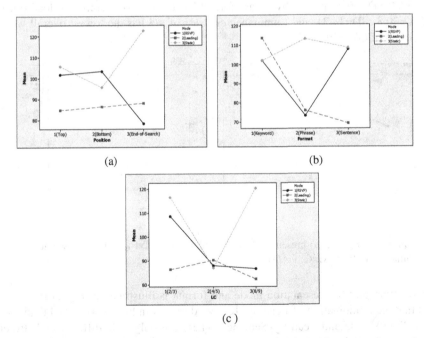

(a)   (b)

(c)

Fig. 2. Interaction plots: (a) presentation mode and position (M×P), (b) presentation mode and format (M×F), and (c) presentation mode and luminance contrast (M×C) for UIS

Table 4. Regression results based on model-selection for UIS

Model	R^2	R^2_{Adj}	C	Kolmogorov-Smirnov	P-value
(1) M,P,F,C,M×P,M×F,M×C	0.92	0.64	218.91	0.149	0.122*
(2)M,P,S,F,C,M×P,M×F, M×C	0.94	0.63	212.59	0.135	>0.150*
(3)M,F,C,M×F,M×C	0.75	0.47	235.97	0.116	>0.150*
(4)M,S,F,C,M×F,M×C	0.78	0.43	236.87	0.085	>0.150*
(5)M,P,F,C,M×P,M×F	0.78	0.43	236.97	0.101	>0.150*

Note: "*" indicates that Kolmogorov-Smirnov test doesn't violate normality at $\alpha=0.05$.

3.3   Overall Workload

NASA-TLX is used to evaluate task load including mental demand, physical demand, temporal demand, performance, effort, and frustration level for each task. The overall workload (OW) is defined as the weighted mean of importance for the pair wise comparison of six subscales. Summary statistics of overall workload is shown in Table 5. It indicates Static Mode has the lowest overall workload (mean of OW=29.3, SD=19.3), Top position has the lowest overall workload (mean of OW=29.1, SD=9.2), Presentation speed of 80WPM has the lowest overall workload (mean of OW=30.4, SD=16.2), phrase-by-phrase format has the lowest overall workload (mean of OW=30.8, SD=14.3), and Luminance contrast of 4/5 has the lowest overall workload (mean of OW=29.2, SD=17.2).

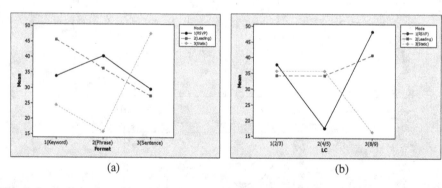

(a)   (b)

Fig. 3. Interaction plots: (a) presentation mode and format (M×F), and (b) presentation mode and luminance contrast (M×C) for OW

Interaction plot of presentation mode and format is illustrated in Fig. 3(a). It indicates that the combination of Leading×Keyword results in higher workload than ones of Leading×Phrase and Leading×Sentence. There are only little differences between Leading and RSVP interacted with Sentence. The combination of Static×Phrase has the lowest overall workload in which it performs best among all combinations. Interaction plot of presentation mode and luminance contrast is illustrated in Fig. 3(b). There is only little difference among the combinations of Leading, RSVP and Static modes interacted with luminance contrast of 2/3, however, Static mode interacted with luminance contrasts of 8/9 and RSVP mode interacted with luminance contrasts of 4/5 have lower workloads out of other combinations. In summary, there is the lowest overall workload for Static×Phrase and inverse, there is highest overall workload for Static×Sentence. In dynamic mobile ad displays, there are the lower overall workloads of Leading×Sentence and RSVP×Sentence than others. The speed of 80 WPM is recommended for dynamic mobile ad displays.

4   Conclusion

Our experiment shows that the empirical study of the position of mobile text ad, moving speed, segmented format, and luminance contrast interacted with three presentation modes affecting significantly comprehension performance, user satisfaction, and overall workload. The main results obtained are the following: (1) interaction effects of presentation mode and position (M×P), and presentation mode and speed (M×S) are important on comprehension performance, (2) interaction effects of presentation mode and position (M×P), presentation mode and format (M×F), and presentation mode and luminance contrast (M×C) are important on user interface satisfaction, (3) interaction effects of presentation mode and format (M×F), and presentation mode and luminance contrast (M×C) are also important on overall workload. The condition of Static mode and End-of-Search position plays an important role on comprehension performance and has the consistently highest user satisfaction. However, the condition of RSVP and End-of-Search position performs the worst comprehension performance and has the lowest user satisfaction. In summary, the interaction effects between text advertising visual structures have to be taken into account for the user-centered usability of mobile text advertising presentation.

Table 5. Summary statistics of overall workload (OW)

Factor	Level	n	Mean	SD	Min	Q_1	Q_2	Q_3	Max
Mode	RSVP	9	34.6	18.2	7.4	20	39.3	42.2	65.2
	Leading	9	36.5	11.7	20.7	23.7	38.5	45.2	51.1
	Static	9	29.3	19.3	9.6	16.3	23.0	37.8	64.4
Position	Top	9	29.1	9.2	17.0	20.7	28.9	37.8	40.7
	Bottom	9	36.8	14.2	16.3	25.9	40.7	45.2	55.6
	End-of-Search	9	34.4	23.5	7.4	14.1	23.7	51.1	65.2
Speed	80WPM	6	30.4	16.2	7.4	20.0	31.9	40.7	50.4
	170WPM	6	43.5	13.0	28.9	34.8	40.4	51.1	65.2
	260WPM	6	32.7	14.4	16.3	20.7	31.5	45.2	51.1
Format	Keyword	9	34.7	18.1	9.6	20.0	37.8	45.2	65.2
	Phrase	9	30.8	14.3	14.1	17.0	28.9	40.7	51.1
	Sentence	9	34.9	18.1	7.4	23.0	38.5	42.2	64.4
Luminance Contrast	2/3	9	36.0	14.0	14.1	23.7	38.5	42.2	55.6
	4/5	9	29.2	17.2	7.4	17.0	25.9	34.8	64.4
	8/9	9	35.1	18.7	9.6	20.7	39.3	50.4	65.2

References

1. Hart, S.G., Staveland, L.E.: Development of NASA-TLX (Task Load Index): Results of Empirical and Theoretical Research. In: Hancock, P.A., Meshkati, N. (eds.) Human Mental Workload, pp. 239–250 (1988)
2. Interactive Ad Bureau, A Mobile Advertising Overview, pp. 4–6 (2008), http://www.iab.net
3. Interactive Ad Bureau, IAB Internet Ad Revenue Report, pp. 8–10 (2008), http://www.iab.net
4. Juola, J.F., Tiritoglu, A., Pleunis, J.: Reading Text Presented on a Small Display. Applied Ergonomics 26(3), 227–229 (1995)
5. Juola, J.F., Ward, N.J., McNamara, T.: Visual Search and Reading of Rapid Serial Presentations of Letter Strings, Words and Text. J. Exper. Psychol:General 111, 208–227 (1982)
6. Laarni, J.: Search for Optimal Methods of Presenting Dynamic Text on Different Types of Screens. In: ACM International Conference Proceeding Series, vol. 31, pp. 219–222 (2002)
7. Lin, Y.L., Chen, Y.W.: Effects of Ad Type, Position, Animation Length, and Exposure Times on Click-Through Rate of Online Advertisings. Computers & Industrial Engineering 57(2), 580–591 (2009)
8. Mobile Marketing Association, Mobile Advertising Guidelines, pp. 3–10 (2008), https://mmaglobal.com/
9. Muter, P.: Interface design and optimization of reading of continuous text. Cognitive Aspects of Electronic Text Processing, 161–180 (1996)
10. Wang, A.H., Fang, J.J., Chen, C.H.: Effects of VDT Leading-Display Design on Visual Performance of Users in Handling Static and Dynamic Display Information Dual-tasks. International Journal of Industrial Ergonomics 32, 93–104 (2003)

Consideration of the Effect of Gesture Exaggeration in Web3D Communication Using 3DAgent

Toshiya Naka[1,2] and Toru Ishida[2]

[1] Panasonic Corporation, 1006 Ohaza-kadoma, Kadoma, Osaka, 571-8501 Japan
[2] Graduate School of Informatics Kyoto University, Yoshida Honmachi, Sakyoku,
Kyoto, 606-8501, Japan
naka.tosiya@jp.panasonic.com, naka.toshiya.25w@st.kyoto-u.ac.jp

Abstract. In this paper, we focused on the characteristic gestures which producing the sense of realism and intimacy in web communication using 3DAgent, and proposed the gesture exaggeration mechanical model which representing the "reservoir (Tame)" or "deciding actions (Kime)" effectively in Anime and Kabuki. By analyzing some tens of gestures including the natural motion and exaggerating one which had same start and end positions, we obtained the following results. The degree of exaggeration of behavior can be expressed mechanically by the integral value of the joint torque. The ratio of the torque value GER between the portion containing the exaggerated behavior and other position has value within the certain range from 0.4 to 0.6. This value can be used as an indicator in determining the good balanced gesture exaggeration. Moreover, we found that the result could also be seen in the case of exaggeration gestures used effectively such as the speech and presentation of famous persons, so we could determine the gesture exaggeration by GER.

Keywords: CG Agent, Nonverbal communication, Gesture, Interaction.

1 Introduction

According to the rapidly development of internet technologies, many new web services using the variety of multi-modal technologies are born and they rapidly go into commodity. The advantages for users using these new web communication tools are freed from the hassle by reducing physical and spatial distance. On the other hand, it becomes obvious problem of the digital divide which including the inability to understand the manners of operation or anonymity and privacy are not strictly protected. Under these background, to avoid the problem of privacy and anonymity by mediating agents, web3D communication using humanoid CG agent with real gestures, facial expressions and even has voices has been proposed shown in figure 1 as the means of easy and natural communication. It has been recognized that they had usefulness for the educational uses, tutoring or guide and animation [1]. In order to spread and further improve the quality of communication by the 3DAgent, it is important to reproduce actuality such as the sense of intimacy and realism through sharing of the facilities between user and 3DAgent, than the reality on the appearance

S. Yamamoto (Ed.): HIMI/HCII 2013, Part III, LNCS 8018, pp. 511–520, 2013.

and behavior such as facial expression. As the example in real world, it is often seen the case that Disney characters and pantomime who can increase the presence by the motion with exaggeration and strong emphasis to achieve the sharing the virtual space with 3DAgent, than to faithfully reproduce the natural movement. In this paper, we focused on the characteristic gestures which enhancing actuality in communication using 3DAgent and proposed a dynamic model of gesture exaggeration which used effectively such as Anime and Kabuki's "deciding action (called Kime)" or "reservoir (called Tame)". We also verified the similarity with gesture exaggeration which used effectively in the speech and presentations of attracting many people.

2   Related Works

With respect to the previous research on the communication between human and agents, it has been the long history in the field of psychology about the role of non-verbal information such as gestures and facial expressions, and it well known that they are much more important than verbal information [2, 3]. The previous studies on the representation of the body language, Nishida et al studied that the higher expression of emotion was very significant factor and the simply reproduction of the human behavior and facial expressions by capturing were not enough [4] and Laban studied for the systematic classification of the quantitative physical characteristics of the dance [5]. However many psychological researches were using based on the subjective evaluation approaches and few cases were classified in the systematic manner to evaluate the effect of the non-verbal mechanism quantitatively. On the other hand, there was the areas of sports biomechanics and kinematics where were many researches of quantitative analysis of human behavior. Koike et al estimated the trajectory of motion of the upper arm with joint torque from EMG changes in using neural networks [6]. And Oyama et al analyzed the mechanism of motion control from the comparison between the predicted value and the locus of movement of the hand movement between two points into the model predictive and feedback control theory [7]. But in previous works in this field were not intended for the target of communication purposes but they were limited for specific sports. There were studies on the effect of CG agents whose gestures in web communication such as Nakano et al assigned according to the sentence of conversation, such as emotion, multiple gestures and nods [9]. And Cassell defined the auto generated gesture of CG agents according to the context of the conversation [10]. We also found with respect to the characteristic gesture of certain trends that there was the advantage which was given to the storage of the gestures, and the superiority of interests and good feeling, but we did not find the formulation of such rules completely [11]. In this paper, we will discuss the mechanism by analyzing exaggerated gestures in web3D communication.

3   Analysis of Gesture Exaggeration

In the communication with 3DAgent, the important factors which enhance the sense of intimacy and realism for users are the reproduction of emotional facial expressions and posture or desire and emotional changes which expressed by gestures. For example in the performance such as Kabuki, dance and pantomime which using the purpose of directing the climax scenes, some exaggerating gestures are frequently used effectively such as "best pose (called Mie)" , "deciding pose (called Kime)" or "reservoir (called Tame)". Furthermore, in the speech of B. Obama and S. Jobs as the techniques of conversation and persuasion which attracting attention recently, some behaviors such as spreading their hands over exaggerated or having "reservoir pose (Tame)" when emphasizing to point some object are used effectively. We call these special gestures by "gesture exaggeration" which is used to enhance users to transform the information having difficulty only by the verbal communication and we analyzed the effect of its mechanism by using the proposed model shown in figure 2.

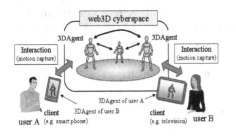 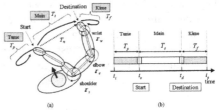

Fig. 1. Web3D communication using 3DAgents

Fig. 2. Mechanical gesture exaggeration model

3.1   Definition of Gesture Exaggeration

In the communication using 3DAgent with the special gestures, we analyzed by the following approaches. In the first step, we found the rule of exaggeration by collecting some tens of gestures which had same start and end positions, and compared the relevance of the physical quantity and the degree of exaggeration. In the next step, we verified the similarity between its rules using the same manner of analyzing the exaggerating gestures used effectively in the speech and presentation. The mechanical model of gesture exaggeration is shown in figure 2. Figure 2-a shows the motion of moving to destination from the start position of the right hand and figure 2-b shows the relationship with the motion in the time domain. In this model, each gesture T_p and T_f is the motion to exaggerate the behavior applied to before the starting position and after the target position of the desired action T_s. We assume that T_s has different path from the trajectory of the motion as natural path T_n. In the communication, this exaggerated gestures T_p has very significant role and the behavior of "reservoir pose (Tame)" of such as Kabuki and speech, T_f is used as the motion of "deciding pose (Kime)", T_s changes both its trajectory and moving speed, too.

3.2   Analysis of Gesture Exaggeration

We constructed the 3DAgent's gesture evaluation system in order to quantitatively analyze the gesture exaggeration [11], and we showed the main components of the evaluating system in figure 3. In figure 3, we will track the gesture to evaluate and convert the time series data of each joint angle of the skeletal model. Within the system, we can quantify the gestures using the evaluating function and dynamics analysis algorithm such as kinetics. We calculate the torque fluctuation for each joint using the data of 3DAgents joint angle data and the body parameters.

Data Structure of Gesture Exaggeration. In this system, we defined the origin O_w of the world coordinate system of 3DAgents hierarchy as shown in figure 4, and set the *humanoid root* as the top level hierarchy in the base of spine joint. The lower layer was followed by shoulder, elbow and wrist. Shoulder joint has three degrees of freedom $\theta_5, \theta_6, \theta_7$, and each wrist and elbow having two degrees of freedom θ_8, θ_9 and θ_{10}, θ_{11} respectively. Each joints gesture of 3DAgent was represented by $\theta(t)$ in time series of the rotational angle with the local coordinate system xyz. Figure 4-a shows an example of shoulder joint angle data and velocity, and $\theta(t)$ shows (dashed line) with the measured angular velocity (axis y) (solid line). In figure 4-b, the hatched "T_p reservoir" is corresponding to the motion of "T_f (deciding pose)" of the mechanical model of exaggerated gesture which mentioned in chapter 3.

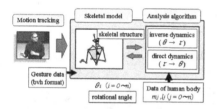

Fig. 3. Overall structure of evaluation system of gesture exaggeration

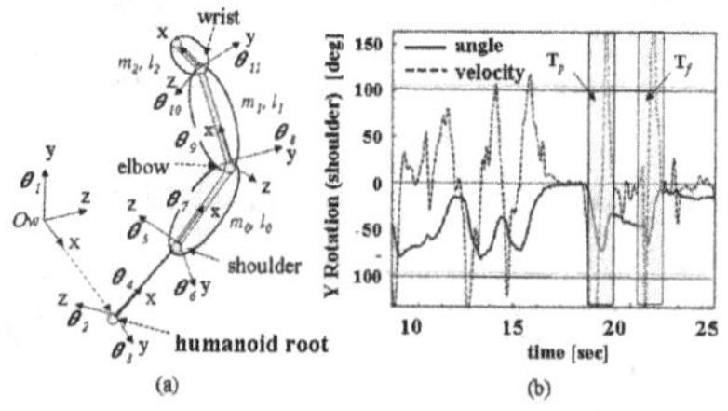

Fig. 4. Skeletal structure of left arm and rotational data with its velocity

Joint Torque of Gesture Exaggeration. We obtained joint torque τ by using joint angle θ of link structure in figure 2 as shown in equation 1. The general dynamic model was defined by equation 1 and we used *Lagrange function* to analysis of each torque calculation detailed below.

$$\tau = M(\theta)\,\theta'' + C(\theta, \theta')\,\theta' + g(\theta) \tag{1}$$

In this equation θ is time series data of $[\theta_1, \theta_2, \cdots \theta_{11}]$ and M shows *Inertia matrix*, C shows *Coriolis force*, g is *gravity term*, and θ' and θ'' are *angular velocity* and *acceleration* of each joint. In addition, we use the total amount of torque value T_n which is obtained by integrating from t_s of start time through t_e, the sum of squares of total time derivative of torque applied to each joint defined by equation 2.

$$T_n = \int_{ts}^{te} \left\{ (d\tau\,{}^x/_{dt})^2 + (d\tau\,{}^y/_{dt})^2 + (d\tau\,{}^w/_{dt})^2 \right\} dt \tag{2}$$

Calculating the torque value by *Lagrange method* is defined as follows.

   Step-1: We define the generalized coordinates $(i = 0 \sim n)$ θ_i of mechanical joint angles of the model structure shown in figure 3.

Step-2: *Lagrange function L* of each link structure is given by the following equation 3.

$$L = \sum_{0 \le i \le n} \{ (\text{Kinetic energy of link } i) - (\text{Potential energy of link } i) \} \quad (3)$$

Step-3: *Lagrange equation* of motion Qi is given by the following equation 4.

$$Q_i = \frac{d}{dt}\left(\frac{\partial L}{\partial \theta'_i}\right) - \frac{\partial L}{\partial \theta_i} \qquad \text{where} \quad i = 0 \sim n \quad (4)$$

Equation of motion Qi can be written in the following non-linear ordinary differential equations 5 (the general formula is given by equation 3).

$$Q_i = \sum_{j=i}^{n}\sum_{k=0}^{j} trace\left[\frac{\partial T_j}{\partial \theta_k} J_j \frac{\partial T_j}{\partial \theta_i}\right]\ddot{\theta}_k + \sum_{j=i}^{n}\sum_{k=0}^{j}\sum_{l=0}^{j} trace\left[\frac{\partial_2 T_j}{\partial \theta_k \partial \theta_l} J_j \frac{\partial T_j}{\partial \theta_i}\right]\dot{\theta}_k \dot{\theta}_i - \sum_{j=i}^{n} m_j g^T \frac{\partial T_j}{\partial \theta_i} S_j$$

$$\text{where} \quad i = 0 \sim n \quad (5)$$

Qi becomes torque τ_i in case of rotational motion, the first term of the right side shows the term of angular velocity, the second term is section of *centrifugal force*, and third term is term related to *Coriolis force* and *gravity*. T_j is the coordinate transformation matrix to convert the world coordinates of the local coordinate system j-th joint. J_i is the *inertia tensor* of the second link j, m_i is the mass of the i-th link. T is the *gravity vector*, and S_j denotes the *position vector* of center of mass of the second link j.

Step-4: We approximate by the elliptic cylinder of each link as Ji, and used for a constant inertia matrix density distribution. However, the center of gravity is located at the origin of the length of elliptic cylinder 2d, and x-axis located in the length direction y and z axis is in a direction perpendicular. Tensor inertia J of the link is given by equation 3-6 below.

$$J = \begin{bmatrix} d^2 m/3 & 0 & 0 & d/2 \\ 0 & a^2 m/2 & 0 & 0 \\ 0 & 0 & b^2 m/2 & 0 \\ d/2 & 0 & 0 & 1 \end{bmatrix} \quad (6)$$

4   Experiments and Results

We performed the experiments with the following approach for the purpose of quantitative analysis of the effects of exaggerated gestures in communication with 3DAgent described in section 3.

4.1   Experimental Conditions and Exaggerated Gesture Classification

Firstly, we gathered and analyzed the special gestures of exaggeration such as Kabuki, Anime and effectively used gestures such as speech and presentation in the real world from the viewpoint of characteristics and frequency which each gesture was used. We selected each gesture showing an example of conversation techniques and instruction. We showed some example gestures in figure 5 [11].

1. Having the same start and end position, these motions move six directions to the inward and outward of the body, and up and down or back and forth around shoulder joint with upper arm (Totally 18 actions showed in figure 5-i, ii and iii), including both exaggerated behavior such as "deciding pose" or "reservoir".
2. In Kabuki's, theaters and entertainments gestures, exaggerating and/or deformed pose for "deciding pose called Kime which is using left hand and holding motion on bending elbow called "Nage Mie". (Totally seven actions such as figure 5-iv).
3. Gestures of upper arms such as "Taikyoku Ken" and Karate pose which are accompanied with "gradual reservoir" (Totally five actions). Especially including exaggerated behavior with "decided (called Kime)" before or after main motion.
4. Exaggeration gestures used effectively in the speech of S. Jobs and B. Obama. They were selected in order to verify the similarity between motions of above listed gestures and totally seven gestures showed in figure 5-v.

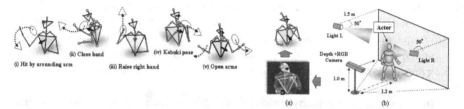

Fig. 5. Examples of the exaggerating gestures   **Fig. 6.** Motion tracking system

We showed the conditions of tracking gestures which were used in our experiment in figure 6. In the following experiments, we asked actors to reproduce each gesture exaggeration and tracked each action by using the video cameras which have the function of depth value, and the resolution of capturing images had 640 × 480 pixels and 30 frames/sec frame rate. We have converted to three dimensional $\theta(t)$ of joint angle data of skeletal structure from captured moving images [11].

4.2   Analysis of Gesture Exaggeration

In the first step, we got the results that have been analyzed for the exaggerated gesture of type A which classifyed in 4.1 by adding "T_f deciding pose" and "T_p reservoir pose" in the dynamic model of figure 2 described in section 3. The orbit T_s slightly changed both in speed and trajectory. Using the torque value of each joint which obtained by equation 3-1, we verified to compare with natural gesture and exaggerated one which had same strating position and destination. We showed in figure 7, an example of actual measurement of upper arm (joint torque value of the motion of group A) which described in section 4.1. In figure 7-a, the first half of about five to seventeen seconds is the gesture moving arm in the horizontal right direction of standing position naturally, and extend forward by moving the left (inside the body) at the end. It shows the smooth torque variation when the series of motion which carried out naturally. Further, in order to compare this motion, the action between about 18 to 32 seconds showed the torque variation obtained from equation 3-1, which has same start and target position but has exaggerated gestures T_p and (gesture exaggeration) T_f before and after them intentionally. In addition, in the following next 18 to 20 seconds which is hatched gray in figure 7-a, it has been measured that torque of exaggerated action of "T_p reservoir pose" and "T_f deciding pose" and torque of T_s which changed due to the movement of the right direction. Furthermore, after changing the torque of T_s which gesture of left direction is measured in about 29 to 30 seconds. The torque value associated with the gesture exaggeration "T_f decided pose" measured in about 30 to 32 seconds. Whereas the integral values of torque of these two is 1123.1 Nm of natural gesture, the exaggerated behavior is about three times 3813.5 Nm. The torque of the upper arm of another exaggerated behavior is shown in figure 6-b which moving right arm to right beside in horizontal direction, stretching before then and spreading his hands of exaggareting gesture "T_f deciding pose" with natural standing position. About seven to nine seconds of hatched portion shows the torque which generated by exaggerated gesture "T_p reservoir pose". And the torque value when open arms in 9 to 14 seconds which associated with the moiton of exaggeration is measured "T_f deciding". And the change in torque of "T_f deciding" to extend the right arm forward action is shown in 18 to 28 seconds of "T_p reservoir" action.

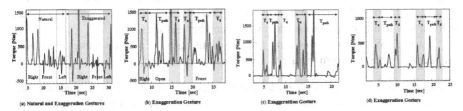

Fig. 7. An example of torque valiation of an exaggeration gesture

The integrated torque value of each exaggerated gesture was 1114.1 Nm and 1275.0 Nm each, T_f became 687.9 Nm and T_a was 934.4 Nm. These results would be occurred from the difference in the degree of emphasis of exaggeration. We also analyzed the motions with both group B and C which mentioned 4.1 and we showed in figure 7-c the torque values of exaggerated gesture of most typical twisting action of Kabuki's "best looking (Mime)" which deciding pose with right hand twist in front of the body. Fiqure 7 shows an example of joint torque of the arm. There is the torque of exaggerated gesture "T_p reservoir pose" about five to six seconds which hatched portion in this figure. And the torque change of the motion which putting forward right hand measured about seven to eight seconds. Furthermore occurred in about eight to nine seconds, the change of torque twist while stretching before "T_f deciding". On the other hand, showed the torque value of exaggerated behavior of another Kabuki's "best looking" after 12 seconds that had "T_p reservoir" for about 12 to 15 seconds near the body with both hands. and about after 15 to 18 seconds was the torque value of exaggerated motion to extend the arm. It was shown the similar trend in other motions which were used in our experiment that the characteristics of integratiing value and characteristic of the joints torque in time domain as shown in figure 7. This tendency to increase both the integral value and the maximum value of the torque was observed in natural gestures. We considered that it was happened to be chosen for the experimental gestures with the emphasis on continuity and good balance. Integrated value of the torque of exaggerating gestures like "T_f decided (Kime)" and "T_p reservoir (Tame)" of two types of figure 7-c became 1078.7 Nm of T_p , 1437.6 Nm of T_f and T_f was 2524.1 Nm.

From these experiments, we found that the exaggeration gestures of "T_f deciding pose" and "T_p reservoir pose" significantly reflected in the difference of the integral values of torque than the difference of each time interval (time between start time t_s and end time t_e) . In addition, there was the tendency to increase the integral value of torque proportionately of exaggerated gesture which putting more strong force as "best looking (Mie)". Figure 7-c showed the example of group C which we analyzed the motion of both arms in Taikyokuken. Compared with other gesture exaggeration, figure7-d was an example that had the characteristics of slow (angular velocity) movement of exaggeration, and including the motion of exaggeration of "decided pose (Kime)" before and after the main action. In the figure 7-d, the hached in gray portion was the moving parts of exaggeration "T_f deciding" and "T_p reservoir". We found that the absolute amount of torque was closely related with the angular velocity (angular acceleration) in the mechanical model of exaggerated gesture described in 4.1 and the ratio of the motion betwwen exaggerating part of T_p , T_f and T_s and rest of them was maintained close tendency with another gestures.

Study 1. We got the following findings with respect to quantitative analysis of exaggerated behavior from the above mentioned experimental results:

— The degree of exaggeration used in our experiment could be compared with the integral value of the torque between them rather than the total time of motion between target position t_e and the starting position t_s of the dynamic model described in Section 4.1. This tendency increased in proportion to the degree of exaggeration. It was also possible to compare the degree of exaggeration in the ratio of integral value of T_f , T_p and exaggerated motion T_s.
— For the exaggerated operation group A to C which were classified in 4.1, there was a similar trend in the joint torque variation and high correlation with the degree of operation of the torque integral value of exaggerated gesture.

4.3   Effective Exaggerated Gestures in Speech

In this section, we examined as the experiment in step two to find the similarity with the exaggeration models described so far (the analysis results of the gesture exaggeration in 4.2) and the gestures which was used effectively such as speech and presentation that was classification group D described in section 4.1.

Similarity with exaggerated gestures in speech. From the experimental results mentioned in 4.2, we found that there was the higher correlation with integral values of joint torque of "reservoir T_p" or "T_f decided" and parts of T_s. We have discussed the quantitative relationships such as the ratio and balance of them. The total torque of the gestures exaggeration would increase the degree of exaggeration by adding "T_f deciding pose" or "T_p reservoir", which reflecting the strong intention of user. In addition, the degree of exaggeration could be expressed with the value of the integral torque, and we will propose the index *GER* (Gesture Exaggeration Ratio) shown in equation 7. In the equation 7 each T_p, T_f and T_s is the integral value of the calculated torque of exaggerated gesture which determined by the equation 2, and W is the weighting factor. Generally speaking the ratio of the integrated value of the torque of the logarithm of equation 2 is smaller, the torque value of the desired behavior of T_p and T_f is greater. Otherwise we can say that exaggerated T_s is smaller, as the greater the value of *GER*.

$$GER = - W \log_2 \left[\frac{Ts}{Tp + Tf} \right] \qquad (7)$$

Study 2. We showed in figure 9, the horizontal axis was the total time from the start to destination of each motion and we put the value of *GER* for all exaggerated motions which classified in chapter 4.1 in the vertical axis. The propotional factor of fiqure 9 was 3.6. In addition, there was the similar gestures in accordance with the rules shown in figure 9, ▲ mark showed with respect to the gesture exaggeration used effectively in speech and presentation of famous persons which classified group D. The ratio of the logarithm of *GER* of equation 7 showed the values within the range of 0.4 to 0.6. This range was an indicator that determined the motion of well balanced exaggeration.

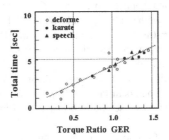

Fig. 8. Relationship between GER and total time of exaggerating gestures

5   Conclusion

In this paper, we focused on the characteristic exaggerated gestures of 3DAgents in web communication and validate the rule of the transmission of the information. And we have examined the similarity of the motions of exaggeration which used effectively in speech of attracting many audiences. The final goal of our study will find new rules to analyze the key factors which producing a sense of intimacy and realism in web communications by 3DAgent. As the initial approach, we proposed the mechanical model of exaggerating motion which used effectively such as Anime and

Kabukis characteristic gestures as "deciding (Kime)" or "reservoir (Tame)". Using the proposed model and collecting some tens of exaggerated gestures which have same start and end positions, we evaluated them by comparing with natural motions. We could represent the degree of exaggeration of motion by the integral value of the mechanical joint torque. Also the *GER* ratio of torque values of the motion between including exaggeration such as "deciding (Kime)" or "reservoir (Tame) " and other motions were within the certain range from 0.4 to 0.6 which regardless of the total time of motion, and we found it could be an indicator to determine the well balanced exaggerating gesture. Furthermore, this result could be confirmed in the exaggerated gestures used effectively in speech and presentation by the famous persons and determined the exaggeration by using *GER* values. In our consideration, it was possible to verify the regularity of the certain characteristic about the exaggerated gestures. In the future, it is necessary to validate the model of averaged balancing exaggeration gestures by increasing the parameter type and motions.

References

1. Ishizuka, M.: Interface / Media by a lifelike agents. PSJL 48(3), 257–263 (2007)
2. Kanda, T., Miyashita, T., Osada, T., Haikawa, Y., Ishiguro, H.: Analysis of Humanoid Appearances in Human-robot Interaction. IEEE Transactions on Robotics 24(3), 725–735 (2008)
3. Reeves, B., Nass, C.: The Media Equation: How People Treat Computers, Television and New Media Like Real People and Places. University of Chicago Press (1996)
4. Nishida, T., Jain, L., Faucher, C. (eds.): Modelling Machine Emotions for Realizing Intelligence: Foundations and Applications. SIST. Springer (2010)
5. Laban, R.V.: Mastery of Movement. Princeton Book Co. Pub. (1988)
6. Koike, Y., Kawato, M.: Estimation of Arm Posture in 3D Space from Surface EMG Signals using a Neural Network Model. IEICE Transactions on Information and Systems E-77D(4), 368–375 (1994)
7. Oyama, T., Uno, Y.: Estimation of a Human Planned Trajectory from a Measured Trajectory. Systems and Computers in Japan 37(9), 1–11 (2006)
8. Garrett, W., Kirkendall, D.: Exercise and Sport Science. Lippincott Williams & Wilkins (2000)
9. Nakano, A., Hoshino, J.: Composite Conversation Gesture Synthesis using Layered Planning. Systems and Computers in Japan 38(10), 58–68 (2007)
10. Cassell, J., Pelachaud, C., Badler, N., Steedman, M., Achorn, B., Becket, T., Douville, B., Prevost, S., Stone, M.: Animated Conversation: Rule-Based Generation of Facial Expression, Gesture and Spoken Intonation for Multiple Conversational Agents. In: Proceedings of SIGGRAPH, pp. 413–420 (1994)
11. Naka, T., Ishida, T.: Web-based nonverbal communication interface using 3DAgents with natural gestures. In: Jacko, J.A. (ed.) HCII 2011, Part II. LNCS, vol. 6762, pp. 565–574. Springer, Heidelberg (2011)

The Relationship between *Kansei* Scale for Uniqueness of Products and Purchase Motivation

Yusuke Ohta and Keiko Kasamatsu

Department of Industrial Art, Graduate School of System Design,
Tokyo Metropolitan University, Tokyo, Japan
{ota-yusuke,kasamatu}@sd.tmu.ac.jp

Abstract. The purpose of this study was to compose *Kansei* Scale on Uniqueness Products (KSUP) which evaluates the uniqueness of products, and to clarify relations between uniqueness of products and the consumer's purchase motivation. The evaluated products were humidifiers. We examined *Kansei* elements consisted uniqueness of humidifier, and relationships between *Kansei* elements of uniqueness and purchase motivation. As the result of present study, it was indicated suggested that the KSUP on humidifier consisted of *"Feeling of nondaily life"* and *"Reminiscent"*. In addition, *"Feeling of nondaily life"* showed a tendency to have a high positive correlation with purchase motivation than *"Reminiscent"*. It is expected that the KSUP will become one of the most effective indexes used in product development and that it will help designers develop more attractive products that are in line with consumer needs.

Keywords: *Kansei,* Uniqueness, Purchase motivation, Product design.

1 Background

Kano (1984) proposed the concepts of the "must-be quality" and "attractive quality." In order to increase the attractive quality of a product, it is necessary to include a Kansei value in the product. It is possible to offer a better product to consumer by incorporating elements that consumer feel are attractive and by producing products that are reviewed highly by them.

The appearance of a product is one of the factors that determine its attractiveness; attractiveness has a significant impact on consumers. If the appearance of a product is characteristic or unique, it is easy to catch the attention of the consumer, and thus, he/she becomes interested in the product. The AIDMA (Attention, Interest, Desire, Memory, and Action) model shows the process involved in human consumption behavior. The appearance of products has an influence on "Attention" and "Interest" as per the AIDMA model. Therefore, it is desirable that the appearance is unique.

The Kansei elements that are related to the uniqueness of products and the scale on the uniqueness of products aid in the design of an attractive product.

Besemer & O'Quin (1986) investigated product creativity and developed the Creative Product Semantic Scale (CPSS), based on the Creative Product Analysis

S. Yamamoto (Ed.): HIMI/HCII 2013, Part III, LNCS 8018, pp. 521–530, 2013.
© Springer-Verlag Berlin Heidelberg 2013

Matrix (CPAM theory) (Besemer & Treffinger, 1981). The validity of CPSS was verified by studying various products, such as T-shirts (Besemer & O'Quin, 1986), chairs (Besemer & O'Quin, 1999), and livingware (Besemer & O'Quin, 1989). Besemer (2000) stated that CPSS is available to predict the purchase of the product.

Ohta & Kasamatsu (2012) proposed scale for measuring the uniqueness of products, called the "Kansei Scale for Uniqueness of Products" (KSUP). Ohta & Kasamatsu extracted Kansei elements related to the uniqueness of products and derived five factors. They are as follows: "Feeling of non-daily life", "Captivated", "Cutting-edge", "Legerity", and "Interesting & Suggestive". Particularly, it was assumed that uniqueness of home electronics was influenced by "Feeling of non-daily life" and "Captivated".

Attention and interest as per the AIDMA model were influenced by the uniqueness of the products. Additionally, uniqueness affects "action." Therefore, using the KSUP in the product development leads to an increase in the attractiveness of the product and facilitates the consumer's purchase motivation.

2   Purpose

The purpose of this study was to compose *Kansei* Scale on Uniqueness Products (KSUP) for the humidifier which evaluates the uniqueness of products, and to clarify relations between uniqueness of products and the consumer's purchase motivation. We examined *Kansei* elements consisted uniqueness of humidifier, and relationships between *Kansei* elements of uniqueness and the reason of purchase motivation.

3   Experimental Method

The evaluated products were five types of humidifiers (H1~H5). These products were released in the past ten years, and the choice was made in such a way that there was no bias in shape, color, and year of release. The features of the five humidifiers were

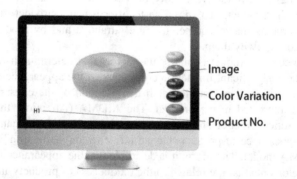

Fig. 1. Sample of PC view

unified on vaporizer type, and its size was up to 16.5 square meters. The images of products were presented on a 24-inch display screen (Fig.1).

Fifty-one participants (Average: 23.5 ages, SD: 1.69 ages) rated the evaluation items for each image on the 7-point scale using Semantic Difference (SD) Method. There were 31 evaluation items broken down as: 14 items extracted by brainstorming about "uniqueness," 13 items selected according to the CPSS of the "Novelty" dimension, 12 items regarding purchase motivation, and 1 item with the comprehensive evaluation of "Unique." Table 1 shows 31 evaluation items.

Table 1. 31 evaluation items

Evaluation Items			
Want to show	— Want to conceal	Fresh	— Overused
Fine	— Coarse	Novel	— Predictable
Reminiscent	— Non-Reminiscent	Unusual	— Usual
Individual	— Public	Original	— Commonplace
Good	— Bad	Startling	— Stale
Delicate	— Rugged	Astonishing	— Commonplace
Interesting	— Boring	Astounding	— Common
Attractive	— Unattractive	Unexpected	— Expected
Well-crafted	— Crude	Trendsetting	— Warmed over
Eccentric	— Conventional	Revolutionary	— Average
New	— Old	Radical	— Old hat
Distinctive	— Ordinary	Want to buy	— Not want to buy
Surprising	— Customary	Want to use	— Not want to use
Shocking	— Ordinary	Easy to use	— Hard to use
Exciting	— Dull	UNIQUE	— Non-UNIQUE
Zippy	— Bland		

The participants were made to give presence or absence of humidifier, the reasons for their evaluations of "uniqueness", determine whether the product was known, and 13 purchase motivation items of the reason for "Want to buy". Participants rated the evaluation items for each items on the 7-point scale (from -3 to 3). Table 2 shows 13 reasons of purchase motivation items.

Table 2. 13 reasons of purchase motivation items

Evaluation Items	
High performance	Get sympathy with others and interest from others
Good design	Keep not get bored
Not drawn much attention	Good texture and material
Look high-class	Have an impact
New feature included	Can express the way I am
Other people not have much	Can express myself in the future
Match my room interior	

4   Results

4.1   Factor Analysis

Factor analysis by maximum likelihood method (promax method) was used to identify a sensitivity factor about "UNIQUE" of humidifier. Object variable were selected 26 items that were excepted "UNIQUE", "Attractive", "Want to buy", "Easy to use ", "Want to use" from the inside of 31 items. As the result, 3 factors were obtained, cumulative contribution ratio was about 74.8 %. Table 3 shows factor loadings.

Factor 1 included 15 items of "Unique", "Novel", "Astonishing" and so on. Factor 2 included 10 items of "Radical", "Want to show", "Good" and so on. Factor 3 included 1 item of "Reminiscent". From the above, 3 Factor were given meaning names, Factor 1: *"Feeling of non-daily life"*, Factor 2: *"Smartness & Cutting-edge"*, Factor 3: *"Reminiscent"*.

Table 3. Result of factor analysis

		Factor loading		
Feeling of nondaily life	Unique	.913	.706	.696
	Novel	.911	.639	.587
	Astonishing	.904	.609	.589
	Individual	.885	.663	.752
	Surprising	.880	.549	.409
	Unusual	.876	.626	.679
	Original	.875	.692	.678
	Shocking	.874	.613	.577
	Unexpected	.864	.495	.510
	Interesting	.861	.725	.447
	Eccentric	.851	.650	.743
	Astounding	.837	.641	.549
	Revolutionary	.834	.692	.730
	Startling	.817	.501	.488
	Exciting	.812	.778	.493
Smartness & Cutting-edge	Radical	.789	.841	.400
	Want to show	.727	.824	.342
	Good	.561	.815	.240
	Well-crafted	.584	.805	.331
	Trendsetting	.786	.803	.634
	New	.784	.801	.368
	Fresh	.788	.793	.383
	Fine	.434	.748	.290
	Delicate	.366	.704	.248
	Zippy	.103	.174	.087
Reminiscent	Reminiscent	.147	.060	.264
Cumulative contribution ratio (%)		62.004	70.499	74.818

4.2   Multiple Regression Analysis

Multiple regression analysis to identify a sensitivity factor about "UNIQUE" of humidifier by 3 factors what were obtained using factor analysis. The multi collinearity by VIF was not confirmed. Multiple regression analysis using the step wise method was conducted. The dependent variable was "UNIQUE", and independent variable was 3 factor *"Feeling of nondaily life"*, *"Smartness & Cutting-edge"*, *"Reminiscent"*. As a result, it was provided below a multiple regression equation (1).

Uniqueness = 0.333 + *"Feeling of nondaily life"* × 1.289 + *"Reminiscent"* × 0.524

$$(R^2 = 0.791) \qquad (1)$$

KSUP-score for five products were calculated using equation (1). As the results, each score for five products were below;
    H1:2.05, H2:0.45, H3:-0.27, H4:0.44, H5:-0.98.

4. 3   *Kansei* Scale on Uniqueness for Five Humidifiers

Figure 2 shows distribution map on five products by factor score of factor analysis. The x axis was set to the factor score of *"Feeling of nondaily life"*, and the y axis was set to the factor score of *"Reminiscent"*. The factor score of both *"Feeling of nondaily life"* and *"Reminiscent"* on H1 were the highest of other products. The factor score of *"Feeling of nondaily life"* on H2 was similar to it on H4, although the factor score of *"Reminiscent"* on H2 was higher than it on H4. The factor score of *"Reminiscent"* on H3 was similar to it on H2, although the factor score of *"Feeling of nondaily life"* on H3 was lower than it on H2 and H4. The factor score of both *"Feeling of nondaily life"* and *"Reminiscent"* on H5 were the lowest of other products.

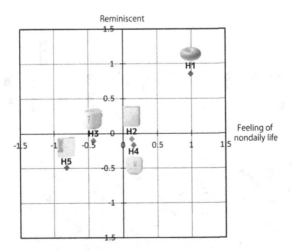

Fig. 2. Distribution map on five humidifiers by KSUP

4. 4   Relationships between Uniqueness and Consumer's Purchase Motivation

We examined the relationships between an item score of "Want to buy" and uniqueness by *"Feeling of nondaily life"* and *"Reminiscent"*. The x axis was set to the factor score of *"Feeling of nondaily life"* (Fig. 3(a)) and *"Reminiscent"* (Fig. 3(b)). The y axis was an item score of "Want to buy". The products with high *"Feeling of nondaily life"* or *"Reminiscent"* was a trend towards higher ratings for "Want to buy". However, this tendency is clearly *"Feeling of nondaily life"* than *"Reminiscent"*.

Then, the correlation coefficient among "UNIQUE", "Attractive" and "Want to buy" was calculated on five products. There were significant high correlation coefficient between "Attractive" and "Want to buy" (r=.753), and between "UNIQUE" and "Attractive" (r=.691).

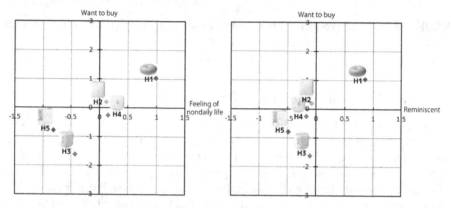

(a) *"Feeling of nondaily life"* and   "Want to buy"   (b) *"Reminiscent"* and   "Want to buy"

Fig. 3. Uniqueness and "Want to buy"

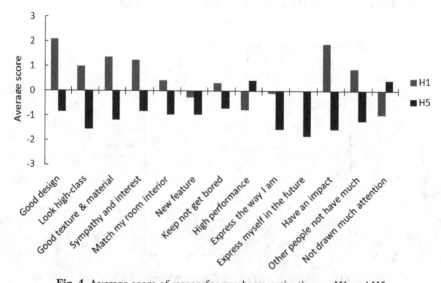

Fig. 4. Average score of reason for purchase motivation on H1 and H5

Next, we examined the relationship between purchase motivation and reason for purchase motivation on high and low uniqueness score of humidifier. Figure 4 shows average score of reason for purchase motivation items on H1 and H5. H1 was focused on as high humidifier of uniqueness, and H5 was as low. H1 with high evaluation score of uniqueness was also high "Want to buy" score. "Good design", "Have an impact", "Good texture and material", "Get sympathy with others and interest from others" were obtained high evaluation as reason of purchase motivation items. In contrast, H5 with low evaluation score of uniqueness was also low "Want to buy" score. "Look high-class", "Can express myself in the future", "Can express the way I am", "Have an impact" were obtained low evaluation as reason for purchase motivation items.

5   Discussion

The *Kansei* elements which consisted uniqueness of humidifier were examined by factor analysis.   As the result of analysis, it was considered that the KSUP on humidifier was consisted of *"Feeling of nondaily life"* and *"Reminiscent"*. This result was different from some results of Ohta and Kasamatsu's (2012); uniqueness scale of home electronic products was constituted of *"Feeling of nondaily life"* and "Smartness". The appearance reminiscent of something was strongly related to uniqueness than "Smartness" in the humidifier. Comparing the coefficients of multiple regression equation, the coefficient of *"Feeling of nondaily life"* was larger than it of *"Reminiscent"*. Therefore, it was indicated that uniqueness of humidifier was strongly influenced by *"Feeling of nondaily life"*.

"Feeling of nondaily life" and *"Reminiscent"* bore almost proportionate relationship to "Want to buy" from the results of relationships between uniqueness and purchase motivation. Especially, factor score of *"Feeling of nondaily life"* and *"Reminiscent"* of H1 was higher than other products. The evaluation of "Want to buy" was high also. When the appearance of product was seen, H1 had round shapes and shiny texture compared with other products. The shape of H1 was rare, and it was not seen to general humidifier and home electric appliance. H5 was noticeable that appearance seems to be a humidifier. In view of this, it was easy to feel uniqueness more and to lead with purchase motivation when a humidifier did not seem to be a humidifier and a general home electric appliance. It was considered that the attractive product and purchase motivation were related closely because there was strongly correlation between "Attractive" and "Want to buy". There was correlated to "UNIQUE" and "Want to buy", but the correlation coefficient between them was lower than it between "Attractive" and "Want to buy". Moreover, the score of uniqueness on H3 was higher than it on H5, on the other hand, the score of "Want to buy" on H5 was higher than it on H3. Therefore, the relations of uniqueness and purchase motivation for humidifier were not strong as relations of attractiveness and purchase motivation. However, it was suggested that uniqueness of humidifier might influence to purchase motivation.

The reason for purchase motivation items was different depending on the level of uniqueness. The reasons for purchase motivation, i.e. goodness of design, strongly impression, goodness of texture and material, and getting sympathy and interest were affected in products with high uniqueness. This means that "Appearance design" consisted by shape, color and texture and "User's mind" that wants to sympathy from people around by possessing influenced to increase purchase motivation of humidifier.

6   The Proposal of a System Which Utilized KSUP

On the basis of above results, we proposed the system which used for R&D (Research and development) at manufacturers and EC (e-commerce) shop for consumer.

The designer gets feedback from consumer's *Kansei* and needs in R&D. Consequently, the designer can create the unique products which suit consumer's *Kansei* and the other needs. KSUP can be used for product research such as a monitor survey at in-house. It is possible to score the degree of uniqueness by KSUP. The designer will be able to understand how consumers feel the uniqueness of the product. The designer will need to modify the design of product when the uniqueness expressed by designer is different from it of consumer.

Therefore, it was considered that this system will serve the information as the support system for designer. Figure 5 shows usage model on proposal system for designer.

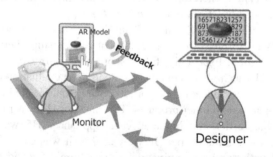

Fig. 5. Usage model on proposal system for designer

Moreover, KSUP can evaluate uniqueness of products that have been on sale. A consumers' evaluation can compare their rating of others by numerical value or visual diagram by this system. They can recognize their degree of sensitivity objectively and visibly. Displaying a degree of uniqueness and a distribution map leads purchase motivation to consumers before buying.

Therefore, it was considered that this system will serve the information to choice products by their Kansei as the support decision-making system for consumer. Figure 6 shows usage model on proposal system for consumer.

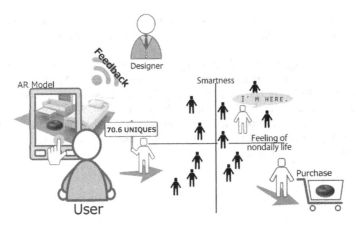

Fig. 6. Usage model on proposal system for consumer

7   Conclusion

The purpose of this study was to compose *Kansei* Scale on Uniqueness Products (KSUP) which evaluates the uniqueness of products, and to clarify relations between uniqueness of products and the consumer's purchase motivation. We examined on five kinds of humidifiers using evaluation experiment. As the result of this study, it was indicated that the KSUP on humidifier consisted of "*Feeling of nondaily life*" and "*Reminiscent*". In addition, "*Feeling of nondaily life*" showed a tendency to have a high positive correlation with purchase motivation than "*Reminiscent*". Moreover, it was considered that the uniqueness of humidifier was influenced by two reasons for purchase motivation which "Appearance design" consisted by shape, color, texture and strong impression and "User's mind" that want to empathize with others by possession after buying mainly.

It is expected that the KSUP will become one of the most effective indexes used in product development and that it will help designers develop more attractive products that are in line with consumer needs. In the future, if consumer as well as designer utilizes the KSUP and a system that could give feedback to designers can be suggested, it will help them design products that are closer to the consumer's affectiveness.

References

1. Kano, N., Seraku, N., Takahashi, F., Tsuji, S.-I.: Affective Quality and Must-Be Quality. The Japanese Society for Quality Control 14(2), 147–156 (1984) (in Japanese)
2. Hall, S.R.: Advertising Handbook. General Books, CA (1986)
3. Besemer, S., O'Quin, K.: Analyzing creativeproducts: Refinement and test of a judginginstrument. Journal of Creative Behavior 20, 115–126 (1986)
4. Besemer, S., Treffinger, D.J.: Analysis ofcreative products: Review and synthesis. Journalof Creative Behavior 15, 158–178 (1981)

5. Besemer, S.P.: Creative Product AnalysisMatrix: Testing the model structure and acomparison among products—three novel chairs. Creativity Research Journal 11, 333–346 (1998)
6. Besemer, S., O'Quin, K.: Confirming thethree-factor Creative Product Analysis Matrixmodel in an American sample. Creativity Research Journal 12, 287–296 (1999)
7. Besemer, S.P.: To buy or not to buy:Predicting the willingness to buy from creativeproduct variables. Korean Journal of Thinking and Problem Solving 10, 5–18 (2000)
8. Ohta, Y., Kasamatsu, K.: Proposal for a *Kansei*Index related to the Uniqueness of a Product. In: The 2012 Applied Human Factors and Ergonomics Conference Proceedings, pp. 6984–6992. The Printing House, Inc. (2012)

Timing and Basis of Online Product Recommendation: The Preference Inconsistency Paradox

Amy Shi, Chuan-Hoo Tan, and Choon Ling Sia

City University of Hong Kong, Hong Kong,
{yanishi2,ch.tan,iscl}@city.edu.hk

Abstract. Online retailers employ recommendation agents (RAs) to provide product recommendations with the objectives of not only to support consumers' decision-making but also to influence their decisions of product choice. However, some empirical studies have found that product recommendations are not always well accepted by consumers. While one cause for the non-acceptance might be the poor personalization of the product recommendations as suggested by prior studies, another plausible cause would be the failure in providing a product recommendation in the wrong way and/or at the wrong time. Building on the theoretical lens of Preference Inconsistency Paradox, this study seeks to investigate how a RA could offer recommendations based on product reviews (i.e., the basis of a recommendation) and at the juncture when consumers are most receptive to (i.e., the timing). A controlled laboratory experiment was subsequently conducted. The results reveal that the basis and time of recommendations could lead to varying impacts on a consumer's decision satisfaction and decision difficulty. Implications for research and practice are discussed.

Keywords: product recommendation, preference inconsistency paradox, recommendation timing, recommendation source.

1 Introduction

Research on recommendation agent (RA), i.e., a software agent that makes product recommendations to individual consumers, is increasingly abundant due to its potentials of not only to assist a consumer in making shopping decisions but also to influence his/her choice of product [1]. It is increasingly cautioned that an unsuitable recommendation may cause a consumer to ignore that recommendation or in certain cases, result in a behavioral backslash: a consumer intentionally contradicts that recommendation [2]. It is added in the marketing literature that a recommendation or an advertisement at the wrong timing would not only lower its persuasiveness but also lead to negative attitude formation [3-5]. Taken together, we argue that a consumer denying a recommendation could be due to the failure in providing a product recommendation in the wrong way (i.e., the basis of recommendation) and/or at the wrong time (i.e., the timing of recommendation).

S. Yamamoto (Ed.): HIMI/HCII 2013, Part III, LNCS 8018, pp. 531–539, 2013.
© Springer-Verlag Berlin Heidelberg 2013

In term of the basis of recommendation, we propose the consideration of third-party generated product information, such as product reviews written by product experts (thereafter terms as expert reviews) and those written by end-consumers after consumption of a product (thereafter terms as consumer reviews). It is increasingly suggested by extant literature that product reviews play an important role in influencing a consumer's purchase decision-making behavior [6, 7].

In term of the timing of recommendation, prior studies have predominantly and implicitly focused on one instant of recommendation provision, which is toward the end of a decision-making process (or just before a decision is made). For example, in the work of [2], which focused on examining the provision of recommendations after preferences are defined. It is not clear what if recommendation comes in the earlier stage of decision process would be well received.

To form theoretical predictions on how a RA could provide recommendation (i.e., the basis) and the instant of providing it (i.e., the timing), we anchor on the theoretical lens of Preference Inconsistency Paradox (PIP). PIP posits that when a consumer is formulating the consideration set, he/she has a tendency to increase more product alternatives to form a large consideration set [8, 9] with the prospective of not missing any good product options; however, when he/she is prompted to make an explicit purchase decision, he/she tends to be troubled not only by a large rather than a small consideration set and also the need to have an easy-to-justify choice [10-12]. A controlled laboratory experiment was subsequently conducted. This research contributes to the extant literature by explicitly examine the issue of how a RA could provide recommendations that could reduce a consumer's decision difficulty and at the same time increase his decision satisfaction.

2   Theoretical Background and Research Model

2.1   Preference Inconsistency Paradox

PIP is based on the view of consumer behavior in a two-stage product decision process. The two stages are (1) forming a consideration set and, subsequently, (2) selecting a product alternative from that consideration set [8, 13, 14]. PIP suggests that there is a discrepancy in a consumer's preferences during the two stages [11, 14].

When a consumer is forming the consideration set, he/she has the preference for having more product alternatives, leading to a large consideration set [8]. For instance, consumers prefer larger assortment rather than smaller assortment when choosing among assortments [11, 15], because people like to have a wider choice selection [16, 17].

Preference inconsistency emerges when a consumer progresses to the stage of making a final product choice. In this stage, a consumer is not interested in increasing the size of consideration set and due to the large consideration set, he/she is troubled by the considerable number of product alternatives. The reason is that a large consideration set increases the demand for cognitive resources to evaluate the product alternatives. Additional effort is required to evaluate alternatives in the larger consideration set, which could result in a cognitive overload [18-20]. Suggested by the need-for-justification paradigm, a consumer needs to focus on finding a good justification/reason for selecting a product alternative among all the options in the consideration set [21].

2.2   Research Framework and Hypothesis Development

The research framework is depicted in Figure 1. As depicted, we seek to assess the impacts of recommendation timing (before search vs. after choice) and basis of recommendation (consumer review vs. expert review) on a consumer's decision satisfaction and decision difficulty in the context of an online shopping website. At the "before search" timing point, which is in the consideration-set-formation stage, a recommendation is presented when a consumer first accesses the online shopping website. At the "after choice" timing point, a recommendation is presented after a consumer has considered some alternatives and made a preliminary choice but before final confirmation of the decision.

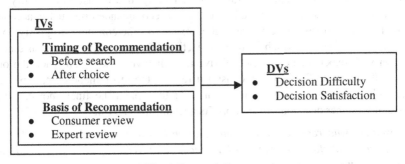

Fig. 1. Research Framework

Decision difficulty refers to the complexities encountered by a consumer during the decision-making process [22, 23]. Decision difficulty comes from various sources at different decision-making stages [24]. At the consideration-set-formation stage, knowledge uncertainty and preference uncertainty are major sources of decision difficulty [25]. A recommendation would be perceived to be helpful at this stage because it could provide product knowledge and aid a consumer's preference construction. Thus, it is less likely that the recommendation would increase a consumer's decision difficulty.

However, at the stage of final choice making, choice conflict and need-for-justification are the main sources of decision difficulty. PIP suggests that when a consumer is making the final choice, it would be more difficult to choose from a large consideration set than from a small one. If a product recommendation is presented "after choice", more cognitive effort is required to solve the choice conflict between the recommended product and a consumer's preliminary choice. The recommendation would compel that consumer to re-evaluate alternatives and re-justify his choice, which increases the demand on consumers' cognitive resources. As a result, a higher decision difficulty is associated with the recommendation presented after search. Therefore, we posit:

H1: Consumers who receive a recommendation presented "after choice" will have higher decision difficulty compared to those who receive a recommendation presented "before search."

Decision satisfaction measures the extent that a consumer perceives a decision to be acceptable [26, 27]. Decision satisfaction is viewed as an antecedent of repeated purchase, loyalty and system usage [26, 28]. Therefore, enhancing a consumer's decision satisfaction is of great importance. We propose that a consumer who receives the recommendation based on expert review would be more satisfied with the decision than an individual who receives the recommendation based on consumer review. Decision satisfaction is not only based on the decision outcome but also on how consumers justify the decision [29]. Compared with consumer review, which is mainly individual consumer's product opinion based on personal usage, expert review, focusing on product attribute information (such as performance, features and reliability) that is easier to quantify and measure, is more objective to be relied on [30]. If a recommended product is accepted by a consumer, expert review serves as a good reason for the consumer to justify comparing to consumer review which is more subjective [31]. It is found that a consumer's satisfaction with expert-made choices relative to their own varies even when the outcomes are the same [32]. Even if a consumer refuses the recommendation, expert review provides a good support for that consumer to explain the final choice, which would result in higher decision satisfaction. As a result, we suggest:

H2: Consumers who receive the recommendation based on expert review will have higher decision satisfaction compared to those who receive the recommendation based on consumer review.

3   Research Methodology

A 2×2 controlled laboratory experiment was conducted in this study. The operationalization of decision satisfaction and decision difficulty was adopted from prior studies [33, 34]. 88 students from a public university in China participated in the experiment. The participants' average age was between 21 and 23 years old; 27 (30.7%) were male and 61 (69.3%) were female. They were randomly assigned to one of the four treatments to minimize the effects of individual differences on the results and there were 22 participants per treatment group. Participants were told to make purchase choices from four product categories (i.e., cell phone, digital camera, laptop and Mp3 player). They were paid about $6 U.S. for each hour of the experiment task.

The experiment was conducted in a computer lab with PCs in groups of 6-12 participants. Participants were required to make a choice from each product category store. Real product data was used in the experiment. When performing the purchase task of a product category, a participant began with a pre-questionnaire regarding his/her knowledge about the product category. Then he/she entered the search page of the online store. He/she could add one or more options into the consideration set by clicking "add into shopping cart." Finally, he/she needed to make a choice by clicking the "buy" button in the shopping cart, and then to click "confirm" for confirmation of final choice. After a post-questionnaire, he/she moved on to making decision for the next product category.

Recommendation timing was manipulated at two timing points: before search and after choice. For the "before search" treatment, a recommendation was presented in a pop-up window when a participant began to search products at the screening page. For the "after choice" treatment, a recommendation was presented when a participant clicked the "buy" button in the shopping cart and before confirmation. These two timing points are chosen to make sure that the presentation of recommendation could be well manipulated at different stages of decision-making.

For the manipulation of basis of recommendation, the recommendation based on consumer review consisted of a title of "Other consumers recommend this product to you," attribute information of the recommended product and several positive consumer reviews. The recommendation based on expert review page included a title of "expert recommends this product to you," attribute information of the recommended product and expert review.

The sequence of the purchase tasks in the four product categories was controlled by randomly assigning task sequences to participants. Recommended product was controlled by randomly recommending a product. Other control variables included perceived knowledge of the product category and perceived task involvement.

4   Data Analysis

Participants' individual characteristics, such as age, gender, computer experience and online shopping experience, were controlled by randomization. Further checks indicated that there is no significant differences among participants in all four treatments in terms of age ($F=1.083$, $p>0.1$), computer experience ($F=0.78$, $p>0.1$), and online shopping experience ($F=2.17$, $p>0.05$). There was no significant difference across the treatment groups in terms of gender ratio, based on the Kruskal-Wallis test ($\chi2=0.648$, $p>0.1$).

Manipulation checks were conducted to ensure that our manipulation was successful. Recommendation timing manipulation was verified by asking the participants to rate on a seven-point Likert scale regarding when they saw the pop-up recommendation (1 means at the beginning of the task and 7 means after making a preliminary decision). Comparing the mean ratings obtained from participants of before search condition and participants of after choice condition (i.e., 1.00 and 6.59 respectively) yielded a highly significant result ($t=45.45$, $p<0.001$). Recommendation source manipulation was checked by asking the participants to rate on a seven-point Likert scale whether they thought the recommendation was mainly based on personal usage experience. Comparing the mean ratings obtained for the consumer recommendation and expert recommendation conditions (i.e., 5.41 and 3.86 respectively) yielded a highly significant result ($t=7.65$, $p<0.001$). As a result, our manipulation of the two independent variables was successful.

Because each participant had four purchase tasks (i.e., cell phone, digital camera, laptop and Mp3 player), our data have a two-level structure with purchase tasks at level 1 and subjects at level 2. In order to control the subjects' variation in the two-level structure data, multi-level linear regression analyses are conducted. Data were analyzed by using the multi-level xtreg module in Stata (release 10.0).

The results are depicted in Table 1. Full models were tested and there was no interaction effect. The results suggested that the timing of recommendation significantly influenced the consumers' decision difficulty and basis of recommendation significantly influenced the consumers' decision satisfaction. It is shown that consumers had significantly lower decision difficulty if the recommendation came at the stage of forming the consideration set than if the recommendation comes at the stage of making the final choice; and they reported significantly higher decision satisfaction if the recommendation was based on expert review than the one based on consumer review. Therefore, H1 and H2 are both supported.

Table 1. Data Analysis Results

	Decision Difficulty (DV)			Decision Satisfaction (DV)		
	Coefficient	Std. Error	Z	Coefficient	Std. Error	Z
Manipulated Independent Variables						
Recommendation Source (0-expert; 1-consumer)	-0.08	0.30	-0.26	-0.56	0.20	-2.82**
Recommendation Timing (0- after choice; 1-before search)	-0.97	0.30	- 3.24***	0.10	0.20	0.48
Recommendation Source * Recommendation Timing	0.26	0.42	0.62	0.36	0.28	1.29
Control Variables						
Product_cellphone	0.12	0.15	0.82	-0.12	0.12	-0.98
Product_digital camera	-0.07	0.15	-0.46	-0.21	0.13	--1.85
Product_laptop	-0.09	0.16	0.55	-0.22	0.13	-1.73
Knowledge	-0.03	0.05	-0.53	0.08	0.04	2.20*
Involvement	0.03	0.04	0.69	0.10	0.04	2.65**
Recommendation Quality	0.003	0.09	0.03	0.03	0.07	0.41
Intercept	2.88	0.34	8.56***	5.04	0.25	20.12***
Log likelihood	-517.47			-418.27		

*p<.05; **p<.01;***p<.001

5   Discussion and Conclusion

This study investigates how a RA could provide recommendations based on product reviews and at the right timing to yield higher decision satisfaction and lower decision difficulty. The results suggest that a product recommendation presented after choice would result in a consumer experiencing greater decision difficulty than the one presented before search. As suggested by PIP, at the stage of making final choice from the consideration set, a consumer has the inclination to minimize decision complexity and reach an easy-to-justify decision, the recommendation at this stage would bring choice conflict between the recommended product and his/her preliminary choice, which increases the demand on that consumer's cognitive effort and causes higher decision difficulty.

It is also found that the basis of recommendation significantly influences a consumer's second-stage decision: making the final choice. Higher decision satisfaction is associated with recommendation based on expert review than recommendation based on consumer review. While the justification for a choice is seen as an important factor in understanding consumer choice and decision satisfaction [21, 35], the recommendation based on expert review assist a consumer to have better reasons for his decision.

Like any other studies, this research suffers from several limitations that readers should take into account when interpreting the findings. First, while the nature of the products would affect consumer decision-making process and the effectiveness of product recommendation, further studies could be conducted to investigate the impact in other product categories, such as experience products/service (e.g., hotels, restaurants). Second, the cultural context of this study may limit the external validity. Without considering the impact of cultural characteristics, this study was conducted in a university of a collectivistic country. The findings might be influenced by cultural factors, such as consumers' preference for expert review. Future research could investigate the impact of recommendation basis and timing in different cultural contexts.

This study contributes to several schools of literature. First, it contributes to the RA literature by examining the impact of product review as basis of recommendation. Although RA is important in online retailing, the truth is that many are not making the most of the opportunities. As the rejection of recommendation might be a result of insufficient evidences of product superiority and not persuasive enough to be relied on [4], we compared the impact of recommendations based on expert review and consumer review. The understanding of employing third-party product review provides valuable implications in RA and electronic commerce literature. Second, this study contributes to recommendation timing literature by considering a consumer's preference inconsistency at two stages of decision-making: preferring larger consideration set when forming the consideration set and, making an easy-to-justify choice from the formed consideration set. While prior studies have mainly focused on one instant of recommendation provision, we compared two timing points and found that recommendation at the second stage of decision-making would bring higher decision difficulty to consumers. Third, while previous consumer research validated the existence of PIP, this study moves forward by drawing from the paradox to study RAs. It contributes to the PIP literature by indicating that consumers' preference inconsistency could be leveraged in understanding consumer behavior, such as the acceptance of online product recommendation.

Our study also provides practical implications for online merchants. First, in order to increase online shoppers' decision satisfaction, online merchants should provide good reasons for them to justify. Recommendations with expert review could be a better solution, compared to consumer review. Second, practitioners should avoid providing late recommendation when consumers are making final choice from a set of considered options. Recommendation at the choice-making stage may increase consumers' decision difficulty, which would have negative impacts on consumers' online shopping, such as reactance and a behavioral backlash that would result in consumers' purchase abandonment.

References

1. Häubl, G., Murray, K.B.: Double agents. MIT Sloan Management Review 47, 8–12 (2006)
2. Fitzsimons, G.J., Lehmann, D.R.: Reactance to Recommendations: When Unsolicited Advice Yields Contrary Responses. Market Sci. 23, 82–94 (2004)
3. Ha, L.: Observations: Advertising clutter in consumer magazines: Dimensions and effects. J. Advertising Res. 36, 76–84 (1996)
4. Chan, J.C.F., Jiang, Z.H., Tan, B.C.Y.: Understanding Online Interruption-Based Advertising: Impacts of Exposure Timing, Advertising Intent, and Brand Image. IEEE T. Eng. Manage 57, 365–379 (2010)
5. Ho, S.Y., Bodoff, D., Tam, K.Y.: Timing of Adaptive Web Personalization and Its Effects on Online Consumer Behavior. Inform Syst. Res. 22, 660–679 (2011)
6. Chen, Y., Xie, J.: Third-Party Product Review and Firm Marketing Strategy. Market Sci. 24, 218–240 (2005)
7. Chen, Y.B., Xie, J.H.: Online consumer review: Word-of-mouth as a news element of marketing communication mix. Manage Sci. 54, 477–491 (2008)
8. Kahn, B.E., Lehmann, D.R.: Modeling Choice among Assortments. J. Retailing 67, 274–299 (1991)
9. Broniarczyk, S.M., Hoyer, W.D., McAlister, L.: Consumers' perceptions of the assortment offered in a grocery category: The impact of item reduction. J. Marketing Res. 35, 166–176 (1998)
10. Iyengar, S.S., Lepper, M.R.: When choice is demotivating: Can one desire too much of a good thing? Journal of Personality and Social Psychology 79, 995–1006 (2000)
11. Chernev, A.: Decision focus and consumer choice among assortments. J. Consum Res. 33, 50–59 (2006)
12. Chernev, A.: Product assortment and individual decision processes. Journal of Personality and Social Psychology 85, 151–162 (2003b)
13. Gensch, D.H., Javalgi, R.G.: The Influence of Involvement on Disaggregate Attribute Choice Models. J. Consum Res. 14, 71–82 (1987)
14. Moe, W.W.: An empirical two-stage choice model with varying decision rules applied to Internet clickstream data. J. Marketing Res. 43, 680–692 (2006)
15. Bulbul, C.: When consumers choose to restrict their options: Influence of concrete and abstract regret on choice set size preference. Graduate School of Business Administration, vol. Ph. D, p. 86. New York University, New York (2007)
16. Botti, S., Iyengar, S.S.: The Psychological Pleasure and Pain of Choosing: When People Prefer Choosing at the Cost of Subsequent Outcome Satisfaction. Journal of Personality and Social Psychology 87, 312–326 (2004)
17. Bown, N.J., Read, D., Summers, B.: The lure of choice. Journal of Behavioral Decision Making 16, 297–308 (2003)
18. Huffman, C., Kahn, B.E.: Variety for Sale: Mass customization or mass confusion? J. Retailing 74, 491–513 (1998)
19. Jacoby, J., Speller, D.E., Berning, C.K.: Brand Choice Behavior as a Function of Information Load: Replication and Extension. The Journal of Consumer Research 1, 33–42 (1974)
20. Malhotra, N.K.: Information Load and Consumer Decision Making. The Journal of Consumer Research 8, 419–430 (1982)
21. Simonson, I.: Choice Based on Reasons: The Case of Attraction and Compromise Effects. The Journal of Consumer Research 16, 158–174 (1989)
22. Dhar, R.: Consumer preference for a no-choice option. J. Consum Res. 24, 215–231 (1997)

23. Greenleaf, E.A., Lehmann, D.R.: Reasons for Substantial Delay in Consumer Decision Making. The Journal of Consumer Research 22, 186–199 (1995)
24. Luce, M.F., Payne, J.W., Bettman, J.R.: Emotional Trade-off Difficulty and Choice. JMR, Journal of Marketing Research 36, 143 (1999)
25. Bettman, J.R., Luce, M.F., Payne, J.W.: Constructive consumer choice processes. The Journal of Consumer Research 25, 187–217 (1998)
26. Meuter, M.L., Ostrom, A.L., Roundtree, R.I., Bitner, M.J.: Self-service technologies: understanding customer satisfaction with technology-based service encounters. The Journal of Marketing 64, 50–64 (2000)
27. Devaraj, S., Fan, M., Kohli, R.: Antecedents of B2C Channel Satisfaction and Preference: Validating e-Commerce Metrics. Inform Syst. Res. 13, 316–333 (2002)
28. Hoyer, W.D.: An Examination of Consumer Decision Making for a Common Repeat Purchase Product. The Journal of Consumer Research 11, 822–829 (1984)
29. Hsee, C.K.: Elastic Justification: How Tempting but Task-Irrelevant Factors Influence Decisions. Organizational Behavior and Human Decision Processes 62, 330–337 (1995)
30. Bickart, B., Schindler, R.M.: Internet forums as influential sources of consumer information. J. Interact Mark 15, 31–40 (2001)
31. Sela, A., Berger, J.: Justification and Choice. Advances in Consumer Research 36, 27–27 (2009)
32. Burson, K.A., Botti, S.: Choice Satisfaction Can Be the Luck of the Draw. Advances in Consumer Research 36 (2009)
33. Bottomley, P.A., Doyle, J.R., Green, R.H.: Testing the reliability of weight elicitation methods: Direct rating versus point allocation. JMR, Journal of Marketing Research 37, 508 (2000)
34. Steenkamp, J.-B., Van Trijp, H.: Attribute Elicitation in Marketing Research: A Comparison of Three Procedures. Marketing Letters 8, 153–165 (1997)
35. Kivetz, R., Zheng, Y.H.: Determinants of justification and self-control. J. Exp. Psychol. Gen 135, 572–587 (2006)

Research on the Measurement of Product Sales with Relation to Visual Planning for Commercial Websites

Chu-Yu Sun

Graduate School of Applied Design & Department of Animation and Game Design,
Shu Te University of Science and Technology
spancy@seed.net.tw

1 The Experimental Design of This Study

This research is utilizes 2*2 dual factor grouping research design (between – subjects designs) and, based on the planning for versions of commercial websites, takes 24 front page commercial items and 24 non-front page commercial items as its sample, thus there are 48 samples in total. These 48 sample items are divided into 2 groups and independent T test methodology is utilized. Items are divided into the 2 groups according to whether or not they are on the front page or not, and the variables employed are "click through rate" and "purchase rate" in order to investigate the sales effectiveness for the visual planning of online sale item presentation. The time observation times are based on the commercial website's front page sales cycle. Information and data are collected once a month.

The sample volume is derived from the webpage template for the front page and 4*6, or 24 commercial items are displayed. In all, non-front page web pages display 10 commercial items, and these are compiled in the background information database and the all of the non-front page versions of front page advertisement items of the same season are found in order to perform examination.

2 Experiment Content

This study delves into its topic from the perspective of visual design and observes front pages which give priority to readability in terms of visual appearance in order to determine whether or not they can fulfill their function in promoting sales to the utmost. Background information is compiled for the study's data, and, based on this, the number of click throughs and reader volume for the page. We further compare these figures with the click through rates of non-front pages. In addition, this research looks at whether or not products with high click through rates are the same ones as those with high purchase rates. This directly influences strategies for visual planning, and this is the main emphasis for this study's examination.

S. Yamamoto (Ed.): HIMI/HCII 2013, Part III, LNCS 8018, pp. 540–545, 2013.

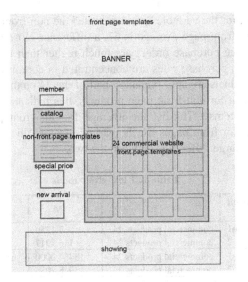

Fig. 1. 24 commercial website front page templates

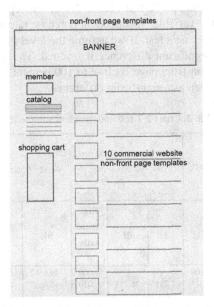

Fig. 2. 10 commercial website non-front page templates

3   Experiment Analysis

After data undergoes quantitative analysis and the independent sample T test compares average values. This study first find from Figure 1, which groups total values that, with respect to the averages for front pages (group 1) and non-front pages, which number 48 in total, for the variable "purchase rate" the non-front page (group 2) average is 117, and the front page average is 67, a difference close to 100 percent. This shows non-front page purchase orders are much higher than those of front page orders, indicating high purchase rates are concentrated in certain commercial products. Secondly, these products are approximately half of the 24 on the front page. In terms of standard deviation for non-front page products, this indicates a situation similar to that of front page items. Thirdly, the average for non-front pages (group 2) was 13,949 and 13,454 for front pages for the variable factor "click through rate," showing there was not a large difference between the two.

Table 1. T test group totals

front page & non-front page templates		n	M	SD	SE
purchase rat	group1	commercial products 24	67.1250	46.6610	9.5246
	group 2	commercial products 24	116.7917	75.8992	15.4929
click through rate group1		commercial products 24	13454.0000	6538.6585	1334.6981
	group2	commercial products 24	13948.7083	5425.3800	1107.4511

For the independent sample T test (Table 2 T test-independent sample chart) this study first examines the variable "independent purchase rate and significance is found to be .100 through a Levene's test. If we assume the level of significance for variance reaches .009 (< .05), significant difference is reached. This proves the difference between front page and non-front page is close to 100 percent for the variable "purchase rate," and this can be seen as a significant difference.

Table 2. Chart 2 T test-independent sample test chart

	equal variances assumed Levene Statistic		t-test Mean equal						95% Confidence Interval for Mean	
	f-test	Sig.	t	df	Sig. two-taile d	SE	SD	Lower Bound	Upper Bound
purchase rat equal variances assumed equal variances not assumed	2.818	-100	- 2.731 -2.731	46 38.213	.009 .010	-49.6667 -49.6667	18.1865 18.1865	-86.2741 -86.4765	-13.0992 -12.8568
click through rate equal variances assumed equal variances not assumed	2.311	-135	-2.85 -2.85	46 44.486	.777 .777	-494.7083 -494.7083	1734.32 00	-3985.7140 -3988.9239	2996.2973 2999.5072

4   Research Results

The primary results of this research are as follows:

1. The "click through rate" and "purchase rate" of non-front page items was higher than that of front page items.   The "purchase rate" for non-front page was close to twice that of front page items concerning purchase averages.
2. Both front page and non-front page are found to be average for "click through rate."
3. For "purchase rate" non-front page and front page present a state of average dichotomy; orders concentrated around approximately half of (12) products.

5   Conclusion and Suggestions

Research suggestions

1. This research finds that rates for front pages are lower than those of non-front pages, and asserts this is not because the front pages in commercial websites are functionally ineffective. Rather, it is due to the post-IPO phenomenon related to front pages. This means the front page is intended to create purchase intention in the browser and make the consumer click through to the page of the product he or she would like to buy. The background information from the "Index Page" belonging to the research website indicates that the items purchased are often concentrated in the first 1 to 3 webpages after the front page in terms of quantity. While not many purchases are made from the front page, the click through rate on the first layer, or front page, certainly has an influence on second layer rates on the non-front pages. This means design strategies for front page visual planning should focus on the image of the product's abstract quality, as well as creating consumer recognition. Design strategies for the front page should not concern themselves with the description and marketing of the actual product, or habitually use sales discounts as a strategy.
2. The Index Page information flow technology does not present an impediment to a browser arriving a web page like it did in the past. For this reason, the click through rate for front page and non-front page was the same.   This indicates in terms of visual planning, in addition to emphasizing the actual description and sale of the item in the non-front page, it is also necessary in local operations to strengthen the products image with respect to abstract quality as with the front page in order to advance consumer recognition and turn this to consumer ideas and actions.
3. The research website's background information number and frequency of orders are concentrated in websites one to three pages removed from the front page. This echoes consumer psychology in which consumers are more interested in the product and not too concerned about the price, and this fact leads this study to suggest, from the perspective of visual design, that the front page emphasize the product's abstract added value; design should be undertaken to best represent this abstract value with the goal of raising click through rates by maximizing the advantage of

having consumers see the front page first. In addition, this experiment finds orders and purchase rates are concentrated in non-front page products. It is suggested the main products for that season be placed on these pages as this would be beneficial to the improvement of sales performance.

References

Ahn, H.J.: A new similarity measure for collaborative filtering to allevative the new user cold-starting problem. International Journal of Information Sciences 178(1), 42–49 (2008)

Boyd, D.M.: Social network sites: Definition, history, and scholarship. Journal of Computer-Mediated Communication 13(1), 215–228 (2007)

Castells, M.: The Internet Galaxy: Reflections on The Internet, Business, and Society. Oxford University Press, NY (2001)

Chafkin, M.: Analyze This. Says Google. Inc. (2006)

Ledford, J.L.: Google Analytics. Wiley Publishing, Indiana (2009)

Safko, L.: The Social Media Bible: Tactics, Tools &; Strategies for Business Success. Sons, Inc., Hoboken (2009)

ThelWell, M.: Web log file analysis: Backlinks and queries. Asilb Proceeding 53(6), 218–221 (2001)

Tsai, S.M., Zhuang, W.Y.: Data mining for library borrowing history records based on the weighted sliding window model. Journal of Computers 17(4), 85–91 (2006)

Wang, S.: Multi-dimensional Resolution Programs and User Website Finding Techniques. MA thesis, Central University Institute of Information Engineering (1989)

Li, S.: Webpage Based Network Management Information Systems. MA thesis, Chinan University Institute of Information Management (1989)

Li, S.: Research on Influence of Index Webpage on Provider-Customer Relations. MA thesis, Chung Yuan Christian University Institute of Information Management (1991)

Li, J.: Research on Webpage Design Principles. MA thesis, National Yunlin University of Science and Technology Institute of Industrial Design 47(3), 351–358 (1996)

Lin, X.: Application of Google Analytics in Digital Archives Website Measurement Analysis. Journal of Educational Media and Library Sciences 47, 351–358 (2010)

Lin, Z.: Research on Integrated Model for the Diffusion of Information Technology-the Case of MPR. Chung Yuan Journal 27, 21–31 (1999)

Lin, J.: Webpage Information Mining Technique Import Website Operator Research-the Case of Import Website Classification Index Services. MA thesis, National Chengchi University Information Management Institute (1991)

Qiu, J.: Web Design. Science Press, China (2010)

Zhou, G., Meiyi, G., Xiaoyuan, S.: Electronic Commerce Meets the Challenges and Opportunities of the N Generation. DrMaster Press, Taipei (2001)

Xu, J.: Research on the Influence of Webpage Style and Visual Elements on Design Evaluation-Enterprise Websites as Example. MA thesis, Jiao Tong University Institute of Applied Arts (2001)

Li, X.: The Era of Community by R. Theobald. Fang Chi, Taipei (2000)

Zhang, Y.: Scalable Feature Selection Using Fuzzy Ranking Analysis for the Automatic Classification of Web Pages. MA thesis, National Taiwan University of Science and Technology (1989)

Xiao, S.: Exploration of Web Interface Usability and Image Research. MA thesis, National Cheng Kung University Department of Industrial Design (1991)

Zhong, Y.: Analysis of Online Search Language. MA thesis, National Jiao Tong University Information Engineering Institute (1991)

Luan, B., Siren, C., Kaiyoang, L.: E-Commerce, 6th edn. Tsang Hai Publishing, Taipei (2009)

Online Sources

http://www.enquiro.com/marketing-monitor/
Web-Analytics-Comparison-Google-VisiStat.asp (2010/11)

http://www.webanalyticsassociation.org/ (2011/11)

http://www.useit.com/alertbox/991113.html (2011/11)

http://www.techbang.com.tw/?p=24058 (2011/12)

http://www.fuland.cn/seo-training/seo-index.htm (2011/12)

http://www.ls.ntu.edu.tw/news/contents.htm (2011/12)

http://www.lib.tku.edu.tw/internet/internet.htm (2011/12)

http://www.searchenginewatch.com/ (2011/12)

http://www.wordtracker.com (2011/12)

http://searchenginewatch.com (2011/12)

Part V
Decision Support

Burglary Crime Analysis Using Logistic Regression

Daniel Antolos[1], Dahai Liu[1], Andrei Ludu[2], and Dennis Vincenzi[3]

[1] Department of Human Factors and Systems Department
[2] Department of Mathematics
[3] Department of Aeronautics, World Wide Campus Embry-Riddle Aeronautical University
Daytona Beach, Florida, 32114
antolosd@my.erau.edu, {dahai.liu,ludua,vincenzd}@erau.edu

Abstract. This study used a logistic regression model to investigate the relationship between several predicting factors and burglary occurrence probability with regard to the epicenter. These factors include day of the week, time of the day, repeated victimization, connectors and barriers. Data was collected from a local police report on 2010 burglary incidents. Results showed the model has various degrees of significance in terms of predicting the occurrence within difference ranges from the epicenter. Follow-up refined multiple comparisons of different sizes were observed to further discover the pattern of prediction strength of these factors. Results are discussed and further research directions were given at the end of the paper.

Keywords: Logistic regression, crime analysis.

1 Introduction

Crime analysis studies certain characteristics of crime and the motives of the persons who committed them developed some form of pattern. Since 1990s, crime analysis has been focused on study the relationship between crime occurrence with human related factors such as personality [17], psychological characteristics[1][4] [7], and factors include peer influence and peer pressure, provocation and anger, boredom and thrill, alcohol and drugs, and money were found to be possible motivators for crimes [5]. Besides the human factors, it has been found that crime activity may have strong correlations to a number of environmental variables that lead to pattern for the occurrence of the crime. For example, how does a criminal, such as a burglar, determine when and where they will target a residence. Nee and Meenaghan [8] found that burglars acted on crime using an almost habitual decision-making process that allow them to navigate quickly and effectively around their world. Pitcher and Johnson [11] showed that a burglar's action is more of a forging and heuristic process when selecting targets. It has been found that burglars consider factors such as the specific period of time for the crime, selection of the target, whether or not the target has been successful in the past and what the terrain is in regards to concealment, ingress and egress. Many factors such as familiarity of the target area [8], distance [14], roadways

S. Yamamoto (Ed.): HIMI/HCII 2013, Part III, LNCS 8018, pp. 549–558, 2013.

and barriers [9] and repeat victimizations on the same target area [15] have been found to play a role in the burglary crime commitment.

Utilizing information attained from historical data, researchers and law enforcement were able to develop models to target the burglar utilizing the characteristics of the crime, such as location, time of day, and day of week [12][13]. Spatial and temporal analysis has been the primary means of determining criminal activity patterns based on the environment and the impact of the behavior upon the environment [6][10]. Burglary behavior and target selection is believed to be predictable by certain characteristics. By identifying these characteristics and analyzing their influences in the decision making process of the criminal one can develop a means to identify potential targets probability that criminal will attempt to target in the future. In turn this will allow law enforcement to focus resources on exploiting key information necessary to reduce or eliminate the criminal threat to a great extent. Although there are many studies that utilize spatial and temporal factors [13][16], but very limited studies represent a combination of factors to predict the probability of crime occurrence with regard to a crime epicenter. This study is intended to address this issue by utilizing a logistic regression model to determine the probability of targeting based on specific conditions of factors

2   Method

2.1   Data Collection

The data were collected from filed police reports from the year 2010 by the local police department. The current crime rate of 7.70 percent resulting in one in thirteen people of having the likelihood of being victimized via burglary, theft, or motor vehicle theft within the city concerning property crime provided enough data to support the study. The data was comprised of the time and date of the offense, approximate start and finish time of the offense, and the street address of the offense.

2.2   Variables

The independent variables for this study were based on prior studies in crime mapping and analysis, including time of day (category data), day of the week (discrete), repeat victimization (the occurrence of the offense at the same residence following the initial offense over the calendar year, category data, 0 or 1), connectors (the amount of access streets, pathways or bridges relative to the targeted residence that allows access to a multi-lane street, discrete variable) and barriers (physical structures that will disrupt or block an individual's egress from a targeted residence, discrete variable).

The dependent variable was the probability of occurrence of crime by the distance from the crime epicenter.

2.3   Model

The logistic regression function denoted as

$$y = f(x) = 11 + e{-z} \tag{1}$$

With

$$z = \alpha + \beta 1 X 1 + \beta 2 X 2 \dots \beta k X k \tag{2}$$

With $y = f(x)$ being the dependent variable and X_i being the independent variables.

   The street addresses from the data were mapped and the coordinates of each incident was determined by developing a grid reference system. By annotating the amount of events per grid, an epicenter can be determined based on the concentration of events within each grid. Incremental diameter circles of 1km were applied from the epicenter to categorize the distance from the established epicenter. This was accomplished by plotting every address in Google Earth and Maps effectively providing the pictorial depiction of the data. The following equations denote the weighted coordinates for the epicenter

$$(i) = \frac{\sum_{j=1}^{n} \sum_{i=1}^{n} i\, v(i,j)}{\sum_{j=1}^{n} \sum_{i=1}^{n} v\,(i,j)} \tag{3}$$

$$(j) = \frac{\sum_{j=1}^{n} \sum_{i=1}^{n} j\, v(i,j)}{\sum_{j=1}^{n} \sum_{i=1}^{n} v\,(i,j)} \tag{4}$$

With i and j being the coordinates and $v(i,j)$ as the number of incidents in the grid as the weights.

   Once the addresses were mapped in Google Maps, the amount of barriers and connectors associated with each targeted residence can be determined in combination with Google Earth. A major street system was defined as a multi-lane street with or without a physical medium that can be accessed by turning immediately with the flow of traffic as governed by the local traffic laws. Adjacent neighborhoods were defined by neighborhoods that can be accessed via foot path or connecting residence street systems. Finally it was determined which residences were repeated targets within the given year. This was accomplished from observing the data and annotating which residences were targeted more than once over the course of 2010.

   The processed data was then input into SPSS in order to run inferential statistics to determine if any of the variables were significant ($p < 0.05$) prior to conducting a binary logistic regression. A binary logistic regression was conducted utilizing a majority portion ($N = 600$) of the information to determine the probability of observed variables and their relation to a burglary event within certain ranges to the epicenter.

   For the validation of the logistic model, a Wald chi-square statistic was utilized to determine the significance of the individual regression coefficients and whether or not they are having some effect upon the regression model. The goodness-of-fit statistic to determine the fit of the logistic model was done utilizing the Hosmer-Lemeshow and supplemental R^2 to determine the proportion of the variation in the dependent variable that can be explained by predictors in the model. The resultant probabilities from the model were then revalidated with the actual outcome to determine if the high probabilities are associated with the events in comparison to the incremental one km radii. This was determined by utilizing a measure of association, more specifically a Somer's D statistics.

3   Results

All the events were categorized based on location within the a central Florida city by developing a 1 (km) x 1 (km) grid system to quantify the amount of activity within each cell. Figure 1 illustrates the mapped burglary events with the grid system.). Figure 2 shows that the epicenter was determined to be at 9.10 units along the x-axis and 7.30 units along the y-axis of the grid system.

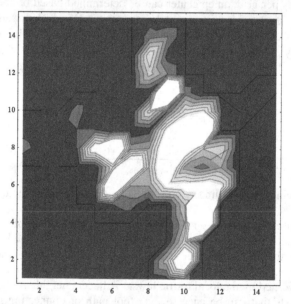

Fig. 1. Graphical representation of grid plotted burglary events depicted utilizing a white hot rendering to show higher concentration in comparison to the low concentration of events as depicted in dark color

A sequence of models were built and tested, starting from one kilometer radius with an increment of one kilometer until the model became insignificant. An overall model evaluation was conducted to determine if the model provided a better fit to an observed data set in comparison to a intercept-only model, or null model which serves as a baseline comparison due to the lack of predictors. It was found the regression models of "one km radii and else", "two km radii and else", and "three km radii and else" were statistically significant. "Four and greater kilometers" radii was not significant. Table 1 illustrates the results for the three significant models.

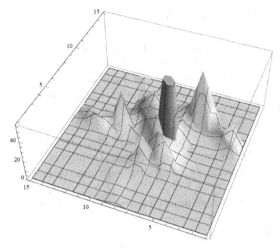

Fig. 2. Graphical representation of epicenter where 9.10 units of x-axis and 7.30 units of y-axis where identified as the epicenter of all the burglary activity in a 3-D rendering

Table 1. Comparison between Logistic Model vs. constant-only model

Radii comparison	< km Sample	> km Sample	α	$\chi 2$ testing p value
1 km to > 1 km and greater	23	568	3.207	p < 0.001
< 2 km to > 2 km and greater	132	459	1.246	p < 0.001
< 3 km to > 3 km and greater	283	308	0.085	p < 0.001

Classification tests were conducted of the model to determine the ability of the model accurately predicting the placement of the burglary events as they relate to the radii with which they are associated. The results are depicted in Table 2. Results showed that all the significant models could accurately classify the burglary events in the comparison groups, however overall classification capability of the model diminished as the comparison sizes became close to each other as the radii increased.

Table 2. Classification by radii

Radii Comparison	< km Sample	> km Sample	< km (%)	> km (%)	Overall (%)
< 1 km to > 1 km and greater	23	568	0	100	96.1
< 2 km to > 2 km and greater	132	459	0	100	77.7
< 3 km to > 3 km and greater	283	308	80.6	59.7	69.7

To determine the effects of the individual IVs, a statistical analysis was conducted to determine the significance of the individual regression coefficients. The regression coefficients, Wald statistics, and odds ratios for each of the five predictors were calculated and tested. The results are shown in Table 3. According to the Wald criterion only certain predictors associated per radii comparisons predicted the event of burglary activity. For the three comparison models, connecters were found significant at 1 km with $P[\chi^2(1)>25.286]<0.001$, 2 km $P[\chi^2(1)>3.905]=0.048$, and 3 km $P[\chi^2(1)>9.019]=0.003$; Barriers were found to be significant at 2 km and 3 km comparison models with $P[\chi^2(1)>7.656]=0.006$ and $P[\chi^2(1)>66.692]<0.001$. The rest of the independent variables were not found to be significant for these three models. Table 3 illustrates the significant effect for the individual variables.

Table 3. Significant predictors within the models

Radii	Variables	B	Wald	d.f.	p
1km	Connectors	2.162	25.286	1	0.000
2km	Connectors	0.33	3.905	1	0.048
2km	Barriers	-0.251	7.656	1	0.006
3km	Connectors	-0.404	9.019	1	0.003
3km	Barriers	-0.692	66.692	1	0.000

Table 4. Comparison between Logistic Model vs. constant-only model on 1km band

Radii	Samples within radii	Sample outside radii	Constant α	P value
1 to 2 km	23	109	1.556	$p < 0.001$
2 to 3 km	109	151	0.326	$p = 0.003$
3 to 4 km	151	82	-0.611	$p < 0.001$
4 to 5 km	82	136	0.506	No significance
5 to 6 km	136	45	-1.106	$p < 0.001$
6 to 7 km	45	9	-1.609	$p < 0.001$
7 to 8 km	9	32	1.003	$p < 0.001$
8 to 9 km	32	4	-2.015	P=0.007

Furthermore, in order to test the sensitivity of small scale of 1 km radii on the prediction of the crime occurrence, eight different models on scale of 1km band (1-2km, 2-3km, etc.) was constructed. It was found that even the small scales, the predictors, as a set; reliably distinguish between the different radii as they increase by one kilometer from the epicenter to the nine kilometer radius. Results of the nine different models are illustrated in Table 4.

Classification varied by kilometer comparison being relatively strong from one to four kilometers and five to nine kilometers with results ranging from 74% to 83%, except for the two to three kilometer comparison resulting in 53%. These classifications depict the ability of the models to correctly classify the events per the kilometer radii based on the five independent variables.

According to the Wald criterion, only certain predictors associated per radii comparisons predicted the event of burglary activity. Connector and barriers were significant predictors from one to three kilometers from the epicenter and from five to six kilometers. Repeat victimization was only significant within one to two kilometers and day of week from five to six kilometers.

4   Discussions

This study utilized logistic regression models to predict the probability of burglary activities with respect to the event density epicenter. The predictors of time of day, day of the week, connectors, barriers, and repeat victimization were selected. Results showed that certain variables such as connectors and barriers had significant effects when observed in certain radii size comparisons; however there was variation in the predictors of time of day, day of week, and repeat victimization.

For the models for the radii size comparison of one kilometer to the remaining, two kilometers to the remaining, and the three kilometers to the remaining data population were found to be significant, the bigger radii were insignificant for the prediction. As shown with additional analysis with individual factors and smaller scale model comparison, it was found that the results have a large degree of variability, which produce a wide range of probabilities for the occurrence prediction. A number of factors could be attributed to this variability.

One, the burglaries in the local population area has a large degree of randomness, due to the nature of tourism for the city and weather conditions. As a result, the burglary events in the different radii comparison groups the variation between the data continued to become too great to determine any significance within the time of day and day of the week predictors.

Secondly, Nee and Meenaghan (2006) found that burglars had multiple reasons for committing a crime; money, thrill, and to support a drug habit could be the majority of reasons. However, they found that the individual would search out an area when the need to commit the crime had to satisfy one of the aforementioned reasons, which can be best described as stochastic. It is possible that there might be no discernible pattern or set of circumstances that would allow the burglar to target a specific residence. In our study, the data was compiled from all burglary activities within the lcoal area, which implies that the decisions of multiple burglars could involve with other factors, causing the complexity for predicting the occurrence accurately.

In this study, the level of detail associated with repeat victimization was not explored precisely. Based on the layout of the local area, the repeat victimization was often not the action of the same offender but of different burglars to generate an effect of repeat victimization. The addition of multiple offenders within a given area without prior knowledge and history of the targeted location cause the deviation from the pattern generation for this factor.

Furthermore, there is a massive single lane road system that interconnects neighborhoods of local area, essentially eliminating the need for the multi-lane road system for egress from a targeted location. The size of the neighborhoods in local area also affords additional concealment by allowing a burglar to access different areas effectively expanding the area searched by law enforcement following a crime and reducing detection. The unique features of connectors and barriers for the local area might lead to its significance for the model.

Hammond and Young [3] showed that crime will effectively reduce as it expands from the identified epicenter, consistent with the findings from our study. However one has to keep in mind that the identified epicenter was calculated based on all empirical data. Based on observation the majority of the crime took place in a high demographic area that is characteristic of low economical and financial income which results in 15% of the population falling below the poverty level. This is greater than the national average as reported by the 2009 U.S. Census Bureau report. By incorporating all the data from local police department, it eliminated significant effects that would normally be demonstrated by specific types of demographic, economics, and financial influences, as Haddad and Moghadam [2] showed that isolating a specific demographic and economics associated with a particular area would yield stronger results when determining the contributors associated with burglary. The mixture of data from different areas could lead to some diminishing patterns for the crime.

5   Conclusions

The study used logistic regression to investigate the factors associated with burglary activity for a local city. It was found that only repeat victimization, connectors, and barriers were significant in determining a burglary probability at certain radii ranges. Further analysis and discussion suggests that the size of the observation area of city and other factors must be refined to strengthen the predictive model. It is believed that the local police department would benefit from this study by utilizing the model within a more constrained area observing the same factors as described in this study. Applying the procedures and model as discussed in this study within a one kilometer area with a 100 meter radii incremental comparison, will provide the resolution required for predictive analysis.

The limitation of this study also pertains to the method itself. Logistic regression model is limited to identifying the probability of burglary activity. It only provides information as it relates to the likelihood of burglary activity within certain radii distances of the cluster's epicenter. This model will not identify specific locations, specifically residences, but will encompass the roads associated with an identified area in turn contributing to the police department patrol plan to deter or capture burglary suspects.

Given the conclusion that smaller geographic areas are required for stronger time and space analysis, connectors and barriers potentially no longer will be influential given the observation the burglar will remain in a neighborhood they too utilize for residence. On the contrary, connectors and barriers can be further refined to determine the amount of association the targeted residence has with the actual residence of the described offender. Overall greater detail needs to be incorporated into a study that will utilize the predictors of time of day, day of the week, connectors, barriers, and repeat victimization. As demonstrated by this study encompassing a wide range of data over a large area with no refinement will yield insignificant results. This study can further be refined to observe smaller clusters of activity; this will allow law enforcement professionals to focus patrol efforts within a one kilometer residential

In reference to utilizing this study for other modes such as other law enforcement activities or IED pattern analysis and prediction the same approach can still be utilized when specific targeted areas of interest are identified based on activity and proximity to one another. The reduction of the observed area along with detailed analysis of the events within that given area will increase the significance of the predictors as well as develop an accurate prediction model.

References

1. Gottfredson, M., Hirschi, T.: A General Theory of Crime. Stanford University Press, Stanford (1990)
2. Haddad, G.R.K., Moghadam, H.M.: The socioeconomic and demographic determinants of crime in Iran (a regional panel study). European Journal of Law and Economics 32(1), 99–114 (2011)
3. Hammond, L., Youngs, D.: Decay functions and criminal spatial processes: Geographical offender profiling of volume crime. Journal of Investigative Psychology and Offender Profiling 8(1), 90–102 (2011)
4. Horney, J.: An alternate psychology of criminal behavior. Criminology 44, 1–16 (2006)
5. Kai, Y.T., Heng, M.A., Bullock, L.M.: What provokes young people to get into trouble: Singapore stories. Preventing School Failure 51(2), 13–17 (2007)
6. Jing, W., Tao, Z.: Analysis of decision tree classification algorithm based on attribute reduction and application in criminal behavior. In: Pro. of 2011 3rd Conference on Computer Research and Development (ICCRD), Shanghai, China, March 11-13, pp. 27–30 (2011)
7. Mischel, W., Shoda, Y.: A cognitive-affect system theory of personality: Reconceptualizing situations, dispositions, dynamics, and invariance in personality structure. Psychological Review 102(2), 246–268 (1995)
8. Nee, C., Meenaghan, A.: Expert decision making in burglars. Brit. J. Criminol. 46, 935–949 (2006)
9. Peeters, M.P.: The influence of physical barriers on the journey-to-crime of offenders. Netherlands Institute for the Study of Crime and Law Enforcement, The Netherlands (2007)

10. Pillai, G., Kumar, R.: Simulation of human criminal behavior using clustering algorithm. In: Proc. of International Conference on Computational Intelligence and Multimedia Applications (ICCIMA 2007), vol. 4, pp. 105–109 (2007)

11. Pitcher, A., Johnson, S.: Exploring theories of victimization using a mathematical model of burglary. Journal of Research in Crime and Delinquency 48(1), 83–109 (2011)

12. Ratcliffe, J.H.: The hotspot matrix: a framework for the spatio-temporal targeting of crime reduction. Police Practice and Research 5(1), 5–23 (2004)

13. Ratcliffe, J.H., McCullagh, M.J.: The perception of crime hot spots: a spatial study in Nottingham. In: LaVigne, N. (ed.) PERF/Crime Mapping Research Center, U.K., Washington, DC, ch. 6 (1998)

14. Rengart, G.F.: The journey to crime. In: Bruinsma, G., Elffers, H., Willem, J., de Keijser (eds.) Punishment, Places, and Perpetrators: Developments in Criminology and Criminal Justice Research, pp. 169–181. Willan Publishing, UffculmeCullompton (2004)

15. Sagovsky, A., Johnson, S.D.: When does repeat burglary victimization occur? The Australian and New Zealand Journal of Criminology 40(1), 1–26 (2007)

16. Short, M.B., D'Orsogna, M.R., Brantingham, P.J., Tita, G.E.: Measuring and modeling repeat and near-repeat burglary effects. Journal of Quantitative Criminology 25(3), 325–339 (2009)

17. Sterzer, P.: Born to be criminal? What to make of early biological risk factors for criminal behavior. The American Journal of Psychiatry 167(1), 56–60 (2010)

Using Video Prototyping as a Means to Involve Crisis Communication Personnel in the Design Process: Innovating Crisis Management by Creating a Social Media Awareness Tool

Joel Brynielsson, Fredrik Johansson, and Sinna Lindquist

Swedish Defence Research Agency, SE-164 90 Stockholm, Sweden
firstname.lastname@foi.se

Abstract. Social media is increasingly used for all kinds of everyday communication, with vast amounts of user-generated content being continuously generated and published. The data provides a new form of information source that can be exploited for obtaining additional knowledge regarding a subset of the population. Although it might be difficult to organize and assess individual text fragments, valuable insights contributing to the overall situational awareness can also be gained through acquiring social media texts and analyzing statistical properties in the data in near real-time. One such avenue of approach which is currently being developed is to analyze the text content linguistically and extract measures regarding the overall feelings and attitudes that people express in relation to an ongoing crisis. To make use of this kind of new information requires the algorithms and the resulting statistics to be designed and presented according to operational crisis management needs. In this paper, we describe the involvement of crisis management stakeholders in a series of user-centered activities in order to understand the needs, and design a useful tool. In particular, video prototyping has been used as method for quickly capturing a first explicit design idea based on real life experience, that could later be used for further generalization and tool design.

1 Introduction

The overall objective of the EU research project Alert4All is to improve the effectiveness of alert and communication towards the population during crises. One component in the Alert4All vision is for the command and control (C2) personnel to be able to monitor social media to find out how people perceive the crisis and how they react to—or not react to—communicated alert messages. Hence, the aim of the Alert4All screening of new media (SNM) tool is to enhance situational awareness [3] among crisis management personnel with regard to public opinions and citizen alertness, based on on-line web content from Twitter, blogs, and other social media. [2,4,8] Monitoring public perception of communicated alert messages has been identified as a particularly important application area for the tool. In this way, new alert messages can be tailored based

S. Yamamoto (Ed.): HIMI/HCII 2013, Part III, LNCS 8018, pp. 559–568, 2013.

on the estimated receiver susceptibility, i.e., how well previous messages have been received by a particular group of people. Designing such a tool is difficult since the relevant C2 stakeholders are busy people who are often on standby 24/7, and are also hesitant to alter daily procedures that are in operative use. This paper describes the activities with and the experiences from involving key personnel to bring about an informed user-centered design of the SNM tool.

The remainder of the paper is structured as follows. Section 2 provides a brief introduction to sentiment analysis and its potential for contributing to crisis management. Then, Section 3 outlines the research design, and Section 4 discusses the workshop series. Next, Section 5 summarizes the major findings from the workshop series, and Section 6 presents the resulting design considerations. Finally, Section 7 concludes the paper.

2   Social Media Awareness

Sentiment analysis, also referred to as opinion mining, has received much research attention during the last decade. Various interpretations of the term exist, but here we use the definition given by Liu [6] who considers sentiment analysis to be the computational study of opinions, sentiment, and emotions expressed in text. Affect analysis, also known as emotion classification, can be considered to be a sub-problem of the broader sentiment analysis problem [1].

Most research on sentiment analysis focuses on classifying a linguistic unit (such as a sentence or a document) as having a positive, negative, or neutral opinion towards the topic of the text. The topic is often assumed to be known in advance (e.g., by having a dataset containing only reviews of a particular movie), but it can also be part of the sentiment analysis task to find out toward which target or topic a specific sentiment is directed. Significantly less research exists on affect analysis, where one instead of only extracting a positive or negative sentiment (and potentially also the strength of the sentiment), also extracts people's emotions, such as "anger" or "fear." From this perspective, affect analysis can be considered a more fine-grained sentiment analysis task.

As a crisis management method, new media web screening is typically used for determining the state of various clusters of people. Here, state refers to, e.g., an emotional state that can be detected by analyzing new media text content linguistically with regard to sentiment, e.g., that persons are upset, happy, ignorant, etc. The relevant clusters of people refer to sections of the population that, in some relevant sense, resemble each other in some way, i.e., when disseminating a warning message one can use web screening to investigate whether tourists, elderly, immigrants, etc., have really been targeted by the message or if one should use another communication channel or perhaps reformulate the message in order to obtain better coverage or perhaps convey the information differently. Hence, social media awareness for crisis management requires a purposeful combination of data acquisition and sentiment analysis.

3   Methodology

To come up with an informed, useable, and useful design, it is important to acquire relevant information from the users of the intended design, whether it is a system or an interactive device. [9] The users are considered "domain experts," as they are experts at their own work in their own context, such as working as operators in a C2 center. That is not to say that they are the best to tell others about what they do, since there might be—and often is—a discrepancy between what you do and what you say you do. Therefore it is important to find methods to really make users give away what they actually know about their domain. It should also be noted that the acquirement of user input regarding a design serves to enrich the designers' and developers' design work, not to explicitly telling them what to do. That is, the users are experts within their domain, and the designers and developers are experts within their domain, i.e., design and development.

There are a variety of ways to get user input on a design, depending on the users and their context, the designers and their context, and in what stage a design is. In our case, the intended users of the SNM tool are commanders and operators working in C2 operating centers during a crisis. The users accessible for the Alert4All project and the workshop series are those that are part of the Alert4All advisory board which represents several European countries and C2 related professions. The SNM tool designers and developers also have different backgrounds from working in different European countries at organizations that differ regarding their focus on research vs. industry. Hence, when it comes to the people involved, language, culture and knowledge differences had to be taken into consideration when planning the user-centered activities. To make use of and draw upon the advisory board domain expertise, and to minimize the risk of language and cultural barriers to become problematic, the workshop was conducted using a variety of engaging design methods such as sticky note sessions, storyboarding, video prototyping, etc. These methods emphasize talking, writing, drawing, and filming as being different expressions that would help the participants to inform one another and also to inform the design itself. [5] In the end, the video prototyping activity turned out to be instrumental for the design end result, and will therefore be covered in more detail.

Video prototyping [7] as a concept can be described as a method to illustrate and communicate design ideas. The video prototype creation is done group wise as a mutual effort, which makes the video a shared artifact showing a joint design idea. It is based on real life stories and experiences told by the users, which makes the design idea explicit, focused, and detailed, rather than general. The explicitness is of importance to become concrete in the user-centered prototyping. Generalizations come later in the design process. Furthermore, it is a "quick and dirty" method, since you describe the design idea through a scenario using a storyboard and then shoot the video sequences in the order they should appear in the video. It means that there is no editing, which makes the video prototype rough as an instant sketch or prototype. Also, it is a useful method for "show and tell," since the design ideas are contextualized through the video and will appear the same over and over again. Hence, when watched together it is always possible to criticize the design and give feedback. To summarize, one can think of video prototypes as user-generated contextualized design sketches, where design generalizations and realizations come later in a follow-up design process involving designers and developers.

4   Workshop Series

Throughout the duration of the Alert4All project, the advisory board has been brought together every tenth month at three occasions to provide feedback to the project, which has been utilized for obtaining three types of feedback: 1) a pre-study, 2) a design workshop, and 3) a validation exercise.

4.1   Pre-study

In June 2011, the advisory board met for the first time in Stockholm in Sweden in order to identify key factors to be considered for the design of a crisis management social media screening tool [8]. The participants' had different experiences from more or less similar events which were shared among them. Of particular interest was to discuss the assumptions underlying the Alert4All project as a whole, and the SNM tool in particular. Using a series of sticky note sessions, the participants confirmed that the ideas underlying the envisioned SNM tool is not something that they are used to or practicing in today's work, but that the SNM tool could probably be an important tool given the right type of implementation.

4.2   Design Workshop

In March 2012, a design workshop involving the advisory board was held in Munich in Germany in order to answer the following questions related to the further design of the SNM tool:

- What kinds of emotional states are relevant to consider operationally, i.e., what public emotions do the advisory board members consider to be interesting to know about in order to make an informed decision in a C2 situation?
- How would the advisory board members prefer to have the result of the screening presented?

Before the workshop, a two-page scenario description (based on the validated overall Alert4All scenario description) was compiled. The scenario contained a trigger incident and consequential incidents, namely a water reservoir dam wall breach followed by a leakage of a chemical substance, an explosion, fire, and finally infrastructure damage. The participants were asked to prepare by reading this scenario and envisioning the course of events that might emerge in such a situation.

After getting familiarized with each other, the workshop context, and the assumptions underlying the project in general, and the SNM tool in particular, the first sticky note session was introduced. Divided into three groups, the participants were asked to individually think of and write down the types of emotional states that they considered relevant to consider operationally, i.e., what public emotions that would, in their opinion, be interesting to know about in order to make an informed decision in a C2 situation. Many notes were written and discussed in a clustering session where the group participants came to agree on a number of overall emotions/expressions that it would be interesting to know about. The group results were later synthesized into a smaller set of relevant emotions according to Section 5.

As a basis for the video prototyping activity, the advisory board then discussed how to make use of the envisioned awareness that could emerge as a result of using the SNM tool, i.e., they addressed questions regarding how one would want public perceptions to be presented in order for the information to be useful for making informed C2 decisions. A main conclusion from this discussion was that emergency management largely consists of performing actions in order to bring a situation into a, in some sense, better situation, i.e., what you want to have presented in the graphical user interface is how the situation is right now in terms of emotions relative to some attributes that you can actually do something about. For example, people might be anxious about the lack of food, which could be brought into a new situation by sending out information with regard to places to find food. Here, "anxiety" is the emotion to be looked for, and "food" is the attribute that the emotion targets. After that a new situation might occur where people are less anxious about the food, but perhaps have become angry about being neglected by politicians, which could potentially be targeted by sending out a second message, and so forth. As a consequence, quantification of the involved variables (emotions and attributes) was another main conclusion that the group saw as an important aspect that the SNM interface needs to take into account.

A most productive part of the workshop followed where the participants came up with how to incorporate the above described aspects (moving between states, and quantification) in a video prototype by making use of colored circles taking both dimensions (attribute vs. emotion) into account, showing a snapshot for each time slot to be considered. That is, the timeline was thought of as being discretized based on certain events such as when the crisis occurs, when a message has been sent out, etc. In Figure 1 six such snapshots can be seen. Here, the pink circles represent the attribute "environment," the orange circles represent the attribute "health," and so forth. Looking further, one can see that the public initially (i.e., after 10 and 20 minutes which is depicted in the first two snapshots) is concerned about the environment attribute, while later (i.e., after 30 and 60 minutes as depicted in the third and fourth snapshot) becomes angry regarding the environmental damages, and finally (i.e., after 2 and 3 hours according to the last two snapshots) becomes content with the development. Also, one can notice that the health attribute varies in size, indicating that the public's initial (after 10 minutes) fairly small concern successively develops into a more substantial concern after 30 minutes (the third snapshot). All in all, the result from the video

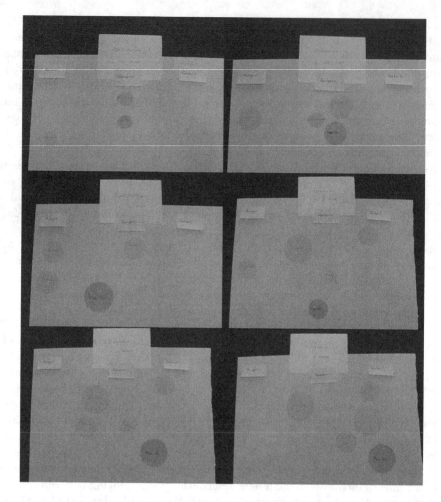

Fig. 1. Screenshots from the video prototype

prototyping activity was a success in that the participants became really involved in actually producing a video prototype describing aspects of the functionality and design that they agreed on being the most important to take into account for a future SNM tool to be used within emergency management.

4.3   Validation Exercise

Finally, in January 2013 the advisory board met for the third time in Bilbao in Spain in order to see and validate a first prototype system. Through a guided walk-through and the possibility to play around with the system, it turned out and was concluded that the many dimensions had to be visualized through several charts as can be seen in Figure 2 rather than trying to capture all relevant aspects in one single chart (as was the case in the shown prototype system).

5 Summary of Workshop Findings

Trying to summarize the main findings from the workshop series, it can be seen that the advisory board members agree on that there are recent events where the SNM would have been beneficial for obtaining better situation awareness (both the Utøya shootings and the London riots were mentioned). Despite this, there was initially skepticism in some of the workshop groups for making use of such tools during a crisis. Somewhat unexpectedly, no privacy considerations were mentioned, but instead the skepticism was based on the potential unreliability of the sources and the collected data ("we are acting on facts, not emotions"). Although the groups could see a clear potential for enhancing the situational awareness among crisis management staff with regard to public opinions and citizen alertness, this aspect was by some of the advisory board members seen as less interesting than the possibility to use the citizens as providers of information (e.g., by having them sending images or videos from the crisis area).

Moving on to the clusters of emotions, emotion states, or moods, the exact naming of the clusters differed amongst the workshop groups but common aspects and a clear theme could be recognized. One such finding is that one can look at many of the suggested emotion states as being somewhere on a continuous scale between a positive and a negative extreme. All groups have mentioned fear, anger, and anxiety as being important negative emotions (although the exact vocabulary has not been the same in all groups). In general, the negative emotions can be seen as more important than the positive ones from a crisis management perspective, but both aspects can be interesting for obtaining a better awareness of the overall picture, and to more clearly see how emotions have changed over time. There has also been a consensus on that active/action-oriented emotions is of larger concern than the passive ones, since the alert messages should be formed in a way that helps people take the correct action.

In terms of visualization, many of the groups have mentioned a need for an adaptive GUI that allows for various kinds of representations. The groups agreed on that it should be possible to see a quantification of emotional states within the posts, and also how these emotions vary over time (most importantly relative to the sent alert messages). Many of the advisory board members also expressed a request to see how the posts are distributed geographically. An interesting aspect that was mentioned in some of the groups is the wish to see the attribute or emotion target of the posts, i.e., to see not only the emotions but also the "theme" or target which the emotion is expressed towards (such as the "food situation"). Related to this is the need to be able to search for specific concepts or terms related to crises, such as "chemical" or "gas." Additionally, the groups wanted the ability to drill down to the actual posts, in order to see not only the overall picture, but also the individual posts.

6 Design Result

The SNM tool design consists of two parts: 1) a data acquisition part in which the user can decide what keywords, sources, etc., to use when retrieving posts

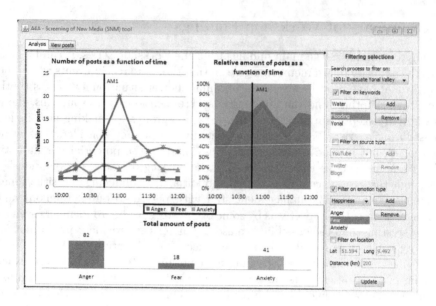

Fig. 2. The SNM data analysis tab gives the operator the possibility to visualize the screening results from a number of statistical viewpoints

related to a crisis, and 2) a data analysis part to be used for analyzing the retrieved posts to become aware of the development of the situation. In the following, we only consider the data analysis part of the tool, since this is the part of the tool that serves to enhance the users' situational awareness. The GUI for the data analysis part comprises an analysis tab according to Figure 2 and a view posts tab according to Figure 3. The main part of the data analysis tab consists of three charts which are meant to provide complementary views of the acquired data and citizens' reactions to communicated alert messages. The top left chart shows the emotional change in the absolute amount of collected posts over time, while the top right chart gives information about the relative change for the same time period. The bottom bar chart gives an aggregated view of the emotional distribution, summarized over the selected time period. As is shown to the right, a number of filtering selections are available for adjusting what data to display in the charts. Several search processes can be initiated during a crisis (e.g., keywords can be added as a new alert message is sent out), so the user has to select which search process to analyze. The user can also choose to only include collected posts containing special keywords of interest (e.g., flooding), or to include only some sources in the analysis. Finally, the user can select which emotions to include in the analysis and has the possibility to include only posts geo-positioned within a certain geographical area of interest. The communicated alert messages are displayed in the charts so that it becomes easy to see if there are emotional changes as reactions to communicated alert messages.

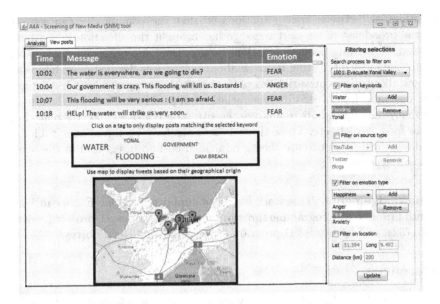

Fig. 3. The second tab gives the operator an alternative view to visualize the underlying data more focusing on the content of the underlying data/posts

The user can obtain an overall view of the situation by using the analysis tab, but in addition to this the user is also able to obtain a deeper understanding of peoples' emotions (e.g., what their emotion targets are). This kind of view is provided by switching to the view posts tab. In this tab, the user can see the collected posts matching the filtering selections and their associated emotions (as classified by an affect analysis algorithm). A tag cloud is displayed in the middle, showing the most frequently used terms within the posts, where the size of the words corresponds to their frequency. Finally, there is also a map in which the geo-positioned posts are aggregated based on their geographical position. By zooming into the map or clicking on a cluster, the individual posts are displayed.

7   Conclusions

The most important finding from the video prototyping activity is that crisis management largely concerns the work of exercising command and control in order to bring a crisis situation into some kind of better situation, and subsequently continuing to perform relevant actions until the crisis has ceased. It follows that situational awareness ought to be defined in terms of the parameters that define the situation, and that also can be affected in order to reach a more desirable situation. For the case of alert and communication, it turned out that the situation therefore needs to be quantified along three dimensions: time, emotions, and attributes. Especially important for the time dimension is to distinguish between crisis situations so that the commander can see how, e.g., the broadcast of an alert message has brought the situation into a better situation. Regarding people's emotions, anger, fear, and positive emotions were deemed the most interesting to know about, i.e., it was deemed more interesting to know about different variations of the negative emotions whilst less interesting to distinguish between different variations of positive moods. Lastly, often an emergency manager wants to analyze the situation relative to a certain attribute such as food, health, etc. These three dimensions have been fundamental for the tool design which is currently being implemented and integrated in the overall Alert4All system.

Acknowledgements. This work has been supported by the European Union Seventh Framework Programme through the Alert4All research project (contract no 261732), and by the R&D program of the Swedish Armed Forces.

References

1. Abbasi, A., Chen, H.: Affect intensity analysis of dark web forums. In: Proceedings of the Fifth IEEE International Conference on Intelligence and Security Informatics (ISI 2007), New Brunswick, New Jersey, pp. 282–288 (May 2007)
2. Artman, H., Brynielsson, J., Johansson, B.J.E., Trnka, J.: Dialogical emergency management and strategic awareness in emergency communication. In: Proceedings of the Eighth International Conference on Information Systems for Crisis Response and Management (ISCRAM 2011), Lisbon, Portugal (May 2011)
3. Endsley, M.R.: Toward a theory of situation awareness in dynamic systems. Human Factors 37(1), 32–64 (1995)
4. Johansson, F., Brynielsson, J., Narganes Quijano, M.: Estimating citizen alertness in crises using social media monitoring and analysis. In: Proceedings of the 2012 European Intelligence and Security Informatics Conference (EISIC 2012), Odense, Denmark, pp. 189–196 (August 2012)
5. Lindquist, S.: Perspectives on Cooperative Design. Ph.D. thesis, Royal Institute of Technology, Stockholm, Sweden (2007)
6. Liu, B.: Sentiment analysis and subjectivity. In: Indurkhya, N., Damerau, F.J. (eds.) Handbook of Natural Language Processing, Machine Learning & Pattern Recognition, 2nd edn., vol. 2. Chapman & Hall, CRC Press, Taylor and Francis Group, Boca Raton, Florida (2010)
7. Mackay, W.E., Ratzer, A.V., Janecek, P.: Video artifacts for design: Bridging the gap between abstraction and detail. In: Proceedings of the ACM Conference on Designing Interactive Systems (DIS 2000), Brooklyn, New York, pp. 72–82 (August 2000)
8. Nilsson, S., Brynielsson, J., Granåsen, M., Hellgren, C., Lindquist, S., Lundin, M., Narganes Quijano, M., Trnka, J.: Making use of new media for pan-european crisis communication. In: Proceedings of the Ninth International Conference on Information Systems for Crisis Response and Management (ISCRAM 2012), Vancouver, Canada (April 2012)
9. Schuler, D., Namioka, A. (eds.): Participatory Design: Principles and Practices. Lawrence Erlbaum Associates, Inc., Hillsdale (1993)

Service Evaluation Method for Managing Uncertainty

Koji Kimita[1], Yusuke Kurita[2], Kentaro Watanabe[3],
Takeshi Tateyama[2], and Yoshiki Shimomura[2]

[1] Dept. of Management Science, Tokyo University of Science, Tokyo, Japan
`kimita@ms.kagu.tus.ac.jp`
[2] Dept. of System Design, Tokyo Metropolitan University, Tokyo, Japan
`{kurita-yusuke,tateyama}@sd.tmu.ac.jp,`
`yoshiki-shimomura@center.tmu.ac.jp`
[3] Center for Service Research, National Institute of Advanced Industrial Science and Technology, Tokyo, Japan
`kentaro.watanabe@aist.go.jp`

Abstract. A service is mainly produced by human capabilities and their interaction, and therefore, the process for the service production includes a lot of uncertainties caused by human factors. In order for service organizations to cope with these uncertainties, in this study, the concept of the modular architecture is applied to the service organization. Especially, this study proposes a method to determine teams consisting of human resources based on the concept of the modular service organization. The effectiveness of this method is demonstrated by the application to a hotel service.

Keywords: Service Engineering, Uncertainty, Design Structure Marix.

1   Introduction

Service is nowadays regarded as a way to achieve the "sustainability" of businesses in manufacturing companies. Long-term and strong relationship with customers can be realized by providing services in combination with a product throughout its lifecycle. In addition, recently, a rapid rise has occurred in expectations that engineering and scientific approaches will bring dramatic improvements in the design and production of services [1]. Indeed, now that the service industry accounts for some 70% of the workforce and Gross Domestic Product (GDP) in Japan [2], it is obvious that the service industry must see dramatic improvement in productivity. According to this background, there is a critical need to establish a method to design and evaluate services from scientific and engineering viewpoints.

On the other hand, the authors of this paper have conducted conceptual research on design services from the viewpoint of engineering. This series of research is called Service Engineering [3-5]. Its objective is to provide a fundamental understanding of services as well as concrete engineering methodologies that can be used to design and evaluate services. The goal of this study is to develop a way of achieving customer satisfaction as a change in the state of the customer of the service. More specifically, procedures for modeling and analyzing human activities and human behaviors are

S. Yamamoto (Ed.): HIMI/HCII 2013, Part III, LNCS 8018, pp. 569–578, 2013.

formed and a computer-aided design (service CAD) software system [5] using those procedures is developed.

A service is mainly produced by human capabilities and their interaction. In order to implement a service designed by the service CAD, therefore, it is important for the service organization to manage uncertainties caused by human factors. To solve this problem, this study aims to propose a method to determine a service organization in consideration of uncertainties. In the proposed method, the concept of the modular architecture is applied to the service organization. The effectiveness of this method is demonstrated by the application to a hotel service.

2   Scope of This Study

2.1   Definition of a Service

Service Engineering is a new engineering discipline with the objective of providing a fundamental understanding of services as well as concrete engineering methodologies to design and evaluate services. In Service Engineering, service is defined as an activity between a service provider and a service receiver to change the state of the receiver [3-5]. Note that the term "service" is used in a broad sense, and, thus, the design target includes not only intangible human activities but also tangible products.

According to the definition, a receiver is satisfied when his/her state changes to a new desirable state. Since the value of a service is determined by the receiver, service design should be based on the state change of the receiver. For design purposes, it is necessary to find a method to express the state changes of the receiver. The target receiver's state in service design is represented as a set of parameters called receiver state parameters (RSPs) [3-5]. RSPs are changed by "service contents" and "service channels," as shown in Figure 1. Service contents are materials, energy, or information that directly changes the receiver's state. Service channels transfer, amplify, and control the service contents.

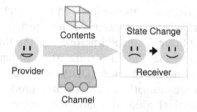

Fig. 1. Definition of a service [3-5]

2.2   Definition of an Uncertainty

Since a service is mainly produced by human capabilities and their interaction, the production process includes a lot of uncertainties. These uncertainties influence on the service quality and efficiency, and therefore, many researches have been conducted in order to manage them. In the ergonomics, for example, some studies classify uncertainties from the viewpoint of human errors (for example [6]), and then, propose methods to prevent them. While these studies mainly focus on provider's human activities, Frei proposed the five types of variability introduced by customers [7].

An uncertainty is represented as uncontrolled stochastic variations with the mathematics of probability, and therefore, is distinct from imprecision [8]. For example, in a service process, uncertainties include human capability variations, customer preference variations and so on. In order to cope with these uncertainties, it is crucial to assess the expected size of variations and determine target range. On the other hand, imprecision is used for the state where a certain variable may potentially assume any value with in a possible rang; the final value will emerge from a process. For example, some customer requirements are ambiguous before offering a service; the service provider make these requirements more detail through the service process.

According to this concept, in this study, uncertainty is defined as uncontrolled stochastic variations. Especially, this study focuses on variations of functional inputs and/or outputs among human resources.

3 Service Evaluation Method for Managing Uncertainty

3.1 Overview

Since a service production process includes a lot of uncertainties caused by human capabilities, the service organization needs to have the adaptability for flexible changes in managing these uncertainties. However, addressing the changes requires much more complex interactions among relevant human resources; these types of interactions involve tremendous coordination efforts. To solve this problem, in this study, the concept of the modular architecture is applied to the service organization. Especially, this study proposes a method to determine teams consisting of human resources based on the concept of the modular service organization. In the modular product, each component can be changed independently without influences on the other components. Since teams within a modular service organization can be regarded as the components in a modular product, it is assumed that changes in managing the uncertainties could be addressed within a relevant team. As a result, it could be possible to reduce coordination efforts for managing uncertainties.

In the proposed method, first, the degree of the uncertainties is evaluated from the viewpoint of the information content proposed in the axiomatic design. According to the information content, subsequently, teams within the service organization are specified in order to reduce coordination efforts for managing uncertainties. For the specification of teams, this study adopts the Design Structure Matrix. The remainder of this section introduces the relevant works: Axiomatic Design and Design Structure Matrix.

Axiomatic Design. Axiomatic design proposes fundamental design principles. It is a methodology about how to use fundamental principles during the mapping process among the domains of the design world [9]. The principle defines the elements that have respective domains: customer needs (CNs), functional requirements (FRs), design parameters (DPs), and process variables (PVs) (see Figure 2).

In the design process, CNs in the customer domain are converted into FRs in the functional domain. FRs are a minimum set of independent requirements that completely characterize the functional needs of the design solution. FRs are embodied into DPs in the physical domain, and then DPs determine PVs in the process domain to produce and/or control the DPs.

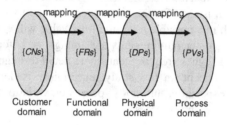

Fig. 2. Four domains of the design world [9]

In axiomatic design, this mapping process is evaluated according to an axiom called the Information Axiom [9], which is stated formally as:

Minimize the information content.

Information is defined in terms of the information content I that is related to the probability of satisfying a given FR. In the Axiomatic Design, the information content is determined by the two ranges: the system range and design range. Figure 3 illustrates these two ranges graphically.

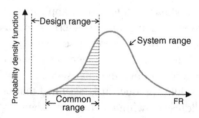

Fig. 3. Relationships among design range, system range, and common range

The system range is plotted as a probability density function versus the specified FR. The design range, on the other hand, represents a target range of the FR. The overlap between the design range and system range is called the common range, and therefore this is the only region where the design requirements are satisfied. Consequently, the area under the common range divided by the area under the system range is equal to the probability of achieving the design objective. As a result, the information content I is expressed as the following equation.

$$I = log\ (A_{sr}/A_{cr}) \tag{1}$$

where

A_{sr} denotes the area under the system range

A_{cr} is the area of the common range

Design Structure Matrix. The design structure matrix (DSM) (e.g. [10]) is becoming a popular representation and analysis tool for system modelling. A DSM displays the relationships between elements of a system. As shown in Figure 4, a DSM is a square matrix with identical row and column labels. An off-diagonal mark represents an element's dependence on another. Reading across a row reveals what other elements are provided by the element in that row. Scanning down a column reveals what other elements the element in that column depends on. For example, in Figure 3, element B provides input to elements A, C, D, F, H, and I, and it depends on outputs from elements C, D, F, and H.

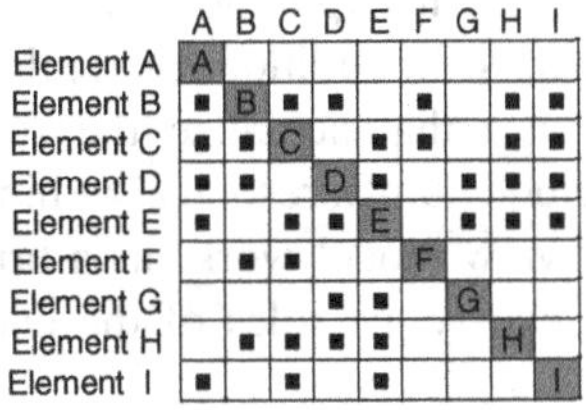

Fig. 4. Example of Design Structure Matrix [10]

DSMs are classified into two main categories: static DSMs and time-based DSMs. Static DSMs represent system elements, such as components of a product architecture or groups in an organization. Static DSMs are usually analyzed with clustering algorithms. In time-based DSMs, on the other hand, the order of the rows and columns indicates a flow through time. Therefore, time-based DSMs represent characteristics of a process sequence, such as feedforward and feedback. Time-based DSMs are typically analyzed using sequencing algorithms.

This study adopts the clustering algorithms in static DSMs. These algorithms are generally clustering along the diagonal marks by reordering the rows and columns of the DSM. Clustering requires several considerations. The foremost objective is to maximize interactions between elements within clusters while minimizing interactions between clusters.

3.2 Procedure of the Proposed Evaluation Method

Step 1: Extraction of customer requirements. Since value in a service is always determined by customers, this method begins with the extraction of customer requirements. For the extraction of customer requirements, in this step, a persona is described. The persona is a tool to give a simplified description of a customer and works as a compass in a design process [11]. According to this persona, subsequently, a scenario is developed to clarify the context in which the service is received. The scenario is described in the form of a state transition graph, since the purpose of receiving a service is to change the customer's state into a more desirable one. The customer's state is represented as a set of parameters called state parameters (SPs) [3-5]. SPs represent the internal/external state of a customer and have a causal relationship. From the SPs, RSPs, which correspond to target requirements in the service design [3-5], are extracted.

Step 2: Development of a realization structure for each customer requirement. In this step, the designers determine a realization structure for each customer requirement, which is represented as an RSP. In this method, we adopt the view model [3-5] as the modeling method for describing the realization structure.

A view model is described in terms of the functional relationships among RSPs, functions and entities. It is assumed that contents that realize customer requirements in a service are comprised of various functions [3-5]. These functions are expressed by function names (FNs) as lexical expressions and function parameters (FPs) as target parameters of the functions. In addition, the realization structure is associated with entities and their attributes that actualize the functions in the view model. Entities in the view model include human resource within a service organization.

As shown in Figure 5, the view model works as a bridge from an RSP to entities and thus allows designers to clarify the roles of the entities in consideration of the RSP.

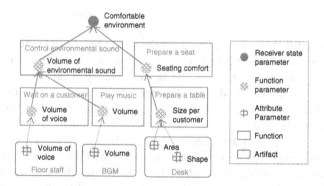

Fig. 5. Example of the view model (a restaurant service) [3-5]

Step 3: Evaluation of uncertainties among human resources. This method focuses on uncertainties with regard to functional inputs and/or outputs among human resources. Therefore, first, the designers develop a functional input-output model based on the view models described in Step 2. In the functional input-output model, FPs correspond to the inputs and/or outputs; FNs are represented as lexical expressions of functions that convert the inputs into the outputs. In addition, entities in the view models are decomposed into human resources so that each human resource can take responsibility for a single function. Next, the designers estimate uncertainties of the inputs and/or outputs represented as FPs. In this method, an uncertainty of an FP is evaluated from the viewpoint of the information content that is defined in the Axiomatic Design [9]. Namely, the information content is evaluated by the system range and design range of corresponding FPs, and then is replaced by a number, for example 5 (large), 3 (normal), 1 (small).

Step 4: Specification of teams within a service organization. Next, the designers specify teams that consist of human resources. For the specification, a DSM is developed according to the inputs and/or outputs developed in the previous step. The DSM in which elements correspond to human resources is described using the numbers that represent the information content of the FP. According to the numbers in the matrix, a clustering of off-diagonal elements is conducted. In this method, the clustering for specifying teams is carried out on the basis of the following assumptions.

1. The difficulty of managing uncertainties is proportional to the amount of the information content. Managing the large amount of the information content requires more attention and/or more time between relevant human resources.
2. It is easier for teams to manage uncertainties within the same team rather than across different teams. In order to manage uncertainties, human resources need to have sufficient communication to share the information content. Human resources belonging in the same team easily communicate with each other rather than ones belonging in the different teams.
3. It is easier for teams to manage uncertainties in smaller human resources rather than large ones. The fewer human resources take part in a team, the easier the team will facilitate managing uncertainties.

Based on these assumptions, the equation proposed by Fernandez [12] is adopted as the evaluation formula of the clustering. This formula aims to minimize the coordination cost among teams in a product development project. In this method, the formula is applied to the service design in order to find teams that minimize coordination cost.

The formula first calculates a coordination cost for each human resource in the DSM, and then the sum of the coordination costs for each resource provides a total coordination cost. Equations 2-3 show the coordination cost for a human resource i.

If both human resource i and j are in any cluster k;

$$\text{Coordination Cost(human resource}_i) = \sum_{j=1}^{size}\big(\text{DSM}(i,j) + \text{DSM}(j,i)\big) * \sum_{k=1}^{Cl} \text{cl\_size}(k)^{pow\_cc} \quad (2)$$

If no k cluster contains both human resource i and j;

$$\text{Coordination Cost(human resource}_i) = \sum_{j=1}^{size}\big(\text{DSM}(i,j) + \text{DSM}(j,i)\big) * size^{pow\_cc} \quad (3)$$

where;

$size$	is the size of the DSM: the number of human resources in the DSM
$\text{DSM}(i,j)$	is the number of the information content between human resource i and j. Note that when $i = j$, $\text{DSM}(i,j) = 0$, $\text{DSM}(j,i) = 0$
Cl	is the maximum number of clusters (set to the number of human resources in this analysis)

cl_size   is the number of human resources contained in cluster k

pow_cc   is a parameter that controls the type of penalty assigned to the size of the cluster in the coordination cost (set to 2 in this analysis)

The total coordination is expressed as Equation 4. This objective function is the expression that the algorithm attempts to minimize.

$$\text{Total Coordination Cost} = \sum_{i=1}^{size} \text{Coordination Cost(human resource}_i) \tag{4}$$

According to the result of the DSM, finally, teams in the service organization can be specified based on clusters in the DSM. Each team is not necessarily corresponding to an actual department or division in the organization, but corresponding to a unit to conduct the management of uncertainties.

4   Application

In this chapter, the proposed method is demonstrated in an application to a hotel service. The purpose of this application is to determine teams in the organization of the hotel service providers.

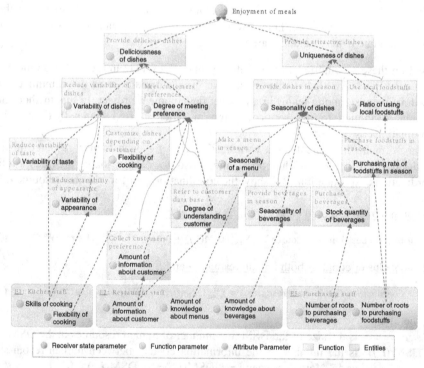

Fig. 6. The view model for "Enjoyment of meals"

In this application, first, RSPs, which correspond to target customer requirements in this service, were defined. As a result, "Enjoyment of meals", "Atmosphere of guest rooms", "comfort of services" and "Flexibility of services" were determined as RSPs. Next, realization structures were developed for these RSPs. Figure 6 shows an example of the view model for "Enjoyment of meals". Functions that realize "Enjoyment of meals" were decomposed into detailed functions, for example "Provide delicious dishes" and "Provide attractive dishes", and then entities, for example "Kitchen staff" and "restaurant staff", were associated with these functions.

These view models were subsequently converted into functional input-output models, and then, entities in the view models were decomposed into human resources so that each human resource took responsibility for a single function. With regard to the inputs and/or outputs among human resources, uncertainties were estimated from the viewpoint of the information content. In this application, the subjective assessment was carried out in order to evaluate the information content, and then, the information contents were rated on a three-point scale, from 1 (small) to 5 (large).

Next, for the specification of teams, a DSM was developed according to the functional input-output models; the DSM was described using the numbers that represent the information content. According to the numbers in the DSM, the clustering of off-diagonal elements was conducted. As a result, eight clusters of human resources were specified as shown in Figures 7 (a)-(h). Each cluster corresponds to a team in the service organization. For example, team (a) includes four kind of human resources that take responsibility for functions, such as "F26: Purchasing foodstuffs" and "F8: Planning beverages". These human resources originally belonged to the entities "Purchasing staff" and "Restaurant staff" respectively.

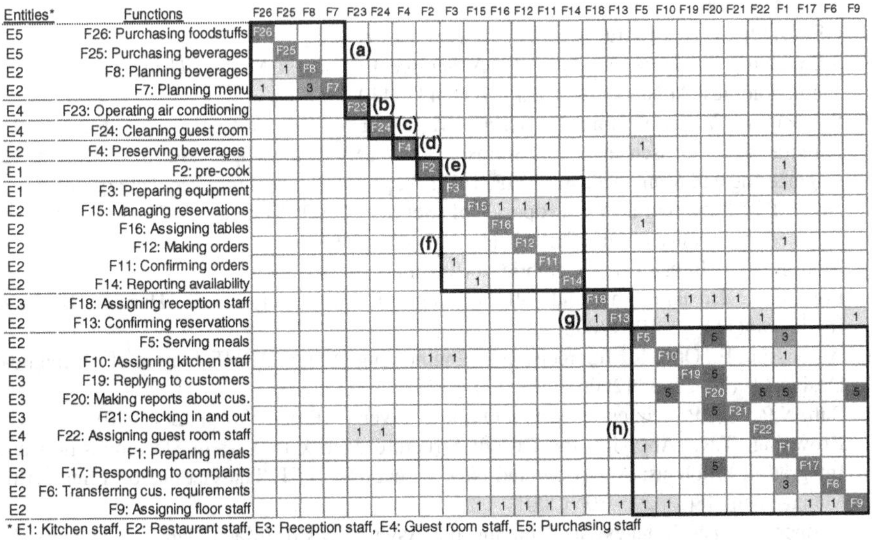
Entities*
Functions
F26 F25 F8 F7 F23 F24 F4 F2 F3 F15 F16 F12 F11 F14 F18 F13 F5 F10 F19 F20 F21 F22 F1 F17 F6 F9
E5 F26: Purchasing foodstuffs
E5 F25: Purchasing beverages
E2 F8: Planning beverages
E2 F7: Planning menu
E4 F23: Operating air conditioning
E4 F24: Cleaning guest room
E2 F4: Preserving beverages
E1 F2: pre-cook
E1 F3: Preparing equipment
E2 F15: Managing reservations
E2 F16: Assigning tables
E2 F12: Making orders
E2 F11: Confirming orders
E2 F14: Reporting availability
E3 F18: Assigning reception staff
E2 F13: Confirming reservations
E2 F5: Serving meals
E2 F10: Assigning kitchen staff
E3 F19: Replying to customers
E3 F20: Making reports about cus.
E3 F21: Checking in and out
E4 F22: Assigning guest room staff
E1 F1: Preparing meals
E2 F17: Responding to complaints
E2 F6: Transferring cus. requirements
E2 F9: Assigning floor staff
(a)
(b)
(c)
(d)
(e)
(f)
(g)
(h)
* E1: Kitchen staff, E2: Restaurant staff, E3: Reception staff, E4: Guest room staff, E5: Purchasing staff

Fig. 7. DSM clustering result of the hotel service

5   Summary

This study proposed a method to determine teams consisting of human resources based on the concept of the modular service organization. In the application, the proposed method is applied to a hotel service, and then, the eight teams, as shown in Figures 7 (a)-(h), were specified. For example, team (h) includes ten kinds of human resources that take responsibilities for functions, such as "F5: Serving meals", "F19: Replying to customers", and "F20: Making reports about customers". Since the information contents of outputs from these functions relatively large, i.e. 3 or 5, managing uncertainties regarding these functions will impose high coordination costs on relevant human resources. Therefore, it is effective for the human resources to manage the uncertainties within the same team rather than across different teams. In addition, since the information contents of inputs and/or outputs among the eight teams are relatively small, i.e. 1, it is enable for each team to carry out the management of uncertainties independently. Therefore, the proposed method is useful for determining teams in consideration of coordination efforts for managing uncertainties. In this application, however, uncertainties were estimated by the subjective assessment. Future works therefore include further applications about evaluation of the information content. In addition, feasibilities of teams result from the proposed method need to be validated.

References

1. Spohrer, J., Maglio, P.: The Emergence of Service Science: Toward systematic service innovations to accelerate co-creation of value. Production and Operations management 15, 329–343 (2006)
2. OECD: OECD.Stat Extracts, http://www.oecd.org
3. Shimomura, Y., Hara, T., Arai, T.: A Service Evaluation Method Using Mathematical Methodologies. Annals of the CIRP 57(1), 437–440 (2008)
4. Shimomura, Y., Tomiyama, T.: Service Modeling for Service Engineering. In: Arai, E., Kimura, F., Goossenaerts, J., Shirase, K. (eds.) Knowledge and Skill Chains in Engineering and Manufacturing. IFIP, vol. 168, pp. 31–38. Springer, Heidelberg (2005)
5. Arai, T., Shimomura, Y.: Proposal of Service CAD System -A Tool for Service Engineering-. Annals of the CIRP 53(1), 397–400 (2004)
6. Reason, J.T.: Human Error. Cambridge University Press (1990)
7. Frei, F.X.: Breaking the trade-off between efficiency and service. Harvard Business Review 84(11), 92–101 (2006)
8. Antonsson, E., Otto, K.: Imprecision in Engineering Design. ASME Journal of Mechanical Design 117(B), 25–32 (2006)
9. Suh, N.P.: The Principles of Design. Oxford University Press, New York (1990)
10. Browning, T.R.: Applying the Design Structure Matrix to System Decomposition and Integration Problems: A Review and New Directions. IEEE Transactions on Engineering Management 48(3), 292–306 (2001)
11. Cooper, A.: The Inmates Are Running the Asylum. SAMS/Macmillan, Indianapolis, IA (1999)
12. Fernandez, C.I.G.: Integration analysis of product architecture to support effective team co-location. ME thesis, MIT, Cambridge, MA (1998)

On Services and Insights of Technology Intelligence System

Seungwoo Lee, Minhee Cho, Sa-Kwang Song, and Hanmin Jung

Department of Computer Intelligence Research, Korea Institute of Science and Technology Information, 245 Daehak-ro, Yuseong-gu, Daejeon, 305-806, Korea
{swlee,mini,esmallj,jhm}@kisti.re.kr

Abstract. The importance of technology strategy in business is getting emphasized as global technology competition is being rapidly intensified. To achieve successful business, nothing is more important than timely establishment of proper technology strategy. The process of establishing technology strategy is technology planning, which should be supported by technology intelligence (TI). To reduce the cost of manual technology intelligence activities, we suggest an automated technology intelligence system which can support whole steps of technology planning systematically. We examined what decision should be made and what information is required in each step. And then, we suggested seven services and their explicit insights which have a specific role at each step of technology planning. Considering recent growth of mobile environment of users, we implemented our system running on tablet PCs.

Keywords: technology planning, strategy planning, technology intelligence, knowledge acquisition, information analytics, insight.

1 Introduction

As business and technology environment rapidly changes and global technology competition is being gradually intensified, the importance of technology strategy as well as business strategy (or strategic management) is getting emphasized. Business strategy identifies the objectives of a particular organization (institution or company) and defines the plans and actions to achieve the objectives [1], while technology strategy defines the objectives, strategies and tactics related to development and application of technologies within an organization [2]. To achieve successful business, nothing is more important than timely establishment of proper technology strategy in addition to business strategy. That is, an organization should continue to discover emerging and promising technologies for its business and make a timely plan of when and how to acquire such technologies. This process of establishing technology strategy is technology planning, which should be supported by technology intelligence (TI). Technology intelligence includes a wide variety of activities such as gathering, analyzing and forwarding information on new technologies to support technology planning and decision-making of an organization [3].

S. Yamamoto (Ed.): HIMI/HCII 2013, Part III, LNCS 8018, pp. 579–587, 2013.

To perform proper technology planning, each organization needs to perform active, continuous and objective technology intelligence activities. However, these activities require many human resources including domain experts and cost too much for small and medium-sized enterprises (SMEs) to come up with. Some analytics tools such as SAS[1] or VantagePoint[2] provide useful analytic functionalities for technology intelligence, but they require a user to learn advanced skills for correct usage of them and to prepare his or her own source data to be analyzed. Furthermore, those tools do not support the whole steps of technology planning systematically. On the other hand, existing information retrieval systems like Google Search[3] (or Google Scholar Search[4]) provide a cheap means of finding technical literature such as papers and patents, but they have a certain limit to their usefulness because they just list up too many results. So, this paper suggests an automated technology intelligence service which can be used with ease like existing information retrieval systems and can support the whole steps of technology planning systematically.

The rest of this paper is organized as follows. In Section 2, we surveys related work to analytics for technology intelligence and then we explore the steps of technology planning in Section 3. We investigate what is needed for each step of technology planning and suggest processes for knowledge acquisition in Section 4, and then define services for technology intelligence in Section 5. We finally conclude in Section 6.

2   Related Work

Gartner[5] pronounces the list of promising technologies every year. Information analytics organizations such as Gartner usually surveys and investigates promising technologies from many domain experts across the whole world through Delphi method [4], and therefore many researchers and companies refer to and rely on their pronouncement. However, it costs quite much and there are also some criticisms that the result of survey depends on subjective opinions of experts participated in the survey.

More objective analytics may be obtained from data. There have recently been some approaches which perform and provide analytics from data, beyond a typical search paradigm. Google Scholar Search and Microsoft Academic Search[6] analyze and serve researchers' specialties, research topics and research network such as co-authorship and citation relationship and paths from publication data such as papers and patents. However, they are so far focusing on network analytics of researchers and organizations, not analytics for technology planning. On the other hand, Recorded Future[7] tries to analyze and predict future events. It continually collects public Web

---

[1]   http://www.sas.com
[2]   http://www.thevantagepoint.com
[3]   http://www.google.com
[4]   http://scholar.google.com
[5]   http://www.gartner.com
[6]   http://academic.research.microsoft.com
[7]   http://www.recordedfuture.com

content such as online news, blogs, public niche sources, government web sites, and financial databases, etc., analyzes them to identify references to entities and events, and visualizes insights for better understanding of complex relationships and issues.

Because technology planning is an important issue for enhancing global competencies of each country, there have been performed several government-funded research projects about information analytics for business and technology intelligence. US government has supported *FUSE* (Foresight and Understanding from Scientific Exposition) project [5], the goal of which is to enhance inter-disciplinary, converged competitiveness by managing vast amounts and kinds of literature with a single, established system while also developing an automated method to support systematic and successive evaluation of technological potential based on information identified in the literature. EU also has supported a similar project, *CUBIST* (Combining and Uniting Business Intelligence with Semantic Technology) [6], which aims to develop an enhanced Semantic Web search platform to allow business-related users to better understand large and heterogeneous data. These two projects commonly have started from 2011 and combine explicit metadata used by most services with implicit metadata hidden within text documents, in order to effectively find technological potential. However, *FUSE* mainly focuses on quantitative analysis based on scientometrics while *CUBIST* mainly focuses on qualitative analysis based on Text Mining and Semantic Web technologies. Korea has also supported similar project, *InSciTe* (Intelligence from Science & Technology) [7], which aims to provide technological policy makers, researchers, and small and medium-sized enterprises with technology intelligence services. *InSciTe* has focused on analytics of technological potential and levels of research agents. In this paper, we extend the *InSciTe* to support the whole steps of technology planning systematically.

3   Technology Planning Steps

Technology planning in an organization is generally carried out through the following five steps (see Fig.1): (1) selection and understanding of an emerging and promising technology; (2) understanding of core or strategic element technologies of the emerging and promising technology; (3) understanding of technical competitiveness and competitors; (4) establishment of technology strategy; (5) execution of technology strategy [8][9].

Among these steps, the first four steps require information to support decision-making by executives of an organization and such information should be acquired through technology intelligence. So, we need to examine what decision should be made and what information is required in the first four steps.

The first step should suggest an emerging and promising technology suitable for a given organization or researcher. To do this, we should also analyze the network of related technologies and evaluate the emergence of each technology and how the technology is promising. The promising degree of a technology could be computed by considering its element technologies and related products [10].

In the second step, core or strategic element technologies of the emerging and promising technology should be determined. To do this, we need to disassemble the selected technology in the previous step into its element technologies and should evaluate the importance of each element technology.

The third step should identify leading researchers and organizations and evaluate technological levels of them in the view of the selected technology and its element technologies.

Finally, the fourth step should determine development order and acquisition method of element technologies. To do this, we need to evaluate maturity and dependency between element technologies.

1.   Selection and understanding of an emerging and promising technology
(What is the technology?)

2.   Understanding of core and strategic element technologies
(What technologies are core or strategic?)

3.   Understanding of technical competitiveness and competitors
(What are distinctive technical competencies?)

4.   Establishment of technology strategy
(When and how to acquire the technologies?)

5.   Execution of technology strategy
(How can technology strategies be implemented?)

Fig. 1. Five steps of technology planning

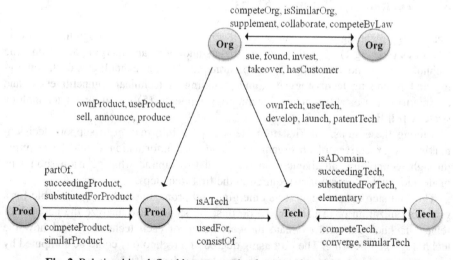

Fig. 2. Relationships defined between technology, product, and organization

4   Knowledge Acquisition

From the steps of technology planning described in the previous section, we can get aware of the fact that core knowledge needed for technology planning should be composed of technology, product and organization. Here, technology includes technical areas, product types, materials, and substances, and product indicates commodities implemented by applying technologies, including intangible ones such as services [11]. Product is a very important element for technology planning because it is a mirror of technologies applied to it.

There exist various and useful relationships between these three entities for technology planning (see Fig. 2) and we can define and classify them by the technology planning steps [12]. For example, all relationships between technologies such as *isA-Domain* (is a domain of), *similarTech* (is a similar technology to), *competeTech* (is a competing technology with), and *converge* and some relationships between product and technology such as *isATech* (is a technology of; e.g., *smart phone* is a technology of *iPhone4*) and *consistOf* (consists of or implements; e.g., *iPhone4S* consists of *speech recognition*) could be used for technology intelligence at the first step.

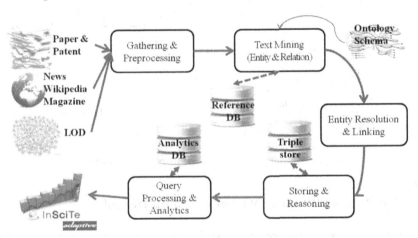

Fig. 3. Overall processes of knowledge acquisition for technology intelligence

- **Lumia 900** is one of the first **Windows Phone device** to support a **4G networking** technology.
- … both **Nokia** and its partner **Microsoft** to flog the new **Lumia smartphone**, which runs **Windows Phone**, …
- … **Samsung Electronics** on Thursday unveiled a new **tablet PC** named the **Galaxy Tab** …
- … that **Samsung's Galaxy Tab tablet** is not a copy of **Apple's** popular **iPad**, …

Fig. 4. The text examples excerpted from news articles

The core of technology intelligence system is to extract and make knowledge from technical literature such as papers, patents, news, magazines, and other technical Web documents in automated way. Natural language processing, text mining, and semantic web technology play important roles to do this. Fig. 3 shows the overall processes from gathering of technical literature to query processing. Linked Open Data (LOD) is utilized for resolving and linking same entities. Fig. 4 shows some example excerpts from news articles. Bold and underlined phrases indicate entities – technologies, products, and organizations – to be recognized and extracted. To correctly recognize these entities, we need to secure enough authority data by entity types because contexts of the entities are often not enough to recognize their types. For example, 'Windows Phone' occurs twice but its contexts are not enough to recognize that it is a *product* of *mobile operating system* unless we are aware of that in advance. Based on the extracted entities, relationships between those entities are recognized and extracted by applying pattern-based rules [13]. Fig. 5 shows the relationships extracted from the example text of Fig. 4. The double-line-boxed entities indicate product, single-line-boxed ones indicate technology, and dotted-line-boxed ones indicate organization. The extracted entities and their relations are converted into semantic triples through URI (Uniform Resource Identifier) assignment and resolution [12][14].

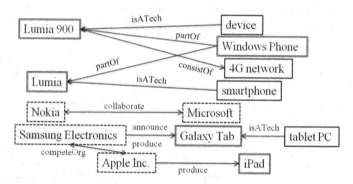

Fig. 5. The examples of entities and their relations extracted

5   Technology Intelligence Services and Insights

Now, we suggest which services and what insights an automated technology intelligence system should provide to support the steps of technology planning described in Section 3. Insight indicates the meaning entailed by a service result and will help users to well understand each service result.

The first step can be supported by technology navigation and technology trend services. *Technology navigation* provides exploration of network composed of technologies, products and organizations with relationships among them. It helps users to understand technologies by exploring the relationships. *Technology trend* analyzes and provides growth stage and speed of emerging technologies in technology life cycle. These services can provide users with insights such as commercialization and opportunity – promising degree – of emerging technologies.

The second step can be supported by element technology and convergence technology services. *Element technology* service discovers which element technologies compose a given technology and the growth stage and speed of each element technology. *Convergence technology* service identifies convergeable technologies with a given technology. These services can provide users with insights such as what is core or strategic among the element technologies and converge-ability of a given technology.

The third step can be supported by agent level and agent partner services. *Agent level* service compares organizations by their development levels of a given technology. It helps users to understand technological competitiveness of each organization and to identify technology competitors. *Agent partner* service identifies and recommends collaboration candidates among leading organizations. These services can provide users with insights such as competition or collaboration degree among organizations in the view of a given technology.

The fourth step can be supported by *technology roadmap* service. This service analyzes dependencies among element technologies and can provide users with insights such as which order and how to acquire each element technology.

Fig. 6 shows the technology intelligence services and their flows by the technology planning steps. After the fourth step, all the analyzed results are piled into a report to provide users.

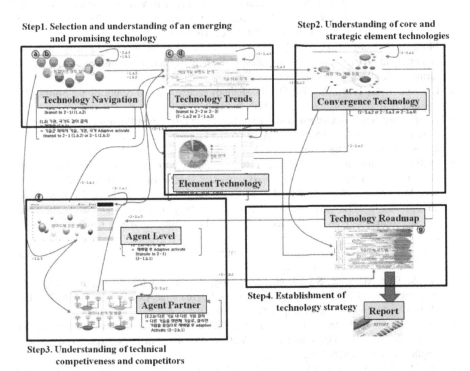

Fig. 6. Service flows by technology planning steps

6   Conclusion

Technology planning is a process of establishing technology strategy and should be supported by technology intelligence (TI). To reduce the cost of manual technology intelligence activities, we suggest an automated technology intelligence system which can be used with ease like existing information retrieval systems and can support whole steps of technology planning systematically. Technology planning has five steps among which first four steps can be supported by a TI system. We examined what decision should be made and what information is required in each step. We then suggested seven services and insights which have a specific role at each step of technology planning. As the number of mobile users is rapidly growing, we implemented our system running on Android tablet PCs. In the future, we will try to compare ours to FUSE and CUBIST outcomes after they are accessible publically.

References

1. Lamb, R.B.: Competitive Strategic Management. Prentice-Hall, NJ (1984)
2. Floyd, S.W., Wolf, C.: Technology Strategy. In: Narayanan, V.K., O'Connor, G.C. (eds.) Encyclopedia of Technology and Innovation Management, pp. 125–128. John Wiley & Sons Ltd., West Sussex (2010) ISBN-978-1-405-16049-0
3. Mortara, L., Kerr, C., Probert, D., Phaal, R.: Technology Intelligence-Identifying threats and opportunities from new technologies, University of Cambridge Institute for Manufacturing (2007) ISBN-978-1902546513
4. Linstone, H.A., Turoff, M.: The Delphi Method: Techniques and Applications. Murray Turoff and Harold A. Linstone (2002) ISBN 0-201-04294-0
5. FUSE, Foresight and Understanding from Scientific Exposition Program - Broad Agency Announcement (BAA) IARPA-BAA-10-06, http://www.iarpa.gov/Programs/ia/FUSE/solicitation_fuse.html (last accessed at March 1, 2013)
6. CUBIST, Combining and Uniting Business Intelligence with Semantic Technology Project, http://www.cubist-project.eu/ (last accessed at March 1, 2013)
7. Lee, M., Lee, S., Kim, J., Seo, D., Kim, P., Jung, H., Lee, J., Kim, T., Koo, H.K., Sung, W.K.: InSciTe Advanced: Service for Technology Opportunity Discovery. In: International Semantic Web Conference (ISWC 2011) – Semantic Web Challenge, Germany (2011)
8. Lee, J.J., Bae, J.T.: Dimension and Contents of Technology Strategy, lecture note MGT532 of KAIST (2001) (in Korean)
9. Lee, S., Cho, M., Song, S.K., Hong, S.C., Jung, H.: Strategy for Developing Technology Planning Support System. In: Proceedings of International Conferences on AST, EEC, MMHS, and AIA 2012, China, pp. 190–193 (2012)
10. Kim, J., Hwang, M., Jeong, D.H., Jung, H.: Technology Trends Analysis and Forecasting Application based on Decision Tree and Statistical Feature Analysis. Expert Systems with Applications 39, 12618–12625 (2012)
11. Cho, M., Lee, S., Song, S.K., Hong, S.C., Jung, H.: Infrastructure for supporting R&D planning system. In: JIST 2012, Japan (2012)

12. Lee, S., Song, S.K., Cho, M., Hong, S.C., Jung, H.: Knowledge construction strategy for technology intelligence system. In: Proceedings of the Korean Society for Internet Information Conference, Korea (2012) (in Korean)
13. Chun, H.W., Jeong, C.H., Shin, S.H., Seo, D.M., Hwang, M.N., Jang, H.J., Park, W.C., Park, J.W., Lee, S., Choi, S.P., Jung, H.: Information Extraction for Technology Trend Analysis. International Journal on Advances in Information Sciences and Service Sciences (on reviewing)
14. Kim, P., Kim, T., Lee, S., Jung, H., Sung, W.K.: OntoURIResolover: URI Resolution Service using Multiple Ontologies. In: International Semantic Web Conference (ISWC 2011) – Semantic Web Challenge, Germany (2011)

Sales Strategy Mining System with Visualization of Action History

Haruhi Satonaka and Wataru Sunayama

Graduate School of Information Sciences, Hiroshima City University
{haruhi,sunayama}@sys.info.hiroshima-cu.ac.jp

Abstract. Recently, sales data of a store is called POS (Point of Sales) data. POS data set of items that each customer purchased is highly expected to be utilized for creating new sales strategies. Though POS data is generally analyzed by data mining techniques, the results do not contain the fact why the customers purchased the items. Therefore, customers moving history in a store is important because such data is directly connected to the reason why they have bought items. However, it was difficult to obtain moving history data. In this paper, Sales Strategy Mining system that supports users to create new sales strategies with customers moving history is proposed. Moving history data is combined with POS data and visualized on the interface effectively. According to the experimental results, the system was effective to create new various sales strategies.

Keywords: Sales Strategy Mining, Moving History, Data Mining, and Data Visualization.

1 Introduction

These days, sales data of a store has become to be used for data mining. Sales data of a store is called "Point Of Sales (POS) data". POS data contains set of items that each customer purchased. Though POS data is generally analyzed by data mining techniques, the results do not contain the fact why the customers purchased the items. Therefore, customers moving history from the entrance to a register in a store is important because such data is directly connected to the reason why they have bought items. However, it was difficult to obtain moving history data. Therefore, sales strategies have been considered by combining subjective analysis by observing customer actions with objective analysis by POS data.

In this paper, Sales Strategy Mining system that supports users to create new sales strategies with customers moving history is proposed. Moving history data is combined with POS data and visualized on the interface effectively. Moving history data is acquired by "Radio Frequency IDentification (RFID) tag" attached to shopping carts. Interface of the system visualizes moving history on a store map. Users can examine moving history and POS data such as areas that customers passed, areas that customers purchased, and areas that customers passed and purchased.

S. Yamamoto (Ed.): HIMI/HCII 2013, Part III, LNCS 8018, pp. 588–597, 2013.

2   Sales Strategy Mining Framework

In this section, a framework for sales strategy mining as Figure 1 is described. This framework has a mining system and five steps to create a new strategy as below:

1. Input conditions: Conditions the user inputs to shrink customers are described.
2. Output customer features: Best 3 and worst 3 areas of each display options, passed, purchased, and pp-ratio, are described.
3. Customer features: A user describes interpretation of the input conditions as in (1).
4. Action features: A user describes interpretation of the output customer features based on the visualized interface and the descriptions in (2).
5. Strategy creation: A user describes a new strategy based on the customers image and their behaviors interpreted by the descriptions in (3) and (4).

This procedure employs a mining system that outputs some patters or features of customers according to input conditions to shrink customer data. Ordinal mining system includes only first two steps of the procedure as the rounded area in Figure 1. So users try and error to find new strategies with ambiguous thought. Therefore, three steps are added to lead users to new strategies by showing what to think. Of course, users may have some intentions to shrink data initially. However, it is not easy to find and think new strategies, so users should input many kinds of inputs at random or blindly in some cases. Step 3) is interpretation of things what the user input, or what the input stands for. This phase is a kind of self-examination. Step 4) is interpretation of things what the outputs stand for. The features of outputs should be well examined in this phase. Finally, interpretations of Step 3) and Step 4) are combined and the relationship between the inputs and the outputs are interpreted in the Step 5). Interpretation means understanding of customer actions, so new strategy comes from such deep recognition.

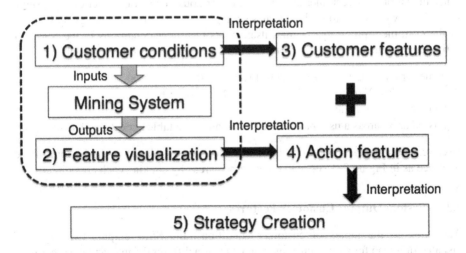

Fig. 1. Framework for sales strategy mining

3   Sales Strategy Mining System

In this section, a system that supports sales strategy mining, called Sales Strategy Mining System (SSM) as in Figure 1 is described. The SSM requires POS and customers' moving history data and outputs their moving and purchasing patterns. This system is based on the framework for sales strategy mining in the last section. That is, while the system mainly outputs features of customers' moving patterns, the system also supports interpretations of the inputs and the outputs by preparing text areas. The details are described in the following subsections.

3.1   Preparation: Inputs of the SSM

The SSM requires a store map and customers data as the input. The store map should include a geometrical map of the store and each item category of each area in the map. This is used for visualizing calculated customer patterns. The customer data contain individual customer information, POS and moving history. Individual information is used for shrinking customer data, such as time for entering the store, gender, sum of sales and passed areas. POS data are sets of baskets what customers bought. This data is connected to the store map, so that the system can identify areas each customer took items to purchase. Moving history is time series data of each customer. Moving history data is collected using a Radio Frequency IDentification (RFID) tag attached to each cart. Customers moving histories, coordinates data from a store entrance to a casher, are collected second by second to visualize customers' behavior and relationship between purchased items and passed areas.

3.2   User Input: Customer Conditions

Since the number of customer data becomes enormous in general, a user of the system, an analyzer who wants to find new sales strategies, has to shrink data to grasp features of the customers precisely. Then, a user inputs customer conditions to the SSM for shrinking customer data. In the prototype system, four conditions are available.

- Time for entering the store: 10:00-, 11:00-, 12:00-, ... , 18:00-
- Sum of sales (Yen): 0-, 2000-, 4000-, 6000-, 8000-, 10000-
- Gender: male, female
- Passed area: areas a user passed such as breads, vegetables, meats, and so on.

Users can input these conditions by using check boxes placed at the bottom of the interface as in Figure 2. Users can input passed areas by clicking each area directly.

3.3   System Output: Customer Features

According to the inputs of customer conditions, the SSM outputs two types of visualization map for shrunk customer data. One is a differential map and the other is an individual data including purchased items and a moving history map.

Figure 3 shows an example of the differential map. The output interface has three output options, passed, purchased, and ratio of purchased among passed, to visualize each area in the output map. These buttons are placed at the low part of Figure 3 as "Passed," "Purchased," and "PP-Ratio."

-passed: visualize passed areas where the customers walked through
-purchased: visualize purchased areas where the purchased items are located in the map
-ratio of purchased among passed: visualize purchasing ratio over passed

In order to visualize each area, differential values between all customers and shrunk customers are calculated. As for the "passed" option, the differential value (passed(A) for shrunk customers − passed(A) for all customers) is calculated. This difference means the features only for the customers who matched with the input conditions. Then, based on this differential value, each area is colored by red or blue. If an area has the positive value, that area is painted in red, and the negative painted in blue.

By seeing the differential map, users can find which areas are more passed, purchased, or have large purchasing ratio intuitively. These output become features of shrunk customers by the input conditions.

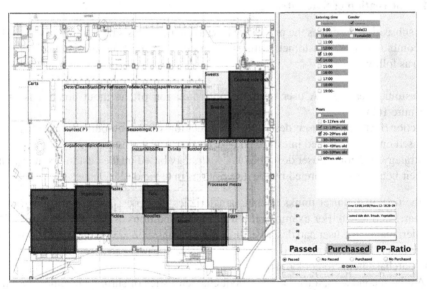

Fig. 2. Differential map for shrunk customers (positive areas are bold framed because of the gray scale image)

The other output is individual information that includes a purchased items list and a moving history map as in Figure 4. Pushing "ID Data" button in the low part of Figure 3 shows this output. Users can see each concrete moving history of each customer from the entrance to the exit on the store map. By clicking the "+" or "-" buttons in the low part of Figure 3, users can see all of shrunk customers' history. Purchased item lists are

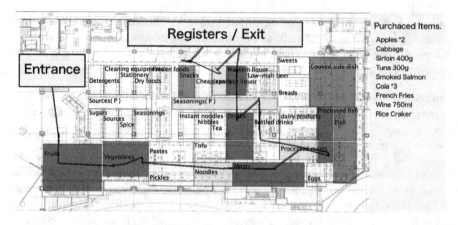

Fig. 3. Moving history map of a customer

also output at the right side of Figure 4. So users can confirm tendencies from individual moving histories and purchased items.

3.4   3Creation of Sales Strategy

This subsection describes the procedure how to create "sales strategy" (Figure 1(5)) by the combination of "Customer features" (Figure 1(3)) and "Action features" (Figure 1(4)) as follows.

1. Customer features: A user describes interpretation of the input conditions as in Figure 1(1).
2. Action features: A user describes interpretation of the output customer features based on the visualized interface and the descriptions in Figure 1(2).
3. Strategy creation: A user describes a new strategy based on the customers image and their behaviors interpreted by the descriptions in (1) and (2).

As the first step, a user thinks about characteristics to express a set of customers who are narrowed down. For example, if a user input conditions as "Entering time: 17-20, Gender: male," the user can describe "business persons who are in the way to home." If a user input "Entering time: 14-16, Gender: female," the user can describe " housewives who purchase items to cook dinner."

As the second step, a user thinks about characteristics of shrunk customers moving histories and purchased items.

For example, if a user noticed a characteristic of products sold well or not, the user can interpret the fact as "They didn't purchase many retort pouches, and they purchased brief food of the cooking such as side dishes well." If a user noticed a movement pattern of customers, the user can interpret the fact as "They always pass the liquor area after the snack area."

Finally, a user thinks of the concrete images of the customers from the two interpretations, "Customer features" and "Action features".

For example, if a user interpreted "Customer features" as " housewives who purchase items to cook dinner " and "Action features" as "The customers didn't bought meat so much, though many of them pass the meat area," a sales strategy "we should show recipes and sample images of meat dishes" can be created.

4   Strategy Creation Experiment

We conducted an experiment to verify whether the SSM can support to create new strategies or not.

Test subjects were 20 university students who majors information sciences. They used the SSM for creating new strategies by using real data of 625 customers of a day. Each test subject used the SSM for 30 minutes. As a comparative system, half of the test subject used SSM without functions related to moving history; two options (purchased, and ratio of purchased among passed) on the visualization map and the moving history map were eliminated from the original SSM. That is, strategies from the proposed SSM come from POS and moving history data, and ones with the comparative SSM come from POS data only.

Test subjects were instructed to be a manager of the store. They were told to create new strategies to raise the sum of sales. By using the assigned system, they instructed to created strategies in thirty minutes.

Table 1 shows the numbers of created strategies. The median of the proposed system was 3 and the one of the comparative system was 4. The number became larger in the comparative system because the proposed system had much information to see and the test subjects had to continue trial and errors.

Table 1. Numbers of created strategies

Test Subject No.	1	2	3	4	5	6	7	8	9	10
Proposed	6	3	2	1	1	4	3	3	3	5
Test Subject No.	11	12	13	14	15	16	17	18	19	20
Comparative	5	5	4	4	3	3	3	14	1	5

Table 2 and Table 3 show the first created sales strategies by each test subject. Many of the test subjects who used the proposed system included keywords related to layout and customer movements, and the ones who used the comparative system didn't. That is, the test subjects who used the proposed system could create strategies from another viewpoints related to moving histories. This is confirmed by the fact that all the subjects who used the proposed system used the functions to refer movement histories of customers.

On the other hand, many of the test subjects who used the comparative system had created strategies about price down. This is because they were easy to notice areas that customers did not purchase items.

Table 2. Created first strategies of the test subject who used the proposed system (Underlined words denote keywords related to layout and customer movements.)

Test Subject No.	Created Sales Strategy
1	Snacks, seasonings area should be placed on the route to fish, vegetables and meats areas.
2	Breads area should be placed at the entrance.
3	Limited-time sale for meats is required.
4	Pickles corner should be placed near the liquors area.
5	Frozen foods, bottled drinks and side dish areas should be adjacent.
6	Cheap side dish area should be placed between meats and fish areas.
7	Cheap lunch packs are required in the morning.
8	Nibbles for drinks should be placed near liquors area.
9	Breads and bottled drinks areas should be adjacent.
10	Meats and frozen areas should be adjacent.

Table 3. Created first strategies of the test subject who used the comparative system

Test Subject No.	Created Sales Strategy
11	Advertisement of limited-time sale for unsold items is required.
12	Sales for frozen food and some other cooked items are required.
13	An area for lunch is required.
14	Areas that include good-selling items should be dispersed.
15	Fish area should be expanded and recipes using fish should be distributed.
16	Liquor sale for housewives is required.
17	Packages that can be a meal should be supplied.
18	Sweets area should be expanded.
19	Areas of pickles and meats should be exchanged.
20	Light meals sale should be held in the morning.

Table 4. Created first strategies of the test subject who used the proposed system

	Proposed	Comparative
Suggestion of changing layout	8/10	4/10
Suggestion Considering customer movements	5/10	2/10
Suggestion of sales (Price down)	3/10	6/10
Suggestion related to stocks on display stands	4/10	5/10

Table 4 shows the number of test subjects classified into four strategy types. The subjects of the proposed SSM created strategies related to suggestion of changing layout the most, while the ones of the comparative created related to suggestion of sales (price down). In addition, subjects of the proposed SSM used the moving history positively. Therefore, moving history was effectively used and marketing strategies about the layout were created easily with the proposed SSM. On the other hand, the test subject of the comparative system could create strategies from another viewpoints.

Finally, Table 5 shows the ratio of used functions related to moving history by the test subject who used the proposed system. As a result, about 30% of functions used by the test subjects were related to moving history. Since the test subjects who used the proposed system were positively used the functions, moving history was effective to create new strategies.

Table 5. The Ratio of used functions related to moving history by the test subject who used the proposed system

Input condition for passed sales areas	13.12%
Change mode in the output interface (passed, purchased, and ratio of purchased among passed)	16.12%
Other functions	70.76%

In these experiments, the test subjects were not managers but students. The created strategies may not be executed actually because created ones were not considered the real store conditions. However, many strategies were easily created from various viewpoints especially from customer movements. Therefore, it was verified that the SSM system could support users to create sales strategies based on the combination of objective characteristics, POS data and moving history.

5   Related Work

A study assists to find interesting patters in the rules by POS (Hamuro, 2001). However, data mining only using POS data has limitation of analysis. Analyzers are hard to grasp why customers buy items from POS data only.

Recently, moving history of customers can be obtained by RFID tags and related techniques. Studies moving history data were not matured and have many possibilities to create new strategies (Yada, 2011; Miyazaki, 2011). For instance, as a research of considering the layout of a shopping center exist (Eppli, 1994), layouts of stores also must be considered using such moving history.

Although many data mining techniques have been studied, there is few works that connects outputs of the system and human interpretation. The proposed system also supports the process from outputs to interpretation. Visualization is a good method to grasp the results of data mining (Faloutsos, 1995; Ko, 2012). Animated visualization system (Beyer, 2006; Nishikido, 2010) is also intended to support interpretation. However, instructions must be needed to understand what to do as the next step. Concrete and certain steps must lead to any goals to accomplish.

6　Conclusions

In this paper, Sales Strategy Mining system that supports users to create new sales strategy is proposed. The SSM supplies the interface that visualizes objective data calculated from POS data and customers moving history. According to the experimental results, it was confirmed that the proposed system could support creating sales strategies based on various viewpoints especially on moving history.

In the future, it is expected that the SSM system will be utilized by real store managers. SSM system can support managers to create meaningful sales strategies more and more. The managers gain profit from the sales strategies. Moreover, the store will be comfortable for customers. Consequently, SSM system will be important system for managers and customers.

References

1. Hamuro, Y., Katoh, N., Yada, K., Yano, T.: Discovering Purchase Association among Brands from Purchase History. In: Conference paper in Industrial Electronics, pp. 114–117 (2001)
2. Yada, K.: String analysis technique for shopping path in a supermarket. Journal of Intelligent Information Systems 36(3), 385–402 (2011)
3. Miyazaki, S., Washio, T., Yada, K.: Analysis of Residence Time in Shopping Using RFID Data – An Application of the Kernel Density Estimation to RFID. In: Proceedings of the 2011 IEEE 11th International Conference on Data Mining Workshops, pp. 1170–1176 (2011)
4. Eppli, M.J., Benjamin, J.D.: The Evolution of Shopping Center Research: A Review and Analysis. Real Estate Research 9(1), 5–32 (1994)
5. Faloutsos, C., Lin, K.I.: FastMap: a fast algorithm for indexing, data-mining and visualization of traditional and multimedia datasets. In: Proceedings of the 1995 ACM SIGMOD International Conference on Management of Data, pp. 163–174 (1995)

6. Ko, S., Maciejewski, R., Jang, Y., Ebert, D.S.: MarketAnalyzer: An Interactive Visual Analytics System for Analyzing Competitive Advantage Using Point of Sale Data. In: Eurographics Conference on Visualization (EuroVis), vol. 31(3), pp. 1245–1254 (2012)
7. Beyer, D., Hassan, A.E.: Animated Visualization of Software History using Evolution Storyboards. In: Proceedings of the 13th Working Conference on Reverse Engineering, pp. 199–210 (2006)
8. Nishikido, T., Sunayama, W., Nishihara, Y.: Valuable Change Detection in Keyword Map Animation. In: Proceedings of the 22nd Canadian Conference on Artificial Intelligence, pp. 233–236 (2009)

An Automatic Classification of Product Review into Given Viewpoints

Yuki Tachizawa, Makoto Oka, and Hirohiko Mori

Tokyo City University, 1-28-1 Tamadutumi, Setagaya Tokyo, Japan
{g1281817,moka,hmori}@tcu.ac.jp

Abstract. Product reviews on the web sites help not only consumers to purchase products but also developers to analyze consumers' needs. Because huge amount of the reviews are presented on the various sites, however, it is a hard task for them to read and to find only the reviews which match their viewpoint that they focus on. Though, to overcome this issue, many researchers in the field of the natural language processing tried to find review sites, classification of reviews according to their viewpoints does not have been succeeded because the corpus for classification must be needed and building it takes a lot of cost. In this paper, we propose a method to build the corpus for each type of products automatically and also propose a method for automatic classification of method of the review. In our method of classification, we focused on the property of review by extending the Tf-Idf. As the classificatoin results contained many errors of classifications in the similar viewpoints, we built the improved method. In this method, we divided the classification process into two-stage. As the result, we could classify reviews by over 80 point.

Keywords: human engineering, classification, text mining.

1 Introduction

In those days, due to the development of the Internet, we can get much valuable information about many kinds of products and a lot of people can get not only the official information but also the users' subjective reviews of the products. As product reviews contain the feedbacks of using them, it is useful for the consumers in purchasing the items. Such kinds of information are also useful for the developers of the products because, to develop new products, they must grasp the users' feedback. However, it is a hard task to read all reviews and to find the reviews which contain the information that they are interested in. For example, when a reader is interested in the design of the digital camera, the reviews are written from various kinds of viewpoints, such as design, picture quality, portability and so on. Though it should be useful if computer extracts only the reviews which much the users viewpoints he/she focuses on, it is difficult to analyze them by the computers because the reviews are written in free forms sentences.

S. Yamamoto (Ed.): HIMI/HCII 2013, Part III, LNCS 8018, pp. 598–606, 2013.

Many researchers in the field of the natural language processing tried to classify reviews [1][2][3], few researches has been succeeded so far, because, to do so, the corpuses customized for each products are required and it is very hard to build each corpus for each product manually. a.

In this paper, we, first, propose a method of automatically building of the corpus for each product using some review site as learning data to build the corpus. We also propose two classification of methods of the reviews using the corpus.

2   Classification

In this section we describe how to classify review articles in our system. At first, we describe the method of building the corpus automatically. Second, we describe the method of calculating the weight of words. This weight was obtained from the corpus. And it show how much the word has association with each viewpoint. Finally, we describe two method of classifier by using weight that we suggest.

2.1   Method of Automatically Building of the Corpus

Corpus is a gallery of the sample text. We picked out characteristics of the viewpoint from this corpus and use characteristics for a classification. As mentioned above, building corpus needs a lot of cost. Here we propose a method to build the corpus automatically.

In those days, rating sites attract somebody's attention. Because of this, reviews that are written in such sites drastically increased. Among these sites,   we focus on the site that have templates for reviews. Template means that user dose not write review all in all but write about viewpoints that are made up by the site.

In this experimentation, we adopted "Kakaku.com" as site for corpus. Because lots of people use "Kakaku.com", it has many reviews about various products. And it preliminarily made up some viewpoints for a writer. (Fig.1) Figure 1 is the review about camera. The underline parts are viewpoints that are prepared beforehand. Our system collects reviews to a clue in this every viewpoint.

Fig. 1. Review of kakau.com

2.2   Weight for Classify

We use the degree of association with each evaluation of words for classification. Here, the degree of association with each evaluation call weight and describe method of count up the weight of word.

Tf-idf is agenerally used to classify documents. This weight is a statistical measure used to evaluate how important a term is for a document. The importance increases proportionallyby the number of times a term appears in the document but is offset by the frequency of the word in the corpus. We show the expression of Tf-ifd(Eq.1).

$$Tf\,idf_{i,j} = tf_{i,j} \times idf_{i,j}$$
$$tf_{i,j} = \frac{the\ count\ of\ appearance\ of\ term\ i\ in\ category\ j}{the\ count\ of\ all\ terms\ in\ category\ j}$$
$$idf_{i,j} = \log\left(\frac{number\ of\ documents}{the\ number\ of\ documents\ containing\ term\ i}\right) \dots \quad (1)$$

Here, Tf-value is the term frequency in one corpus. Idf-value is the inverse document frequency of term over a collection of among some corpus. Thus, it is the bias of appearance of terms among some documents. Tf-Idf-value is weight which multiplied Tf-value by Idf-value about term.

Table 1 shows the Tf-idf values of the words in each category for the digital single-lens reflex camera. Looking at these results, while the values of the words that appear frequently, such as "design" for the design category, "hold and shooting" for the portability category are too high, the word of "shoulder bag" which should have a high value for the category of "portability" is approximately zero value. Such results caused because Tf-Idf requires many sentences in the document such as articles of newspapers, books, and academic papers, as important terms must be appeared frequently. On the other hand, a product review is not long enough to get the frequency of the important terms. As the result, specific words have too significant effects. It means that certain sentence has been classified in specific evaluation viewpoint when that sentence contains specific word by necessity, and we can find that general Tf-idf does not work well for the classification of review articles.

Table 1. Example of TfIdf-values

category / wrods	design	image quality	operability	battely	portability	functionality	LCD	feelings of hold
design	28.15	0.00	0.39	0.06	0.45	0.08	0.21	1.39
hold	2.67	0.80	0.48	17.66	4.62	0.94	0.31	13.11
shooting	0.45	7.52	4.92	15.22	1.75	10.51	7.91	2.88
do	18.49	21.81	20.21	27.51	14.75	18.29	21.15	17.85
...								
fatigue	0.00	0.00	0.00	0.00	0.11	0.00	0.05	0.32
sensing	0.00	0.00	0.00	0.06	0.00	0.06	0.00	0.00
shoulder bag	0.00	0.00	0.00	0.00	0.39	0.00	0.00	0.00
error	0.00	0.00	0.06	0.06	0.00	0.00	0.00	0.00

We, therefore, extend Tf-Idf to solve this problem and to use to classify reviews. The new weight can be calculated as follows (Eq.2).

$$W_{i,j} = \left(\frac{Tf\,idf_{i,j}}{\sum_{k=1}^{n} Tf\,idf_{i,k}}\right)^2 \times \alpha$$

$$\begin{cases} \text{if } 0.1 > max\left(Tf\,idf_{i,1}, Tf\,idf_{i,2}, \ldots, Tf\,idf_{i,j}\right) \times 10^2\,\alpha = 1 \\ \ldots \\ \text{if } max\left(Tf\,idf_{i,1}, Tf\,idf_{i,2}, \ldots, Tf\,idf_{i,j}\right) \times 10^2 > 5\alpha = 9 \ldots \end{cases} \qquad (2)$$

The first term of expression (1) makes the weight of the bias of appearance of terms strong. The denominator is summarized value of all categories of Tf-idf values about the term. So, the first term represents square of rate of term i about category j of Tf-idf value. The second term of expression (1), α gives a certain level of weight to term which is low appearance frequency in the extreme. And it adjusts the weight of term which high appearance frequency expressly. (2) is the expression to determine the alpha. Alpha determined depending on the maximal value of Tf-idf among all category. And we configured that it is step function.

Table 2 shows the new weight of the words for each category as same as a table 1(Table 2). Comparing to Table 1, the results has been improved and the extended Tf-idf can be said to work well for the classification of the review articles.

Table 2. Example of new weight

category / wrods	design	image quality	operability	battely	portability	functionality	LCD	feelings of hold
design	8.24	0.00	0.12	0.02	0.13	0.02	0.06	0.41
hold	0.59	0.18	0.11	3.91	1.02	0.21	0.07	2.91
shooting	0.08	1.32	0.87	2.68	0.31	1.85	1.39	0.51
do	1.04	1.23	1.14	1.55	0.83	1.03	1.19	1.00
...								
fatigue	0.00	0.00	0.00	0.00	0.68	0.00	0.33	1.99
sensing	0.00	0.00	0.00	0.53	0.00	0.47	0.00	0.00
shoulder bag	0.00	0.00	0.00	0.00	3.00	0.00	0.00	0.00
error	0.00	0.00	0.47	0.53	0.00	0.00	0.00	0.00

When compared with Table 1, weight of design fall and weight of shoulder bag rise. The problem of Tf-Idf is solved.

2.3 Morphological Analysis

Though there is a space between words in English, there is no space in Japanese language. So, in processing natural language in Japanese, it is required to divide a sentence into each word. Chasen is a Japanese morphological analysis software based on support vector machines. It cut up Japanese language that is no separated to morpheme unit and we can obtain the information about the word class, its antetype and so on (Figure 2.) The first line is an input to Chasen in Japanese, which means "I am alumnus of Tokyo City University". From the second line, the first rows show information of divided term. The second and third rows shows the antetype of the term presented in first row, and the forth rows show the word class.

In this method, we utilize the antetype of the noun, verb, adjective and adjective to classify the documents.

```
私は、東京都市大学の卒業生である。
私	ワタシ	私	名詞-代名詞-一般
は	ハ	は	助詞-係助詞
、	、	、	記号-読点
東京	トウキョウ	東京	名詞-固有名詞-地域-一般
都市	トシ	都市	名詞-一般
大学	ダイガク	大学	名詞-一般
の	ノ	の	助詞-連体化
卒業生	ソツギョウセイ	卒業生	名詞-一般
で	デ	だ	助動詞	特殊・ダ	連用形
ある	アル	ある	助動詞	五段・ラ行アル	基本形
。	。	。	記号-句点
EOS
```

Fig. 2. Output of Japanese morphological analysis "Chasen"

2.4 Classification

Here, we explain how we classify with the weight. When we presuppose that each category express $\{C_1, C_2, C_3, \ldots, C_i\}$ and sentence express $\{S_1, S_2, S_3, \ldots, S_j\}$ and words are contained sentence express $\{W_1, W_2, W_3, \ldots, W_k\}$ and the weight which the word k has about category i express $V_{i,n}$, the classification result $\hat{C}$ get decided by following expression.(Eq.3)

$$
\begin{aligned}
f(A, j) &= V_{A,1} + V_{A,2} + V_{A,3} + \cdots + V_{A,n} \\
&= \sum_{k=1}^{n} V_{A,k} \\
\hat{C} &= \arg\max_{C_i} f(i, j) \\
&= \arg\max_{C_i} \sum_{l=1}^{n} V_{A,l} \ldots
\end{aligned}
\tag{3}
$$

$f(A, j)$ is total of weight of category A about sentence j.

This expression computes total of each category's weight of words which are included in object sentence and adopts the category that is the highest total weight as result.

3 Experiment

To evaluate our system, we used the review articles of the digital camera in "kakaku.com" to build the corpus and adopted our system to ones in "amazon.com." We made 50 evaluation data about the category of "design", 50 about "image quality", 50 about "operability", 26 about "battery", 50 about "portability", 50 about "functionality," and 50 about "LCD".

3.1   Result

Table 3 indicates the result of classification by our method. As F-values of most of viewpoints are over 80, it can be said that the weight in our approach is good for classifications of the reviews. Here, "image quality" and "functionally" are fewer than 70. When we watch a careful result (Table 4), there were many errors for the classification between the "image quality" and the "functionally", between "portability" and "hold", and between "image quality" and "LCD".

Table 3. Accuracy of our method of classification

	Presision(%)	Recall(%)	F-value(%)
design	84	88	85
image quality	71	66	68
operability	86	88	86
battely	92	100	95
portability	72	96	82
functionality	85	58	68
LCD	73	92	81
feelings of hold	88	64	74
totality	80	80	80

Table 4. A classification result of our method of classification

	design	image	opera···	battely	porta···	func···	LCD	hold	answer
design	44	1	0	0	2	0	0	3	50
image	2	33	0	1	0	0	14	0	50
operability	2	0	44	0	3	1	0	0	50
battely	0	0	0	26	0	0	0	0	26
portability	0	0	0	0	48	1	0	1	50
functionality	1	12	6	0	0	29	2	0	50
LCD	0	0	1	0	0	3	46	0	50
hold	3	0	0	1	13	0	1	32	50
output	52	46	51	28	66	34	63	36	

3.2   Consideration

Though we could obtain the good results by proposed our method as a whole, there are many errors between some of the viewpoints.

Analizing the results in detail, the same terms which characterize the categories are contained over two categories. For example, the term of "the image quality" is contained in both categories of "image quality" and "LCD", because the reviewers sometimes evaluated "LCD" from its quality. In this way, the appearance frequency of the word come close in each other.

Analizing results also show that some errors were caused by the ambigious meaning of terms. As, for example, we a Japanese word "Motsu" that have both meanings of "carry" and "have", the term "Motsu" must have large weight values in both categories of "portability" and "feeling of hold". However, in our method of classification, the weight of "Motsu" only in the category "feeling of hold" was large while the one in the category "portability" was small.

Here, note that the terms such as "Motsu" are useful to distinguish among a combined category of "feeling of hold" and "portability" and another categories.

4   Improved Classfication

In the above consideration, we mentioned the current problems of the system. To drawback them, we improved the way of   the classification.

4.1   Improved Method

When we try to classify something, we sometimes divide them into some big categories roughly before classifying them into the detail categories. Our improved system mimics this way and adopts two-stage classification, which is as follows:

1. The system makes some groups of the categories. This process is done be the cluster analysis using the frequency of each term.
2. The importance weights of appeared terms for each big category are calculated.
3. Using the importance weights, the review articles are classified in to the big groups.
4. The importance weights of appeared terms for the small categories are calculated, considering each big group as one entire articles.
5. The terms which have the close importance weights over the multiple categories are eliminated.
6. The classification into the small categories is done in the same manner as above.

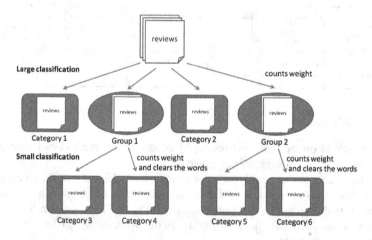

Fig. 3. Flowing of the method of improved classification

As a result of step 1, "image quality" and "LCD" ,"Feeling of hold" and "Portability", "operability" and "functionally"   were got together. Most of word that were problem about mistake in near evaluation viewpoints in hindsight of step 5.

5   Experiment II

To compare the results between the experiment I and II, we used the same data.

5.1   Result

The table 5 shows that, comparing with the experiment I, the whole results are improved and, especially, the F-values of the categories whose results were not obtained the good results, such as the categories of "image quality", "portability", "functionality", "LCD", and "feelings of hold" are raised. It can be said, therefore, the two-stage classification drawback the problem of the first manner of the classification.

Table 5. Accuracy of improved classification

	Presision(%)	Recall(%)	F-value(%)
design	84	88	85
image quality	72	74	72
operability	89	84	86
battely	92	100	95
portability	82	92	86
functionality	81	62	70
LCD	79	92	85
feelings of hold	84	78	80
totality	83	83	83

Table 6. A classification result of improved classfication

	design	image	opera···	battely	porta···	func···	LCD	hold	answer
design	44	1	0	0	1	0	0	4	50
image	2	37	0	1	0	0	10	0	50
operability	2	0	42	0	3	3	0	0	50
battely	0	0	0	26	0	0	0	0	26
portability	0	0	0	0	46	1	0	3	50
functionali	1	13	4	0	0	31	1	0	50
LCD	0	0	1	0	0	3	46	0	50
hold	3	0	0	1	6	0	1	39	50
output	52	51	47	28	56	38	58	46	376

5.2   Consideration

By the two-stage classification, we could improve the precision of classification between the similar viewpoints. Eliminating the terms which appear frequently in multiple categories, however, causes another problem and, eventually causes another type of the classification error. In this process, too many terms were eliminated including some important terms. For example, the review sentence "The feeling of holding this camera is comfortable" was not classified into the "Hold" category but into the "Portability", because the term "hold" and "comfortable" were removed and only the term "feeling" remained. To solve this problem, another parameter in addition to the frequency should be considered in removing redundant terms.

6   Consideration the of Two Methods

We found the new calcuration manner of the importance weights and the two-stage classification succeeded to classify of review articles. This manner should be able to adopt to the classification of another small documents. But some problems is still left to solve.

One is how to deal with compound nouns. In our method, a compound noun are treated as a aggregate of words and theie weights are calculated independently. For example, when the words "Vari-angle LCD monitor function" are contained in the article, it is classified into the "LCD" category because the weight of term "LCD" have a large value for the "LCD" category, while the article should be classified into the category "function." If we can identify "Vari-angle LC monitor function" as a one compound norn and give one weight value to it, this article would be classified into the category "function." To solve this problem, we need to develop some manners to identify compund nouns.

The second is that, when an article includes a word which has extreme high weight for one category, it is classified into the category because of too strong affect of the word. To refine the calculation method of weight may solve this problem .

7   Conclusion

In this paper, we propose a method to build the corpus and also propose a method for automatic classification of the review articles. Our system works out over 80% accuracy in classification.

In our method we use only the frequency of the appeared word to classify reviews. But, only with values, it should be difficult to get the result of the classification more precisely. Now, we are considering to utilize sentence structures. Especially, using the grammatical modification relations would be contribute to more precious.

8   Future Works

In our method we use only he appearance frequency information of the word. But, only with this information, it is difficult to raise classification precision. We assume that we use information of modification relation to raise classification precision.

About the compound noun, we would identify it and give heaviness by different methods of words.

References

1. Kaji, N., Kitsuregawa, Y.: The automatic collection of evaluation sentences from an HTML document galaxy. Natural Language Processing Association (2004)
2. Suzuki, M.: The automatic classification of the text with difference of the word frequency between categories. Journal of Japan Industrial Management Association (2008)

User Needs Search Using Text Mining

Yukiko Takahashi and Yumi Asahi

Shizuoka University,
3-5-1 Johoku Naka-ku Hamamatsu 432-8561 Japan
ne210026@gmail.com, tyasahi@ipc.shizuoka.ac.jp

Abstract. In recent years, people came to write the opinion of them by social networking service, such as a twitter, mixi, a blog. However, it is the present conditions that we cannot analyze it though we can watch a lot of opinions. Answer to choice is important, but opinion in a free writing conveys a thought concretely. From it, the authors considered using text mining in the spot. By doing text mining, it can enumerate frequent appearance word and we can know user's needs. The width of the analysis thereby spreads. For example, those who say a specific word find out in what kind of tendency it is. The authors can think about the product development that we matched with each user from there. In addition, it can compare the opinion by various approaches. In this way, Text mining is an effective way to take advantage of user's voice.

Keywords: text mining, frequently-appearing word, free writing.

1 Introduction

Recently, a huge amount of information has been accumulated by the development of the information technology on the Internet. Therefore, Companies can get the data that can be used for the business. For example, the questionnaire data, the complaint data, and the opinion on electronic bulletin board, etc.

Especially, the number of users who are using SNS (Social Networking Services) such as "mixi" and "Twitter" increasing in recent years. There are so many opinions on the internet with the online population increasing. However, getting this information and analyzing it by the people is beyond the human capacity.

Recently, the technique for analyzing this information has been noted in recent years. [1-3] this information is written by free description, so, the technique is required capacity of analyzing it.

To solve the problems, A lot of excellent open source software about morphological analysis such as "Chasen" and "MeCab" were developed to a practical level and it released all over the world. Applying the search index, such as text mining to it is usuful can lead to a difference with other companies.

Japanese text mining is more difficult than English text mining. So, companies are not positive to do it. But you may obtain information that cannot have been placed from the information, such as helping product development choices help to describe what this kind of freedom, but the improvements. Text mining is a technique also

S. Yamamoto (Ed.): HIMI/HCII 2013, Part III, LNCS 8018, pp. 607–615, 2013.

needed to help [4] business. In this paper, we pick up the awareness of products users by analyzing the free text description. And we show this work help to applying user's awareness on product development. We will describe the analysis as an example of using the word-of-mouth large site about cosmetic trick for that.

2   About Text Mining

2.1   Outline of Text Mining

Text-mining-Analysis is a technique that consists of two data mining "natural language processing" and "natural language processing" text mining.

Natural language processing allows the computer to understand natural language that humans use. On the other hand Data mining is a technique to find the correlation between the items and patterns from data from the statistical processing. We examine the association with frequently-appearing word and the anteroposterior words, we can obtain useful information from the opinion of the user.

To examine the relevance of such words and frequent words or melody, it is possible to obtain useful information from the opinions of the user.

Text analysis discussion has been made in the field [5], the language model is used in research, such as automatic summarization and automatic translation of the original document. Recently, we have also established a new word, such as text mining to dig a meaning that valuable information from a large amount of text data.

Text mining is a general term for any technique to obtain the knowledge to analyze the data from a large number of documents in other words.

Text mining is divided into sentences word by word, and sees their relationships.

Text mining is performed through the following steps [6]

1. Morphological processing is divided into sentences written in natural language: morphological analysis
2. Handle the unwanted words such as auxiliary verbs and particles for analysis or create a synonym: unification of synonyms, such as after an unnecessary processing
3. Process of analyzing the dependency relation with words: parsing
4. You can analyze the frequency and number of occurrences, co-occurrence, clustering, and attribute analysis:

Is often carried out after the above one, working up to 4-2 is repeated while confirming the results.

2.2   Example of Text Mining

I'll explain using an example. This time we will analyze the opinions of users free description listed in the user ranking site @ cosme [7] as an example. Until now, the cosmetics industry market was higher advertising expenses and selling expenses. There was a tendency to a leading manufacturer was able to spend a large amount of advertising expenses, create a brand image sold. With the advent of @ cosme, users can now just have to know what to buy goods before the evaluation, however. This @ cosme review that was ever written by the user is more than of 10.4 million (as of February 2013) to understand the high level of interest that is a site dedicated to information on cosmetic @ cosme are 20 000 domestic and international We handle more than a few cosmetic information 200 000 1,000 brands, products. Total Monthly review search page is also called Mon PV / about 250 million, found this site that you have used to buy cosmetics how In. [8]

This time I found out where a popular product has been evaluated or examined a comment (with 2013/2/22) Popularity Index # 1 of lotion.

3   Morphological Analysis

3.1   Outline of Morphological Analysis

First, morphological analysis is carried out. And (Morpheme) is a technical term used in linguistics morpheme, which is the smallest unit of a string of meaning. And morphological analysis of the work is that adding information such as part of speech then divided into units of morphological and sentence. Based on a dictionary and grammar of natural language understanding, the statement is divided into morphemes, morphological analysis system to grant mechanically and each part of speech information. Free software is relatively good precision morphological analyses have been published a few, but this time use MeCab [8] as the soft morphological analysis.

Free description to understand human-read let this be understood by the computer even easier is by no means easy. Shaking notation, because problems such as synonym occur. Same meaning but not aggregated together, "Maintenance", "inspection", for example as a result of [6]. In Japanese, to extract the semantic information from character units who were each word, a phrase that is good. Since there is no habit of "segmentation" to insert a space between words such as English, in Japanese, it always remains ambiguity toward separation into words but not uniquely determined.

Because many morphological analyzers allow the user to register to add items to the dictionary, we can increase the accuracy of the analysis to enhance the dictionary function, however. Research stochastic language model using a probability model using the information on frequency of occurrence of each morpheme from the text data a number of [9] is advanced, in recent high precision more than 95% has been achieved further.

First, morphological analysis is carried out. And (Morpheme) is a technical term used in linguistics morpheme, which is the smallest unit of a string of meaning. And morphological analysis of the work is that adding information such as part of speech then divided into units of morphological and sentence. Based on a dictionary and grammar of natural language understanding, the statement is divided into morphemes, morphological analysis system to grant mechanically and each part of speech information. Free software is relatively good precision morphological analyses have been published a few, but this time use MeCab [8] as the soft morphological analysis.

Free description to understand human-read let this be understood by the computer even easier is by no means easy. Shaking notation, because problems such as synonym occur. Same meaning but not aggregated together, "Maintenance", "inspection", for example as a result of [6]. In Japanese, to extract the semantic information from character units who were each word, a phrase that is good. Since there is no habit of "segmentation" to insert a space between words such as English, in Japanese, it always remains ambiguity toward separation into words but not uniquely determined.

Because many morphological analyzers allow the user to register to add items to the dictionary, we can increase the accuracy of the analysis to enhance the dictionary function, however. Research stochastic language model using a probability model using the information on frequency of occurrence of each morpheme from the text data a number of [9] is advanced, in recent high precision more than 95% has been achieved further.

3.2   Example of Morphological Analysis

Let's make the first real morphological analysis.Morphological analysis is carried out following three processes.

- Analysis and words: hit or split where
- Infer the POS: POS shed
- Estimation and semantic: Identify the ambiguous word on the notation

I'll need to determine a word boundary than English and Japanese, unlike English As I said before. Are increasingly step of the analysis compared to morphological analysis of Japanese and English grammar as well because there is a fluctuation in addition to it.

期待を裏切らない良い商品でした

↓

期待	を	裏切ら	ない	良い	商品	でし	た
noun	postpositional particle	verb	auxiliary verb	adjective	noun	auxiliary verb	auxiliary verb

Fig. 1. Examples of morphological analysis

Table 1. Frequently-appearing word to skin toner

Words	Frequency
Skin	116
Vitamin	47
Smell	46
Pores	39
Dryness	35

As a result of the analysis to proceed free of such description, frequent words became as shown in Table 1. Increase the data available the more frequent data word has been ranked the top five this time since there were little 458 statements and the number of free description of the analysis.

The results of this analysis there are many opinions about the skin, the appearance frequency is more than twice the vitamin of the 2-position. This analysis is not impossible is also essential because it is compatible with skin lotion for user comments. Morphological analysis is the analysis of only this is difficult because it is to separate the text, leading to the following analysis, skin, vitamins, aroma, pores, it can be seen from here, at least, for drying on lotion first place this It is that many users who are interested in this product.

If this alone is what makes skin, etc. I do not know whether you are what you comment on any fragrance but. Parsing or other analysis is subsequent to that step become necessary.

4   About Syntactic Analysis

4.1   Outline of Syntactic Analysis

Must be formatted according to certain rules of each comment is text mining. I cannot obtain a significant analysis this normalization has not been properly carried out. The need for it is this parsing.

Parsing is to be analyzed as a unit clause, sentence structure sentences free description. In English, that phrase structure parsing in order to enter a space between is easy. For Japanese, the syntax used to analyze the relationship between the receiving units according to the clause is common, however. A clause, in which the separated units meaningful Japanese. In Japanese, any one clause in the sentence, is characterized in accordance with the relationship and receive one of the following clauses of the clause at least.

And dependency is that of the relationship and phrases and clauses. For example, "Who is the what-what-" "I like candy" of each word are connected by the relationship between the word if. You can find the most important information what is good and what is bad by this [6], in the free description.

Parsing I know that the most important step in conducting a text mining from this.

Fig. 2. Diagram showing the dependency relations

You are the ones who translated the Japanese "It was a good commodity that did not do the reverse of what one is expected to do." On the figure. Here is separated for each clause were separated by one word in FIG. I found that "Do not betray → expected" from here referred to as "goods → good."

5   For Co-occurrence Frequency of Words

And co-occurrence (collocation) means that there is a word that appears adjacent to another particular word. Co-occurrence frequency is in the field of research which has been widely used vocabulary as a guide to know the relationship between words.

You will be as shown in Figure 3 and analyzed from the Japanese of "It was a good commodity that did not do the reverse of what one is expected to do." Are using so far.

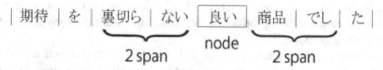

Fig. 3. Based on co-occurrence analysis diagram

Determine the co-occurrence analysis (node) and central Italian first keyword. Here you select the word or anxious, with the most frequent word appears in the morphological analysis. Specify the number of words before and after the node at the center from there. And this time I did because I wanted to know 2pan two words before and after. When you place this node is the "good" that is, "was" "goods" "no" "betrayed" is the word co-occurrence.

It cannot be said that this analysis alone, however. At the first analysis is essential for understanding the co-occurrence relation in this sentence all the words in the entire text of "good" came out, I turned off the noise. Can be determined between the two words is that there is a strong relationship between the words if there is a high degree of respect and frequent "good".

Working to truncáte the noise when then examines the co-occurrence frequency. It is the task of co-occurrence relation checks whether there ie.

Whether or not there is a co-occurrence relations, as judgment, it is intended that the value T in corpus linguistics statistically. T value, the statistical analysis is an index which is used for example, when performing a test of the difference between the average values. This is corpus linguistics is widely used as an index to determine the presence or absence of co-occurrence relations. T value formula is the following. [10]

Value T = (measured value - mean) / Square root of actual measurement value

"The square root of the measured value" in the denominator represents the approximate value of the standard deviation about the words co-occur with language center here.

In corpus linguistics it is considered as equal to or greater than 1.65, the co-occurrence of two terms is no coincidence. There is a co-occurrence relation if there is more than 1.65 T value based on corpus linguistics, this time you shall make any sense.

Based on the above results, we analyzed node co-occurrence as a "flavor" in third place with "skin" of first place in the morphological analysis is in Tables 2 and 3. I chose because it was concerned about why I chose the "smell" of third place on the aroma and how it is written, whether it is good or bad.

Table 2. Co-occurrence relation for the "skin"

rank	Term	Before	After	measured value	Square root of actual measurement value	mean	T
1	Adhesion	0	6	6	2.449489743	0.315217391	2.320802782
2	Puffily	0	6	6	2.449489743	0.315217391	2.320802782
3	Softly	1	3	4	2	0.210144928	1.894927536
4	Change	0	4	4	2	0.210144928	1.894927536
5	Trouble	0	4	4	2	0.210144928	1.894927536

Table 3. Co-occurrence relation for "aroma"

rank	Term	Before	After	measured value	Square root of actual measurement value	mean	T
1	Geranium	5	2	7	2.645751311	0.104619565	2.606208832
2	good	5	0	5	2.236067977	0.074728261	2.202648483
3	Essential oil	5	0	5	2.236067977	0.074728261	2.202648483
4	very	2	2	4	2	0.059782609	1.970108696
5	Lavender	4	0	4	2	0.059782609	1.970108696
6	like	1	2	3	1.732050808	0.044836957	1.706164179
7	heal	1	2	3	1.732050808	0.044836957	1.706164179

I know that there are many users who have said that using this lotion for the "skin" from here is going to be "moist" "plump". For "fragrance" is ranked 1, 3, 5 is a word for the components of the scent, I found that you have the most impressive in terms of geranium is this lotion among them. We found that the high interest of the user other words, from the fact that only a positive image of the word, such as "healing", "like" or "good", this product has been successful with respect to flavor.

These results may be easier to see the relationship to FIG.

6   Conclusion

Relationship and businesses to make use of text mining. I am what text mining and business are inseparable, even one I mentioned. Thing the user's feedback is essential to planning When a product. Business performs a variety of methods for obtaining it.

But user surveys that are often used in it, which can be heard for each item that you want to know themselves. From there I choose to give age and occupation, the choice of the user, such as a description of its contents is freedom. To process the information obtained from the trouble and how to obtain information will vary greatly from these but any important information.

Information in the information age and the choices can be obtained from there to aggregate the number of graphs, etc., for example. This low degree of difficulty as soon as I can use a computer. Free description is hard to analyze the language of the user is a drawback, however. It takes time and effort people are going to analyze one by one comment read. Have knowledge of the personal computer, unlike when you aggregate choice because it requires a specialized program on your computer but also trying to do. And when the difference between the aggregate of the choices, the analysis of the description is to do in-house human freedom that can accommodate it means that it is limited.

Often not the company itself can ask any money but there may be voices that I thank analysis specialist companies. Analysis of free writing companies that can not only do many rough few people who can be fully in-house analysis by which the aggregate of the choices can be. The problem is that many companies have not been able to successfully reflect the opinions of the description field of freedom that is. The more difficult and complex software that can parse for Japanese is particularly complex.

Does not change that you should not not get information from text they are also there, such as comments on the product is written in such as electronic bulletin board monitor and have them actually use the products also, in various ways.

Making a text mining is the most important thing for the company. Is likely to provide tremendous benefits even in business activities, the text mining technology, is expected to have on future research and application.

7   Future Outlook

In this study, we describe the basics of text mining of user ranking sentences lotion. The image was found of interest to users, products resulting from frequent word, it is a small part. What of the product user or was attracted. Also, where the hate was has not yet been identified to like something.

Text mining is to use a personal computer, a time-consuming analysis of the text, quick easy viewing. While using it anymore CEEB model, to capitalize commentary, business, and text mining in this analysis is a difficult challenge in the future there is a demand.

References

1. Tsukide, N., Ishizaki, S.: Impression extraction system of free answer sentence to TV program.- Analysis of free answer sentence by the Internet questionnaire survey. Association for Natural Language Processing the sixth Meeting Annual Rally Announcement Thesis Collection, pp. 249–251 (2000)
2. Pang, B., Lee, L., Vaithyanathan, S.: Thumbs up? sentiment classification using machine-learning techniques. In: Proceedings of the Conferenceon Empirical Methods in Natural Language Processing (EMNLP), pp. 76–86 (2002)
3. Turney, P.D.: Thumbs up? thumbs down? Semanticorientation applied to unsupervised classificationof reviews. In: Proceedings of the 40th Annual Meeting ofthe Association for Computational Linguistics (ACL), pp. 417–424 (2002)
4. Kinmei, T., Murakami, S., Nagata, M., Otsu, T., Yamanishi, K.: Language and statistics of psychology. Iwanami Shoten Publisher (2003)

5. Ishimura, Y., Hasegawa, T., Watabe, I., Satou, M.: Text mining- Case introduction. Japanese Society for Artificial Intelligence Magazine 16(2), 192–200 (2001)
6. Asano, H.: Introduction to questionnaire survey, pp. 107–117 (2011)
7. @cosme, http://www.cosme.net/
8. MeCab,
   http://mecab.googlecode.com/svn/trunk/mecab/doc/index.html
9. Kita, K.: Probabilistic language model. The University of Tokyo-Publication association (1991)
10. Barnbrook, G.: Language and computers: A practical introduction to the computer analysis of language. Edinburgh University Press, Edinburgh (1996)

Finding a Prototype Form of Sustainable Strategies for the Iterated Prisoners Dilemma

Mieko Tanaka-Yamawaki and Ryota Itoi

Department of Information and Knowledge Engineering, Graduate School of Engineering,
Tottori University, 101-4 Koyamacho-Minami, Tottori, 680-8552 Japan
mieko@ike.tottori-u.ac.jp

Abstract. We deal with a multi-agent model of the iterated prisoners' dilemma with evolvable strategies, originally proposed by Lindgren that allows elongation of genes represented by one-dimensional binary arrays, by means of three kinds of mutations: the duplication, the fission, and the point mutation, and the strong strategies are set to survive according to their performance at every generation change. The actions that the players can choose are assumed to be either cooperation (represented by C) or defection (represented by D). We conveniently use {0,1} instead of {D,C}. Each player has a strategy that determines the player's action based on the history of actions chosen by both players. Corresponding to the history of actions, represented by a binary tree of depth m, a strategy is represented by the leaves of that tree, an one-dimensional array of length 2^m. We have performed extentive simulations until many long genes are generated by mutations, and by evaluating those genes we have discovered that the genes of high scores are constructed by 3 common quartet elements, [1001], [0001], and [0101]. Furthermore, we have found that the strong genes commonly have the element [1001 0001 0001 0001] that have the following four features:

(1) never defects under the cooperative situation, represented by having '1' in the fourth element of the quartet such as [***1],
(2) retaliates immediately if defected, represented by having '0' in the first element and the third element in the quartet such as [0*0*],
(3) volunteers a cooperative action after repeated defections, represented by '1' in the first element of the genes,
(4) exploits the benefit whenever possible, represented by having '0' in the quartet such as [*0**].

This result is stronger and more specific compared to [1**1 0*** 0*** *001] reported in the work of Lindgren as the structure of strong genes.

1 Introduction

In designing a system, we often ignore the necessity for individual based on the idea that a specific necessity for individual may not apply to the others. However, a design for everybody sometimes satisfies nobody's need. Given a sufficient speed and capacity of today's computers, we are now in the position to put the necessity for individual into a computer.

S. Yamamoto (Ed.): HIMI/HCII 2013, Part III, LNCS 8018, pp. 616–624, 2013.
© Springer-Verlag Berlin Heidelberg 2013

Based on this thought, we have been studying the game theory simulations and the prediction of the price fluctuation using multi agent models in which the individual setting is allowed for each agent. We have discovered the fact that an evolutional program to simulate a game theory, in order to create a set of better strategies to win the game by examining the past rewards acquired by the players corresponding to the history of actions by both players, can be immediately converted into a program for predicting the next price by changing a small number of commands. For the sake of short term prediction, those elements must be considered independent of the prices. However, it is extremely difficult to incorporate into the program the elements other than the prices, such as human expectations and social conditions. Those elements are to be digested into the market prices after a long time, but it takes a while before they become reflected in the market prices.

In this paper, we consider a model of two-player-game in which strategies of the two players evolve by learning the performance in the past. We adopt a model of iterated prisoners' dilemma with evolving strategies originally proposed by Lindgren and perform extensive amount of simulations until a novel strategy stronger than TFT or Pavlov, by considering the past actions of the both players to the depth 5. This particular strategy is characterized by the 4 features such as, (1) cooperative by nature (2) reasonable (3) generous (4) cool

2   Iterated Prisoners' Dilemma

The prisoners' dilemma is defined by the payoff structure of both players shown in Table 1. We assume the players have only two ations to choose, to cooperate (C, hereafter) or todefect (D, hereafter). There are four parameters R, P, S, T which are set tp satisfy S < P < R < T and S + T < 2R. The key point of the situation under which the two players are set in this model is the better choice for individual results in the worst choice of both. For example, if we assume B cooperates, A's rational choice is to defect because R < T. However, even if we assume B defects, A's rational choice is still to defect because S < P. Thus A is supposed to defect whatever B chooses. The situation is the same for B. Thus both A and B end up with choosing to defect. However, the payoff P is smaller than R. How can they choose the better option of mutualo cooperation ?

Table 1. The payoff table of the prisoners' dilemma(S<P<R<T and S+T<2R)

(A's payoff, B's payoff)	B's action is C	B's action is D
A's action is C	(R, R)	(S, T)
A's action is D	(T, S)	(P, P)

The poor soluion (P,P) is inevitable for a single game, unless they promise to start with the cooperative actions. When they repeat the game by starting with the cooperative actions, then the best choice for both of them is to continue to cooperate except the last match. Because onece each of them defects, then the opponent will retaliate in the next match. Therefore if they know the time to end the repeated game, they will defect at the last match. For this reason, the iterated prisoners dilemma game (abbreviated as IPD, hereafter) is played without fixing the time to end. In such a game, a particular strategy called Tit-For-Tat (TFT, hereafter) wins over the other strategies. In general, good strategies including the TFT, share the following three features:

(1) to cooperate as long as the opponent cooperates
(2) to retaliate immediately if defected
(3) to offer cooperation after continuous defections.

However, it has been known that the Pavlov strategy (PAV, hereafter) is better than the TFT under a certain condition. The PAV keeps the same action after getting T or R which are the good payoff, and changes the action from the pervious one after getting S or P which are the poor payoff. This strategy is stronger than the TFT in a model allowing errors in actions in which the player chooses an opposite action from the one chosen by the strategy [7].

This situation is depicted in an example shown in Table 2. In this case, both (TFT,TFT) and (PAV, PAV) begin the game from the cooperative relationships at the time t=1. Suppose if an error occurs at t=2 in the second player, then the TFT pair immediately fall into pose if an error occurs at t=2 in the second player, then the TFT pair immediately fall into (C, D) a series of (C, D) and (D, C), while the PSV pair can recover the original cooperative situation of (C, C). Thus the TFT is not always the best under errors.

Table 2. Actions of the TFT/PAV pair when the second player commits an error at t=2

Time t	(TFT,TFT)	(PAV,PAV)
1	(C, C)	(C, C)
2	(C, 'D')	(C, 'D')
3	(D, C)	(D, D)
4	(C, D)	(C, C)
5	(D, C)	(C, C)

3   Evolvable Strategies in the IPD

In the framework of the artificial life (ALIFE), a new scheme of searching for the better strategies was preseted in Ref. [6] in a multi-agent model of evolvable strategies, in which the strategies grow like genes. Here the strategies are represented by one-dimensional binary strings.

The two actions, the cooperation and the defection, {D,C}, are represented by {0,1}. Each player has a strategy that determines the player's action based on the history of actions chosen by both players in each game. Corresponding to the history of actions, represented by a binary tree of depth m, a strategy is represented by the leaves of that tree, an one-dimensional array of length 2^m. It is convenient to set the two edges of the binary tree to have 0 in the left edges and 1 in the right edges.

For example there are four strategies repsresented by [00], [01], [10], [11], for m=1 corresponding to a model to simply count the opponent's previous action as the history. The strategy [00] is called as ALLD because only D is chosen irrelevant to the opponent's past action. Likewise, [11] is called as ALLC. The strategy [01] is the TFT because D is chosen only when the opponet's action of the immediate past is D. Likewise the strategy [10] is called as anti-TFT (abbreviated as ATFT).

If we count the actions of both players as the history, that is the case of m=2 and the corresponding strategy becomes a binary string of length 4. For example, a strategy [1001] chooses C if the past actions of both players are the same, i.e., both C or both D, and chooses D if the past actions of both players were not the same, i.e., when one player's action was C, the other player's action was D. This corresponds to the PAV. A strategy [0101] is the same as [01] because D is chosen for the opponent's defective action and C is chosen for the opponent's cooperative action irrelevent to the past action of the other side. Likewise, the strategy [0000] is the same as [00]. A strategy represented by [0001] chooses C only when the past actions of both sides were C. We call this strategy as the retaliation-oriented TFT (abbreviated by RTFT).

For larger m, the history and the corresponding strategy can be written as $h_m = (a_m, ..., a_2, a_1)_2$ and $S_m = [A_1 A_2 ... A_n]$ for $n = 2^m$. An example of the strategy for the case of m=3 represented by a string of 10010001 is shown in Fig. 1. Out of all the possible strategies, good ones are chosen by employing the genetic algorithm. The typical job-flow of this mecahnism is illustrated in Fig.2.

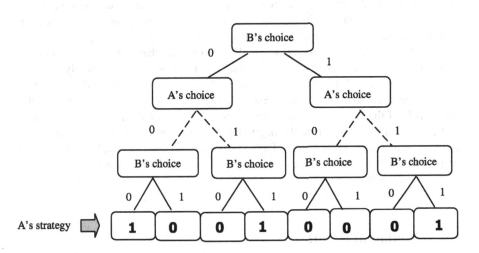

Fig. 1. A strategy of length 8 and a binary tree of the history of depth 3

Starting from the initial population of agents, which could be the entire set of possible strings or a randomly sampled subset of the entire set, pairs of agents play the IPD of indefinite length. After all the agents playing the game with all the other agents, their total payoff are counted and their population is renewred according to the

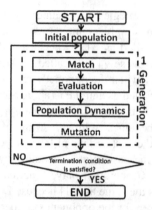

Fig. 2. The Job-flow of the evolvable IPD simulation

population dynamics explained below. Subseqeuently the mechanism of three types of mutation, (1) point mutation (2) doubling, and (3) fission, are applied in order to grow the strategy strings to create new patterns and the new lengths that the previous generation did not know.

We have followed the senario written by Lindgren [6], except for the two points: the first point is the stochastic ending of IPD, and the second point is that we have performed extensive amount of simulations. As a result, we have discovered the type of gene structure of sustainable strategies in more specific manner compared to [1**1 0*** 0*** *001] suggested in Ref.[6]. The reason that we have chosen the stochastic ending is as follows. It is well known that the defective action is the optimum choice for a single-time PD. If the players know the ending time, they are bound to choose to defect (if they are rational), because the situation at the last match is exactly the same as the single match. If the players know their choice to defect at the n-th match, they do not have to consider the effect of their current choice on the later games. In other words, IPD of the length n is equivalent to the IPD of the length n-1, if their choices of the last game are fixed from the beginning and they cannot avoid taking the defective choice at the (n-1)-th match. Thus the players are bound to take the defective choice throughout the IPD, if they know the time to end the iteration of the games. In the IPD game with stochastic ending, on ther other hand, the players do not know the time of ending and they have to consider which action to choose each time.

4   Simulation Result

We have run our program by the following conditions. We have tried two different initial conditions to start the simulation. The first type consists of the four m=1 strategies , [00], [01], [10], and [11] with equal polulations of 250 each, and the second type consists of 1000 random sequences of length 32. Either case, the total population of agents is kept unchanged from the initial value of 1000 throughout the simulation. The number of simulations are 50 for the first type and 40 for the second type. The rate of point mutation, the duplication rate, and the split rate are are set to be 2×10^{-5}, 10-6,

10-6, the same as in Ref. [6]. We also assume the rate of error, i.e., with which the opposite action prescribed by the gene is executed, to be 0.01. The payoff parameters in Table 1 are also chosen to be S=0, P=1, R=3, and T=5.

The length of each game is not fixed in order to avoid the convergence to the ALLD dominance, but the end of the game is announced with the probability of 0.005.

We show simulation results of the Type I initial populations in Fig. 3 in which the horizontal axis shows the generation and the vertical axis shows the population of strategies. Both cases exhibit drastic changes of dominating stratesies as the generation increases.

An interesting feature is observed in Fig. 3. Namely, the [01] (=TFT) dominance followed by the [1001] (=PAV) dominance, then the [0001] (RTFT) dominance comes and the [01] dominance. This particular pattern is observed in 37 examples out of 50 independent runs of the first type initial condition, and this triplet pattern of TFT=>PAV=>RTFT is sometimes repeated for many generations. However, as the length of the genes reaches the size of 16 or 32, this triplet pattern disappear and the [1001000100010001] dominates.

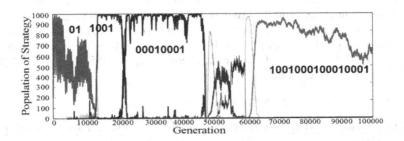

Fig. 3. The TFT-PAV-RTFT triplet is observed in the Type I condition

Fig.4 is an example of the triplet pattern of TFT-PAV-RTFT repeated for three cycles. Fig.5 shows a case of the triplet pattern washed away by the emergence of the longer and the stronger strategies.

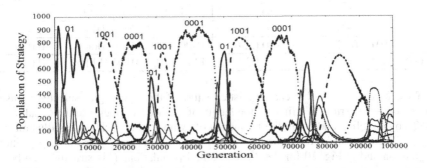

Fig. 4. An example of the TFT-PAV-RTFT triplet repeated by 3 times

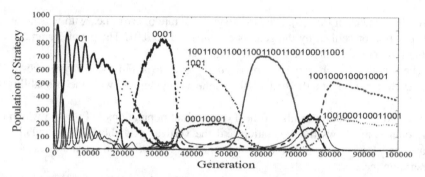

Fig. 5. A collapse of the triplet by the emergence of longer strategies

5   Evaluation of the Sategies

We try to quantify the degree of sustainability of those strategies by means of a fitness parameter W_i defined by the accumulated sum of population throughout the total generation. The 8153 strategies emerged in the 45 simulations of Type I initial condition and the 11753 strategies emerged in the 50 simulations of Type II initial condition are sorted in the descending order of W_i in Table 3. The strategies having positive values of fitness are chosen as 'good' strategies and selected for further analysis. The number of 'good' strategies, satisfying the of the positive fitness condition, was 340 out of 8153 for the case of Type I initial condition, and 785 out of 11753 for the case of Type II initial condition.

Table 3. Evaluation of the strategies

Type I initial strategies(fixed)		Type II initial strategies(random)	
Strategy	W_i	Strategy	W_i
1101 1001	0.123	1011	0.078
0101 1001	0.077	0000 0011	0.070
1101 0110	0.064	1101 1010	0.059
1010 0011	0.050	1001 1001	0.049
1101 0100	0.047	1101 1011 1101 1011	0.045
1001 0001 0001 0001	0.041	0001 0011	0.038
0001 1011	0.040	1101 0101 0001 1001	0.036
0100 1001	0.039	1101 1101 0000 0111	0.032
1101 0111	0.029	1000 0000 0100 0001	0.029
1001 1011 1001 1011	0.028	1111 0101 0101 1110	0.027

We search for a possible characteristic feature of those strategies selected by using the goodness criterion. We first set the length of all those strategies to the equal length (=32), by doubling and count the frequency of symbol '1' at each site, as illustrated in Fig. 8. The rates of '1' for all the 32 sites are shown in Fig. 9 for the Type I initial population and in Fig. 10 for the Type II initial population. This structure can be assumed to be the prototype strategy. The result shows that both Type I and Type II derived the same structure of [1001 0001 0001 0001].

Fig. 6. Compute the rate of occurrence of '1' at each site

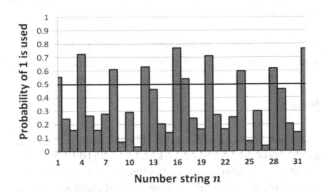

Fig. 7. The rates of '1' at each site of total 32 sites for Type I initial population

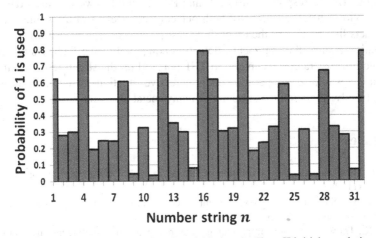

Fig. 8. The rates of '1' at each site of total 32 sites for Type II initial population

6   Discussion

Based on the result of our simulations, 'good' strategies who survive longer with larger population compared to the others have a common prototype gene structure of
[1001 0001 0001 0001]. Moreover, this result was irrelevant to the initial population.
This gene structure is characterized by the following 4 features.

1. cooperate if the opponent cooperates (This feature is seen in common to   [***1 ***1 ***1 ***1], TFT,   PAV,   and [1**1 0*** 0*** *001], etc.)
2. immediately retaliate if defected (This feature is seen in common to [0*0* 0*0* 0*0* 0*0* 0*0*], TFT,   PAV,   but not in [1**1 0*** 0*** *001].)
3. generous
   This feature is seen in common to [1*** **** **** ****], PAV, and
   [1**1 0*** 0*** *001], but not in TFT. Also, the structure [1*** **** **** ****] has an advantage over PAV for being more robust against ALL-D due to longer term of patience.
4. coolness
   This feature is in common to [*0** *0** *0** *0**] having 0 against the opponent's cooperative action. TFT,   [1**1 0*** 0*** *001] do not have such a feature.

7   Conclusion

We have performed extensive simulations of IPD and analyzed to determine the prototype structure of 'good' genes having a structure of [1001 0001 0001 0001]. Although this is a specific example of the structure of strong gene, [1**1 0*** 0*** *001], suggested in Ref. [6], our analysis have reached much stronger specification of the gene structure of the strategy 'better' than TFT. This prototype consists of two types of quartets corresponding to PAV and RTFT. In other words, this strategy acts like the Pavlov when the actions of both players were 'Defect' at the game before the last, but acts like RTFT for the other three cases. This strategy has stronger tendency of retaliation against the opponent's defection compared to the Pavlov strategy. The advantage of this strategy compared to TFT is based on the structure of starting with '1', which helps to offer cooperation under defective situations, which is considered to be a key to solve the dilemma structure of many social problems.

References

1. Novak, M.A., Sigmund, K.: Evolution of indirect reciprocityby image scoring. Nature 393, 573–576 (1998)
2. Roberts, G., Sherratt, T.N.: Development of cooperative rela-tionship through increasing investment. Nature 394, 175–178 (1998)
3. Yao, X., Darwen, P.: How important is your requtation in amultiagent environment. In: IEEE-SMC 1999, pp. 575–580 (1999)
4. Axelrod, R.: The Evolution of Cooperation (1984)
5. Tanaka-Yamawaki, M., Murakami, T.: Effect of reputation on the formation of cooperative network of prisoners. In: Nakamatsu, K., Phillips-Wren, G., Jain, L.C., Howlett, R.J. (eds.) New Advances in Intelligent Decision Technologies. SCI, vol. 199, pp. 615–623. Springer, Heidelberg (2009)
6. Lindgren, K.: Evolutionary Phenomena in Simple Dynamics; Articial Life II, pp. 295–312. Addison-Wesley (1990)
7. Nowak, M.A., Sigmund, K.: A strategy of win-stay, lose-shift that outperforms tit-for-tat in Prisoner's Dilemma. Nature 364, 56–58 (1993)

The Study to Clarify the Type of "Otome-Game" User

Misaki Tanikawa and Yumi Asahi

Department of Systems Engineering, Shizuoka University
3-5-1 Johoku Naka-ku Hamamatsu 432-8561, Japan
sleeplus0716@gmail.com, asahi@sys.eng.shizuoka.ac.jp

Abstract. The authors use the Marketing Science.And the one of the authors study to clarify the type of "Otome-game"user. "Otome-game" users have many kinds of liking or desire.So it is difficult for makers to create products that match with the demands of users.By this research, users and makers will be able to trade at the suitable type of demands. So the auther will research the market of the "Otome-game". The data that is collected by marketing research is analyzed by SPSS.

Keywords: Marketing Science, Otome-game, Japanese culture, User Analysis,SPSS.

1   Introduction

I research to clarify the types of "Otome game" users, using marketing science.

1.1   What Is Otome Game?

"Otome game" means love simulation game for women in Japanese. The word "Otome " means a young girl, and this word also suggests a virgin indirectly.

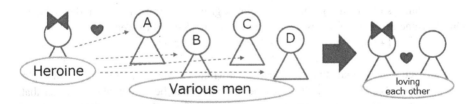

Fig. 1. Explanation of   Otome game

Otome game is a game genre like novel. Each one has own story. The player of the game handles a girl who is the heroine of the story. The player can change heroine's name. Of course, the player can change it into her name.And the heroine meets handsome men of various characters in the game. She fall in love with one of them. As a result, the player who handles the heroine can enjoy virtual love with the man in the game. This story of the game branches when the heroine chooses one of the men. The

S. Yamamoto (Ed.): HIMI/HCII 2013, Part III, LNCS 8018, pp. 625–631, 2013.

number of the branches in a game is same as the number of the men in the game, so the player can fall in love with each man. This is like a romance novel which can choose heroine's partner.

Fig. 2. Play screen of Otome game (This game was made from TECMO KOEI HOLDINGS CO.,LTD. Haruka naru Toki no Naka de5)

The game screen usually displays the background image and the character images.This shows the player the heroine's field of vision. The girl who is in the lower left is a heroine of the game. In the text box on her right side, her or the others words are displayed. The name of the speaker is displayed on the text box. Their conversation basically advances by pushing the button. The player plays the game by reading this conversation like reading a novel. At that time, the characters' dialogs recorded by voice actors are played. Sound effect and background music are also played. As a result, the player will experience the story with sense of presence.

1.2   Situation in Today's Japanese Market

Otome game is one of the game genres that is growing significantly in today's Japan. Otome game market is forecasted to become about 15.6 billion yen in 2012. The market in 2011 is 14.6 billion yen. This is 30 percent extra compared with 2010. [1]

The history of Otome game goes back until 1994. But at that time, the game genre was not well known, that state continued for a while. However, a product had an explosive sales in 2002. Hereafter, Otome game has become to be known at once. After that, the products which became a big hit continued in 2006 and 2008. In 2010 Otome game came to be known more because famous product had been animated. More over, in 2011, an animated product did smash hit. To promote CD products related to the animation work, a lot of flags and the posters were located at JR Ikebukuro station. In 2013, promoting posters were posted at 13 JR stations nationwide. At first, Otome game was known by only a part of the game industry. However today, it is known by many people and was grown to very popular genre in Japan. In addition, if a product becomes big hit, a lot of related products are sold, such as CDs, Goods, or events.

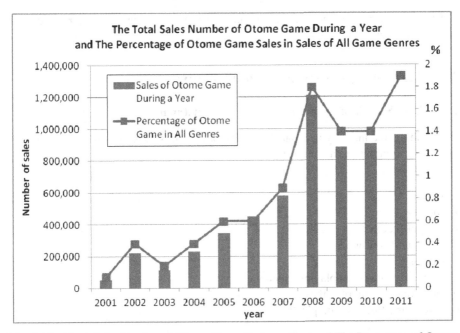

Fig. 3. The Total Sales Number of Otome Game During a Year and The Percentage of Otome Game Sales in Sales of All Game Genres

These graphs show two kinds of numbers about sales of Otome game industry between 2001 and 2011. Blue bar graph and left vertical line show the total sales number of Otome game during a year. Red line graph and right vertical line show the percentage of Otome game in all genres of game. These graphs also shows Otome game market is growing in Japan. Especially, because the percentage has been increase, it is clear that Otome game is known by people who did not play these games gradually.

Recently, Otome game is also released in foreign countries. In 2012, Voltage Inc. began the service "A Prince's Proposal" for North America. The company already had purveyed the service "Pirates in Love", Otome game for North America. This took 21st place by the App store entertainment category of North America in August 2012. And in Asia, this took 1st place by the App store entertainment category of Singapore in same month. Moreover, another product of Voltage Inc. "My Forged Wedding" took 2nd place in same record. From above, it can be said that the acknowledgment level of Otome game in foreign countries is rising.

1.3   Purpose of Research

As can be seen from above, the market of Otome game has expanded every year. However, today in Japan, Otome game industry do not enough analyze the user. Then, to search for "Needs requested from the otome game now", I decided to analyze the otome game user.

So, to search for the needs that are required for Otome game, the author decided to analyze the users.

2   Marketing Research of Otome Game

2.1   User Survey of Game Industry in Present Japan

Today, the game industry in Japan surveys a lot of points of various users for marketing. Those contents are as follows.[2]

- Sex
- Age
- Job
- Annual Income
- Terminal Environment
- Genres
- Why did you started playing video game?
- How long do you play the game in a day?
- How many titles do you play?

And the following items are investigated in the social network game industry.

- The number of having smartphones
- The number of having feature phones
- The number of users who use two platforms (Mobage and GREE)
- Utilization of other platforms
- Rate of users paying
- Rate of users paying
- Average of rate of paying
- Genres which users pay
- payment method
- Influence on expense for other leisure by paying to social network game

A large amount of item is surveyed, although only small points are surveyed about Otome game. The author thinks that to survey the users of Otome game, different points of view are necessary. The points are various liking or desire of each user, because they are the most important points in Otome game.

"The evolution and trends of Otome game" was researched by Aya Higuchi and Yukiko Takahashi, who belong to School of Network and Information, Senshu University in Japan. The following survey results came out from their research. They analyzed the comments of the " Otome Game of the Year" user questionnaire Freem Ltd. has made on the Internet. They used the aggregate of 2009. They analyzed the number of each word in whole comments that was constituted by 43339 words rather than contents of each comment. They choose 11 words related to the game, and compared the comments including these words. As a result, the number of comments including 11 items was 644. The number of the comments about the story of the game was 179. The next place was the comments about the characters of the game, the number was 105. These two numbers are quite different. And, the percentage of the comments about the story is 27.8% in comments about 11 items. This survey results shows lively interest of the users to the story.

However, Otome game industry has not investigated users' needs for story of the game. Moreover, relationship of the story and the users also has not been investigated. From the above it is clear that, Otome game industry needs the user surveys which are distinctive and thoroughly.

2.2   User Survey of Otome Game

Then, how investigate the users? One is survey of the attitudes types of the user to the story because the story is especially interested by the users. The author insists that there are two types of attitude of the user to the story of Otome game. So most important question is this:

"When you play the Otome game, which is your attitude type, 'empathize' or 'overlook'? If your attitude is not in these two types, please tell me your attitude."

"empathize" and "overlook" are the grouping of the users which the author insists. There are 3 features of the "empathize" type.

- She empathize the heroine in the game.
- She change heroine's name.
- She is permissive with the character of the heroine.

"Overlook" type has 4 features.

- She regards that the player and the heroine are different separate person.
- he plays the game as if she reads a novel.
- She do not change heroine's name.
- She is severe to the character of the heroine.

The most important point in these two types of attitude is that "is she permissive with or severe to the heroine?" But in Japanese Otome game industry, sometimes this distinction is mistaken. Why the distinction of the two types is important? The author thinks that, when a company which remembers incorrect user type promotes a product, they will choose incorrect users to promote.

There is a product which clearly shows relation between heroine and story. It is "Haruka naru Toki no Naka de 5" an Otome game produced by TECMO KOEI HOLDINGS CO.,LTD. in 2011. This work has history for 15 years as a popular Otome game series. However, in Amazon.com, this work was evaluated 2.5 points in five point full marks. 340 reviews were written to regular version of this work. 31 people evaluated 5 points, 83 people did 4 points, 53 people did 3 points, 72 people did 2 points, and 101 people did 1 point.

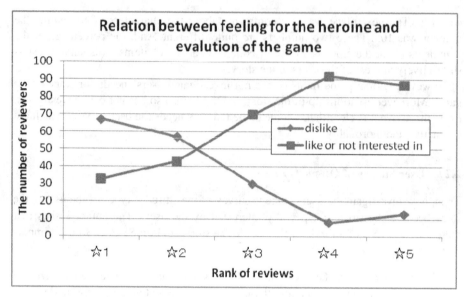

Fig. 4. Relation between feeling for the heroine and evalution of the game

This graph shows that if the player hate the heroine of the game, she do not admit the value of the story of the game.On the other hand, if the player like the heroine, she also prize the story.The blue line shows the number of the people who said dislike the heroine.And the red line shows the number of the people who like the heroine,or who is not interested in her.

The author also researched a lot of element that compose "Otome-game" such as character, the voice actor, graphic art, back ground music, game system, bonus for purchaser, media mix or mobile products.

3   Development in the Future

As mentioned 1-2, Otome game market is expanding overseas. Especially, Voltage, Inc. has already released a service in North America. So this area is one of the large markets of the game industry.[3]

"Famitsu white book of Game 2012" published by Enterbrain Inc. announced as follows. The game market in 2011 are 1 trillion 910 billion yen in North America, Europe 1 trillion 5400 billion yen, 760.4 billion yen in Japan, China, 533 billion yen, 315 billion yen in Korea, India is 20.5 billion yen. This is to say that, the market in North America is as twice and a half large as Japan, and the market in Europe is as twice large as Japan.

Because the game released by Voltage Inc. took high rank in App store ranking, the author thinks there are demands of the Otome game overseas, and expects Otome game can spread from Japan to the world.

To create Otome games which can play overseas, the author thinks the user survey which is adapted to each region is important. Hereafter I would like to do it.

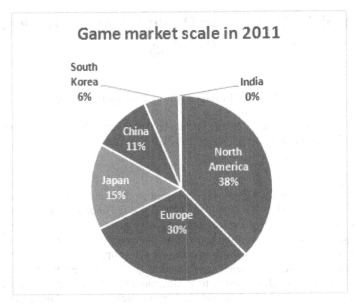

Fig. 5. Game market scale in 2011

References

1. Yano Econimic Research Institute Investigation result 2012 concerning the Otaku market (2012)
2. Seed Planning, Inc. Smart phone game user trend analysis investigation of Mobage. GREE (2012)
3. ENTERBRAIN, Inc. Famitsu white book of Game 2012 (2012)

A Method for Developing Quality Function Deployment Ontology

Ken Tomioka, Fumiaki Saitoh, and Syohei Ishizu

Aoyama Gakuin University, 5-10-1 Fuchinobe, Sagamihara City, 252-5258, Japan
c5612129@aoyama.jp, {saitoh,ishizu}@ise.aoyama.ac.jp

Abstract. It is important to provide developed products in accord with customer needs to the market. We usually use QFD (Quality Function Deployment) to assure the quality fit for the customer needs. We can check the completeness of the qualities which are necessary to realize the customer needs by QFD, and compute importance of qualities in terms of QA. Supporting tools for QFD make quality table and compute importance of qualities. Moreover, QFD tools with ontologies are developed to treat hierarchy of qualities. However in real QFD, we cannot deploy without technical knowledge of design and manufacturing engineers. The relationships among the qualities sometimes change by product mechanisms of technical condition and we must consider various conditions when we perform horizontal deployment. Thus, we need a supporting tool that can represent logical restrictions of incorporating product mechanism. Our main aim of this paper is to propose a methodology of QFD based on logical restrictions and propose a supporting tool for QFD.

Keywords: Decision support systems, Ontology, Quality Function Deployment, Logical restrictions, Formalization.

1 Introduction

It is important for surviving company to supply developed products in accord with customer needs to the market. QFD (Quality Function Deployment) is utilized to assure the quality in accord with the customer needs. QFD is a table to show the relationships among qualities from required quality to quality elements and parts quality. We can check for leaks of quality elements and parts qualities those are necessary to realize the required quality by QFD. Also, we can compute importance of quality elements and parts qualities in terms of QA of required quality. System tools of making quality table and of computing importance are developed for supporting QFD. Furthermore, supporting QFD tools with ontologies (especially taxonomy) are developed to treat hierarchy of qualities [1].

However, in the actual deployment of quality function we must deploy with investigating relationships among qualities by technical knowledge of design engineers and manufacturing engineers. The relationships among the qualities sometimes change by product mechanisms of technical condition. In fact, we work out same required quality, in which case conditions of quality deployment may change by method for

S. Yamamoto (Ed.): HIMI/HCII 2013, Part III, LNCS 8018, pp. 632–638, 2013.

selecting product mechanisms. Also, we sometimes apply horizontal deployment of QFD (called horizontal deployment as against vertical deployment of QFD) to utilize improvements of quality deployment of a product to the other product. We must consider whether we can apply the improvements of one product to the other product or not by various conditions about the improvements. We need a supporting tool that can express not only straightforward relationships between qualities but relationships based on logical restriction of considering product mechanism.

The supporting system for ontologies (Protégé etc.) can define not only taxonomy between concepts but properties of concepts and can infer the class members based on the logical restrictions with properties. The supporting tools for quality audit by the use of the ontology editor protégé are researched [3], [4].

One of our main purposes of this paper is to propose methodology of QFD based on logical restrictions (product mechanism etc.) and propose a supporting tool for QFD. In this paper, first we formalize ontology of quality deployment and propose methodology of quality deployment based on logical restrictions. Next, we propose methodology of horizontal deployment of an improvement case with same formalization.

2   Formalization of Parts Deployment from Required Quality (QFD Ontology)

In this chapter, we introduce a formalization of basic type of QFD ontology which is deployed from required quality to quality of parts as shown in Figure 1. This QFD ontology consists of logical restrictions depend on the engineering mechanism of the product. The following is the steps for QFD from required quality to quality of parts.

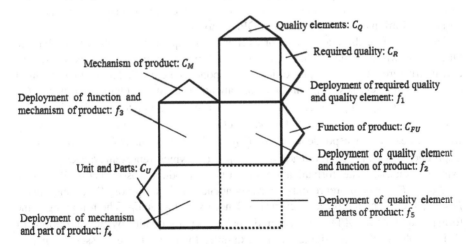

Quality elements: C_Q

Required quality: C_R

Mechanism of product: C_M

Deployment of required quality and quality element: f_1

Deployment of function and mechanism of product: f_3

Function of product: C_{FU}

Deployment of quality element and function of product: f_2

Unit and Parts: C_U

Deployment of quality element and parts of product: f_5

Deployment of mechanism and part of product: f_4

Fig. 1. Quality function deployment

Step1. We deploy from the required quality to quality element. We make relationships between required quality and quality element. Where quality element means quality that is defined in product planning. We usually call it as quality table.

Step2. We deploy from quality element to function of product, and make relationships between quality element and function of product. In this step, we clarify the main function of the product in order to attain planned quality.

Step3. We deploy from function of product to mechanism of product, and make relationships between function and mechanism of product. Mechanism of product is structure to perform function of product. In this step, we clarify the engineering mechanism by which the function of product will be realized.

Step4. We deploy from mechanism of product to parts of product, and make relationships between mechanism and parts of product. In this step, we clarify the parts which are needed to perform function of product by the engineering mechanism.

Step5. We deploy from quality element to parts of product, and make relationships between quality element and parts. In this step, we clarify quality attributes in parts level in order to satisfy quality attributes of product.

Next we introduce a formalization of QFD ontology according to the above steps. In ontology editor, especially in ontology editor protégé, ontology is defined by the classes as concepts and properties of classes as the relationships among the other classes. Properties link two classes. There are two types of class definition. One is direct definition of class, and the other is defined by the logical restriction by use of the other classes and the properties. In the ontology editor protégé, we can infer the classes according to the latter definition of the classes. The definition of the classes is called restriction. Protégé is equipped with inference functions which reclassify class based on restrictions.

QFD ontology is composed of properties and class hierarchy of quality information (required quality, quality element, function of product, mechanism of product and parts). We introduce a formalization of QFD ontology.

First we define the classes and properties of the qualities which are involved in QFD as shown in Table 1. Quality class C is formalized and each class has hierarchical structure. We termed properties "correspondence exists". The formalization of required quality classes is C_R, and the formalization of quality element classes is C_Q. We made $f_1 \subset C_R \times C_Q$ which represents properties correspondence exists C_Q on C_R. The formalization of function of product classes is C_{FU}. We made $f_2 \subset C_Q \times C_{FU}$ which represents correspondence exists C_{FU} on C_Q. The formalization of mechanism of product classes is C_M. We made $f_3 \subset C_{FU} \times C_M$ which represents correspondence exists C_M on C_{FU}. The formalization of parts of product classes is C_U. We made $f_4 \subset C_M \times C_U$ which represents correspondence exists C_U on C_M, and made $f_5 \subset C_U \times C_Q$ which represents correspondence exists C_Q on C_U. The following is the formalized steps of QFD from required quality to parts quality by the definitions of QFD ontology of a gas lighter as an example. First, we make classes of quality information of a gas lighter and formalized. The formalization of required quality class of a gas lighter is $C_{R(G)}$. The formalization of quality element class of a gas lighter is $C_{Q(G)}$. The formalization of function class of a gas lighter is $C_{FU(G)}$.

The formalization of mechanism class of a gas lighter is $C_{M(G)}$. The formalization of parts class of a gas lighter is $C_{U(G)}$.

Step 1. We clarify the required quality of a gas lighter $C_{R(G)}$, and next we deploy $C_{R(G)}$ to C_Q in accord with property $f_1 \subset C_{R(G)} \times C_Q$. We will get quality element classes $C_{Q(G)}$ which relate to $C_{R(G)}$ next as lows. $C_{Q(G)} = \{x | x \in C_Q, \exists y \in C_{R(G)}, (x,y) \in f_1\}$.

Step 2. We deploy $C_{Q(G)}$ to C_{FU} in accord with property $f_2 \subset C_{Q(G)} \times C_{FU}$ in order to clarify the function of a gas lighter to realize important design quality. We will get function classes of a gas lighter $C_{FU(G)}$ which relate to $C_{Q(G)}$ next as follows. $C_{FU(G)} = \{x | x \in C_{FU}, \exists y \in C_{Q(G)}, (x,y) \in f_2\}$.

Step 3. We deploy $C_{FU(G)}$ to C_M in accord with property $f_3 \subset C_{FU(G)} \times C_M$ in order to realize function of a gas lighter. We must consider logical condition $p_{C_M}(x)$ about mechanism of the product which shows the proposition function for the mechanism $x \in C_M$. This means that whether we can use other mechanisms of product or not when we select one mechanism of product. Therefore, we will get mechanism classes of gas lighter $C_{M(G)}$ which relate to $C_{FU(G)}$ next as follows. $C_{M(G)} = \{x | x \in C_M, \exists y \in C_{FU(G)}, (x,y) \in f_3, p_{C_M}(x)\}$.

Step 4. We deploy $C_{M(G)}$ to C_U in accord with property $f_4 \subset C_{M(G)} \times C_U$ in order to consider parts of gas lighter which compose mechanism of gas lighter. We will get parts of oil lighter $C_{U(G)}$ which relate to $C_{M(G)}$ next as follows. $C_{U(G)} = \{x | x \in C_U, \exists y \in C_{M(G)}, (x,y) \in f_4\}$.

Step 5. We define $C_{U(G)}$ to deploy parts of a gas lighter. This $C_{U(G)}$ is the set of parts of a gas lighter which relate to $C_{M(G)}$. We perform inference function of Protégé. Protégé can infer $C_{Q(G)}, C_{FU(G)}, C_{M(G)}$, and $C_{U(G)}$ based on the above steps 1 to 4. As a result, we get $C_{U(G)}$ as shown in Figure 2.

In this way, we can construct QFD ontology of product and deploy from required quality to parts of product by restrictions and inference functions.

3   Formalization of Horizontal Deployment

In this chapter, we introduce a formalization of method for performing horizontal deployment on difference in the mechanism of gas lighter and oil lighter as an example. The steps of performing horizontal deployment are similar to deploying from required quality to parts of product (chapter 2). However we adopt technology of oil lighter to gas lighter, required quality will greatly change. So, we must check required qualities in every level.

We assumed that ontology of gas and oil lighter are also already constructed. First, we formalized classes of quality information of oil lighter. The formalization of required quality, quality element, function, mechanism and parts of oil lighter are $C_{R(O)}, C_{Q(O)}, C_{FU(O)}, C_{M(O)}, C_{U(O)}$ respectively. Also, we use formalization of classes and properties (as shown in Table 1).

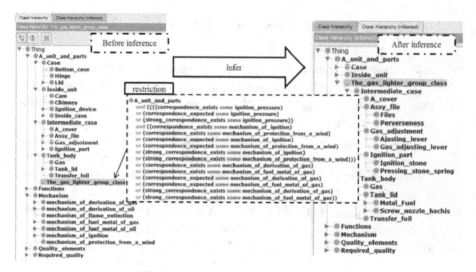

Fig. 2. Parts deployment of a gas lighter

Table 1. Formalization of classes and properties

Class	Formalization	Gas lighter
Requirement Quality Class	C_R	$C_{R(G)}$
Quality Elements Class	C_Q	$C_{Q(G)}$
Function of product Class	C_{FU}	$C_{FU(G)}$
Mechanism of product Class	C_M	$C_{M(G)}$
Parts of product Class	C_U	$C_{U(G)}$
Property		Formalization
Correspondence exists C_Q on C_R		$f_1 \subset C_R \times C_Q$
Correspondence exists C_{FU} on C_Q		$f_2 \subset C_Q \times C_{FU}$
Correspondence exists C_M on C_{FU}		$f_3 \subset C_{FU} \times C_M$
Correspondence exists C_U on C_M		$f_4 \subset C_M \times C_U$
Correspondence exists C_Q on C_U		$f_5 \subset C_U \times C_Q$

Let q_R is a required quality of gas lighter. The following is the steps for horizontal development of q_R of gas lighter to oil lighter.

Step 1. We must clarify the required quality of oil lighter $C'_{R(O)} = C_{R(O)} \cup \{q_R\}$ because required quality greatly changed by technology of oil lighter. Next, we deploy $C'_{R(O)}$ to C_Q in accord with property $f_1 \subset C'_{R(O)} \times C_Q$. We will get quality element classes $C'_{Q(O)}$ which relate to $C'_{R(O)}$ next as follows. $C'_{Q(O)} = \{x | x \in C_Q, \exists y \in C'_{R(O)}, (x, y) \in f_1\}$.

Step 2. We deploy $C'_{Q(O)}$ to C_{FU} in accord with property $f_2 \subset C'_{Q(O)} \times C_{FU}$ in order to clarify the function of oil lighter to realize important design quality. We will get function classes of oil lighter $C'_{FU(O)}$ which relate to $C'_{Q(O)}$ next as follows. $C'_{FU(O)} = \{x | x \in C_{FU}, \exists y \in C'_{Q(O)}, (x, y) \in f_2\}$.

Step 3. We deploy $C'_{FU(O)}$ to C_M in accord with property $f_3 \subset C'_{FU(O)} \times C_M$ in order to realize function of oil lighter. We must consider logical tion $p_{C_M}(x)$. We will get mechanism classes of oil lighter $C'_{M(O)}$ which relate to $C'_{FU(O)}$ next as follows. $C'_{M(O)} = \{x | x \in C_M, \exists y \in C'_{FU(O)}, (x, y) \in f_3, p_{C_M}(x)\}$.

Step 4. We deploy $C'_{M(O)}$ to C_U in accord with property $f_4 \subset C'_{M(O)} \times C_U$ in order to consider parts of oil lighter which compose mechanism of oil lighter. We will get parts of oil lighter $C'_{U(O)}$ which relate to $C'_{M(O)}$ next as follows. $C'_{U(O)} = \{x | x \in C_U, \exists y \in C'_{M(O)}, (x, y) \in f_4\}$.

Step 5. We define $C'_{U(O)}$ in order to deploy parts of oil lighter. This $C'_{U(O)}$ is the set of parts of oil lighter which relate to $C'_{M(O)}$. We perform inference function of Protégé. Protégé can infer $C'_{R(O)}$, $C'_{Q(O)}$, $C'_{FU(O)}$, $C'_{M(O)}$ and $C'_{U(O)}$ based on the above step 1 to 4. As a result, we get as shown in Figure 3.

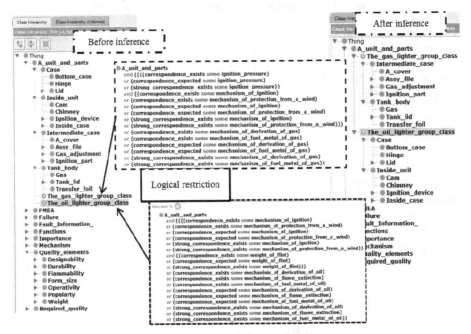

Fig. 3. Parts deployment of oil lighter

In this way, we can construct QFD ontology and perform horizontal deployment by logical restrictions and inference functions.

4   Conclusion

In this study, we introduced a methodology for constructing QFD ontology based on the formalization, and proposed a supporting tool for QFD. QFD ontology can deploy from required quality to parts of product, and perform horizontal deployment. Also, we will develop a methodology of new product development because horizontal deployment of the past products to the new product is similar to the development of new products. The development of new products needs the technology of other products and new technology. Therefore, QFD ontology will contribute to develop a new product by logical restrictions and inference functions proposed in this paper.

References

1. Nomaguchi, Y., Yamadaoka, S., Fujita, K.: Design Methodology and Ontology Building. Nihon Kikai GakkaiSekkeiKogaku 16(06), 232–235 (2006)
2. Tomioka, K., Saitoh, F., Ishizu, S.: Construction of Quality Function Deployment Ontology Involving Logical Restriction among Qualities. In: Proceedings of Asia Network Quality Congress 2012 (ANQ 2012), vol. 10,
3. Gehrmann, A., Ishizu, S.: Improving management system audits by knowledge sharing with ontologies. JASMIN 16(4), 51–65 (2008)
4. Gehrmann, A., Ishizu, S.: Ontology based auditing in complex organizations. In: ICQ 2005, Tokyo (2005)
5. Ishizu, S., Gehrmann, A., Minegishi, J., Nagai, Y.: Ontology-driven decision support systems for management system audit. ISSS (2008)
6. Ishizu, S., Gehrmann, A., Nagai, Y., Inukai, Y.: Rough ontology: Extension of ontologies by rough sets. In: Smith, M.J., Salvendy, G. (eds.) HCII 2007. LNCS, vol. 4557, pp. 456–462. Springer, Heidelberg (2007)

Integrating the Anchoring Process with Preference Stability for Interactive Movie Recommendations

I-Chin Wu and Yun-Fang Niu

Department of Information Management, Fu-Jen Catholic University
510 Chung Cheng Rd, Hsinchuang, Taipei County 24205 Taiwan
icwu.fju@gmail.com

Abstract. Many e-commerce sites employ collaborative filtering techniques to provide recommendations to customers based on the preferences of similar users. However, as the number of customers and products increases, the prediction accuracy of collaborative filtering algorithms declines because of sparse ratings. In addition, the traditional recommendation approaches just consider the item's attributes and the preference similarities between users; however, they are not concerned that users' preferences may be developed as their familiarity with or experiences during choice or preference elicitation grows. In this work, we propose an anchor-based hybrid filtering approach to capture the user's preferences of movie genres interactively and then achieve precise recommendations. To conduct this experiment, we recruited 30 users with different types of preference stabilities for movie genres. The experimental results show that the proposed anchor-based hybrid filtering approach can effectively filter out the users' undesired movie genres, especially for the user who has unstable movie genre preferences. The results suggest that the factor of the stability of users' preferences can be considered for developing effective recommendation strategies.

Keywords: Anchoring process, Genre-based fuzzy inference, Hybrid filtering, Interactive recommendation, Preference stability.

1 Introduction

Recommendation techniques are widely utilized in electronic commerce because of their potential commercial values. The collaborative filtering (CF) approach has been widely used in a large number of diverse applications [1] and enables websites to recommend products based on the preferences of peers whose interests are similar to those of the target user. GroupLens [8] and MovieLens [6] are two well-known collaborative recommendation systems that recommend news and movies respectively. Although CF offers a promising way to expand a user's profile of interests, it cannot overcome the problems of cold-start and sparse ratings (i.e., an individual can only vote for a small fraction of all items). The problem is usually resolved by employing hybrid methods, i.e., by combining content-based and CF techniques [1][4]. This hybrid filtering approach applies CF as the primary algorithm and triggers the

S. Yamamoto (Ed.): HIMI/HCII 2013, Part III, LNCS 8018, pp. 639–648, 2013.

content-based filtering algorithm to make a recommendation. Common research problems in recommendation systems (RSs) are as follows.

- **The cold-start problem:** Cold-start refers to the time in which a new product is introduced into the market and thus has no previous ratings information are available either for computing the correlations or training the models [5][8].
- **The rating sparsity problem:** Generally, most commercial RSs employ a large set of items and customers. Thus, the user-item rating matrix will be extremely sparse and also contain a few co-rated items by users [11]. When we use this sparse matrix to calculate similarity and make predictions, the results will be inaccurate.
- **Preference development problem:** In most exiting RSs, users' preferences are predicted by analyzing the relationship between product ratings and users (Cheung, et al., 2003). Recent research studies have shown that a user's preference is correlated with his/her personality and prior knowledge [7][10]. However, a few researchers have considered how the stability of users' preferences will influence their decision making processes. Accordingly, considering the stability of the users' preferences to provide effective recommendations is worth investigating.

To tackle the aforementioned problems, we propose an anchor-based hybrid filtering (AHF for short) approach in order to take advantage of content-based and CF approaches in an effort to learn the user's movie genre preferences and then provide effective recommendations. Moreover, the user's preferences develop according to the growth in his/her familiarity with or experience of a specific product or service [9][12]. Thus, the user's preferences are likely to be stable over time, and the user is likely to be well aware of his/her preferences [9][12]. As mentioned previously, we can conclude that when the user's experience increases, the user's preferences become increasingly more stable. Accordingly, the anchoring process in the presented iMovie system is designed to determine how the stability of the user's preferences influences the recommendation results.

2   The Research Objectives and Movie Preference Types

2.1   The Research Objectives

The research objectives in this work are addressed as follows. Initially understanding the user's movie preferences is difficult due to the low numbers of ratings that have being collected in the system (application). Thus, we inferred the user's preference for movie genres via a series of interactive anchoring processes. Theoretically, we used the Analytic Hierarchy Process (AHP) [13], a well-known multi-criteria evaluation approach, to filter out undesirable movie genres and then identify the user's movie preferences for specific genres. Note that the contrast effect of the anchor theory has been applied in the AHP model to learn the user's movie preferences during the interactive process. Basically, any systematic shift in judgment away from an anchor is known as the contrast effect. Furthermore, we proposed an anchor-based hybrid filtering approach to tackle the problem of sparse ratings. Namely, after obtaining the anchor point of the user, we will utilize the result to calculate the user's genre-based preference and then create the genre-based profile. Note that the genre-based fuzzy inference approach is executed in the back-end system to recommend movies to the user based on his/her genre-based profile [14].

To investigate the issue of preference stability, we defined movie preference (MP) types based on the user's stability of movie genres, i.e., stable and unstable preferences for movie genres. The recommendation strategies are designed based on the user's MP type to see if the user's stability for movie genres will influence the recommendation results. We defined the genre-based movie preference types based on Simonson (2005)[12] and Kwon et al. (2009)[9] to extract the user's stability of preference to genres of movies. Researchers in the customer decision making area pointed out that the consumers often do not have well-defined pre-existing preferences that are merely revealed when they make choices among available products or services [3]. In this work, we measured the user's preference stability based on the user's variants of movie genres, which are introduced as follows.

Stable Preference: When the users have stable preferences, they are highly predictable if their preferences are revealed well [9]. Accordingly, we could infer the users' movie preference based on their previous records. Both the content-based filtering and anchor-based hybrid filtering (AHF) approaches would be effective.

Unstable Preference: It is difficult to customize the offers for the users who have unstable preferences [9]. Thus, the personalized content-based filtering approach would not be suitable for this type of user [2]. Therefore, a more elaborate approach to predict users' movie genre preferences is required. The proposed AHF approach may lead to a much better effect on recommendation results while people have unstable preferences for movie genres.

3   The Anchor-Based Hybrid Approach for Recommendations

3.1   Genre-Based User Movie Preference Modeling

Users have to rate at least fifty movies which they have seen initially. Based on the ratings, the recommendation system will infer the user's initial preference of movie genres. According to the result of the first rating, we use the genre-based fuzzy inference filtering approach (*G-Fuzzy* for short) which is similar to the content-based filtering approach to predict the ratings of a movie [14]. The method is described as follows.

User Preference Modeling: A movie may belong to more than one genre, for example, Toy Story III belongs to the animation, adventure, and comedy genres. Each user's movie preferences (*UP*) are expressed as a set of movie genres with associated scores, as shown in Eq. (1).

$$Genre_{userx,j} = \frac{\sum_{k=1}^{n_j} r_k}{n_j} \tag{1}$$

where r_k denotes the ratings for movies belonging to genre j , and n_j is the number of movies that belong to the jth *genre*. Thus, $Genre_{j, user\,i}$ means the xth user's average movie preference for $genre_j$. Accordingly, the *UP* of $user_x$ can be expressed as $UP_{user_x}=(Genre_{x,1}, Genre_{x,2}, \cdots, Genre_{x,n})$

3.2   The Anchoring Process

During the anchoring process, an AHP method is applied to calculate the weights of genres for adjusting the user's genre-based profile. In addition, the stability of the user's preference can be evaluated after iterations of interaction result.

Initially, we selected three movies, and then two of the three movies will be an anchor item and a target item respectively at each round, as shown in Fig. 1. Note that we adopted the contrast effect of the anchor theory. We sorted the scores of genres in ascending order in the user's genre-based profile first. We selected the movie of a genre type with the highest score, $genre^h$, and two movies of genre types with the lowest scores, $genre_{l1}$ and $genre_{l2}$, based on the user's original *UP*. Then, we asked the user to make a pair-wise comparison between the most favorite genre type of movie, i.e., the genre with the highest score, and the last two undesired genres of movies, i.e., the last two genres with the lowest scores. In this work, the size of the pair-wise comparison matrix is three which is based on the number of evaluation movies. Then, the relative weights of genres of movies can be calculated. Through a series of comparisons, we can filter out the genres which may not interest to the user and identify the genres which may interest the user. After the pair-wise comparisons at each round, the result may keep the same order of preferences for movie genres as the last round. If it dose, we will not change the anchor movie in the next round. Otherwise, we will select as the anchor the genre with the highest weight in the previous round.

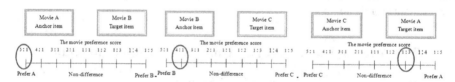

Fig. 1. The Pair-wise Comparisons (the First Round)

3.3   Adjust the User's Genre-Based Profile

The relative weights of genres of movies will be calculated based on the results of the anchoring process. The user's *UP* will be adjusted at each round. By adjusting the genre's score for each user, we filtered out the genres that are not of interest to users. After computing the movies' weights by AHP method, we normalized the user's genre-based profile. We used Equation (2) to normalize the user's genre-based profile.

$$GR_i = \frac{r_i}{\sum_{i=1}^{n} r_i}, \tag{2}$$

Where r_i is the rating of genre i, n is the total number of genres, and GR_i denotes the rating of genre i, which is normalized.

After normalizing the user's genre-based profile, the genres which are selected during the anchoring process were multiplied by the weights which are generated from AHP, as shown in Equation (3). In order to maintain the relative order of genres which are not selected, the unselected genre's score was multiplied with the highest weights.

$$pw_j = GR_j \times w_j \tag{3}$$

GR_j is the normalized rating of genre j, w_j is the weight of the genre j derived from AHP evaluation results and pw_j denotes the proportional weight of the genre j.

4   Experimental Process

4.1   The Dataset

The front-end recommender system, iMovie, is built for collecting users' ratings on movies. We recruited the subjects who are interesting in watching movies in their leisure time. Thirty students at Fu-Jen Catholic University (Taipei) performed the rating and evaluation tasks. For the back-end database, we used one of the Movie-Lens's data sets, collected by the GroupLens research group at the University of Minnesota. MovieLens data sets have proven useful for the algorithm research of the recommender system, which contains 943 users, 1682 movies of 100,000 ratings and has been used in numerous collaborative filtering publications (http://www.grouplens.org/node/12). Notably, we adopted the genre-based fuzzy inference approach to build the model for recommending movies to users.

4.2   The Evaluation Metric

We used the *Genre preference ratio* to evaluate the effectiveness of the presented *Anchor-based Hybrid Filtering* approach in comparison with the *Genre-based Fuzzy Inference* approach. The metric aims to examine if the proposed approach can help subjects identify favorite or undesired genres of movies, and is introduced below.

Genre Preference Ratio (GPR): The genre preference ratio evaluates the percentage of recommended movies genres that fit the subject's favor or undesired movie genres. There are two types of GPR: favorite GPR (denoted as f_g) and undesirable GPR (denoted as d_g). Both types of GPR are calculated by Equation (4) to evaluate the effectiveness of filtering results based on the proposed anchoring process.

$$GPR = \frac{|\text{\# of movies with favorite (undesired)genres}|}{|\text{Total number of recommended movies}|} \tag{4}$$

Note that we will examine how many favorite or undesired genres of movies are preserved or filtered out in the subject's genre-based profile. Basically, the higher the number of favorite movie genres and the lower the number of undesired movie genres preserved in the profile, the better the approach is. Accordingly, we denoted the number (#) of favor and undesired genres of movies as #_f_g and #_d_g, respectively.

5   Experimental Results

5.1   Evaluation of the Subjects' Preference Stability

We used the *Pearson Correlation Coefficient* to evaluate the stability of our subjects. When the correlation coefficient is above or equal to 0.8, there is a strong relationship with the subject's preference over time. On the contrary, there is the relatively weaker relationship with the subject's preference over time when it is below 0.8. Therefore, we separated the stability into the stable status (stability >= 0.8) and the unstable status (stability < 0.8). Table 1 shows that the average stability of all subjects is 0.7768. For stable preference subjects, the average stability is 0.8692 with 77% of subjects, whereas for unstable preference subjects, the average of stability is 0.5142 with 23% of subjects. It shows that a higher proportion of the subjects belongs to the group with a higher stability of movie-genre preferences.

Table 1. The Stability Values of Subjects

Subjects	Stability	Ratio of subjects
All subject	0.7768	100%
Stable subject	0.8692	77%
Unstable subject	0.5124	23%

5.2   Experiment 1: The Genre-Based Fuzzy Inference Approach

Fig. 2 and Fig. 3 show the results of genre preference filtering by the *Genre-based Fuzzy Inference (G-Fuzzy)* approach under various numbers of neighborhoods. The observations are given as follows.

The Results of Stable Subjects: Fig. 2 shows that the *G-Fuzzy* approach make it easier to select a higher number of subjects' preferred movie genres, but will select a higher number of subjects' undesirable movie genres when we increase the number of neighbors from 5 to 25. Overall, the number of neighbors at 15 or 20 achieves the best performance for stable subjects.

The Results of Unstable Subjects: These results are similarly to the results of subjects with a highly stability of genre preference of movies. Fig. 3 shows that the G-Fuzzy approach make it easier to select a higher number of subjects' preferred movie genres, but will select a higher number of subjects' the subjects' undesirable movie genres when we increase the number of neighbors form 5 to 30. Overall, the number of neighbors at 15 achieves the best performance for unstable subjects. Furthermore, this result shows that the approach is more effective for filtering out undesirable movie genres for subjects with unstable movie preferences than those with stable ones. That is, it will not select the four most undesirable genres of movies as that of stable users, as shown in Fig. 2.

Discussions: Fig. 2 and Fig. 3 show that the *G-Fuzzy* approach has good performance for stable or unstable user groups when numbers of neighborhoods are 15 or 20.

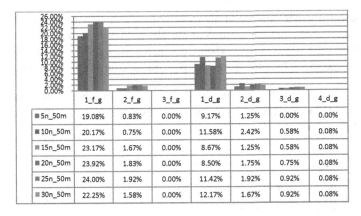

	1_f_g	2_f_g	3_f_g	1_d_g	2_d_g	3_d_g	4_d_g
■ 5n_50m	19.08%	0.83%	0.00%	9.17%	1.25%	0.00%	0.00%
■ 10n_50m	20.17%	0.75%	0.00%	11.58%	2.42%	0.58%	0.08%
■ 15n_50m	23.17%	1.67%	0.00%	8.67%	1.25%	0.58%	0.08%
■ 20n_50m	23.92%	1.83%	0.00%	8.50%	1.75%	0.75%	0.08%
■ 25n_50m	24.00%	1.92%	0.00%	11.42%	1.92%	0.92%	0.08%
■ 30n_50m	22.25%	1.58%	0.00%	12.17%	1.67%	0.92%	0.08%

Fig. 2. The GPRs of the Genre-based Fuzzy Inference Approach of Stable Users

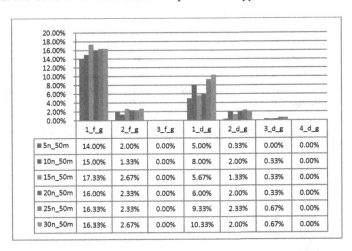

	1_f_g	2_f_g	3_f_g	1_d_g	2_d_g	3_d_g	4_d_g
■ 5n_50m	14.00%	2.00%	0.00%	5.00%	0.33%	0.00%	0.00%
■ 10n_50m	15.00%	1.33%	0.00%	8.00%	2.00%	0.33%	0.00%
■ 15n_50m	17.33%	2.67%	0.00%	5.67%	1.33%	0.33%	0.00%
■ 20n_50m	16.00%	2.33%	0.00%	6.00%	2.00%	0.33%	0.00%
■ 25n_50m	16.33%	2.33%	0.00%	9.33%	2.33%	0.67%	0.00%
■ 30n_50m	16.33%	2.67%	0.00%	10.33%	2.00%	0.67%	0.00%

Fig. 3. The GPRs of the Genre-based Fuzzy Inference Approach of Unstable Users

5.3   Experiment 2: The Anchor-Based Hybrid Filtering Approach

Fig. 4 and Fig. 5 show the results of genre preference filtering by the *Anchor-based Hybrid Filtering (AHF) approach* under various numbers of neighborhoods. The observations are given as follows.

The Results of Stable Subjects: Fig. 4 shows that the *AHF* approach make it easier to select a higher number of subjects' favorite movie genres. It also makes it easier to select a lower number of subjects' undesirable movie genres when we increase the number of neighbors from 5 to 30. Overall, the number of neighbors at 15 achieves the best performance for stable subjects.

The Results of Unstable Subjects: Fig. 5 shows that the *AHF* approach makes it easier to select a higher number of subjects' favorite movie genres. It also makes it easier to select a lower number of subjects' undesirable movie genres when we increase the number of neighbors form 5 to 30. The results for unstable users are somewhat different from stable users as shown in Fig. 5 and Fig. 4. That is, the numbers of neighbors at 20, 25, or 25 achieve the best performance for the unstable subjects.

Discussions: Fig. 4 and Fig. 5 show that the *AHF* approach also has good performance for stable or unstable user groups. Interestingly, it is especially good for users with unstable preferences.

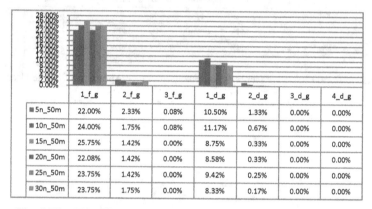

	1_f_g	2_f_g	3_f_g	1_d_g	2_d_g	3_d_g	4_d_g
■ 5n_50m	22.00%	2.33%	0.08%	10.50%	1.33%	0.00%	0.00%
■ 10n_50m	24.00%	1.75%	0.08%	11.17%	0.67%	0.00%	0.00%
■ 15n_50m	25.75%	1.42%	0.00%	8.75%	0.33%	0.00%	0.00%
■ 20n_50m	22.08%	1.42%	0.00%	8.58%	0.33%	0.00%	0.00%
■ 25n_50m	23.75%	1.42%	0.00%	9.42%	0.25%	0.00%	0.00%
■ 30n_50m	23.75%	1.75%	0.00%	8.33%	0.17%	0.00%	0.00%

Fig. 4. The GPRs of the Anchor-based Hybrid Approach of Stable Users

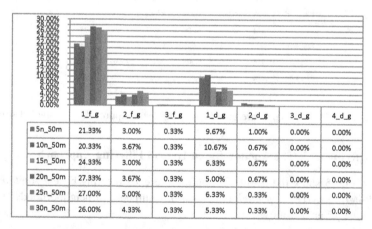

	1_f_g	2_f_g	3_f_g	1_d_g	2_d_g	3_d_g	4_d_g
■ 5n_50m	21.33%	3.00%	0.33%	9.67%	1.00%	0.00%	0.00%
■ 10n_50m	20.33%	3.67%	0.33%	10.67%	0.67%	0.00%	0.00%
■ 15n_50m	24.33%	3.00%	0.33%	6.33%	0.67%	0.00%	0.00%
■ 20n_50m	27.33%	3.67%	0.33%	5.00%	0.67%	0.00%	0.00%
■ 25n_50m	27.00%	5.00%	0.33%	6.33%	0.33%	0.00%	0.00%
■ 30n_50m	26.00%	4.33%	0.33%	5.33%	0.33%	0.00%	0.00%

Fig. 5. The GPRs of the Anchor-based Hybrid Approach of Unstable Users

5.4   Comparing Results of Groups with Different Stability

According to the evaluation results, we discovered that the number of neighbors at 15 can achieve the best performance for the two approaches on average. We set the number of neighbors at 15 to analyze the performance of the experiments. The discussions are summarized as follows.

Observation 1: The GPR of the *AHF* approach is better than the *G-Fuzzy* approach for selecting subjects' most favorite genres of movies for both stable and unstable user groups, as shown in Fig. 6. It indicates that the proposed *AHF* approach is good for helping subjects select movies which will be of interest to them.

Observation 2: The *AHF approach* achieves the best performance for the subjects who have unstable preferences for movie genres, as shown in Fig. 6. Some of the cases show that it has good performance at selecting two or three genres which are relevant to the subjects' preferences. Similarly, some of cases also show that the anchoring processes can effectively filter the subjects' undesired movie genres, especially for subjects who have unstable preferences. The *AHF approach* can also achieve good performance for subjects with unstable movie genres preferences. The *G-Fuzzy* approach achieves the worst performance for subjects with unstable movie genres preferences.

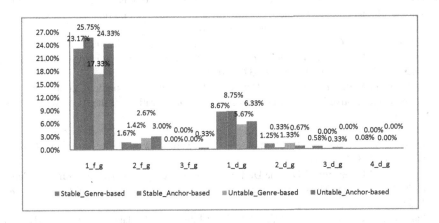

Fig. 6. The GPRs of Two Approaches for Stable and Unstable User Groups

6   Conclusions and Future Works

A series of experiments were conducted in this research to preliminarily evaluate our research questions. The experimental results show that the proposed *Anchor-based Hybrid Filtering* approach can effectively capture the user's preferences and filter out their undesired movie genres. In addition, the approach can produce effective recommendations, especially for the user who has unstable movie genre preferences. We will continue evaluating whether applying the proposed anchor-based approach in the front-end *iMovie* system can precisely recommend movies. We will have an in-depth analysis for applying different recommendation strategies by considering the users' preference stabilities.

References

1. Adomavicius, G., Tuzhilin, A.: Toward the Next Generation of Recommender Systems: A Survey of The State-of-the-Art and Possible Extensions. IEEE Transitions Knowledge and Data Engineering 17(6), 734–749 (2005)
2. Arora, N., Dreze, X., Ghose, A., Hess, J.D., Iyengar, R., Jing, B., Joshi, Y., Kumar, V., Lurie, N., Neslin, S., Sajeesh, S., Su, M., Syam, N., Thomas, J., John Zhang, Z.: Putting One-to-One Marketing to Work: Personalization, Customization, and Choice. Marketing Letter 19(3-4), 305–321 (2008)
3. Bettman, J.R., Luce, M.F., Payne, J.W.: Constructive Consumer Choice Processes. Journal of Consumer Research, 187–217 (1998)
4. Burke, R.: Hybrid Recommender Systems: Survey and Experiments. User Modeling and User-Adapted Interaction 12(4), 331–370 (2002)
5. Cheung, K.W., Kwok, J.T., Law, M.H., Tsui, K.C.: Mining Customer Product Ratings for Personalized Marketing. Decision Support Systems 35(2), 231–243 (2003)
6. Dahlen, B.J., Konstan, J.A., Herlocke, J.L., Good, N., Borchers, A., Riedl, J.: Jump-starting MovieLens: User Benefits of Starting a Collaborative Filtering System with "Dead Data". University of Minnesota. Technical Report, 98–017 (1998)
7. Hu, R., Pu, P.: A Comparative User Study on Rating vs. Personality Quiz based Preference Elicitation Methods. In: Proceedings of the 13th International Conference on Intelligent User Interfaces (IUI 2009), pp. 367–372 (2009)
8. Konstan, J., Miller, B., Maltz, D., Herlocker, J.L., Gordon, L., Riedl, J.: GroupLens: Applying Collaborative Filtering to Usenet News. Communications of the ACM 40(3), 77–87 (1997)
9. Kwon, K., Cho, J., Park, Y.: Influences of Customer Preference Development on the Effectiveness of Recommendation Strategies. Electronic Commerce Research and Applications 8(5), 263–275 (2009)
10. Rentfrow, P.J., Gosling, S.D.: The Do Re Mi's of Everyday Life: The Structure and Personality Correlates of Music Preferences. Journal of Personality and Social Psychology 84, 1236–1256 (2003)
11. Sarwar, B., Karypis, G., Konstan, J., Reidl, J.: Item-based Collaborative Filtering Recommendation Algorithms. In: Proceedings of 10th International Conference on World Wide Web (WWW 2001), Hong Kong, pp. 285–295 (2001)
12. Simonson, I.: Determinants of Customers' Responses to Customized Offers: Conceptual framework and research Propositions. Journal of Marketing 69(1), 32–45 (2005)
13. Saaty, T.L.: A Scaling Method for priorities in Hierarchical Structure. Journal of Mathematical Psychology 15(3), 234–281 (1977)
14. Wu, I.C., Hwang, W.H.: A Genre-based Fuzzy Inference Approach for Effective Filtering of Movies. Intelligent Data Analysis 17(6) (2013)

Application of Ethno-Cognitive Interview and Analysis Method for the Smart Communication Design

Ayako Yajima[1,3], Haruo Hira[2], and Toshiki Yamaoka[3]

[1] Smart City Unit Fujitsu Ltd.
[2] SI Unit Fujitsu Ltd.
17-25, Shinkamata 1-chome, Ota-ku, Tokyo 144-8588 Japan
[3] Department of design and Information Science Faculty of Systems Engineering
yajima.ayako@jp.fujitsu.com

Abstract. In recent years, the problem with which the world is faced has arisen by many complex problems being intermingled by change of global environment and a resident life. We are holding various subject, such as an increase in world population, economic growth of a newly emerging country, global warming, a natural disaster, low birthrate and longevity and so on. In March 11 2011, a huge earthquake disaster has occurred and we had to stop having to change consciousness how a better life and a life should be realized with safe relief.

This research was applied as the technique of finding out about a subject and needs. As a result, it turned out that it is applicable as the technique of the ability to grasp and visualize needs and the subject of an employee or residents which are end users.

Keywords: smart community, Ethnography, Cognitive Psychology Interview Social and Field Innovation, residents.

1   Introduction

In recent years, the form where end users, such as diversification of a network connection terminal, Cloud's progress are provided with the environment which surrounds ICT is changing from product to service as an immaterial thing. Therefore we called for new worth of an end user viewpoint and offer of service. On the other hand, in a systems development scene, the present condition which is not utilized although the customer introduced the system has been seen.

Holding the dissatisfaction people who use "cannot use" even if a customer replaces by spending a large amount of expense, and advancing daily business has encountered the scene which the bad influence has produced besides original business. We needed to enable it to supply the system which a customer satisfies, and we have to need about interview and analysis method which can be understood with customer's demand at the time of interviewing both IT vender and the customer. There are three skills for interviewing.

S. Yamamoto (Ed.): HIMI/HCII 2013, Part III, LNCS 8018, pp. 649–657, 2013.

1. Skill which grasps and extracts a customer's demand
2. Skill which analyzes a customer's demand
3. Skill which defines a demand of the customer who found out

Then, we tried whether the operating grasp interview technique used in the case of a systems configuration could be used for the subject and needs extraction in modern society.

2   The Developed Interview and Analysis Method

In terms of the subject of a requirement definition in IT vendor, it is said that the quality improves 82%. But the method and neither an interview for neither demand extraction nor its methodology improves. Further, about 25% of the systematic measure is taken for the requirements engineering included to quality [1]. From these result, it is important whether it can advance arranging and visualizing a customer's demand from these results, and taking agreement. We fixed the method of that interview skill and analytic procedure that is required for demand extraction.

2.1   The Difference between Our Method and Conventional Method

The technique which we developed was in order to hear usual action focusing on the person of the spot which is actually using the system. At IT vender, they have developed the technique for hearing it focusing on a function. About our interview technique, the developed technique can acquire not functional and non-functional requirements but the information called requirements. That is they are about feeling of those who exist especially in the adjacent spaces of a system and its environment, sensitivity, as much as possible. Moreover, we usually interviewed for participant who belongs to the information system section. But the information section doesn't grasp about present condition of an on-site section's reality. The problem is that customer doesn't write requirement [2]. Therefore, we need to show a way concretely rather than the conventional technique.

Table 1. The difference between our technique and conventional technique

	Stance	Scope	Focus
The conventional technique	Operation of a system Usability	Information system section	Structural-interview, Direct question
Ethno-Cognitive interview and analysis method	The adjacent space, feeling, sensitivity which suuround a system	Field All Users that use systems	Semi-structural interview Story telling

2.2   Structure of Ethno-Cognitive Interview and Analysis Method

This method consists of two phases. The 1st phase is drawing inforamtion from participant (Interview phase). The 2nd phase is analysing the acquired contents of an interview(Analysis phase).

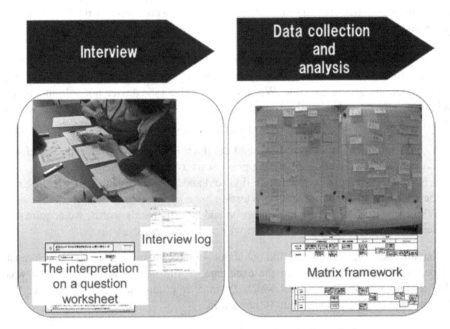

Fig. 1. Ethno-Cognitive Interview and analysis method

2.3   Outline of Ethno-Cognitive Interview and Analysis Method

"Ethno-Cognitive" is coined word, Ethnography and Cognitive Psychology. This method contains two methodologies. One is an ethnographic interview [3] and it defines what should be done with three open questions (Descriptive question/Structural question/Comparison Question). In cultural anthropology, we applied the theory of understanding people's action by a different cultural identification from oneself. Another is a view of Cognitive psychology [4] and it is a view which predicts and interprets cognitive activities (consciousness, memory, study, thinking, etc.). By using this interview technique, we can find out about information a shot time and efficiently about the operating actual condition as much as possible. And we can do visualization of a customer's on-site subject.

2.4   The Feature of Ethno-Cognitive Interview and Analysis Method

In this section, we explain the merit of our technique of each phase.

2.4.1   The Feature of Interview Technique

We pursued the ease of hearing it by combining the theory of social science, psychology, and cultural anthropology, in order to be able to find out about talks including the culture of people's action background or its people. And we put emphasis on finding out about the talk, included the culture of the background for that people act. Furthermore, we perform finding out from many viewpoints to an interview candidate's one action and thought. It enables it to interpolate the utterance of the portion depending on ambiguous memory.

For applying this interview technique, we use a "question worksheet" with emphasis on actual condition grasp of business. And it centers upon three view points, human relations, space, and time. We can find out about the device not only in a regulation operating process but the spot, the consciousness, and the real intention which are a foregone conclusion efficiently.

— Various interview tools were fixed and the interview was systematized. Therefore, anyone can find out about operating grasp or an awareness if the issues
— It is effective as an interview which finds out about the information for creating not the interview for general hypothesis testing but a hypothesis.
— While repeating an open-ended question and a participant's words, we acquire the device in their working place and the way of true business.

By having such a feature, it can find out about people's relation and action which must be performed by cooperating, or the exchange of information in detail. And it was able to find out about the idea which an interview candidate did not notice, the person's true feeling, or the hint to future action.

2.4.2   The Feature of Data Collecting and Analsis Technique

The qualitative data obtained at the interview is immediately text-ized after the end of an interview. Because we prepared the matrix framework, an interview candidate can look through what kind of problem there is. Moreover, he can understand the priority (dignity) of the issue which should be solved from an analysis result.

For applying this analysis technique, we use a kinds of three "matorix framework" with emphasis on actual plobelm and needs. There are the following merits by using these frameworks.

— We can understand the content for the acquired information structurally in accordance with the future and a time series in the past and now.
— When told about a problem, we can visualize whether those problems originated in which process and arose
— From the scene, saying "BA", such as the place of work, one's post, a team, the priority of needs can be caught according to the purpose.

By having these matrixes, the analyzed contents can take out the measure of the issue to solve with being based on these features. Moreover, it can drop to the action level that a theme is decided and works by what kind of structure concretely.

2.5   The Tools Used by Ethno-Cognitive Interview and Analysis Method

We prepared the auxiliary tool which can be used in each stage from interviewing to analysis. We describe explanation of the main tools and an application effect below.

1) Question worksheet
This is a tool certainly used at the time of ethno-cognitive intervew implementation.
   They used these kinds of question worksheets when they understand an interview participant's operating background using two or more viewpoints. By useing these sheets, they can acquire the information on the seeds which lead to truly needed solution. In this interview, In this interview, they do not hear something to hear and to know directly. We prepared that there are six kinds of unique question worksheets.
   These question worksheets consist on including two more aspect such as aspect of interpersonal relationship axis, time axis and space axis.

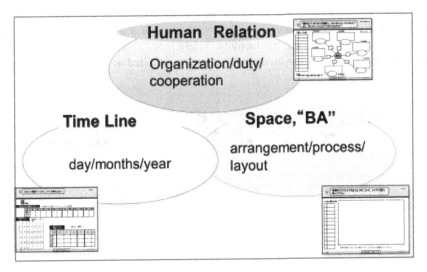

Fig. 2. Main of original question worksheets

2) Analysis matrix
These are used in order to interpret and analyze the narration obtained at the interview.

2-1) The overall matrix framework which catches the contents acquired at the interview
It is a matrix framework which they catch in the following viewpoints about contents acquired at the interview based on a time-axis.

— Thinking inside(potential)
— Action(actual)
— Height of a viewpoint (stance of an interview participant's utterance)

They use in combination with a question worksheets, inorder for the contents to hear this matrix framework during the time of an interview design, or an interview and to reduce a leak. As a result, they can interview by within time.

2-2) Subject arrangement matrix framework

In overall matrix framework, we are present from the past and read the contents by which the content, such as a reason, problem institution, negative feeling, were plotted. Furthermore, an analyzer's viewpoint and experience value are put in and it is tied up the subject relevant to which stakeholder it is.

This framework extracts a subject from the viewpoint of an operating process to a customer and a stakeholder.

2-3) Needs arrangement matrix framework

In overall matrix framework, we treat the mapped contents which are evaluation, influence and feeling, an intention from the present to the future. A needs arrangement matrix framework sets up the level of a customer, the whole company, head offices, a section, an employee, in order to catch of which calss they are needs on a vercical axis.

When trying to an in-company improvement or the measure of operating improved quality, we apply this viewpoint. The horizontal axis of a matrix is a value quality label. For example, there are productivity, safety, cost, service, quantity and so on. They discern in which value element the contents acquired at the interview have an effect.

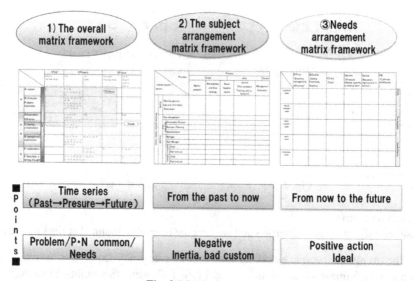

Fig. 3. Matrix framework

2.6   Procedure of Ethno-Cognitive Interview and Method

This technique is the interview method of advancing a question flexibly according to a partner's narration, writing int mutually showing original question worksheet before an interview participant. We interview by three persons, interviewer, interview partcipant and the choronicler who performs a supplementary question and follows up an interviewer when hearing it and preventing a leak. Moreover, the interviewer memorizes beforehand the point which can check whether it is that the contents about which the partner is speaking consider whether it is action in the talk of which time axis. After the end of an interview, and while their memory is fresh as much as possible, we create an interview log. Based on the interview they extrct a subject and needs and develop th to the purpose, means, and measure which agreed at the spot as much as possible.

Then, we explain an analytic procedure. At first, we use a whole arrangement matrix table and map an interview log in this matrix. The told contents examine whether it is mapped by which position of the future in the past and now. And are the told contents saying whether to talk about the consciousness and the action background related to both a problem or needs? Moreover, an analyzer judges whether it is talking about expectation or the future to change.

3   Case Study : Trial to End User Investigation of Ethno-Cognitive Interview Methos

In this section, we tried on end user investigation using ethno-cognitive interview and analysis method.

3.1   Purpose

We performed verification from how to use a technique that was how the person used that tecnique. In order to consider about new services how to offer the information for customer, we investigated the information dissemination method in an end user's viewpoint and its thought. We clarified consciousness of as opposed to consider and business which leads to the customer satisfaction which the employee itself has, and the improvement in sales, and tried improvement in demand quality.

3.2   Scope and Procedure

We interviewed from many employee of headquaters at the the supermarcket. Concretely, we heard global inagesm such as business for a store to mainly manage, organization, and a role. It took about 1 or 1.5 hours per each. The second time, we interviewed to the chief buyer of head office, and the person in change of a store. We were heard about their service of contents, woking hours, thinking every day and is carrying out by implications. It took about 2 or 2.5 hours per each. After the end of an interview, we changed the contets of the interview into the text from the sound immediately after the end of an interview. Next, we use the overall matrix framework and arranged about contents. Then we argued about the cause of the contents deeply by the problem arrangement matrix, considering thcontexts that what the problem occur and why they feel nagative mind etc.

Although we explain validation methodology below. In the interview phase, we noted the point what kind of contents are easy to gain, in how to hear this interview.

Moreover, we investigated whether there would be any difference by the case where it use matrix or not use while analysing the data.

3.3   Result

By using this interview, the information acquired most was related with relation that has shifted behavior between sections. Then we grasped the action which is finite or not finite and also understand the reason for acting. In analysis phase, we compared the contents of analysis the case that matrix framework is used or not. The following results were that

We got a lot of voice which desires efficiency in which head office wants to offer goods collectively.

— And there was a needs which desires each store and production of a goods concept that store and a buyer reflect their experience and consciousness on goods.

As a result, it's obvious that we could visualize about gap which contained about the strategy of goods or store process for sale between head office and store. For using the needs matrix framework, although it was very important claim from customer for sales and degree of satisfaction of store. But it has understood that information tends to be postponed.

3.4   The Effect Using the Ethno-Cognitive Interview Method

It is using various tool s and matrix framework from an interview to analysis, we were able to catch structurally the contents of an interview told individually, in an early end-user's requirement process. By using such a method, about the quality of the demand, the domain could be caught and quality was able to be efficiently considered towards the solution measure, catching the contents comprehensively. And we are the view-points of those who are performing business and were able to catch the present condition and thought on many sides. Those who do not know business well were also able to catch concrete contents by including the viewpoint of ethnography or cognitive psychology in an interview design. Also using a matrix framework, we were able to tie the information acquired at the interview to analysis, while we had been realistic.

In particular, quality and quantity of Talked contents were able to improve when using the matrix framework.

4   Conclusion

We developed Ethno-cognitive interview and analysis method and tried that technique from interview to analysis whether it can be used for end-user's behavior and their thought of behavior. So we have begun to apply in order to extract the subject of regional vitalization and a measure. From now on, we will perform subject extraction for the business solution and town planning of elderly people's life.

And we aim at that this technique can be used as the innovation technique in a smart city.

References

1. Information-technology Promotion Agency Japan Reservation of demand quality in which a software engineering manager task part- The vital point of IT attacked from the super-upper stream The 2nd edn. (2006)
2. Japan Information Technology Service Industry Association Technology-Trends investigation in the information service industry (2009),
   http://www.jisa.or.jp/committee/2009
3. Spradley, J.P.: The ethnographic Interview. Wadsworsh Pub. Co. (1997)
4. Yajima, A., Shiino, Y., Yamaoka, T.: Understanding the business realities: An interview technique which can visualize the job problems. In: Kurosu, M. (ed.) HCD 2011. LNCS, vol. 6776, pp. 449–457. Springer, Heidelberg (2011)

Author Index

Abe, Koji   III-203
Aehnelt, Mario   III-413
Ahram, Tareq   II-3
Akakura, Takako   III-63, III-79
Alfaris, Anas   III-287
Al-Omar, Mashael   I-169
Altmüller, Tobias   II-223
Amaba, Ben   II-3
Amemiya, Tomohiro   II-189, III-203
Andersen, Anders   II-337
Antolos, Daniel   III-549
Aoki, Kazuaki   III-297
Aoki, Kunio   III-238
Aquino Junior, Plinio Thomaz   I-484
Arima, Masahiro   II-443
Arima, Michitaka   II-443
Armsdoff, Gregory B.   II-163
Asahi, Yumi   I-284, I-449, III-607,
   III-625
Asao, Takafumi   I-3, I-89, I-117, I-584,
   I-594, I-620, II-291

Bader, Sebastian   III-413
Bagnasco Gianni, Giovanna   III-258
Bai, Ming-Yao   I-151
Banahatti, Vijayanand   I-505
Barot, Vishal   III-277
Barricelli, Barbara Rita   III-258
Battiste, Henri   II-13
Battiste, Vernol   I-269, II-76, II-136,
   II-606
Bay, Susanne   II-22
Bolton, Albanie   III-3
Bonacin, Rodrigo   II-530
Bortolotto, Susanna   III-258
Brauner, Philipp   II-22, III-423
Brynielsson, Joel   III-559
Byer, David   II-347

Cahier, Jean-Pierre   I-465
Campbell, Stuart A.   II-453
Canter, Maria   III-9
Carlson, Paul   II-66
Castronovo, Sandro   II-460

Chamberlain, Alan   I-411
Chan, Alan H.S.   I-650
Chan, Ken W.L.   I-650
Chang, Wen-Chih   I-421
Chang, Wen-Te   I-567
Chen, An-Che   II-363
Chen, Chien-Hsiung   II-355
Chen, Chi-Hsiung   III-433
Chen, Hao   I-177
Chen, Shih-Chieh   II-355
Chen, Wei-Ting   I-421
Cheung, Ho Cheung   I-197
Chiang, Zun-Hwa   I-567, II-363
Chiappe, Dan   II-13, II-606
Chin, Cherng   I-197
Chiu, Min-Chi   I-12, I-151
Cho, Minhee   III-579
Cho, Vincent   III-443
Choi, Sung-Pil   I-250, II-32
Choi, William   II-13
Cholewiak, Roger W.   II-46
Chun, Hong-Woo   II-32
Coleti, Thiago Adriano   I-338
Correa, Pedro Luiz Pizzigati   I-338
Corsar, David   II-153
Cox, Andrew   I-169
Crabtree, Andy   I-411
Craig, Paul   II-66
Cui, Peng   I-177

Dahal, Sirjana   I-635
Damrongrat, Chaianun   II-39
Dao, Quang   II-136
Davies, Mark   I-411
Del Giudice, Katie   III-475
Depradine, Colin   II-347
Djamasbi, Soussan   I-576, II-235
Doherty, Shawn   III-25

Ebbesson, Esbjörn   I-187
Ebuchi, Eikan   II-85
Edwards, Peter   II-153
Egawa, Koichi   II-421
Eibl, Maximilian   III-336

Elliott, Linda R.   II-46
Elrod, Cassandra C.   III-450
Enami, Toshihiro   I-20
Endo, Yuji   III-210
Enokida, Susumu   I-584
Erickson, John   I-295
Eschenbrenner, Brenda   III-16
Everard, Andrea   II-245

Fechtelkotter, Paul   II-3
Fernández Robin, Cristóbal   I-213
Fernando, Owen Noel Newton   II-373
Flachsbart, Barry   III-450
Foo, Schubert   II-373
Frederick-Recascino, Christina   III-25
Fujita, Kinya   III-297
Fukaya, Junpei   I-30
Fukuzumi, Shin'ichi   I-614
Furuta, Takehiro   III-79
Furuya, Tadasuke   II-56

Georgiou, Andrea   II-66
Ghosh, Sanjay   I-37
Glover, Kevin   I-411
Go, Kentaro   I-55
Gossler, Thomas   II-22
Grigoleit, Tristan   I-269, II-540
Grossman, Elissa   I-221
Groten, Marcel   III-423
Guo, Yinni   III-457
Gürlük, Hejar   II-143

Hadhrawi, Mohammad K.   III-287
Hagiwara, Yoichi   II-411
Hale, Kelly S.   III-475
Hall, Richard H.   III-33
Hall-Phillips, Adrienne   I-576
Hamaguchi, Takashi   II-507
Harada, Tomohiro   III-137
Harrison, Robert   III-277
Hashimoto, Satoshi   III-297
Hattori, Kiyohiko   III-137
Hayashi, Naruhiro   III-195
Hayashi, Yoshiki   III-157
Hayashi, Yuki   III-43
Hein, Michael   II-66
Herms, Robert   III-336
Herron, Meghann   II-252
Higham, Tiana M.   II-76
Hilgers, Michael G.   III-450

Hills, Martina M.   I-660
Hira, Haruo   III-649
Hirano, Ryo   I-305
Hiraoka, Toshihiro   II-470
Hirasawa, Naotake   I-143, III-467
Hirashima, Tsukasa   III-147, III-165, III-175
Hirayama, Makoto J.   II-261
Hirose, Michitaka   II-85, III-238, III-248
Hirota, Koichi   II-189, III-203
Hiyama, Atsushi   II-85
Holzinger, Andreas   II-325
Honda, Ayumi   II-92
Honda, Takumi   III-238
Horie, Yoshinori   II-577
Horiguchi, Tomoya   III-147
Horikawa, Shigeyuki   II-430
Hosono, Naotsune   II-269
Hou, Cheng-yu   II-363
Hsiao, Chih-Yu   I-48
Hsiao, Wen-Hsin   II-355
Huang, Kuo-Chen   I-567
Huang, Lihua   II-173
Huang, Li-Ting   I-322
Hung, Che-Lun   I-197
Hwang, Mi-Nyeong   II-32
Hwang, Myungkwon   I-357, I-524

Ichikawa, Yoshihiro   III-137
Ihlström Eriksson, Carina   I-187
Iinuma, Masahiro   II-285
Iizuka, Shigeyoshi   I-55
Ikeda, Mitsuru   II-39
Ikeda, Tsunehiko   II-291
Ikei, Yasushi   II-189, III-203
Inaba, Toshiyuki   II-269
Inagaki, Toshiyuki   II-548
Inoue, Hiroaki   II-308
Inoue, Shuki   I-545
Ishida, Kenji   I-584
Ishida, Toru   III-511
Ishii, Yutaka   I-431
Ishikawa, Takahiro   I-584
Ishizu, Syohei   I-494, II-181, III-632
Isogai, Satoshi   I-439
Ison, David C.   II-585
Itai, Shiroh   III-195, III-210
Ito, Sadanori   III-362
Ito, Takuma   II-480
Ito, Teruaki   III-307

Ito, Yoshiteru   II-430
Itoh, Makoto   II-490, II-548
Itoi, Ryota   III-616
Iwasawa, Shoichiro   III-362

Jahkola, Olli   III-391
Jang, Hyunchul   II-100
Jeong, Chang-Hoo   II-32
Jeong, Do-Heon   I-357, I-524
Jingu, Hideo   I-614
Jinnai, Akihito   I-594
Johansson, Fredrik   III-559
Johnson, Nathan   II-383
Johnson, Walter   II-136
Johnston, Matthew   III-475
Jones, Brian M.   II-245, II-383
Jones, Matt   I-411
Joshi, Anirudha   I-37
Jung, Hanmin   I-250, I-357, I-524, II-32,
    III-579
Jung, Sung-Jae   II-32
Jung, Wondea   II-524

Kaewkiriya, Thongchai   III-53
Kamata, Minoru   II-480
Kamiya, Tosirou   III-362
Kamo, Hiroyuki   III-317
Kanai, Hideaki   II-39
Kanamori, Haruki   III-63
Kanbe, Takehiro   III-165
Kanegae, Hiroki   III-326
Kaneko, Shun'ichi   I-107
Kang, Yen-Yu   II-355, III-70
Kao, Chih-Tung   I-604
Karashima, Mitsuhiko   II-497
Karslen, Randi   II-337
Karwowski, Waldemar   II-3
Kasai, Torahiko   III-238
Kasamatsu, Keiko   I-614, III-521
Kastler, Leon   I-203
Katagiri, Yurika   I-347
Katayama, Tsuyoshi   II-558
Kato, Shin   II-548
Kawakami, Hiroshi   II-470
Kawase, Masashi   II-490
Kido, Nobuki   I-620
Kim, Anna   II-100
Kim, Jinhyung   I-357, I-524
Kim, Lee-Kyum   II-110
Kim, Sang Kyun   II-100

Kim, Sun-Tae   II-110
Kim, YoungEun   III-219
Kimita, Koji   III-485, III-569
Kimura, Naoki   II-507
Kinoe, Yosuke   II-275
Kirste, Thomas   III-413
Kiso, Hiroaki   I-614
Klack, Lars   II-325
Klomann, Marcel   I-316
Kobayashi, Daiji   I-62
Kobayashi, Takuto   I-449
Koeda, Masanao   I-72
Kojima, Shota   II-291
Koltz, Martin T.   II-163
Komachi, Yushi   II-261
Kometani, Yusuke   III-79
Komine, Shohei   I-80
Konbu, Yuki   I-72
Kosaka, Hiroaki   II-515
Kotani, Kentaro   I-3, I-89, I-117, I-584,
    I-594, I-620, II-291
Koteskey, Robert   II-136
Kring, Jason   III-25
Krüger, Frank   III-413
Kuraya, Naomi   II-261
Kuriiwa, Hidetaka   I-30
Kurita, Yusuke   III-485, III-569
Kuwata, Hironori   III-495

Lachter, Joel   II-136
Lai, Chen-Chun   I-197
Lai, Chih-Hsiang   III-501
Lan, Kang-Hua   III-433
Lau, Candy   III-443
Lea, Bih-Ru   II-116
Lee, Cheng-Lung   I-151
Lee, Juihsiang   I-456
Lee, MiGyung   III-219
Lee, Seung Jun   II-524
Lee, Seungwoo   I-357, I-524, II-32,
    III-579
Lee, Tae-Young   II-110
Liang, Po-Jui   I-322
Liao, Gen-Yih   I-322
Liao, Yu-Hsiang   III-70
Lin, Miaokun   I-628
Lin, Ya-Li   III-501
Lindholm, David   III-89
Lindquist, Sinna   III-559
Liskey, Devin   III-25

Littlepage, Glenn   II-66
Liu, Dahai   III-25, III-549
Liu, You-Jia   I-48
Liuska, Markus   II-124
Lockwood, Nick S.   I-635, III-33
Loiacono, Eleanor T.   I-213, I-628
Long, Yoanna   II-173
Ludu, Andrei   III-549
Luna, Ronaldo   III-182
Lwin, May O.   II-373

Ma, Xiaoyue   I-465
Maeda, Kazushige   III-165
Maeshiro, Tetsuya   I-475
Mahr, Angela   II-460
Makkonen, Emmi   II-124
Maniwa, Hiroki   I-89
Manthey, Robert   III-336
Marayong, Panadda   II-163
Marumo, Yoshitaka   II-558
Masiero, Andrey Araujo   I-484
Masuda, Yukinori   III-203
Matsumoto, Kazunori   I-157
Matsuzaki, Keita   II-490
McCary, Eric   I-97
McCoy, Scott   I-213, II-245
McLeod, Alister   II-198
Meske, Christian   III-342
Miki, Hiroyuki   I-329, II-269
Milde, Jan-Torsten   I-316
Miles, Jim   II-76
Mirchi, Tannaz   II-13
Miwa, Yoshiyuki   III-195, III-210
Miyajima, Fumihiro   II-269
Miyashita, Mariko   II-85
Miyata, Mitsuru   II-285
Miyazaki, Yoshinori   III-157
Mizukoshi, Asahi   III-118
Mizutani, Makoto   II-291
Mochizuki, Makoto   II-568
Moffett, Rick   II-66
Mogawa, Takuya   I-494
Mohamad, Radziah   I-400
Moody, Gregory D.   I-213, II-391
Morales, Gregory   II-606
Morandini, Marcelo   I-338
Moreira, Waldomiro   II-530
Mori, Hirohiko   I-30, I-126, I-642,
    III-118, III-495, III-598
Mori, Yuki   I-107

Morodome, Hiroki   I-117
Mort, Greg R.   II-46
Mortimer, Bruce J.P.   II-46
Müller, Christian   II-460
Munch-Ellingsen, Arne   II-337

Nagamatsu, Takashi   II-421
Nagata, Mizue   I-276
Nah, Fiona Fui-Hoon   II-116, III-99
Nair, Vikram   I-505
Naito, Wataru   I-55
Naka, Toshiya   III-511
Nakagawa, Hironobu   II-421
Nakagawa, Seiji   I-594
Nakajima, Ai   III-108
Nakamura, Atsushi   II-400
Nakamura, Yohei   I-305
Nakanishi, Miwa   I-80, I-305, I-439,
    II-400
Nakano, Atsushi   I-126
Nakano, Yukiko I.   III-43
Nakatani, Momoko   I-347
Nakatsu, Robbie   I-221
Nakayama, Koichi   II-92
Nam, SangHun   III-219
Narumi, Takuji   III-238, III-248
Nauerby, Tom   III-89
Nazir Ahmad, Mohammad   I-400
Nelson, John D.   II-153
Ngo, Mary K.   II-540
Nieminen, Marko   III-381
Nieminen, Mika P.   III-352
Nino, Yoshiaki   III-175
Nish, Hiroko   III-195
Nishiguchi, Hiromi   II-497
Nishijima, Masaru   II-269
Nishimura, Hiromitsu   I-133
Nishimura, Ryota   II-596
Nishimura, Takuichi   III-401
Nitsche, Marcus   I-230, I-240
Niu, Yun-Fang   III-639
Noborio, Hiroshi   I-72
Nobuta, Satoshi   I-515
Noda, Masaru   II-131, II-507, II-515
Nouh, Mariam   III-287
Novaes, Tharsis   I-338
Nürnberger, Andreas   I-230, I-240

O'Connor, Ryan   II-136, II-163, II-606
Oehlmann, Ruediger   III-126

Ogawa, Yuji   III-43
Oh, Yong-Taek   II-100
Ohneiser, Oliver   II-143
Ohno, Takehiko   I-347
Ohta, Yusuke   III-521
Ojima, Chika   II-275
Oka, Makoto   I-30, I-126, I-642, III-118, III-495, III-598
Okada, Masaaki   II-490
Okubo, Masashi   I-515, I-534
Okuya, Yujiro   III-203
Omori, Nao   III-228
Onimaru, Hiroyuki   II-85
Ooba, Yutaro   I-30
Osada, Takuya   III-175
Oshima, Chika   II-92
Otsuka, Asuka   I-594

Papangelis, Konstantinos   II-153
Park, Eric   II-163
Park, JinWan   III-219
Park, Sangkeun   I-250
Pedanekar, Niranjan   I-505
Peters, Clara   I-357
Petersson Brooks, Eva   III-89
Pietras, Nadine   I-524
Pittman, Rodney   II-46
Proctor, Robert W.   III-457

Qin, Erwa   II-173

Rallapalli, Shashank   III-99
Rallapalli Venkata, Pavani   III-99
Rathnayake, Vajira Sampath   II-373
Reeves, Stuart   I-411
Remy, Sekou L.   I-365
Ritter, Marc   III-336
Roberts, Zach   II-136, II-606
Robles, Jose   II-163
Rorie, Conrad   II-606
Runge, Simone   III-423
Runonen, Mikael   III-352
Ruscher, Gernot   III-413

Saga, Ryosuke   I-545, III-53
Saito, Takafumi   II-56
Saito, Yuichi   II-548
Saitoh, Fumiaki   I-494, II-181, III-632
Sajjad, Mazhar   I-357, I-524
Sakamoto, Takafumi   II-301

Sakata, Mamiko   I-534, III-362
Sakurada, Takeshi   II-411
Sakurai, Yuri   II-275
Salvendy, Gavriel   III-457
Sanchez, Abel   III-287
Sanchez, Karen   II-13
Sasaji, Kazuki   I-555
Sasaki, Takashi   II-189
Sato, Hiroyoki   III-137
Sato, Keiji   III-137
Satonaka, Haruhi   III-588
Savoy, April   II-198
Sawadaishi, Yuya   III-137
Scherp, Ansgar   I-203
Schuh, Günther   III-423
Seals, Cheryl D.   III-3
Seki, Masazumi   II-85
Sheng, Hong   I-635, III-33
Shi, Amy   III-531
Shibata, Maho   II-291
Shida, Masakuni   III-175
Shigeyoshi, Hiroki   I-545
Shih, Ling-Hung   I-567
Shimada, Mika   I-669
Shimohara, Katsunori   I-259, III-362
Shimomura, Yoshiki   III-485, III-569
Shin, Jinseop   I-250
Shin, Sungho   I-250
Shiozaki, Hikari   II-430
Shiozu, Yurika   I-259
Shirazi, Farid   II-207
Shively, Jay   II-606
Shunji, Shimizu   II-308
Sia, Choon Ling   III-531
Siau, Keng   I-295
Siio, Itiro   II-124
Silva, Hector I.   I-269
Sim, Paul   II-163
Song, Sa-Kwang   I-250, I-357, I-524, II-32, III-579
Soufi, Basil   I-375
Sripada, Somayajulu   II-153
Stieglitz, Stefan   III-342
Storz, Michael   III-336
Strybel, Thomas Z.   I-269, II-13, II-76, II-136, II-163, II-540, II-606
Sugaya, Takahiro   I-133
Sugihara, Kota   III-175
Sugiyama, Seiji   II-596
Sugiyama, Tetsuya   II-291

Sumi, Kaoru   I-276
Sun, Chu-Yu   III-267, III-540
Sunayama, Wataru   III-588
Susuki, Naoyuki   I-642
Suto, Hidetsugu   III-126
Suzuki, Anna   I-62
Suzuki, Hironori   II-558
Suzuki, Keisuke   II-568
Suzuki, Michio   II-269
Suzuki, Noriko   III-362
Suzuki, Satoshi   I-3, I-89, I-117, I-584,
   I-594, I-620, II-291
Suzuki, Takayuki   I-133

Tachizawa, Yuki   III-598
Takada, Shota   II-470
Takadama, Keiki   I-555, III-137
Takahashi, Yuichi   II-217
Takahashi, Yukiko   III-607
Takahashi, Yuzo   III-372
Takeda, Kazuhiro   II-507
Takemori, Kouki   I-555
Takeuchi, Yugo   II-301
Takiguchi, Kenta   I-642
Tamano, Ken'iti   I-545
Tan, Chuan-Hoo   III-531
Tanaka, Hiroshi   I-133
Tanaka, Jiro   III-317
Tanaka, Takahiro   III-297
Tanaka, Takayuki   I-107
Tanaka, Tetsuo   I-157
Tanaka-Yamawaki, Mieko   III-616
Tang, Han   I-177
Tanikawa, Misaki   III-625
Tanikawa, Tomohiro   III-238, III-248
Tateyama, Takeshi   III-569
Telaprolu, Venkata Rajasekhar   III-99
Terawaki, Yuki   I-383
Terwilliger, Brent A.   II-585
Tolmie, Peter   I-411
Tomimatsu, Kiyoshi   III-108
Tomioka, Ken   III-632
Tomita, Yutaka   II-269
Tomoto, Takahito   III-63, III-79, III-147
Tonidandel, Flavio   I-484
Toriizuka, Takashi   II-577
Tripathi, Sanjay   I-37
Tsai, Nien-Ting   I-12
Tsang, Steve Ngai Hung   I-650
Tsuji, Hiroshi   I-545, III-53

Tsutsui, Masato   III-228
Tyllinen, Mari   III-352, III-381

Ueda, Yusuke   I-284
Ueki, Mari   II-291
Ueno, Takuya   II-443
Ueno, Tsuyoshi   I-545
Ueoka, Ryoko   III-228
Uesaka, Makoto   II-430
Umata, Ichiro   III-362
Urban, Bodo   III-413
Urokohara, Haruhiko   I-143

Valtolina, Stefano   III-258
Vartiainen, Matti   III-391
Velaga, Nagendra   II-153
Vijaykumar, Santosh   II-373
Vincenzi, Dennis A.   II-585, III-549
Vu, Kim-Phuong L.   I-269, I-660, II-13,
   II-76, II-136, II-163, II-252, II-540,
   II-606

Wada, Chikamune   II-285
Wada, Takahiro   II-596
Wang, Man-Ying   I-604
Wang, Mao-Jiun J.   I-48
Wang, Zhiyu   I-177
Watabe, Takayuki   III-157
Watanabe, Kentaro   III-401, III-485,
   III-569
Watanabe, Tomio   I-431, III-307, III-326
Wen, Chia-Ching   II-363
Wesugi, Shigeru   II-315
Wilkowska, Wiktoria   II-325
Wilson, E. Vance   II-235
Winslow, Brent   III-475
Wu, Dezhi   II-391
Wu, Hsin-Chieh   I-12, I-151
Wu, I-Chin   III-639

Xu, Yingquing   I-177

Yajima, Ayako   III-649
Yamada, Ryuta   I-30
Yamagishi, Misako   I-614
Yamaguchi, Tomohiro   I-555, III-137
Yamaguchi, Toshikazu   I-449
Yamamoto, Katsumi   II-490
Yamamoto, Michiya   II-421, III-326
Yamamoto, Sakae   II-217

Yamamoto, Sho   III-165
Yamamoto, Tomohito   II-430
Yamanaka, Mami   II-430
Yamane, Masaru   III-326
Yamaoka, Toshiki   III-649
Yamashita, Tsubasa   I-534
Yanagimoto, Hidekazu   I-669
Yang, Ruijiao (Rachel)   I-576
Yang, Shiqiang   I-177
Yao, Tsun-Hsiung   III-267
Yazawa, Yuuki   II-558
Yokoyama, Shin'ichi   II-490
Yoneya, Nanami   I-62
Yonezaki, Katsuhiko   I-259
Yoshida, Kan   III-175

Yoshida, Yuta   III-165
Yoshimura, Akane   I-669
Yoshino, Shizuki   I-157
You, Manlai   I-456
Yu, Wen-Bin   III-182

Zempo, Hideo   I-393
Zeshan, Furkh   I-400
Zets, Gary A.   II-46
Zhang, Chenghong   II-173
Zhang, Jingyaun   I-97
Zhang, Ran   II-223
Zhu, Yu   III-457
Ziccardi, Jason   I-269, II-136, II-606
Ziefle, Martina   II-22, II-325, III-423